The Guide to the
PROFESSIONAL CONDUCT OF SOLICITORS

Sixth Edition
1993

The Guide to the PROFESSIONAL CONDUCT OF SOLICITORS

Sixth Edition
1993

Editorial Board

Stephen Hammett, *Solicitor, Prince Evans, Law Society Council member, Chairman of the Standards and Guidance Committee*
Peter A. Verdin, LL.B., *Solicitor, Healds, Law Society Council member, member of the Standards and Guidance Committee*
Christopher W. Hughes, LL.B., *Solicitor, Wragge & Co., member of the Standards and Guidance Committee*

General Editor

Nicola Taylor, B.A., *Solicitor, the Law Society's Professional Ethics Division*

THE LAW SOCIETY

113 Chancery Lane, London WC2A 1PL

First published as
A Guide to the Professional Conduct and Etiquette of Solicitors,
Sir Thomas Lund CBE, 1960
A Guide to the Professional Conduct of Solicitors, 1974
The Professional Conduct of Solicitors, 1986
The Professional Conduct of Solicitors (updated), 1987
The Guide to the Professional Conduct of Solicitors, 1990

This 6th edition published by

THE LAW SOCIETY

113 Chancery Lane
London WC2A 1PL

© The Law Society 1993
All rights reserved
ISBN 1 85328 169 7

Typeset and printed by Eyre & Spottiswoode Ltd,
London and Margate

Contents

PART II - INTERNATIONAL ASPECTS OF PRACTICE

Page

Page

Page

PART VII - DISCIPLINARY PROCESS

CONTENTS

Foreword

It is my pleasure to welcome you to the sixth edition of the Guide.

Most readers will be familiar with previous editions and will already have a thorough knowledge of the high standards of conduct with which solicitors must comply. For some readers, however, this will be their first introduction to the Guide which has now become a set text for students of the Legal Practice Course, and I particularly welcome them.

Whether or not you are a new reader of the Guide, I urge you to observe the rules and principles of conduct and to be vigilant to ensure that others do so. It is only through the maintenance of high standards by individuals that justice will be served, the public will be protected and the profession as a whole will thrive.

Issues of professional conduct are central to all the current debates on the future of the legal profession - legal aid, contingency fees, rights of audience, the Compensation Fund and multi-disciplinary practice.

I am particularly pleased to see a greater emphasis on the international aspects of legal practice in this edition.

The profession owes a debt of gratitude to the Editorial Board: Stephen Hammett, Peter Verdin and Christopher Hughes for their hard work in producing this edition.

I recommend the Guide to you.

Mark H Sheldon
President
The Law Society

June 1993

Introduction

Changes in this edition

It is three years since the fifth edition of the Guide appeared in 1990. The changes in the new edition fall into three main categories. First, there are substantive re-formulations of some of the Principles and Commentaries, such as those on change in composition of the firm and on a fee-earner leaving a firm (both in Chapter 3), and on agreeing costs with another party (in Chapter 18). Second, there are changes which reflect changes in the legislative framework, statutory rules, Council statements and other published guidance. Third, there has been a comprehensive reorganisation of the material in the Guide.

Keeping up to date

The Guide sets out the requirements of professional conduct for solicitors as at 8th February 1993. Subsequent changes will be published in the issues of the Professional Standards Bulletin, from Bulletin no. 9 onwards. These should be kept with the Guide.

Changes in the way the Guide is organised

An innovation in this edition is that a new Chapter 1 has been added, explaining the various types of provision appearing in the Guide. It is hoped that this will dispel some of the mystery surrounding the complex series of interlocking provisions which govern the professional conduct of solicitors.

In the hope of making the Guide easier to use, the material has been radically reorganised. In previous editions of the Guide the number of appendices had grown so large that these outweighed the chapters themselves. Much important material, hidden away in appendices, was not readily accessible to the user of the Guide. The decision has now been taken to move all the appendices from the back of the Guide and to annex them to the individual chapters, so that, so far as possible, all material on the same subject now appears together.

Courts and Legal Services Act 1990

The Courts and Legal Services Act 1990 has made possible important innovations in the provision of legal services. The first multi-national partnerships between solicitors and registered foreign lawyers were set up in January 1992. The Courts and Legal Services Act has extended the Sex Discrimination Act 1975 and the Race Relations Act 1976 so as to cover the instruction of counsel; and has made major amendments to the Solicitors Act 1974, including the introduction of a streamlined procedure for the issue, expiry and renewal of practising certificates. Production of the Guide itself has been affected by the need to put some of the material through the complex procedures of Schedule 4 to the Courts and Legal Services Act.

Administration of Justice Act 1985

Section 9 of the Administration of Justice Act 1985 came into force on 1st January 1992, permitting solicitors to practise in corporate form. The first 'recognised body' (incorporated practice) received recognition in May 1992.

New practice rules

The Solicitors' Practice Rules 1990 introduced two principal innovations - Rule 15 on client care, and Rule 16 which made the CCBE Code of Conduct binding on solicitors doing cross-border work in the European Community.

The Solicitors' Publicity Code 1990 has further liberalised the rules on advertising. The Solicitors' Introduction and Referral Code 1990 has already been substantially amended to cover contractual referrals of conveyancing work. The Employed Solicitors Code 1990 has extended the work employed solicitors are permitted to do for third parties.

All the statutory rules and codes have been amended to cover multi-national partnerships.

New accounts rules

A complete new set of accounts rules - the Solicitors' Accounts Rules 1991, the Solicitors' Accounts (Legal Aid Temporary Provision) Rule 1992 and the Accountant's Report Rules 1991 - came into force on 1st June 1992. They include new provisions on unpaid counsel's, agents' and experts' fees, stakeholder money, deposit interest and test checks on controlled trust accounts.

New regulations

The regulations governing continuing professional development (formerly known as continuing education) have been completely restructured as from 1st November 1992. These regulations are in the Guide for the first time.

Lord Donaldson, before he was succeeded by Sir Thomas Bingham, issued new regulations governing appeals and other applications to the Master of the Rolls, and these regulations are printed in full in the Guide.

New guidance and practice information

There have been a number of new Council statements and other guidance, for which space has had to be found in the Guide. The subjects include freedom of choice of solicitor, the supervision of solicitors' clerks, claims to specialisation, advertisements for the arrangement of mortgages, home income plans, production orders under the Police and Criminal Evidence Act 1984 and access to recordings of a child witness's statement.

The written professional standards, dealing with information on costs for clients, were re-launched in May 1991, and now appear in Chapter 13.

New practice information (which is included in the Guide where it relates closely to issues of conduct) covers subjects as diverse as solicitors going on the court record in the name of a multi-national partnership, and good practice guidelines on the recruitment and supervision of employees undertaking investment business.

New chapters

There are new chapters dealing with particular areas of practice, such as conveyancing, property selling and insolvency practice. The former chapter on the solicitor and the court is now entitled 'Litigation, advocacy and alternative dispute resolution'.

There are also new chapters covering the anti-discrimination code, legal aid, legal expenses insurance, multi-national legal practices, cross-border practice in the European Community and the indemnity rules.

Most of the material in the former chapter on law centres, advice services and duty solicitor schemes now appears in Chapter 4 on employed practice.

Plans for the future

It is ironic that the Law Society's initiatives in deregulating solicitors' practice have produced an ever-increasing number of new codes, rules, Council statements and committee guidance. In this edition of the Guide, the Editorial Board has tried to demonstrate that this structure, though complex, is not as impenetrable as might at first appear. However, the ultimate aim of the Editorial Board, in the spirit of deregulation, is the abolition of the distinction between statutory rules and non-statutory guidance. In this way the Guide could eventually become a unified but flexible code of conduct for solicitors. Users of the Guide are invited to see the changes in the 1993 edition as a step towards that goal.

PART I—SOLICITORS IN PRACTICE

Chapter 1

The rules and principles of professional conduct

1.01 Practice Rule 1

Principle

'A solicitor shall not do anything in the course of practising as a solicitor, or permit another person to do anything on his or her behalf, which compromises or impairs or is likely to compromise or impair any of the following:

(a) the solicitor's independence or integrity;

(b) a person's freedom to instruct a solicitor of his or her choice;

(c) the solicitor's duty to act in the best interests of the client;

(d) the good repute of the solicitor or of the solicitors' profession;

(e) the solicitor's proper standard of work;

(f) the solicitor's duty to the Court.'

Solicitors' Practice Rules 1990, Rule 1

Commentary

1. Rule 1 sums up, in the form of a practice rule, the basic principles of conduct governing the professional practice of solicitors. The basic principles stem from the ethical duties imposed on solicitors by the common law. The words of the rule speak for themselves, and should be given a common-sense interpretation. The principles set out in the rule are the bedrock of solicitors' practice, and solicitors should always refer to Rule 1 if they have an ethical problem.

2.   The Principles and Commentaries and other material in the chapters of the Guide, as well as the Council statements and other guidance material in the annexes, represent the Council's interpretation of the basic principles summarised in Rule 1, as applied to the various circumstances arising in the course of a solicitor's practice. Where two or more of the Rule 1 principles come into conflict, the determining factor in deciding which principle should take precedence must be the public interest, and especially the interests of the administration of justice (see Annex 1B).

3.   'Solicitors' in the Guide means solicitors of the Supreme Court of England and Wales, forming one of the two branches of the English and Welsh legal profession (the other branch being barristers). A rule identical to Rule 1 of the Practice Rules appears as Rule 3 of the Solicitors' Overseas Practice Rules 1990, making it clear that the basic principles apply to English and Welsh solicitors wherever they practise.

1.02   Behaviour outside legal practice

Principle

A solicitor is an officer of the Court, and should conduct himself or herself appropriately.

Commentary

1.   A solicitor, whether practising or not, is an officer of the Court. Certain standards of behaviour are required of a solicitor, as an officer of the Court and as a member of the profession, in his or her business activities outside legal practice and even in his or her private life. Disciplinary sanctions may be imposed if, for instance, the solicitor's behaviour tends to bring the profession into disrepute.

2.   When solicitors are acting on their own behalf, whether in conveyancing, litigation or any other legal matter, they are expected to observe the same standards of conduct as are required in the course of practice.

1.03 Sources

Principle

The requirements of solicitors' professional conduct derive from both statutory and non-statutory sources. The latter include Law Society guidance on conduct, which is treated as authoritative by the Adjudication and Appeals Committee, the Solicitors' Disciplinary Tribunal and the Court.

Commentary

1. Statutory provisions which regulate solicitors' professional conduct are:

    (a) the Solicitors Act 1974, the Administration of Justice Act 1985 and the Courts and Legal Services Act 1990;

    (b) other statutes, such as the Financial Services Act 1986;

    (c) orders, rules and regulations made under statute, such as:

    – the Solicitors' Remuneration Order 1972 (see Annex 14A);

    – the Solicitors' Practice Rules 1990 (see Annex 1A);

    – the Civil Legal Aid (General) Regulations 1989 (see Principle 5.03);

    (d) codes and guidance made under statutory rules, such as:

    – the Solicitors' Publicity Code 1990 (see Annex 11A);

    – the Council guidance on the form of private client letter (see Annex 26E);

    (e) principles, rules and codes applied under statutory rules, such as:

    – the Securities and Investments Board's Ten Principles (see Annex 26C);

    – Part 7 of the Financial Services (Conduct of Business) Rules 1990 (see Annex 26D);

    – the CCBE Code of Conduct for Lawyers in the European Community (see Annex 10B).

2. Non-statutory sources are:

    (a) the common law, which has developed and elaborated the basic principles of conduct;

(b)   Law Society guidance on conduct, including:

–   the Principles and Commentaries in the Guide;

–   the code of practice on the avoidance of race and sex discrimination (see Chapter 7);

–   the written professional standards on information on costs for clients (see Chapter 13);

–   other material in the Guide, such as Chapter 27 on the accounts rules;

–   the Council direction on submitting draft contracts to more than one prospective purchaser (see Annex 24A);

–   the Council requirement on the Association of British Insurers' Code of Practice for Intermediaries (see Annex 24B);

–   the International Bar Association's International Code of Ethics, adopted by the Council as the basic code for solicitors practising outside the jurisdiction (see Annex 9B);

–   Council statements, such as that on solicitors taking defamation proceedings against complainants (see Annex 30C);

–   Council guidance, such as that on dealing with unqualified conveyancers (see Annex 24F);

–   guidance issued by the Standards and Guidance Committee, such as the guidance on commissions (see Annex 14C);

(c)   decisions of the Adjudication and Appeals Committee, the Solicitors' Disciplinary Tribunal and the Court.

3.   The nomenclature of each item of non-statutory guidance on conduct (Principle, Commentary, Council direction, Council statement, guidance, professional standard, etc.) to some extent reflects the importance placed by the Council on compliance, and the nature of the obligations placed on solicitors by each item.

4.   The statutory and non-statutory bases of conduct are closely intertwined:

(a)   A statutory rule may be based on a common law ethical requirement, such as Practice Rule 10 on receipt of commissions from third parties (see Annex 1A).

(b)   Non-statutory guidance may be based on an interpretation of statutory rules, such as the guidance on claims to specialisation and particular expertise (see Annex 11D).

(c)   Practice Rule 1 (see Principle 1.01) sums up, in the form of a statutory rule, the basic principles of conduct derived from the common law.

(d)   If a change in non-statutory guidance amounts to an alteration in the rules as to the conduct required of solicitors in exercising a right of audience or right to conduct litigation, the new guidance requires to be approved by the Lord Chancellor and the four designated judges under section 29 of the Courts and Legal Services Act 1990.

5.   The requirements of professional conduct should not be confused with the requirements of the general law of contract or tort, or the requirements of the criminal law, even though the requirements of conduct may in some cases follow or closely parallel the general legal requirements. For the effect of the general law on solicitors, reference should be made to the appropriate authorities, including *Cordery on Solicitors* (currently the 8th edition, Butterworths).

6.   Some items appearing in the annexes, whilst closely connected with conduct requirements, are reproduced in the Guide for information rather than as requirements of conduct. These are designated as 'practice information'. An example is Annex 7A on equal opportunities in solicitors' firms.

1.04   Keeping abreast of changes

Principle

Changes in the statutory rules and non-statutory guidance governing solicitors' professional conduct are published from time to time by the Law Society.

Commentary

1.   *The Guide to the Professional Conduct of Solicitors* ('the Guide') is now published about every three years. It originated in 1960 as *A Guide to the Professional Conduct and Etiquette of Solicitors* by Sir Thomas Lund. This is the 6th edition.

2.   The *Professional Standards Bulletin* ('the Bulletin'), among its other functions, acts as a supplement to the Guide, in that it contains new Law Society rules and Council statements, as well as other guidance material. The Bulletin appears about three times a year. Users of the Guide are advised to keep the issues of the Bulletin, commencing with Bulletin no.9, with their copy of the Guide.

3. The *Gazette*, the weekly journal of the Law Society, announces forthcoming rule changes, and reproduces or summarises major new requirements of professional conduct.

4. The Law Society's Professional Ethics Division gives written or telephone advice on the requirements of professional conduct. If necessary, an opinion can be sought from the Standards and Guidance Committee or the Standards and Guidance Casework Committee. Advice can almost always be given on a confidential basis.

1.05   The Law Society

Principle

The Law Society, established under Royal Charter, is a voluntary body representing English and Welsh solicitors, as well as exercising statutory functions in the regulation of solicitors.

Commentary

1. The Law Society has its origins in The Society of Gentlemen Practisers in the Courts of Law and Equity, founded in 1739. The present organisation was founded in 1826 as The Law Institution, and a Royal Charter was granted to it in 1831 as The Society of Attorneys, Solicitors, Proctors and others, not being Barristers, practising in the Courts of Law and Equity in the United Kingdom.

2. The present Royal Charter of the Society dates from 1845, and there are supplemental Charters dated 1872, 1903, 1909 and 1954. The name was changed to The Law Society by the supplemental Charter of 1903.

3. The 1845 Royal Charter recites the purposes of the Society as 'promoting professional improvement, and facilitating the acquisition of legal knowledge'.

4. Important functions in the regulation of solicitors' practices are given to the Law Society and its Council by the Solicitors Act 1974, the Administration of Justice Act 1985 and the Courts and Legal Services Act 1990.

5. For international purposes the Society adopts the style 'The Law Society of England and Wales'.

Annex 1A

Solicitors' Practice Rules 1990

(with consolidated amendments to 1st June 1992)

Rules dated 18th July 1990 made by the Council of the Law Society with the concurrence of the Master of the Rolls under section 31 of the Solicitors Act 1974 and section 9 of the Administration of Justice Act 1985, regulating the English and Welsh practices of solicitors, registered foreign lawyers and recognised bodies and, in respect of Rule 12 only, regulating the English and Welsh and overseas practices of such persons in the conduct of investment business in or into any part of the United Kingdom.

Rule 1 (Basic principles)

A solicitor shall not do anything in the course of practising as a solicitor, or permit another person to do anything on his or her behalf, which compromises or impairs or is likely to compromise or impair any of the following:

(a) the solicitor's independence or integrity;

(b) a person's freedom to instruct a solicitor of his or her choice;

(c) the solicitor's duty to act in the best interests of the client;

(d) the good repute of the solicitor or of the solicitors' profession;

(e) the solicitor's proper standard of work;

(f) the solicitor's duty to the Court.

Rule 2 (Publicity)

Solicitors may at their discretion publicise their practices, or permit other persons to do so, or publicise the businesses or activities of other persons, provided there is no breach of these rules and provided there is compliance with a Solicitors' Publicity Code promulgated from time to time by the Council of the Law Society with the concurrence of the Master of the Rolls.

Rule 3 (Introductions and referrals)

Solicitors may accept introductions and referrals of business from other persons and may make introductions and refer business to other persons, provided there is no breach of these rules and provided there is compliance with a Solicitors' Introduction and Referral Code promulgated from time to time by the Council of the Law Society with the concurrence of the Master of the Rolls.

Rule 4 (Employed solicitors)

(1)   Solicitors who are employees of non-solicitors shall not as part of their employment do for any person other than their employer work which is or could be done by a solicitor acting as such, save as permitted by an Employed Solicitors Code promulgated from time to time by the Council of the Law Society with the concurrence of the Master of the Rolls.

(2)   Solicitors who are employees of multi-national partnerships shall not be regarded as "employees of non-solicitors" for the purpose of this rule.

Rule 5 (Offering services other than as a solicitor)

(1) (*Application of the rule*)

This rule applies only to such services as may properly be offered as part of a solicitor's practice.

(2) (*Prohibition in respect of certain services*)

Solicitors shall not by themselves or with any other person set up, operate, actively participate in or control any business, other than a solicitor's practice or a multi-national partnership, which offers any of the following services:

(a)   the conduct of any matter which could proceed before any court, tribunal or inquiry, whether or not proceedings are commenced;

(b)   advocacy before any court, tribunal or inquiry;

(c)   instructing Counsel;

(d)   acting as executor or trustee;

(e)   drafting any will;

(f)   giving legal advice;

(g)   property selling;

(h)   investment business as defined in the Financial Services Act 1986;

(i)   any activity reserved to solicitors (whether solely or together with other persons) by the Solicitors Act 1974 or any other statute; or

(j)   drafting legal documents other than those comprised in the above sub-paragraphs.

(3) (*Safeguards for the public*)

Where a solicitor by himself or herself or with any other person without breach of paragraph (2) of this rule operates, actively participates in or controls any business, other than a solicitor's practice or a multi-national partnership, which offers any service which may properly be offered as part of a solicitor's practice, the solicitor shall ensure:

(a)   that the name of that business has no substantial element in common with the name of any practice of the solicitor;

(b)   that the words "solicitor(s)", "attorney(s)" or "lawyer(s)" are not used in connection with the solicitor's involvement with that business;

(c)   that any clients referred by any practice of the solicitor to that business are informed in writing that, as the customers of that business, they do not enjoy the statutory protection attaching to clients of a solicitor; and

(d)   that, where that business shares premises or reception staff with any practice of the solicitor, all customers of the business are informed in writing that, as customers of that business, they do not enjoy the statutory protection attaching to clients of a solicitor.

(4) (*Exceptions*)

(a)   The prohibition in paragraph (2) of this rule shall not apply to a business consisting of a management consultancy or a company secretarial service and which offers none of the services specified in that paragraph save the drafting of documents under sub-paragraph (2)(j) and the giving of legal advice, provided such drafting or advice is ancillary to the main purpose of the business.

(b)   The prohibition in paragraph (2) of this rule shall not apply to prevent a solicitor who is qualified as a lawyer of a jurisdiction other than England and Wales, patent agent, trade mark agent or European patent attorney from having a separate practice as such; and such a practice shall not be subject to the provisions of sub-paragraphs (3)(a) and (b) of this rule.

(4A) (*Multi-national partnerships*)

(a)   Where all or any of the principals of a multi-national partnership have a separate legal practice as foreign lawyers:

    (i)   neither the prohibitions in paragraph (2)(a) to (j) of this rule nor the safeguards in paragraph (3)(a) to (d) of this rule shall apply in relation to the separate legal practice; but

    (ii)   all the principals of the multi-national partnership shall ensure:

        (A)   that any clients referred by the multi-national partnership to the separate legal practice are informed in writing that, as clients of that practice, they do not enjoy the statutory protection attaching to clients of a multi-national partnership, and

        (B)   that, where the separate legal practice shares premises or reception staff with the multi-national partnership, all clients in England and Wales of the separate practice are informed in writing that, as clients of that practice, they do not enjoy the statutory protection attaching to clients of a multi-national partnership.

(b)   Notwithstanding paragraphs (2) and (5)(a) of this rule, a registered foreign lawyer will not be in breach of these rules by virtue of setting up, operating, actively participating in or controlling a business outside England and Wales, provided:

    (i)   the registered foreign lawyer's involvement in the business is not in breach of his or her own professional rules;

(ii)   the registered foreign lawyer's solicitor partners play no role in setting up, operating, actively participating in or controlling the business; and

(iii)   the business does not offer in England and Wales any of the services set out in paragraph (2)(a) to (j) of this rule.

(5) (*Explanatory provisions*)

(a)   This rule applies whether the business concerned is in England and Wales or outside the jurisdiction; but nothing in this rule prevents the setting up outside the jurisidiction of a practice complying with Rules 8 or 9 of the Solicitors' Overseas Practice Rules 1990.

(b)   No part of this rule applies to a solicitor solely by virtue of the fact that:

(i)   the solicitor is a non-executive director of a company; or

(ii)   the solicitor, as the employee of a non-solicitor, does work permitted by virtue of Rule 4 of these rules.

(c)   A separate practice as a notary public operated by a solicitor in conjunction with his or her practice as a solicitor shall not be regarded as a business "other than a solicitor's practice" for the purpose of this rule.

(6) (*Transitional provisions*)

(a)   Until three years after the coming into force of the Solicitors' Incorporated Practice Rules 1988, no part of this rule shall apply:

(i)   to a wholly owned executor and trustee company or nominee company already providing services before the coming into force of those rules; or

(ii)   to a wholly owned company to provide company secretarial services already providing services before 9th June 1988.

(b)   Until 1st September 1993 no part of this rule shall apply to any business already providing services before 11th December 1986 without putting the solicitor in breach of the Solicitors' Practice Rules 1936/72 (as amended).

Rule 6 (Prohibition against acting for seller and buyer, or for lender and borrower in a private mortgage)

(1)   Without prejudice to the general principle of professional conduct that a solicitor shall not accept instructions to act for two or more clients where there is a conflict between the interests of those clients, a solicitor or two or more solicitors practising in partnership or association shall not act for both seller and buyer on a transfer of land for value at arm's length, or for both lessor and lessee on the grant of a lease for value at arm's length, or for both lender and borrower in a private mortgage at arm's length.

(2)   Provided no conflict of interest appears, and provided the seller or lessor is not a builder or developer selling or leasing as such, and provided the solicitor or any solicitor practising in partnership or association with that solicitor is not instructed to negotiate the sale of the property concerned, the rule set out in paragraph (1) of this rule shall not apply if:

(a)   the parties are associated companies; or

(b)   the parties are related by blood, adoption or marriage; or

(c)   both parties are established clients (which expression shall include persons related by blood, adoption or marriage to established clients); or

(d)   on a transfer of land, the consideration is less than £5,000; or

(e)   there is no other solicitor or other qualified conveyancer in the vicinity whom either party can reasonably be expected to consult; or

(f)   two associated firms or two offices of the same firm are respectively acting for the parties, provided that:

   (i)   the respective firms or offices are in different localities; and

   (ii)   neither party was referred to the firm or office acting for him or her from an associated firm or from another office of the same firm; and

   (iii)   the transaction is dealt with or supervised by a different solicitor in regular attendance at each firm or office.

(3)   In this rule:

(a)   "association" refers to a situation where two or more firms of solicitors have at least one common principal; and where either firm is a recognised body "principal" means a director or member of that body, or the beneficial owner of any share in the body held by a member as nominee, or the body itself; and

(aa)   "firm of solicitors" includes a multi-national partnership; and

(b)   "private mortgage" means any mortgage other than one provided by an institution which provides mortgages in the normal course of its activities.

Rule 7 (Fee sharing)

(1)   A solicitor shall not share or agree to share his or her professional fees with any person except:

    (a)   a practising solicitor;

    (b)   a practising foreign lawyer (other than a foreign lawyer whose registration in the register of foreign lawyers is suspended or whose name has been stuck off the register);

    (c)   the solicitor's *bona fide* employee, which provision shall not permit under the cloak of employment a partnership prohibited by paragraph (6) of this rule; or

    (d)   a retired partner or predecessor of the solicitor or the dependants or personal representatives of a deceased partner or predecessor.

(2)   Notwithstanding paragraph (1) of this rule a solicitor who instructs an estate agent as sub-agent for the sale of properties may remunerate the estate agent on the basis of a proportion of the solicitor's professional fee.

(3)   The exceptions set out in paragraphs 2 to 9 of the Employed Solicitors Code shall where necessary also operate as exceptions to this rule but only to permit fee sharing with the solicitor's employer.

(4)   A solicitor who works as a volunteer in a law centre or advice service operated by a charitable or similar non-commercial organisation may pay to the organisation any fees or costs that he or she receives under the legal aid scheme.

(5)   For the purposes of sub-paragraph (1)(d) above, the references to a retired or deceased partner shall be construed, in relation to a recognised body, as meaning a retired or deceased director or member of that body, or a retired or deceased beneficial owner of any share in that body held by a member as nominee.

(6)   (a)   A solicitor shall not enter into partnership with any person other than a solicitor, a registered foreign lawyer or a recognised body.

    (b)   A recognised body shall not enter into partnership with any person other than a solicitor or a recognised body.

    (c)   In this paragraph, "solicitor" means a solicitor of the Supreme Court of England and Wales.

(7)   A solicitor shall not practise through any body corporate except a recognised body, or save as permitted under Rule 4 of these rules.

Rule 8 (Contingency fees)

(1)   A solicitor who is retained or employed to prosecute any action, suit or other contentious proceeding shall not enter into any arrangement to receive a contingency fee in respect of that proceeding.

(2)   Paragraph (1) of this rule shall not apply to an arrangement in respect of an action, suit or other contentious proceeding in any country other than England and Wales to the extent that a local lawyer would be permitted to receive a contingency fee in respect of that proceeding.

Rule 9 (Claims assessors)

(1)   A solicitor shall not, in respect of any claim or claims arising as a result of death or personal injury, either enter into an arrangement for the introduction of clients with or act in association with any person (not being a solicitor) whose business or any part of whose business is to make, support or prosecute (whether by action or otherwise, and whether by a solicitor or agent or otherwise) claims arising as a result of death or personal injury and who in the course of such business solicits or receives contingency fees in respect of such claims.

(2)   The prohibition in paragraph (1) of this rule shall not apply to an arrangement or association with a person who solicits or receives contingency fees only in respect of proceedings in a country outside England and Wales, to the extent that a local lawyer would be permitted to receive a contingency fee in respect of such proceedings.

Rule 10 (Receipt of commissions from third parties)

(1)   Solicitors shall account to their clients for any commission received of more than £20 unless, having disclosed to the client in writing the amount or basis of calculation of the commission or (if the precise amount or basis cannot be ascertained) an approximation thereof, they have the client's agreement to retain it.

(2)   Where the commission actually received is materially in excess of the amount or basis or approximation disclosed to the client the solicitor shall account to the client for the excess.

(3)   This rule does not apply where a member of the public deposits money with a solicitor who is acting as agent for a building society or other financial institution and the solicitor has not advised that person as a client as to the disposition of the money.

Rule 11 (Name of a firm)

(1)   The name of a firm of solicitors shall consist only of the name or names of one or more solicitors, being present or former principals together with, if desired, other conventional references to the firm and to such persons; or a firm name in use on 28th February 1967; or one approved in writing by the Council of the Law Society.

(1A)   The firm name used by a multi-national partnership shall consist only of the name or names of one or more lawyers, being present or former principals of *either* the multi-national partnership *or* a predecessor legal practice, together with, if desired, other conventional references to the firm and to such persons; or a name approved in writing by the Council as the name of the multi-national partnership or of a predecessor legal practice.

(2)   This rule shall not apply to the name of a recognised body.

Rule 12 (Investment business)

(1)   Without prejudice to the generality of the principles embodied in Rule 1 of these rules, solicitors shall not in connection with investment business:

  (a)   be appointed representatives; or

  (b)   have any arrangements with other persons under which the solicitors could be constrained to recommend to clients or effect for them (or refrain from doing so) transactions in some investments but not others, with some persons but not others, or through the agency of some persons but not others; or to introduce or refer clients or other persons with whom the solicitors deal to some persons but not others.

(2)   Notwithstanding any proviso to Rule 5 of these rules, solicitors shall not by themselves or with any other person set up, operate, actively participate in or control any separate business which is an appointed representative.

(3)   Where a solicitor, authorised to conduct investment business, is required by the rules of the relevant regulatory body to use a buyer's guide, the solicitor shall use a buyer's guide in a form which has been approved by the Council of the Law Society.

(4)   This rule shall have effect in relation to the conduct of investment business within or into any part of the United Kingdom.

(5)   In this rule "appointed representative", "investment" and "investment business" have the meanings assigned to them by the Financial Services Act 1986.

Rule 13 (Supervision and management of an office)

(1)   Solicitors shall ensure that every office where they or their firms practise is and can reasonably be seen to be properly supervised in accordance with the following minimum standards:

  (a)   Every such office shall be attended on each day when it is open to the public or open to telephone calls from the public by:

    (i)   a solicitor who holds a practising certificate and has been admitted for at least three years; or

    (ii)   in the case of an office from which no right of audience or right to conduct litigation is exercised and from which no exercise of any such right is supervised, a registered foreign lawyer who is a principal of the firm and who has been qualified in his or her own jurisdiction for at least three years;

    who shall spend sufficient time at such office to ensure adequate control of the staff employed there and afford requisite facilities for consultation with clients. In the case of a firm in private practice such solicitor may be a principal, employee or consultant of the firm, provided that the firm must have at least one principal who is a solicitor who has been admitted for at least three years, or alternatively, in the case of a firm none of whose principals exercise any right of audience or right to conduct litigation or supervise or assume responsibility for the exercise of any such right, a foreign lawyer who has been qualified in his or her own jurisdiction for at least three years;

(b)   Every such office shall be managed by one of the persons listed below who shall normally be in attendance at that office during all the hours when it is open to the public or open to telephone calls from the public:

    (i)   a solicitor holding a current practising certificate;

    (ii)   a Fellow of the Institute of Legal Executives confirmed by the Institute as being of good standing and having been admitted as a Fellow for not less than three years;

    (iia)   in the case of an office from which no right of audience or right to conduct litigation is exercised and from which no exercise of any such right is supervised, a registered foreign lawyer who is a principal of the firm;

    (iii)   in the case of an office dealing solely with conveyancing, a licensed conveyancer; or

    (iv)   in the case of an office dealing solely with property selling and surveying, a chartered surveyor or person holding another professional qualification approved by the Council under Rule 14 of these rules.

(2)   In determining whether or not there has been compliance with the requirement as to supervision in paragraph (1) of this rule, account shall be taken of, *inter alia*, the arrangements for principals to see incoming mail.

(3)   Where daily attendance or normal attendance in accordance with sub-paragraphs (1)(a) or (1)(b) of this rule is prevented by illness, accident or other sufficient or unforeseen cause for a prolonged period, suitable alternative arrangements shall be made without delay to ensure compliance.

(4)   A solicitor's employee who would not otherwise qualify under sub-paragraph (1)(b) of this rule to manage an office and who was 50 years of age or more on 9th May 1975 and had at that date been continuously employed in connection with the practice of that solicitor for not less than 20 years shall, provided he or she exercised the duty of management at that date, be entitled to continue to do so until retiring or attaining the age of 70 years, whichever first happens.

(5)   In this rule:

    (a)   references to a principal shall be construed, in relation to a recognised body, as references to a director of that body;

    (b)   in paragraph (2) of this rule, "principals" shall be construed, except in relation to a firm none of whose principals exercise any right of audience or right to conduct litigation or supervise or assume responsibility for the exercise of any such right, as referring to principals who are solicitors; and

    (c)   "right of audience" and "right to conduct litigation" shall be construed in accordance with Part II and section 119 of the Courts and Legal Services Act 1990.

Rule 14 (Structural surveys and formal valuations)

Solicitors may not provide structural surveys or formal valuations of property unless:

(a) the work is carried out by a principal or employee who is a chartered surveyor or who holds another professional qualification approved by the Council; and

(b) the appropriate contribution has been paid to the Solicitors' Indemnity Fund.

Rule 15 (Client care)

(1) Every principal in private practice shall operate a complaints handling procedure which shall, *inter alia*, ensure that clients are informed whom to approach in the event of any problem with the service provided.

(2) Every solicitor in private practice shall, unless it is inappropriate in the circumstances:

(a) ensure that clients know the name and status of the person responsible for the day to day conduct of the matter and the principal responsible for its overall supervision;

(b) ensure that clients know whom to approach in the event of any problem with the service provided; and

(c) ensure that clients are at all relevant times given any appropriate information as to the issues raised and the progress of the matter.

(3) Notwithstanding Rule 19(2) of these rules, this rule shall come into force on 1st May 1991.

Rule 16 (Cross-border activities within the European Community)

(1) In relation to cross-border activities within the European Community solicitors shall, without prejudice to their other obligations under these rules or any other rules, principles or requirements of conduct, observe the rules codified in articles 2 to 5 of the CCBE Code of Conduct for Lawyers in the European Community adopted on 28th October 1988, as interpreted by article 1 (the preamble) thereof and the Explanatory Memorandum and Commentary thereon prepared by the CCBE's Deontology Working Party and dated May 1989.

(2) In this rule:

(a) "cross-border activities" means:

(i) all professional contacts with lawyers of member states of the European Community other than the United Kingdom; and

(ii) the professional activities of the solicitor in a member state other than the United Kingdom, whether or not the solicitor is physically present in that member state; and

(b) "lawyers" means lawyers as defined in Directive 77/249 of the Council of the European Communities dated 22nd March 1977 as amended from time to time.

Rule 17 (Waivers)

In any particular case or cases the Council of the Law Society shall have power to waive in writing any of the provisions of these rules for a particular purpose or purposes expressed in such waiver, and to revoke such waiver.

Rule 18 (Application and interpretation)

(1) (*Application to solicitors*)

These rules shall have effect in relation to the practice of solicitors whether as a principal in private practice, or in the employment of a solicitor or of a non-solicitor employer, or in any other form of practice, and whether on a regular or on an occasional basis.

(1A) (*Application to registered foreign lawyers*)

(a)   For the avoidance of doubt, neither registration in the register of foreign lawyers, nor anything in these rules or in any other rules made under Part II of the Solicitors Act 1974 or section 9 of the Administration of Justice Act 1985, shall entitle any registered foreign lawyer to be granted any right of audience or any right to conduct litigation within the meaning of Part II and section 119 of the Courts and Legal Services Act 1990, or any right to supervise or assume responsibility for the exercise of any such right.

(b)   A registered foreign lawyer shall do nothing in the course of practising in partnership with a solicitor which, if done by a solicitor would put the solicitor in breach of any of these rules or any other rules, principles or requirements of conduct applicable to solicitors.

(c)   A registered foreign lawyer shall do nothing in the course of practising as the director of a recognised body which puts the recognised body in breach of any of these rules, or any other rules, principles or requirements of conduct applicable to recognised bodies.

(2) (*Interpretation*)

In these rules, except where the context otherwise requires:

(a)   "arrangement" means any express or tacit agreement between a solicitor and another person whether contractually binding or not;

(b)   "contentious proceeding" is to be construed in accordance with the definition of "contentious business" in section 87 of the Solicitors Act 1974;

(c)   "contingency fee" means any sum (whether fixed, or calculated either as a percentage of the proceeds or otherwise howsoever) payable only in the event of success in the prosecution of any action, suit or other contentious proceeding;

(d)   "firm" includes a sole practitioner or a recognised body;

(da)   "foreign lawyer" means a person who is a member, and entitled to practise as such, of a legal profession regulated within a jurisdiction outside England and Wales;

(db)   "multi-national partnership" has the meaning given in section 89 of the Courts and Legal Services Act 1990;

(e)   "person" includes a body corporate or unincorporated association or group of persons;

(ea)   "principal in private practice" includes a recognised body;

(f)   "recognised body" means a body corporate for the time being recognised by the Council under the Solicitors' Incorporated Practice Rules from time to time in force;

(fa)   "registered foreign lawyer" means a person registered in accordance with section 89 of the Courts and Legal Services Act 1990; and "register" and "registration" are to be construed accordingly;

(g)   "solicitor" means a solicitor of the Supreme Court of England and Wales and, except in Rule 7(6) of these rules, also includes a firm of solicitors or a recognised body; and

(h)   words in the singular include the plural, words in the plural include the singular, and words importing the masculine or feminine gender include the neuter.

Rule 19 (Repeal and commencement)

(1)   The Solicitors' Practice Rules 1988 are hereby repealed.

(2)   These rules shall come into force on 1st September 1990.

Annex 1B

Guidance — freedom of choice of solicitor — Practice Rule 1

The Standards and Guidance Committee has been concerned by reports of restrictions being placed on a person's freedom to instruct a solicitor of his or her choice and has issued the following guidance:

Rule 1 of the Solicitors' Practice Rules 1990 provides (in part) that:

'A solicitor shall not do anything ... likely to compromise or impair...

(b)   a person's freedom to instruct a solicitor of his or her choice;

(c)   the solicitor's duty to act in the best interests of the client...

(f)   the solicitor's duty to the Court.'

Where two or more of the Rule 1 principles come into conflict the determining factor in deciding which principle should take precedence must be the public interest and especially the interests of the administration of justice.

The Standards and Guidance Committee wishes to point out two instances where, in its view, acting in accordance with Rule 1(c) (client's best interests) would bring the solicitor into conflict with Rule 1(b) (person's freedom of choice of solicitor) and where the public interest demands that Rule 1(b) (person's freedom of choice of solicitor) take precedence:

1.   A solicitor would breach Rule 1 (and be guilty of unprofessional conduct) if he/she were to pass on to another person any requirement by his/her client that that person instruct a solicitor other than the solicitor of that person's choice. A solicitor should cease to act for any client whom he/she knew to have made such a requirement direct to the other side, unless the client agreed to retract the requirement.

   It would, for example, be wrong for solicitor X, acting for a landlord, to require that a prospective tenant use a solicitor other than solicitor Y because solicitor X (or his landlord client) knew that solicitor Y had already advised another prospective tenant that a lease contained unfavourable terms.

2.   A solicitor would also breach Rule 1 if he/she were to pass on to another person any requirement by his/her client that the other person's solicitor must agree not to act for other parties in other matters.

   It would, for example, be wrong for solicitor X, acting for a defendant in litigation, to offer a settlement which included a provision that the plaintiff's solicitor Y refrain from acting for other plaintiffs against the defendant in other, future matters. Equally, it would be wrong for solicitor Y to accept any such restriction.

Where a solicitor has received information which has been disclosed under compulsion pursuant to any rule or order during discovery for which he/she has given the usual undertakings or implied undertaking to the Court, and where such information has not been referred to in open court, the solicitor must ensure that the undertakings are not breached.

22nd August 1990

Chapter 2

Requirements of practice

2.01 The need to hold a practising certificate

Principle

'No person shall be qualified to act as a solicitor unless —

(a) he has been admitted as a solicitor, and

(b) his name is on the roll, and

(c) he has in force a certificate issued by the Society in accordance with the provisions of this Part authorising him to practise as a solicitor (in this Act referred to as a "practising certificate").'

Solicitors Act 1974, section 1

Commentary

1. The definition of 'unqualified person' in section 87 of the Solicitors Act 1974 includes a solicitor without a practising certificate. Thus, a solicitor, even if he or she is not in practice, who wishes to undertake any of the acts prohibited to unqualified persons by sections 20-22 and 23-24, must hold a practising certificate (see Annex 2A). A solicitor who performs such acts without a practising certificate could be prosecuted under the Act and would also be liable to disciplinary proceedings.

2. The acts reserved to *inter alia* solicitors by sections 20-22 and 23-24 of the Act or by other statutory or non-statutory provisions, and for which a solicitor would require a practising certificate, include:

(a) acting (or practising) as a solicitor;

(b) conducting litigation as a solicitor (see also Courts and Legal Services Act 1990, section 28);

(c) appearing as an advocate before a court or tribunal (see also Courts and Legal Services Act 1990, section 27);

(d) drawing or preparing certain legal documents for or in expectation of any fee, gain or reward; these documents include instruments relating to any legal proceeding, contracts for the sale of land, certain instruments of conveyance or transfer relating to real or personal estate, and papers upon which to found or oppose a grant of probate or letters of administration;

(e) making an application or lodging a document for registration at the Land Registry for or in expectation of any fee, gain or reward;

(f) administering an oath (see Solicitors Act 1974, section 81);

(g) instructing counsel (see also the Bar's Code of Conduct, Annex 21B).

3. Certain categories of persons are exempt from some or all of the provisions of 20-22 and 23-24 of the Solicitors Act 1974, such as barristers, notaries public, Scottish solicitors, licensed conveyancers, trade mark agents, patent agents and certain public officers. Sections 27(10), 28(6) and 55(1) of the Courts and Legal Services Act 1990 give certain exemptions to those granted rights of audience or litigation and to approved probate bodies.

4. Section 1A of the Solicitors Act 1974 provides that any solicitor employed in private practice in connection with the provision of any legal services must have a practising certificate. This provision is interpreted as covering consultants and locums as well as assistant solicitors. A person who, during employment in private practice, applies to be admitted as a solicitor, needs to apply simultaneously for a practising certificate if that employment is to continue.

5. The Master of the Rolls has held that section 1A does not prohibit the employment in private practice of a solicitor whose practising certificate has been suspended. Such a person must not be held out as a solicitor, and can only do work which may be done by a solicitor's clerk.

6. Costs in respect of work done by an 'unqualified person' (including a solicitor who does not hold a practising certificate) are not recoverable by that person or any other person (see Solicitors Act 1974, section 25 in Annex 2A). However, a solicitor who pays money on behalf of a client while acting without a practising certificate is not prevented thereby from recovering that money. It appears that, where work has been billed in the name of a firm at least one of whose members held a practising certificate at the time the work was done, the fact that the partner or employee who actually did the work was uncertificated would not prevent the firm from recovering the costs (see *Hudgell Yeates & Co. v. Watson* [1978] Q.B. 451). In the case of legal aid work, however, where a legal aid certificate is issued in the name of an individual solicitor, the Legal Aid Board is likely to refuse payment if that solicitor was uncertificated. Sections 27(10) and 28(6) of the Courts and Legal Services Act 1990 give exemption from section 25 of the Solicitors Act to those granted rights of audience or litigation.

7. Law Society rules provide that certain functions can only be carried out by a solicitor if he or she has a practising certificate. These functions are: supervising or managing an office which is open to the public or open to telephone calls from the public (see Practice Rule 13(1)(a) and (b) in Annex 1A); and authorising the withdrawal of money from a client account (see Accounts Rule 11(6) in Annex 27B). In private practice, such a solicitor would in any case need to have a practising certificate by virtue of section 1A of the Solicitors Act 1974 (see Commentary 4 above). However, solicitors in employed practice need to be aware of these provisions in the rules.

8. A solicitor who does not hold a practising certificate should qualify the description 'solicitor' by the addition of words such as 'not practising' or 'uncertificated' in any case where such a description might mislead people into thinking that he or she is qualified to act as a solicitor, e.g. in the context of carrying out the type of services which might be provided by a solicitor.

9. An uncertificated solicitor in the employment of a non-solicitor employer must not be described as 'solicitor' on notepaper used for legal professional business, unless the description can properly be qualified by the addition of words such as 'not practising' or 'uncertificated' (see Principle 4.01). All solicitors employed in private practice must hold a practising certificate (see Solicitors Act 1974, section 1A and Commentary 4 above). A completely retired consultant who plays no part in the provision of any legal services can appear on the notepaper of a practice as 'consultant', but only with the addition of such explanatory words as 'retired non-practising solicitor' or 'retired uncertificated solicitor' (see also Publicity Code, paragraph 7(a) in Annex 11A).

10. An uncertificated solicitor may describe himself or herself as 'solicitor' in situations where there is no implication that he or she is entitled to practise as a solicitor, e.g. in the context of the authorship of a book. When witnessing documents, an uncertificated solicitor may use the description 'solicitor' provided that the document is not required to be witnessed by a practising solicitor.

11. By Rule 2 of the Solicitors' Overseas Practice Rules 1990, a solicitor practising as such outside England and Wales must hold a practising certificate.

2.02   Issue and renewal of practising certificates

Principle

Practising certificates are issued by the Law Society under Part I of the Solicitors Act 1974 and are renewable annually.

Commentary

Application procedure

1. Applications for and the issue of practising certificates are regulated by the Solicitors Act 1974, sections 9-18 and the Practising Certificate Regulations 1976. The regulations (see Annex 2C) are made under section 28 of the Act by the Master of the Rolls with the concurrence of the Lord Chancellor and the Lord Chief Justice. Applications for a practising certificate must be made by the solicitor on the form issued by the Law Society (Form PCR1). Care should be taken to complete the form correctly; false or reckless statements made on the form can lead to disciplinary proceedings.

Practising certificate fee

2. With the application for a practising certificate a solicitor must send to the Society the requisite fee. This fee is fixed annually under section 11(1) of the Solicitors Act 1974 by the Master of the Rolls with the concurrence of the Lord Chancellor and the Lord Chief Justice.

3. The practising certificate year runs from 1st November to 31st October.

4. There are certain provisions for payment of a reduced practising certificate fee:

    (a) A reduced fee is payable by solicitors whose gross income from practice as a solicitor or from employment in connection with the provision of any legal services has not exceeded £5,000 in the year ending 31st March preceding the commencement of the practising certificate year for which a practising certificate is sought.

    (b) A reduced fee is also payable by Crown prosecutors.

    (c) In general there is no reduction for applications during the course of the practising certificate year; however, there are reduced rates for certain such applications by newly qualified solicitors and by solicitors returning to practice after a break.

5. An additional fee of £50 is payable by any solicitor subject to section 12(1)(ee) of the Solicitors Act 1974 (late accountants' reports) — see section 12A in Annex 2A, and Principle 2.03.

Compensation Fund contributions

6.   In addition to the practising certificate fee, a solicitor must with his or her application pay the annual contribution to the Solicitors' Compensation Fund (see Chapter 29 and Solicitors Act 1974, Schedule 2). The amount of the annual contribution is determined by the Council of the Law Society.

7.   A solicitor is wholly exempt from payment of the annual contribution to the Compensation Fund in respect of his or her first three practising certificates. In respect of the next three practising certificates issued to that solicitor, the amount of the annual contribution is reduced to one-half. A solicitor who has not held or received clients' money during the practising certificate year prior to that for which a practising certificate is sought, and who has not held or received clients' money through a recognised body (incorporated practice), pays a reduced annual contribution. Crown prosecutors are exempted from payment.

8.   The Council can also impose a further contribution to the Compensation Fund, known as a special levy (see Solicitors Act 1974, Schedule 2). The special levy is payable only by those solicitors who have held or received clients' money during the practising certificate year prior to that for which a practising certificate is sought. As with the annual contribution, solicitors are exempt from making payment in respect of their first three practising certificates and pay only one-half of any levy in respect of their next three practising certificates. Crown prosecutors are exempted

Evidence of Indemnity Fund contributions

9.   On applying for a practising certificate, a solicitor must either:

(a)   satisfy the Society, by attaching to his or her application the appropriate proof of compliance, that he or she has complied with the Solicitors' Indemnity Rules (whether by payment of the required contributions to Solicitors Indemnity Fund Limited or by submission of a valid direct debit mandate); or

(b)   satisfy the Society that he or she is not subject to the Indemnity Rules (e.g. because he or she is not in private practice as a principal); or

(c)   satisfy the Society that he or she is exempt from the Indemnity Rules by claiming the benefit of the exemption in Rule 9.1 (see Annex 28B); or

(d)   satisfy the Society that he or she is exempt from the Indemnity Rules by claiming the benefit of an individual waiver of the Indemnity Rules, details of which must be supplied.

The Society must be satisfied that the appropriate evidence has been provided for each practice of the solicitor. A solicitor who is a director of a recognised body has to provide evidence of compliance by the recognised body, as well as evidence of compulsory top-up cover where required (see

Rule 13 of the Solicitors' Incorporated Practice Rules in Annex 3C). For the Solicitors' Indemnity Rules generally, see Chapter 28 and Annexes 28B and 28C.

Issue or refusal of certificates

10. In most cases, a solicitor who applies for a practising certificate is entitled to receive one as of right, provided that his or her application complies with the Practising Certificate Regulations 1976. However, in certain circumstances, the Society has a discretion to refuse to issue a certificate, or to issue one subject to conditions (see Solicitors Act 1974, section 12 in Annex 2A, and Principle 2.03). If the Society refuses to issue a new certificate, an existing certificate will expire as soon as the replacement date has passed (see Commentary 11). If the replacement date has already passed, the existing certificate will expire immediately upon the Society taking the decision not to issue a new certificate.

Annual renewal or withdrawal of certificates

11. Every practising certificate bears the 'replacement date' of the 31st October next after it is issued. By that date, application must be made for a new certificate if required. If the replacement date has passed, and a solicitor has made no application for a new certificate, the Society may withdraw the solicitor's existing certificate (see Solicitors Act 1974, section 14).

2.03 Refusal of a practising certificate, or imposition of conditions

Principle

In certain cases, set out in section 12(1) of the Solicitors Act 1974, the Law Society has discretion to refuse a practising certificate or to issue a certificate subject to conditions.

Commentary

1. The full text of section 12 appears in Annex 2A. Where section 12 applies, an applicant must give six weeks' notice to the Society of his or her intention to apply for a practising certificate, unless the Master of the Rolls orders otherwise. This notice must be given on the appropriate form (Form PCR5) and in most cases must be accompanied by a certificate of fitness (Form PCR4) signed by two practising solicitors.

2. In the majority of applications under section 12(1)(a) (first application) or 12(1)(c) (application after a lapse of 12 months or more) the requirement

for the certificate of fitness will be waived. Applications under these paragraphs are considered by the Standards and Guidance Casework Committee if a period of five years or more has elapsed since the applicant qualified or last held a practising certificate, or if it appears that the applicant may have practised uncertificated. A condition requiring completion of a number of courses of continuing professional development is frequently imposed where the applicant has not been in practice during the intervening period.

3.   Applications made under other paragraphs of section 12(1) are considered by the Solicitors Complaints Bureau. One common area where section 12 applies is where a solicitor has been invited by the Society to give an explanation in respect of his or her conduct and has failed to give an explanation which the Society finds sufficient and satisfactory. The solicitor must accordingly give the requisite six weeks' notice to the Society of his or her intention to apply for a practising certificate and the Society must then decide whether to refuse to issue a certificate or to issue a certificate subject to conditions. Conditions commonly imposed include the delivery of half-yearly accountant's reports, or that the solicitor must practise only in approved partnership or approved employment.

4.   The attention of solicitors is drawn to section 12(1)(ee), under which the Society's discretion to refuse a practising certificate, or to impose conditions, arises when a solicitor is late with his or her accountant's report. Section 12A(1) imposes an additional fee in such circumstances.

5.   An appeal against the refusal by the Society to issue a practising certificate, or against the imposition by the Society of conditions, lies to the Master of the Rolls (see Solicitors Act 1974, section 13, and also Annex 2E).

6.   In certain cases, the Society may impose conditions on a practising certificate during the currency of the certificate (see Solicitors Act 1974, section 13A in Annex 2A).

2.04   Limitations on practice for newly qualified solicitors

Principle

A solicitor cannot normally practise as a sole principal until he or she has been admitted for three years. At least one of the partners in a firm must normally have been admitted for at least three years.

Commentary

1. A solicitor who has been admitted less than three years does not qualify to supervise an office open to the public or open to telephone calls from the public, under Rule 13(1)(a) of the Solicitors' Practice Rules 1990 (see Annex 1A and Principle 3.02). In the case of private practice, the duty of supervision can be fulfilled by an assistant solicitor or consultant rather than a principal, but at least one principal in the practice must be a solicitor who has been admitted for at least three years.

2. The rule makes specific provision for multi-national partnerships and for recognised bodies (incorporated practices).

3. It should be noted that Practice Rule 13 applies to employed practice as well as to private practice, where an employed solicitor is practising from an office open to the public or open to telephone calls from the public. This applies particularly to solicitors employed by law centres and other non-commercial advice services (see paragraph 7 of the Employed Solicitors Code 1990 in Annex 4A). It could also apply to solicitors employed by certain commercial legal advice services and regulatory bodies (see paragraphs 8 and 9 of the Code).

2.05   Special qualifications for investment business and insolvency practice

Principle

For a solicitor to carry on investment business or to act as an insolvency practitioner, it is not sufficient to hold a practising certificate — further qualification is also required.

Commentary

1. For a solicitor to carry on investment business within the meaning of the Financial Services Act 1986, the solicitor's firm must either hold an investment business certificate from the Law Society, or have authorisation from another appropriate regulator such as FIMBRA. Sole practitioners, recognised bodies (incorporated practices), multi-national partnerships and, in restricted circumstances, employed solicitors may apply for an investment business certificate, as well as firms of solicitors (see also Chapter 26).

2. To act as an insolvency practitioner within the meaning of the Insolvency Act 1986 a solicitor must, as an individual, hold a certificate of authorisation from the Law Society (see also Chapter 23).

2.06   Continuing professional development

Principle

Solicitors admitted after 1st August 1987 are subject to the compulsory continuing professional development scheme.

Commentary

1. The present scheme for continuing professional development was introduced on 1st November 1992. The requirements are set out in the Training Regulations 1990, relevant extracts from which appear in Annex 2F.

2. The ways in which the requirements can be satisfied are set out in the code of practice for compliance with continuing professional development obligations (see Annex 2G).

3. The requirements of the scheme apply to solicitors who are in legal practice or employment, whether or not they hold a practising certificate.

4. From 1st November 1994, the scheme will apply to solicitors admitted on or after 1st November 1982. From 1st November 1998 the scheme will apply to the whole profession.

2.07   Notification of practice address(es)

Principle

'**For the purpose of facilitating the service of notices and other documents, every solicitor who has in force, or has applied for, a practising certificate shall give notice to the Society of any change in his place or places of business before the expiration of 14 days from the date on which the change takes effect.**'

Solicitors Act 1974, section 84(1)

2.08   Practice rules

Principle

Under section 31 of the Solicitors Act 1974 the Council of the Law Society

makes rules governing the professional practice, conduct and discipline of solicitors.

Commentary

1. Section 31 is set out in Annex 2A.

2. The Solicitors' Practice Rules 1990 (see Annex 1A), made by the Council with the concurrence of the Master of the Rolls, govern a number of aspects of solicitors' practice, as follows:

    (a) *Rule 1* sums up the basic principles of conduct governing the professional practice of solicitors (see Principle 1.01).

    (b) *Rule 2* deals with publicity, and requires compliance with the Solicitors' Publicity Code 1990 (see Chapter 11 and Annex 11A).

    (c) *Rule 3* deals with the acceptance and the making of introductions and referrals, and requires compliance with the Solicitors' Introduction and Referral Code 1990 (see Chapter 11 and Annex 11B).

    (d) *Rule 4* prohibits solicitors in the employment of a non-solicitor employer from being employed to do professional work for persons other than the employer, except as permitted by the Employed Solicitors Code 1990 (see Chapter 4 and Annex 4A).

    (e) *Rule 5* deals with offering services other than as a solicitor — sometimes known as 'hiving off' (see Chapter 3).

    (f) *Rule 6* prohibits acting for both seller and buyer in a conveyancing transaction, or for both lender and borrower in a private mortgage (see Chapter 24).

    (g) *Rule 7* deals with partnership and with sharing fees generally (see Chapters 3 and 14).

    (h) *Rule 8* prohibits contingency fee arrangements in respect of contentious proceedings (see Chapter 14).

    (i) *Rule 9* prohibits arrangements and associations with claims assessors (see Chapter 11).

    (j) *Rule 10* deals with the receipt of commissions from third parties (see Chapter 15 and Annex 14C).

    (k) *Rule 11* deals with the name of a firm (see Principle 3.10).

    (l) *Rule 12* deals with arrangements in connection with investment business, and governs all solicitors doing investment business, whether or not they have an investment business certificate from the Law Society (see Chapter 26).

    (m) *Rule 13* deals with the supervision and management of solicitors' offices (see Chapter 3).

(n) *Rule 14* deals with structural surveys and formal valuations (see paragraph 25.39 in Chapter 25).

(o) *Rule 15* deals with client care (see Chapter 13).

(p) *Rule 16* deals with cross-border activities in the European Community, and requires compliance with the CCBE Code of Conduct (see Chapter 10 and Annex 10B).

3. The Law Society's guidance on conduct, although not made under statute, is treated as authoritative by the Adjudication and Appeals Committee, the Solicitors' Disciplinary Tribunal and the Court, and is therefore regarded as binding on solicitors (see Principle 1.03). Non-statutory guidance includes the code of practice on the avoidance of race and sex discrimination (see Chapter 7), the written professional standards on information on costs for clients (see Chapter 13), the Principles and Commentaries and other material in the chapters of the Guide, and the Council statements and other guidance in the annexes.

4. If a change in the Solicitors' Practice Rules, or in non-statutory guidance, amounts to an alteration in the rules as to the conduct required of solicitors in exercising a right of audience or right to conduct litigation, the alteration requires to be approved by the Lord Chancellor and the four designated judges under section 29 of the Courts and Legal Services Act 1990.

5. The Solicitors' Overseas Practice Rules 1990, made by the Council with the concurrence of the Master of the Rolls, regulate the professional conduct of solicitors practising as such outside England and Wales (see Chapter 9 and Annex 9A).

6. The Solicitors' Incorporated Practice Rules 1988, made by the Council under section 9 of the Administration of Justice Act 1985 with the concurrence of the Master of the Rolls, regulate incorporated practices (see Chapter 3 and Annex 3C). The Practice Rules, Overseas Practice Rules and Investment Business Rules, as well as non-statutory guidance, apply to a recognised body (incorporated practice) as they apply to a solicitor.

7. The Solicitors' Investment Business Rules 1990, made by the Council with the concurrence of the Master of the Rolls under section 31 of the Solicitors Act 1974 and under paragraph 6 of Schedule 15 to the Financial Services Act 1986, regulate the investment business activities of firms which have been issued with an investment business certificate by the Law Society (see Chapter 26 and Annex 26B).

8. Rule 18(1A) of the Solicitors' Practice Rules 1990 applies the Practice Rules themselves, as well as non-statutory guidance, to registered foreign lawyers practising in a multi-national partnership. The Investment Business Rules apply to a multi-national partnership. An incorporated practice of solicitors and registered foreign lawyers is regulated in the same way as an incorporated practice of solicitors.

2.09   Accounts rules and accountants' reports

Principle

Solicitors are required to comply with accounts rules made under section 32 of the Solicitors Act 1974, and to submit an annual accountant's report under section 34 of the Act.

Commentary

1.   Sections 32-34 of the Solicitors Act 1974 appear in Annex 27A.

2.   Under section 32 the Council, with the concurrence of the Master of the Rolls, has made the Solicitors' Accounts Rules 1991, which are arranged as follows (see Annex 27B):

   (a)   Part I governs client accounts, dealings with clients' money, and accounting records for client accounts and clients' money;

   (b)   Part II governs controlled trust accounts, dealings with controlled trust money, and accounting records for controlled trust accounts;

   (c)   Part III deals with deposit interest, and is designed to ensure that clients receive interest on money held by their solicitor in certain specified circumstances;

   (d)   Part IV deals with the inspection of accounts by the Law Society; and

   (e)   Part V applies the rules to recognised bodies (incorporated practices) and to registered foreign lawyers, as well as exempting certain public officers from the rules.

3.   Other rules made by the Council with the concurrence of the Master of the Rolls to regulate solicitors' accounts are:

   (a)   the Solicitors' Accounts (Legal Aid Temporary Provision) Rule 1992, which deals with the treatment of payments from the Legal Aid Board (see Annex 27C);

   (b)   Rule 13 of the Solicitors' Investment Business Rules 1990, which deals with bills relating to discrete investment business (see Annex 26B);

   (c)   Rules 12-16 of the Solicitors' Overseas Practice Rules 1990 (see Annex 9A), which regulate, in relation to solicitors practising outside England and Wales, dealings with and accounting records for clients' money and trust money, the treatment of deposit interest, the investigation of accounts by the Law Society, and the submission of accountants' reports. Rule 9(3) of the Overseas Practice Rules applies Rules 12-16 to certain solicitors practising through overseas corporations. A model form of accountant's report for overseas practices appears at Annex 27F.

4. Under section 34 of the Solicitors Act 1974 the Council has made the Accountant's Report Rules 1991, which regulate the submission and content of accountants' reports (see Annex 27D).

5. For a detailed commentary on the Solicitors' Accounts Rules and the Accountant's Report Rules, see Chapter 27.

2.10 Compensation Fund rules

Principle

The Council of the Law Society makes rules about the Solicitors' Compensation Fund, which is maintained and administered under section 36 of the Solicitors Act 1974.

Commentary

1. Grants from the Compensation Fund may be made to relieve loss resulting from the dishonesty of a solicitor or a solicitor's employee, or hardship resulting from failure by a solicitor to account for money which has come to his or her hands. Under section 36 (see Annex 29A), the Council has made the Solicitors' Compensation Fund Rules 1975. The rules do not relate to the conduct of solicitors, but to claims for grants out of the Compensation Fund (see Annex 29B). For details of the Compensation Fund scheme, see Chapter 29.

2. Under paragraph 6 of Schedule 2 to the Administration of Justice Act 1985, grants from the Compensation Fund may be made to relieve loss resulting from the dishonesty of an officer or employee of a recognised body (incorporated practice), or hardship resulting from failure by a recognised body to account for money which has come into its possession. Rule 14 of the Solicitors' Incorporated Practice Rules (see Annex 3C) requires each share-owner of a recognised body to execute a 'Compensation Fund covenant' to reimburse the Law Society, if required to do so, in respect of certain grants made out of the Compensation Fund.

3. Under paragraph 6 of Schedule 14 to the Courts and Legal Services Act 1990, grants from the Compensation Fund may be made to relieve loss resulting from the dishonesty of a registered foreign lawyer practising in a multi-national partnership, or hardship resulting from failure of such a registered foreign lawyer to account for money which has come to his or her hands. The Solicitors' Compensation Fund (Foreign Lawyers' Contributions) Rules 1991, made by the Council under paragraph 7 of Schedule 14 with the concurrence of the Master of the Rolls, relate to the contributions required of registered foreign lawyers (see Annex 8B).

2.11   Indemnity rules

Principle

Under section 37 of the Solicitors Act 1974 the Council has made rules which establish the Solicitors' Indemnity Fund, provide for the Fund to be managed and administered by Solicitors Indemnity Fund Limited, and require principals in private practice to make annual contributions to the Fund.

Commentary

1. Under section 37 the Council, with the concurrence of the Master of the Rolls, has made the Solicitors' Indemnity (Enactment) Rules 1992 and the Solicitors' Indemnity Rules 1992 (see Annex 28B).

2. The rules provide for compulsory indemnity cover for solicitors who are principals in private practice, and their employees, against the risks of professional negligence claims. For details of the scheme, see Chapter 28.

3. Solicitors need to consider whether the compulsory cover is sufficient having regard to the requirements of their own practice and whether they need voluntary top-up cover from the commercial market.

4. The Solicitors' Indemnity Rules apply to multi-national partnerships and to registered foreign lawyers in partnership with solicitors as they apply to solicitors' practices and to solicitor principals. For details, see Chapter 28.

5. The Solicitors' Indemnity Rules are applied to recognised bodies (incorporated practices) by the Solicitors' Indemnity (Incorporated Practice) Rules 1991 (see Annex 28C). Rule 13 of the Solicitors' Incorporated Practice Rules 1988 (see Annex 3C) provides for compulsory top-up cover for certain recognised bodies.

6. The Employed Solicitors Code 1990 governs employed solicitors who in the course of their employment act for clients other than the employer. The code contains requirements on professional indemnity cover (see Annex 4A):

    (a) paragraph 1(f) is of general application and requires certain information to be given to clients;

    (b) paragraph 7(a)(v) prescribes the indemnity cover required for law centres, charities and other non-commercial advice services;

    (c) paragraph 8(b) prescribes the indemnity cover required for commercial legal advice services.

7. Rule 17 of the Solicitors' Overseas Practice Rules 1990 prescribes the indemnity cover required by solicitors practising outside England and Wales (see Annex 9A).

2.12   Waivers and other dispensations

Principle

All the rules affecting the conduct of solicitors, apart from the Solicitors' Accounts Rules, contain power for the Council of the Law Society to grant waivers. The Training Regulations also contain a power for the Society to grant waivers. Waivers must be in writing, and may be revoked by the Society.

1. The effect of a waiver is to modify the rule to which it applies so that, subject to the terms of the waiver and any conditions attached to it, the rule does not apply to the solicitor to whom the waiver is granted. Consequently, the Adjudication and Appeals Committee or the Solicitors' Disciplinary Tribunal would be bound by the terms of a waiver when considering any complaint against the solicitor.

2. There are no longer any general waivers of the rules. Most of the former general waivers have been consolidated with the rules, to which reference should be made.

3. For the expiry or continuance of waivers of previous practice rules now repealed, see the Council statement on waivers in Annex 2H.

4. Other dispensations which the Council is empowered to grant under the primary legislation or under the rules include:

    (a) dispensation under section 34(1) of the Solicitors Act 1974 or paragraph 8(1) of Schedule 14 to the Courts and Legal Services Act 1990 from the obligation to submit an accountant's report;

    (b) approval under the Solicitors' Accounts Rules 1991 to draw money from a client account (Rule 8(2)) or controlled trust account (Rule 17);

    (c) approval of the name of a practice under Rule 11 of the Solicitors' Practice Rules 1990, Rule 10 of the Solicitors' Overseas Practice Rules 1990 or Rule 22(4) of the Solicitors' Incorporated Practice Rules 1988.

5. Applications for waivers and other dispensations under the primary legislation or under the rules are normally heard by the Standards and Guidance Committee, the Standards and Guidance Casework Committee or the Indemnity Casework Committee. Applications for waivers of the Training Regulations in respect of continuing professional development are normally heard by the Post-Qualification Casework Committee.

6. For the Council's powers to delegate its functions, see section 79 of the Solicitors Act 1974, which is set out in Annex 2A. For the terms of reference of the Standards and Guidance Committee, see Annex 2B.

2.13   Statutory requirements as to remuneration

Principle

There are important statutory provisions governing solicitors' remuneration.

Commentary

1.   Remuneration for non-contentious business is governed by sections 56-58 and 67-75 of the Solicitors Act 1974, and by the Solicitors' Remuneration Order 1972 (see Annex 14A).

2.   Remuneration for contentious business is governed by sections 59-75 of the Solicitors Act 1974.

3.   See further Chapter 14 and Annex 14F.

2.14   Enforcement of rules and principles

Principle

The rules and principles are binding on all solicitors and are enforceable by the Adjudication and Appeals Committee, the Solicitors' Disciplinary Tribunal and the Court.

Commentary

1.   Complaints of alleged breaches are usually made to the Solicitors Complaints Bureau, but may be made direct to the Solicitors' Disciplinary Tribunal. Any person may make a complaint. For an account of the disciplinary process, see Chapters 30 and 31.

2.   A solicitor who is or may be in breach of the rules may wish to seek advice from:

   (a)   Professional Ethics, which is almost always able to advise on a confidential basis;

   (b)   members of the Solicitors' Assistance Scheme (see Annex 2I) — the addresses of members in or near a solicitor's home town, or in a completely different part of the country, may be obtained from Professional Ethics;

   (c)   the Lawyers' Support Group, who offer help to lawyers who need assistance with an alcohol problem — see the list of useful addresses at the end of the Guide.

3.   The Master of the Rolls hears appeals and applications under a number of statutes, rules and regulations. The Master of the Rolls (Appeals and Applications) Regulations 1991 are set out in full in Annex 2E.

2.15   Right to make a complaint

Principle

A solicitor must not accept instructions which at any stage involve any agreement whereby the Solicitors Complaints Bureau is precluded from investigating the conduct of a solicitor or a solicitor's clerk.

Commentary

1.   It is unbefitting conduct for a solicitor to seek to preclude his or her client or former client from reporting that solicitor's conduct to the SCB.

2.   It is also improper for a solicitor acting for either party to a dispute to accept instructions to offer a settlement on similar terms.

3.   For breaches of undertaking, see also Principle 19.15.

4.   See also the Council statement on solicitors taking defamation proceedings against complainants (Annex 30C).

2.16   The roll of solicitors

Principle

The roll of solicitors of the Supreme Court is kept by the Law Society.

Commentary

1.   Arrangements for the keeping of the roll of solicitors are governed by sections 6-8 of the Solicitors Act 1974, and by the Solicitors (Keeping of the Roll) Regulations 1989 (see Annex 2D) made under section 28 of the Act.

2.   Solicitors who do not hold practising certificates are required to confirm annually that they wish to remain on the roll. The regulations provide for a notice to be sent to such solicitors, who must pay a fee of £15 if they wish to remain on the roll. If such solicitors do not indicate their wish to remain on the roll within a given period, notice of intention to remove the solicitor's name will be given before removal.

Annex 2A

Solicitors Act 1974

sections 1-1A, 12-12A, 13A, 20-22, 23-25, 31 and 79
(as amended by the Courts and Legal Services Act 1990)

---

1. *Qualifications for practising as solicitor*

No person shall be qualified to act as a solicitor unless -

(a)   he has been admitted as a solicitor, and

(b)   his name is on the roll, and

(c)   he has in force a certificate issued by the Society in accordance with the provisions of this Part authorising him to practise as a solicitor (in this Act referred to as a "practising certificate").

1A.   *Practising certificates: employed solicitors*

A person who has been admitted as a solicitor and whose name is on the roll shall, if he would not otherwise be taken to be acting as a solicitor, be taken for the purposes of this Act to be so acting if he is employed in connection with the provision of any legal services -

(a)   by any person who is qualified to act as a solicitor;

(b)   by any partnership at least one member of which is so qualified; or

(c)   by a body recognised by the Council of the Law Society under section 9 of the Administration of Justice Act 1985 (incorporated practices).

12.   *Discretion of Society with respect to issue of practising certificates in special cases*

(1)   Subject to subsections (2) and (3), this section shall have effect in any case where a solicitor applies for a practising certificate -

(a)   for the first time; or

(b)   not having held a practising certificate free of conditions since the date of his admission; or

(c)   when, on what would be the commencement date for the certificate, if it were granted, a period of twelve months or more will have elapsed since he held a practising certificate in force; or

(d)   after the Tribunal has ordered a penalty or costs to be paid by him or that he be reprimanded; or

(e)   after he has been invited by the Society to give an explanation in respect of any matter relating to his conduct and has failed to give an explanation in respect of that matter which the Council regard as sufficient and satisfactory, and has been notified in writing by the Society that he has so failed; or

(ee)   when, having been required by section 34(1) to deliver an accountant's report to the Society, he has not delivered that report within the period allowed by section 34(2); or

(f)   when, having been suspended from practice, the period of his suspension has expired; or

(g)   when, having had his name removed from or struck off the roll, his name has been restored to the roll; or

(h)   while he is an undischarged bankrupt; or

(i)   after having been adjudged bankrupt and discharged or after having entered into a composition with his creditors or a deed of arrangement for the benefit of his creditors; or

(j)   while he is a patient as defined by section 94 of the Mental Health Act 1983 (which relates to the judge's functions in relation to the patient), or while he is a person as to whom powers have been exercised under section 104 of the Mental Health Act 1959 or section 98 of the said Act of 1983 (which relates to the judge's powers in cases of emergency); or

(k)   after having been committed to prison in civil or criminal proceedings; or

(l)   after having had given against him any judgment which involves the payment of money, not being a judgment -

   (i)   limited to the payment of costs; or

   (ii)   as to the whole effect of which upon him he is entitled to indemnity or relief from some other person; or

   (iii) evidence of the satisfaction of which has been produced to the Society.

(2)   Where a practising certificate free of conditions is issued by the Society under subsection (4) to a solicitor in relation to whom this section has effect by reason of any such circumstances as are mentioned in paragraph (d), (e), (ee), (f), (g), (i), (k) or (l) of subsection (1) then, except in the case of any circumstances of whose existence the Society is unaware at the time the certificate is issued, this section shall not thereafter have effect in relation to that solicitor by reason of those circumstances.

(3)   Where a solicitor's practising certificate is suspended by virtue of section 15(1) by reason of his suspension from practice and the suspension of his practising certificate is terminated unconditionally under section 16(4) or (5), then, notwithstanding subsection (1) (f), this section shall not thereafter have effect in relation to that solicitor by reason of that suspension from practice and the expiry of the period of that suspension.

(4)   In any case where this section has effect, the applicant shall, unless the Society or the Master of the Rolls otherwise orders, give to the Society not less than six weeks before he applies for a practising certificate notice of his intention so to apply and subject

to subsections (6) and (7), the Society may in its discretion—

(a)   grant or refuse the application, or

(b)   decide to issue a certificate to the applicant subject to such conditions as the Society may think fit.

(4A) Without prejudice to the generality of subsection (4)(b) -

(a)   conditions may be imposed under that provision for requiring the applicant to take any specified steps that will, in the opinion of the Society, be conducive to his carrying on an efficient practice as a solicitor; and

(b)   conditions may be so imposed (whether for the purpose mentioned in paragraph (a) or otherwise) notwithstanding that they may result in expenditure being incurred by the applicant.

(5)   Where the Society decides to issue a certificate subject to conditions, it may, if it thinks fit, postpone the issue of the certificate pending the hearing and determination of any appeal under section 13(2) (b).

(6)   The Society shall not refuse an application by a solicitor for a practising certificate in a case where this section has effect by reason only -

(a)   that he is applying for the first time; or

(b)   that he has not held a practising certificate free from conditions since the date of his admission;

and, in a case falling within paragraph (b), the certificate shall not be made subject to any conditions binding on the applicant in respect of any period more than three years after the date on which the first practising certificate issued to him had effect.

(7)   Where a solicitor applies for a practising certificate in a case where this section has effect by reason only of any such circumstances as are mentioned in paragraph (h), (k) or (l) of subsection (1) and an appeal has been made to the appropriate court against the order or judgment in question, the Society shall not refuse the application before the determination of that appeal, unless in the opinion of the Society the proceedings on that appeal have been unduly protracted by the appellant or are unlikely to be successful.

12A.   *Additional fee payable by certain solicitors on applying for practising certificates*

(1)   Where a solicitor applies for a practising certificate at a time when section 12 has effect in relation to him by reason of the circumstances mentioned in section 12(1)(ee), he shall pay an additional fee to the Society when making his application.

(2)   The amount of that additional fee -

(a)   shall be fixed by order of the Master of the Rolls made with the concurrence of the Lord Chancellor and the Lord Chief Justice; and

(b)   shall be designed to provide reasonable compensation to the Society for the additional cost of dealing with such applications.

13A. *Imposition of conditions while practising certificates are in force*

(1)　Subject to the provisions of this section, the Society may in the case of any solicitor direct that his practising certificate for the time being in force (his "current certificate") shall have effect subject to such conditions as the Society may think fit.

(2)　The power to give a direction under this section in the case of any solicitor shall be exercisable by the Society at any time during the period for which his current certificate is in force if -

(a)　in the event of an application for a practising certificate being made by him at that time, section 12 would have effect in relation to him by reason of any such circumstances as are mentioned in paragraph (d), (e), (ee), (k) or (l) of subsection (1) of that section; or

(b)　[repealed]

(c)　he has entered into a composition with his creditors or a deed of arrangement for the benefit of his creditors; or

(d)　he has been charged with, or convicted of -

(i)　an offence involving dishonesty or deception; or

(ii)　a serious arrestable offence (as defined by section 116 of the Police and Criminal Evidence Act 1984).

(3)　Subject to subsection (4), the conditions specified in a direction under this section shall have effect as from the time when the solicitor concerned is notifed of the Society's decision to give the direction.

(4)　The Society may, if it thinks fit, provide in a direction under this section that the conditions specified in the direction shall not have effect pending the hearing and determination of any appeal under subsection (6).

(5)　Where there is pending against any judgment or order an appeal by a solicitor which, if successful, would result in subsection (2) no longer being applicable to him, the Society shall not give a direction under this section in his case so long as the appeal is pending, unless in the opinion of the Society the proceedings on that appeal have been unduly protracted by him or are unlikely to be successful.

This subsection does not apply to the exercise of the Society's powers under this section by virtue of subsection (2)(d).

(6)　A solicitor in whose case a direction is given under this section may appeal to the Master of the Rolls against the decision of the Society within one month of being notified of it.

(7)　On an appeal under subsection (6), the Master of the Rolls may -

(a)　affirm the decision of the Society; or

(b)　direct that the appellant's current certificate shall have effect subject to such conditions as the Master of the Rolls thinks fit; or

(c)　by order revoke the direction; or

(d)　make such other order as he thinks fit.

(8)　Subsection (4A) of section 12 shall apply for the purposes of subsection (1) of this section as it applies for the purposes of subsection (4)(b) of that section.

20. *Unqualified person not to act as solicitor*

(1)   No unqualified person shall -

(a)   act as a solicitor, or as such issue any writ or process, or commence, prosecute or defend any action, suit or other proceeding, in his own name or in the name of any other person, in any court of civil or criminal jurisdiction; or

(b)   act as a solicitor in any cause or matter, civil or criminal, to be heard or determined before any justice or justices or any commissioners of Her Majesty's revenue.

(2)   Any person who contravenes the provisions of subsection (1):

(a)   shall be guilty of an offence and liable on conviction on indictment to imprisonment for not more than two years or to a fine or to both; and

(b)   shall be guilty of contempt of the court in which the action, suit, cause, matter or proceeding in relation to which he so acts is brought or taken and may be punished accordingly.

(3)   A person exempted from the provisions of section 23(1) by virtue of section 23(2) or (3) of this Act or section 55 of the Courts and Legal Services Act 1990 may, in any non-contentious or common form probate business, apply for a grant of probate or for letters of administration or oppose such an application without committing an offence under this section.

(4)   In subsection (3) "non-contentious or common form probate business" has the same meaning as in section 128 of the Supreme Court Act 1981.

[NOTES

1.   Section 27(10) of the Courts and Legal Services Act 1990 provides that section 20 shall not apply in relation to any act done in the exercise of a right of audience and section 28(6) of that Act provides that section 20 shall not apply in relation to any act done in the exercise of a right to conduct litigation.

2.   Section 9(3) of the Administration of Justice Act 1985 provides that, notwithstanding section 24(2) of the Solicitors Act 1974, section 20 shall not apply to a recognised body (i.e. an incorporated practice recognised under section 9).]

21. *Unqualified person not to pretend to be a solicitor*

Any unqualified person who wilfully pretends to be, or takes or uses any name, title, addition or description implying that he is, qualified or recognised by law as qualified to act as a solicitor shall be guilty of an offence and liable on summary conviction to a fine not exceeding the fourth level on the standard scale.

22. *Unqualified person not to prepare certain instruments*

(1)   Subject to subsections (2) and (2A), any unqualified person who directly or indirectly -

(a)   draws or prepares any instrument of transfer or charge for the purposes of the Land Registration Act 1925, or makes any application or lodges any document for registration under that Act at the registry, or

(b)   draws or prepares any other instrument relating to real or personal estate, or any legal proceeding,

shall, unless he proves that the act was not done for or in expectation of any fee, gain or reward, be guilty of an offence and liable on summary conviction to a fine not exceeding level 3 on the standard scale.

(2)   Subsection (1) does not apply to -

(a)   a barrister or duly certificated notary public;

(aa)   a registered trade mark agent drawing or preparing any instrument relating to any invention, design, trade mark or service mark;

(ab)   a registered patent agent drawing or preparing any instrument relating to any invention, design, technical information, trade mark or service mark;

(b)   any public officer drawing or preparing instruments or applications in the course of his duty;

(c)   any person employed merely to engross any instrument, application or proceeding;

and paragraph (b) of that subsection does not apply to a duly certificated solicitor in Scotland.

(2A) Subsection (1) also does not apply to any act done by a person at the direction and under the supervision of another person if -

(a)   that other person was at the time his employer, a partner of his employer or a fellow employee; and

(b)   the act could have been done by that other person for or in expectation of any fee, gain or reward without committing an offence under this section.

(3)   For the purposes of subsection (1)(b), "instrument" includes a contract for the sale or other disposition of land (except a contract to grant such a lease as is referred to in section 54(2) of the Law of Property Act 1925 (short leases)), but does not include -

(a)   a will or other testamentary instrument;

(b)   an agreement not intended to be executed as a deed other than a contract that is included by virtue of the preceding provisions of this subsection;

(c)   a letter or power of attorney; or

(d)   a transfer of stock containing no trust or limitation thereof.

(3A) In subsection (2) -

"registered trade mark agent" has the same meaning as in section 282(1) of the Copyright, Designs and Patents Act 1988; and "registered patent agent" has the same meaning as in section 275(1) of that Act.

(4)   A local Weights and Measures Authority may institute proceedings for an offence under this section.

[NOTES

1.   Section 11(4) of the Administration of Justice Act 1985 provides that section 22(1) shall not apply to any act done by a licensed conveyancer in the course of the provision of any conveyancing services if he is not precluded from providing those services as a licensed conveyancer by any conditions imposed as mentioned in section 16(3)(a) of the Administration of Justice Act 1985.

2.   Section 27(10) of the Courts and Legal Services Act 1990 provides that section 22 shall not apply in relation to any act done in the exercise of a right of audience and section 28(6) of that Act provides that section 22 shall not apply in relation to any act done in the exercise of a right to conduct litigation.

3.   Section 9(3) of the Administration of Justice Act 1985 provides that, notwithstanding section 24(2) of the Solicitors Act 1974, section 22(1) shall not apply to a recognised body (i.e. an incorporated practice recognised under section 9).

4.   Section 9(4) of the Administration of Justice Act 1985 provides that section 22(1) shall not apply to any act done by an officer or employee of a recognised body if -

'(a)   it was done by him at the direction and under the supervision of another person who was at the time an officer or employee of the body; and

(b)   it could have been done by that other person for or in expectation of any fee, gain or reward without committing an offence under the said section 2...'

5.   For the exemption, in certain circumstances, from section 22(1) of a licensed conveyancers' incorporated practice and its officers and employees see section 32(4) and (5) of the Administration of Justice Act 1985.]

23.   *Unqualified person not to prepare papers for probate etc.*

(1)   Subject to subsections (2) and (3), any unqualified person who, directly or indirectly, draws or prepares any papers on which to found or oppose -

(a)   a grant of probate, or

(b)   a grant of letters of administration,

shall, unless he proves that the act was not done for or in expectation of any fee, gain or reward, be guilty of an offence and liable on summary conviction to a fine not exceeding the first level on the standard scale.

(2)   Subsection (1) does not apply to -

(a)   a barrister;

(b)   a duly certificated notary public;

(c)   the Public Trustee;

(d)   the Official Solicitor;

(e)   any institution which -

(i)   is authorised by the Bank of England, under Part I of the Banking Act 1987, to carry on a deposit taking business; and

(ii)   satisfied the conditions mentioned in subsection (2A);

(f)   any building society which -

(i)   is authorised to raise money from its members by the Building Societies Commission under section 9 of the Building Societies Act 1986; and

(ii)   satisfied those conditions;

(g)   any insurance company which -

(i)   is authorised under section 3 or 4 of the Insurance Companies Act 1982; and

(ii)   satisfied those conditions;

(h)   any subsidiary (as defined by section 736(1) of the Companies Act 1985) of a body falling within paragraph (e), (f) or (g) -

(i)   whose business, or any part of whose business, consists of acting as trustee or executor; and

(ii)   which satisfied those conditions.

(2A) The conditions are that the body is a member of, or otherwise subject to, a scheme which -

(a)   has been established (whether or not exclusively) for the purpose of dealing with complaints about the provision of probate services; and

(b)   complies with such requirements as may be prescribed by regulations made by the Lord Chancellor with respect to matters relating to such complaints.

(3)   Subsection (1) also does not apply to -

(a)   any act done by an officer or employee of a body corporate at a time when it is exempt from subsection (1) by virtue of any of paragraphs (e) to (h) of subsection (2) or by virtue of section 55 of the Courts and Legal Services Act 1990 (preparation of probate papers etc); or

(b)   any act done by any person at the direction and under the supervision of another person if -

(i)   that other person was at the time his employer, a partner of his employer or a fellow employee; and

(ii)   the act could have been done by that other person for or in expectation of any fee, gain or reward without committing an offence under this section.

(4)   For the avoidance of doubt, where a person does any act which would constitute an offence under subsection (1) but for an exemption given to him by this section or by or under any other enactment, he shall not be guilty of an offence under section 22 by virtue of having done that act.

[NOTES

1.   Section 55(10) of the Courts and Legal Services Act 1990 states that the provisions of section 23(1) shall not apply to any person to whom exemption from those provisions is granted by an approved body. Section 55(4) provides that 'an approved body' means a professional or other body approved by the Lord Chancellor under Schedule 9 to the 1990 Act.

2.   Section 9(3) of the Administration of Justice Act 1985 provides that, notwithstanding section 24(2) of the Solicitors Act 1974, section 23(1) shall not apply to a recognised body (i.e. an incorporated practice recognised under section 9).

3.   Section 9(4) of the Administration of Justice Act 1985 provides that section 23(1) shall not apply to any act done by an officer or employee of a recognised body if -

'(a)   it was done by him at the direction and under the supervision of another person who was at the time an officer or employee of the body; and

(b)   it could have been done by that other person for or in expectation of any fee, gain or reward without committing an offence under the said section 23.']

24.   *Application of penal provisions to body corporate*

(1)   If any act is done by a body corporate, or by any director, officer or servant of a body corporate, and is of such a nature or is done in such a manner as to be calculated to

imply that the body corporate is qualified or recognised by law as qualified to act as a solicitor -

(a)   the body corporate shall be guilty of an offence and liable on summary conviction to a fine not exceeding the fourth level on the standard scale, and

(b)   in the case of an act done by a director, officer or servant of the body corporate, he also shall be guilty of an offence and liable on summary conviction to a fine not exceeding the fourth level of the standard scale.

(2)   For the avoidance of doubt it is hereby declared that in sections 20, 22 and 23 references to unqualified persons and to persons include references to bodies corporate.

[NOTE

Section 9(3) of the Administration of Justice Act 1985 provides that, notwithstanding section 24(2), sections 20, 22(1) and 23(1) shall not apply to a recognised body (i.e. an incorporated practice recognised under section 9) and that nothing in section 24(1) shall apply in relation to such a body.]

25.   *Costs where unqualified person acts as solicitor*

(1)   No costs in respect of anything done by an unqualified person acting as a solicitor shall be recoverable by him, or by any other person, in any action, suit or matter.

(2)   Nothing in subsection (1) shall prevent the recovery of money paid or to be paid by a solicitor on behalf of a client in respect of anything done by the solicitor while acting for the client without holding a practising certificate in force if that money would have been recoverable if he had held such a certificate when so acting.

(3)   For the avoidance of doubt, where a person does an act which would be an offence under section 23 were it not for the provisions of section 54 or 55 of the Courts and Legal Services Act 1990, this section does not apply in relation to that act.

[NOTE

Section 27(10) of the Courts and Legal Services Act 1990 provides that section 25 shall not apply in relation to any act done in the exercise of a right of audience and section 28(6) of that Act provides that section 25 shall not apply in relation to any act done in the exercise of a right to conduct litigation.]

31.   *Rules as to professional practice, conduct and discipline*

(1)   Without prejudice to any other provision of this Part the Council may, if they think fit, make rules, with the concurrence of the Master of the Rolls, for regulating in respect of any matter the professional practice, conduct and discipline of solicitors.

(2)   If any solicitor fails to comply with rules made under this section, any person may make a complaint in respect of that failure to the Tribunal.

(3)   Where, under Schedule 4 to the Courts and Legal Services Act 1990 (approval of certain rules in connection with the grant of rights of audience or rights to conduct litigation), the Master of the Rolls approves any rule made under this section he shall be taken, for the purposes of this section, to have concurred in the making of that rule.

(4)   Subsection (3) shall have effect whether or not the rule required to be approved under Schedule 4 of the Act of 1990.

[NOTES

1.   By virtue of section 89(3) of the Courts and Legal Services Act 1990 the power to make rules under section 31 is also exercisable in relation to registered foreign lawyers.

2.   By virtue of section 9(2)(f) of the Administration of Justice Act 1985 rules made under section 31 may be made to have effect in relation to a recognised body (i.e. an incorporated practice recognised under section 9).]

79.   *Committees and sub-committees*

(1)   Subject to any provision to the contrary made by or under any enactment, the Council may arrange for any of its functions (other than reserved functions) to be discharged by -

(a)   a committee of the Council;

(b)   a sub-committee of such a committee; or

(c)   an individual (whether or not a member of the Society's staff).

(2)   Where, by virtue of subsection (1)(a), any of the Council's functions may be discharged by a committee, the committee may arrange for the discharge of any of those functions by -

(a)   a sub-committee of that committee; or

(b)   an individual (whether or not a member of the Society's staff).

(3)   Where, by virtue of subsection (1) or (2), any of the Council's functions may be discharged by a sub-committee, the sub-committee may arrange for the discharge of any of those functions by a member of the Society's staff.

(4)   Subsections (2) and (3) shall have effect subject to any contrary direction given by the Council.

(5)   Subject to any direction given by the Council under subsection (4), subsection (3) shall have effect subject to any contrary direction given by the committee concerned.

(6)   Any power given by subsection (1), (2) or (3) may be exercised so as to impose restrictions or conditions on the body or individual by whom the functions concerned are to be discharged.

(7)   A committee of the Council, and any sub-committee of such a committee, discharging functions delegated under this section may include persons other than-

(a)   members of the Council;

(b)   members of the Society;

(c)   solicitors.

(8)   The majority of the members of any such committee or sub-committee may be persons who may be included by virtue of subsection (7).

(9)   The number and term of office of the members of such a committee and the number of those members necessary to form a quorum, shall be fixed by the Council.

(10)   Subject to any restriction or condition imposed by the Council, the number and term of office of the members of such a sub-committee and the number of those members necessary to form a quorum, shall be fixed by the committee concerned.

(11) The validity of any proceedings of such a committee or sub-committee shall not be affected by any casual vacancy among its members.

(12) In this section "reserved functions" means -

(a)   the function of making rules or regulations under sections 2, 31, 32, 34, 36 or 37 or under section 9 of the Administration of Justice Act 1985 (incorporated practices);

(b)   the function of setting fees or financial contributions under paragraph 2(1) of Schedule 2 or section 8(2) or under paragraph 6 of Schedule 2 to the Administration of Justice Act 1985.

Annex 2B

Law Society's General Regulations 1987

regulation 41 — terms of reference of Standards and Guidance Committee
(with consolidated amendments to 5th November 1992)

The terms of reference of the Standards and Guidance Committee are:

(1)   to formulate policy in all matters relating to professional conduct, standards and quality of work;

(2)   to keep under review the Solicitors' Practice Rules, the Solicitors' Publicity Code, the Solicitors' Introduction and Referral Code, the Solicitors' Accounts Rules, the Solicitors' Trust Accounts Rules, the Accountant's Report Rules, the Solicitors' Accounts (Deposit Interest) Rules, the Solicitors' Compensation Fund Rules, the Solicitors' Compensation Fund (Foreign Lawyers' Contributions) Rules, the Solicitors' Investment Business Rules, the Solicitors' Overseas Practice Rules, the Solicitors' Incorporated Practice Rules, the Employed Solicitors Code, the Solicitors' Indemnity (Incorporated Practice) Rules and the Solicitors' Indemnity Rules (and any other subordinate legislation in force relating to the professional practice, conduct and discipline of solicitors, registered foreign lawyers and recognised bodies) together with standards of professional conduct and to be responsible for updating "The Professional Conduct of Solicitors";

(3)   to provide guidance and advice to members of the profession and to members of the public in all matters within the terms of reference of the Committee, the Adjudication Committee or the Investigation Committee;

(4)   to deal with all:

(a)   applications for waivers under the Solicitors' Practice Rules, the Solicitors' Indemnity Rules, the Solicitors' Overseas Practice Rules, the Solicitors' Investment Business Rules and the Solicitors' Incorporated Practice Rules;

(b)   applications under Rule 8(2) of the Solicitors' Accounts Rules;

(c)   applications under Rule 11 of the Solicitors' Practice Rules, Rule 10 of the Solicitors' Overseas Practice Rules and Rule 22(4) of the Solicitors' Incorporated Practice Rules;

(d)   applications under Rule 16(1) of the Solicitors' Overseas Practice Rules; and

(e)   applications for dispensation under section 34(1) Solicitors Act 1974 and paragraph 8(1) of Schedule 14 to the Courts and Legal Services Act 1990;

(5)   to implement, supervise and keep under review the operation and management of:

(a)   compulsory professional indemnity cover for solicitors, registered foreign lawyers and recognised bodies; and

(b)   other indemnity cover for solicitors ancillary to compulsory professional indemnity cover;

(6)   to keep under review all other matters relating to professional indemnity cover;

(7)   to keep under review the issue of remuneration certificates under the Solicitors' Remuneration Order 1972 and under Rule 8(7)(c) of the Matrimonial Causes (Costs) Rules 1979;

(8)   to review from time to time the rules of professional conduct governing professional practitioners (whether in the legal profession or not) who are not solicitors in England and Wales;

(9)   to exercise the powers conferred by Rules 4 and 5 of the Solicitors' Investment Business Rules 1990 to issue or refuse to issue, suspend, withdraw or impose conditions on certificates of authorisation issued by the Law Society under the Financial Services Act 1986 in circumstances where it appears that there is no issue of conduct;

(10)   to exercise the powers of the Council under Rule 14 of the Solicitors' Investment Business Rules 1988;

(11)   to exercise the powers of the Council under sections 12(1)(a) and 12(1)(c) Solicitors Act 1974;

(12)   to deal with all notices of application for restoration to the Roll of names of former solicitors under the provisions of section 8(2) Solicitors Act 1974;

(13)   to keep the Roll of solicitors under section 6 Solicitors Act 1974 and to compile and maintain records and statistical information relating to the solicitors' profession generally and to each individual solicitor whether a member of the Society or not;

(14)   to keep under review the issue of practising certificates;

(15)   to remove from the Roll the names of solicitors who make application under the provision of section 8(1) Solicitors Act 1974, consulting as appropriate with the Adjudication and Appeals Committee;

(16)   to exercise the powers of the Council under the Keeping of the Roll Regulations made under section 28(3A) Solicitors Act 1974;

(17)   to keep under review the administrative procedures for dealing with accountants' reports;

(18)   to approve qualifications for surveyors and valuers for the purposes of Rule 14 of the Solicitors' Practice Rules 1990;

(19)   to maintain a register of foreign lawyers for the purposes of section 89 of the Courts and Legal Services Act 1990 and deal with all applications for registration thereunder;

(20)   to determine under paragraph 2(2) of Schedule 14 to the Courts and Legal Services Act 1990 whether a legal profession is one which is so regulated as to make it appropriate for solicitors to enter into multi-national partnerships with members of the profession and for members of that profession to be officers of recognised bodies;

(21) to deal with all applications for registration under paragraph 2(2) of Schedule 14 to the Courts and Legal Services Act 1990;

(22) under paragraph 2(3) of Schedule 14 to the Courts and Legal Services Act 1990 to impose conditions upon the registration of foreign lawyers at initial registration;

(23) to cancel the registration of any person in the register of foreign lawyers in accordance with paragraph 3(4) of Schedule 14 to the Courts and Legal Services Act 1990, or upon his or her becoming ineligible under section 89(1) of the Act for inclusion in the register, or where on an application for a renewal of registration he or she has failed to comply with the application requirements under paragraph 2(1) and (4)(b) of Schedule 14 to the Act;

(24) to exercise all the powers of the Council and the Society under the Solicitors' Incorporated Practice Rules (except Rules 10 and 15(g));

(25) to approve from time to time forms required under Rule 12(3) of the Solicitors' Practice Rules 1990, the Accountant's Report Rules 1986 and 1991, the Solicitors' Overseas Practice Rules 1990, section 89 of and Schedule 14 to the Courts and Legal Services Act 1990, the Foreign Lawyers Registration Regulations 1991, the Solicitors' Indemnity Rules 1991 and Rules 4(1), 4(4) and 10(5)(a) of the Solicitors' Investment Business Rules 1990; and

(26) to exercise the powers of the Council under the Solicitors' Accounts Rules in relation to the inspection of solicitors' accounts for the purpose of monitoring compliance and to keep the exercise of these powers under review.

Annex 2C

Practising Certificate Regulations 1976

Made on the 25th May 1976 by the Master of the Rolls with the concurrence of the Lord Chancellor and the Lord Chief Justice under section 28 of the Solicitors Act 1974.

Part I — Introductory

1. These Regulations may be cited as the Practising Certificate Regulations 1976, and shall come into force on 1st September 1976, on which date the Practising Certificate Regulations 1966 and any amendments thereto shall cease to have effect.

2. (1) The Interpretation Act, 1889, shall apply to the interpretation of these Regulations as it applies to the interpretation of an Act of Parliament.

(2) In these Regulations "applicant" means an applicant for a practising certificate, "the Society" means The Law Society and a form referred to by number means the form so numbered in the Schedule of these Regulations.

Part II — Application for practising certificates

3. Every applicant shall deliver at the Society's Hall, either by post or in person or by his agent, a written application in Form PCR1, correctly completed by the applicant and signed by him personally:

Provided that on receipt of a statutory declaration in Form PCR2 the Society may at its discretion on the ground of the illness or absence abroad of the applicant or on any other ground deemed by the Society to be sufficient, either unconditionally or subject to such conditions as the Society may think fit, dispense with the necessity for personal signature by the applicant and accept an application signed by a partner of his or by some other competent person approved by the Society.

4. When the application is delivered there shall at the same time be paid to the Society:

    (a)   the fee payable in respect of the certificate under section 11(1) of the Solicitors Act 1974; and

    (b)   any annual contribution to the Compensation Fund and any special levy payable by the applicant under paragraph 2 of Schedule 2 to the Solicitors Act 1974.

Part III — Form and issue of practising certificate

5.　　Every practising certificate shall be in Form PCR3 duly endorsed with any conditions imposed on its grant by the Council of the Society.

6.　　Every practising certificate shall be sent by post to the applicant at the place of business first named by him in his application or to such other address as he may state in writing to the Society.

Part IV — Notice of intention to apply for practising certificate in special cases

7. (1) Subject to paragraph (2) and (3) of this Regulation and except where the Society or the Master of the Rolls otherwise orders, a solicitor to whom section 12(1) of the Solicitors Act 1974 applies, shall, not less than six weeks before applying for a practising certificate, give notice of his intended application by delivering at the Society's Hall, either by post or in person or by his agent:

(a)　　a certificate of fitness in Form PCR4 completed by two practising solicitors to whom the applicant is personally known and of whom only one may be his partner, former partner, employer, or fellow-employee and neither shall be his relative, employee, fellow-employee junior in rank or a person to whom the said section 12(1) applies;

(b)　　a notice in Form PCR5;

(c)　　if the said section 12(1) applies to the applicant by virtue of paragraph (h) or (i) thereof, a completed questionnaire in Form PCR6 or Form PCR7 as appropriate;

(d)　　if the said section 12(1) applies to the applicant by virtue of paragraph (j) thereof, an office copy of any order, direction or authority made or given in relation to the applicant under Part VIII of the Mental Health Act 1959.

(2)　　A solicitor to whom the said section 12(1) applies who wishes to obtain leave to give less than six weeks' notice of his intention to apply for a practising certificate must include in Form PCR5 a statement of the grounds on which he seeks such leave.

(3)　　The Society may dispense with compliance with paragraph (1)(a) of this Regulation in such cases and to such extent as it considers appropriate.

Part V — Variation to the forms

8.　　The forms set out in the Schedule to these Regulations shall be used wherever applicable, with such variations as the Master of the Rolls may from time to time require for the purpose of giving effect to these Regulations and to the provisions of the Solicitors Act 1974 relating to practising certificates.

SCHEDULE

[Note: The Schedule does not appear in this Annex as the forms contained therein are regularly updated and would soon be out of date. Current forms are available from the Practising Certificates Section.]

Annex 2D

Solicitors (Keeping of the Roll) Regulations 1989

(with consolidated amendments to 1st February 1991)

Made on the 17th January 1989 by the Master of the Rolls with the concurrence of the Lord Chancellor and the Lord Chief Justice under section 28 of the Solicitors Act 1974 as amended by section 8 and Schedule 1 paragraph 8 of the Administration of Justice Act 1985.

Part I — Preliminary

1.   These Regulations may be cited as the Solicitors (Keeping of the Roll) Regulations 1989 and shall come into effect on 1st February 1989.

2.   The Interpretation Act 1978 applies to the interpretation of these Regulations and, unless the context otherwise requires, expressions defined there or in the Solicitors Act 1974 have the same meanings when used in the Regulations.

3.   In the Regulations, a form referred to by letter and number means the form so lettered and numbered in the Schedule hereto.

Part II — Annual Enrolment

4.   Not later than the first day of April in every year, the Secretary-General may enquire in Form KR1 or in a form to like effect of every solicitor without a practising certificate whether that solicitor wishes to have his name retained on the Roll and require that solicitor to pay a fee of £15.00 in respect of retention of that solicitor's name on the Roll provided that no such fee shall be payable by any solicitor whose name has been on the Roll for fifty years, or for such shorter period as the Society, with the concurrence of the Master of the Rolls, may determine.

5.   The Society may remove from the Roll the name of any solicitor who replies on Form KR1 stating that he does not wish to have his name retained on the Roll or who applies by way of Form KR2 or in a form to the like effect.

6.   Subject to Regulation 7, the Society may remove from the Roll the name of a solicitor who fails, within 56 days of the sending to him by the Secretary-General of Form KR1, or a form to like effect, to return to the Society Form KR1 duly completed and to pay the fee.

7. The name of any solicitor shall not be removed from the Roll in accordance with Regulation 6 above unless:

(a) The Society is satisfied that there are no outstanding complaints against the solicitor concerning his professional conduct and that there are no proceedings pending against him before the Supreme Court or the Solicitors' Disciplinary Tribunal; and

(b) 21 days have elapsed following the date, whichever is the latest, of

(i) the sending by the Secretary-General to the solicitor of Form KR6 or a form to like effect giving notice of intention to remove the solicitor's name from the Roll; and

(ii) the publication by the Society in the Law Society's Gazette of notice of intention to remove the solicitor's name from the Roll; and

(iii) the display in the Society's Hall of notice of intention to remove the solicitor's name from the Roll.

8. Upon the removal from the Roll of the name of any solicitor in accordance with this Part, the Secretary-General shall give that former solicitor notice in Form KR3 or in a form to like effect and cause similar notice to be published in the London Gazette and the Law Society's Gazette.

9. The Society may remove from the Roll the name of any solicitor who has died.

10. Service of all notices and other documents under this Part shall be effected in accordance with the provisions of section 84 of the Solicitors Act 1974 or to the last known address held by the Society.

Part III — Restoration of Name on the Roll

11. An application to the Society by a former solicitor whose name has been removed from the Roll by virtue of these Regulations that his name be restored to the Roll shall be made by way of Form KR4 or in a form to the like effect and the applicant shall pay to the Society the fee prescribed by the Council under the provisions of Section 8 of the Solicitors Act 1974 as amended by Schedule 1 paragraph 3 of the Administration of Justice Act 1985.

Part IV — Change of Name on the Roll

12. Where the name of a solicitor is changed in consequence:

(a) in the case of a woman, of marriage; or

(b) in any case of the acquisition of a title,

the Society may make the appropriate change to the Roll upon production to the Society of evidence of the change which is satisfactory to the Society.

13. (a) An application by a solicitor that his name be changed upon the Roll in circumstances other than those mentioned in Regulation 12 shall be made to the Society by way of Form KR5 or in a form to the like effect.

(b) The application shall be supported by a Deed Poll or a statutory declaration by the applicant providing satisfactory evidence of the change of name.

14.   Upon receipt of an application under Regulations 12 and 13 the Society shall:

(a)   display in the Society's Hall and make public in such other manner as the Society thinks fit particulars of the applicant, the nature of his application, his present private and business addresses, the date of his admission and every address at which he formerly practised as a solicitor;

(b)   give notice of such particulars to any solicitor or firm of solicitors with whom the applicant might in the opinion of the Society be confused if the proposed change were made.

Part V — Appeal to the Master of the Rolls

15.   Any person aggrieved by the removal of his name from the Roll or refusal by the Society to grant his application for removal of his name from the Roll, or restoration of his name to the Roll or change of his name on the Roll under these Regulations may, within 28 days of the notice of the Society's decision, appeal to the Master of the Rolls in accordance with the Regulations as to Applications and Appeals to the Master of the Rolls 1964.

SCHEDULE — (FORMS)

FORM KR 1 — Enquiry as to Retention of Name on the Roll

[Form KR1 is sent out to solicitors by the Law Society and is not reproduced here.]

Solicitors (Keeping of the Roll) Regulations 1989 (as amended)

FORM KR 2   Regulation 5

Application to the Law Society for Removal of Name
at Solicitor's own Request

I,   (a)   of (b)

hereby apply to the Society that my name be removed from the roll.

1.   I was admitted a solicitor on the.............................day of.........................(c).

2.   I wish my name to be removed from the roll.

3.   I am not aware of any disciplinary proceedings brought or to be brought against me in my capacity of solicitor and do not know of any cause for such proceedings to be brought and I am not in breach of any of the rules.

I solemnly and sincerely declare that the facts set out herein and in the replies to any questionnaire lodged herewith are true.

And I make this solemn declaration conscientiously believing the same to be true and by virtue of the Statutory Declarations Act 1835.

DECLARED at

on the..day of ....19........

Before me,

                        Solicitor/Commissioner for Oaths

(a)   Full name of applicant

(b)   Address of applicant

(c)   Date of admission

FORM KR 3 — Notice of Removal of Name from the Roll

[Form KR3 is sent out to former solicitors by the Law Society and is not reproduced here.]

Solicitors (Keeping of the Roll) Regulations 1989 (as amended)

FORM KR 4 Regulation 11

Application to the Law Society to Enter on the Roll of Solicitors a Name Previously Removed by Virtue of these Regulations

I, (a) of (b)

hereby apply to the Society that my name be entered on the roll of solicitors (the roll).

1. I was admitted a solicitor on the (c) ....day of ....19..........

2. On the (d)...........day of ....19 .... my name was removed from the roll.

3. My name was removed from the roll (e)

    (i) at my own request; or

    (ii) because I failed to reply to a request under Regulation 4 of the above Regulations; or

    (iii) because I failed to pay the prescribed fee under Regulation 4.

4. I wish my name to be restored to the roll for the following reasons: (f)

I solemnly and sincerely declare that the facts set out herein and in the replies to any questionnaire lodged herewith are true.

And I make this solemn declaration conscientiously believing the same to be true and by virtue of the Statutory Declarations Act 1835.

DECLARED at

on the...day of ....19........

Before me,

Solicitor/Commissioner for Oaths

(a) Full name of applicant
(b) Address of applicant
(c) Date of admission
(d) Date on which name was removed from the roll
(e) Delete whichever is not applicable
(f) State reasons for applying for restoration

Footnote — For applicants for restoration after striking-off, see s.7 of the Solicitors Act 1974 and The Solicitors (Disciplinary Proceedings) Rules 1985.

Solicitors (Keeping of the Roll) Regulations 1989 (as amended)

FORM KR 5   **Regulation 12 & 13**

Application to the Law Society for Change of Name on the Roll

I,   (a)   of (b)

hereby apply to the Society that my name be changed on the roll of solicitors (the roll).

1.   My name is at present shown on the roll as (c)...

2.   My name as I desire it to be shown on the roll in future is (d) ....

3.   I am at present practising [under the style of ....] and intend to [continue so to do] [alter such style to..](e).

4.   I was admitted as a solicitor on (f) ....

5.   My place(s) of business has/have been at (g) ....and my proposed business address(es) is/are (h) ....

6.   My private address(es) is/are...

7.   I (enclose with this application) (shall produce to the Society before the Society shall effect any change of name upon the roll) the following evidence of change of name:

(i)...

I solemnly and sincerely declare that the facts set out herein and in the replies to any questionnaire lodged herewith are true.

And I make this solemn declaration conscientiously believing the same to be true and by virtue of the Statutory Declarations Act 1835.

DECLARED at

on the..day of ....19........

Before me,

                    Solicitor/Commissioner for Oaths

(a)	Full name of applicant	(f)	Date of admission
(b)	Address of applicant	(g)	State all past and present business
(c)	Full name of applicant as shown on the roll		addresses where practicable
(d)	Full name of applicant as desired to be shown on the roll in future	(h)	State proposed business address
		(i)	Complete paragraph specifying evidence
(e)	Strike out words in square brackets which are not applicable and complete as necessary		of change of name being either a deed poll or a statutory declaration by the applicant

---

FORM KR 6 — Notice of Intention to Remove Name from the Roll

[Form KR6 is sent out to solicitors by the Law Society and is not reproduced here.]

Annex 2E

Master of the Rolls (Appeals and Applications) Regulations 1991

Dated 14th January 1991

Made by the Master of the Rolls under sections 8(5), 28(5), 41(5) and 49(7) of the Solicitors Act 1974, Schedule 2 paragraph 2(4) of the Administration of Justice Act 1985 and Schedule 14 paragraph 17(4) of the Courts and Legal Services Act 1990, and to provide the procedure for appeals and applications under the Law Society's Training Regulations 1989, the Law Society's Training Regulations 1990 and the Law Society's Qualified Lawyers Transfer Regulations 1990.

Part I — Preliminary

1. (i) Save as hereinafter provided these regulations come into force on the 1st day of February 1991, whereupon the regulations as to applications and appeals to the Master of the Rolls dated 26th February 1964, 29th July 1966 and 1st May 1975 cease to have effect.

(ii) Insofar as these regulations apply to rights of application under the Training Regulations 1990 these regulations shall not come into force until the coming into force of the Training Regulations 1990.

(iii) Insofar as these regulations apply to appeals under Schedule 14 of the Courts and Legal Services Act 1990 these regulations shall not come into force until the coming into force of section 89 of the said Act.

2. (i) The Interpretation Act 1978 applies to these regulations in the same manner as it applies to an Act of Parliament.

(ii) In these regulations, unless the context otherwise requires:

(a) "the Act" means the Solicitors Act 1974;

(b) "the Council" means the Council of the Law Society;

(c) "Master of the Rolls" includes any judge of the Supreme Court appointed to exercise the relevant functions of the Master of the Rolls under section 73 of the Courts and Legal Services Act 1990;

(d) "the Society" means the Law Society;

(e) "the Tribunal" means the Solicitors' Disciplinary Tribunal.

Part II — Scope of the regulations and powers of the Master of the Rolls

3.   These regulations apply to appeals and applications made to the Master of the Rolls in the following circumstances:

(i)   an application under regulation 7(6)(ii) of the Training Regulations 1989 or regulation 6(4)(ii) of the Training Regulations 1990 in respect of a decision of the Society upon an application for review of its decision to refuse to issue a certificate of enrolment; such application to be made within three months of the applicant receiving notification of the Society's decision upon the application for review; in respect of which application the Master of the Rolls is empowered by the said regulation to:

(a)   affirm the decision of the Society; or

(b)   direct the Society to issue a certificate of enrolment to the applicant;

(ii)   an application under regulation 62(3)(ii) of the Training Regulations 1989 in respect of a decision of the Society upon an application for review of its decision under regulation 62(2) to:

(a)   cancel enrolment;

(b)   prohibit entry into articles;

(c)   refuse to register articles;

(d)   discharge articles;

(e)   prohibit attendance at a recognised course for the Solicitors' First Examination or the Final Examination;

(f)   prohibit an attempt at any examination the applicant is required to pass pursuant to regulation 60 or 61 of the said regulations; or

(g)   oppose admission as a solicitor;

such appeal to be made within three months of the applicant receiving notification of the Society's decision upon the application for review;

in respect of which application the Master of the Rolls is empowered by regulation 62(3)(ii) of the said regulations to:

(a)   affirm the decision of the Society; or

(b)   make such other order as the Master of the Rolls thinks fit;

(iii)   an application under regulation 62(3)(iv) of the Training Regulations 1989 in respect of a decision of the Society on an application for the removal of a prohibition or sanction imposed under regulation 62(2) of the said regulations;

such application to be made within three months of the applicant receiving notification of the Society's decision on the application;

in respect of which application the Master of the Rolls is empowered by regulation 62(3)(iv) of the said regulations to:

(a)   affirm the decision of the Society; or

(b)   make such other order as the Master of the Rolls thinks fit;

(iv)   an application under regulation 22(3)(ii) of the Training Regulations 1990 in respect of a decision of the Society upon an application for review of its decision under regulation 22(2) of the said regulations to:

(a)   cancel enrolment;

(b)   prohibit entry into a training contract;

(c)   refuse to register a training contract;

(d)   discharge a training contract;

(e)   prohibit attendance at a Legal Practice Course;

(f)   prohibit attendance at a Professional Skills Course; or

(g)   oppose admission as a solicitor;

such application to be made within three months of the applicant receiving notification of the Society's decision upon the application for review;

in respect of which application the Master of the Rolls is empowered by regulation 22(3)(ii) of the said regulations to:

(a)   affirm the decision of the Society; or

(b)   make such other order as the Master of the Rolls thinks fit;

(v)   an application under regulation 22(3)(iv) of the Training Regulations 1990 in respect of a decision of the Society on an application for the removal of a prohibition or sanction imposed under regulation 22(2) of the said regulations;

such application to be made within three months of the applicant receiving notification of the Society's decision on the application;

in respect of which application the Master of the Rolls is empowered by regulation 22(3)(iv) of the said regulations to:

(a)   affirm the decision of the Society; or

(b)   make such other order as the Master of the Rolls thinks fit;

(vi)   an application under regulation 16(2)(b) of the Qualified Lawyers Transfer Regulations 1990 in respect of a decision of the Society upon an application for review of its decision under regulation 16(1) of the said regulations to:

(a)   prohibit an attempt at the Qualified Lawyers Transfer Test;

(b)   refuse to recognise periods of employment as compatible with articles of training; or

(c)   oppose admission as a solicitor;

such application to be made within three months of the applicant receiving notification of the Society's decision upon the application for review;

in respect of which application the Master of the Rolls is empowered by regulation 16(2)(b) of the said regulations to:

(a)   affirm the decision of the Society; or

(b)   make such other order as the Master of the Rolls thinks fit;

(vii)   an application under regulation 16(2)(d) of the Qualified Lawyers Transfer Regulations 1990 in respect of a decision of the Society on an application for the removal of a prohibition or sanction imposed under regulation 16(1) of the said regulations;

such application to be made within three months of the applicant receiving notification of the Society's decision on the application;

in respect of which application the Master of the Rolls is empowered by regulation 16(2)(d) of the said regulations to:

(a)   affirm the decision of the Society; or

(b)   make such other order as the Master of the Rolls thinks fit;

(viii) an appeal under regulation 7(3) of the Solicitors' Admission Regulations 1989 in respect of the refusal or failure of the Society to issue a certificate of satisfaction under regulation 7(1) of the said regulations;

in respect of which appeal the Master of the Rolls is empowered by regulation 7(3) of the said regulations to make such recommendations to the Society with regard to the issue of a certificate as the Master of the Rolls thinks fit;

(ix)   an appeal under section 13(1) of the Act in respect of the refusal or neglect of the Society to issue a practising certificate on application duly made otherwise than in a case where section 12 of the Act has effect;

in respect of which appeal the Master of the Rolls is empowered by section 13(1) of the Act to make such order, including an order for the payment of costs by the Society to the applicant or by the applicant to the Society, as may be just;

(x)   an appeal under section 13(2) of the Act in respect of a decision of the Society made in the exercise of its powers under section 12 of the Act to refuse to issue a practising certificate or to issue a certificate subject to conditions, such appeal to be made within one month of the appellant being notified of the Society's decision;

in respect of which appeal the Master of the Rolls is empowered by section 13(4) of the Act to:

(a)   affirm the decision of the Society;

(b)   direct the Society to issue a certificate to the applicant free from conditions or subject to such conditions other than training conditions or indemnity conditions as the Master of the Rolls may think fit;

(c)   direct the Society not to issue a certificate;

(d)   order the suspension of a certificate which has been issued; or

(e)   make such other order as the Master of the Rolls thinks fit;

(xi)   an application under section 12(4) of the Act, for an order that the applicant may be at liberty to give less than six weeks' notice of his or her intention to apply for a practising certificate;

in respect of which appeal the Master of the Rolls may make such order as the Master of the Rolls thinks fit;

(xii) an appeal under section 16(5) of the Act in respect of an order of the Society, on an application under section 16(3) for the termination of the suspension of the appellant's practising certificate, that the suspension be terminated subject to conditions, or the refusal of any such application;

in respect of which appeal the Master of the Rolls is empowered by section 16(5) of the Act to:

(a)   affirm the decision; or

(b)   terminate the suspension either unconditionally or subject to such conditions as the Master of the Rolls may think fit;

(xiii) an appeal under section 13A(6) of the Act in respect of a direction of the Society made in exercise of its powers under section 13A of the Act that the appellant's current practising certificate shall have effect subject to a condition or conditions, such appeal to be made within one month of the appellant being notified of the Society's decision;

in respect of which appeal the Master of the Rolls is empowered by section 13(7) of the Act to:

(a)   affirm the decision of the Society;

(b)   direct that the appellant's current certificate shall have effect subject to such conditions as the Master of the Rolls thinks fit;

(c)   revoke the direction by order; or

(d)   make such other order as the Master of the Rolls thinks fit;

(xiv) an appeal under section 13B(7) of the Act in respect of a direction by the Society made in exercise of its powers under section 13B(1) or (4) of the Act that the appellant's practising certificate be suspended or that the suspension of the appellant's practising certificate be continued, such appeal to be made within one month of the appellant being notified of the direction;

in respect of which appeal the Master of the Rolls is empowered by section 13B(8) of the Act to:

(a)   affirm the suspension;

(b)   direct that the appellant's certificate shall not be suspended but shall have effect subject to such conditions as the Master of the Rolls thinks fit;

(c)   by order revoke the direction; or

(d)   make such other order as the Master of the Rolls thinks fit;

(xv) an appeal under section 41(3) of the Act in respect of a decision of the Society upon an application to employ or remunerate a person disqualified from practising as a solicitor by reason of the fact that:

(a)   his or her name has been struck off the roll;

(b)   he or she is suspended from practising as a solicitor;

(c)   his or her practising certificate is suspended whilst he or she is an undischarged bankrupt; or

(d)   there is a direction in force under section 47(2)(g) of the Act prohibiting the restoration of his or her name to the roll except by order of the Tribunal;

in respect of which appeal the Master of the Rolls is empowered by section 41(3) of the Act to:

(a)   confirm the refusal or the conditions, as the case may be; or

(b)   grant a permission under section 41 of the Act for such period and subject to such conditions as the Master of the Rolls thinks fit;

2E

(xvi) an appeal under section 49(1)(a) of the Act in respect of a decision of the Tribunal upon an application made under section 43(3) of the Act for the revocation of an order made by the Tribunal in respect of the employment of a clerk; such appeal to be made within 28 days from the pronouncement of the findings and order;

in respect of which appeal the Master of the Rolls is empowered by section 49(4) of the Act to make such order as the Master of the Rolls may think fit;

(xvii) an appeal under section 49(1)(a) of the Act in respect of a decision of the Tribunal on an application under section 47(1)(d), (e) or (f) of the Act:

    (a)   by a solicitor who has been suspended from practice for an unspecified period, by order of the Tribunal, for the termination of that suspension;

    (b)   by a former solicitor whose name has been struck off the roll to have his or her name restored to the roll; or

    (c)   by a former solicitor in respect of whom a direction has been given under section 47(2)(g) prohibiting the restoration of his or her name to the roll except by order of the Tribunal, to have his or her name restored to the roll; such appeal to be made within 28 days of the pronouncement of the findings and order;

in respect of which appeal the Master of the Rolls is empowered by section 49(4) of the Act to make such order as the Master of the Rolls may think fit;

(xviii) an appeal under section 8(4) of the Act in respect of a decision of the Society on the application of a former solicitor whose name is not on the roll because it has been removed from it, to have his or her name entered on the roll;

in respect of which appeal the Master of the Rolls may make such order as the Master of the Rolls thinks fit;

(xix) an appeal under regulation 15 of the Solicitors (Keeping of the Roll) Regulations 1989 in respect of the removal of a person's name from the roll, or the refusal by the Society to grant an application for the removal of a solicitor's name from the roll or change of a solicitor's name on the roll in accordance with the said regulations; such appeal to be made within 28 days of the applicant being notified of the Society's decision;

in respect of which appeal the Master of the Rolls may make such order as the Master of the Rolls may think fit;

(xx) an appeal under paragraph 2 of Schedule 2 to the Administration of Justice Act 1985 in respect of the refusal of the Council to grant recognition to a body corporate under section 9 of the said Act, such appeal to be made within one month of the applicant being notified of the Society's decision;

in respect of which appeal the Master of the Rolls is empowered by paragraph 2 of Schedule 2 to the said Act to:

    (a)   direct the Council to grant recognition of the body in question under section 9 of the said Act; or

    (b)   affirm the refusal of the Council;

and to make such order as to the payment of costs by the Council or by that body as the Master of the Rolls thinks fit;

(xxi) an appeal under paragraph 2 of Schedule 2 to the Administration of Justice Act

1985 by virtue of Rule 17(2) of the Solicitors' Incorporated Practice Rules 1988 where recognition of a body corporate under section 9 of the said Act has been neither granted nor refused by the Council within three months of the date on which the application for recognition was received;

in respect of which appeal the Master of the Rolls may make such order as the Master of the Rolls thinks fit;

(xxii) an appeal by a foreign lawyer under paragraph 14 of Schedule 14 to the Courts and Legal Services Act 1990 in respect of:

> (a)   the refusal of the Society to refuse to register or to renew the registration of a foreign lawyer;

> (b)   the refusal of the Society to terminate the suspension of the registration of a foreign lawyer on an application made by the foreign lawyer under paragraph 12 of the said schedule;

> (c)   the failure of the Society to deal with any application by a foreign lawyer for registration, renewal of registration or the termination (under paragraph 12(2) of the said schedule) of a suspension within a reasonable time; or

> (d)   any condition imposed by the Society under paragraph 2(3), 12(2) or 13 of the said schedule;

appeals set out in (a), (b) or (d) above to be brought within the period of one month beginning with the date on which the Society notifies the applicant of its decision on his or her application;

in respect of which appeal the Master of the Rolls is empowered by paragraph 14(3) of the said schedule to make such order as the Master of the Rolls thinks fit;

(xxiii) an appeal under paragraph 17(1)(a) of Schedule 14 to the Courts and Legal Services Act 1990 in respect of:

> (a)   an order of the Tribunal on an application under paragraph 15(2)(d) of the said schedule by a foreign lawyer whose name has been struck off the register by order of the Tribunal to have his or her name restored to the register, or the refusal of any such application; or

> (b)   an order of the Tribunal on an application under paragraph 15(2)(e) of the said schedule by a foreign lawyer whose registration has been suspended for an indefinite period by order of the Tribunal for the termination of that suspension, or the refusal of any such application;

in respect of which appeal the Master of the Rolls may make such order as the Master of the Rolls thinks fit.

4.   These regulations shall not apply to appeals under Rule 6 of the Solicitors' Investment Business Rules 1990, in respect of which the procedures are set out in the said rules.

Part III — Procedure for appeals and applications

5.   The appellant or applicant shall lodge with the Clerk to the Master of the Rolls:

> (a)   a petition signed by the appellant or applicant asking for the appropriate relief

and setting out the circumstances in which the appeal or application is made and the matters of fact upon which the appellant or applicant relies in support of the appeal or application; and

(b)   a statutory declaration verifying the facts stated in the petition; and

(c)   in the case of an appeal against a decision of the Tribunal, copies of all documents referred to at the hearing before the Tribunal;

and shall within two days of lodging the said documents with the Clerk to the Master of the Rolls lodge copies at the Society's offices.

6.   The Master of the Rolls may appoint a time for hearing any appeal or application made to the Master of the Rolls, allowing normally six weeks from the date of the filing of the petition before the appeal or application is heard, but an earlier date may be appointed on request.

7.   On the hearing of the appeal or application the appellant or applicant and the Society may appear in person, or by solicitor or counsel or, in the case of a body corporate, by a director.

8.   On the hearing of the appeal or application the strict rules of evidence shall not apply.

9.   Any order made by the Master of the Rolls shall be signed by the Master of the Rolls and shall be filed with the Society by the Secretary to the Master of the Rolls. The Society shall take such action as is necessary to give effect to the order.

Annex 2F

Training Regulations 1990

extracts relating to continuing professional development

Made on the 12th day of July 1990 as amended on the 31st day of January 1991 and the 9th day of July 1992 by the Council of the Law Society under sections 2 and 80 of the Solicitors Act 1974 with the concurrence of the Lord Chancellor, the Lord Chief Justice and the Master of the Rolls.

PART I — INTRODUCTORY

2. Interpretation and definitions

(3) In these Regulations:

> "continuing professional development" means a course, lecture, seminar or other programme or method of study (whether requiring attendance or not) that is relevant to the needs and professional standards of solicitors and complies with guidance issued from time to time by the Society.

PART VI — CONTINUING PROFESSIONAL DEVELOPMENT (CPD)

35. Application of Part VI

This Part shall apply:

(a) on 1st November 1992 to solicitors admitted after 1st August 1987;

(b) on 1st November 1994 to solicitors admitted on or after 1st November 1982;

(c) on 1st November 1998 to all solicitors.

36. CPD requirement during first three years after admission

A solicitor must in the first three years following admission attend such continuing professional development courses as the Society may prescribe.

37. CPD requirement during first months after admission

A solicitor who has been admitted after this Part has come into force must undertake one hour of continuing professional development for each whole month in legal practice or employment between admission and the next 1st day of November.

38. CPD requirement in first three complete years of legal practice or employment and subsequent years

(1)   A solicitor must in each of the first three complete years in legal practice or employment commencing with the 1st day of November immediately following admission undertake 16 hours of continuing professional development.

(2)   A solicitor must in each subsequent three year period undertake 48 hours of continuing professional development.

39. CPD requirement for solicitors admitted before 3rd November 1989

Solicitors admitted on or before 2nd November 1989 must undertake 48 hours of continuing professional development in each successive three year period the first of which commences as follows:

> (a)   on 1st November 1992 for solicitors admitted on or after 2nd August 1987 and on or before 2nd November 1989;
>
> (b)   on 1st November 1994 for solicitors admitted on or after 1st November 1982 and on or before 1st August 1987;
>
> (c)   on 1st November 1998 for solicitors admitted on or before 31st October 1982.

40. Obligation to keep record

A solicitor must keep a record of such continuing professional development undertaken to comply with these regulations and produce the records to the Society on demand.

41. CPD undertaken pre-admission

A solicitor who has undertaken continuing professional development between the expiry of articles or a training contract and the date of admission shall be credited with the relevant number of hours for the purpose of Regulations 37 and 38 provided that at the time of undertaking the continuing professional development an application for admission in accordance with admission regulations current at that time had been lodged with the Society and a record kept in accordance with Regulation 40.

42. Suspension

If a solicitor does not work for any period in legal practice or employment in England and Wales the application of this Part is suspended for that period.

43. Part-time working

If a solicitor works part-time in legal practice or employment the requirements under this Part are reduced on the basis that in each year one hour of continuing professional development must be undertaken for every two hours per week worked.

PART VII — GENERAL

44. Waiver of Regulations

In any particular case the Society has power to waive in writing any of the provisions of these Regulations and to revoke such waiver.

Annex 2G

Code of practice for compliance with continuing professional development obligations

guidance issued under regulation 2(3) of the Training Regulations 1990

(A)   Solicitors are reminded of their responsibility under Practice Rule 1. Failure to keep up to date with developments in law and practice relating to their work could compromise or impair their proper standard of work contrary to paragraph (e) of that Rule.

(B)   Over and above that general professional responsibility there are compulsory requirements for continuing professional development (CPD) which are set out in the Training Regulations 1990. Details of how these requirements may be satisfied are set out below:

1.   To obtain the maximum advantage from CPD, training activities should be relevant to the current or foreseeable future needs of the solicitor or the firm. Solicitors, and those with training responsibilities in their firms or organisations, are encouraged to review their professional development periodically, using the training record supplied by the Society. Care should be taken that solicitors retain the flexibility, through possession of a range of skills, to move to different areas of work where necessary to meet clients' changing needs.

2.   At least 25% of the requirement to undertake CPD will be undertaken by participation in courses offered by providers authorised by the Society requiring attendance for one hour or more. 'Attendance' means attendance at the complete course. 'Course' includes face-to-face sessions forming part of a course otherwise delivered by an authorised distance-learning provider.

3.   Up to 25% of the requirement may be undertaken by writing law books or articles in legal journals, by legal research which is of use beyond the particular case and results in the production of a precedent, practice note or other form of written guidance, or by production of a dissertation counting towards a qualification recognised by the Law Society, or by undertaking courses offered by an authorised provider delivered by audio/visual means.

4.   Up to 50% of the requirement may be fulfilled by undertaking distance-learning courses offered by authorised providers where there is provision for the answering of enquiries or for discussion. This proportion may be increased to up to 75% where the distance-learning course requires participants' work to be assessed or 100% where the course involves both examination and the production of a dissertation.

THE GUIDE TO THE PROFESSIONAL CONDUCT OF SOLICITORS 1993

'Distance-learning' courses may be delivered by correspondence, video and audio cassettes, television or radio broadcasts and computer based learning programmes.

5.   It is important to appreciate that solicitors most often get into difficulty because of lapses of case or office management and poor communication with clients rather than through ignorance of law or procedure. The Society therefore recommends that at least 25% of the requirement should be fulfilled by undertaking training in practical skills such as communication and other aspects of management. Such training is particularly important before solicitors take on managerial responsibilities.

6.   To count towards compliance the activity should be at an appropriate level and contribute to a solicitor's general professional skill and knowledge and not merely advance a particular fee-earning matter.

7.   In-house training is valuable in that it can be more easily made relevant to the needs of the solicitor or the firm. Account should be taken of the importance of contact with practitioners from other firms thereby increasing awareness of different approaches to similar problems. This is best achieved by attendance at external courses and conferences but may also be achieved by a firm or group of firms inviting outsiders to attend internal training events.

8.   The preparation or delivery of a training course is a very effective means of learning. Solicitors involved in the delivery of any course forming part of the process of qualification or post admission training may count two hours CPD for each hour in which they are involved on the first occasion the course runs. If the course is repeated only the time involved in presenting the course may be counted. Where a solicitor is involved in preparation (whether or not they are involved in the presentation of the course) the solicitor may count the actual time spent in the preparation up to 25% of the requirement to undertake CPD.

9.   For the development of practical skills, courses requiring delegates' active participation, for example through workshops, role-plays, etc., will be more effective than more traditional lecture based courses. Solicitors attending such courses, when noting their training record, may add 25% to the actual time of the course. No specific application to the Society by either the solicitor or the provider of the course is required.

10.   Solicitors should take note of those areas of law and practice which the Society indicates are of particular current importance. Statements will appear in the Law Society's Gazette from time to time indicating any additional credit which may be given to undertaking CPD in these areas.

11.   Under Regulation 42 of the Training Regulations 1990 the CPD requirement is suspended for the length of time a solicitor is not in legal practice or employment. The dates of and reasons for the suspension should be noted on the Training Record.

On return to legal employment the solicitor will be required to undertake two hours of CPD for every complete month from the date of return to the following 31st October up to a total of 16 hours for that CPD year. Where a solicitor has been admitted for three or more complete years a new three-year period will start from the 1st November following his/her return to legal practice or employment.

12.   The requirement to undertake CPD is automatically adjusted pro rata where a solicitor is working part-time on the basis that one hour per annum of CPD should be undertaken for every two hours per week worked. No specific application to the Society is required but the dates of and reasons for the variation should be noted on the Training Record.

November 1992

Annex 2H

Council statement on waivers

The new practice rules

1.   The Solicitors' Practice Rules 1990 came into effect on 1st September 1990.

General waivers

2.   There are no general waivers of the Solicitors' Practice Rules 1990, and there were no general waivers of the Solicitors' Practice Rules 1988. All general waivers of previous practice rules expired on 31st August 1988.

Individual waivers of previous practice rules

3.   All individual waivers of the Solicitors' Practice Rules 1936/72, the Solicitors' Practice Rules 1975 and the Solicitors' Practice Rules 1987 were (unless subject to a prior time limit) continued as like waivers of the Solicitors' Practice Rules 1988 with an expiry date of 31st August 1990. Solicitors are of course at liberty to seek new waivers to replace those which expired on that date.

Waivers of the 1988 practice rules

4.   Of waivers of the Solicitors' Practice Rules 1988 granted since 1st September 1988, some will have expired due to a time limit expressed in the waiver. Some, although having no time limit, will now no longer be necessary because of changes in the practice rules, and in such cases the waivers concerned should be regarded as having expired.

5.   All other waivers of the Solicitors' Practice Rules 1988 granted since 1st September 1988 are hereby continued as like waivers of the Solicitors' Practice Rules 1990 with an expiry date of 31st August 1992 (unless subject to a prior time limit).

The overseas practice rules

6.   The Solicitors' Overseas Practice Rules 1990 also came into effect on 1st September 1990. All waivers of the Solicitors' Overseas Practice Rules 1987 are hereby continued as like waivers of the Solicitors' Overseas Practice Rules 1990 with an expiry date of 31st August 1992 (unless subject to a prior time limit).

3rd September 1990

Annex 2I

Solicitors' Assistance Scheme — practice information

Solicitors who find themselves in difficulties or potential difficulties and for one reason or another prefer not to consult the Law Society or a member of the Society's Council can approach a member of this Scheme.

The Scheme was set up in 1972 to help solicitors who may find themselves in difficulties and who would like to have guidance and advice from an experienced, independent and sympathetic solicitor on a confidential basis. Difficulties might include those of a financial nature, those of a personal nature — such as divorce — or simply those where the solicitor is no longer able to cope with the pressures of practice.

The Scheme is administered by the Society's Professional Ethics Division, which is quite separate from the Solicitors Complaints Bureau. The SCB does, of course, circulate the list of Scheme members as it is often those who find themselves in the SCB's hands who most need help in resolving their problems. All those invited to provide an explanation with regard to their conduct are automatically sent a list of Scheme members by the SCB.

Members are normally nominated by local law societies and are neither officers nor council members of the local society. They are asked to withdraw from the Scheme if they take such an office.

The Scheme is operated on a completely confidential solicitor/client basis. No charge is made for an initial interview, but thereafter it is open to the individual Scheme member (or his or her firm) to make a more formal arrangement with the solicitor concerned. The Law Society does not give any guidance as to charges, or at what stage these should be made, but prefers to leave the matter to the discretion of Scheme members according to circumstances.

Consultations can vary from a telephone call to a series of interviews, and some solicitors in trouble prefer to contact a Scheme member outside their own area.

Often solicitors find that being able to talk about their problems to an understanding and objective listener who is also a fellow practitioner, rather than seeking specific advice, can help them reach decisions more easily.

Others may find that Scheme members can best help by acting as a source of referral to specialist help, e.g. to the Lawyers' Support Group who help with alcohol and drug abuse problems. Some Scheme members are able to offer help and advice regarding disciplinary proceedings, and details are available from Professional Ethics.

Scheme members who feel that they would like advice on a conduct related matter are welcome, as are all solicitors, to contact Professional Ethics. If they are uncertain as to whom reference should be made, Professional Ethics may be able to help in this respect.

Professional Ethics is always pleased to receive comments and views from Scheme members so that the Scheme can be kept up to date with the needs of members of the profession.

Solicitors in difficulties are reminded that they can also themselves contact Professional Ethics on a confidential basis.

Revised January 1993

Chapter 3

Private practice

3.01 Responsibility for supervision of staff

Principle

A solicitor is responsible for exercising proper supervision over both admitted and unadmitted staff.

Commentary

1. The duty to supervise staff covers not only employees but also independent contractors engaged to carry out work on behalf of the firm, e.g. consultants, locums, solicitors' clerks.

2. A solicitor cannot escape responsibility for work carried out by the firm by leaving it entirely to his or her staff, however well qualified.

3. This general principle of professional conduct is supplemented by the provisions of Rule 13 of the Solicitors' Practice Rules 1990 (see Annex 1A).

4. Guidance on solicitors' responsibilities for the supervision of clerks exercising rights of audience under section 27 of the Courts and Legal Services Act 1990 is contained in Annex 3H.

5. Law Society good practice guidelines on the recruitment and supervision of employees undertaking investment business are to be found in Annex 26I.

6. Sections 41-44 of the Solicitors Act 1974 (see Annex 3A) impose restrictions on the employment of certain persons by a solicitor. Permission must be obtained from the Society by the solicitor if he or she wishes to employ any person who, to the solicitor's knowledge, is disqualified from practising as a solicitor by reason of having been struck off the roll, suspended from practice, or by reason of being an undischarged bankrupt. Further, under section 43, the Solicitors' Disciplinary Tribunal have the power to order that no solicitor shall employ a named clerk without permission from the Society. Solicitors can check with the Records Office whether an order restricting the employment of a clerk is in existence, or whether a solicitor has been struck off.

3.02 Standards of supervision and management

Principle

Solicitors shall ensure that every office where they or their firms practise is and can reasonably be seen to be supervised and managed in accordance with Rule 13 of the Solicitors' Practice Rules 1990.

Commentary

1. Rule 13 (see Annex 1A) sets out the minimum standards of supervision and management in relation to a solicitor's office when it is open to the public or open to telephone calls from the public. The rule requires daily supervision of an office by a solicitor who has been admitted for at least three years. An office must be managed on a full-time basis by a solicitor or other suitably qualified person as defined in the rules.

2. Examples of offices which are normally considered to be open to the public include building society agencies, consulting rooms, annexes, property selling or financial services departments where those offices are separate from the main office, as well as any office through which appointments with clients are made. However, an office used purely for administrative purposes and through which there is no contact with clients is not open to the public. Nor would an office dealing exclusively with the affairs of a single client normally be subject to the requirements of the rule. In determining whether or not an office is open to the public, no distinction should be drawn between existing and potential clients.

3. It is recognised with regard to the management provisions in Rule 13(1)(b) that managers are entitled to take normal holidays. Therefore a breach of this rule would not necessarily occur merely by virtue of the office not being managed during such holidays. However, steps must be taken to ensure that adequate supervision of the office is maintained throughout the manager's absence.

4. Rule 17 of the Solicitors' Practice Rules 1990 gives the Council a power to grant waivers. A solicitor seeking a waiver must satisfy the Council that the circumstances of his or her application are sufficiently exceptional to justify a departure from the requirements of Rule 13. In addition, it is the Council's practice to seek the views of the appropriate local law society when considering applications for waivers.

5. In some circumstances the Council may grant waivers limited as to time. These circumstances could include, for example, the death or unexpected absence of a manager or supervisor. Save in exceptional cases, these waivers will not be renewed on expiry; consequently solicitors to whom such waivers are granted will be required to bring their arrangements into compliance with the rules on or before the expiry of the waiver.

6.   If a sole principal wishes to practise from more than one office (including a consulting room) and does not propose to employ a person qualified to manage each office in accordance with Rule 13(1)(b), he or she should consult Professional Ethics as to the possibility of a waiver being granted. The Council are not prepared to grant waivers in this category to sole principals practising from more than two offices, save in very exceptional circumstances.

7.   A solicitor who practises from a conventional office and also from home must include both addresses in his or her application for a practising certificate and must comply with Rule 13 in respect of both addresses. The rule also applies where a solicitor practises exclusively from his or her home. However, a solicitor who uses his or her home for an occasional interview cannot be said to be practising from home and consequently need not comply with the rule in relation to his or her home address.

8.   A solicitor must have been admitted for three years or more before he or she is entitled to practise as a sole principal and supervise his or her own office which is open to the public. See also Principle 2.04.

3.03   Absence of sole principal

Principle

A sole principal should make suitable arrangements for the running of the practice during a period of absence.

Commentary

1.   When a sole principal is absent from the office for whatever reason, (holiday, sickness, etc.) he or she owes a continuing duty to clients to ensure that the practice will be carried on with the minimum interruption to clients' business. Consequently, he or she must make adequate arrangements for the practice (including the client account) to be administered during the period of absence. The degree of supervision required must depend upon the circumstances but regard must be had to Rule 13(1) of the Solicitors' Practice Rules 1990. Because it is reasonable to plan for holiday periods, a waiver would not normally be available for such a period.

2.   If a solicitor has not made adequate arrangements in advance to meet unforeseen circumstances, difficulties will arise in the conduct of the clients' affairs and in the administration of the solicitor's own business. For example, an accountant's report must be submitted, a practising certificate must be applied for and indemnity cover must be obtained notwithstanding a solicitor's absence. Consequently, a sole principal should have an

arrangement with another solicitor (who is of sufficient seniority and who holds a practising certificate) to supervise the sole principal's practice until such time as the sole principal returns. Further, the sole principal should notify his or her bankers in advance of these arrangements so that the incoming solicitor can operate the client and office accounts of the principal.

3.   Before any responsibilities or duties are assumed by the incoming solicitor, Solicitors Indemnity Fund Limited should be notified of the position. Cover will normally remain in force against the risks of professional negligence. Insurers writing top-up cover or excess cover for both the sole principal's practice and the practice of the incoming solicitor should be notified immediately of the arrangements that have been made. Unless the absence of the principal is likely to be of short duration, clients of the practice should be informed as should the Records Office.

4.   If the absence of the principal lasts beyond the period covered by his or her practising certificate, the principal may sometimes arrange with the Records Office for another solicitor to complete the application for a practising certificate; only if the principal continues to hold a practising certificate can his or her name appear on the professional stationery.

5.   If a sole principal decides to cease to practise, he or she must inform clients of the fact so that they may instruct other solicitors. Failure to inform clients could amount not only to an act of negligence but also to unbefitting conduct leading to disciplinary action. Guidance for solicitors considering retirement is contained in Annex 3I.

3.04   Arrangements on death of sole principal

Principle

A sole principal should make a will containing adequate provision for the running of the practice after his or her death.

Commentary

1.   Clear instructions should be left by the sole principal to ensure that the executors are able to make arrangements immediately after his or her death to appoint a solicitor of sufficient seniority to run the practice, pending its disposal.

2.   Although it is not essential to appoint a solicitor as executor, this would greatly facilitate the running of the practice. The will should include an authority for the solicitor-executor to purchase the practice if he or she desires.

3. An executor who is not a solicitor may not sign cheques on the client account of the deceased's practice.

4. In view of the provisions of Rule 9 of the Solicitors' Incorporated Practice Rules 1988 (Annex 3C) it is advisable for a solicitor shareholder in a recognised body to appoint a solicitor as executor in respect of his or her shares.

5. If no appointment of a suitable solicitor-manager is made, the Law Society may intervene in accordance with the provisions contained in Schedule 1 to the Solicitors Act 1974. The powers of intervention are available where the Council of the Law Society have reason to suspect dishonesty on the part of the personal representatives, where there has been undue delay on the part of the personal representatives, or where the Schedule applied to the sole principal before his or her death. To avoid ensuing difficulties to clients following intervention, every effort should be made by the personal representative to find a solicitor-manager. In cases of difficulty, the honorary secretary of the local law society may be able to help.

6. If a sole principal dies intestate, those entitled to apply for a grant of letters of administration to the estate strictly have no right to take active steps in administering the estate until so authorised. However, in these circumstances the prospective administrators are encouraged to nominate a manager for the practice before the grant is obtained.

7. Where there is a failure, within a reasonable time of death, to apply for a grant of representation in respect of the estate of a deceased sole principal (whether under a will or an intestacy) the court has power to protect the interests of the clients. In exercise of the discretion conferred by section 116 of the Supreme Court Act 1981, the court can make an order for a grant in respect of the deceased solicitor's estate in favour of a nominee or nominees of the Law Society. The grant may be general or limited depending on the circumstances and the power is in addition to that conferred on the Law Society by paragraph 11 of Schedule 1 to the Solicitors Act 1974.

3.05 Obligations of a solicitor-manager

Principle

Where a manager is appointed in respect of a deceased solicitor's practice, he or she must comply personally with all professional obligations in relation to the practice.

Commentary

1. When appointed, the manager effectively becomes sole principal of a new practice and must therefore comply with all the rules of professional conduct, including Rule 13 of the Solicitors' Practice Rules, in relation to that new practice. Detailed guidance is contained in Annex 3F.

2. The manager should take care to ensure that confidential information relating to the clients of the deceased sole principal is kept confidential and that any conflict of interest is avoided. (For conflict of interests see Chapter 15.)

3.06 Bankruptcy

Principle

Bankruptcy of a solicitor automatically suspends his or her practising certificate.

Commentary

Guidance for practitioners who become bankrupt or enter into voluntary arrangements with creditors is contained in Annex 3J (see Commentary 3 to Principle 12.17).

3.07 Solicitors who retire from full-time practice

Principle

Solicitors who retire from full-time practice but continue to practise on a part-time or *ad hoc* basis, or act as consultant with a firm, must continue to comply with all relevant provisions of the Solicitors Act 1974, the Solicitors' Practice Rules 1990 and all the requirements of professional conduct generally.

Commentary

1. For detailed guidance reference should be made to the guidance for retiring solicitors (Annex 3I), which also contains guidance for professional trustees who continue to hold monies in that capacity.

2. The Solicitors (Keeping of the Roll) Regulations 1989 (Annex 2D) require

solicitors who do not hold practising certificates to confirm annually that they wish to remain on the roll. Guidance is contained in Annex 3I.

3.08 Need to hold a practising certificate

Principle

Every solicitor who is a principal in private practice or who is employed in private practice in connection with the provision of any legal services must hold a practising certificate.

Commentary

1. The requirement to hold a practising certificate applies to assistants, associates, consultants and locums (see Commentary 4 to Principle 2.01).

2. It should be noted that where a partner fails to hold a practising certificate, not only will he or she commit serious breaches of the Solicitors Act 1974 and the Solicitors' Practice Rules, but also the partnership will be rendered illegal. This has the effect of dissolving the partnership under section 34 of the Partnership Act 1890 (see *Hudgell Yeates & Co.* v. *Watson* [1978] Q.B. 451; and the appropriate authorities on partnership law). Under Rule 2 of the Overseas Practice Rules solicitors who practise outside England and Wales are required to hold current practising certificates. For multi-national practices see Chapter 8.

3.09 Partnerships

Principle

A solicitor shall not enter into partnership with any person other than a solicitor, a registered foreign lawyer or a recognised body. See Rule 7(6) of the Solicitors' Practice Rules 1990.

Commentary

1. Solicitors practising outside England and Wales must comply with the Solicitors' Overseas Practice Rules 1990. Under Rule 8(2) of these rules it is possible for such solicitors, subject to any relevant overseas law or local rules, to enter into a partnership with a lawyer of another jurisdiction or an English barrister (see Annex 9A).

2. A recognised body shall not enter into partnership with any person other than a solicitor or a recognised body.

3.10   Name of a practice

Principle

'The name of a firm of solicitors shall consist only of the name or names of one or more solicitors, being present or former principals together with, if desired, other conventional references to the firm and to such persons; or a firm name in use on 28th February 1967; or one approved in writing by the Council of the Law Society.'

Solicitors' Practice Rules 1990, Rule 11(1)

Commentary

1.   The 'name' of a solicitor means the solicitor's full surname, or full surname plus other names and/or initials. 'Conventional references' encompasses such terms as 'and Co.' or 'and Partners'. Whilst a sole practitioner could use 'and Co.', it would not be proper for a sole practitioner to use terms such as 'and Partners' or 'and Associates' unless the practice did formerly have more than one principal.

2.   Rule 11(1) of the Solicitors' Practice Rules governs the practice name used by a sole practitioner as well as that used by a firm of solicitors. Rule 11(2) contains similar provisions for the name of a multi-national practice. The name of a recognised body (incorporated practice) is governed by Rule 22 of the Solicitors' Incorporated Practice Rules 1988. The name of an overseas practice is governed by Rule 10 of the Solicitors' Overseas Practice Rules 1990.

3.   Applications for Council approval of a name other than one permitted by the rules should be made to Professional Ethics, and are normally considered by the Standards and Guidance Casework Committee.

3.11   A solicitor's name on firm's notepaper

Principle

Solicitors must comply with the provisions of the Solicitors' Publicity Code 1990 when naming partners and staff on the firm's stationery and in other publicity.

Commentary

1.   The full text of the Code is contained in Annex 11A.

2.   For the descripton on notepaper of a former partner who has completely retired from practice, see Commentary 9 to Principle 2.01.

3.   The status of non-partners must be indicated for avoidance of doubt whenever a situation of inadvertent holding out might otherwise arise. In the opinion of the Council a printed line is not in itself sufficient to distinguish partners from non-partners in a list.

4.   If a salaried partner's name appears on headed notepaper of a firm in the list of partners, he or she will be treated by the Law Society as a full partner and as holding or receiving clients' money irrespective of whether that partner can operate the client account. This is so even if the partner's name appears on the notepaper under a separate heading of 'salaried partners'. Thus he or she will be required to deliver an annual accountant's report. The salaried partner must accept responsibility for the books of the firm and for any breach of the Solicitors' Accounts Rules 1991, even if he or she is not permitted access to the books.

5.   A salaried partner whose name appears on headed notepaper of a firm in the list of partners, whether or not separately designated as a salaried partner, is thereby held out to the public as a principal in private practice. Thus he or she must comply with the Solicitors' Indemnity Rules 1992.

6.   The Publicity Code states at section 1(c) that publicity must not be inaccurate or misleading in any way. The Solicitors' Disciplinary Tribunal have held that it is improper for two sole principals to hold themselves out as being in partnership when that was not in fact the case.

3.12   Joint and several responsibility of partners in conduct

Principle

As a matter of conduct a partner is *prima facie* responsible for the acts or omissions of the firm and this extends to the acts or omissions of staff.

Commentary

1.   If a partner is not personally involved in an act of unbefitting conduct (other than a breach of the Accounts Rules) this fact will be taken into account by the Solicitors Complaints Bureau when deciding whether to institute disciplinary action against all or some only of the partners.

2.   Where one partner (or an employee of the firm) has committed acts of
      dishonesty entitling clients to make claims against the other partners,
      Solicitors Indemnity Fund Limited should be notified as well as the
      Solicitors Complaints Bureau.

3.   Every partner is personally responsible for complying with the rules
      relating to solicitors' accounts and the delivery of an annual accountant's
      report. Therefore, if the book-keeping is left to one partner or to an
      employee, all the partners will be liable to disciplinary action if there is a
      failure to comply with the rules. The nature of the disciplinary action will
      depend upon the seriousness of the breach and the extent to which the
      partner concerned knew or should have known of the breach.

4.   See Principle 3.01 for responsibility for supervision of staff.

3.13   Change in composition of the firm

Principle

**Where there has been an alteration to the composition of the firm, all
clients of the firm who may be affected must be informed promptly.**

Commentary

1.   All clients for whom the firm is acting currently are likely to be affected by
      a material change to its composition. Whether a change in the composition
      of a firm amounts to a material change would depend on the circumstances.
      A partner leaving a small firm (for example a four partner firm) would
      almost always amount to a material change but a partner leaving a large
      firm (for example 20 partners or more) would not normally do so.

2.   The departure of a partner would affect all the clients for whom that partner
      was acting as fee-earner and all the clients whose matters he or she was
      responsible for supervising. The departure of a partner who was in charge
      of a branch office might be material for all the clients using that office.
      Clients whose wills or deeds are held by the firm are likely to be affected if
      those documents are moved. If provisions in a will or deed are affected —
      for example, where unnamed partners of the firm or its successor are
      appointed executors or trustees and there is no clear successor firm — it is
      likely to be appropriate to seek instructions to vary the appointment.

3.   Where a firm amalgamates with another firm the Principle requires that
      clients affected should be notified of the amalgamation. Where two or more
      firms amalgamate and have previously been acting for clients who have
      conflicting interests, the new firm must cease to act for both clients unless
      it is able to continue to act for one with the consent of the other (see
      Principle 15.03 and guidance on amalgamations in Annex 15A).

4. A solicitor who acquires or retains the 'goodwill' of a firm does not thereby acquire or retain any automatic right to continue to act for its clients, who are always free to instruct other solicitors. However, a sale or transfer of goodwill may, as a matter of law, restrict what the transferor may do in the way of competition. This may mean that he or she has entered voluntarily into legal obligations which affect the method by which clients can be notified. Whilst nothing in this Principle should be taken to override any contractual obligation on the part of any partner, contractual obligations between partners will not absolve the partners from their obligation to fulfil the duties they owe to clients as a matter of professional conduct. Care should be taken to ensure that partnership deeds and other agreements do not put obstacles in the way of the proper discharge of duties to clients.

5. The principle, set out in Rule 1(b) of the Solicitors' Practice Rules 1990, that a client is free to instruct a solicitor of his or her own choice, applies equally where the firm, in effect, ceases to exist, e.g. when a new firm takes over from a firm which has ceased to practise or an existing firm is dissolved and the partners divide into two new firms. It would not be proper for the new firm to take over clients' business, including papers or money previously held, without the clients being notified as soon as possible. Prompt notification by a letter is therefore essential, as is an agreement between the solicitors concerned as to the contents of such a letter. It is a useful practice for the letter to state the amount standing to the credit of that particular client's account. The letter may add that, unless instructions are received to the contrary within a specified time, the writer will continue to deal with the client's affairs in accordance with instructions given to the previous firm. It is a matter for the new firm to decide whether to notify clients for whom no current work is in progress and for whom no money or original documents of value are held. For a specimen letter see Annex 3G.

6. Where the partners disagree about the arrangements for notifying clients of a material change in the composition of the firm, there is no rule of conduct which prevents one or more partners (subject to Commentary 3) separately notifying all the clients of the firm. This notification should be a short factual statement informing the clients of the change as the result of a dissolution of the partnership, and may give the new practising addresses of each partner. The letter could include an invitation to contact that solicitor if he or she could be of assistance to the client, but solicitors should have regard to Commentary 3. If the client is invited to instruct a particular firm, there should also be a statement that the client is free to instruct a solicitor of his or her choice.

7. Quite apart from the requirements of this Principle, Rule 15 of the Solicitors' Practice Rules 1990 requires that solicitors ensure that clients know the name and status of the person responsible for the day to day conduct of the matter in which they have instructed the practice, and the principal responsible for its overall supervision. Therefore, where a fee-earner having conduct of a matter leaves a firm, the client in question

should be informed, preferably in advance, and told the name and status of the person who is to take over his or her matter. If the client enquires where the fee-earner will be found the information should not be withheld from the client unless there are good reasons for withholding the information, or at the request of the fee-earner.

8.   Solicitors who are authorised by the Law Society to conduct investment business are reminded of their obligation under the Solicitors' Investment Business Rules to notify the Financial Services Section of any change in the composition of the firm.

9.   The Records Office must also be notified if an alteration to the composition of a firm results in a change in any solicitor's practising address (Solicitors Act 1974, section 84(1)).

3.14   Fee-earner leaving a firm

Principle

It is not in itself misconduct for a solicitor, whether partner or employee, to write to clients of a firm after leaving that firm, inviting their instructions. However, nothing in this Principle can absolve the solicitor from any legal obligations arising out of his or her former contract of employment or partnership agreement.

Commentary

1.   Sometimes a solicitor leaving a firm will have entered into restrictive covenants in a partnership deed or contract of employment, which could have the effect of preventing him or her from approaching the firm's clients or former clients. Where there is a breach of such a contractual term, enforcement is a matter for the courts, and not for the Solicitors Complaints Bureau, which cannot adjudicate on contractual obligations between partners, or between employers and employees.

2.   Where a solicitor is subject to restrictive covenants which might prevent him or her from acting for clients of the firm, there may be rare cases where to enforce such a covenant in particular circumstances would act against the best interest of the client. If a solicitor having conduct of a matter of some complexity leaves the firm at a crucial stage in the proceedings and it is necessary for the proper conduct of the client's case that he or she should continue to act, an agreement to a transfer should be sought as early as possible and should not be withheld against the client's interest. For transfer of papers see Principle 12.18.

3.   A solicitor who ceases to be a partner or employee in a firm is entitled to advertise his or her new firm provided there is no breach of the Solicitors'

Practice Rules or the Solicitors' Publicity Code. An example of a breach of the Publicity Code would be where a solicitor makes direct comparison between the services provided by his or her new firm and those of the firm he or she has left.

4. As a matter of law, it is a breach of contractual duty for an employee or partner to copy, remove or memorise a list of client addresses for the purpose, after leaving a firm, of inviting clients to transfer their instructions, or to approach clients whilst still in partnership or employment and invite them to transfer instructions at a later date. This would not prevent a solicitor informing clients that he or she was shortly to leave the firm.

5. Solicitors employing a former partner or employee of another firm may need to bear in mind that acts done in breach of legal obligations with the authority of the new employer may give rise to a right of action by the employee's previous firm. This applies whether an employee is a solicitor or a non-solicitor.

6. Care should be taken to ensure that there is no breach of Rule 1 of the Solicitors' Practice Rules on the part of either a solicitor leaving a firm or its remaining principals, as might happen where any pressure is placed on clients to transfer instructions or remain with the firm, or where there is an unseemly and public dispute about the right to accept a client's instructions or where a firm refuses without justification to transfer papers at the client's request.

3.15 Offering services other than as a solicitor

Principle

A solicitor may be involved in a wide range of activities which relate to the legal work carried out by his or her practice. Some of these activities must be carried on as part of the solicitor's practice. Rule 5 of the Solicitors' Practice Rules 1990 sets out a list of such activities, together with certain exceptions to the rule (Annex 1A).

Commentary

1. The purpose of the rule is to ensure that the public are always fully protected in their dealings with solicitors. Thus the rule prevents practising solicitors from having an interest in a business which is not a solicitor's practice, but which offers services which are considered to be central to a solicitor's practice. The rule has no effect on solicitors who are not practising as such.

2.   Rule 5(1) provides that the rule applies only to such services as may properly be offered by a solicitor as part of his or her practice. For example, a solicitor may operate a separate business as a greengrocer without being in breach of the rule.

3.   Rule 5(2) lists the activities that a practising solicitor may not offer, other than through a solicitor's practice. Examples of these prohibited activities include property selling, investment business, legal advice, and will drafting.

4.   Rule 5(4) contains important exceptions to Rule 5(2). Rule 5(4)(a) provides that the prohibition in Rule 5(2) shall not apply to a business consisting of a management consultancy or a company secretarial service and which offers none of the services specified in that paragraph save the drafting of documents under sub-paragraph 5(2)(j) and the giving of legal advice, provided such drafting or advice is ancillary to the main purpose of the business. Nor do the rules prevent a solicitor who is qualified as a lawyer of a jurisdiction other than England and Wales, patent agent, trademark agent or European patent attorney from practising as such; and such a practice shall not be subject to the provisions of Rule 5(3).

5.   Rule 5(3) sets out the conditions that should be met when a solicitor, through a separate business, offers services (not being those prohibited by Rule 5(2)) which he or she could offer as part of his or her practice. The safeguards are intended to lessen any confusion that may be caused by the solicitor's involvement. For example, the name of the separate business should have no substantial element in common with the name of any practice of the solicitor.

6.   Rule 5 applies whether the business concerned is in England and Wales or outside the jurisdiction; but nothing in the rule prevents the setting up outside the jurisdiction of a practice complying with Rules 8 or 9 of the Solicitors' Overseas Practice Rules 1990 (see Annex 9A).

7.   No part of Rule 5 applies to any solicitor *solely* by virtue of the fact that:

(i)   the solicitor is a non-executive director of a company; or

(ii) the solicitor, as the employee of a non-solicitor, does work permitted by virtue of Rule 4 of the Solicitors' Practice Rules 1990.

8.   The rule does not apply to a separate practice as a notary public operated by a solicitor in conjunction with his or her practice.

9.   Rule 5(6)(a) contains transitional provisions for wholly owned executor and trustee companies or nominee companies. Until three years after the coming into force of the Solicitors' Incorporated Practice Rules 1988 ('SIPR') no part of Rule 5 shall apply to a wholly owned executor and trustee company or nominee company already providing services before the coming into force of those rules, i.e. providing services before 1st January 1992. Previous guidance relating to existing wholly owned

executor, trustee and nominee companies was that they could operate as separate businesses if all the profits went to the firm, and that the name of the company could be similar to the firm of solicitors controlling it. Now that the SIPR are in force no new companies may be set up which are not recognised bodies, and from the expiration of the transitional period on 31st December 1994, existing companies may be operated only as part of the solicitor's practice, regulated by SIPR (see Principle 3.16 and Annex 3D).

10. Again, until 1st January 1995, no part of Rule 5 shall apply to a wholly owned company set up to provide company secretarial services which was already providing those services before 9th June 1988.

11. Until 1st September 1993 Rule 5 shall not apply to any business which was already providing services before 11th December 1986 without putting the solicitor in breach of the Solicitors' Practice Rules 1936/72 (as amended). See Annex 3E.

3.16   Service companies

Principle

Solicitors may, subject to conditions, form service companies.

Commentary

1. The formation of a service company to carry out necessary administrative functions concerned with the running of the practice, e.g. the provision of staff, hiring premises, furniture and equipment and general maintenance, is permitted, provided membership of the company is limited to members or partners of the firm, admitted solicitors holding practising certificates, retired partners of the firm and dependants of retired or deceased partners.

2. The books of the company must be made available where the Council of the Law Society require an inspection of the accounts under the Solicitors' Accounts Rules 1991.

3.17   Incorporated practices

Principle

Solicitors may practise in corporate form, subject to compliance with the Solicitors' Incorporated Practice Rules 1988 ('SIPR') and other rules and principles of conduct applying to solicitors' incorporated practices and to individual solicitors.

Commentary

1. On 1st January 1992 section 9 of and Schedule 2 to the Administration of Justice Act 1985 ('AJA') (see Annex 3B), came into force. On the same date the SIPR were also brought into force. The combined effect of the AJA and the SIPR is to allow solicitors to practise in corporate form, provided the incorporated practice is recognised by the Law Society. An incorporated practice recognised by the Law Society under section 9 of the AJA is known as a recognised body. An information pack on incorporated practices is available from Professional Ethics.

2. Schedule 2 to the AJA applies provisions in the Solicitors Act 1974 to recognised bodies. On 1st January 1992 the Solicitors' Incorporated Practices Order 1991 was made. This statutory instrument applies provisions in other statutes applying to solicitors, to recognised bodies, sometimes with modifications. The combined effect of the Schedule and the statutory instrument is to place a recognised body, for practical purposes, in the same position as a solicitor or partnership of solicitors, and to lay on it similar legal requirements.

3. Rule 8 of the SIPR provides that a recognised body's registered office must be in England and Wales and at its place of business or one of its places of business. A recognised body could practise overseas as well as in England and Wales, subject, of course, to local law and compliance with the Solicitors' Overseas Practice Rules.

4. The SIPR do not apply to a corporate practice conducted entirely outside England and Wales. For corporate practice overseas see Chapter 9.

5. Rule 3 of the SIPR provides that a recognised body must be managed and controlled by solicitors or other recognised bodies, or by such persons together with one or more registered foreign lawyers ('RFLs').

6. Rule 4 of the SIPR provides that only solicitors with practising certificates and RFLs may be directors of a recognised body. At all times at least one of the directors must be a solicitor. A recognised body cannot be a director. Rule 3 makes it clear that the company secretary need not be a solicitor or an RFL.

7. Rule 5 of the SIPR contains three fundamental provisions:

    (a)   Only solicitors with practising certificates, RFLs and other recognised bodies may be shareholders of a recognised body.

    (b)   A shareholder may not hold shares for others save as a nominee, for a solicitor, an RFL or a recognised body. A shareholder may not create any charge or other third party interest over his or her shares.

    (c)   At least one share must be held by a solicitor or recognised body; thus no recognised body can be comprised only of RFL members.

8.   Under section 9 of the AJA, rules governing the conduct of solicitors have been applied to recognised bodies. Rule 12 of the SIPR provides that all the principles and requirements of conduct affecting solicitors apply also to recognised bodies.

9.   The Solicitors' Indemnity Rules are applied to recognised bodies, with certain adaptations, by the Solicitors' Indemnity (Incorporated Practice) Rules 1991 (see Annex 28C). In addition, Rule 13 of the SIPR requires a recognised body which is a limited company to obtain top-up insurance over and above that provided by the Solicitors' Indemnity Fund, to a specified level.

10.   Recognised bodies must, on initially obtaining recognition and on renewing recognition, pay a contribution to the Compensation Fund. Recognised bodies which have held clients' money may also be required to pay a further contribution (see paragraph 6 of Schedule 2 to the AJA).

11.   Solicitors and RFLs who are directors or share owners of a recognised body have a separate obligation to pay the individual annual contributions to the Compensation Fund payable by solicitors or RFLs. If the recognised body (or another recognised body in which it owns shares) has held or received clients' money, such solicitors and RFLs will pay the annual contribution at the full rate for solicitors or RFLs. They will not, however, be required to pay any special levy unless they have held or received clients' money as individuals.

12.   Rule 14 of the SIPR requires each member of and each beneficial owner of a share in a recognised body to submit to the Council a covenant under seal to reimburse the Society, if so required, in respect of a grant made out to the Fund in circumstances where the Society has been unable to recover the amount from the recognised body or the defaulting party. A specimen Compensation Fund covenant is contained in the information pack (see Commentary 1).

13.   Solicitors may wish to incorporate part, but not all, of a practice; for example trustee and executor functions, and/or the property selling and/or financial services departments of the practice. The rules allow this. If the share owners are the same as the partners then the firm and the recognised body will normally be treated as one practice for the purpose of the Indemnity Rules, i.e. only one contribution, based on one gross fee return, will be payable, but additional top-up insurance, if required, is not

available from the Solicitors' Indemnity Fund. The ability to incorporate only part of the practice will be important to those firms having or wishing to set up separate executor, trustee or nominee companies. Such companies must be recognised bodies unless they are able to take advantage of the transitional provisions in Rule 5(6) of the Solicitors' Practice Rules 1990. For details regarding hived off businesses and Rule 5 of the Solicitors' Practice Rules see Principle 3.15.

14. The full text of the SIPR is set out in Annex 3C.

Solicitors Act 1974

sections 41-44 — restrictions on employment of certain persons
(as amended by the Courts and Legal Services Act 1990)

41. *Employment by solicitor of person struck off or suspended*

(1)   No solicitor shall, except in accordance with a written permission granted under this section, employ or remunerate in connection with his practice as a solicitor any person who to his knowledge is disqualified from practising as a solicitor by reason of the fact that -

(a)   his name has been struck off the roll, or

(b)   he is suspended from practising as a solicitor, or

(c)   his practising certificate is suspended while he is an undischarged bankrupt.

(1A) No solicitor shall, except in accordance with a written permission granted under this section, employ or remunerate in connection with his practice as a solicitor any person if, to his knowledge, there is a direction in force under section 47(2)(g) in relation to that person.

(2)   The Society may grant a permission under this section for such period and subject to such conditions as the Society thinks fit.

(3)   A solicitor aggrieved by the refusal of the Society to grant a permission under subsection (2), or by any conditions attached by the Society to the grant of any such permission, may appeal to the Master of the Rolls who may -

(a)   confirm the refusal or the conditions, as the case may be; or

(b)   grant a permission under this section for such period and subject to such conditions as he thinks fit.

(4)   If any solicitor acts in contravention of this section or of any conditions subject to which a permission has been granted under it, the Tribunal or, as the case may be, the High Court shall order -

(a)   that his name be struck off the roll; or

(b)   that he be suspended from practice for such period as the Tribunal or the court thinks fit.

(5)   The Master of the Rolls may make regulations about appeals to him under subsection (3).

42.   *Failure to disclose fact of having been struck off or suspended*

(1)   Any person who, while he is disqualified from practising as a solicitor by reason of the fact that -

> (a)   his name has been struck off the roll, or
>
> (b)   he is suspended from practising as a solicitor, or
>
> (c)   his practising certificate is suspended while he is an undischarged bankrupt,

seeks or accepts employment by a solicitor in connection with that solicitor's practice without previously informing him that he is so disqualified shall be guilty of an offence and liable on summary conviction to a fine not exceeding level three on the standard scale.

(1A) Any person -

> (a)   with respect to whom a direction is in force under section 47(2)(g); and
>
> (b)   who seeks or accepts employment by a solicitor in connection with that solicitor's practice without previously informing him of the direction,

shall be guilty of an offence and liable on summary conviction to a fine not exceeding level three on the standard scale.

(2)   Notwithstanding anything in the Magistrates' Courts Act 1980, proceedings under this section may be commenced at any time before the expiration of six months from the first discovery of the offence by the prosecutor, but no such proceedings shall be commenced except by, or with the consent of, the Attorney General.

43.   *Control of employment of certain clerks*

(1)   Where a person who is or was a clerk to a solicitor but is not himself a solicitor -

> (a)   has been convicted of a criminal offence which discloses such dishonesty that in the opinion of the Society it would be undesirable for him to be employed by a solicitor in connection with his practice; or
>
> (b)   has, in the opinion of the Society, occasioned or been a party to, with or without the connivance of the solicitor to whom he is or was clerk, an act or default in relation to that solicitor's practice which involved conduct on his part of such a nature that in the opinion of the Society it would be undesirable for him to be employed by a solicitor in connection with his practice,

an application may be made to the Tribunal with respect to that person by or on behalf of the Society.

(2)   The Tribunal, on the hearing of any application under subsection (1), may make an order that as from such date as may be specified in the order no solicitor shall, except in accordance with permission in writing granted by the Society for such period and subject to such conditions as the Society may think fit to specify in the permission, employ or remunerate, in connection with his practice as a solicitor, the person with respect to whom the application is made.

(3)   An order made by the Tribunal under subsection (2) may, on the application of the Society or of the person with respect to whom the application for the order was made, be revoked by a subsequent order of the Tribunal; and where in the opinion of the Tribunal no prima facie case is shown in favour of an application for revocation, the Tribunal may refuse the application without hearing the applicant.

(4)   The Tribunal, on the hearing of any application under this section, may make an order as to the payment of costs by any party to the application.

(5)   Orders made under this section and filed with the Society may be inspected by any solicitor during office hours without payment but shall not be open to the inspection of any person other than a solicitor.

(6)   [Repealed]

(7)   For the purposes of this section an order under Part I of the Powers of Criminal Courts Act 1973 discharging a person absolutely or conditionally shall, notwithstanding anything in section 1C of that Act, be deemed to be a conviction of the offence for which the order was made.

44. *Offences in connection with orders under section 43(2)*

(1)   Any person who, while there is in force in respect of him an order under section 43(2), seeks or accepts any employment by or remuneration from a solicitor in connection with that solicitor's practice without previously informing him of that order shall be guilty of an offence and liable on summary conviction to a fine not exceeding £50.

(2)   Where an order is made under section 43(2) in respect of any person and that order is one -

(a)   against which no appeal has been made or which has been confirmed on appeal; and

(b)   which has not been revoked under section 43(3),

then, if any solicitor knowingly acts in contravention of that order or of any conditions subject to which permission for the employment of that person has been granted under it, a complaint in respect of that contravention may be made to the Tribunal by or on behalf of the Society.

(3)   Any document purporting to be an order under section 43(2) and to be duly signed in accordance with section 48(1) shall be received in evidence in any proceedings under this section and be deemed to be such an order without further proof unless the contrary is shown.

(4)   Notwithstanding anything in the Magistrates' Courts Act 1980, proceedings under subsection (1) may be commenced at any time before the expiration of six months from the first discovery of the offence by the prosecutor, but no such proceedings shall be commenced, except with the consent of the Director of Public Prosecutions, by any person other than the Society or a person acting on behalf of the Society.

[NOTE

For the application of section 44 to a recognised body (i.e. an incorporated practice recognised under section 9 of the Administration of Justice Act 1985) see paragraphs 12 and 16(1)(d) of Schedule 2 to the Administration of Justice Act 1985.]

Annex 3B

Administration of Justice Act 1985

section 9 — incorporated practices
(as amended by the Courts and Legal Services Act 1990)

(1)   The Council may make rules:

(a)   making provision as to the management and control by solicitors or solicitors and one or more registered foreign lawyers of bodies corporate carrying on businesses consisting of the provision of professional services such as are provided by individuals practising as solicitors or by multi-national partnerships;

(b)   prescribing the circumstances in which such bodies may be recognised by the Council as being suitable bodies to undertake the provision of any such services;

(c)   prescribing the conditions which (subject to any exceptions provided by the rules) must at all times be satisfied by bodies corporate so recognised if they are to remain so recognised; and

(d)   regulating the conduct of the affairs of such bodies.

(2)   Rules made by the Council may also make provision:

(a)   for the manner and form in which applications for recognition under this section are to be made, and for the payment of fees in connection with such applications;

(b)   for regulating the names that may be used by recognised bodies;

(c)   as to the period for which any recognition granted under this section shall (subject to the provisions of this Part) remain in force;

(d)   for the revocation of any such recognition on the grounds that it was granted as a result of any error or fraud;

(e)   for the keeping by the Society of a list containing the names and places of business of all bodies corporate which are for the time being recognised under this section, and for the information contained in any such list to be available for inspection;

(f)   for rules made under any provision of the 1974 Act to have effect in relation to recognised bodies with such additions, omissions or other modifications as appear to the Council to be necessary or expedient;

(g)   for empowering the Council to take such steps as they consider necessary or expedient to ascertain whether or not any rules applicable to recognised bodies by virtue of this section are being complied with;

(h)   for the manner of service on recognised bodies of documents authorised or required to be served on such bodies under or by virtue of this Part.

(3)   Notwithstanding section 24(2) of the 1974 Act (application of penal provisions to bodies corporate), sections 20, 22(1) and 23(1) of that Act (prohibition on unqualified person acting as solicitor, etc.) shall not apply to a recognised body; and nothing in section 24(1) of that Act shall apply in relation to such a body.

(4)   Section 22(1), or (as the case may be) section 23(1), of that Act shall not apply to any act done by an officer or employee of a recognised body if:

(a)   it was done by him at the direction and under the supervision of another person who was at the time an officer or employee of the body; and

(b)   it could have been done by that other person for or in expectation of any fee, gain or reward without committing an offence under the said section 2 or (as the case may be) under the said section 23.

(5)   A certificate signed by an officer of the Society and stating that any body corporate is or is not, or was or was not at any time, a recognised body shall, unless the contrary is proved, be evidence of the facts stated in the certificate; and a certificate purporting to be so signed shall be taken to have been so signed unless the contrary is proved.

(6)   Schedule 2 (which makes provision with respect to the application of provisions of the 1974 Act to recognised bodies and with respect to other matters relating to such bodies) shall have effect.

(7)   Subject to the provisions of that Schedule, the Lord Chancellor may by order made by statutory instrument subject to annulment in pursuance of a resolution of either House of Parliament provide for any enactment or instrument passed or made before the commencement of this section and having effect in relation to solicitors to have effect in relation to recognised bodies with such additions, omissions or other modifications as appear to the Lord Chancellor to be necessary or expedient.

(8)   In this section:

"the 1974 Act" means the Solicitors Act 1974;

"the Council" and "the Society" have the meaning given by section 87(1) of the 1974 Act;

"multi-national partnership" means a partnership whose members consist of one or more registered foreign lawyers and one or more solicitors;

"recognised body" means a body corporate for the time being recognised under this section; and

"registered foreign lawyer" means a person who is registered under section 89 of the Courts and Legal Services Act 1990.

(9)   Any rules made by the Council under this section shall be made with the concurrence of the Master of the Rolls.

Annex 3C

Solicitors' Incorporated Practice Rules 1988

(with consolidated amendments to 1st June 1992)

Rules dated 17th June 1988 made by the Council of the Law Society with the concurrence of the Master of the Rolls under section 9 of the Administration of Justice Act 1985, Part II of the Solicitors Act 1974 and schedule 15 paragraph 6 of the Financial Services Act 1986, regulating the incorporated practices of solicitors and registered foreign lawyers in England and Wales and overseas.

1. Interpretation

In these Rules, except where the context otherwise requires:

(1) (a) 'the Act' means the Administration of Justice Act 1985;

(b) 'authorised insurers', 'the Council', 'practising certificate', 'the roll' and 'the Society' shall have the meanings assigned to them in the Solicitors Act 1974;

(c) 'firm' means an unincorporated partnership consisting of solicitors or recognised bodies or both, or a multi-national partnership and includes also a solicitor who is a sole practitioner;

(ca) 'foreign lawyer' and 'registered foreign lawyer' shall have the meanings assigned to them by section 89 of the Courts and Legal Services Act 1990;

(d) 'indemnity rules' means rules made under section 37 of the Solicitors Act 1974 and section 9 of the Act;

(e) 'member' means a person who agrees to become a member of a body corporate and whose name is entered in its register of members;

(ea) 'multi-national partnership' means an unincorporated partnership consisting of one or more registered foreign lawyers and one or more solicitors;

(f) 'person' includes a body corporate;

(g) 'recognised body' means a body corporate for the time being recognised by the Council under these Rules as being a suitable body to undertake the provision of professional services such as are provided by individuals practising as solicitors or by multi-national partnerships;

(h) 'solicitor' means a person qualified to act as a solicitor under section 1 of the Solicitors Act 1974;

(i) 'Solicitors Indemnity Fund' means the Fund established under the Solicitors' Indemnity Rules 1987.

(2) A reference to a Rule is a reference to one of the Solicitors' Incorporated Practice Rules 1988.

(3) A reference to any provision of an Act of Parliament includes a reference to any statutory modification or re-enactment of that provision for the time being in force.

(4) Words importing the masculine gender include the feminine and the neuter, words in the singular include the plural and words in the plural include the singular.

2. Requirement as to recognition by the Council

(1) Subject to the provisions of these Rules, a body corporate may carry on business consisting of the provision of professional services such as are provided by individuals practising as solicitors or by multi-national partnerships provided that before commencing any such business such body corporate shall have been recognised by the Council as being a suitable body to undertake the provision of such services and providing that at all times while carrying on such business it remains so recognised.

(2) A recognised body may carry on only such business as is referred to in paragraph (1) of this Rule.

3. Management and control

A recognised body shall at all times be managed and controlled by solicitors or recognised bodies, or by such persons together with one or more registered foreign lawyers provided that there shall be no breach of this Rule where the secretary of a recognised body is not a solicitor, a registered foreign lawyer or a recognised body.

4. Directors

A recognised body shall not have as a director any person who is not a solicitor or a registered foreign lawyer; provided that at all times at least one of the directors shall be a solicitor.

5. Shares

(1) A recognised body shall not have as a member any person who is not a solicitor, a registered foreign lawyer or a recognised body.

(2) (a) (i) Subject to paragraphs (4) and (5) of this Rule a member of a recognised body shall not hold any share in the body for another person save as nominee for a solicitor, a registered foreign lawyer or a recognised body who or which is himself or itself a member or officer of the recognised body or for a solicitor or registered foreign lawyer who is working in the practice of the body or for a receiver appointed under section 99 of the Mental Health Act 1983 in respect of any such solicitor or registered foreign lawyer; and

(ii) at all times at least one share in the body must be so held either by a member who or which is a solicitor or a recognised body and who or which beneficially owns that share; or by a member who or which holds that share as nominee for a solicitor or for a recognised body or for a receiver appointed under section 99 of the Mental Health Act 1983 in respect of a solicitor.

(b)   A member of a recognised body shall disclose to the body the nature and extent of any interests in shares registered in his name and the persons by whom such interests are held. The recognised body shall maintain a record of the identity of all persons, other than the member in whose name a share is registered, holding such interests. The record shall be kept in respect of each person on it for at least three years from the date on which that person ceased to hold any interest in any share in the body.

(c)   A member of a recognised body shall not create any charge or other third party interest (save as permitted by sub-paragraph (a) of this paragraph) over any share in the recognised body.

(3)   In paragraphs (4) and (5) of this Rule references to the beneficial owner of a share do not include a person in whose name that share is registered and who beneficially owns that share.

(4)   (a)   Where a member of a recognised body dies the recognised body shall ensure that any shares registered in his name at the time of his death are within twelve months of his death registered in the name of a solicitor or a recognised body or (where permitted by paragraph (2)(a)(i) of this Rule) a registered foreign lawyer or (where the recognised body is a company limited by shares) are acquired by the recognised body itself.

(b)   A solicitor, a registered foreign lawyer or a recognised body who or which is the personal representative of a deceased member of or beneficial owner of a share in a recognised body may elect to be entered in the register of members of the recognised body but no member shall hold any share as personal representative for longer than twelve months from the date of the death of the deceased.

(c)   Where a beneficial owner of a share in a recognised body dies, a member may notwithstanding sub-paragraph (2)(a) of this Rule, continue to hold such share for the personal representative of the deceased for a period of not longer than twelve months from the date of the death; provided that voting rights shall only be exercised in respect of any share held in reliance on this sub-paragraph where the only personal representative in respect of the deceased beneficial owner's interest in the share is a solicitor, a registered foreign lawyer or a recognised body.

(5)   (a)   Where one of the following specified events happens, to a member of or a beneficial owner of a share in a recognised body, that is to say: (where such member or beneficial owner is a solicitor) his name is struck off or removed from the roll or his practising certificate is suspended (including automatic suspension on bankruptcy) or withdrawn; or (where such a member or beneficial owner is a registered foreign lawyer) his name is struck off the register or his registration is suspended (including automatic suspension on bankruptcy, or on striking off or suspension in his own jurisdiction) or cancelled; or (where such a member or beneficial owner is a recognised body) its recognition is revoked or expires (including automatic expiry on liquidation, making of an administration order or appointment of an administrative receiver);

then -

(i) where the specified event happens in respect of a member, any share registered in his name may, notwithstanding paragraph (1) of this Rule, remain so registered for a period of not longer than six months from the date of the specified event; provided that no voting rights shall be exercised in respect of any such share while it remains so registered; and

(ii) where the specified event happens in respect of a beneficial owner of a share, a member may, notwithstanding sub-paragraph (2)(a) of this Rule, continue to hold such share for the beneficial owner or, as the case may be, his trustee in bankruptcy or liquidator for a period of not longer than six months from the date of the specified event; provided that no voting rights shall be exercised in respect of any share held in reliance on this sub-paragraph.

(b) A solicitor or registered foreign lawyer who is the trustee in bankruptcy or liquidator of a member of or a beneficial owner of a share in a recognised body may elect to be entered in the register of members of the recognised body but no member shall hold any share as trustee in bankruptcy or liquidator for longer than six months from the date of the bankruptcy order or winding-up order as the case may be.

(6) A member of a recognised body shall not exercise any voting rights in respect of any share held in breach of any part of this Rule and the chairman of a meeting shall not accept any vote tendered in breach of this paragraph or paragraph (7) of this Rule.

(7) For the purpose of attending and voting at meetings a member of a recognised body shall not appoint as a proxy or corporate representative any person other than a solicitor who is a member or officer of or who is working in the practice of, or a registered foreign lawyer who is a member or director of, (a) the recognised body or (b) a recognised body which is itself a member of the recognised body.

(8) A recognised body shall so far as possible ensure that its members comply with this Rule and Rule 6.

6. Mental health

A recognised body shall not have as a director a solicitor or registered foreign lawyer while he is a patient as defined by section 94 of the Mental Health Act 1983 or while he is a person as to whom powers have been exercised under section 98 (emergency powers) of that Act and no voting rights shall be exercised in respect of any shares registered in the name of or beneficially owned by such a solicitor or registered foreign lawyer.

7. Proper service to clients

A recognised body shall at all times remain able to provide a proper service to its clients.

8. Registered office

The registered office of a recognised body shall be in England and Wales and at the place of business or one of the places of business of the body.

9.   Conditions which must at all times be satisfied

(1) The following conditions shall at all times be satisfied by a recognised body and where any condition fails to be satisfied by a recognised body the recognition of the body by the Council shall expire:

   (a)   a recognised body shall be registered in England and Wales under the Companies Act 1985 as an unlimited company having a share capital or as a company limited by shares;

   (b)   a recognised body which is an unlimited company shall retain its status as an unlimited company, save where the Council consents to the body being re-registered as limited by shares under the Companies Act 1985;

   (c)   a recognised body shall, notwithstanding sub-paragraphs (4)(c) and (5)(a) of Rule 5, at all times have at least one member holding a share or shares in the circumstances set out in Rule 5(2)(a)(ii) of these rules and able to exercise voting rights in respect of at least one share in the body, except that the recognition of a body shall not expire solely because:

   (i)   the practising certificate of any member is withdrawn due to non-renewal under Section 14(5) of the Solicitors Act 1974 provided that a new practising certificate is issued within two months of such expiry; or

   (ii)   the death of a member has left a recognised body with no member able to exercise voting rights in respect of at least one share in the body provided (a) that within three months of the death the recognised body has at least one member able to exercise such voting rights, and (b) that until proviso (a) has been fulfilled either at least one share in the body is beneficially owned by a solicitor or a recognised body or the only personal representative in respect of at least one share in the body is a solicitor or a recognised body.

(2) The recognition of a recognised body shall expire where a winding-up order or an administration order under Part II of the Insolvency Act 1986 is made with respect to the body or where a resolution for voluntary winding-up is passed with respect to the body or where a person is appointed administrative receiver of the body.

10. Revocation of recognition

The Council may revoke the recognition of a recognised body if that recognition was granted as a result of any error or fraud.

11. [Repealed]

12. Application of principles and requirements of conduct to recognised bodies

All the principles and requirements of conduct affecting solicitors shall apply in all respects *mutatis mutandis* to recognised bodies.

13. Top-up insurance

(1) A recognised body which is a company limited by shares shall insure with authorised insurers against the losses referred to in paragraph (3) of this Rule over and above the maximum indemnity provided from time to time by the Solicitors Indemnity Fund.

(2) The insurance required by paragraph (1) of this Rule shall provide, over and above that maximum indemnity, a minimum cover of either £500,000 on an each and every claim basis or £2,000,000 per annum on an aggregate basis.

(3) The losses against which a recognised body is required to insure under this Rule are all losses arising from claims in respect of civil liability incurred in the practice of the recognised body by the recognised body or by any of its officers or employees or former officers or employees or by any solicitor or registered foreign lawyer who is or was a consultant to or associate in the body's practice or is or was working in the practice as an agent or a *locum tenens*; save that a recognised body shall not be required to insure against losses arising from claims of a type excluded, by the indemnity rules applicable from time to time to recognised bodies, from being afforded indemnity by the Solicitors Indemnity Fund.

(4) The insurance required by paragraph (1) of this Rule shall cover the insured in respect of:

(a) any claim first made or intimated during the period of insurance, and

(b) any claim arising out of circumstances notified to the insurer during the period of insurance as circumstances which might give rise to a claim.

(5) A recognised body which is required to insure under this Rule shall each twelve months after recognition is granted to it under these Rules, or at any other time when so required by the Council, submit to the Council evidence of compliance with this Rule.

14. Compensation Fund covenant

(1) Each member of and each beneficial owner of a share in a recognised body shall submit to the Council, in such form as the Council may from time to time prescribe, a covenant under seal (referred to in these Rules as a 'Compensation Fund covenant') that he or it will jointly and severally with the other members of and beneficial owners of any shares in the body reimburse the Society, when required to do so by the Council, in respect of any grant made out of the Compensation Fund under paragraph 6 of Schedule 2 to the Act where:

(a) such grant is made in consequence of some act or default of the recognised body or any of its officers or employees; and

(b) at the time of such act or default the covenantor is or was a member of or a beneficial owner of a share in the recognised body;

provided that a member or a beneficial owner of a share shall only be required to reimburse the Society to the extent that the Society has been unable to recover the amount of the grant from the recognised body or the officer or employee committing the act or default or the personal representative, trustee in bankruptcy or liquidator or any such person.

(2) The Compensation Fund covenant shall include a covenant by the covenantor that

before transferring any share or transferring a beneficial interest in any share or holding any share as nominee he or it will ensure that the intended transferee or beneficial owner submits a Compensation Fund covenant to the Council.

(3)   A recognised body shall not enter in its register of members any person until that person has submitted a Compensation Fund covenant to the Council and shall so far as possible ensure that all beneficial owners of any shares submit such a covenant to the Council.

15. Applications for recognition

A body corporate seeking recognition under these Rules shall submit to the Council:

(a)   a completed application signed by all the members and directors of the body (in the case of a member which is a recognised body two directors of that body shall sign on its behalf save that where a body has only one director that director shall sign on its behalf) in such form as the Council may from time to time prescribe, which application shall include:

   (i)   the names and addresses of all solicitors who are members of the body, and (separately designated) the names and addresses of all registered foreign lawyers who are members of the body;

   (ii)   the names and registered offices of all recognised bodies who are members of the body;

   (iii) the nature and extent of the interest held in any share by any person other than the member in whose name the share is registered and the identity of the person by whom such interest is held (including, separately designated, the identity of any such person who is a registered foreign lawyer);

   (iv)   the names and addresses of all directors of the body (including, separately designated, all directors who are registered foreign lawyers);

   (v)   the name, the registered office and any other proposed place or places of business of the body;

   (vi)   a statement as to whether the body is a company limited by shares or an unlimited company;

   (vii) reasonably sufficient information in respect of any of the matters referred to in Rule 16(2) except such information as has been provided by the body in a previous application under this Rule;

   (viii) a declaration:

      (a)   that the body complies with Rules 3-6, 8, 9 and 22 and that its members comply with Rules 5 and 6; and

      (b)   that the memorandum and articles of association of the body are such as to enable the body (i) to continue to comply with Rules 3-6 and (ii) so far as possible to ensure continued compliance by its members with Rules 5 and 6;

(b)   evidence of compliance with the indemnity rules applicable from time to time to recognised bodies;

(c)   in the case of a body which is a company limited by shares, evidence of compliance with Rule 13 (top-up insurance);

(d)   Compensation Fund covenants by all the members of the body and by all the beneficial owners of any shares in the body;

(e)   a copy of the certificate of incorporation of the body;

(f)   any other documentation or information which the Council may require;

(g)   such fee as the Council may from time to time prescribe in connection with such applications.

16.   Grants and refusals of recognition

(1)   Where a body corporate has applied for recognition in accordance with Rule 15 the Council may recognise the body as a suitable body to undertake the provision of professional services such as are provided by individuals practising as solicitors or by multi-national partnerships where the Council is satisfied:

(a)   that the body complies with Rules 3-6, 8, 9 and 22 and that its members comply with Rules 5 and 6;

(b)   that the body complies with the indemnity rules applicable from time to time to recognised bodies; and

(c)   that, in the case of a body which is a company limited by shares, it complies with Rule 13 (top-up insurance).

(2)   Without prejudice to the generality of the Council's discretion under paragraph (1) of this Rule the Council may refuse to recognise a body where:

(a)   a director or member of the body is or has been a director or member of a recognised body which has been the subject of an order or direction under paragraphs 18 or 21 of Schedule 2 to the Act or the recognition of which has been revoked under Rule 10 of these Rules or has expired under Rule 9 of these Rules; or

(b)   a director or member has been the subject of an order under section 47(2)(a)-(c) of the Solicitors Act 1974 or Schedule 14 paragraph 15(4)(a)-(c) of the Courts and Legal Services Act 1990;

(c)   the powers conferred by Part II of Schedule 1 to the Solicitors Act 1974 have been exercised in respect of the body or in respect of a firm or recognised body of which a director or member of the body applying for recognition is or has been a principal or a director or member as the case may be; or

(d)   a director or member:

     (i)   has been convicted of a criminal offence involving fraud, dishonesty or violence; or

     (ii)   has had a bankruptcy order made against him or has made a composition or arrangement with his creditors or has made a proposal for a voluntary arrangement under Part VIII of the Insolvency Act 1986 or is or has been a director of a company in respect of which an administration order under Part II of the Insolvency Act 1986 or a winding-up order has been made or in respect of which a resolution for voluntary winding up has been passed or which has made a proposal for a voluntary arrangement under Part I of the Insolvency Act 1986 or in respect of which a person has been appointed receiver or administrative receiver; or

(iii) has had an order made against him which is not a bankruptcy order but which has the same or a similar effect under the law in force in any territory outside England and Wales;

(iv) has been struck off or suspended from practice as a lawyer of a jurisdiction other than England and Wales; or

(e) for any other reason the Council thinks it proper in the public interest not to recognise the body.

17. Requirements on refusal; right of appeal if recognition neither granted nor refused within specified period

(1) Where the Council refuses an application for recognition it shall notify the applicant of the refusal and of the grounds on which it has been refused.

(2) Where the Council has within three months beginning with the date when an application for recognition was received by the Council neither granted nor refused recognition, an appeal to the Master of the Rolls may be brought under paragraph 2 of Schedule 2 to the Act as if the application had been refused by the Council. For the purpose of calculating the period of three months referred to in this paragraph time shall not run in August.

18. Duration of recognition

(1) Every recognition granted under these Rules shall, subject to paragraph (2) of this Rule, remain in force until the end of the third 31st May next after that recognition is granted except where prior to that time the recognition expires under Rule 9 or is revoked.

(2) Where an application is made in accordance with Rule 15 by a body which at the date of the application is already recognised under these Rules and the Council has neither granted nor refused a new recognition by the time when the body's existing recognition would, apart from this paragraph, expire in accordance with paragraph (1) of this Rule, the existing recognition shall not expire at that time but shall continue in force until a new recognition is granted or refused.

19. Duty to notify the Society of certain matters and to provide items required by the Council

(1) A recognised body shall notify the Society in writing:

(a) not less than 28 days before the change is implemented, of any change in the body's name, registered office or principal office if different from its registered office;

(b) forthwith of any change:

(i) in the body's members, directors, or place or places of business other than those referred to in sub-paragraph (a) of this paragraph;

(ii) with respect to the interests held in any share in the body by a person other than the member in whose name the share is registered and in the identity of the person by whom any such interest is held;

(c) forthwith of any of the occurrences referred to in Rule 9(2) or where a condition referred to in Rule 9(1) ceases to be satisfied.

(2)   The Council may (in order to ascertain whether or not any of these Rules or other rules, principles or requirements of conduct applicable to recognised bodies by virtue of these Rules or section 9 of the Act are being complied with) at any time by written notice require a recognised body or an officer or member of the body to submit to the Council any report, certificate, audit or other documentation or information which the Council may require and the recognised body or the officer or member as the case may be shall submit such item to the Council within such period as may be reasonably determined by the Council.

20.   Certificate of recognition

Where the Council recognises a body under these Rules it shall issue to the body a certificate of recognition which shall state:

(a)   the name and registered office of the recognised body;

(b)   the dates of granting and expiry of recognition; and

(c)   whether the body is a company limited by shares or an unlimited company.

21.   List of recognised bodies

The Society shall maintain a list containing the name, registered office and other place or places of business of every body for the time being recognised by the Council under these Rules, which list shall be available for inspection by the public.

22.   Name

(1)   The name of a recognised body shall consist only of one or more of the following:

(a)   the name or names of one or more solicitors, registered foreign lawyers or recognised bodies who are members or former members of the body;

(b)   the name or part of the name of any predecessor firm or recognised body in practice at the time of the formation of the body provided that such name did not infringe Rule 11 of the Solicitors' Practice Rules 1990 (or any rule for the time being replacing that Rule) or this Rule;

(ba)   in the case of a recognised body which has at least one registered foreign lawyer as a director, member or beneficial owner of a share, the name or part of the name of a predecessor legal practice which was in practice at the time of the formation of the body, provided that such name consisted of the name or names of present or former principals and conventional references to such persons and to the practice;

(c)   other conventional references to any such person, firm or body as is referred to in sub-paragraphs (a), (b) and (ba) of this paragraph;

(d)   conventional references to the body such as 'and Company';

(e)   the word 'solicitor' or 'solicitors';

(f)   in the case of a recognised body which has at least one registered foreign lawyer as a director, member or beneficial owner of a share:

(i)   the words 'solicitor(s)' and 'registered foreign lawyer(s)'; or

(ii)   the word 'solicitor(s)' together with words denoting the countries or jurisdictions of qualification of those registered foreign lawyers and their professional qualifications;

provided that in any such name the constituent elements must be placed in order, with the largest category first; and provided that there must be no breach of the principle set out in paragraph 14(b) of the Solicitors' Publicity Code (use of the word 'lawyer(s)').

(2)   The name of a recognised body must include the name of at least one solicitor, foreign lawyer or recognised body included by virtue of sub-paragraphs (1)(a), (b) or (ba) of this Rule.

(3)   The name of a recognised body which is a company limited by shares must have 'limited' or 'ltd.' as its last word except that the name of a body which has its registered office in Wales may have '*cyfyngedig*' or '*cyf.*' as its last word.

(4)   Notwithstanding paragraphs (1) and (2) of this Rule the Council may approve in writing some other name for a recognised body.

23.   Requirement to state certain matters on stationery, etc.

(1)   The names of all the directors of a recognised body shall be stated either on the body's stationery or in a list of the names of all the directors maintained at the body's registered office provided that in the latter case the body's stationery must state that such a list of all the directors' names is open to inspection at the body's registered office and must state the address of that office.

(1A) In the case of a recognised body which has at least one registered foreign lawyer as a director, member or beneficial owner of a share, there must, in addition to paragraph (1) of this Rule, also be compliance with paragraph 7(b) of the Solicitors' Publicity Code.

(2)   A recognised body which is a company limited by shares shall comply with Chapter I (appearance of company name and other particulars on stationery, etc.) of Part XI of the Companies Act 1985.

(3)   On the stationery of a recognised body which is an unlimited company it shall be stated, either as part of the body's name or otherwise, that the body is a body corporate.

(4)   Where a recognised body which is an unlimited company is a partner in partnership with a solicitor or another recognised body it shall be stated on the stationery of the partnership, either as part of the body's name or otherwise, that the recognised body is a body corporate except where this is so stated on a list of the names of all the partners maintained by the partnership at its principal place of business in pursuance of section 4(3) of the Business Names Act 1985.

24.   Duty of officers; application of Rules, etc., to officers, members, employees, etc.

(1)   It is the duty of a solicitor who or a recognised body which is an officer of a recognised body, or a registered foreign lawyer who is a director of a recognised body to take all reasonable steps to ensure compliance by any recognised body of which he or it is an officer with these Rules and any rules, principles or requirements of conduct applicable to recognised bodies by virtue of these Rules or section 9 of the Act.

(2)   A solicitor who is an officer, member or employee of or who is otherwise working in the practice of a recognised body, or a recognised body which is an officer or member of a recognised body, or a registered foreign lawyer who is a director or member of a recognised body, shall not by any act or omission by himself (or itself) or with any other person cause, instigate or connive at any breach of these Rules or any rules, principles or requirements of conduct applicable to recognised bodies by virtue of these Rules or section 9 of the Act and, for the avoidance of doubt, it is confirmed that a solicitor who is an officer, member or employee of or who is otherwise working in the practice of a recognised body remains personally subject to all the rules, principles and requirements of conduct affecting solicitors.

25. Waivers

In any particular case or cases the Council shall have power to waive in writing any of the provisions of these Rules for a particular purpose or purposes expressed in such waiver and to revoke such waiver.

26. Commencement

These Rules shall come into force on the coming into force of section 9 of the Administration of Justice Act 1985.

Annex 3D

Guidance — Practice Rule 5(6)(a) — transitional provisions for executor, trustee and nominee companies and companies providing company secretarial services

---

Commencement of the Incorporated Practice Rules

Rule 5 of the Solicitors' Practice Rules 1990 (offering services other than as a solicitor) ('Rule 5') is affected by the commencement of the Solicitors' Incorporated Practice Rules 1988 ('SIPR'), which came into force on 1st January 1992, together with section 9 of the Administration of Justice Act 1985. Paragraph (6)(a) of Rule 5 provides a transitional period, under which certain companies wholly owned by solicitors are exempted from the rule for a period of three years from the commencement date of the SIPR.

Three-year transitional period

The companies which have the benefit of the transitional period are executor and trustee companies and nominee companies already providing services before the commencement of the SIPR, and companies already providing company secretarial services before 9th June 1988. In respect of such companies the three-year transitional period started to run from 1st January 1992.

New trustee and nominee companies

However, executor and trustee companies and nominee companies which were not already providing services before the commencement of the SIPR became subject to Rule 5 from 1st January 1992. Any such company newly providing services from or after that date must be a recognised body.

(*Extract from Gazette notice of 27th November 1991, revised February 1993*)

Annex 3E

Guidance — Practice Rule 5(6)(b) — transitional provisions for companies providing services before 11th December 1986

Rule 5(6)(b) of the Solicitors' Practice Rules 1990 provides a transitional period for any business which was already providing services before 11th December 1986 without putting the solicitor in breach of the Solicitors' Practice Rules 1936/72 (as amended). Rule 1 of these rules is set out below as this is the rule which could most readily have been breached by a solicitor operating a separate business. It should be noted that the Solicitors' Practice Rules 1936/72 were repealed by the Solicitors' Practice Rules 1987.

Rule 1, Solicitors' Practice Rules 1936/72 (as amended)

(1) Subject to paragraph (2) of this Rule a solicitor shall not obtain or attempt to obtain professional business by:

(a) directly or indirectly without reasonable justification inviting instructions for such business, or

(b) doing or permitting to be done without reasonable justification, anything which by its manner, frequency or otherwise advertises his practice as a solicitor, or

(c) doing or permitting to be done anything which may reasonably be regarded as touting.

(2) In the interests of informing the public of the services provided by particular solicitors and the profession as a whole, a solicitor shall be entitled to advertise his practice in accordance with guidance published from time to time by the Council.

Revised January 1993

Annex 3F

Guidance — managers appointed following the death of a sole practitioner

1. The manager of the practice must have been admitted for more than three years and must hold a current practising certificate. When appointed, he or she must personally exercise control over the staff of the deceased principal and must supervise the office in accordance with Rule 13 of the Solicitors' Practice Rules 1990. During this period the manager will conduct the practice for the personal representative and pay the profits, less any remuneration agreed to be paid to him or her, to the estate. Arrangements for remuneration of the manager are a matter between the manager and the personal representatives. The personal representatives are entitled to the professional profits earned during this period. Only in exceptional circumstances should these arrangements continue beyond the executor's year. Any manager who considers that the arrangement should continue after this time must contact the Law Society for guidance.

2. The manager must arrange for the stationery of the practice to be changed so that his or her name appears on the letterheads as if he or she were the sole principal. If so desired he or she may be described as the manager of the firm.

3. The manager must inform the clients of the practice of the arrangements made. Further, Solicitors Indemnity Fund Limited and other insurers concerned (i.e. those providing excess and top-up cover) should be advised so that proper insurance cover can be provided for the solicitor-manager. The Records Office must also be notified and informed of these arrangements.

4. Fresh books of account must be opened immediately following the death of the principal and these should be kept as the solicitor-manager's books until the practice is diposed of. The solicitor-manager may arrange with the bank for the opening of a new separate bank account for client account purposes. This is because the sole principal's client account will be frozen until such time as a grant of representation is obtained. The bank may allow the new account to be overdrawn to the extent of the sum standing to the credit of the sole principal's client account. No further monies should be paid into this latter account, and reimbursement will be made from it to the new account on the grant of representation.

5. For the purposes of the Solicitors' Account Rules 1991 the sum overdrawn must not exceed the sum held in the sole principal's client account. Further it is only possible to withdraw sums from this new account on behalf of an individual client to the extent of the funds held therein and in the sole principal's client account for that individual client. A similar arrangement can be made for office account

purposes. Although the practice of banks in these circumstances may differ in minor respects, the solicitor-manager will be responsible for ensuring compliance with the requirements of the bank concerned. In cases of doubt, the solicitor-manager may refer the matter to the Law Society.

6. Client's money received after the date of death should be placed in the new account, operated by the solicitor-manager. The solicitor-manager must supply an accountant's report in respect of the practice from the date of death of the sole principal and must use his or her best endeavours to ensure that the personal representatives supply an accountant's report up to the date of death. This requirement must be in addition to a separate report supplied by the solicitor-manager where he or she has held clients' money in respect of his or her own practice.

7. The manager should consider his or her position in relation to the Financial Services Act 1986. An investment business certificate which has been issued to a sole principal lapses with the death of the sole principal. Therefore the manager must apply for an investment business certificate in his or her own name if he or she intends to conduct investment business. This is so even when the manager holds separate authorisation in relation to another practice. Applications for an investment business certificate should be made to the Financial Services Section. Alternatively, authorisation to conduct investment business may be obtained from a self-regulating organisation or the Securities and Investments Board.

8. Once the personal representatives of the deceased sole principal have obtained a grant of representation they have the power to sell the practice for the benefit of the estate. If the solicitor-manager purchases the practice from the personal representatives, he or she must not act for the personal representatives and must insist that they be independently advised in this transaction. The Records Office must be informed of the arrangements for the disposal or sale of the practice.

Revised January 1993

Annex 3G

Guidance — specimen letter where a firm ceases to practise as such and clients are required to be given a choice of solicitor

(see Commentary 5 to Principle 3.13)

J & Co
64 High Street
Craxenford

Dear ....

I write to inform you that Mr J and I have agreed to dissolve our partnership and will each be setting up our own practice on 31st May.

Mr J will continue to practise from this address as J & Co.

I will be practising at 25 Market Street, Craxenford as A & Co.

Please let us know as soon as possible which of us you wish to act for you. You are, of course, free to instruct any solicitor of your choice.

It would be helpful if you could complete and sign the attached form and return it to this address preferably before 31st May. We will then be able to deal with your papers in accordance with your instructions.

For your information, we currently hold your will, as well as [£15,000] (balance of sale proceeds of your former home), in our client account in your name.

Your will and other papers will remain in safekeeping at this address and your money will remain on our client account, until we receive your instructions, or until [1st June]. If we have not heard from you by then, J & Co will assume responsibility for your papers, and hold your money on their client account until they hear from you.

Yours sincerely

I wish *Mr J/Mr A/........................(+other firm — please specify) to act for me, and instruct you to deal with my matters, papers and money accordingly.

Signed......................................

*   Please delete as appropriate.

+   If you wish to instruct another firm, we will ask you to settle any outstanding account first.

Annex 3H

Guidance — solicitors' clerks — rights of audience—solicitors' supervision responsibilities

Solicitors' clerks have a common law right of audience in chambers in the High Court and by long custom and usage they are heard in chambers in the county court. The Courts and Legal Services Act now gives statutory recognition to the position. Section 27(2)(e) gives a person a right of audience in chambers in the High Court or a county court where:

'he is employed (whether wholly or in part), or is otherwise engaged, to assist in the conduct of litigation and is doing so under instructions given (either generally or in relation to the proceedings) by a qualified litigator'.

This provision makes it clear that a person instructed by a solicitor to appear in chambers may be either an employee of the solicitor or an independent contractor.

The Standards and Guidance Committee wishes to remind solicitors that under Principle 3.01 of the Guide a solicitor is responsible for exercising supervision over both admitted and unadmitted staff. The duty to supervise extends to independent contractors as much as to employees. Commentary 1 to Principle 3.01 makes it clear that solicitors remain responsible for work carried out by their firm and that this extends to the acts or omissions of their staff, which term would include an independent contractor as well as an employee.

Accordingly, as a matter of a professional conduct, when instructing an unadmitted person (whether an employee or an independent contractor) to appear in chambers in the High Court or the county court, a solicitor should:

— be satisfied that the person is responsible and competent to carry out the instructions;

— give the person sufficiently full and clear instructions to enable him or her to carry out those instructions properly;

— afford appropriate supervision.

Solicitors' attention is drawn to section 27(4) which explicitly preserves the power of any court to refuse to hear a person who would otherwise have a right of audience before the court for reasons which apply to him or her as an individual. Thus a court could refuse to hear a person who was incompetent or irresponsible but should such a situation arise in relation to a solicitor's clerk whether or not an employee, his or her principal may be called upon to give an explanation.

Updated January 1993

Annex 3I

Guidance — retiring solicitors, including solicitors who are professional trustees

Solicitors considering retirement have a number of decisions to make in relation to their professional position. These notes are intended to provide some basic information which may help in making these decisions.

There are a several options open to retiring solicitors — to continue to hold a practising certificate and perhaps to act as a consultant for a firm to do occasional or part-time work; to cease holding a practising certificate but remain on the roll, or to have their name removed from the roll altogether.

The need to hold a practising certificate

The Solicitors Act 1974 ('the Act') restricts certain activities to solicitors with practising certificates and lays down requirements for those who wish to act as solicitors.

The definition of 'unqualified person' in section 87 of the Act includes a solicitor without a practising certificate. Thus, a solicitor, even if he or she is not in practice, who wishes to undertake any of the acts prohibited to unqualified persons by sections 20-22 and 23-24, must hold a practising certificate. A solicitor who performs such acts without a practising certificate could be prosecuted under the Act and would also be liable to disciplinary proceedings.

Principle 2.01 in the Guide and the accompanying commentary detail the acts reserved to *inter alia* solicitors by sections 20-22 and 23-24 of the Act or by other statutory or non-statutory provisions, for which a solicitor would require a practising certificate.

Section 1A of the Act provides that any solicitor employed in private practice in connection with the provision of any legal services must have a practising certificate. This provision is interpreted as covering consultants and locums as well as assistant solicitors.

The following are some of the common questions raised by solicitors who wish to retire:

Can I hold myself out as a solicitor if I do not have a practising certificate?

If you remain on the roll but do not hold a practising certificate, you may, nevertheless, describe yourself as a solicitor provided that in doing so you are not by implication holding yourself out as qualified to practise as a solicitor. For example, if you have written a book there would be no objection to being described on the title page as a solicitor even though you hold no practising certificate. By contrast, if you went into a business which provided services of any type which solicitors might provide you should qualify the description 'solicitor' by the addition of words such as 'non-practising' or 'uncertificated' in order to avoid misleading people into thinking that you are qualified to act as a solicitor.

Do I need a practising certificate if I am a consultant with a firm?

If you remain as a consultant with your firm then a practising certificate will be required if you play any part in the provision of legal services.

However, if you are completely retired and play no part in the provision of any legal services your name can appear on a firm's notepaper as 'consultant' without the need for a practising certificate if qualified by such explanatory words as 'retired non-practising solicitor' or 'retired uncertificated solicitor'.

What do I need to do if I wish to practise on my own account, or on a part-time or *ad hoc* basis?

If you continue to practise, albeit on a part-time or purely occasional basis, you must comply with all relevant provisions of the Act, with the Solicitors' Practice Rules and with the requirements of professional conduct generally. In particular, it should be noted that you must comply with the Solicitors' Accounts Rules and the Solicitors' Indemnity Rules.

Where you wish to do work as a solicitor without remuneration only for personal friends, relatives, companies wholly owned by your family, or registered charities, you should retain your practising certificate but you will not need to make contributions to the Indemnity Fund provided that you tell your clients in writing that you are not covered by the Solicitors' Indemnity Fund. See Rule 9 of the Solicitors' Indemnity Rules 1992. However, if you do work for persons other than those specified you must take out indemnity cover.

If you decide to go into practice on your own account you will have to consider whether you need to apply to the Law Society for an investment business certificate (see Chapter 26 in the Guide). Guidance on the question of authorisation may be obtained from Professional Ethics and application forms for certificates may be obtained from the Financial Services Section.

What are the requirements if I am a consultant with a firm?

1. You will need a practising certificate (see above).

2. A solicitor who acts as a consultant to a firm will be covered by that firm's indemnity cover for work carried out on behalf of the firm. However, see above as to the position if you are also practising on your own account.

3. A consultant will be covered by the firm's investment business certificate. However, see above as to the position if you are also practising on your own account.

What work can I undertake without a practising certificate?

If you wish to give legal advice (e.g. to friends or relatives) you must make it clear to the person concerned that you are not a practising solicitor and cannot give advice or do any work on their behalf as such, and that as a non-practising solicitor you are not insured against professional indemnity risks. As indicated above, an uncertificated solicitor may not undertake any of the reserved activities under sections 20-22 and 23-24 of the Act.

If you are uncertificated you cannot be authorised by the Law Society to conduct investment business. Carrying on investment business without authorisation is a criminal offence under the Financial Services Act 1986.

If you are uncertificated you cannot hold clients' money within the meaning of the Solicitors' Accounts Rules and you would be strongly advised against holding other people's money in any uncertificated capacity. The position of a solicitor who is a professional trustee is dealt with below.

Can I still administer oaths?

Without a practising certificate you cannot administer oaths under the Act. Under section 81 of the Act, solicitors holding current practising certificates have the powers of commissioners for oaths. Section 113 of the Courts and Legal Services Act 1990 provides that solicitors with practising certificates can also use the title 'Commissioner for Oaths'.

Some solicitors hold separate commissions granted by the Lord Chancellor and some of the older commissions do allow the holder to act as a commissioner without also holding a current practising certificate as a solicitor. If in doubt, the commission itself should be looked at to determine its scope.

Whom should I notify about my retirement?

On retiring from practice, you should notify the Records Office. You should also deliver a final accountant's report to Accountants' Reports.

If you are a sole practitioner, your date of retirement and the name of any successor practice should be notified to Solicitors Indemnity Fund Limited ('SIF Ltd') forthwith. You will receive free run-off cover thereafter, subject only to the standard deductible provisions in force at the date of your retirement. There is an option to buy out the deductible for the run-off cover period and quotes can be obtained direct from SIF Ltd.

If you cease to practise before the start of the new indemnity year (i.e. 1st September), you will not be required to make any further contributions to the Indemnity Fund. However, if you cease to practise after 1st September and/or there is a succession to your practice after this date you will be liable for the full contribution to the Fund in respect of that indemnity year. If you are likely to incur problems in closing your practice by 1st September, you should contact the Professional Indemnity Section to determine whether any dispensation might be available.

If you are a partner, your retirement should be notified to SIF Ltd forthwith. There will be no adjustment to the contribution due from the practice in respect of the indemnity year in which your retirement occurs. If you retire after the firm's gross fee certificate has been submitted to the Fund in March, your retirement can be taken into account in calculating the forthcoming contribution (due on 1st September) but only if the change is notified in writing to SIF Ltd by 31st July.

Claims which occur following the retirement of a partner are usually dealt with under the cover of the continuing partnership.

It should be noted that the indemnity year ends on 31st August whereas the practising certificate year ends on 31st October. A solicitor who continues to practise until the end of the practising certificate year will have practised two months into the next indemnity year and will be liable to pay the full contribution for that indemnity year unless, in an exceptional situation, a waiver is granted.

What are the requirements for notifying clients?

If a sole principal decides to cease to practise, he or she must inform clients of the fact so that they may make arrangements to instruct other solicitors. In other circumstances where there has been an alteration to the composition of the firm, all clients of the firm who may be affected must be informed promptly. Detailed guidance is to be found in Principle 3.13 of the Guide.

Do I still need to retain my name on the roll?

If you do not remain on the roll you may not describe yourself as a solicitor, or a 'retired solicitor', although such designation as 'former solicitor' is acceptable.

If you remain on the roll but do not practise as a solicitor, you still have an obligation not to behave in a manner unbefitting a solicitor, either in your business or private life, and you are subject to the jurisdiction of the Adjudication and Appeals Committee and the Solicitors' Disciplinary Tribunal.

If you no longer wish to hold a practising certificate, you will be asked to decide whether you wish to retain your name on the roll. Under the Solicitors (Keeping of the Roll) Regulations 1989, an enquiry form will automatically be despatched annually at the beginning of March to the last recorded address held on the Society's records.

If you wish to remain on the roll you should complete the enquiry form and forward it to the Society with the appropriate annual enrolment fee, currently set at £15.00. You should also ensure that the Records Office is kept informed of your current address so that you can be sent renewal forms.

You can request the removal of your name from the roll on the same enquiry form. Application for restoration to the roll, subsequent to removal in accordance with the Solicitors (Keeping of the Roll) Regulations, is relatively straightforward. Any information that you require on this can be obtained from the Records Office.

All solicitors on the roll are entitled to free Law Society membership. Those who are not currently members of the Law Society will need to complete a membership proposal form, and will need to find an existing member to support the application. Forms may be obtained from the Records Office. The *Gazette* is not provided free of charge unless the solicitor has a practising certificate. Non-practising solicitors may take out an annual subscription for the *Gazette* and enquiries may be made of the subscriptions department.

What are the requirements if I wish to continue to act as a professional trustee?

It is the view of the Professional Standards and Development Directorate that a retired solicitor who continues to hold monies as a professional trustee will be holding clients' money or controlled trust money as the case may be.

To do this a solicitor must have a practising certificate. Indemnity cover must also be in place unless Rule 9 of the Solicitors' Indemnity Rules 1992 applies and/or a waiver of the rules has been obtained. Such a waiver and the exemption contained in Rule 9 will not be available to a solicitor who is charging for his or her services. For further information, contact the Professional Indemnity Section.

The obligation to deliver an accountant's report extends to a solicitor who is holding controlled trust money, even if the solicitor holds no clients' money. In limited circumstances a dispensation from this requirement may be granted. Accountants' Reports should be contacted for information about obtaining a dispensation.

A solicitor who wishes to retire as a professional trustee and not hold a practising certificate should cease to act, or charge, as a professional trustee.

Revised January 1993

Annex 3J

Guidance — sole practitioners who become bankrupt or enter into a voluntary arrangement with creditors

I am a sole practitioner having financial difficulties. What will happen if I:

(a) become bankrupt;

(b) enter into a voluntary arrangement with my creditors?

Bankruptcy

If you become bankrupt, section 15 of the Solicitors Act 1974 will operate automatically to suspend your practising certificate. If this happens you can apply for the suspension to be terminated by writing to the Solicitors Complaints Bureau ('SCB').

Should you be successful in having the suspension terminated, the SCB, through its Adjudication and Appeals Committee, has a discretion to impose conditions on your certificate. Conditions would undoubtedly be attached and these would inevitably require you to enter an approved partnership or employment within a firm.

Your bankruptcy would also be grounds for an intervention under Schedule 1 to the Solicitors Act 1974. An intervention would be inevitable unless you could find someone willing to take over your practice or enter into partnership with you, presupposing your practising certificate is reinstated.

If you do find yourself in a situation where bankruptcy seems probable, you should start to consider what arrangements you can make for your practice to amalgamate or for your clients to be taken over by another firm. It is worth bearing in mind that the cost of any intervention would ultimately be charged to you which would only add to your indebtedness.

When you are discharged from your bankruptcy, the SCB still has a discretion to impose conditions on your practising certificate and will in all probability impose similar conditions to those which it would impose on a bankrupt solicitor until you have had the chance to re-establish yourself.

Voluntary arrangement

Unlike bankruptcy, entering into a voluntary arrangement with creditors does not operate to suspend the practising certificate. However, the SCB would again have the power to impose a condition on your current practising certificate to the effect that you practise only in approved employment or partnership.

Again, a voluntary arrangement would give the SCB powers to intervene in your practice, but these powers would only be exercised where there is no alternative or where there is evidence that clients' money is at risk.

The SCB recognises the fact that a voluntary arrangement is intended to keep creditors at bay and that this will only be achieved if there is a reasonable prospect of their receiving money from you. The purpose of the arrangement, therefore, would be defeated if an intervention occurred.

If you cease to practise

The economic climate may make it impossible for you to find a partner or to sell your practice. If you reach the decision that you must cease to practise, you should give your clients as much notice of your intention as possible so that they can find another solicitor. It may be possible to agree with another local firm that they will take over all your clients but it must be made clear to the clients that they do have the freedom to choose any solicitor they wish.

You will need to write to all your clients and ask them to let you know what they would like you to do with their files and similarly to all those on whose behalf you hold wills, deeds and other documents. Where clients' matters need urgent attention you should ensure that the files are handed over without delay. Arrangements with your clients' new solicitors should be made with regard to the payment of any outstanding costs due to you. On a practical note, you should ensure that you get a receipt in respect of all papers which are handed over.

It is almost inevitable that you will be left with some files which are unclaimed by the clients and you should make proper arrangements for them to be stored where confidentiality can be assured. If the files are old, it may be possible to destroy them. Annex 12C in the Guide has some helpful notes on this subject.

Finally, you must not overlook your obligation to file a final accountant's report once you cease to hold clients' money. Your accountant's report will fall due within six months of the date you cease to hold clients' money. You must also inform the Solicitors Indemnity Fund Limited and the Records Office of your decision to cease practice.

Financial assistance

If you and your family are in severe financial difficulties, it may be worth contacting the Solicitors Benevolent Association at 1 Jaggard Way, Wandsworth Common, London SW12 8SG, as it may be able to offer some financial help.

Other help

If you need to talk over your problems on a confidential basis with another practising solicitor, you may wish to get in touch with Professional Ethics who can refer you to a Solicitors' Assistance Scheme member.

January 1993 (based on an article published in the Gazette on 8th April 1992.)

Chapter 4

Employed solicitors

4.01 General principles

Principle

A solicitor employed by a non-solicitor is subject to the same principles of professional conduct as a solicitor in private practice.

Commentary

1. For the purpose of this chapter, 'employed solicitor' means a solicitor employed by a non-solicitor. This chapter does not attempt to cover all conduct requirements governing employed solicitors — who are subject to the same rules and principles as solicitors in private practice — but highlights certain important requirements some of which only apply to employed solicitors.

2. The relationship between an employed solicitor and his or her employer is that of solicitor and client and therefore an employed solicitor must comply with the Solicitors' Practice Rules 1990 — in particular the Employed Solicitors Code 1990 referred to in Practice Rule 4(1) — and the general principles of professional conduct. For the Employed Solicitors Code see Annex 4A.

3. An employed solicitor is personally bound by undertakings given in the course of his or her professional duties. In particular, Principle 19.10 on undertakings and its Commentary should be noted.

4. An employed solicitor should not, when acting in the capacity of a solicitor (rather than, for example, as secretary to a company or local authority) communicate with third parties who are represented by a solicitor, except with that solicitor's consent; any communication should be made through the solicitor acting for the third party (see Principle 20.02).

5. An employed solicitor requires a practising certificate in the following circumstances unless, in the case of (c) and (d), that solicitor is supervised by and acting in the name of a certificated solicitor:

    (a)   where the solicitor is held out (either on stationery or otherwise) as a solicitor for the employer, whether in a legal department or otherwise;

    (b)   in administering oaths; the solicitor must also comply with the requirements of the Solicitors Act 1974, section 81(2) (see Principle 18.08);

    (c)   in doing any of the acts prohibited to unqualified persons by the Solicitors Act 1974, save where there are statutory exceptions such as for certain work carried out by non-certificated solicitors employed by a local authority (see Local Government Act 1972, section 223);

    (d)   in instructing counsel;

    (e)   where the solicitor appears before a court or a tribunal and in so appearing places reliance on his or her right of audience as a solicitor.

6.   A justices' clerk acting as such is not practising as a solicitor; therefore the requirement in Commentary 5(d) will not apply.

7.   An employed solicitor may use the stationery of, or stationery including the name of, his or her employer for professional work provided:

    (a)   either the letterhead or the signature makes it clear that the stationery is being used by a solicitor on legal professional business and that the solicitor is responsible for the contents of the letter; and

    (b)   the stationery is being used for the business of the non-solicitor employer or for third parties in circumstances permitted by Practice Rule 4.

8.   An employed solicitor may, when acting as such, use a style of stationery or description which appears to hold that solicitor out as a principal or solicitor in private practice. The Solicitors' Indemnity Fund would not cover work done by an employed solicitor acting as such, and there would be no obligation to comply with the Solicitors' Indemnity Rules; but see Commentary 3 to Principle 4.04.

9.   The address of a company's legal department is the place (or one of the places) where the solicitor practises and must therefore be notified to the Records Office as a practising address of the solicitor.

10.   Employed solicitors who do not have offices open to the public are not required to comply with Rule 13 of the Solicitors' Practice Rules 1990. However, an employed solicitor will be answerable in conduct for the acts of staff assisting in his or her practice as a solicitor.

11.   An employed solicitor's obligation to pay counsel's fees is dealt with in Commentary 6 to Principle 21.08.

4.02　Accounts rules and accountants' reports

Principle

Employed solicitors who receive or hold clients' money must comply with the Solicitors' Accounts Rules 1991 ('the Accounts Rules') and the Accountant's Report Rules 1991 ('the Accountant's Report Rules'), and will be required to contribute to any special levy for the Compensation Fund.

Commentary

1.　A solicitor receiving a cheque made out in his or her favour on behalf of an employer is receiving clients' money and must deal with it in accordance with the Accounts Rules. Even if a cheque is simply endorsed over to the employer, the solicitor will need to keep a record (see Rule 11 of the Accounts Rules) and submit an accountant's report.

2.　An in-house accountant may not prepare an accountant's report for an employed solicitor (see Rule 3(1)(c) of the Accountant's Report Rules).

3.　When only a small number of transactions are undertaken or a small volume of client money is handled in a year, a dispensation from the obligation to deliver an accountant's report may be sought from Accountants' Reports.

4.　A solicitor who receives only his or her employer's money may be well advised to ensure that all cheques are made payable to the employer.

5.　A solicitor acting in the course of his or her employment as:

(a)　a public officer;

(b)　an officer of statutory undertakers; or

(c)　an officer of a local authority

need not comply with the Accounts Rules (see Rule 30 of the Accounts Rules).

4.03　Acting for third parties

Principle

'Solicitors who are employees of non-solicitors shall not as part of their employment do for any person other than their employer work which is or could be done by a solicitor acting as such, save as permitted by an Employed Solicitors Code promulgated from time to time by the Council of

the Law Society with the concurrence of the Master of the Rolls.'

Solicitors' Practice Rules 1990, Rule 4(1)

Commentary

1. The Employed Solicitors Code 1990 is set out in Annex 4A.

2. The code governs the conduct of solicitors in the course of their practice as employees of non-solicitor employers. Paragraph 1 sets out general principles. Paragraphs 2-9 deal with specific circumstances where an employed solicitor, in the course of his or her employment, may act for persons or bodies other than the employer. Save as permitted by the code, employed solicitors may not, in the course of their employment, act for third parties.

4.04   Separate private practice

Principle

An employed solicitor may act for private clients, including fellow employees, outside the course of the solicitor's employment.

Commentary

1. For details regarding arrangements for the introduction of clients, see the Introduction and Referral Code set out in Principle 11.03 and Annex 11B.

2. An employed solicitor must not act for private clients where there is any conflict between the interests of the private clients and the interests of the solicitor's employer.

3. An employed solicitor who also practises privately as a solicitor, is a principal in private practice. In such circumstances contribution must be made to the Solicitors' Indemnity Fund. (For details of the Solicitors' Indemnity Rules see Chapter 28.)

4. An employed solicitor who carries on a private practice from home must take care not to breach the provisions of Rule 13 of the Solicitors' Practice Rules 1990. The requirements regarding supervision and management of an office 'when it is open to the public or open to telephone calls from the public' have the following implications:

    (a) as regards supervision, a solicitor or a partner must have been admitted for at least three years;

(b)   telephone calls can only be taken, or members of the public seen in the solicitor's absence, if the requirements for management and supervision of the office are met by a partner or employee with the necessary qualifications. However, the use of an answerphone when the solicitor is not at home would not breach Rule 13.

5.   An employed solicitor also practising privately who holds or receives clients' money must comply with the Accounts Rules and the Accountant's Report Rules. Details are to be found in Chapter 27.

6.   An employed solicitor who also carries on private practice on his or her own account may agree to reimburse his or her employer for that proportion of the solicitor's salary and of the employer's other overhead expenses which is attributable to any private practice work carried out in the employer's time, on the employer's premises and/or with the assistance of staff and materials provided by the employer. It will be the responsibility of the solicitor in such cases to ensure that this allowance for overheads is properly computed; otherwise there could be a breach of Practice Rule 7 (fee-sharing).

4.05   Industrial action

Principle

It is not improper for an employed solicitor to strike or take other industrial action, but the solicitor must have regard to his or her duties to the court and third parties.

Commentary

Before deciding to take industrial action a solicitor must:

(a)   ensure that no party for whom the solicitor is acting in the course of his or her employment is prejudiced by the action in any crucial way, e.g. by a failure to meet limitation periods;

(b)   ensure that steps are taken to cover all court engagements;

(c)   ensure that there is compliance with any professional undertaking given by him or her as a solicitor;

(d)   at the earliest possible time take reasonable steps to notify persons who may be affected by the proposed action.

4.06   Costs recovered from third parties

Principle

An employed solicitor, in putting forward a claim for costs against a third party, must have regard to the proper indemnity basis for costs.

Commentary

1.   Where an employed solicitor acts for his or her employer, there is no presumption that it is any cheaper to employ a solicitor in-house than to retain a solicitor in private practice. The court will therefore normally regard it as proper for an employed solicitor's bill to be drawn on the usual principles applicable to a solicitor in private practice. There may, however, be special cases where it is quite clear that a bill drawn on this basis would improperly remunerate the employer and should therefore be disallowed (see *Henderson* v. *Merthyr Tydfil U.D.C.* [1900] 1 Q.B. 434 and *Re Eastwood (deceased)* [1975] Ch. 112). There seems no reason in principle why such an approach should not also be applicable to non-contentious business, or to matters where the employed solicitor is acting for someone other than the employer.

2.   Under certain circumstances the Employed Solicitors Code permits an employed solicitor to act for someone other than the employer, as part of the solicitor's employment. In such cases there will be no breach of Practice Rule 7 when the solicitor accounts to the employer for costs paid either by the client or by the client's opponents or other third parties (see Rule 7(3)).

4.07   Direct access to client

Principle

A solicitor employed as the senior legal adviser of a company or a local authority must have direct access to the board of the company or to the council and committees of the authority whom he or she is advising.

Commentary

1.   A solicitor employed in this position should seek to ensure that his or her terms of employment provide for such access.

2.   'Direct access' does not mean that all instructions and advice must pass directly to and from the council, committee or board, but the solicitor must have direct access where necessary.

4.08 Law centres and other non-commercial advice services

Principle

A solicitor employed by a law centre, a Citizen's Advice Bureau or similar non-commercial organisation may, in accordance with paragraph 7 of the Employed Solicitors Code 1990, advise and act for members of the public; the solicitor must comply in all respects with the Practice Rules, the code, and other principles of conduct.

Commentary

1. At a law centre or other non-commercial advice service, not only is advice given, but casework (including legal proceedings) may be handled. Solicitors employed in connection with the provision of such services are practising from offices which must be regarded as open to the public and must comply with Rule 13 of the Solicitors' Practice Rules 1990. The difficulties for law centres in complying with Rule 13 have resulted in frequent applications for waivers of Rule 13.

2. A solicitor employed by a non-commercial advice service is obliged to hold a current practising certificate and to comply in all respects with the Solicitors' Accounts Rules 1991 (see Principle 4.02).

3. As a solicitor employed by a non-commercial advice service is not employed in private practice, he or she is outside the scope of the Solicitors Indemnity Fund in respect of legal services provided there. An advice service within the meaning of paragraph 7 of the Employed Solicitors Code must effect insurance against any professional negligence in accordance with paragraph 7(a)(v).

4. A service may be offered through an honorary legal adviser scheme or rota scheme. Solicitors participating in these schemes, and their firms, must comply with the Solicitors' Introduction and Referral Code 1990 (see Annex 11B).

5. A solicitor who works as a volunteer for a non-commercial advice service may pay to the organisation any fees or costs he or she receives under the Legal Advice and Assistance ('green form') Scheme (see Rule 7(4) of the Solicitors' Practice Rules 1990). He or she must also have the benefit of indemnity cover through Solicitors Indemnity Fund Limited unless exempted by a waiver.

4.09   Commercial legal advice services

Principle

A solicitor who is the employee of a commercial organisation providing a telephone legal advice service may advise enquirers in accordance with paragraph 8 of the Employed Solicitors Code 1990; the solicitor must comply in all respects with the Practice Rules, the code, and other principles of conduct.

Commentary

Where the service is open to telephone calls from the public the solicitor must comply with Practice Rule 13.

Annex 4A

Employed Solicitors Code 1990

(with consolidated amendments to 1st January 1992)

Code dated 18th July 1990 promulgated by the Council of the Law Society with the concurrence of the Master of the Rolls under Rule 4 of the Solicitors' Practice Rules 1990, regulating the practices of employed solicitors.

1. General

(a) This code applies to solicitors employed by non-solicitor employers in the course of the solicitor's employment with such a non-solicitor employer. This code does not apply to any private practice of such solicitors. The code sets out the principles to be followed when an employed solicitor, as part of his or her employment, acts for a person other than the employer in accordance with the provisions of the code.

Multi-national partnerships

(aa) Nothing in this code applies to a solicitor employed by a multi-national partnership.

Conflict of interest

(b) Despite anything in this code employed solicitors must not act in any situation where they would be precluded from acting by an actual or potential conflict of interest.

Practice Rules

(c) Nothing is this code should be taken as sanctioning conduct inconsistent with the principle of the solicitor's independence as embodied in Rule 1 of the Solicitors' Practice Rules 1990 or with any other provisions of those rules.

Best interests of client

(d) The solicitor should, before accepting instructions to act for persons other than the employer in accordance with this code, consider whether the employer is able by way of insurance or otherwise to indemnify the client adequately in the event of a claim against the solicitor for which the employer would be vicariously liable.

ANNEX 4A: EMPLOYED SOLICITORS CODE 1990

Confidentiality

(e) Where an employed solicitor is acting for a person other than the employer in accordance with this code any information disclosed to the solicitor by the client is confidential and cannot be disclosed to the employer without the express consent of the client.

Indemnity

(f) The solicitor must ensure at the outset of the matter that the client has been made aware of the insurance position in that the solicitor is not covered by the Solicitors' Indemnity Fund in relation to professional negligence, and that the client receives or has received notice in writing of the position.

2. Fellow employees

Where it is not prohibited by the principles set out in paragraph 1 above, and subject to provisos (i)-(iv) below, an employed solicitor may act for:

(a)   a fellow employee;

(b)   a director, company secretary or board member of the solicitor's employer;

(c)   an employee, director, company secretary, board member or trustee of a related body of the employer within the meaning of paragraphs 5(a) or 6(b) below;

(d)   a contributor to a programme or periodical publication, broadcast or published by the solicitor's employer (or by a related body within the meaning of paragraphs 5(a) or 6(b) below), but only where the contributor is a defendant or potential defendant in a defamation case; and

(e)   in conveyancing transactions, where acting in accordance with this code for any person in sub-paragraph (a) to (c) above, the employed solicitor may also act for a joint owner/buyer and for a mortgagee;

provided in every case that:

(i)   the matter relates to or arises out of the work of the employee, director, company secretary, board member, trustee or contributor in that capacity; and

(ii)   the matter does not relate to a claim arising as a result of a personal injury to the employee, director, company secretary, board member or trustee; and

(iii) the solicitor is satisfied that the employee, director, company secretary, board member, trustee or contributor does not wish to instruct some other solicitor or other qualified conveyancer; and

(iv)   there is no charge to the employee, director, company secretary, board member, trustee or contributor in relation to the solicitor's costs insofar as they are not recoverable from any other source.

3. Associations

A solicitor who is the employee of an association may act for a member provided:

(a)   the membership of the association is limited to persons engaged or concerned in a particular trade, occupation or activity or otherwise having a community of interest; and

THE GUIDE TO THE PROFESSIONAL CONDUCT OF SOLICITORS 1993

(b)   the association is one formed *bona fide* for the benefit of its members and not formed directly or indirectly for the benefit of the solicitor or primarily for securing assistance in legal proceedings; and

(c)   there shall be no charge to the member in non-contentious matters; and in contentious matters the association shall indemnify the member in relation to the solicitor's costs and disbursements insofar as they are not recoverable from any other source.

4.   Insurance

(a)   A solicitor who is the employee of an insurer subrogated to the rights of an insured in respect of any matter may act on behalf of the insurer in relation to that matter in the name of the insured, and if he or she does so may:

(i)   act on behalf of the insured in relation also to uninsured losses in respect of the matter;

(ii)   act in proceedings both for the insured and for a defendant covered by another insurer where the insurers have agreed an apportionment of liability; and/or

(iii) act in the matter on behalf of the employer and another insurer in the joint prosecution of a claim.

(b)   A solicitor who is the employee of a legal expenses insurer may handle on behalf of an insured a claim (other than a personal injury claim) the value of which does not exceed the "no costs" limit from time to time in operation in the county court, provided the insured gives specific consent.

5.   Related bodies

(a)   An employed solicitor may act for:

(i)   the employer's holding, associated or subsidiary company;

(ii)   a partnership, syndicate or company by way of joint venture in which the employer and others have an interest;

(iii) a trade association of which the employer is a member;

(iv)   a club, association, pension fund or other scheme operated for the benefit of employees of the employer.

(b)   Sub-paragraphs (a)(i) and (ii) above do not apply to local government.

6.   Local government

A solicitor employed in local government may act:

(a)   for another public body or statutory officer to which the employer is statutorily empowered to provide legal services; or

(b)   for a company limited by shares or guarantee of which the employer or nominee of the employer is a shareholder or guarantor in pursuance of its statutory powers and of which the solicitor or an officer of the employer is a director or secretary; together with any wholly owned subsidiary or associated companies of such a company; provided that in the case of a company limited by shares the majority of the shares are owned by either the employer or by the employer together with other public bodies; or

(c)   for lenders in connection with new mortgages arising from the redemption of mortgages to the local authority, provided:

    (i)   no employed solicitor or other employee acts on behalf of the borrowers; and

    (ii)   the borrowers are given the opportunity to be independently advised by a solicitor or other qualified conveyancer of their choice; or

(d)   in non-contentious matters for a charity or voluntary organisation whose objects relate wholly or mainly to the employer's area, provided there is no charge to the charity or organisation.

7.   Law centres, charities and other non-commercial advice services

(a)   A solicitor who is the employee of a law centre or advice service operated by a charitable or similar non-commercial organisation may give advice to and otherwise act for members of the public, provided:

    (i)   no funding agent has majority representation on the body responsible for the management of the service, which body must remain independent of central and local government; and

    (ii)   no fees are charged save:

        (A) under the legal aid scheme; or

        (B) where the organisation indemnifies the client in relation to the solicitor's costs insofar as they are not recoverable from any other source; and

    (iii) all fees earned and costs recovered by the solicitor are paid to the organisation for furthering the provision of the organisation's services; and

    (iv) the organisation is not described as a law centre unless it is a member of the Law Centres Federation; and

    (v)   the organisation effects indemnity cover reasonably equivalent to that available to solicitors from the Solicitors' Indemnity Fund.

(b) Sub-paragraph (a) above does not extend to an association formed for the benefit of its members.

8.   Commercial legal advice services

A solicitor who is the employee of a commercial organisation providing a telephone legal advice service may advise enquirers, provided:

(a)   subject to paragraph 4(b) above, the advice comprises telephone advice only, together with a follow up letter to the enquirer when necessary; and

(b)   the solicitor is satisfied that there is indemnity cover reasonably equivalent to that available to solicitors from the Solicitors' Indemnity Fund.

9.   Government departments and regulatory bodies

A solicitor who is the employee of a government department or a regulatory body may in carrying out the functions of the employer give legal advice to other persons and in the case of statutory functions may act generally for such persons.

10. Interpretation

In this code:

(a)   all words have the meanings assigned to them in Rule 18 of the Solicitors' Practice Rules 1990;

(b)   "act" includes the giving of legal advice;

(c)   "holding company" and "subsidiary company" have the meanings assigned to them by the Companies Act 1985 (as amended by the Companies Act 1989) and two companies are "associated" where they are subsidiary companies of the same holding company; and

(d)   save in paragraph 1, references to a solicitor's employer include the employer's holding, associated or subsidiary company; and references to an employee include references to an employee of such holding, associated or subsidiary company.

Chapter 5

Legal aid

5.01 The duty to advise

Principle

A solicitor is under a duty to consider and advise the client on the availability of legal aid where the client might be entitled to assistance under the Legal Aid Act 1988.

Commentary

1. This chapter deals with the conduct issues arising out of legal aid work. Solicitors should refer to the current *Legal Aid Handbook* for practical guidance on the application of all the legal aid regulations.

2. Failure to advise clients of their rights under the Legal Aid Act can amount to unbefitting conduct and may also lead to a claim in negligence against a solicitor for breach of duty owed to the client.

3. If the client is eligible for legal aid but no application is made for legal aid, it is prudent to keep a record on the client's file of the reasons for not making an application.

4. The duty to advise applies not only at the outset of the retainer but, as the matter proceeds. It is the duty of a solicitor to ensure that any material change of which he or she becomes aware in the client's means is at once taken into consideration in the context of eligibility for legal aid.

5. Where a solicitor considers that legal aid is likely to be available to the client, the availability of an emergency certificate should also be borne in mind. A solicitor who commences work without legal aid cover runs the risk of being unable to recover his or her pre-certificate costs.

6. Legally aided clients must be treated in the same way as privately funded clients and the same standards of care apply.

5.02   Costs — civil legal aid

Standard (e) written professional standards states:

'Where clients are legally aided they should be informed at the outset of a case and at appropriate stages thereafter:

    (i)   **of the effect of the statutory charge on the case;**

    (ii)   **that if they lose the case they may still be ordered by the court to contribute to their opponent's costs even though their own costs are covered by legal aid;**

    (iii)   **that even if they win their opponent may not be ordered to pay the full amount of their costs and may not be capable of paying what they have been ordered to pay;**

    (iv)   **of their obligations to pay any contribution assessed and of the consequences of any failure to do so.'**

5.03   Confidentiality — civil legal aid — exceptions to general principles

Principle

In certain circumstances in legally aided cases, a solicitor may be under a duty to report information to the Legal Aid Board concerning the client which is confidential and/or privileged.

Commentary

1.   The Area Director of the Legal Aid Board (under regulation 19 of the Legal Advice and Assistance Regulations 1989) can require a solicitor to give information to the Area Director and the solicitor shall not be precluded by reason of any privilege from disclosing the information to the Area Director.

2.   Where a solicitor believes that:

    (a)   the assisted person has required his or her case to be conducted unreasonably so as to incur unjustifiable expense;

    (b)   has intentionally failed to comply with any provision made under the Legal Aid Act concerning information to be furnished by the client;

    (c)   in furnishing information has knowingly made a false statement or representation,

    then the solicitor must report this to the Area Director (see regulation 67 of the Civil Legal Aid (General) Regulations 1989). Where the solicitor is uncertain as to whether it would be reasonable to continue acting for the assisted person, the solicitor must report the circumstances to the Area Director.

3. If solicitors wish to refuse to act for a legally aided client or to give up the case after being selected for it, there is a duty to report the reasons to the Area Director (regulation 69 of the Civil Legal Aid (General) Regulations 1989).

4. Solicitors must report to the Area Director where assisted persons decline a reasonable settlement offer or a payment into court (regulation 70 of the Civil Legal Aid (General) Regulations 1989).

5. Privilege and confidentiality are specifically overridden by regulation 73 of the Civil Legal Aid (General) Regulations 1989, which provides that solicitors shall not be precluded by reason of any privilege, from providing any information or giving any opinion which the Area Director or the area committee require under the Legal Aid Act or the legal aid regulations.

5.04   Confidentiality — criminal legal aid

Principle

Where the client is legally aided in a criminal matter the duty to disclose all relevant information remains with the client. However, if the solicitor becomes aware of information which indicates that the client's circumstances have changed, or that the client did not disclose relevant information at the outset, the solicitor must advise the client that unless the client informs or permits the solicitor to inform the clerk to the justices or the appropriate officer in the Crown Court, the solicitor will have to cease acting.

5.05   Termination of retainer — lien

Principle

On termination of the retainer a solicitor should, subject to his or her lien, deliver to the client any papers and property to which the client is entitled or hold them to his or her order, and account for all of the client's funds which are not subject to the Legal Aid Board's statutory charge.

Commentary

1. A lien will arise over a client's papers and documents delivered to a solicitor in his or her professional capacity for work done prior to the issue

of a legal aid certificate where the client has not paid the pre-certificate costs. Consequently, a solicitor will be able to retain all papers, including those relating to work done under a legal aid certificate. However, the Society recommends that where proceedings are continuing the solicitor's papers should be released to the successor solicitor subject to the receipt of a satisfactory undertaking as to the costs already incurred. For guidance on ownership of documents see Annex 12B.

2.   Where there are no outstanding pre-certificate costs and the client is legally aided, the Society takes the view that a solicitor's costs covered by a legal aid order or certificate are secure. It follows that it would be inappropriate to call for a professional undertaking from the successor solicitor as to payment of costs.

3.   A solicitor acting in legally aided matters may call for an undertaking from the successor solicitor either:

    (a)   to return the papers promptly at the end of the matter to enable a bill of costs to be drawn up; or

    (b)   that the successor solicitor will include the former solicitor's costs in a bill to be taxed, collect those costs and pay them over to the former solicitor.

5.06   Court and 24-hour duty solicitor schemes

Principle

A solicitor who provides police station advice as a duty solicitor or representation at a magistrates' court is bound by Parts VII and VIII of the Legal Aid Board Duty Solicitor Arrangements 1992 as to the scope of service to be provided including paragraphs 51 (defendant's right to instruct other solicitor) and 60 (continued instructions). The arrangements are contained in the current *Legal Aid Handbook*.

Commentary

1.   The Legal Aid Board Duty Solicitor Arrangements 1992 provide for the duty solicitor schemes at magistrates' courts and the provision of 24-hour duty solicitor arrangements for suspects at police stations. The responsibility for the scheme at individual courts or police stations is with local duty solicitor committees consisting of local solicitors and others such as the clerk to the justices, a justice of the peace and lay members. Regional committees made up of representatives of all local duty solicitor committees in a region, justices of the peace, justices' clerks, lay members and representatives of the police and probation services have a general duty to implement and monitor the provision of both court and 24-hour duty solicitors.

2.   Solicitors may attend at court or police stations, have clients referred to them by court officers and others, may directly approach defendants at court and subsequently act for the client at their office in the usual way.

3.   Solicitors wishing to become duty solicitors should apply ' to the administrator of their local committee. The legal aid area office can inform them of the identity of the appropriate administrator.

Chapter 6

Legal expenses insurance

6.01 Acceptance of referrals from legal expenses insurers

Principle

Solicitors may accept referrals from legal expenses insurers to act for the insured provided they comply with provisions of the Solicitors' Introduction and Referral Code 1990.

Commentary

1. The solicitor's principal duty is to the insured, not the legal expenses insurer but the insured has a duty to mitigate loss and keep the insurer informed of progress. The solicitor should remind the client of these obligations when necessary. Consequently, the referred client must be dealt with in the same manner as any private client.

2. Solicitors must not enter into any arrangement in which the insurer insists that a particular solicitor must act. By virtue of Rule 1 of the Solicitors' Practice Rules 1990 and the Solicitors' Introduction and Referral Code 1990 (see Annex 11B) the client has the right to instruct a solicitor of his or her choice. However, the client's right to instruct a solicitor of his or her choice may have been modified by the terms of the insurance policy.

3. It is a breach of the Solicitors' Introduction and Referral Code for solicitors to reward introducers by the payment of commission or otherwise.

4. Solicitors should make clear to the insured that the responsibility for the payment of the solicitor's costs remains with the insured and if for any reason the insurer refuses to make a payment for costs, the solicitor will look to the insured for payment.

5. For details of information that should be given at the outset of the retainer see Chapter 13.

6.02   Confidentiality

Principle

A solicitor has a duty of confidentiality to the insured client.

Commentary

1.   The solicitor's duty of confidentiality is the same as in a privately funded matter but the insured client will normally be under an obligation to disclose relevant matters to the insurer.

2.   A solicitor must obtain specific consent from the insured client before allowing the legal expenses insurer to inspect the file. The client should be reminded of his or her duties to the insurer when consent is sought.

6.03   Termination of retainer by legal expenses insurer or the solicitor

Principle

The retainer with the insured client is not terminated when an insurer refuses to fund a matter further. Only the insured client or the solicitor can terminate the retainer. If funding is withdrawn a solicitor has an obligation to advise as to the availability of legal aid or otherwise advise as to costs if the insured wishes to continue as a private client.

Commentary

As a matter of law, subject to any provisions within the policy, where the insurer decides not to continue funding the proceedings, the normal position as to ownership of papers in the solicitor's possession should apply (for guidance on ownership of documents see Annex 12B).

6.04   Solicitors employed by legal expenses insurers

Principle

'Solicitors employed by a legal expenses insurer may with the insured's specific consent handle a claim (other than a personal injury claim) on the

client's behalf provided that the value of the claim does not exceed the current county court "no costs" limit.'

Employed Solicitors Code 1990, paragraph 4

Commentary

Further guidance on employed solicitors can be found in Chapter 4.

Chapter 7

Anti-discrimination code

7.01 Code of practice on the avoidance of race and sex discrimination

Principle

Solicitors must not discriminate on grounds of race or sex in their professional dealings with clients, employees, other solicitors, barristers or other persons.

Commentary

1. Solicitors and their staff should deal with all persons with the same attention, courtesy and consideration regardless of race or sex.

2. (a) A solicitor must not discriminate on grounds of race or sex in the selection, treatment or promotion of staff.

    (b) In relation to a position as partner in a firm, solicitors are also reminded of the provisions of section 10 of the Race Relations Act 1976 and section 11 of the Sex Discrimination Act 1975 as amended by section 1(3) of the Sex Discrimination Act 1986.

3. A solicitor is generally free to decide whether to accept instructions from any particular client, but any refusal to act must not be based upon the race, colour, ethnic or national origins, sex or creed of the prospective client.

4. (a) In relation to the instruction of counsel, solicitors are reminded of the provision of section 26A(3) of the Race Relations Act 1976 and section 35A(3) of the Sex Discrimination Act 1975 as inserted by section 64 of the Courts and Legal Services Act 1990.

    (b) Barristers should be instructed on the basis of their skills, experience and ability. Solicitors must not, on the grounds of race or sex, avoid briefing a barrister, and must not instruct barristers' clerks to do so.

(c) Clients' requests for a named barrister should be accepted, subject to the solicitor's duty to discuss with the client the suitability of the barrister and to advise appropriately.

(d) A solicitor has a duty to discuss with the client any requests by the client that only a barrister of a particular racial group or sex be instructed. The solicitor must endeavour to persuade the client to modify instructions which appear to be given on discriminatory grounds. Should the client refuse to modify such instructions, the solicitor should cease to act.

Annex 7A

Equal opportunities in solicitors' firms — practice information

Introduction

It is a widespread practice in commerce, industry and the public sector for employers to have equal opportunities policies to ensure fair practices in employment. The reasons behind the increasing number of such policies are not only because it is fair that employers make an effort to ensure that all parts of their workforce — and of the population outside seeking to join their workforce — have equal access to benefits, but also because it makes good business sense. For instance, the long-term retention of highly trained women who leave to have a baby is a sound commercial step, but policies need to be developed to cater for women's needs. Similarly, with the drop in the number of school leavers in the 1990s, employers will need to be sure that they appeal to all parts of the community, including ethnic minorities, if they are to attract the best candidates. Firms of solicitors are no different from other employers. Equal opportunities will help firms to flourish. The message is: 'Be fair and be business-like: adopt an equal opportunities policy!'

Groups to be covered

All people, white or black, male or female, able-bodied or disabled, should feel that they are covered by an equal opportunities policy. However, it is generally recognised that certain groups in society have more difficulty in making progress than others, and Acts of Parliament have been passed to protect them from discrimination in employment — the Sex Discrimination Act 1975 and the Race Relations Act 1976, for instance, and also legislation relating to disabled people. Women, ethnic minorities and disabled people should, therefore, be in an employer's mind when drawing up an equal opportunities policy. There is plenty of research to show — and many people know from their own experience — that a number of employers have unfavourable assumptions about these groups — for instance, that women are not really suited because of child care responsibilities to become partners in firms, or that clients would not like a black solicitor looking after their affairs. It is to counter actions taken on these assumptions that an equal opportunities policy is necessary.

Contents of an equal opportunities policy

A standard policy for use by firms of solicitors, which can be used as a precedent in developing an equal opportunities policy is set out below. Its form is not unalterable, and firms should feel free to change it according to their own wishes. It has been drawn up in line with recommendations made by the Equal Opportunities Commission and Commission for Racial Equality.

Also listed below are the main pieces of legislation affecting this area, so that firms can know the legislative framework within which they are working.

Implementation and monitoring

It must be stressed that the adoption of an equal opportunities policy does not in itself change anything. It is the implementation which is important, and for these purposes it is vital to monitor how the policy is working. In a small firm, this may be done without unnecessarily detailed, bureaucratic procedures, but in a large firm there will have to be formal mechanisms (such as monitoring of applicants and of appointments by race, sex and disability) to ensure that the policy is being implemented. Monitoring should also show what changes need be made to the policy to ensure its greater success. In addition, a senior person should be appointed in a large firm to oversee the implementation, deal with problems or breaches, and review the policy at fixed intervals (say, annually). Literature on monitoring is available from the Equal Opportunities Commission and the Commission for Racial Equality.

Training

It may also be necessary to undertake training of staff. People's attitudes, and in particular their unconscious attitudes, do not change overnight as a result of the adoption of a new policy. There needs to be sensitive training of staff, in particular of those who are responsible for recruitment, backed with practical written guidance, to ensure that everyone understands the aims and consequences of an equal opportunities policy. When appointing managers, firms should check that they understand and support the policy. The Law Society advises firms as to the organisations which provide training, and the Equal Opportunities Commission, the Commission for Racial Equality and the Royal Association for Disability and Rehabilitation can also advise.

One of the most positive measures which can be taken by a firm is to ensure that the images chosen to represent it — in brochures, videos or other promotional material — are representative of all sections of the community. Women, people from ethnic minorities, and disabled people are more likely to seek employment in a firm if they are assured that they will be welcomed there, and one message they will note is the way that the firm presents itself. Clients from those groups are likely to be attracted in a similar way.

Positive action for women

The Law Society has a report prepared by its Working Party on Women's Careers. A number of proposals are made, some of which are addressed to firms themselves. Full details of these can be obtained from the Law Society, but the main proposals were as follows:

(1) Firms should become more flexible in their working practices, and in particular more flexible in their approach to part-time work, whether based in the office or at home, on a job share basis, by way of consultancy or part-time partner. The full-time career model does not suit many mothers, and there is no reason why use should not be made of their skills in a different way, meeting not only their needs but the needs of firms of solicitors, especially at a time when recruits are scarce. Many women are keen to return to work after the birth of their children on a part-time basis, and much of the work of a firm can be effectively done by a part-timer. Firms should think of the possibility of part-time work whenever a

vacancy arises. Some advisory guidelines for firms on part-time work are set out below.

(2)   Firms should also take into consideration the career needs of their female assistant solicitors by beginning to operate career break schemes and advertising themselves as career break employers. A career break scheme is one where an employer spends some money each year on the individual woman who is temporarily away from work bearing and raising children, while the female employee agrees in return to give a fixed amount of time each year in work to the employer. The purpose is for the woman and the organisation to remain in contact during the child raising years in the expectation of the woman's eventual return. The scheme proposed by the Working Party is that the employer should pay for the woman's practising certificate, her membership of the Law Society, the cost of one training course per year on a subject relevant to her work and the salary for the days during the year that she is employed in the firm; while the employee agrees that in each year of the scheme she will come in to the firm to work for 10 days. Clearly, firms can adapt schemes to their own circumstances. A number of organisations, such as the big banks and the health service, have been operating such retainer schemes for some years, and they are being promoted in other professions.

(3)   Firms should also consider the need for maternity leave and maternity pay of their female partners, whether present or prospective, and ensure that there is adequate provision in their partnership deeds to cover such arrangements. Draft clauses for use by firms have been prepared, and are quoted below for adaptation and use in partnership deeds. It must be remembered that the figures in the clauses are just recommendations, and consideration should also be given to the effect of working at home, part-time work and the treatment of holiday time. Another issue worth considering is the effect of a number of pregnancies.

Finally, firms may also want to consider part-time working for staff, as well as paternity leave and career breaks for men with young childen. It is no longer wise to assume that all responsibility for the care of young children will be borne by women. The firms with the best equal opportunities policies for both sexes will have a competitive edge in attracting the best men and women.

Positive action for ethnic minorities

The Law Society employs an Ethnic Minorities Careers Officer with a specific brief to attract ethnic minority candidates to become solicitors. The objects of the post are to:

(a)   raise the awareness of young people from ethnic minorities to the opportunities within the solicitors' branch of the legal profession, by a programme of visits to schools, polytechnics, universities and colleges of law;

(b)   promote opportunities within the ethnic press, particularly with a view to promoting positive role models;

(c)   explore the possibilities of expanding access law courses as a stepping stone for candidates from ethnic minorities getting on the ladder to higher education and ultimately to becoming solicitors;

(d)   visit large practices and investigate the possibilities of work experience with them for ethnic minority candidates from schools, universities and polytechnics.

It is possible for firms of solicitors to participate in this programme, by themselves contributing to the objects described. In particular, firms can make contact with ethnic minority communities and colleges in their area, and even more importantly can offer places in their offices for vacation work or for access students to gain work experience in a solicitor's office. This may result in longer term connections between the individual on placement and the firm. Firms can also examine their existing practices (such as taking articled clerks only from universities without high ethnic minority numbers, or going on the 'milk round' only to such universities) to see whether or how these practices need to be changed so as to maximise the inclusion of ethnic minorities in target areas for recruitment. It must be remembered that the ethnic minorities are not evenly distributed throughout the higher education system, but concentrated in the main areas of settlement and particularly in certain polytechnics. It is possible to advertise a positive welcome to ethnic minority applicants if they are under-represented in your firm. The Law Society has a Race Relations Committee which looks at all aspects of race relations in the profession. Further enquiries about the programme for ethnic minorities can be made to the Ethnic Minorities Careers Officer at the Society.

Positive action for the disabled

Disability can take many forms, physical and mental. One of the chief measures that an employer can take is to ensure that facilities are available for the employment of disabled people: that premises are accessible to people in wheelchairs or with restricted mobility, that aids are obtained which will enable disabled people to carry out their work and that facilities such as special toilets or car parking facilities are available. There is a wide range of organisations which can provide advice, and sometimes financial assistance, in these matters. For instance, grants may be available through the Government's Disability Resettlement and Disablement Advisory Services. The Communications Division at the Law Society will direct firms to appropriate organisations for advice.

Similar measures can be taken in relation to the employment of disabled people as have been discussed regarding other groups — for instance, the training of staff to promote good working practice between able-bodied and disabled employees, and the use of advertisements which positively welcome disabled people into employment with the firm.

Conclusion

We have shown some of the ways in which firms of solicitors can develop their own equal opportunities policies, and contribute to equal opportunities generally within the profession. It is easy to find reasons for not implementing such a policy; for instance, because it will take time and money, or because you as a manager are not prejudiced; or because there are other minority groups, such as homosexuals, who should also be considered, and other groups after that without end. These are all valid points, but none of them should prevent a start being made. It is true that the implementation of an equal opportunities policy will take time and possibly some money, but this is a small price to pay for a fair employment policy which will make sound business sense by ensuring that the best candidates are recruited to your firm. It may be true that you are not prejudiced, but other people contributing to the recruitment of personnel within your firm might not be as fair-minded, and in any case you may be discriminating against some groups unconsciously, for instance by setting criteria which exclude certain candidates. We have dealt here only with those groups about whom there is existing legislation, but it is possible to develop your own policies to deal with other groups that may suffer discrimination.

Firms are urged to adopt their own policies in the interests of fairness and business sense. Further information can be obtained from the Communications Division.

POLICY ON EQUAL OPPORTUNITIES

1. General statement

The firm is committed to provide equal opportunities in employment. This means that all job applicants and employees will receive equal treatment regardless of sex, marital status, race, colour, nationality, ethnic or national origins, or disability.

It is good business sense for the firm to ensure that its most important resource, its staff, is used in a fair and effective way.

2. Legislation

It is unlawful to discriminate against individuals either directly or indirectly in respect of their race or sex. The Race Relations Act 1976 and the Sex Discrimination Act 1975 are the relevant Acts. Outlines of their main provisions appear below.

Codes of Practice relating to sex and race discrimination have been produced by the Equal Opportunities Commission and the Commission for Racial Equality and have been used as a basis for this policy. There is also a Code of Good Practice on the Employment of Disabled Persons published by the Department of Employment (Training) which is reflected in this policy.

3. Forms of discrimination

The following are the kinds of discrimination which are against the firm's policy:

(a)   direct discrimination, where a person is less favourably treated because of sex, race or disability. An example is if someone is refused promotion on the grounds that he or she is black, disabled, or she is a woman;

(b)   indirect discrimination, where a requirement or condition which cannot be justified is applied equally to all groups but has a disproportionately adverse effect on one particular group. An example is where an age limit for new recruits may exclude many women of that age group because they are unable to apply for the job as a result of family commitments, or the restricting of recruitment to areas where there are few ethnic minorities, or a requirement which is non-essential to the job description which may exclude a disabled person (such as the requirement for a driving licence for a job which is mainly office based);

(c)   victimisation, where someone is treated less favourably than others because he or she has taken action against the firm under one of the relevant Acts (Sex Discrimination Act 1975, Race Relations Act 1976, Equal Pay Act 1970 or the Disabled Persons (Employment) Acts 1944 and 1958).

4. Positive action

Although it is unlawful and against the firm's policy positively to discriminate in favour of certain groups, on the grounds of their race or sex, positive action to enable greater representation of under-represented groups is permitted by law and encouraged by the firm. All job advertisements wherever placed will include the following statement: 'This firm welcomes applications from all sections of the community irrespective of race, sex, or disability' and where appropriate, advertisements will be placed in the ethnic minority and disability press to ensure that all groups are reached in the firm's recruitment practices.

5. Recruitment

The firm will take steps to ensure that applications are attracted from both sexes and all races and from disabled people, and will ensure that there are equal opportunities in all stages of the recruitment process. Job advertisements will contain a brief statement that the firm is an equal opportunities employer as in 4. above, and any publicity relating to the firm and employment with it will make reference to the equal opportunities policy. Where appropriate, staff responsible for recruitment will receive training in equal opportunities, and guidance will be available to all staff.

Promotion within the firm is based solely on merit, and without regard to race, sex or disability.

6. Monitoring and review

This policy will be monitored by the firm to judge its effectiveness. In particular, the firm will monitor the ethnic and sexual composition of its existing staff, and of applicants for jobs, and the number of disabled people within these groups, and will review its equal opportunities policy in accordance with the results shown by the monitoring. If changes are required, the firm will implement them.

7. Disciplinary and grievance procedures

Acts of discrimination or harassment on grounds of sex, race or disability by employees of the firm will result in disciplinary action. Failure to comply with this policy will be treated in a similar fashion, and the policy applies to all who are employed in the firm.

The firm will treat seriously and take action when any employee has a grievance as a result of discrimination or harassment on sexual or racial grounds or on grounds of disability.

THE LEGISLATION

Sex Discrimination Act 1975 (and its amendments, 1986)

This Act makes it unlawful to discriminate directly or indirectly on the grounds of sex or marital status, or to apply requirements or conditions which have a disproportionately disadvantageous effect on people of a particular sex or marital status where these cannot be justified. It also applies to discriminatory employment advertising and makes it unlawful to apply pressure to discriminate or to aid discrimination by another person.

Race Relations Act 1976

This Act makes it unlawful to discriminate directly or indirectly on the grounds of colour, race, nationality (including citizenship) or ethnic or national origin, or to apply requirements or conditions which have a disproportionately disadvantageous effect on people of a particular racial group, and which cannot be justified on non-racial grounds. It also applies to discriminatory employment advertising and makes it unlawful to apply pressure to discriminate or to aid discrimination by another person.

Legislation relating to the disabled

The Disabled Persons (Employment) Acts 1944 and 1958 provide specific provision for the employment of people with disabilities. Under the provisions of the quota scheme employers with more than 20 staff have an obligation to employ at least 3% registered disabled people, and to allocate to registered disabled people vacancies as they occur on the staff until the quota is reached.

The Chronically Sick and Disabled Persons Act 1970 (and its amendments, 1976) impose obligations on employers to provide access to premises and facilities for people with disabilities.

Other legislation

The Equal Pay Act 1970 (and its amendments) establish the right of women and men to equal treatment in relation to contractual terms and conditions of employment when they are employed on the same or broadly similar work, or on work which, though different, is of equal value.

Advisory guidelines on part-time work

(1)   It is advisable that clients be told at the first opportunity on what occasions the part-time solicitor will be available in the office, and whom to contact in an emergency.

(2)   It is a good idea to agree the following matters between a part-time solicitor and the firm at the beginning of the arrangement:

   (a)   the hours worked by the part-time solicitor — and the solicitor should not be made to feel obliged to work more hours than those agreed;

   (b)   the rate of pay, which in the case of an employee should be based on the percentage of hours worked over an equivalent full-timer's contractual hours and salary;

   (c)   terms and conditions of employment regarding holidays and holiday pay, sickness entitlement, pension and National Insurance contributions — or the terms of any consultancy.

(3)   It is best if a solicitor who will be available in the firm during the hours not worked by the part-timer is made responsible for emergencies which may arise during the part-timer's absence, and is acquainted in general terms with the part-timer's caseload and methods of work.

(4)   Try and consider all work as suitable for a part-timer, regardless of client contact or the anticipated demands of a client. A part-timer is unlikely to be happy being given just the undesirable work that no one else wants to do.

(5)   It is best if arrangements are made, by the part-time solicitor and the firm, to ensure that the part-timer is kept up to date in the relevant field of law, by regular reading of the Law Society's *Gazette* and other legal publications and by attendance at courses.

Organisations

Below is a list of organisations which may be of assistance in the field of equal opportunities and the legal profession. For up-to-date addresses, telephone numbers and names of officers, please contact the Communications Division of the Law Society (telephone 071-242 1222).

Law Society's Women's Careers Working Party
Association of Women Solicitors
Equal Opportunities Commission
The Society of Black Lawyers
The Society of Asian Lawyers
The Commission for Racial Equality
The Royal Association for Disability and Rehabilitation

DRAFT MATERNITY CLAUSES FOR PARTNERSHIP DEEDS

Absence through pregnancy

A partner who becomes pregnant shall be entitled to up to six months' leave of absence. Up to 11 weeks may be taken prior to the expected date of confinement but the period of leave may commence earlier if a doctor certifies that it should. Such absence shall not affect her holiday entitlement.

Notification of absence through pregnancy

A partner who becomes pregnant shall give to her other partners as much notice as is reasonable in the circumstances of:

(i)   her expected date of confinement, and

(ii)   the date on which she expects to leave work, and

(iii) the date on which she expects to return to work.

Profit share during absence through pregnancy

If a partner becomes pregnant:

(a)   for the first three months of absence the partner shall be entitled to her full share of profits;

(b)   for the next three months the partner shall be entitled to one-half of her full share of the profits;

(c)   for any further period of absence the partner shall not be entitled to any further share of profits unless such absence arises through sickness (in which case the provisions of this Deed relating to sick leave will apply) or unless otherwise agreed from time to time.

Issued by the Law Society in 1989, references to legislation updated January 1993

PART II—INTERNATIONAL ASPECTS OF PRACTICE

Chapter 8

Multi-national legal practices

8.01 Formation of multi-national legal practices

Principle

Solicitors may practise in England and Wales in partnership and in incorporated practices with registered foreign lawyers.

Commentary

1. The Courts and Legal Services Act 1990 removed the statutory ban on partnerships between solicitors and non-solicitors, subject however to professional rules made by the Law Society. Rule 7 of the Solicitors' Practice Rules 1990 prohibits multi-disciplinary practices. Multi-national legal practices are now permitted, as set out below.

2. The Multi-National Legal Practice Rules 1991 amended the Solicitors' Practice Rules 1990 and other rules to permit and to regulate, as from 1st January 1992, partnerships between solicitors and registered foreign lawyers ('RFLs'). This type of partnership is described in the Courts and Legal Services Act and the Solicitors' Practice Rules as a multi-national partnership ('MNP'). The Solicitors' Incorporated Practice Rules 1988 now permit RFLs to be share-owners and directors of recognised bodies (see Principle 3.17). All the amendments made by the Multi-National Legal Practice Rules are consolidated in the rules as they appear in Annex 1A and the other annexes in the Guide.

3. RFLs are foreign lawyers who are registered by the Law Society under section 89 of and Schedule 14 to the Courts and Legal Services Act 1990.

Section 89 is set out in Annex 8A. The section defines 'foreign lawyer' as a person who is not an English solicitor or barrister but who is a member, and entitled to practise as such, of a legal profession regulated within a jurisdiction outside England and Wales.

4. Before a foreign lawyer may be registered, the Law Society must be satisfied that he or she is a member of a legal profession which is so regulated as to make it appropriate for solicitors to enter into MNPs with members of it, and for members of it to be officers of recognised bodies. Additional requirements for registration are that the professional rules governing the applicant do not prohibit practice in partnership with English solicitors in England and Wales; that the applicant is of good standing with his or her professional body or bodies; and that there are no other circumstances which would make it undesirable to register the applicant. A fee is payable on registration and on the annual renewal of registration.

5. The information in the register of foreign lawyers is public and open to inspection. The entry for each RFL shows his or her full name, title, date of birth, practising address(es), jurisdiction(s) and profession(s), and the date on which renewal of registration is due. In addition, the register shows the name of the practice(s) of each RFL, the RFL's partners if he or she is practising in an MNP, and the RFL's fellow directors if he or she is a director of a recognised body.

6. RFL status does not confer any right of audience or right to conduct litigation in the courts of England and Wales, or any right to undertake activities reserved to solicitors by the Solicitors Act 1974.

7. Solicitors practising wholly outside England and Wales may do so in partnership with lawyers of other jurisdictions, whether they are RFLs or not, and indeed with English barristers practising under the Bar's overseas practice rules. Unless, however, all the partners are solicitors or RFLs, the partnership may not practise in England and Wales. Similarly, a solicitor overseas may practise in corporate form with lawyers of other jurisdictions, whether RFLs or not, unless the corporate practice also wishes to practise in England and Wales, in which case it would need to be a recognised body and have its registered office in England and Wales (see Principle 3.17).

8. An information pack on multi-national legal practices is available from Professional Ethics. This includes two lists: a list of foreign legal professions approved by the Law Society as appropriate for the formation of multi-national legal practices; and a list of foreign regulatory bodies whose rules do not prohibit the formation of multi-national legal practices in England and Wales. Both lists are updated from time to time. Forms of application to become an RFL, and for renewal of registration, are available from the Records Office.

8.02   Regulation of registered foreign lawyers and multi-national legal practices

Principle

Registered foreign lawyers practising in partnership or in recognised bodies with solicitors are subject to the same rules and principles as solicitors, and multi-national legal practices are broadly subject to the same regulation as solicitors' practices.

Commentary

1.   By virtue of section 89(3) of the Courts and Legal Services Act 1990 the Solicitors' Practice Rules, the Solicitors' Publicity Code, the Solicitors' Introduction and Referral Code, the Solicitors' Indemnity Rules, the Solicitors' Accounts Rules, the Accountant's Report Rules and the Solicitors' Investment Business Rules have all been amended so as to extend to RFLs and MNPs those provisions which apply to solicitors and solicitors' firms.

2.   Certain rules contain special provisions in respect of MNPs, in particular Practice Rule 5 (hiving off), Practice Rule 11 (name of a practice) and the Solicitors' Publicity Code. The Solicitors' Overseas Practice Rules prohibit a solicitor practising overseas from sharing fees or entering into partnership with a foreign lawyer whose name has been struck off or suspended from the register. For special provisions relating to indemnity for MNPs with overseas offices see Commentary 7 to Principle 9.01, and Chapter 28.

3.   RFLs are subject to the jurisdiction of the Solicitors' Disciplinary Tribunal, and may be struck off the register, suspended or fined. In addition, an RFL's registration is automatically suspended on the RFL being made bankrupt in England and Wales or overseas, or on the RFL being struck off or suspended from practice in his or her own jurisdiction.

4.   The regulatory powers of the Law Society, such as inspection of accounts and intervention in a practice, are exercisable in respect of MNPs.

5.   All RFLs must pay, on first registration, an initial contribution to the Solicitors' Compensation Fund. On annual renewal of registration, RFLs who have held client's money in the course of their practice in an MNP or recognised body pay an annual contribution to the Compensation Fund, and may be required to pay a special levy. The annual contribution is reduced where an RFL practises mainly from an office or offices outside England and Wales. There is a discretion to reduce or remit an RFL's annual contribution or special levy where the RFL claims, and the Council agrees, that there is a substantial reduction in the risk to the Fund in respect of that RFL's practice because the RFL has alternative cover — see the

Solicitors' Compensation Fund (Foreign Lawyers' Contributions) Rules 1991 in Annex 8B. The Solicitors' Compensation Fund Rules 1975 have been amended to accommodate claims in respect of the act or default of an RFL.

6. The Partnerships (Unrestricted Size) No. 8 Regulations 1991 (S.I. 1991 no. 2729) permit MNPs to have more than 20 partners.

7. Solicitors have traditionally gone on the court record in litigation in the name of their firms. The Lord Chancellor's Department has issued guidance to courts which will enable solicitors to go on the record in the name of an MNP (see Annex 8C).

8. Section 85 of the Solicitors Act 1974 gives protection to solicitors' client accounts against claims by banks, as well as protecting banks against certain claims in respect of client accounts. These protections are extended to client accounts of MNPs by the Registered Foreign Lawyers Order 1992 (S.I. 1992 no. 2831).

9. The Registered Foreign Lawyers Order 1992 (see Commentary 8) extends to MNPs the exemption enjoyed by solicitors' practices under the Banking Act 1987.

10. MNPs may seek authorisation from the Law Society to conduct investment business under the Financial Services Act 1986.

11. The consumer credit licence issued to the Law Society by the Director General of Fair Trading covers MNPs as well as solicitors and recognised bodies.

Annex 8A

Courts and Legal Services Act 1990

section 89 — foreign lawyers: recognised bodies and partnerships with solicitors

___

(1)   The Law Society shall maintain a register of foreign lawyers for the purposes of this section.

(2)   A foreign lawyer who wishes to be registered under this section must apply to the Society in accordance with the requirements of Part I of Schedule 14.

(3)   The power to make rules under -

    (a)   the following provisions of the Solicitors Act 1974 -

        (i)   section 31 (professional practice, conduct and discipline);

        (ii)   section 32 (accounts and trust accounts);

        (iii)   section 34 (accountants' reports);

        (iv)   section 36 (Compensation Fund); and

        (v)   section 37 (professional indemnity); and

    (b)   section 9 of the Administration of Justice Act 1985 (incorporated practices),

shall also be exercisable in relation to registered foreign lawyers.

(4)   Subject to the provisions of Schedule 14, any such power may be exercised so as -

    (a)   to make different provision with respect to solicitors who enter into multi-national partnerships to the provision made with respect to other solicitors;

    (b)   to make different provision with respect to the management and control of recognised bodies by solicitors and registered foreign lawyers to the provision made with respect to the management and control of recognised bodies by solicitors;

    (c)   to make different provision with respect to registered foreign lawyers who are members of multi-national partnerships to the provision made with respect to solicitors; or

    (d)   to make different provision with respect to officers of recognised bodies who are registered foreign lawyers to the provision made with respect to officers of recognised bodies who are solicitors.

(5)   Subject to the provisions of Schedule 14, the Lord Chancellor may by order provide that any enactment or instrument -

(a)   passed or made before the commencement of this section;

(b)   having effect in relation to solicitors; and

(c)   specified in the order,

shall have effect with respect to registered foreign lawyers as it has effect with respect to solicitors.

(6)   An order under subsection (5) may provide for an enactment or instrument to have effect with respect to registered foreign lawyers subject to such additions, omissions or other modifications as the Lord Chancellor sees fit to specify in the order.

(7)   Subject to the provisions of Schedule 14, the Lord Chancellor may by order provide that any enactment or instrument -

(a)   passed or made before the commencement of this section;

(b)   having effect in relation to recognised bodies; and

(c)   specified in the order,

shall, in its application in relation to recognised bodies whose officers include one or more registered foreign lawyers, have effect with such additions, omissions or other modifications as the Lord Chancellor sees fit to specify in the order.

(8)   Schedule 14 shall have effect for the purposes of supplementing this section.

(9)   In this section and in Schedule 14 -

"foreign lawyer" means a person who is not a solicitor or barrister but who is a member, and entitled to practise as such, of a legal profession regulated within a jurisdiction outside England and Wales;

"multi-national partnership" means a partnership whose members consist of one or more registered foreign lawyers and one or more solicitors;

"recognised body" has the same meaning as in section 9 of the Administration of Justice Act 1985 (management and control by solicitors of incorporated practices); and

"registered foreign lawyer" means a foreign lawyer who is registered under this section.

Annex 8B

Solicitors' Compensation Fund (Foreign Lawyers' Contributions) Rules 1991

Rules dated 8th October 1991 made by the Council of the Law Society with the concurrence of the Master of the Rolls under Schedule 14 paragraph 7 of the Courts and Legal Services Act 1990 to regulate the contributions of registered foreign lawyers to the Solicitors' Compensation Fund.

Rule 1 — Interpretation

In these rules:

(a) "the Act" means the Courts and Legal Services Act 1990;

(b) "annual contribution" has the meaning given in Schedule 14 paragraph 7 of the Act;

(c) "the Council" means the Council of the Law Society;

(d) "multi-national partnership" has the meaning given in section 89 of the Act;

(e) "recognised body" has the meaning given in section 9 of the Administration of Justice Act 1985;

(f) "registered foreign lawyer" has the meaning given in section 89 of the Act; and

(g) "special levy" has the meaning given in Schedule 14 paragraph 7 of the Act.

Rule 2 — Remission of annual contribution for RFLs not holding clients' money

Where a registered foreign lawyer has not, at any time during the period specified in the application for renewal of his or her registration, either:

(i) practised as a partner in a multi-national partnership which held or received clients' money; or

(ii) been a director or member of or a beneficial owner of any share in a recognised body which held or received clients' money; or

(iii) been a director or member of or a beneficial owner of any share in a recognised body which directly or indirectly owned any share in another recognised body which held or received clients' money;

the registered foreign lawyer shall not be required to make an annual contribution.

Rule 3 — Reduced annual contribution for RFLs mainly practising overseas

Where a registered foreign lawyer is required to pay an annual contribution, but has, during the period specified in his or her application for renewal of registration, mainly practised from an office or offices outside England and Wales, that annual contribution shall be reduced to one quarter of the full amount determined under Schedule 14 paragraph 7(2)(a) of the Act, rounded to the nearest five pounds.

Rule 4 — Discretion to reduce or remit annual contribution or special levy

Where a registered foreign lawyer who would, apart from this rule, be required to pay an annual contribution or special levy, claims, and the Council agrees, that he or she is so covered in respect of dishonesty or failure to account, whether by a compensation fund other than the Solicitors' Compensation Fund, or by an indemnity fund other than the Solicitors' Indemnity Fund, or by compulsory insurance, that there is a substantial reduction in the risk to the Solicitors' Compensation Fund in respect of his or her practice in comparison with the risk presented by a solicitor practising in a like manner, the Council may reduce that annual contribution or special levy to such amount as the Council thinks fit or to zero.

Rule 5 — Decision on matters to be determined under these rules

The decision of the Council on any matter to be determined under these rules shall be final.

Rule 6 — Commencement

These rules shall come into force on 1st January 1992.

Annex 8C

Solicitors going on record in the name of a multi-national partnership —practice information

The Lord Chancellor's Department has issued the following guidance to courts (Court Business, January 1992):

'From 1st January 1992 solicitors have been entitled to enter into partnerships with registered foreign lawyers. Solicitors who are members of a multi-national partnership may appear on the court record in the name of the partnership.

Sections 66 and 89 of the Courts and Legal Services Act 1990 enable a solicitor practising in England and Wales to enter into partnership with a foreign lawyer. In order to protect clients, the foreign lawyer must be registered with the Law Society and be subject to its regulation. Multi-national partnerships themselves are also subject to special regulation by the Law Society. Registered foreign lawyers are not themselves permitted to conduct litigation in courts in England and Wales although litigation services may be provided through a multi-national partnership. The established practice is for solicitors to appear on the court record in the name of the partnership. The Senior Judiciary have been consulted and are content that this practice should also apply in the case of multi-national partnerships.'

Chapter 9

Practice outside England and Wales

9.01 Rules applicable outside England and Wales

Principle

The Solicitors' Overseas Practice Rules 1990 apply to solicitors practising as such outside England and Wales.

Commentary

1. Throughout this chapter 'solicitor' means a solicitor of the Supreme Court of England and Wales. 'Overseas' means outside England and Wales.

2. The Solicitors' Overseas Practice Rules 1990, together with explanatory notes, are contained in Annex 9A. These rules apply to a solicitor practising as such outside England and Wales. However, they are not an exhaustive statement of the professional obligations of such solicitors. The general principles of professional conduct will apply (see Principle 9.02). The Solicitors' Incorporated Practice Rules 1988 also have effect where a recognised body practises overseas as well as in England and Wales.

3. The Solicitors' Compensation Fund Rules 1975 apply to overseas practice. A claim may be made on the Fund in respect of the dishonesty or failure to account of a solicitor practising overseas.

4. Rule 2 of the Overseas Practice Rules provides that a solicitor who practises as such outside England and Wales must hold a practising certificate. The question whether a solicitor is practising as such is addressed in the explanatory note to the rule.

5. The Overseas Practice Rules contain rules which correspond to certain of the Solicitors' Practice Rules 1990 and associated codes:

    (a) Rule 3 of the Overseas Practice Rules (basic principles) is identical to Rule 1 of the Solicitors' Practice Rules.

(b)   Rule 4 of the Overseas Practice Rules (cross-border activities within the European Community) corresponds with Rule 16 of the Solicitors' Practice Rules, and requires compliance with the CCBE Code of Conduct (see Annex 10B).

(c)   Rule 5 of the Overseas Practice Rules (publicity) states that a solicitor practising outside England and Wales may publicise his or her practice provided that he or she complies not only with the Solicitors' Publicity Code 1990 but also with any restrictions concerning lawyers' publicity in force in the jurisdiction in which publicity is conducted.

(d)   Rule 6 of the Overseas Practice Rules (introductions and referrals) permits solicitors practising outside England and Wales to accept and make introductions and referrals of business, reflecting Rule 3 of the Solicitors' Practice Rules. Assistance may be obtained from the Solicitors' Introduction and Referral Code 1990.

(e)   Rule 7 of the Overseas Practice Rules (solicitors employed by non-lawyer employers) applies the main principle underlying Rule 4 of the Solicitors' Practice Rules.

(f)   Rule 8 of the Overseas Practice Rules (fee-sharing) is the equivalent of Rule 7 of the Solicitors' Practice Rules. Rule 8(1) sets out the persons with whom a solicitor practising outside England and Wales may share professional fees. For partnership, see Principle 9.04.

(g)   Solicitors may practise outside England and Wales through a body corporate without any requirement for the corporate practice to be a recognised body — indeed a corporate practice carried on entirely overseas cannot be a recognised body. Rule 9 of the Solicitors' Overseas Practice Rules (corporate practice) requires that shares in an overseas corporate practice may be owned only by solicitors and other lawyers; that only solicitors and other lawyers may be directors; and that the provisions relating to accounts will apply where solicitors own a controlling majority of shares.

(h)   Rule 10 of the Overseas Practice Rules (name of a solicitor's practice) reflects Rule 11 of the Solicitors' Practice Rules.

(i)   Rule 11 of the Overseas Practice Rules (supervision of offices) reflects the general principle underlying Rule 13 of the Solicitors' Practice Rules that a solicitor must ensure that any office from which he or she practises is properly supervised.

6.   The Solicitors' Accounts Rules 1991 and the Accountant's Report Rules 1991 do not apply to a solicitor practising wholly outside England and Wales. However, the basic requirements of those rules are contained in the Overseas Practice Rules in Rule 12 (solicitors' accounts), Rule 13 (solicitors' trust accounts), Rule 14 (deposit interest) and Rule 16 (accountants' reports). Further assistance may be derived from the rules

which apply in England and Wales. A form of accountant's report applicable to practice outside England and Wales may be found in Annex 27F. Rule 15 of the Overseas Practice Rules (investigation of accounts) empowers the Council to investigate the accounts of a solicitor practising outside England and Wales.

7. Rule 17 of the Overseas Practice Rules (professional indemnity) requires a solicitor practising outside England and Wales to have professional indemnity cover. The extent and amount must be reasonable having regard to the circumstances set out in the rule, subject always to any more onerous requirements of local law or local rules applicable to the solicitor. Rule 17 applies to a practice operating entirely outside England and Wales. Where a firm practises both in England and Wales and overseas the Solicitors' Indemnity Rules, and not Rule 17, will apply to the whole practice, except that in the case of an MNP having fewer than 75% solicitor-principals Rule 17 will apply to any overseas branch offices. (See also Commentary 5 to Principle 28.01.)

8. Rule 19 of the Overseas Practice Rules (waivers) gives the Council power to waive the provisions of the rules in any particular case or cases. A solicitor practising outside England and Wales who finds that the application of any provision of the Overseas Practice Rules causes difficulty in the particular conditions of the jurisdiction in which he or she practises may write to Professional Ethics for guidance and if appropriate make an application for a waiver.

9. Rule 12 of the Solicitors' Practice Rules 1990 (investment business) has effect in relation to the conduct of investment business within or into any part of the United Kingdom. The Solicitors' Investment Business Rules have effect in relation to investment business conducted within or into any part of the United Kingdom by a firm which is authorised by the Law Society under the Financial Services Act 1986. Guidance on the need for authorisation for overseas offices appears in Annex 26G.

10. There is no equivalent in the Overseas Practice Rules to Rule 5 of the Solicitors' Practice Rules (offering services other than as a solicitor). However, a solicitor practising in England and Wales is prevented by Rule 5 from setting up a separate business elsewhere which offers certain core services, set out in Rule 5(2). Similarly, the safeguards in Rule 5(3) would apply to a separate business overseas permitted by the rule. Thus Rule 5 bites on a separate business operated by an overseas firm which also practises in England and Wales, or which has one or more partners who also practise in England and Wales.

9.02   General principles of conduct

Principle

A solicitor remains a solicitor, and thus an officer of the Court, when outside England and Wales, whether elsewhere in the United Kingdom or abroad. The general principles of professional conduct apply to solicitors practising as such outside England and Wales.

Commentary

1. The Principles and Commentaries in the Guide apply to overseas practice as they apply to domestic practice, with any modifications necessitated by local conditions.

2. While Rule 6 of the Solicitors' Practice Rules (acting for seller and buyer) does not apply outside England and Wales, a solicitor practising overseas must not act in any situation where there is a conflict of interest.

3. Rules 8 and 9 of the Solicitors' Practice Rules (contingency fees and claims assessors) do not apply to a practice outside England and Wales. However, a solicitor should not enter into a contingency fee arrangement in respect of proceedings in any jurisdiction where such arrangements are prohibited either by law or by local professional rules.

4. Rule 10 of the Solicitors' Practice Rules (receipt of commissions from third parties) does not in terms apply to a practice outside England and Wales. However, the general principle that a solicitor must account to his or her client for any commission or secret profit applies.

5. The Council have adopted as the basic code for solicitors practising outside England and Wales the International Bar Association's International Code of Ethics (set out in Annex 9B).

9.03   Local law and rules of conduct

Principle

A solicitor outside England and Wales must comply with the requirements of the local law, and must comply, where appropriate, with local requirements as to professional conduct.

Commentary

1. A distinction must be drawn between local law and the rules of conduct of

the local legal professions. A solicitor is in any event bound by the local law of the jurisdiction in which he or she practises.

2. In certain cases, solicitors may have an express obligation to comply with the rules of a local legal profession:

   (a) If local law imposes an obligation on solicitors to observe the rules applicable to a local legal profession, then a solicitor must comply with any such obligation.

   (b) If a solicitor becomes a full member of a local legal profession, whether or not he or she also continues to practise as a solicitor, the rules of conduct applicable to that local profession must be observed (see Rule 18 of the Solicitors' Overseas Practice Rules 1990).

   (c) The rules and principles of solicitors' professional conduct may directly require observance of particular local rules. An example is the obligation to observe local restrictions on publicity (see Solicitors' Publicity Code 1990, paragraph 14(a)(ii), Solicitors' Overseas Practice Rules 1990, Rule 5(2)(b), International Bar Association's Code, Rule 8, and CCBE Code, Article 2.6.1). A further example is Article 4.1 of the CCBE Code, which requires a solicitor who appears before a court or tribunal in another EC member state to comply with the rules of conduct applied before that court or tribunal.

3. In the absence of such an express application of local rules, a solicitor should nevertheless respect the rules of conduct applied to local lawyers. Where the structure and sphere of activity of the local legal profession or professions differ substantially from those of solicitors, it may be inappropriate or impossible for a solicitor who is not a member of any local legal profession to comply in every particular with the rules of conduct applicable to the local profession or professions, or it may be doubtful which rules of conduct should be applied. In such circumstances, the solicitor should observe the standards of conduct applicable to local lawyers to the extent that this can be done without infringing the rules applicable to solicitors and without hindering the proper exercise of his or her profession.

9.04 Partnerships with lawyers of other professions

Principle

Outside England and Wales a solicitor may enter into partnership with a lawyer of a jurisdiction other than England and Wales, or a member of the English Bar, subject to any applicable provisions of the local law or professional rules of conduct (see Rule 8(2) of the Solicitors' Overseas Practice Rules 1990).

Commentary

1. In England and Wales, a solicitor may not practise in partnership with a lawyer of another jurisdiction unless that lawyer is a registered foreign lawyer ('RFL') — see Rule 7(6) of the Solicitors' Practice Rules 1990. Consequently, any overseas partnership between a solicitor and a lawyer who is not an RFL must be kept distinct from any practice of that solicitor in England and Wales.

2. For details as to partnerships between solicitors and RFLs see Chapter 8.

3. Subject to local law and any applicable local rules, a solicitor may enter into partnership outside England and Wales with an English barrister to the extent permitted by the overseas practice rules of the English Bar.

Annex 9A

Solicitors' Overseas Practice Rules 1990

(with consolidated amendments to 1st September 1992)

Rules dated 18th July 1990 made by the Council of the Law Society with the concurrence, where requisite, of the Master of the Rolls under Part II of the Solicitors Act 1974 and section 9 of the Administration of Justice Act 1985, regulating the overseas practices of solicitors and recognised bodies, together with explanatory notes not forming part of the rules.

Rule 1 — Ambit of the rules

(1)   These rules shall have effect in relation to the practice of solicitors, whether or not together with other lawyers, and whether as a principal in private practice, or in the employment of a solicitor, other lawyer, recognised body or other corporate practice, or of a non-lawyer employer, or in any other form of practice, and whether on a regular or an occasional basis.

(2)   Subject always to any requirements of the relevant law or of such local rules as may be applicable to him or her, a solicitor practising as such from an office outside England and Wales shall, in respect of that practice, comply with these rules and not be subject to any other rules made by the Council under sections 31, 32, 34 or 37 of the Act except where it is expressly provided to the contrary in any such rules or in these rules.

Explanatory notes

(i)   These rules are not an exhaustive statement of the professional obligations of solicitors practising outside England and Wales. The Council considers that the principles of professional conduct which apply in England and Wales apply to all solicitors, even where no specific reference to a particular principle appears in these rules. For example, although these rules do not include any equivalent of Rule 10 of the Solicitors' Practice Rules (receipt of commissions from third parties), the general principle that a solicitor must account to his or her client for any commission or secret profit still applies. Similarly, a solicitor must not act in any situation where he or she would be involved in a conflict of interest.

(ii)   The Solicitors' Compensation Fund Rules, made under section 36 of the Act, apply to practices outside England and Wales.

(iii)   The Solicitors' Investment Business Rules and Rule 12 of the Solicitors' Practice

Rules (investment business) apply to the conduct of investment business within or into any part of the United Kingdom.

Rule 2 — Obligation to hold a practising certificate

A solicitor shall not practise as such unless he or she has in force a practising certificate issued by the Law Society.

Explanatory note

The rules are directed at practice carried on by an English solicitor as such from an office outside England and Wales. Whether a person outside the jurisdiction is practising as an English solicitor depends on the circumstances. If a person is practising as a lawyer but with no other legal qualification than as an English solicitor, the presumption is that he or she is practising as such a solicitor. If a person describes him — or herself as an English solicitor in the context of such practice, he or she must be treated as practising as such. If that person is also qualified as a member of another legal profession it is a question of fact and degree in each case whether he or she is practising as an English solicitor or as a member of the other legal profession. A person may be practising as both simultaneously, but will not be practising as an English solicitor when carrying on activities reserved to the local legal profession.

Rule 3 — Basic principles

A solicitor shall not do anything in the course of practising as a solicitor, or permit another person to do anything on his or her behalf, which compromises or impairs or is likely to compromise or impair any of the following:

(a)   the solicitor's independence or integrity;

(b)   a person's freedom to instruct a solicitor of his or her choice;

(c)   the solicitor's duty to act in the best interests of the client;

(d)   the good repute of the solicitor or of the solicitors' profession;

(e)   the solicitor's proper standard of work;

(f)   the solicitor's duty to the Court.

Rule 4 — Cross-border activities within the European Community

(1)   In relation to cross-border activities within the European Community solicitors shall, without prejudice to their other obligations under these rules or any other rules, principles or requirements of conduct, observe the rules codified in articles 2 to 5 of the CCBE Code of Conduct for Lawyers in the European Community adopted on 28th October 1988, as interpreted by article 1 (the preamble) thereof and the Explanatory Memorandum and Commentary thereon prepared by the CCBE's Deontology Working Party and dated May 1989.

(2)   In this Rule:

(a)   "cross-border activities" means:

    (i)   all professional contacts with lawyers of member states of the European Community other than the United Kingdom; and

(ii)   the professional activities of the solicitor in a member state other than the United Kingdom, whether or not the solicitor is physically present in that member state; and

(b)   "lawyers" means lawyers as defined in Directive 77/249 of the Council of the European Communities dated 22nd March 1977 as amended from time to time.

Explanatory note

The Council's view is that a solicitor will fulfil his or her obligations under articles 2 to 5 of the code by observing the corresponding rules, principles and requirements of conduct otherwise applicable to solicitors (including these rules), and in addition articles 2.5 (incompatible occupations), 5.2 (co-operation among lawyers of different member states), 5.3 (correspondence between lawyers), 5.6 (change of lawyer) and 5.9 (disputes among lawyers in different member states), being articles having no such corresponding provision. This view is subject to any authoritative ruling to the contrary at Community level.

Rule 5 — Publicity

(1)   Solicitors may at their discretion publicise their practices or permit other persons to do so, or publicise the business or activities of other persons, provided there is no breach of paragraph (2) of this rule or any other provision of these rules, and provided there is compliance with the Solicitors' Publicity Code from time to time in force.

(2)   No publicity for a solicitor's practice may be conducted in another jurisdiction in any manner that would contravene either:

(a)   the provisions of the Solicitors' Publicity Code; or

(b)   any restrictions in force in that other jurisdiction concerning lawyers' publicity.

For the purposes of this paragraph, publicity shall be deemed to be conducted in the jurisdiction in which it is received. However, publicity shall not be regarded as being conducted in a jurisdiction in which such publicity would be improper if it is conducted for the purpose of reaching persons in a jurisdiction or jurisdictions where such publicity is permitted and its reception in the former jurisdiction is incidental.

Explanatory note

One of the provisions of the Solicitors' Publicity Code is the prohibition on unsolicited visits and telephone calls (paragraph 3). Attention is drawn not only to the corresponding provisions of the CCBE Code of Conduct for Lawyers in the European Community (article 2.6), but also to the International Code of Ethics of the International Bar Association, which the Council has adopted as the basic code of solicitors practising outside the jurisdiction. Rule 8 of the International Code provides: "A lawyer should not advertise or solicit business except to the extent and in the manner permitted by the rules of the jurisdiction to which that lawyer is subject. A lawyer should not advertise or solicit business in any country in which such advertising or soliciting is prohibited."

Rule 6 — Introductions and referrals

Solicitors may accept introductions and referrals of business from other persons and may make introductions and refer business to other persons, provided there is no breach of Rule 3 or any other provision of these rules.

Explanatory note

Assistance on complying with the provisions of Rule 3 can be obtained from the Solicitors' Introduction and Referral Code.

Rule 7 — Solicitors employed by non-lawyer employers

(1)   Solicitors who are employees of non-lawyer employers shall not as part of their employment do for any person other than their employer work which is or could be done by a solicitor acting as such.

(2)   Paragraph (1) of this rule shall not prevent a solicitor from acting for a company or organisation controlled by the employer or in which the employer has a substantial measure of control, or a company in the same group as the employer or which controls the employer.

Explanatory note

A body corporate wholly owned and controlled by lawyers for the purpose of practising law would not be a "non-lawyer employer".

Rule 8 — Fee sharing

(1)   A solicitor shall not share or agree to share his or her professional fees with any person except:

(a)   a practising solicitor (which term includes a recognised body);

(b)   a practising lawyer of another jurisdiction (other than a lawyer whose registration under section 89 of the Courts and Legal Services Act 1990 is suspended or whose name has been struck off the register);

(c)   a member of the Bar of England and Wales acting in accordance with the overseas practice rules of the Bar;

(d)   any body corporate (other than a recognised body) wholly owned and controlled by lawyers for the purpose of practising law;

(e)   the solicitor's bona fide employee; or

(f)   a retired partner or predecessor of the solicitor, or the dependants or personal representatives of a deceased partner or predecessor.

(2)   A solicitor shall not enter into partnership with any person other than those within sub-paragraphs (1)(a) to (c) of this rule.

(3)   In sub-paragraph (1)(f) of this rule, the references to a retired or deceased partner shall be construed, in relation to a recognised body, as including a retired or deceased director or member of that body or to a retired or deceased beneficial owner of any share in that body held by a member as nominee.

Explanatory note

Paragraph (2) of this rule allows a solicitor to be in partnership outside England and Wales with a lawyer of another jurisdiction. However, such a partnership may only practise in England and Wales, or hold itself out as so practising, if all the non-solicitor partners are on the register of foreign lawyers maintained by the Law Society under section 89 of the Courts and Legal Services Act 1990.

Rule 9 — Corporate practice

(1)   A solicitor shall not practise through a body corporate save one in which all the directors and the owners of all the shares are persons within Rule 8(1)(a) to (c) of these rules, or save as permitted under Rule 7 of these rules.

(2)   Notwithstanding Rule 1(2) of these rules, all the provisions of the Solicitors' Incorporated Practice Rules from time to time in force shall have effect where a recognised body practises outside England and Wales.

(3)   Where solicitors own a controlling majority of the shares in a corporate practice other than a recognised body, the provisions of Rules 12 to 16 of these rules shall apply to all solicitors who own shares in and all solicitors who are directors of that corporate practice as if all such solicitors and any other owners of shares and directors were practising in partnership as the principals of that practice.

Explanatory note

A corporate practice operating both in England and Wales and in another jurisdiction needs to comply, in respect of its overseas practice, both with the Solicitors' Overseas Practice Rules and the Solicitors' Incorporated Practice Rules. A corporate practice operating solely outside England and Wales needs to comply with the Solicitors' Overseas Practice Rules but is not eligible for recognition under the Solicitors' Incorporated Practice Rules.

Rule 10 — Name of a solicitor's practice

(1)   The name of a firm of solicitors (which shall include the name used for the practice of a sole practitioner) shall consist only of the name of one or more present or former principals together with, if desired, other conventional references to the firm and to such persons; or a firm name in use on 28th February 1967; or one approved in writing by the Council.

(2)   A similar standard shall apply to any other legal practice (other than a recognised body) of which solicitors form a majority of the partners or own a controlling majority of the shares; save that in the case of a corporate practice the name of an owner of shares or a director shall be treated as the name of a principal.

Explanatory note

The name of a recognised body is governed by the Solicitors' Incorporated Practice Rules.

Rule 11 — Supervision of offices

Solicitors shall ensure that every office from which their practice is carried on is supervised sufficiently to ensure that at all times the practice is properly conducted and the affairs of the clients receive proper attention.

Rule 12 — Solicitors' accounts

(1) (a) A solicitor shall keep any money held by him or her on behalf of clients separate from any other funds (save as provided in sub-paragraph (1)(d) of this rule) and in an account at a bank or similar institution subject to supervision by a public authority.

    (b) All money received by a solicitor for or on behalf of a client shall be paid into such an account forthwith unless the client expressly or by implication agrees that the money shall be dealt with otherwise.

    (c) Any such account in which clients' money is held in the name of the solicitor shall indicate in the title or designation that the funds belong to the client or clients of the solicitor.

    (d) In such account may be kept money held subject to a controlled trust and paid into such account in accordance with Rule 13(1)(a) of these rules.

(2) A solicitor shall at all times keep, whether by written, electronic, mechanical or other means, such accounts as are necessary:

    (a) to record all the solicitor's dealings with money dealt with through any such account for clients' money as is specified in sub-paragraph (1)(a) of this rule;

    (b) to show separately in respect of each client all money received, held or paid by the solicitor for or on account of that client and to distinguish the same from any other money received, held or paid by the solicitor; and

    (c) to ensure that the solicitor is at all times able without delay to account to clients for all money received, held or paid by the solicitor on their behalf.

(3) A solicitor shall not make any payment or withdrawal from money held on behalf of any client except where the money paid or withdrawn is:

    (a) properly required for a payment to or on behalf of the client;

    (b) properly required for or towards payment of a debt due to the solicitor from the client or in reimbursement of money expended by the solicitor on behalf of the client;

    (c) paid or withdrawn on the client's authority; or

    (d) properly required for or towards payment of the solicitor's costs where there has been delivered to the client a bill of costs or other written intimation of the amount of the costs incurred and it has thereby or otherwise in writing been made clear to the client that the money so paid or withdrawn is being or will be so applied.

(4) A solicitor shall not make any payment or withdrawal from money held subject to a controlled trust and kept in an account in accordance with sub-paragraph (1)(d) of this rule except in proper execution of that trust.

(5) Every solicitor shall preserve for at least six years from the date of the last entry therein all accounts, books, ledgers and records kept under this rule.

Explanatory note

Assistance in the keeping of solicitors' accounts may be derived from the Solicitors' Accounts Rules.

Rule 13 — Solicitors' trust accounts

(1)   A solicitor who holds or receives money subject to a controlled trust of which he or she is a trustee shall without delay pay such money either:

(a)   into an account for clients' money such as is specified in Rule 12(1)(a) of these rules; or

(b)   into an account in the name of the trustee or trustees at a bank or similar institution subject to supervision by a public authority, which account shall be clearly designated as a trust account by use of the words "executor" or "trustee" or otherwise, and shall be kept solely for money subject to that particular trust;

provided that a solicitor shall not be obliged to comply with sub-paragraphs (1)(a) or (b) of this rule where money received is without delay paid straight over to a third party in the execution of the trust.

(2)   A solicitor shall at all times keep, whether by written, electronic, mechanical or other means, such accounts as are necessary:

(a)   to show separately in respect of each controlled trust all the solicitor's dealings with money received, held or paid by the solicitor on account of that trust; and

(b)   to distinguish the same from money received or paid by the solicitor on any other account.

(3)   A solicitor shall not make any payment or withdrawal from money held subject to a controlled trust except in proper execution of that trust.

(4)   Every solicitor shall preserve for at least six years from the date of the last entry therein all accounts, books, ledgers and records kept under this rule.

Explanatory note

Assistance in the keeping of trust accounts may be derived from the Solicitors' Accounts Rules.

Rule 14 — Deposit interest

Where a solicitor holds or receives for or on behalf of a client money on which, having regard to all the circumstances (including the amount and the length of the time for which the money is likely to be held and the law and prevailing custom of lawyers practising in the jurisdiction in which the solicitor practises) interest ought, in fairness, to be earned for the client, then, subject to any agreement to the contrary made in writing between solicitor and client, the solicitor shall either:

(a)   deal with that money in such a way that proper interest is earned thereon; or

(b)   pay to the client out of the solicitor's own money a sum equivalent to the interest which would have been earned for the benefit of the client had the money been dealt with in accordance with paragraph (a) of this rule.

Rule 15 — Investigation of accounts

(1)   In order to ascertain whether or not Rules 12 to 14 of these rules have been complied with, the Council may at any time in writing (including by telex or facsimile transmission) require any solicitor to produce at a time and place to be fixed by the Council all necessary documents for the inspection of any person appointed by the Council and to supply to such person any necessary information and explanations, and such person shall be directed to prepare a report on the result of such inspection.

(2)   Any requirement made by the Council of a solicitor under paragraph (1) of this rule shall be deemed to have been received by the solicitor upon proof of its having been delivered at or transmitted to the solicitor's practising address or last known practising address (or, in the case of a recognised body, its registered office).

(3)   Upon being required to do so a solicitor shall produce all necessary documents at the time and place fixed, and shall supply any necessary information and explanations.

(4)   Where a requirement is made by the Council of a recognised body under paragraph (1) of this rule such requirement shall, if so stated in the requirement, be deemed also to be made of any solicitor who is an officer or employee of that recognised body where such solicitor holds or has held client's money or money subject to a controlled trust of which he or she is or was a trustee.

Rule 16 — Accountants' reports

(1)   The accountant's report which a solicitor is required to deliver annually to the Council under section 34 of the Act shall be signed either by a qualified accountant (who may be an accountant qualified in the jurisdiction where the solicitor practises) or by such other person as the Council may think fit.

(2)   Such report shall be based on a sufficient examination of the relevant documents to give the person signing the report a reasonable indication whether or not the solicitor has complied with Rule 12(1) to (4) of these rules during the period covered by the report.

(3)   Such report shall include:

   (a)   the name, practising addresses and practising style of the solicitor and any partners of the solicitor;

   (b)   the name, address and qualification of the person signing the report;

   (c)   an indication of the nature and extent of the examination made of the relevant documents by the said person;

   (d)   a statement to the effect that so far as may be ascertained from the examination the said person is satisfied (if this is indeed the case) that (save for trivial breaches) the solicitor has complied with Rule 12(1) to (4) of these rules during the period covered by the report;

   (e)   a statement of the total amount of money held at banks or similar institutions on behalf of clients on a date during the period under review, which date shall be selected by the accountant and which may be the last day of the period to which the report relates, and of the total liabilities to clients on such date, and an explanation of any difference; and

   (f)   details of any matters in respect of which the said person has been unable so to satisfy him – or herself and any matters (other than trivial breaches) in respect of which it appears to the said person that the solicitor has not complied with Rule 12(1) to (4) of these rules.

(4) The delivery of an accountant's report shall be unnecessary in respect of any period during which the solicitor did not hold or receive money for or on behalf of clients; provided that, except where the solicitor has no practising address outside England and Wales, the solicitor or a solicitor-partner of the solicitor (or, in the case of a recognised body, a director of that body) signs and delivers to the Council a declaration that no such money was held or received during that period.

(5) It shall be unnecessary to deliver an accountant's report until after the end of any period of twelve months ending 31st October during which the solicitor first held or received money for or on behalf of clients, having not held or received any such money in the period of twelve months immediately preceding that period; provided that an accountant's report then delivered includes the period when such money was first held or received.

Explanatory notes

(i) Assistance in the preparation of accountants' reports may be derived from the Accountant's Report Rules. Reference should also be made to section 34 of the Act.

(ii) Where a firm practises both in England and Wales and overseas, it would, if desired, be proper for a single report to be submitted covering both the "domestic" and overseas parts of the practice (provided that, in appropriate cases, there is also a declaration under paragraph (4) of this rule).

Rule 17 — Professional indemnity

(1) A solicitor shall take out and maintain insurance or other indemnity against professional liabilities, or shall be covered by such insurance or other indemnity. The extent and amount of such insurance or other indemnity shall be reasonable having regard to the nature and extent of the risks the solicitor incurs in his or her practice, to the local conditions in the jurisdiction in which the solicitor practises and to the availability of insurance or other indemnity on reasonable terms, but need not exceed the current requirements of any other rules made by the Council under section 37 of the Act.

(2) Paragraph (1) of this rule shall not apply to a solicitor who is the employee of a non-lawyer employer, provided the solicitor fully complies with Rule 7 of these rules in respect of that employment and conducts no professional business as a solicitor outside that employment.

(3) Notwithstanding paragraphs (1) and (2) of this rule, a practice carried on both in England and Wales and in another jurisdiction shall be subject to all other rules made by the Council under section 37 of the Act; save that solicitors who are partners in a multi-national partnership of which fewer than 75% of the principals are solicitors shall be subject to paragraphs (1) and (2) of this rule in respect of any offices outside England and Wales and not any other rules made by the Council under section 37 of the Act.

(4) A recognised body shall be governed in respect of professional indemnity not by this rule but by the indemnity rules applicable from time to time to recognised bodies and by the Solicitors' Incorporated Practice Rules from time to time in force, subject always to any requirements of the relevant law or of such local rules as may be applicable to the recognised body.

(5)   Notwithstanding paragraph (4) of this rule, a recognised body which is subject to Rule 12.18(b) of the Solicitors' Indemnity Rules shall be subject to paragraph (1) of this rule in respect of its offices outside England and Wales.

Explanatory notes

(i)   The statement in paragraph (1) that the extent and amount of insurance or other indemnity need not exceed the current requirements of any other rules made under section 37 of the Act ensures that the requirements of this rule are not more onerous than those of the Solicitors' Indemnity Rules, but the rule is subject to any more onerous requirements of the relevant law or of such local rules as may be applicable to the solicitor (see Rule 1(2) of these rules).

(ii)   Paragraph (3) provides that the Solicitors' Indemnity Rules shall continue to apply to (*inter alia*) a firm of solicitors (or a multi-national partnership of which at least 75% of the principals are solicitors) which has a head office in England and Wales and a branch office overseas.

Rule 18 — Dual qualification

Where a solicitor is qualified as a member of a legal profession of another jurisdiction, nothing in these rules shall affect such duty as may be upon the solicitor to observe the rules of that profession.

Rule 19 — Waivers

In any particular case or cases the Council shall have power to waive in writing any of the provisions of these rules for a particular purpose or purposes expressed in such waiver, and to revoke such waiver.

Rule 20 — Interpretation

In these rules, except where the context otherwise requires:

(a)   the expressions "accounts", "books", "ledgers" and "records" include loose-leaf books and such cards or other permanent documents or records as are necessary for the operation of any system of book-keeping whether written, electronic, mechanical or otherwise;

(b)   "the Act" means the Solicitors Act 1974;

(c)   "another jurisdiction" means a jurisdiction other than England and Wales;

(d)   "controlled trust", in relation to a solicitor, means a trust of which he or she is a sole trustee or co-trustee only with one or more of his or her partners or employees;

(e)   "controlled trust", in relation to a recognised body, means a trust of which it is a sole trustee or co-trustee only with one or more of its officers, partners or employees;

(f)   "controlled trust", in relation to a solicitor or a recognised body, also includes, where that solicitor or recognised body is an officer or employee of a recognised body, a trust of which he, she or it is co-trustee only with one or more other officers or employees of that recognised body or the body itself;

(g) "controlled trust", in relation to a solicitor who is an officer or employee of a corporate practice (other than a recognised body) of which solicitors own a controlling majority of the shares, also includes a trust of which he or she is a sole trustee or co-trustee only with one or more other officers or employees of that corporate practice or the corporate practice itself;

(h) "the Council" means the Council of the Law Society;

(i) "lawyer", except in Rule 4 of these rules, means a member of a regulated legal profession who is entitled to practise as such in the relevant jurisdiction (whether he or she is a member of the legal profession of that jurisdiction or of a different jurisdiction);

(j) "person" includes a body corporate or unincorporated association or group of persons;

(k) "recognised body" means a body corporate for the time being recognised by the Council under the Solicitors' Incorporated Practice Rules from time to time in force as being a suitable body to undertake the provision of professional services such as are provided by individuals practising as solicitors;

(l) "solicitor" means a solicitor of the Supreme Court of England and Wales and shall also be construed as including a firm of solicitors or a recognised body; and

(m) words in the singular include the plural, words in the plural include the singular, and words importing the masculine or feminine gender include the neuter.

Explanatory note

In connection with the definition of "lawyer", in some jurisdictions there may be uncertainty as to whether a particular profession can be regarded as a "regulated legal profession" in view of the differences in legal and professional structures. In case of doubt solicitors are invited to seek guidance from the Law Society.

Rule 21 — Repeal and commencement

(1) The Solicitors' Overseas Practice Rules 1987 are hereby repealed.

(2) These rules shall come into force on 1st September 1990.

Annex 9B

International Code of Ethics of the International Bar Association*

adopted by the Council of the Law Society as the basic code for solicitors practising outside the jurisdiction — 1988 edition

Preamble

The International Bar Association is a federation of National Bar Associations and Law Societies with full or sustaining organisational members and individual members. Most of the full or sustaining organisational members have established Codes of Legal Ethics as models for or governing the practice of law by their members. In some jurisdictions these Codes are imposed on all practitioners by their respective Bar Associations or Law Societies or by the courts or administrative agencies having jurisdiction over the admission of individuals to the practice of law.

Except where the context otherwise requires, this Code applies to any lawyer of one jurisdiction in relation to his contacts with a lawyer of another jurisdiction or to his activities in another jurisdiction.

Nothing in this Code absolves a lawyer from the obligation to comply with such requirements of the law or of rules of professional conduct as may apply to him in any relevant jurisdiction. It is a re-statement of much that is in these requirements and a guide as to what the International Bar Association considers to be a desirable course of conduct by all lawyers engaged in the international practice of law.

The International Bar Association may bring incidents of alleged violations to the attention of relevant organisations.

Rules

1.   A lawyer who undertakes professional work in a jurisdiction where he is not a full member of the local profession shall adhere to the standards of professional ethics in the jurisdiction in which he has been admitted. He shall also observe all ethical standards which apply to lawyers of the country where he is working.

2.   Lawyers shall at all times maintain the honour and dignity of their profession. They shall in practice as well as in private life, abstain from any behaviour which may tend to discredit the profession of which they are members.

---

*Reproduced by the kind permission of the International Bar Association.

3.   Lawyers shall preserve independence in the discharge of their professional duty. Lawyers practising on their own account or in partnership where permissible, shall not engage in any other business or occupation if by doing so they may cease to be independent.

4.   Lawyers shall treat their professional colleagues with the utmost courtesy and fairness.

Lawyers who undertake to render assistance to a foreign colleague shall always keep in mind that the foreign colleague has to depend on them to a much larger extent than in the case of another lawyer of the same country. Therefore their responsibility is much greater, both when giving advice and when handling a case.

For this reason it is improper for lawyers to accept a case unless they can handle it promptly and with due competence, without undue interference by the pressure of other work. To the fees in these cases Rule 19 applies.

5.   Except where the law or custom of the country concerned otherwise requires, any oral or written communication between lawyers shall in principle be accorded a confidential character as far as the court is concerned, unless certain promises or acknowledgements are made therein on behalf of a client.

6.   Lawyers shall always maintain due respect towards the court. Lawyers shall without fear defend the interests of their clients and without regard to any unpleasant consequences to themselves or to any other person.

Lawyers shall never knowingly give to the court incorrect information or advice which is to their knowledge contrary to the law.

7.   It shall be considered improper for lawyers to communicate about a particular case directly with any person whom they know to be represented in that case by another lawyer without the latter's consent.

8.   A lawyer should not advertise or solicit business except to the extent and in the manner permitted by the rules of the jurisdiction to which that lawyer is subject. A lawyer should not advertise or solicit business in any country in which such advertising or soliciting is prohibited.

9.   A lawyer should never consent to handle a case unless:

  (a)   the client gives direct instructions, or

  (b)   the case is assigned by a competent body or forwarded by another lawyer, or

  (c)   instructions are given in any other manner permissible under the relevant local rules or regulations.

10.   Lawyers shall at all times give clients a candid opinion on any case. They shall render assistance with scrupulous care and diligence. This applies also if they are assigned as counsel for an indigent person.

Lawyers shall at any time be free to refuse to handle a case, unless it is assigned by a competent body.

Lawyers should only withdraw from a case during its course for good cause, and if possible in such a manner that the client's interests are not adversely affected.

The loyal defence of a client's case may never cause advocates to be other than perfectly candid, subject to any right or privilege to the contrary which clients choose them to exercise, or knowingly to go against the law.

11.   Lawyers shall, when in the client's interest, endeavour to reach a solution by settlement out of court rather than start legal proceedings.

Lawyers should never stir up litigation.

12.   Lawyers should not acquire a financial interest in the subject matter of a case which they are conducting. Neither should they directly or indirectly, acquire property about which litigation is pending before the court in which they practise.

13.   Lawyers should never represent conflicting interests in litigation. In non-litigation matters, lawyers should do so only after having disclosed all conflicts or possible conflicts of interest to all parties concerned and only with their consent. This Rule also applies to all lawyers in a firm.

14.   Lawyers should never disclose, unless lawfully ordered to do so by the court or as required by statute, what has been communicated to them in their capacity as lawyers even after they have ceased to be the client's counsel. This duty extends to their partners, to junior lawyers assisting them and to their employees.

15.   In pecuniary matters lawyers shall be most punctual and diligent. They should never mingle funds of others with their own and they should at all times be able to refund money they hold for others. They shall not retain money they receive for their clients for longer than is absolutely necessary.

16.   Lawyers may require that a deposit is made to cover their expenses, but the deposit should be in accordance with the estimated amount of their charges and the probable expenses and labour required.

17.   Lawyers shall never forget that they should put first not their right to compensation for their services, but the interests of their clients and the exigencies of the administration of justice.

The lawyers' right to ask for a deposit or to demand payment of out-of-pocket expenses and commitments, failing payment of which they may withdraw from the case or refuse to handle it, should never be exercised at a moment at which the client may be unable to find other assistance in time to prevent irreparable damage being done.

Lawyers' fees should, in the absence of non-applicability of official scales, be fixed on a consideration of the amount involved in the controversy and the interest of it to the client, the time and labour involved and all other personal and factual circumstances of the case.

18.   A contract for a contingent fee, where sanctioned by the law or by professional rules and practice, should be reasonable under all circumstances of the case, including the risk and uncertainty of the compensation and subject to supervision of a court as to its reasonableness.

19.   Lawyers who engage a foreign colleague to advise on a case or to co-operate in handling it, are responsible for the payment of the latter's charges except where there is express agreement to the contrary. When lawyers direct a client to a foreign colleague they are not responsible for the payment of the latter's charges, but neither are they entitled to a share of the fee of this foreign colleague.

20.   Lawyers should not permit their professional services or their names to be used in any way which would make it possible for persons to practise law who are not legally authorised to do so.

Lawyers shall not delegate to a legally unqualified person not in their employ and control any functions which are by the law or custom of the country in which they practise only to be performed by a qualified lawyer.

21.   It is not unethical for lawyers to limit or exclude professional liability subject to the rules of their local bar association and to there being no statutory or constitutional prohibitions.

Chapter 10

Cross-border practice in the European Community

10.01 Legal practice in the European Community

Principle

The rules and principles of professional conduct apply to solicitors who are working in other member states of the European Community in the same way as to solicitors in non-member states, subject, however, to the provisions of European Community law and the CCBE Code of Conduct.

Commentary

1. Chapters 2 and 3 of the Treaty of Rome contain provisions, applicable to the legal profession, for the removal of restrictions on the freedom of nationals of one member state to establish themselves on a permanent basis, or to provide services on an occasional basis, in another member state.

2. A Community Directive to facilitate the effective exercise by lawyers of freedom to provide services was made on 22nd March 1977 (77/249/EEC-O.J./L78/17). This Directive has been implemented in the United Kingdom by the European Communities (Services of Lawyers) Order 1978 (S.I. 1978 no. 1910) which came into effect on 1st March 1979 (see Annex 10A). A note prepared by the CCBE on the application of the Lawyers' Services Directive appears in Annex 10D.

3. A general Directive on the recognition of higher education diplomas was made on 21st December 1988. This Directive among other things facilitates access by lawyers from one member state into the legal profession of another member state. The Directive has been implemented in the U.K. by S.I. 1991 no. 824 in relation to the professions generally. For access to the solicitors' profession in England and Wales it has been implemented by the Law Society's Qualified Lawyers Transfer Regulations 1990. Enquiries about these regulations should be addressed to

184

the Transfer Unit. Enquiries about the implementation of the Directive in other jurisdictions should be addressed to Legal Practice (International).

4. Proposals for a further Directive to facilitate the exercise of the right of permanent establishment of lawyers from one member state in another member state under their home title have been made by the CCBE to the European Commission. Guidance on the state of progress of these proposals is available from Legal Practice (International).

5. A general discussion of the provisions of the law applicable, as at 31st January 1992, to the cross-border practice of lawyers in the EC may be found in *Free Movement of Lawyers* by Hamish Adamson, available from the Law Society Shop.

6. Although the legal profession in England and Wales is divided into barristers and solicitors, it has been agreed between the Law Society and the Bar Council that, as regards business in other member states, the English legal profession should, so far as practicable, be treated as one. Both barristers and solicitors have the same rights with regard to establishment and the provision of services in other member states under the Treaty and the Directives, and are equally recognised as lawyers for all purposes under European Community instruments, including practice before the European Court of Justice and the Court of First Instance. The same applies to practice before the European Commission of Human Rights and the European Court of Human Rights. Lawyers from other member states exercising the right to provide services or to establish themselves in England and Wales must, however, choose whether to practise in the sector of the Bar or of the solicitors' branch of the profession.

7. The CCBE (the Council of the Bars and Law Societies of the European Community) is the officially recognised representative body in the EC for the bars and law societies of the member states. Its objects include the study of all questions affecting the legal profession in the Community and the formulation of solutions designed to co-ordinate and harmonise professional practice. The Law Society is represented on the United Kingdom delegation to the CCBE.

8. In October 1988 the CCBE adopted a Code of Conduct for Lawyers in the European Community, with particular reference to cross-border activities. The Council of the Law Society has ratified the decision of the U.K. delegation to support the Code. The Code, together with the Explanatory Memorandum and Commentary approved in May 1989 by the CCBE for publication, is contained in Annex 10B. Rule 16 of the Solicitors' Practice Rules 1990 and Rule 4 of the Solicitors' Overseas Practice Rules 1990 require solicitors to comply with the CCBE Code in relation to cross-border activities in the EC. A Council statement (see Annex 10C) details some areas of the CCBE Code which have no exact equivalent in the rules governing solicitors generally.

9.   The lawyer's professional identity card, published in 1978 by the CCBE and issued by the bars and law societies of the member states, is officially recognised by the European Court of Justice and by national authorities as *prima facie* proof of the lawyer's right to practise. Solicitors holding practising certificates may obtain the card on application to the Records Office.

10.   The CCBE has set up a Council for Advice and Arbitration to settle disputes between lawyers, and between bars or law societies throughout the Community, on matters such as responsibility for fees. A note on the Council for Advice and Arbitration and on the procedure for dealing with complaints as between lawyers from different member states is contained in Annex 10E.

11.   The term 'cross-border activities' is defined as including all professional contacts with lawyers of other EC member states, and all professional activities in other EC member states (see Article 1.5 of the CCBE Code, Rule 16 of the Solicitors' Practice Rules 1990 and Rule 4 of the Solicitors' Overseas Practice Rules 1990).

Annex 10A

European Communities (Services of Lawyers) Order 1978 (S.I. 1978 no. 1910)

(as amended by S.I. 1980 no. 1964)

Whereas a draft of this Order has been laid before Parliament and has been approved by a resolution of each House of Parliament:

Now, therefore, Her Majesty, in exercise of the powers conferred on Her by section 2(2) of the European Communities Act 1972, is pleased, by and with the advice of Her Privy Council, to order, and it is hereby ordered, as follows:

Citation and commencement

1. This Order may be cited as the European Communities (Services of Lawyers) Order 1978 and shall come into operation on 1st March 1979.

Interpretation

2. In this Order, unless the context otherwise requires -

    "advocate", "barrister" and "solicitor" mean, in relation to any part of the United Kingdom, a person practising in that part as an advocate, barrister or solicitor as the case may be;

    "the Directive" means the European Communities Council Directive no.77/249/EEC to facilitate the effective exercise by lawyers of freedom to provide services;

    "EEC lawyer" means a person entitled to pursue his professional activities under the designation, in Belgium of an avocat-advocaat, in Denmark of an advokat, in Germany of a Rechtsanwält, in France of an avocat, in the Hellenic Republic of a dikigoros, in the Republic of Ireland of a barrister or solicitor, in Italy of an avvocato, in Luxembourg of an avocat-avoué, or in the Netherlands of an advocaat;

    "member State of origin", in relation to an EEC lawyer, means the member State or States in which he is established; and

    "own professional authority", in relation to an EEC lawyer, means an authority entitled to exercise disciplinary authority over him in his member State of origin.

3.   (1) The Interpretation Act 1978 shall apply to this Order as it applies to subordinate legislation made after the commencement of that Act.

(2) Unless the context otherwise requires, any reference in this Order to a numbered article or to the Schedule is a reference to an article of, or the Schedule to, this Order.

Purpose of Order

4.   The provisions of this Order shall have effect for the purpose of enabling an EEC lawyer to pursue his professional activities in any part of the United Kingdom by providing, under the conditions specified in or permitted by the Directive, services otherwise reserved to advocates, barristers and solicitors; and services which may be so provided are hereafter in this Order referred to as services.

Representation in legal proceedings

5.   No enactment or rule of law or practice shall prevent an EEC lawyer from providing any service in relation to any proceedings, whether civil or criminal, before any court, tribunal or public authority (including appearing before and addressing the court, tribunal or public authority) by reason only that he is not an advocate, barrister or solicitor; provided that throughout he is instructed with, and acts in conjunction with, an advocate, barrister or solicitor who is entitled to practise before the court, tribunal or public authority concerned and who could properly provide the service in question.

6.   Nothing in this Order shall enable an EEC lawyer -

(a)   if he is established in practice as a barrister in the Republic of Ireland, to provide in the course of any proceedings any service which could not properly be provided by an advocate or barrister;

(b)   if he is instructed with and acts in conjunction with an advocate or barrister in any proceedings, to provide in the course of those proceedings, or of any related proceedings, any service which an advocate or barrister could not properly provide;

(c)   if he is instructed with and acts in conjunction with a solicitor in any proceedings, to provide in the course of those proceedings, or of any related proceedings, any service which a solicitor could not properly provide.

7.   An EEC lawyer in salaried employment who is instructed with and acts in conjunction with an advocate or barrister in any proceedings may provide a service on behalf of his employer in those proceedings only in so far as an advocate or barrister in such employment could properly do so.

Drawing of documents, etc., not related to legal proceedings

8.   No enactment or rule of law or practice shall prevent an EEC lawyer from drawing or preparing for remuneration:

(i)   in England, Wales or Northern Ireland, an instrument relating to personal estate, or

(ii)   in Scotland, a writ relating to moveable property,

by reason only that he is not an advocate, barrister or solicitor.

9. Nothing in this Order shall entitle an EEC lawyer to draw or prepare for remuneration any instrument, or in Scotland any writ:

    (i)   creating or transferring an interest in land; or

    (ii)   for obtaining title to administer the estate of a deceased person.

Legal aid

10. Services may be provided by an EEC lawyer by way of legal advice and assistance or legal aid under the enactments specified in Part 1 of the Schedule; and references to counsel and solicitors in those and any other enactments relating to legal advice and assistance or legal aid shall be construed accordingly.

Title and description to be used by EEC lawyers

11. In providing any services, an EEC lawyer shall use the professional title and description applicable to him in his member State of origin, expressed in the language or one of the languages of that State, together with the name of the professional organisation by which he is authorised to practise or the court of law before which he is entitled to practise in that State.

Power to require an EEC lawyer to verify his status

12. A competent authority may at any time request a person seeking to provide any services to verify his status as an EEC lawyer.

13. Where a request has been made under article 12, the person to whom it is made shall not, except to the extent (if any) allowed by the competent authority making the request, be entitled to provide services in the United Kingdom until he has verified his status as an EEC lawyer to the satisfaction of that authority.

14. For the purposes of articles 12 and 13, a competent authority is -

    (a)   where the services which the person concerned seeks to provide are reserved to advocates or barristers, or in any case where the person concerned claims to be a barrister established in practice in the Republic of Ireland, the Senate of the Inns of Court and the Bar, the Faculty of Advocates, or the Benchers of the Inn of Court of Northern Ireland, according to the part of the United Kingdom concerned; or

    (b)   where subparagraph (a) does not apply, the Law Society, the Law Society of Scotland, or the Incorporated Law Society of Northern Ireland, according to the part of the United Kingdom concerned; or

    (c)   in any case, any court, tribunal or public authority before which the person concerned seeks to provide services.

Professional misconduct

15. (1) A complaint may be made to a disciplinary authority that an EEC lawyer providing any services has failed to observe a condition or rule of professional conduct referred to in article 4 of the Directive and applicable to him.

    (2) Where a complaint is made under paragraph (1), the disciplinary authority

concerned shall consider and adjudicate upon it in accordance with the same procedure, and subject to the same rights of appeal, as apply in relation to an advocate, barrister or solicitor (as the case may be) over whom that authority has jurisdiction.

(3) For the purposes of this article and article 16, a disciplinary authority is -

(a) where the services in question are reserved to advocates or barristers, or in any case where the person whose conduct is in question is established in practice as a barrister in the Republic of Ireland, an authority having disciplinary jurisdiction over advocates or barristers (as the case may be) in the part of the United Kingdom concerned;

(b) where subparagraph (a) does not apply, an authority having disciplinary jurisdiction over solicitors in the part of the United Kingdom concerned.

16. (1) Where a disciplinary authority finds that an EEC lawyer against whom a complaint has been made under article 15(1) has committed a breach of a condition or a rule of professional conduct mentioned in that article, that authority -

(a) shall report that finding to the EEC lawyer's own professional authority; and

(b) may, if it thinks fit, direct him not to provide services in the United Kingdom, except to such extent and under such conditions (if any) as the disciplinary authority may specify in the direction.

(2) A disciplinary authority may at any time, if it thinks fit, vary, cancel or suspend the operation of a direction given by it under paragraph (1)(b).

17. An EEC lawyer in respect of whom a direction is made under article 16(1)(b) shall not be entitled to provide services in the United Kingdom except as allowed by the direction.

Modification of enactments

18. (1) Without prejudice to the generality of articles 5 and 8, the enactments specified in Part 2 of the Schedule (being enactments which reserve the provision of certain services to advocates, barristers, solicitors and other qualified persons) shall be construed subject to those articles.

(2) Notwithstanding anything in the Solicitors (Scotland) Act 1933, the Solicitors Act 1974 or the Solicitors (Northern Ireland) Order 1976, references to unqualified persons, however expressed, in the enactments specified in Part 3 of the Schedule (being enactments relating to unqualified persons acting as solicitors) shall not include an EEC lawyer providing services within the meaning of this Order.

(3) Nothing in section 42 of the Solicitors (Scotland) Act 1933 shall prevent an EEC lawyer from recovering any remuneration or expenses to which that section applies by reason only that he is not qualified as a solicitor.

N.E. Leigh,

Clerk of the Privy Council.

Schedule

Article 10

PART I

Enactments Relating to the Provision of Legal Advice and Assistance and Legal Aid

Legal Aid and Advice Act (Northern Ireland) 1965 (c.8).
Legal Aid (Scotland) Act 1967 (c.43).
Legal Advice and Assistance Act 1972 (c.50).
Legal Aid Act 1974 (c.4).
Legal Aid, Advice and Assistance (Northern Ireland) Order 1977 (S.I. No. 1252 (N.I.19)).

Article 18(1)

PART II

Enactments Reserving the Provision of Services to Advocates, Barristers, Solicitors, etc.

Solicitors (Scotland) Act 1933 (c.21), section 39.
Magistrates' Courts Act 1952 (c.55), section 99.
Magistrates' Courts Act (Northern Ireland) 1964 (c.21(N.I.)), section 165(1).
County Courts Act 1959 (c.22), section 89.
County Courts Act (Northern Ireland) 1959 (c.25(N.I.)), section 139.
Solicitors Act 1974 (c.47), sections 20, 22.
Solicitors (Northern Ireland) Order 1976 (S.I. No. 582 (N.I.12)), articles 19, 23.

Article 18(2)

PART III

Enactments Relating to Unqualified Persons Acting as Solicitors

Solicitors (Scotland) Act 1933 (c.21), sections 37, 38.
Solicitors Act 1974 (c.47), sections 25(1), 39(1).
Solicitors (Northern Ireland) Order 1976 (S.I. No. 582 (N.I. 12)), articles 25(1), 27.

Annex 10B

CCBE Code of Conduct for Lawyers in the European Community*

with explanatory memorandum and commentary

Code of Conduct for Lawyers in the European Community [October 1988]

Preamble

1.1   The function of the lawyer in society

In a society founded on respect for the rule of law the lawyer fulfils a special role. His duties do not begin and end with the faithful performance of what he is instructed to do so far as the law permits. A lawyer must serve the interests of justice as well as those whose rights and liberties he is trusted to assert and defend and it is his duty not only to plead his client's cause but to be his adviser.

A lawyer's function therefore lays on him a variety of legal and moral obligations (sometimes appearing to be in conflict with each other) towards:

—   the client;

—   the courts and other authorities before whom the lawyer pleads his client's cause or acts on his behalf;

—   the legal profession in general and each fellow member of it in particular; and

—   the public for whom the existence of a free and independent profession, bound together by respect for rules made by the profession itself, is an essential means of safeguarding human rights in the face of the power of the state and other interests in society.

1.2   The nature of rules of professional conduct

1.2.1   Rules of professional conduct are designed through their willing acceptance by those to whom they apply to ensure the proper performance by the lawyer of a function which is recognised as essential in all civilised societies. The failure of the lawyer to observe these rules must in the last resort result in a disciplinary sanction.

---

*Reproduced by the kind permission of the CCBE.

1.2.2   The particular rules of each bar or law society arise from its own traditions. They are adapted to the organisation and sphere of activity of the profession in the member state concerned and to its judicial and administrative procedures and to its national legislation. It is neither possible nor desirable that they should be taken out of their context nor that an attempt should be made to give general application to rules which are inherently incapable of such application.

The particular rules of each bar and law society nevertheless are based on the same values and in most cases demonstrate a common foundation.

1.3   The purpose of the code

1.3.1   The continued integration of the European Community and the increasing frequency of the cross-border activities of lawyers within the Community have made necessary in the public interest the statement of common rules which apply to all lawyers from the Community whatever bar or law society they belong to in relation to their cross-border practice. A particular purpose of the statement of those rules is to mitigate the difficulties which result from the application of 'double deontology' as set out in Art 4 of EC Dir 77/249 of 22 March 1977.

1.3.2   The organisations representing the legal profession through the CCBE propose that the rules codified in the following articles:

—   be recognised at the present time as the expression of the consensus of all the bars and law societies of the EC;

—   be adopted as enforceable rules as soon as possible in accordance with national or Community procedures in relation to the cross-border activities of the lawyer in the EC; and

—   be taken into account in all revisions of national rules of deontology or professional practice with a view to their progressive harmonisation.

They further express the wish that the national rules of deontology or professional practice be interpreted and applied whenever possible in a way consistent with the rules in this code.

After the rules in this code have been adopted as enforceable rules in relation to his cross-border activities the lawyer will remain bound to observe the rules of the bar or law society to which he belongs to the extent that they are consistent with the rules in this code.

1.4   Field of application ratione personae

The following rules shall apply to lawyers of the EC as they are defined by Dir 77/249.

1.5   Field of application ratione materiae

Without prejudice to the pursuit of a progressive harmonisation of rules of deontology or professional practice which apply only internally within a member state, the following rules shall apply to the cross-border activities of the lawyer within the EC. Cross-border activities shall mean:

—   all professional contacts with lawyers of member states other than his own; and

—   the professional activities of the lawyer in a member state other than his own, whether or not the lawyer is physically present in that member state.

1.6   *Definitions*

In these rules:

'home member state' means the member state of the bar or law society to which the lawyer belongs;

'host member state' means any other member state where the lawyer carries on cross-border activities; and

'competent authority' means the professional organisation(s) or authority(ies) of the member states concerned responsible for the laying down of rules of professional conduct and the administration of discipline of lawyers.

2.   General principles

2.1   *Independence*

2.1.1   The many duties to which a lawyer is subject require his absolute independence, free from all other influence, especially such as may arise from his personal interests or external pressure. Such independence is as necessary to trust in the process of justice as the impartiality of the judge. A lawyer must therefore avoid any impairment of his independence and be careful not to compromise his professional standards in order to please his client, the court or third parties.

2.1.2   This independence is necessary in non-contentious matters as well as in litigation. Advice given by a lawyer to his client has no value if it is given only to ingratiate himself, to serve his personal interests or in response to outside pressure.

2.2   *Trust and personal integrity*

Relationships of trust can only exist if a lawyer's personal honour, honesty and integrity are beyond doubt. For the lawyer these traditional virtues are professional obligations.

2.3   *Confidentiality*

2.3.1   It is of the essence of a lawyer's function that he should be told by his client things which the client would not tell to others, and that he should be the recipient of other information on a basis of confidence. Without the certainty of confidentiality there cannot be trust. Confidentiality is therefore a primary and fundamental right and duty of the lawyer.

2.3.2   A lawyer shall accordingly respect the confidentiality of all information given to him by his client, or received by him about his client or others in the course of rendering services to his client.

2.3.3   The obligation of confidentiality is not limited in time.

2.3.4   A lawyer shall require his associates and staff and anyone engaged by him in the course of providing professional services to observe the same obligation of confidentiality.

2.4   Respect for the rules of other bars and law societies

Under Community law (in particular under Dir 77/249 of 22 March 1977) a lawyer from another member state may be bound to comply with the rules of the bar or law society of the host member state. Lawyers have a duty to inform themselves as to the rules which will affect them in the performance of any particular activity.

2.5   Incompatible occupations

2.5.1   In order to perform his functions with due independence and in a manner which is consistent with his duty to participate in the administration of justice a lawyer is excluded from some occupations.

2.5.2   A lawyer who acts in the representation or the defence of a client in legal proceedings or before any public authorities in a host member state shall there observe the rules regarding incompatible occupations as they are applied to lawyers of the host member state.

2.5.3   A lawyer established in a host member state in which he wishes to participate directly in commercial or other activities not connected with the practice of the law shall respect the rules regarding forbidden or incompatible occupations as they are applied to lawyers of that member state.

2.6   Personal publicity

2.6.1   A lawyer should not advertise or seek personal publicity where this is not permitted.

In other cases a lawyer should only advertise or seek personal publicity to the extent and in the manner permitted by the rules to which he is subject.

2.6.2   Advertising and personal publicity shall be regarded as taking place where it is permitted, if the lawyer concerned shows that it was placed for the purpose of reaching clients or potential clients located where such advertising or personal publicity is permitted and its communication elsewhere is incidental.

2.7   The client's interests

Subject to due observance of all rules of law and professional conduct, a lawyer must always act in the best interests of his client and must put those interests before his own interests or those of fellow members of the legal profession.

3.   Relations with clients

3.1   Instructions

3.1.1   A lawyer shall not handle a case for a party except on his instructions. He may, however, act in a case in which he has been instructed by another lawyer who himself acts for the party or where the case has been assigned to him by a competent body.

3.1.2   A lawyer shall advise and represent his client promptly, conscientiously and diligently. He shall undertake personal responsibility for the discharge of the instructions given to him. He shall keep his client informed as to the progress of the matter entrusted to him.

3.1.3   A lawyer shall not handle a matter which he knows or ought to know he is not competent to handle, without co-operating with a lawyer who is competent to handle it.

A lawyer shall not accept instructions unless he can discharge those instructions promptly having regard to the pressure of other work.

3.1.4   A lawyer shall not be entitled to exercise his right to withdraw from a case in such a way or in such circumstances that the client may be unable to find other legal assistance in time to prevent prejudice being suffered by the client.

3.2   Conflict of interests

3.2.1   A lawyer may not advise, represent or act on behalf of two or more clients in the same matter if there is a conflict, or a significant risk of a conflict, between the interests of those clients.

3.2.2   A lawyer must cease to act for both clients when a conflict of interests arises between those clients and also whenever there is a risk of a breach of confidence or where his independence may be impaired.

3.2.3   A lawyer must also refrain from acting for a new client if there is a risk of a breach of confidences entrusted to the lawyer by a former client or if the knowledge which the lawyer possesses of the affairs of the former client would give an undue advantage to the new client.

3.2.4   Where lawyers are practising in association, paras 3.2.1 to 3.2.3 above shall apply to the association and all its members.

3.3   Pactum de quota litis

3.3.1   A lawyer shall not be entitled to make a *pactum de quota litis*.

3.3.2   By *pactum de quota litis* is meant an agreement between a lawyer and his client entered into prior to the final conclusion of a matter to which the client is a party, by virtue of which the client undertakes to pay the lawyer a share of the result regardless of whether this is represented by a sum of money or by any other benefit achieved by the client upon the conclusion of the matter.

3.3.3   The *pactum de quota litis* does not include an agreement that fees be charged in proportion to the value of a matter handled by the lawyer if this is in accordance with an officially approved fee-scale or under the control of the competent authority having jurisdiction over the lawyer.

3.4   Regulation of fees

3.4.1   A fee charged by a lawyer shall be fully disclosed to his client and shall be fair and reasonable.

3.4.2   Subject to any proper agreement to the contrary between a lawyer and his client, fees charged by a lawyer shall be subject to regulation in accordance with the rules applied to members of the bar or law society to which he belongs. If he belongs to more than one bar or law society the rules applied shall be those with the closest connection to the contract between the lawyer and his client.

3.5   Payment on account

If a lawyer requires a payment on account of his fees and/or disbursements such payment should not exceed a reasonable estimate of the fees and probable disbursements involved.

Failing such payment, a lawyer may withdraw from the case or refuse to handle it, but subject always to para 3.1.4 above.

3.6   Fee-sharing with non-lawyers

3.6.1   Subject as after-mentioned a lawyer may not share his fees with a person who is not a lawyer.

3.6.2   This shall not preclude a lawyer from paying a fee, commission or other compensation to a deceased lawyer's heirs or to a retired lawyer in respect of taking over the deceased or retired lawyer's practice.

3.7   Legal aid

A lawyer shall inform his client of the availability of legal aid where applicable.

3.8   Clients' funds

3.8.1   When lawyers at any time in the course of their practice come into possession of funds on behalf of their clients or third parties (hereinafter called 'clients' funds') it shall be obligatory:

3.8.1.1   that clients' funds shall always be held in an account in a bank or similar institution subject to supervision of public authority and that all clients' funds received by a lawyer should be paid into such an account unless the client explicitly or by implication agrees that the funds should be dealt with otherwise;

3.8.1.2   that any account in which the clients' funds are held in the name of the lawyer should indicate in the title or designation that the funds are held on behalf of the client or clients of the lawyer;

3.8.1.3   that any account or accounts in which clients' funds are held in the name of the lawyer should at all times contain a sum which is not less than the total of the clients' funds held by the lawyer;

3.8.1.4   that all clients' funds should be available for payment to clients on demand or upon such conditions as the clients may authorise;

3.8.1.5   that payments made from clients' funds on behalf of a client to any other person including payments made to or for one client from funds held for another client and payment of the lawyer's fees, are prohibited except to the extent that they are permitted by law or have the express or implied authority of the client for whom the payment is being made;

3.8.1.6   that the lawyer shall maintain full and accurate records, available to each client on request, showing all his dealings with his clients' funds and distinguishing clients' funds from other funds held by him; and

3.8.1.7   that the competent authorities in all member states should have powers to allow them to examine and investigate on a confidential basis the financial records of lawyers' clients' funds to ascertain whether or not the rules which they make are being complied with and to impose sanctions upon lawyers who fail to comply with those rules.

3.8.2   Subject as aforementioned, and without prejudice to the rules set out above, a lawyer who holds clients' funds in the course of carrying on practice in any member state must comply with the rules relating to holding and accounting for clients' funds which are applied by the competent authorities of the home member state.

3.8.3   A lawyer who carries on practice or provides services in a host member state may with the agreement of the competent authorities of the home and host member states concerned comply with the requirements of the host member state to the exclusion of the requirements of the home member state. In that event he shall take reasonable steps to inform his clients that he complies with the requirements in force in the host member state.

3.9   Professional indemnity insurance

3.9.1   Lawyers shall be insured at all times against claims based on professional negligence to an extent which is reasonable having regard to the nature and extent of the risks which lawyers incur in practice.

3.9.2.1   Subject as aftermentioned, a lawyer who provides services or carries on practice in a member state must comply with any rules relating to his obligation to insure against his professional liability as a lawyer which are in force in his home member state.

3.9.2.2   A lawyer who is obliged so to insure in his home member state and who provides services or carries on practice in any host member state shall use his best endeavours to obtain insurance cover on the basis required in his home member state extended to services which he provides or practice which he carries on in a host member state.

3.9.2.3   A lawyer who fails to obtain the extended insurance cover referred to in para 3.9.2.2 above or who is not obliged so to insure in his home member state and who provides services or carries on practice in a host member state shall in so far as possible obtain insurance cover against his professional liability as a lawyer whilst acting for clients in that host member state on at least an equivalent basis to that required of lawyers in the host member state.

3.9.2.4   To the extent that a lawyer is unable to obtain the insurance cover required by the foregoing rules, he shall take reasonable steps to draw that fact to the attention of such of his clients as might be affected in the event of a claim against him.

3.9.2.5   A lawyer who carries on practice or provides services in a host member state may with the agreement of the competent authorities of the home and host member states concerned comply with such insurance requirements as are in force in the host member state to the exclusion of the insurance requirements of the home member state. In this event he shall take reasonable steps to inform his clients that he is insured according to the requirements in force in the host member state.

4. Relations with the courts

4.1 Applicable rules of conduct in court

A lawyer who appears or takes part in a case before a court or tribunal in a member state must comply with the rules of conduct applied before that court or tribunal.

4.2 Fair conduct of proceedings

A lawyer must always have due regard for the fair conduct of proceedings. He must not, for example, make contact with the judge without first informing the lawyer acting for the opposing party or submit exhibits, notes or documents to the judge without communicating them in good time to the lawyer on the other side unless such steps are permitted under the relevant rules of procedure.

4.3 Demeanour in court

A lawyer shall while maintaining due respect and courtesy towards the court defend the interests of his client honourably and in a way which he considers will be to the client's best advantage within the limits of the law.

4.4 False or misleading information

A lawyer shall never knowingly give false or misleading information to the court.

4.5 Extension to arbitrators etc

The rules governing a lawyer's relations with the courts apply also to his relations with arbitrators and any other persons exercising judicial or quasi-judicial functions, even on an occasional basis.

5. Relations between lawyers

5.1 Corporate spirit of the profession

5.1.1 The corporate spirit of the profession requires a relationship of trust and co-operation between lawyers for the benefit of their clients and in order to avoid unnecessary litigation. It can never justify setting the interests of the profession against those of justice or of those who seek it.

5.1.2 A lawyer should recognise all other lawyers of member states as professional colleagues and act fairly and courteously towards them.

5.2 Co-operation among lawyers of different states

5.2.1 It is the duty of a lawyer who is approached by a colleague from another member state not to accept instructions in a matter which he is not competent to undertake. He should be prepared to help his colleague to obtain the information necessary to enable him to instruct a lawyer who is capable of providing the service asked for.

5.2.2   Where a lawyer of a member state co-operates with a lawyer from another member state, both have a general duty to take into account the differences which may exist between their respective legal systems and the professional organisations, competences and obligations of lawyers in the member states concerned.

5.3   Correspondence between lawyers

5.3.1   If a lawyer sending a communication to a lawyer in another member state wishes it to remain confidential or without prejudice he should clearly express this intention when communicating the document.

5.3.2   If the recipient of the communication is unable to ensure its status as confidential or without prejudice he should return it to the sender without revealing the contents to others.

5.4   Referral fees

5.4.1   A lawyer may not demand or accept from another lawyer or any other person a fee, commission or any other compensation for referring or recommending a client.

5.4.2   A lawyer may not pay anyone a fee, commission or any other compensation as a consideration for referring a client to himself.

5.5   Communication with opposing parties

A lawyer shall not communicate about a particular case or matter directly with any person whom he knows to be represented or advised in the case or matter by another lawyer, without the consent of that other lawyer (and shall keep the other lawyer informed of any such communications).

5.6   Change of lawyer

5.6.1   A lawyer who is instructed to represent a client in substitution for another lawyer in relation to a particular matter should inform that other lawyer and, subject to 5.6.2 below, should not begin to act until he has ascertained that arrangements have been made for the settlement of the other lawyer's fees and disbursements. This duty does not, however, make the new lawyer personally responsible for the former lawyer's fees and disbursements.

5.6.2   If urgent steps have to be taken in the interest of the client before the conditions in 5.6.1 above can be complied with, the lawyer may take such steps provided he informs the other lawyer immediately.

5.7   Responsibility for fees

In professional relations between members of bars of different member states, where a lawyer does not confine himself to recommending another lawyer or introducing him to the client but himself entrusts a correspondent with a particular matter or seeks his advice, he is personally bound, even if the client is insolvent, to pay the fees, costs and outlays which are due to the foreign correspondent. The lawyers concerned may, however, at the outset of the relationship between them make special arrangements on this matter. Further, the instructing lawyer may at any time limit his personal responsibility to the amount of the fees, costs and outlays incurred before intimation to the foreign lawyer of his disclaimer of responsibility for the future.

5.8   Training young lawyers

In order to improve trust and co-operation amongst lawyers of different member states for the clients' benefit there is a need to encourage a better knowledge of the laws and procedures in different member states. Therefore when considering the need for the profession to give good training to young lawyers, lawyers should take into account the need to give training to young lawyers from other member states.

5.9   Disputes among lawyers in different member states

5.9.1   If a lawyer considers that a colleague in another member state has acted in breach of a rule of professional conduct he shall draw the matter to the attention of his colleague.

5.9.2   If any personal dispute of a professional nature arises amongst lawyers in different members states they should if possible first try to settle it in a friendly way.

5.9.3   A lawyer shall not commence any form of proceedings against a colleague in another member state on matters referred to in 5.9.1 or 5.9.2 above without first informing the bars or law societies to which they both belong for the purpose of allowing both bars or law societies concerned an opportunity to assist in reaching a settlement.

Explanatory Memorandum and Commentary [*May 1989*]

This explanatory memorandum and commentary is prepared at the request of the CCBE standing committee by the CCBE's deontology working party, who were responsible for the drafting of the code of conduct itself. It seeks to explain the origin of the provisions of the code, to illustrate the problems which they are designed to resolve, particularly in relation to cross-border activities, and to provide assistance to the competent authorities in the member states in the application of the code. It is not intended to have any binding force in the interpretation of the code.

The original versions of the code are in the French and English languages. Translations into other Community languages are being prepared under the authority of the national delegations concerned.

1.   Preamble

1.1   The function of the lawyer in society

The Declaration of Perugia, adopted by the CCBE in 1977, laid down the fundamental principles of professional conduct applicable to lawyers throughout the EC. The provisions of Art 1.1 reaffirm the statement in the Declaration of Perugia of the function of the lawyer in society which forms the basis for the rules governing the performance of that function.

1.2   The nature of rules of professional conduct

These provisions substantially restate the explanation in the Declaration of Perugia of the nature of rules of professional conduct and how particular rules depend on particular local circumstances but are nevertheless based on common values.

1.3   The purpose of the code

These provisions introduce the development of the principles in the Declaration of Perugia into a specific code of conduct for lawyers throughout the EC, with particular reference to their cross-border activities (defined in 1.5 below). The provisions of Art 1.3.2 lay down the specific intentions of the CCBE with regard to the substantive provisions in the code.

1.4   Field of application ratione personae

The rules are here stated to apply to all the lawyers of the EC as defined in the Lawyers' Services Directive of 1977. This includes lawyers of the member states which subsequently acceded to the treaty, whose names have been added by amendment to the Directive. It accordingly applies to all the lawyers represented on the CCBE, namely:

Belgium — avocat/advocaat/rechtsanwält;
Denmark — advokat;
France — avocat;
Germany — rechtsanwält;
Greece — dikigoros;
Ireland — barrister, solicitor;
Italy — avvocato, procuratore;
Luxembourg — avocat-avoué/rechtsanwält;
Netherlands — advocaat;
Portugal — advogado;
Spain — abogado;
United Kingdom — advocate, barrister, solicitor.

Although the competence of the CCBE extends only to member states, representatives of the observer delegations to the CCBE from European states which are not members of the Community (Austria, Norway, Sweden, Switzerland, Finland and Cyprus) have participated in the work on the code. It is believed that its provisions are acceptable in those states and it is hoped that the code can be applied as between them and the member states by appropriate conventions. It is also hoped that the code will be acceptable to the legal professions of other non-member states in Europe and elsewhere so that it could also be applied in the same way between them and the member states.

1.5   Field of application ratione materiae

The rules are here given direct application only to 'cross-border activities', as defined of lawyers within the EC. (See also above as to possible extensions in the future to lawyers of other states.) The definition of cross-border activities would, for example, include contacts in state A even on a matter of law internal to state A between a lawyer of state A and a lawyer of state B; it would exclude contacts between lawyers of state A in state A on a matter arising in state B, provided that none of their professional activities takes place in state B; it would include any activities of lawyers of state A in state B, even if only in the form of communications sent from state A to state B.

1.6   Definitions

This provision defines three terms used in the code, 'home member state', 'host member state' and 'competent authority'. The references to 'member state' include, where appropriate, separate jurisdictions within a single member state. The reference to 'the bar or law society to which the lawyer belongs' includes the bar or law society responsible for exercising authority over the lawyer. The reference to 'where the lawyer carries on cross-border activities' should be interpreted in the light of the definition of 'cross-border activities' in Art 1.5.

2.   General principles

2.1   Independence

This provision substantially reaffirms the general statement of principle in the Declaration of Perugia.

2.2   Trust and personal integrity

This provision also restates a general principle contained in the Declaration of Perugia.

2.3   Confidentiality

This provision first restates, in Art 2.3.1, general principles laid down in the Declaration of Perugia and recognised by the ECJ in the *AM & S* case (157/79). It then, in Arts 2.3.2 to 4, develops them into a specific rule relating to the protection of confidentiality. Art 2.3.2 contains the basic rule requiring respect for confidentiality. Art 2.3.3 confirms that the obligation remains binding on the lawyer even if he ceases to act for the client in question. Art 2.3.4 confirms that the lawyer must not only respect the obligation of confidentiality himself but must require all members and employees of his firm to do likewise.

2.4   Respect for the rules of other bars and law societies

Art 4 of the Lawyers' Services Directive of 1977 contains the provisions with regard to the rules to be observed by a lawyer from one member state providing services by virtue of Art 59 of the treaty in another member state as follows:

(a)   activities relating to the representation of a client in legal proceedings or before public authorities shall be pursued in each host member state under the conditions laid down for lawyers established in that state, with the exception of any conditions requiring residence, or registration with a professional organisation, in that state;

(b)   a lawyer pursuing these activities shall observe the rules of professional conduct of the host member state, without prejudice to his obligations in the member state from which he comes;

(c)   when these activities are pursued in the UK, 'rules of professional conduct of the host member state' means the rules of professional conduct applicable to solicitors, where such activities are not reserved for barristers and advocates. Otherwise the rules of professional conduct applicable to the latter shall apply. However, barristers from Ireland shall always be subject to the rules of professional conduct applicable in the UK to barristers and advocates. When these activities are pursued in Ireland 'rules of professional conduct of the host member state' means, in so far as they govern the oral presentation of a case in court, the rules of professional conduct applicable to barristers. In all other cases the rules of professional conduct applicable to solicitors shall apply. However, barristers and advocates from the UK shall always be subject to the rules of professional conduct applicable in Ireland to barristers; and

(d)   a lawyer pursuing activities other than those referred to in para (a) shall remain subject to the conditions and rules of professional conduct of the member state from which he comes without prejudice to respect for the rules, whatever their source, which govern the profession in the host member state, especially those concerning the incompatibility of the exercise of the activities of a lawyer with the exercise of other activities in that state, professional secrecy, relations with other lawyers, the prohibition on the same lawyer acting for parties with mutually conflicting interests, and publicity. The latter rules are applicable only if they are capable of being observed by a lawyer who is not established in the host member state and to the extent to which their observance is objectively justified to ensure, in that state, the proper exercise of a lawyer's activities, the standing of the profession and respect for the rules concerning incompatibility.

In cases not covered by this Directive, the obligations of a lawyer under Community law to observe the rules of other bars and law societies are a matter of interpretation of the applicable provisions of the treaty or any other relevant Directive. A major purpose of the code is to minimise, and if possible eliminate altogether, the problems which may arise from 'double deontology', that is the application of more than one set of potentially conflicting national rules to a particular situation (see Art 1.3.1).

2.5   Incompatible occupations

There are differences both between and within member states on the extent to which lawyers are permitted to engage in other occupations, for example in commercial activities. The general purpose of rules excluding a lawyer from other occupations is to protect him from influences which might impair his independence or his role in the administration of justice. The variations in these rules reflect different local conditions, different perceptions of the proper function of lawyers and different techniques of rule-making. For instance in some cases there is a complete prohibition of engagement in certain named occupations, whereas in other cases engagement in other occupations is generally permitted, subject to observance of specific safeguards for the lawyer's independence.

Arts 2.5.2 and 3 make provision for different circumstances in which a lawyer of one member state is engaging in cross-border activities (as defined in Art 1.5) in a host member state when he is not a member of the host state legal profession.

Art 2.5.2 imposes full observation of host state rules regarding incompatible occupations on the lawyer acting in national legal proceedings or before national public authorities in the host state. This applies whether the lawyer is established in the host state or not.

Art 2.5.3, on the other hand, imposes 'respect' for the rules of the host state regarding forbidden or incompatible occupations in other cases, but only where the lawyer who is established in the host member state wishes to participate directly in commercial or other activities not connected with the practice of the law.

2.6 Personal publicity

The term 'personal publicity' covers publicity by firms of lawyers, as well as individual lawyers, as opposed to corporate publicity organised by bars and law societies for their members as a whole. The rules governing personal publicity by lawyers vary considerably in the member states. In some there is a complete prohibition of personal publicity by lawyers; in others this prohibition has been (or is in the process of being) relaxed substantially. Art 2.6 does not therefore attempt to lay down a general standard on personal publicity.

Art 2.6.1 requires a lawyer not to advertise or seek personal publicity in a territory where this is not permitted to local lawyers. Otherwise he is required to observe the rules on publicity laid down by his own bar or law society.

Art 2.6.2 contains provisions clarifying the question of the place in which advertising and personal publicity is deemed to take place. For example, a lawyer who is permitted to advertise in his home member state may place an advertisement in a newspaper published there which circulates primarily in that member state, even though some issues may circulate in other member states where lawyers are not permitted to advertise. He may not, however, place an advertisement in a newspaper whose circulation is directed wholly or mainly at a territory where lawyers are not permitted to advertise in that way.

2.7 The client's interests

This provision emphasises the general principle that the lawyer must always place the client's interests before his own interests or those of fellow members of the legal profession.

3. Relations with clients

3.1 The acceptance and transmission of instructions

The provisions of Art 3.1.1 are designed to ensure that a relationship is maintained between lawyer and client and that the lawyer in fact receives instructions from the client, even though these may be transmitted through a duly authorised intermediary. It is the responsibility of the lawyer to satisfy himself as to the authority of the intermediary and the wishes of the client.

Art 3.1.2 deals with the manner in which the lawyer should carry out his duties. The provision that he shall undertake personal responsibility for the discharge of the instructions given to him means that he cannot avoid responsibility by delegation to others. It does not prevent him from seeking to limit his legal liability to the extent that this is permitted by the relevant law or professional rules.

Art 3.1.3 states a principle which is of particular relevance in cross-border activities, for example when a lawyer is asked to handle a matter on behalf of a lawyer or client from another state who may be unfamiliar with the relevant law and practice, or when a lawyer is asked to handle a matter relating to the law of another state with which he is unfamiliar.

A lawyer generally has the right to refuse to accept instructions in the first place, but Art 3.1.4 states that, having once accepted them, he has an obligation not to withdraw without ensuring that the client's interests are safeguarded.

3.2   Conflict of interests

The provisions of Art 3.2.1 do not prevent a lawyer acting for two or more clients in the same matter provided that their interests are not in fact in conflict and that there is no significant risk of such a conflict arising. Where a lawyer is already acting for two or more clients in this way and subsequently there arises a conflict of interests between those clients or a risk of a breach of confidence or other circumstances where his independence may be impaired, then the lawyer must cease to act for both or all of them.

There may, however, be circumstances in which differences arise between two or more clients for whom the same lawyer is acting where it may be appropriate for him to attempt to act as a mediator. It is for the lawyer in such cases to use his own judgment on whether or not there is such a conflict of interest between them as to require him to cease to act. If not, he may consider whether it would be appropriate for him to explain the position to the clients, obtain their agreement and attempt to act as mediator to resolve the difference between them, and only if this attempt to mediate should fail, to cease to act for them.

Art 3.2.4 applies the foregoing provisions of Art 3 to lawyers practising in association. For example a firm of lawyers should cease to act when there is a conflict of interest between two clients of the firm, even if different lawyers in the firm are acting for each client. On the other hand, exceptionally, in the 'chambers' form of association used by English barristers, where each lawyer acts for clients individually, it is possible for different lawyers in the association to act for clients with opposing interests.

3.3   Pactum de quota litis

These provisions reflect the common position in all member states that an unregulated agreement for contingency fees (*pactum de quota litis*) is contrary to the proper administration of justice because it encourages speculative litigation and is liable to be abused. The provisions are not, however, intended to prevent the maintenance or introduction of arrangements under which lawyers are paid according to results or only if the action or matter is successful, provided that these arrangements are under sufficient regulation and control for the protection of the client and the proper administration of justice.

3.4   Regulation of fees

Art 3.4.1 lays down a general standard of disclosure of a lawyer's fees to the client and a requirement that they should be fair and reasonable in amount. Art 3.4.2 deals with the question of the machinery for regulating the lawyers' fees. In many member states such machinery exists under national law or rules of conduct, whether by reference to a power of adjudication by the '*Batonnier*' or otherwise. Art 3.4.1 applies the rules of the bar or law society to which the lawyer belongs (see on Art 1.6) unless this has been varied by an agreement between lawyer and client which is in accordance with the relevant law or rules of conduct. It goes on to provide a 'choice of law' rule to deal with cases when the lawyer belongs to more than one bar or law society.

3.5 Payment on account

Art 3.5 assumes that a lawyer may require a payment on account of his fees and/or disbursements, but sets a limit by reference to a reasonable estimate of them. See also on Art 3.1.4 regarding the right to withdraw.

3.6 Fee-sharing with non-lawyers

In some member states lawyers are permitted to practise in association with members of certain other approved professions, whether legal professions or not. The provisions of Art 3.6.1 are not designed to prevent fee-sharing within such an approved form of association. Nor are the provisions designed to prevent fee-sharing by the lawyers to whom the code applies (see on Art 1.4 above) with other 'lawyers', for example lawyers from non-member states or members of other legal professions in the member states such as notaries or *conseils juridiques*.

3.7 Legal aid

Art 3.7 requires a lawyer to inform his client of the availability of legal aid where applicable. There are widely differing provisions in the member states on the availability of legal aid. In cross-border activities a lawyer should have in mind the possibility that the legal aid provisions of a national law with which he is unfamiliar may be applicable.

3.8 Clients' funds

The provisions of Art 3.8.1 reflect the recommendation adopted by the CCBE in Brussels in November 1985 on the need for minimum regulations to be made and enforced governing the proper control and disposal of clients' funds held by lawyers within the Community. In some member states such regulations have not yet been introduced for internal purposes. Art 3.8.1 lays down minimum standards to be observed, while not interfering with the details of national systems which provide fuller or more stringent protection for clients' funds.

The provisions of Arts 3.8.2 and 3.8.3 deal with questions which arise where the rules on clients' funds of more than one member state may be applicable.

3.9 Professional indemnity insurance

Art 3.9.1 reflects a recommendation, also adopted by the CCBE in Brussels in November 1985, on the need for all lawyers in the Community to be insured against the risks arising from professional negligence claims against them.

Again in some member states such an obligation has not yet been introduced for internal purposes. Art 3.9.2 deals with questions which arise when the risks to be insured relate to more than one member state.

4.   Relations with the courts

4.1   Rules of conduct in court

This provision applies the principle that a lawyer is bound to comply with the rules of the court or tribunal before which he practises or appears.

4.2   Fair conduct of proceedings

This provision applies the general principle that in adversarial proceedings a lawyer must not attempt to take unfair advantage of his opponent, in particular by unilateral communications with the judge. An exception however is made for any steps permitted under the relevant rules of the court in question (see also 4.5).

4.3   Demeanour in court

This provision reflects the necessary balance between respect for the court and for the law on the one hand and the pursuit of the client's best interests on the other.

4.4   False or misleading information

This provision applies the principle that the lawyer must never knowingly mislead the court. This is necessary if there is to be trust between the courts and the legal profession.

4.5   Extension to arbitrators etc

This provision extends the preceding provisions relating to courts to other bodies exercising judicial or quasi-judicial functions.

5.   Relations between lawyers

5.1   Corporate spirit of the profession

These provisions, which are based on statements in the Declaration of Perugia, emphasise that it is in the public interest for the legal profession to maintain a relationship of trust and co-operation between its members. However, this cannot be used to justify setting the interests of the profession against those of justice or of clients (see also on Art 2.7).

5.2   Co-operation

This provision also develops a principle stated in the Declaration of Perugia with a view to avoiding misunderstandings in dealings between lawyers of different member states.

5.3   Correspondence between lawyers

In certain member states communications between lawyers (written or by word of mouth) are normally regarded as confidential. This means that lawyers accept that those communications may not be disclosed to others and copies may not be sent to the lawyers' own client. This principle is recognised in Belgium, France, Greece, Italy, Luxembourg, Portugal and Spain. Such communications if in writing are often marked as '*confidentiel*' or '*sous la foi du Palais*'.

In the UK and Ireland the notion of 'confidentiality' is different in that it refers not to such communications between lawyers but to the lawyer's right and duty to keep his client's affairs confidential. However communications between lawyers made in order to attempt to settle a dispute are normally not regarded by a court as admissible evidence and the lawyer should not attempt to use them as evidence. If a lawyer wishes to indicate that he regards a document as such a communication he should indicate that it is sent 'without prejudice'. This means that the letter is sent without prejudice to and under reservation of the client's rights in the dispute.

In Denmark as a general rule, a lawyer has a right and duty to keep his client informed about all important correspondence from a lawyer acting for an opposing party, in practice normally by sending photocopies. This rule applies whether or not the letter is marked 'without prejudice' or 'confidential'. As an exception, lawyers may exchange views — normally by word of mouth only — on a case with a view to finding an amicable settlement, on the mutual understanding that such communications should be kept confidential and not disclosed to the clients. A lawyer is not legally bound by such a confidence, but to break it would prejudice his future participation in such confidential exchanges. Some lawyers do not wish to receive such communication in any form without having the right to inform their clients; in that event they should inform the other lawyer before he makes such a confidential communication to them. As a general rule also, all correspondence between lawyers may be freely produced in court. Normally, however, if such correspondence is marked 'without prejudice' or, even if not so marked, it is clearly of a 'without prejudice' nature, the court will disregard it and the lawyer producing it will be treated as being in contravention of the rules of professional conduct.

In the Netherlands legal recourse based on communications between lawyers may not be sought, unless the interest of the client requires it and only after prior consultation with the lawyer for the other party. If such consultation does not lead to a solution, the advice of the dean should be sought before recourse to law. The content of settlement negotiations between lawyers may not be communicated to the court without the permission of the lawyer for the other party, unless the right to do so was expressly reserved when the settlement proposal in question was made. There is however no general rule preventing a lawyer from sending copies of such communications to his client.

In Germany communications between lawyers are not confidential. The lawyer has an obligation to communicate them to his client and they may be admitted as evidence in court.

These differences often give rise to misunderstandings between lawyers of different member states who correspond with each other. For this reason lawyers should be particularly careful to clarify the basis upon which correspondence with lawyers in other member states is sent and received. In particular a lawyer who wishes to make a confidential or 'without prejudice' communication to a colleague in a member state where the rules may be different should ask in advance whether it can be accepted as such.

5.4   *Referral fees*

This provision reflects the principle that a lawyer should not pay or receive payment purely for the reference of a client, which would risk impairing the client's free choice of lawyer or his interest in being referred to the best available service. It does not prevent fee-sharing arrangements between lawyers on a proper basis (see also on Art 3.6 above).

In some member states lawyers are permitted to accept and retain commissions in certain cases provided the client's best interests are served, there is full disclosure to him and he has consented to the retention of the commission. In such cases the retention of the commission by the lawyer represents part of his remuneration for the service provided to the client and is not within the scope of the prohibition on referral fees which is designed to prevent lawyers making a secret profit.

5.5   *Communication with opposing parties*

This provision reflects a generally accepted principle, and is designed both to promote the smooth conduct of business between lawyers and to prevent any attempt to take advantage of the client of another lawyer.

5.6   *Change of lawyer*

This provision is designed to promote the orderly handing over of the business when there is a change of lawyer. It also reflects the commonly accepted principle in member states that there is some duty on the new lawyer in respect of the settlement of the former lawyer's account. This duty is not, however, generally accepted as being more than a duty to ascertain that arrangements have been made for the settlement.

5.7   *Responsibility for fees*

These provisions substantially reaffirm provisions contained in the Declaration of Perugia. Since misunderstandings about responsibility for unpaid fees are a common cause of difference between lawyers of different member states, it is important that a lawyer who wishes to exclude or limit his personal obligation to be responsible for the fees of his foreign colleague should reach a clear agreement on this at the outset of the transaction.

5.8   *Training young lawyers*

This provision is by way of an exhortation emphasising the general obligation of the members of the legal profession in the EC to ensure that future generations of lawyers in each member state have knowledge of the laws and procedures in other member states.

5.9   *Disputes: lawyers in different member states*

A lawyer has the right to pursue any legal or other remedy to which he is entitled against a colleague in another member state. Nevertheless it is desirable that, where a breach of a rule of professional conduct or a dispute of a professional nature is involved, the possibilities of friendly settlement should be exhausted, if necessary with the assistance of the bars or law societies concerned, before such remedies are exercised.

Annex 10C

Council statement on cross-border activities within the European Community

(see also Annex 10B)

---

1. The Solicitors' Practice Rules 1990 contain a rule (Rule 16 — cross-border activities within the European Community) which carries into effect in practice rule form the Council's ratification of the CCBE Code of Conduct for Lawyers in the European Community.

2. Solicitors will wish to know to what extent their obligations under the Code add to their other obligations under the rules and principles of professional conduct.

3. The Council's view is that a solicitor will fulfil his or her obligations under articles 2 to 5 of the code by observing the corresponding rules, principles and requirements of conduct otherwise applicable to solicitors (incuding the Solicitors' Practice Rules 1990), and in addition articles 2.5 (incompatible occupations), 5.2 (co-operation among lawyers of different member states), 5.3 (correspondence between lawyers), 5.6 (change of lawyer) and 5.9 (disputes among lawyers in different member states), being articles having no such corresponding provision. This view is subject to any authoritative ruling to the contrary at Community level.

18th July 1990, updated January 1993

THE GUIDE TO THE PROFESSIONAL CONDUCT OF SOLICITORS 1993

Annex 10D

CCBE note on the application of the Lawyers' Services Directive no. 77/249/EEC — practice information*

(see also Annex 10A)

The above Directive required Member States to adopt implementing legislation within two years. Implementing legislation has been adopted in all Member States.

It is possible that practical difficulties might arise in the exercise of their professional activities by lawyers in another Member State, particularly in proceedings before courts and tribunals, due to ignorance of the above-mentioned legislation. With a view to avoiding these difficulties the CCBE has prepared the following note as a reminder of the principles involved.

1. Art 4.1 entitles lawyers of EC Member States as described in Art 1.2 to represent clients in proceedings before the courts or public authorities of another Member State under the conditions laid down for lawyers established in that State, with the exception of any conditions requiring residence or registration with a professional organisation in that State.

Art 4.1 concerns the principle of respect for the local rules relating to professional ethics and professional organisation in contentious matters.

Art 4.4 determines the extent of their application in non-contentious activities.

2. Art 5 entitles a Member State to require a lawyer pursuing activities relating to the representation of a client in legal proceedings to do so in conjunction with a lawyer who practises before the judicial authority in question.

All Member States which have adopted implementing legislation have included this requirement.

3. Art 7 entitles the competent authority of the host Member State to request the person providing the services to establish his qualifications as a lawyer.

This requirement involves the local lawyer, who intends to appear in court with an EC lawyer, in first checking that the EC lawyer is entitled to provide services before appearing with him, i.e. that he is in compliance with the requirements of his home country as to his entitlement to practise and is in good standing with his home Bar or Law Society.

---

*Reproduced by the kind permission of the CCBE.

The CCBE identity card, issued by Bars and Law Societies throughout the Community, is a simple method by which a lawyer can establish *prima facie* proof of his right to practise. The Court of Justice of the European Communities accepts this card if it has been validated or revalidated within the previous twelve months.

4.   Having satisfied himself of the credentials of the EC lawyer, the home lawyer should then inform the court in advance of his intention to appear with the EC lawyer under the terms of the order. Not only is this a matter of courtesy, but it also prevents the court being taken unawares and thereby saves any possibility of embarrassment to the EC lawyer, the home lawyer and the client.

Annex 10E

CCBE note on dealing with complaints between lawyers from different member states — practice information*

The CCBE has set up a Council for Advice and Arbitration, the object of which is to help lawyers, particularly in settling their differences by arbitration. All the bars and law societies have received a text of the resolution, and of the rules of procedure.

Its first opinion dealt with the personal financial responsibility of a lawyer who has entrusted a correspondent with a particular matter or sought his advice.

The CCBE found that, in many cases, this rule (which was adopted unanimously) had not been followed, many lawyers complaining that they had undertaken work and incurred costs without being paid by their foreign colleagues.

To help find an amicable and practical solution in each particular case, the CCBE has obtained an undertaking from each of the delegates of the bars and law societies of the Member States of the European Community to provide all possible assistance to lawyers from other Member States who have consulted or entrusted a particular matter to one of their lawyers.

The Secretary-General of the CCBE and of the Council for Advice and Arbitration will therefore send every written and supported complaint to the Delegation of the Member State of the lawyer concerned, subject to one condition, namely that the bar or law society of the correspondent alleges a failure to reply or refusal to pay his fees or disbursements.

The list of authorities in each Member State has been sent to the secretaries of all the bars and law societies by their delegation to the CCBE. These authorities may also receive complaints from foreign lawyers who, by amicable means, want to prevail on their correspondent to be more diligent.

Whether he has been consulted on the law or legal practice of his country or asked to represent the foreign lawyer's client, the correspondent's duty clearly is to meet his colleague's expectations by taking action and keeping him informed.

The authorities designated by the bars and law societies of the Community will help to achieve the desired result by providing their assistance and, in extreme cases, they will have recourse to the appropriate conciliation and arbitration procedures.

[*For further information, contact Legal Practice (International).*]

---

*Reproduced by the kind permission of the CCBE.

PART III – RELATIONSHIP WITH THE CLIENT

Chapter 11

Obtaining instructions

11.01 Basic principles

Principle

It is fundamental to the relationship which exists between solicitor and client that a solicitor should be able to give impartial and frank advice to the client, free from any external or adverse pressures or interests which would destroy or weaken the solicitor's professional independence or the fiduciary relationship with the client.

1. The basic principles governing a solicitor's practice are summed up in Rule 1 of the Solicitors' Practice Rules 1990.

2. A potential client who has been improperly influenced in his or her choice of solicitor cannot be said to have had a free choice. Improper influence can come from the solicitor or from a third party. Where a solicitor has reason to suspect that there may have been improper influence, the solicitor must satisfy himself/herself that the client's freedom of choice has not been restricted.

3. A solicitor must avoid being placed in a position where the solicitor's interests or the interests of a third party to whom the solicitor may owe a duty conflict with the interests of the client. See Chapter 15 in respect of conflicts, and Principles 11.03-11.05 in respect of third party arrangements.

4. A solicitor must not allow clients to override the solicitor's professional judgment, for example by insisting on the solicitor acting in a way which is contrary to law or to a rule or a principle of professional conduct (see Principle 12.02).

11.02 Publicity

Principle

'Solicitors may at their discretion publicise their practices or permit other persons to do so or publicise the businesses or activities of other persons, provided there is no breach of these rules and provided there is compliance with a Solicitors' Publicity Code promulgated from time to time by the Council of the Law Society with the concurrence of the Master of the Rolls.'

Rule 2, Solicitors' Practice Rules 1990

Commentary

1. The Solicitors' Publicity Code 1990 (see Annex 11A) gives details of the way in which solicitors may publicise their practices. Solicitors' publicity should comply with the Business Names Act 1985 and the Consumer Credit Act 1974. Guidance on advertisements for mortgages may be found in Annex 11E.

2. Solicitors' publicity should also comply with the British Code of Advertising Practice (see Annex 11C).

3. The provisions of the Solicitors' Investment Business Rules 1990 apply in relation to investment advertisements. Rule 8(1) relates to solicitors' own advertisements.

4. Solicitors may claim to be specialists or experts in a particular field, provided that they can justify such a claim (see paragraph 2(b) of the Publicity Code). Guidance is contained in Annex 11D.

5. Unsolicited mailshots may be sent and can be targeted. However, there are restrictions on unsolicited telephone calls and visits (see paragraph 3 of the Publicity Code).

6. Publicity as to charges must be clearly expressed (see paragraph 5 of the Publicity Code). Care should be taken where an advertisement offers a discount as it could be open to criticism if there are no clear scales included.

7. A designation of the practice may be used in addition to the firm's name. Such designation must include the word 'solicitor(s)' or in the case of publicity conducted outside England and Wales, the word 'lawyer(s)'. The designation must comply with the general law and must not be inaccurate or misleading (see paragraph 6 of the Publicity Code). For example, the use of the description 'patent agent' is restricted by the Copyright, Designs and Patents Act 1988 and therefore, the designation 'solicitors and patent

agents' may only be used where all the partners are registered patent agents or where the firm is able to satisfy such future conditions prescribed under the Act in relation to mixed partnerships. The designation 'solicitors and patent attorneys' may be used without contravention of the Act.

8. Solicitors may name members of their staff on notepaper subject to the provisions of paragraph 7 of the Publicity Code (see Principle 3.11).

9. A subsidiary practising style is an additional business style (of a type other than that used as the name of a firm) which is used to denote the work of a firm or a department of the firm. Smith, Smith and Smith may use, for their conveyancing department, the style 'Cosy Abodes', but paragraph 9 of the Publicity Code requires that such a style must be used in conjunction with the firm name and the word 'solicitors'. The letterhead could read 'Smith, Smith and Smith, Solicitors — Cosy Abodes'. A subsidiary practising style must not be misleading. It would be misleading for Smith, Smith and Smith to use the style 'Jones Investment Services' for their investment business department if Mr Jones were a non-solicitor financial adviser.

11.03   Introductions and referrals

Principle

'Solicitors may accept introductions and referrals of business from other persons and may make introductions and refer business to other persons, provided there is no breach of these rules and provided there is compliance with a Solicitors' Introduction and Referral Code promulgated from time to time by the Council of the Law Society with the concurrence of the Master of the Rolls.'

Rule 3, Solicitors' Practice Rules 1990

Commentary

1. The Solicitors' Introduction and Referral Code 1990 states the principles to be observed in relation to the introduction and referral of clients to and from solicitors (see Annex 11B). Sections 1 to 3A deal with the introduction of clients to solicitors. Sections 1 and 4 deal with the introduction of clients to third parties.

2. The Introduction and Referral Code applies to all arrangements for the referral of clients, other than introductions and referrals between solicitors, between solicitors and barristers or between solicitors and lawyers of other jurisdictions. Arrangements whereby the solicitor agrees to be paid by a third party to do work for the third party's customers are permitted although these are subject to the additional requirements and restrictions

set out in section 3 of the code in relation to work other than conveyancing and section 3A in relation to conveyancing (see Principle 24.08).

3. Rule 9 of the Solicitors' Practice Rules 1990 prevents solicitors from entering into arrangements with claims assessors in relation to claims for death or personal injury if the claims assessor solicits or receives a contingency fee (see Principle 11.06).

4. Rule 12 of the Solicitors' Practice Rules 1990 makes provision in respect of introductions and referrals in connection with investment business and may restrict some forms of arrangement. In particular, the rule prevents a solicitor from acting as an appointed representative as defined in the Financial Services Act 1986 (see Principle 26.32).

5. In accepting and making referrals in relation to mortgages or investment business, solicitors must also comply with the Council statement on the Financial Services Act 1986: life policies and tied agents (see Principle 24.07 and Annex 24C).

6. Section 2(3) of the Introduction and Referral Code provides that a solicitor must not reward an introducer by the payment of commission or otherwise.

7. There is no objection to an employer recommending to employees the services of a particular solicitor in private practice. However, any arrangement must be in accordance with the Introduction and Referral Code. It would not be proper for a solicitor to act for one of the employees in the knowledge that the employer has made it a condition of employment that the employee should instruct that solicitor.

8. Many insurance policies give the insurers the right to act in the name of the insured in the defence, prosecution or settlement of any claim falling within the policy cover and also to nominate solicitors to provide legal services to the insured. Solicitors are permitted to act on the instructions of insurers who offer this form of policy. It must be recognised that in these circumstances, a solicitor-client relationship is established between the solicitor and the insured. This Commentary applies to indemnity insurance only. It should not be taken as applying to legal expenses insurance, which is dealt with in Principle 6.01.

9. Where solicitors are asked to draft wills by will-writing companies, the Introduction and Referral Code will apply as the testator will be the client and the will-writing company the introducer. Principle 12.05 applies in relation to the testator's instructions and Principle 11.05 will also be relevant.

11.04   Associations

Principle

A solicitor may act for members of a formal or informal association subject to the provisions of the Solicitors' Introduction and Referral Code 1990.

Commentary

1.   Where the costs of an individual are to be paid by the association, the normal solicitor-client relationship will exist with the member client. Where the association for any reason decides not to continue to fund proceedings on its member's behalf, the position as to ownership of documents is governed, as always, by the law. The normal position is set out in Annex 12B. However, if statements were obtained by the association's officials before instructions were sent to the solicitor to act on behalf of the member client, the association may be able to claim ownership of those statements.

2.   A solicitor may be instructed to act in a matter both for an association, club or trade union and for the association's members, or to act for a number of members of the association. The solicitor should be alert to the possibility of conflicting interests arising. In some circumstances, the solicitor should, at the outset, insist on one or more of the parties being separately represented. In other circumstances, the solicitor may be able to act for all the parties but needs to warn them, at the outset, that separate representation may be necessary, at some stage.

3.   Where there is a common interest between one or more individuals, but there is no formal association it may be clear that to arrange for one solicitor to act for all those individuals whose rights are affected could save time and costs. Examples of such circumstances include common claims arising out of an air crash or certain neighbourhood disputes. Any solicitor accepting joint instructions should bear in mind the possibility of conflicting interests between the clients and should warn the prospective clients that at some later stage it may be necessary that each person is separately advised.

4.   The Law Society offers information and co-ordination facilities to firms instructed in the wake of disasters or otherwise involved in multi-party actions. For further information contact the Information Co-ordinator, Legal Practice Directorate.

11.05   Freedom of choice

Principle

A solicitor must not accept instructions knowing that a third party has stipulated that the solicitor must act.

Commentary

1. A breach of this Principle would have the effect of denying the prospective client freedom of choice (see Rule 1(b) of the Solicitors' Practice Rules 1990 and Principle 11.01). Consequently, a solicitor must not act for a borrower where the solicitor knows or ought to know that a condition of the loan is that the solicitor should act for the borrower. In many cases, however, such conditions are imposed without the knowledge of the solicitor. A solicitor who has any doubts should satisfy himself or herself that the third party introductions are not tainted by such objectionable conditions by making enquiries of the prospective client.

2. Some builders seek to impose a condition on the sale of their houses that their solicitor must act for the buyer or that they will select a solicitor to act for the buyer and pay the legal fees. To accept instructions in such circumstances would not only be a breach of Rule 1, but where the solicitor was also acting for both parties, would also be a breach of Rule 6 of the Solicitors' Practice Rules 1990. This rule specifically prohibits the seller's solicitor from acting for the buyer where the seller is a builder or developer selling as such. The fact that the conveyancing is being offered free makes no difference.

11.06   Claims assessors

Principle

A solicitor shall not enter into arrangements with claims assessors in respect of a claim or claims arising from death or personal injury, if the claims assessor solicits or receives a contingency fee.

Commentary

1. Rule 9 of the Solicitors' Practice Rules 1990 makes it clear that the prohibition only relates to claims arising as a result of death or personal injury. Therefore, other types of claims will not be affected by the rule.

2. The rule prevents such arrangements being made with claims assessors

who may be defined as non-solicitors, whose business, or any part of whose business, is to make, support or prosecute claims arising from death or personal injury and who solicit or receive contingency fees in respect of such claims. Contingency fees are defined in Rule 18(2) of the Solicitors' Practice Rules 1990.

3.   As a matter of law, agreements in such situations would be unenforceable, and solicitors would need to be free to advise clients accordingly.

4.   There is no prohibition under Rule 9 where the proceedings take place outside England and Wales if a local lawyer would be able to receive a contingency fee.

Annex 11A

Solicitors' Publicity Code 1990

(with consolidated amendments to 1st January 1992)

Code dated 18th July 1990 promulgated by the Council of the Law Society with the concurrence of the Master of the Rolls under Rule 2 of the Solicitors' Practice Rules 1990, regulating the publicity of solicitors and recognised bodies in England and Wales or overseas, and the publicity of registered foreign lawyers practising in England and Wales.

1. General principles

(a) *Compliance with professional obligations*

Nothing in this code shall be construed as authorising any breach of the Solicitors' Practice Rules, and in particular Rule 1 thereof, or any other professional obligation or requirement.

(b) *Publicity in bad taste*

Solicitors shall not publicise their practices in any manner which may reasonably be regarded as being in bad taste.

(c) *Misleading or inaccurate publicity*

Publicity must not be inaccurate or misleading in any way.

(d) *Statutory requirements*

As a matter of professional conduct the publicity of a solicitor must comply with the general law. Solicitors are reminded, *inter alia,* of the requirements of:

(i) any regulations made under the Consumer Credit Act 1974 concerning the content of advertisements;

(ii) the Business Names Act 1985 concerning lists of partners and an address for service on stationery, etc.; and

(iii) Chapter 1 of Part XI of the Companies Act 1985 concerning the appearance of the company name and other particulars on stationery, etc.

(e)   *Other codes of advertising practice*

No advertisement shall be published which breaches the British Code of Advertising Practice or the IBA Code of Advertising Standards and Practice for the time being in force.

(f)   *Solicitors' responsibility for publicity*

It is the responsibility of solicitors to ensure that all their publicity, and all publicity for their services which is conducted by other persons, complies with the provisions of this code. The responsibility cannot be delegated. Where solicitors become aware of any impropriety in any publicity appearing on their behalf, they must use their best endeavours to have the publicity rectified or withdrawn as appropriate.

2.   Contents of publicity — general

(a)   *Solicitor to be identified*

Every advertisement by a solicitor must bear the solicitor's name or firm name (subject to paragraph 10 below on flag advertising).

(b)   *Claims to specialisation or particular expertise*

It is not improper for a claim to be made that a solicitor (or a registered foreign lawyer) is a specialist, or an expert, in a particular field provided that such a claim can be justified.

(c)   *Success rate*

No publicity may refer to a solicitor's success rate (or that of a registered foreign lawyer practising with the solicitor).

(d)   *Comparisons and criticisms*

No publicity may make direct comparison or criticism in relation to the charges or quality of service of any other identifiable solicitor. However, a solicitor may participate in the preparation of a *bona fide* survey of legal services conducted by a third party which may make comparisons between the charges of or quality of service provided by different solicitors.

(e)   *The Law Society's coat of arms*

The armorial bearings of the Law Society may not appear in a solicitor's publicity.

(f)   *Legal aid logo*

Solicitors willing to undertake legal aid cases may use the legal aid logo in their publicity, but the logo must not be altered in any way. (Photographic copies of the logo can be obtained from the Legal Aid Board.)

(g)   *Judicial appointments*

No mention may be made in any advertisement (including stationery — see paragraph 16 (ii) below) of the fact that a solicitor is a recorder, assistant recorder, deputy registrar, acting stipendiary magistrate or justice of the peace.

3.   Unsolicited visits and telephone calls

Solicitors may not publicise their practices or properties for sale or to let by means of unsolicited visits or telephone calls except:

(i)   by means of a telephone call to a current or former client; or

(ii)   by means of a visit or telephone call to another solicitor or to an existing or potential professional connection; or

(iii)   by means of a visit or telephone call made to publicise a specific commercial property or properties the solicitor has for sale or to let.

4.   Naming clients

Solicitors may name or identify their clients in advertisements for their practices or in the public media, or supply information about their clients to publishers of directories, provided that:

(i)   the client gives consent which, in the case of advertisements and directories, shall be in writing; and

(ii)   any such naming or identification of a client is not likely to prejudice the client's interests.

5.   Statements as to charges

(a)   *Clarity*

Any publicity as to charges or a basis of charging must be clearly expressed. It must be stated what services will be provided for those charges or on that basis of charging. Any circumstances in which the charges may be increased or the basis altered must be stated. It must be clear whether disbursements and VAT are included.

(b)   *Fee from or upwards of a figure*

It is prohibited to state a fee as being from or upwards of a certain figure.

(c)   *Service free of charge*

Publicity may state that a particular service of a solicitor is free of charge, but this must not be conditional on the solicitor or any other person being given any other instructions, or receiving any commission or other benefit, in connection with that or any other matter.

(d)   *Composite fees*

No publicity may quote a composite fee for two or more separate services of a solicitor unless the solicitor is willing if required (i) to quote separate fees for the individual services (which separate fees may not total more than the composite fee), and (ii) to carry out any one only of those services on the basis of such separate fee.

(e)   *Commissions from third parties*

In publicity for conveyancing or other services of a solicitor, fees must not be quoted which are intended to be net fees, i.e. fees which are reduced by the availability of any commission (such as that on an endowment policy). Any fee quoted in such circumstances must be the gross fee, although there is no objection to mentioning that the availability for the benefit of the client of a commission may reduce the net cost of the transaction to the client; provided that, where such mention is made in connection with mortgages, there must be no implication that endowment mortgages are appropriate in all circumstances, and there must be included an indication of the solicitor's willingness to advise as to the appropriate type of mortgage for the client's circumstances.

6.   Designation of a practice

(a)   *Provisions applying to all firms*

A firm may use, in addition to its name, a designation of the practice. Such a designation must include:

(i)   the word 'solicitor(s)'; or

(ii)   as an additional option in the case of publicity conducted outside England and Wales (including the notepaper of an office outside England and Wales), the word 'lawyer(s)'.

The designation must not be misleading, nor must it be based on an area of practice in which a claim to specialisation or particular expertise would be improper (see paragraph 2(b) above). There must be no breach of paragraph 14(b) below on the use of the word 'lawyer(s)'.

(b)   *Additional provisions applying to multi-national practices*

In the case of a practice which has at least one registered foreign lawyer as a partner, director, registered member or beneficial owner of a share, a designation used in publicity conducted in England and Wales (including the notepaper of an English or Welsh office) must include:

(i)   the words 'solicitor(s)' and 'registered foreign lawyer(s)'; or

(ii)   the word 'solicitor(s)' together with words denoting the countries or jurisdictions of qualification of the foreign lawyers who are partners, directors, registered members or beneficial owners of shares in the practice and their professional qualifications.

In the designation, such constituent elements must be placed in order, with the largest category first.

7. Naming partners and staff

(a)   Provisions applying to all practices

(i)   A member of staff (including a partner or director) other than a solicitor who holds a current practising certificate may only be named in a practitioner's publicity, including stationery, if the status of that person is unambiguously stated.

(ii)   The term 'legal executive' may only be used in a practitioner's publicity, including stationery, to refer to a Fellow of the Institute of Legal Executives; and 'trainee solicitor' to refer to a person under articles of training.

(iii)   Practitioners are reminded of the danger of inadvertently holding out persons as partners in a firm by inclusion of both partners' and non-partners' names in a list. The status of non-partners must be indicated for avoidance of doubt whenever a situation of inadvertent holding out might otherwise arise.

(iv)   The following terms, used alone or in combination, will be deemed to indicate that a person is a solicitor holding a current practising certificate, unless it is made clear that the person is not so qualified:

(A)   associate;

(B)   assistant;

(C)   consultant.

(v)   The following terms, used alone or in combination, will be deemed to indicate that a person is not a solicitor holding a current practising certificate, unless a contrary indication appears:

(A)   executive;

(B)   clerk;

(C)   manager;

(D)   secretary;

(E)   paralegal.

(vi)   The appearance against a person's name of an indication that he or she is qualified in a jurisdiction other than England and Wales, or the title licensed conveyancer, or registered foreign lawyer, or the title of any other profession, will be deemed to indicate that the person is not a solicitor holding a current practising certificate, unless a contrary indication appears. (See also paragraph 14(b) below on the use of the word 'lawyer(s)'.)

(b)   *Additional provisions applying to multi-national practices*

(i)   In the case of a practice which has at least one registered foreign lawyer as a partner, director, registered member or beneficial owner of a share, the notepaper of an English or Welsh office of the practice must contain either:

(A) a list of the partners or directors; or

(B) a statement that a list of the partners or directors and their professional qualifications is open to inspection at that office (see also paragraph 1(d)(ii) above, the Business Names Act 1985 and Rule 23 of the Solicitors' Incorporated Practice Rules).

(ii)   Any such list, as well as a list of the partners or directors in any other publicity conducted in England and Wales, must indicate the countries or jurisdictions of qualification of the partners or directors and their professional qualifications.

(iii)   Where the notepaper of an English or Welsh office of the practice includes *neither* a designation of the practice (see paragraph 6(b) above) *nor* a list of the partners or directors, the statement required by sub-paragraph (b)(i)(B) above must also state that the partners or directors are (as the case may be) solicitors and registered foreign lawyers, or describe them in such other terms which, as applied to those partners or directors, would be permitted by paragraph 6(b)(i) or (ii) above. In any such statement or description, the constituent elements must be placed in order, with the largest category first.

(iv)   Sub-paragraph (b)(iii) above does not apply to the notepaper of a recognised body if a designation would merely repeat part of the body's name.

(v)   For the purpose of sub-paragraphs (b)(ii) and (iii) above:

(A) there must be no breach of the principle set out in paragraph 14(b) below on the use of the word 'lawyer(s)'; and

(B) the word 'solicitor(s)' is sufficient in itself to indicate that a solicitor's jurisdiction of qualification is England and Wales.

8. Directory headings

A firm may have an entry or advertisement in a directory or listing under any appropriate heading provided that either:

(i)   the word 'solicitor(s)'; or

(ii)   as an additional option in the case of a directory referring wholly or mainly to practice outside England and Wales, the word 'lawyer(s)' (but see paragraph 14(b) below);

appears *either* in the heading of the directory *or* listing or in a designation of the practice (see paragraph 6 above) appearing in the entry or advertisement itself.

9. Subsidiary practising style

A subsidiary practising style of a type other than that used as the name of a firm may be used in relation to a firm or a part of a firm, provided that it is used in conjunction with the name of the firm and provided that the word 'solicitor(s)' (or, as an additional option in the case of an office outside England and Wales, the word 'lawyer(s)') is also used. (For the use of the word 'lawyer(s)' see paragraph 14(b) below. For the name of a firm see Practice Rule 11 and, in the case of a recognised body, Rule 22 of the Solicitors' Incorporated Practice Rules 1988. For the designation of a practice see paragraph 6 above.)

10. Flag advertising

(a)   For the purpose of this paragraph, 'flag advertising' means advertising conducted by or on behalf of solicitors under the logo of or in the name of a grouping or association including one or more firms of solicitors (or recognised bodies or multi-national partnerships) but without naming the firm or firms whose services are being advertised.

(b)   Any flag advertising must include the word 'solicitor(s)' (or, as an additional option in the case of publicity conducted outside England and Wales, the word 'lawyer(s)') and an address at which the names of all the firms involved are available. (For the designation of a practice see paragraph 6 above. For the use of the word 'lawyer(s)' see paragraph 14(b) below.)

(c)   Notwithstanding anything in this paragraph, notepaper used on legal professional business must include the name of the firm concerned and not merely the name of a grouping or association.

11. Addresses to the court

It is not proper for solicitors to distribute to the press, radio or television copies of a speech or address to any court, tribunal or inquiry, except at the time and place of the hearing to persons attending the hearing to report the proceedings.

12. Professional stationery

(a)   Application of the code to stationery

The provisions of this code apply to a solicitor's letterhead and matter similarly forming part of a solicitor's professional stationery.

(b)   Practising address on stationery

Any stationery used by solicitors for their professional work must include a practising address and not merely a box number. Where a facsimile transmission is being sent, the frontsheet should contain the solicitor's address if this is not contained in some other part of the transmission.

(c)   *Use of client's or employer's stationery and client's or employer's name on solicitor's stationery*

Solicitors may use for their professional work the stationery of, or stationery including the name of, a client or non-solicitor employer, provided that:

(i)   either the letterhead or the signature makes it clear that the stationery is being used by a solicitor on legal professional business and that the solicitor is responsible for the contents of the letter; and

(ii)   the stationery is being used for the business of that client or non-solicitor employer or for third parties in circumstances permitted by Practice Rule 4.

(d)   *Stationery of a recognised body*

The professional stationery of a recognised body and of a partnership which includes a recognised body as a partner must comply with the Solicitors' Incorporated Practice Rules from time to time in force.

13. Professional announcements, advertisements for staff, etc.

Any professional announcement, advertisement for staff, advertisement offering agency services, or any other like advertisement by a solicitor (including any advertisement in the Law Society's Gazette) must comply with the provisions of this code.

14. International aspects of publicity

(a)   No publicity for a solicitor's practice may be conducted in a jurisdiction other than England and Wales in any manner that would contravene either (i) the provisions of this code or (ii) any restrictions in force in that other jurisdiction concerning lawyers' publicity. For the purposes of this paragraph publicity shall be deemed to be conducted in the jurisdiction in which it is received. However, publicity shall not be regarded as being conducted in a jurisdiction in which such publicity would be improper if it is conducted for the purpose of reaching persons in a jurisdiction or jurisdictions where such publicity is permitted and its receipt in the former jurisdiction is incidental.

(b)   Whether in England and Wales or in any other jurisdiction, a solicitor's advertising (including stationery — see paragraph 16(ii) below) must not, except in the expression 'registered foreign lawyer(s)', use the word 'lawyer(s)' to refer to a person's qualification in a member state of the European Community unless the qualification is that of a 'lawyer' as defined in the 1977 Lawyers' Services Directive as from time to time amended.

15. Institutional publicity

(a)   *Institutional publicity by the Law Society*

This code does not apply to publicity by the Law Society, or any body established under the control of the Law Society, concerning the services of solicitors in general or any class or group of solicitors.

(b)   *Institutional publicity by local law societies*

This code does not apply to publicity by a local law society concerning the services of solicitors in general.

(c)   *Publicity naming solicitors*

Where any publicity referred to in (a) and (b) above names individual solicitors or firms, such publicity must comply with this code as if the publication were by individual solicitors.

16. Interpretation

In this code:

(i)   All references to individual practice rules are references to the Solicitors' Practice Rules 1990 and all words have the meanings assigned to them in Rule 18 of those rules; and

(ii)   'advertisement' and 'advertising', except where the context otherwise requires, refer to any form of advertisement and include *inter alia* brochures, directory entries, stationery, and press releases promoting a solicitor's practice; but exclude press releases prepared on behalf of a client.

17. Commencement

This code will come into force on 1st September 1990.

Note: Breaches of the Publicity Code

Where contravention of this code is not serious, the Council encourages local law societies to bring breaches to the attention of the solicitors concerned. Serious or persistent cases should be reported to the Solicitors Complaints Bureau.

Annex 11B

Solicitors' Introduction and Referral Code 1990

(with consolidated amendments to 1st January 1992)

Code dated 18th July 1990 promulgated by the Council of the Law Society with the concurrence of the Master of the Rolls under Rule 3 of the Solicitors' Practice Rules 1990, regulating the introduction of clients to and by solicitors, registered foreign lawyers and recognised bodies practising in England and Wales.

Introduction

(1) This code states the principles to be observed in relation to the introduction of clients by third parties to solicitors or by solicitors to third parties.

(2) The code does not apply to introductions and referrals between solicitors, between solicitors and barristers or between solicitors and lawyers of other jurisdictions.

(3) Non-compliance, evasion or disregard of the code could represent not only a breach of Practice Rule 3 (introductions and referrals) but also a breach of Practice Rule 1 (basic principles) or one of the other practice rules, and conduct unbefitting a solicitor.

(4) Those wishing to advertise the services of solicitors to whom they refer work should be encouraged to publicise their adherence to the code by means of a notice on the following lines:

'We comply with the Solicitors' Introduction and Referral Code published by the Law Society, and any solicitor to whom we may refer you is an independent professional from whom you will receive impartial and confidential advice. You are free to choose another solicitor.'

(5) In this code all references to individual practice rules are references to the Solicitors' Practice Rules 1990 and all words have the meanings assigned to them in Rule 18 of those rules.

(6) The code will come into force on 1st September 1990.

Section 1 : The basic principles

(1) Solicitors must always retain their professional independence and their ability to advise their clients fearlessly and objectively. Solicitors should never permit the requirements of an introducer to undermine this independence.

(2)   In making or accepting introductions or referrals, solicitors must do nothing which would be likely to compromise or impair any of the principles set out in Practice Rule 1:

(a)   the solicitor's independence or integrity;

(b)   a person's freedom to instruct a solicitor of his or her choice;

(c)   the solicitor's duty to act in the best interests of the client;

(d)   the good repute of the solicitor or the solicitors' profession;

(e)   the solicitor's proper standard of work;

(f)   the solicitor's duty to the Court.

(3)   Practice Rule 9 prevents a solicitor from entering into any arrangement with a claims assessor for the introduction of personal injury clients to the solicitor.

(4)   Practice Rule 12 makes provision in respect of introductions and referrals in the field of investment business. In particular the rule prevents a solicitor from acting as an appointed representative as defined in the Financial Services Act 1986.

Section 2 : Introduction or referral of business to solicitors

(1)   Solicitors may discuss and make known to potential introducers the basis on which they would be prepared to accept instructions and the fees they would charge to clients referred.

(2)   Solicitors should draw the attention of potential introducers to the provisions of this code and the relevant provisions of the Solicitors' Publicity Code.

(3)   Solicitors must not reward introducers by the payment of commission or otherwise. However, this does not prevent normal hospitality. A solicitor may refer clients to an introducer provided the solicitor complies with Section 4 below.

(4)   Solicitors should not allow themselves to become so reliant on a limited number of sources of referrals that the interests of an introducer affect the advice given by the solicitor to clients.

(5)   Solicitors should be particularly conscious of the need to advise impartially and independently clients referred by introducers. They should ensure that the wish to avoid offending the introducer does not colour the advice given to such clients.

(6)   Where a tied agent refers to a solicitor a client who is proposing to take out a company life policy, the solicitor should, where necessary, have regard to the suitability of that policy in each particular case.

(7)   Solicitors must ensure that they alone are responsible for any decisions taken in relation to the nature, style or extent of their practices.

(8)   This code does not affect the need for the solicitor to communicate directly with the client to obtain or confirm instructions, in the process of providing advice and at all appropriate stages of the transaction.

(9)   Each firm should keep a record of agreements for the introduction of work.

(10)   Each firm should conduct a review at six-monthly intervals, which should check:

(a)   that the provisions of this code have been complied with;

(b) that referred clients have received impartial advice which has not been tainted by the relationship between the firm and the introducer; and

(c) the income arising from each agreement for the introduction of business.

(11) Where, so far as can be reasonably ascertained, more than 20 per cent of a firm's income during the period under review arises from a single source of introduction of business, the firm should consider whether steps should be taken to reduce that proportion.

(12) Factors to be taken into account in considering whether to reduce the proportion include:

(a) the percentage of income deriving from that source;

(b) the number of clients introduced by that source;

(c) the nature of the clients and the nature of the work; and

(d) whether the introducer could be affected by the advice given by the solicitor to the client.

Section 3 : Solicitor agreeing to be paid by a third party to do work for the third party's customers other than conveyancing work

(1) In addition to the other provisions of this Code the following requirements should be observed in relation to agreements for the introduction of clients/business to solicitors under which the solicitor agrees with the introducer to be paid by the introducer to do work other than conveyancing work for the introducer's customers.

(2) The terms of the agreement should be set out in writing and a copy available for inspection by the Law Society or the Solicitors Complaints Bureau.

(3) The solicitor may agree to be remunerated by the introducer either on a case by case basis or on a hourly, monthly or any other appropriate basis.

(4) The solicitor should ensure that any agreement between the introducer and customer for the provision of services under this section includes:

(a) express mention of the independence of the solicitor's professional advice;

(b) a provision that control of the professional work should remain in the hands of the solicitor subject to the instructions of the client; and

(c) a provision that information disclosed by the client to the solicitor should not be disclosed to the introducer unless the client consents.

Section 3A : Contractual referrals for conveyancing

(1) In addition to the other provisions of this code the following requirements must be observed in relation to agreements for the introduction of clients/business to solicitors under which the solicitor agrees with the introducer to be paid by the introducer to provide conveyancing services for the introducer's customers.

Agreements for referrals

(2) Solicitors may enter into agreements under this section for referrals for

conveyancing services only with introducers who undertake in such agreements to comply with the terms of this code.

(3) Referrals under this section must not be made where the introducer is a seller or seller's agent and the conveyancing services are to be provided to the buyer.

(4) The agreement between the solicitor and the introducer must be set out in writing. A copy of the agreement and of records of the six monthly reviews carried out under paragraph 10 of Section 2 of this code in relation to transactions under the agreement must be retained by the solicitor for production on request to the Law Society or the Solicitors Complaints Bureau.

(5) If the solicitor has reason to believe that the introducer is breaching terms of the agreement required by this section the solicitor must take all reasonable steps to procure that the breach is remedied. If the introducer persists in breaches the solicitor must terminate the agreement in respect of future referrals.

(6) The agreement between the introducer and the solicitor must not include any provisions which would:

(a) compromise, infringe or impair any of the principles set out in Rule 1 of the Solicitors' Practice Rules or any duties owed by the solicitor to the introducer's customer by virtue of the solicitor/client relationship and/or the requirements of professional conduct; or

(b) restrict the scope of the duties which the solicitor owes to the customer in relation to the services agreed to be provided by virtue of the professional relationship between solicitor and client; or

(c) interfere with or inhibit the solicitor's responsibility for the control of the professional work.

Publicity as to conveyancing services

(7) Publicity material of the introducer which includes reference to any service that may be provided by the solicitor must comply with the following:

(a) Any reference to the charge for the conveyancing service must be clearly expressed separately from charges for other services. Any circumstances in which the charges may be increased must be stated. It must be made clear whether disbursements and VAT are or are not included.

(b) The publicity must not suggest that the service is free, nor that different charges for the conveyancing services would be made according to whether the customer takes other products or services offered by the introducer or not.

(c) Charges must not be stated as being from or upwards of a certain figure.

(d) The publicity must not suggest that the availability or price of other services offered by the introducer are conditional on the customer instructing the solicitor.

Notice to customer

(8) Before making a referral the introducer must give the customer in writing:

(a) details of the conveyancing service to be provided under the terms of the referral;

(b)   notification of:

    (i)   the charge payable by the customer to the introducer for the conveyancing services;

    (ii)   the liability for VAT and disbursements and how these are to be discharged; and

    (iii)   what charge if any is to be made if the transaction does not proceed to completion or if the solicitor is unable to continue to act;

(c)   notification of the amount the introducer will be paying to the solicitor for the provision of conveyancing services relating to the customer's transaction;

(d)   a statement to the effect that the charge for conveyancing services will not be affected whether or not the customer takes other products or services offered by the introducer, and that the availability and price of other services will not be affected whether the customer chooses to instruct a solicitor under the referral or decides to instruct another solicitor or conveyancer; and

(e)   a statement to the effect that the advice and service of the solicitor to whom the customer is to be referred will remain independent and subject to the instructions of the customer.

Solicitor's terms of business

(9)   Where a solicitor accepts instructions on referral under this section the solicitor must provide the client with written terms of business which must include:

(a)   details of the conveyancing service to be provided under the referral and if appropriate any other services the solicitor is to provide and on what terms;

(b)   a statement that any advice given by the solicitor will be independent and that the client is free to raise questions on all aspects of the transaction;

(c)   confirmation that information disclosed by the client to the solicitor will not be disclosed to the introducer unless the client consents; but that where the solicitor is also acting for the introducer in the same matter and a conflict of interest arises, the solicitor might be obliged to cease acting.

Definition

(10)   In this section references to a conveyancing service or services include services to be provided to the introducer if the solicitor is also to be instructed to act for the introducer.

Section 4 : Referral of clients by solicitors

(1)   If a solicitor recommends that a client use a particular firm, agency or business, the solicitor must do so in good faith, judging what is in the client's best interest. A solicitor should not enter into any agreement or association which would restrict the solicitor's freedom to recommend any particular firm, agency or business.

(2)   The referral to a tied agent of a client requiring life insurance would not discharge the solicitor's duty to give his/her client independent advice. In such circumstances, any referral should be to an independent intermediary.

(3) If the best interests of the client require it, a solicitor may refer a client requiring a mortgage to a tied agent, provided that the client is informed that the agent offers products from only one company.

(4) In relation to commission received for the introduction of clients' business to third parties, Practice Rule 10 applies.

Annex 11C

British Code of Advertising Practice*

(relevant extracts)

PART A

Preliminary

Scope

1.1 The Code's rules apply to:

— advertisements in newspapers, magazines and other printed publications;

— indoor and outdoor posters and other outdoor advertisements, including aerial advertisements;

— cinema and video-cassette commercials;

— advertisements on viewdata services; and to

— advertising material such as brochures and leaflets, whether these are mailed or delivered directly, or reach their public as inserts in newspapers or other publications, through distribution in shops or at exhibitions, or in other ways.

1.2 The Code's rules do not apply to:

— broadcast commercials;...

— advertisements in media which are principally intended for circulation outside the United Kingdom; or to

— advertisements addressed, either directly or in their professional journals, to members of the medical and allied professions in their professional capacities...

1.3 Communications and material of the following kinds are not regarded as advertisements for the purposes of this Code:

— statutory, public, police and other official notices;

— material published as a matter of record only;

— non-advertising matter (e.g. works of art) exhibited on billboards or other advertising sites used primarily for advertisements;

---

*Reproduced from The British Code of Advertising Practice, 8th edition, December 1988, by the kind permission of the Advertising Standards Authority Limited.

THE GUIDE TO THE PROFESSIONAL CONDUCT OF SOLICITORS 1993

— private correspondence, as distinguished from personalised or individually addressed circulars;

— oral communications, including telephone calls;

— press releases and other public relations material;

— the contents of books and the contents of the editorial columns of the press, even if either of these has the outward semblance of advertising material;

— packages, wrappers, labels, tickets and the like, except to the extent that either

(a) they advertise a sales promotion, or a product other than the one they contain, or are attached to; or

(b) they are depicted in an advertisement; in which case any words, pictures etc. which are reproduced in a legible or otherwise comprehensible manner are subject to the Code on the same basis as the other contents of the advertisement. Material which is *not* shown (e.g. because it is on the opposite side of a pack to that depicted) is not subject to this Code....

Definitions

2. For the purposes of the Code:

— a **product** is anything that is capable of forming the subject matter of an advertisement. It is most often a tangible object of trade, but may also be, for example, a service or facility, an idea, a cause or an opportunity;

(Because products are so various, much of the Code is expressed, for the sake of clarity, in terms most apt in relation to goods. Wherever this is the case, the principles embodied in the rules concerned are to be understood as applying, in all appropriate circumstances, equally to other kinds of product).

— a **consumer** means any person likely to be reached by a given advertisement (and not only a member of the general public, or one of those directly addressed):

— ...references to the **United Kingdom** are to be understood as relating also to the Isle of Man and the Channel Islands;

— **claim** is to be understood as applying to both express and implied claims.

(Other definitions of limited application are explained at appropriate points throughout the Code).

Interpretation

3.1 The opinion of the Advertising Standards Authority on any matter concerning the interpretation of the Code is final.

3.2 Conformity with the Code is assessed in the light of an advertisement's probable effect when taken as whole, and in context. In applying these criteria, particular attention is paid to

— the characteristics of the likely audience for the advertisement;

— the medium by means of which the advertisement is communicated;

— the nature of the advertised product; and

— the nature and content of any associated material made available contemporaneously to consumers by the advertiser.

3.3   The Code is interpreted in the spirit, as well as in the letter.

3.4   The Code does not claim either legal force or legal authority; it is thus inappropriate for its provisions to be construed in the fashion in which a statute or legal document would be construed.

3.5   For the sake of clarity and brevity, many rules in the Code use only masculine and singular forms of words. This is not to be understood as implying the exclusion of women, legal persons or groups of whatever kind from the scope of such rules, to the extent that it is appropriate they be included.

3.6   Advertisements published in languages other than English may present difficulties. Steps have been taken to produce abbreviated versions of the Code in others of the languages spoken in the United Kingdom. Nonetheless it may be impossible in some cases, at present, for ASA or CAP to judge the extent to which an advertisement not in English conforms to the Code.

3.7   There are many statutory rules governing advertising. These are often complicated and professional advice should be sought when in doubt about their application. References in this edition of the Code to statutes and other legislation are believed to be correct at the time of going to print; they should be read in the light of any subsequent modifications, repeals or re-enactments...

Commencement

This edition of the Code comes into force on publication. It replaces all previous editions.

PART B

General Rules

The obligations of the advertiser

1.1   Primary responsibility for observance of this Code falls upon the advertiser, and remains with him even when delegated, for practical purposes, to an advertising agency or other intermediary...

Substantiation

1.2   Before offering an advertisement for publication, the advertiser should have in his hands all documentary and other evidence necessary to demonstrate the advertisement's conformity to the Code. This material, together, as necessary, with a statement outlining its relevance, should be made available without delay if requested by either the Advertising Standards Authority or the Committee of Advertising Practice.

1.3   Whenever conformity with the Code is a matter of judgement rather than evidence, the advertiser should be prepared to explain without delay, when requested to do so, why he believes his advertisement conforms to the Code.

1.4   An advertisement may be found to be in contravention of the Code if the advertiser does not respond, or delays his response, to such requests from the Authority or the Committee.

Confidentiality

1.5 Subject to their overriding duties to the Courts and to officials with statutory powers to compel disclosure, the Authority and the Committee will always respect any request that genuinely private or secret information supplied in support of an advertisement should be treated in confidence.

All advertisements should be legal, decent, honest and truthful

Legality

2.1 Advertisements should contain nothing which is in breach of the law, nor omit anything which the law requires.

2.2 Advertisements should contain nothing which is likely to bring the law into disrepute...

Decency

3.1 No advertisement should contain any matter that is likely to cause grave or widespread offence. Whether offence is likely to be caused and, if so, of what gravity will be assessed in each case in the light of the provisions of A.3.2 above and of the standards of decency and propriety that are generally accepted at present in the United Kingdom.

3.2 Some advertisements, which do not conflict with the preceding sub-paragraph, may nonetheless be found distasteful because they reflect or give expression to attitudes or opinions about which society is divided. Where this is the case, advertisers should carefully consider the effect that any apparent disregard of the sensitivities involved may have upon their reputation and that of their product, and upon the acceptability, and hence usefulness, of advertising generally.

3.3 The fact that a product may be found offensive by some people is not, in itself, a sufficient basis under the Code for objecting to an advertisement for it. Advertisers are urged, however, to avoid unnecessary offence when they advertise any product which may reasonably be expected to be found objectionable by a significant number of those who are likely to see their advertisement.

Honesty

4.1 No advertiser should seek to take improper advantage of any characteristic or circumstance which may make consumers vulnerable; as, for example, by exploiting their credulity or their lack of experience or knowledge in any manner detrimental to their interests.

4.2 The design and presentation of advertisements should be such as to allow each part of the advertiser's case to be easily grasped and clearly understood.

Truthful presentation: general

5.1 No advertisement, whether by inaccuracy, ambiguity, exaggeration, omission or otherwise, should mislead consumers about any matter likely to influence their attitude to the advertised product.

Matters of fact

5.2 1. Whenever an advertisement is likely to be understood as dealing with matters capable of objective assessment upon a generally agreed basis, it should be backed by substantiation as required by B.1.2 above. The adequacy of such substantiation will be gauged by the extent to which it provides satisfactory evidence that the advertisement is both accurate in its material details and truthful in the general impression it creates.

2. No advertisement should claim that the account it gives of any facts is generally accepted, or universally true, if there exists a significant division of informed opinion as to how either the accuracy or the truthfulness of that account may properly be assessed.

3. When a factual claim in an advertisement is said to be supported by the results of independent research, the advertiser should be able to show that those responsible for the research accept as accurate his account of it.

4. Advertisements which contain material of the kinds described below are not to be regarded, for that reason alone, as in conflict with the Code's rules on truthful presentation:

(a) obvious untruths, exaggerations and the like, the evident purpose of which is to attract attention or to cause amusement and which there is no likelihood of consumers misunderstanding;

(b) incidental minor inaccuracies, unorthodox spellings and the like which do not affect the accuracy or truthfulness of the advertisement in any material respect;

(c) accurate descriptions of the contents of books and other media of communication in circumstances in which some of the matter so described cannot itself be substantiated.

(Publishers are urged, nonetheless, to consider carefully the possibility of harm or distress resulting from their acceptance of such advertisements, particularly where these contain material advocating either unproven remedies for disease or disability, or the employment of consumers' resources in risky ventures).

5. When the consumer's response to an advertisement is likely to be directly affected by the appearance of a person whose real-life experiences it describes — as may happen, for example, in connection with a charitable appeal — a model should not be used to represent that person unless the advertiser makes it quite clear that this has been done.

6. On the truthful presentation of comparisons, see B.21 to B.24 below.

Matters of opinion

5.3 The Code's rules on truthful presentation place no constraint upon the free expression of opinion, including subjective assessments of the quality or desirability of products, provided always that:

— it is clear what is being expressed is an opinion;

— there is no likelihood of the opinion or the way it is expressed misleading consumers about any matter in respect of which objective assessment, upon a generally accepted basis, is practicable (if there is, the provisions of 5.2 above apply);

— the advertiser is ready to fulfil his obligations under B.1.3 above (substantiation);

— the advertisement is in conformity with B.3 above (decency); and

— so far as commercial advertisers are concerned, the Code's rules on fair competition are observed (see B.21 to B.24 below).

Truthful presentation: political claims

6.1 To the extent that any advertisement:

— expresses an opinion on a matter which is the subject of controversy; and

— that controversy involves issues within the areas, broadly defined, of public policy or practice;

then neither that opinion, nor any evidence which the advertisement may include in support or explanation of it, is subject to the provisions of this Code on truthful presentation, except as provided in the remainder of this paragraph.

6.2 Assertions of fact and expressions of opinion which are 'political' in the sense of the preceding sub-paragraph will be required to conform to the provisions of B.5 above if they are made in the context of an appeal for funds or are directly linked to the offer of any product in return for payment.

6.3 All advertisements which contain 'political' claims should:

— be readily recognisable as advertisements;

— cause no confusion as to the identity or status of the advertiser; and

— whenever such information is not otherwise readily accessible, state the advertiser's address or telephone number.

Truthful presentation: quotation of prices

[The following paragraph is retained in this edition of the Code in the form in which it appeared in the Seventh Edition. This is done pending the introduction of a new Code on Price Indications (to be made under the Consumer Protection Act 1987) which was close to completion as this edition of BCAP went to press. To the extent that any of the provisions of the forthcoming Code prove to be incompatible with what follows, they will override the corresponding provisions of this paragraph with immediate effect.]

7.1 The provisions of this paragraph apply to advertisements of all kinds. Where appropriate, therefore, 'price' is to be understood as meaning 'charge', 'fee', etc., and references to the sale of goods are to be understood as being applicable also to the provision of services, facilities etc. in return for payment.

7.2 The Code makes no general requirement that the cost to the consumer of an advertised product should be stated in an advertisement...

7.3 When any indication of cost is given in an advertisement, regard should be paid to the provisions of the following four sub-paragraphs.

Clarity

1.   If reference is made in an advertisement to more than one product, or more than one version of a single product, it should be clear to which product or version any quoted price relates.

2.   If a product is illustrated, and a price quoted in conjunction with the illustration, advertisers should ensure that what is illustrated can be purchased for the price shown.

Inclusiveness

3.   Except when those addressed by an advertiser are likely to be able to recover VAT, prices should normally be quoted inclusive of VAT. When prices are quoted exclusive of VAT, that fact should be stated with no less prominence than the prices themselves. The same principles apply in the case of other taxes and duties.

4.   When an advertised product cannot be purchased unless the consumer is willing to make associated purchases from the advertiser (e.g. where a case has to be purchased with a camera), the price of the advertised product should normally be quoted on a basis which includes such unavoidable costs. Where it is impracticable to include such costs in the quoted price, because, for example, they are variable while the price of the advertised product is not, the consumer's liability to pay them should be stated with no less prominence than the price of the advertised product itself.

On price comparisons, see B.21 and especially B.21.3 below.

Truthful presentation: use of 'free'

8.1   When a product is advertised as being 'free', incidental costs which will necessarily be incurred in acquiring it, and which are known to (or can be accurately assessed by) the advertiser, should be clearly indicated; and when such incidental costs exceed those that would typically arise if a comparable product was *bought* from a comparable source, the product advertised should not be described as free.

8.2   Advertisers should not seek to recover the cost to them of a product which they describe as free:

—   by imposing additional charges they would not normally make;

—   by inflating any incidental expenses they may legitimately recover (e.g. cost of postage); or

—   by altering the composition or quality, or by increasing the price, of any other product which they require to be bought as a pre-condition of the consumer obtaining the 'free' product.

8.3   Except in the context of a free trial, the word 'free' should not be used if payment for an advertised product is only deferred.

8.4   Any offer which consists in the giving without cost of one product on condition that another is paid for should normally be temporary, otherwise if such a combination offer is continuous, the use of the word 'free' may become misleading.

Truthful presentation: use of 'up to...' and 'from...'

9.   Expressions such as 'up to x miles per gallon' and 'prices from as low as y' should

not be used if, as a result, consumers may be misled about the extent to which the benefits claimed are in practice attainable by them or are available to them.

Truthful presentation: testimonials and other indications of approval

10.1 In this paragraph 'testimonial' embraces any reference made by an advertiser to the favourable opinion of another in circumstances in which the consumer is likely to give added credence to that opinion because of the ostensible independence of the person or institution said to hold it.

10.2 Except when the opinion quoted is available in a published source, in which case a full reference should be made available on request, the advertiser should be able to provide substantiation for a testimonial in the form of a signed and dated statement, containing any words which appear in the advertisement in the form of a direct quotation, and with an address at which the author of the statement may be contacted.

10.3 Testimonials should not be used unless the advertiser has good reason to believe that they represent the genuine and informed opinion of those giving them.

10.4 A testimonial may become misleading if the formulation of the product concerned, or its market environment, changes significantly after the date on which the testimonial was given. As a general rule, therefore, testimonials should relate only to the product as currently offered.

10.5 The fact that a testimonial is given by a person or body independent of the advertiser is not, in itself, sufficient to demonstrate the accuracy or truthfulness of any claim it may contain about a product; and advertisers should be prepared to provide objective substantiation for such claims in the normal way (see B.1 and B.5 above). They should also ensure that, in all other respects, what is quoted by way of testimonial in an advertisement conforms to this Code.

10.6 When fictitious characters in an advertisement express satisfaction with the advertiser's product, care should be taken to avoid consumers confusing them (or their ostensible experiences) with real people or their experiences.

10.7 Advertisers are reminded that testimonials by persons named or depicted in an advertisement may be employed only when the consent of these persons has been obtained in advance (see further B.17 below).

Royal approval

10.8 Attention is drawn to the provisions governing the use of the Royal Arms and Cypher, and references to the Queen's Award to Industry. (Details may be obtained from the offices of the Lord Chamberlain and the Queen's Award to Industry respectively.)

10.9 The Royal Warrant does not imply either personal endorsement or use of the product concerned by H.M. The Queen (or such other royal person on whose behalf the warrant is issued) and no suggestion that it does should appear in any advertisement.

Truthful presentation: recognisability of advertisements

11. An advertisement should always be so designed and presented that anyone who looks at it can see, without having to study it closely, that it is an advertisement.

Truthful presentation: identity of advertisers

12.1 Except in respect of:

— 'political' advertisements (see B.6 above)...

the Code makes no requirement that the name or address of an advertiser be given in an advertisement....

12.2 When an advertiser *is* named in an advertisement, the way in which this is done should not be such as to cause confusion about his identity or mislead as to his status or qualifications.

12.3 In some cases there may be a legal requirement that an advertisement names the advertiser. Advertisers are advised to seek professional advice on this point....

Switch selling

14.2 An advertisement may be regarded as misleading if an advertiser's salesmen seriously disparage or belittle the article advertised, recommend the purchase of a more expensive alternative, indicate unreasonable delays in obtaining delivery or otherwise seek to put difficulties in the way of its purchase.

> *All advertisements should be prepared with a sense of responsibility to the consumer and to society*

Fear and distress

15.1 Without good reason, no advertisement should play on fear or excite distress.

15.2.1 When an appeal to fear is properly made in an advertisement — as, for instance, when it is made with the object of encouraging prudent behaviour — the fear evoked should not be disproportionate to the risk addressed.

15.2.2 An advertisement should excite distress only in circumstances in which the seriousness and importance of the subject matter unarguably warrant such an approach. Distress should never be occasioned merely in pursuit of an attempt to attract attention, or to shock.

Violence and anti-social behaviour

16.1 Advertisements should neither condone nor incite to violence or anti-social behaviour.

16.2 Advertisements for weapons and for items, such as knives, which offer the possibility of violent misuse, should avoid anything, in copy or in illustration, that may encourage such misuse.

Protection of privacy and exploitation of the individual

17.1 1. Except in the circumstances noted in paragraphs 17.2 to 17.5 below, advertisements should not portray or refer to any living persons, in whatever form or by whatever means, unless their express prior permission has been obtained.

2. 'Refer' in the preceding sub-paragraph embraces reference to a person's

possessions, house etc. in any manner which unambiguously identifies their owner to prospective readers of the advertisement.

17.2 The circumstances in which a reference or portrayal *may* be acceptable in the absence of prior permission, are the following:

— generally, when the advertisement contains nothing which is inconsistent, or likely to be seen as inconsistent, with the position of the person to whom reference is made, and when it does not abrogate his right to enjoy a reasonable degree of privacy;

— in the special case of advertisements the purpose of which is to promote a product such as a book or film, when the person concerned is the subject of that book, film etc.

A complaint from a person represented that an advertisement falling within either of these exclusions is nonetheless offensive, harmful or humiliating, will be weighed by ASA or CAP when deciding whether the advertisement concerned is within the spirit of the Code.

The applicability of these two exceptions to the general rule is further considered in sub-paragraphs 17.3 to 17.5 below.

17.3 It follows from the above that complaints from those who occupy positions or exercise trades or professions which necessarily entail a high degree of public exposure, such as actors, sportsmen and politicians, can be entertained only:

— when it can reasonably be argued that the advertisement concerned suggests some commercial involvement on their part which is of a kind likely to be generally perceived as inconsistent with their status or position; or

— when the effect of the advertisement is to substantially diminish or to abrogate their right to control the circumstances or terms upon which they may exploit their name, likeness or reputation on a commercial basis.

17.4 The use of crowd or background shots, in which individuals or their possessions, houses etc. are recognisable, is not regarded under the Code as inconsistent with the right of such individuals to enjoy a reasonable degree of privacy, provided that there is nothing in the depiction which is defamatory, offensive or humiliating. Advertisers should be ready to withdraw any advertisement in respect of which they receive a reasonable objection on such grounds from a person affected.

17.5 Advertisements in which reference may properly be made to members of the Royal Family include:

— those which incorporate a reference to royal approval which satisfies the provisions of B.10.8 and B.10.9 above;

— those for which express permission has been granted by the Lord Chamberlain's office;

— those for, or depicting, products such as stamps or commemorative items which have received royal approval; and

— advertisements for books, films, articles and the like which deal with a member or members of the Royal Family.

17.6 It is not regarded as contrary to the principle set out in 17.1 above for unsolicited advertising material to be addressed to a consumer personally.

17.7 References to individuals with whom the advertiser is personally acquainted, and which he has no reason to suppose will be resented, are not regarded as infringements of the privacy of such individuals, but should be withdrawn if any reasonable objection is received.

17.8 Advertisers should seek to avoid unnecessary offence to the susceptibilities of those connected in any way with deceased persons depicted or referred to in any advertisements....

Safety

19.1 As a general rule, advertisements should not show or advocate dangerous behaviour or unsafe practices except in the context of the promotion of safety. Exceptions may be permissible, in circumstances in which emulation is unlikely. Special care should be taken with advertisements directed towards or depicting children or young people....

Children

20. Advertisements should contain nothing which is likely to result in physical, mental or moral harm to children, or to exploit their credulity, lack of experience or sense of loyalty....

All advertisements should conform to the principles of fair competition generally accepted in business

Comparisons

[The following paragraph is retained in this edition of the Code in the form in which it appeared in the Seventh Edition. This is done pending the introduction of a new Code on Price Indications (to be made under the Consumer Protection Act 1987) which was close to completion as this edition of BCAP went to press. To the extent that any of the provisions of the forthcoming Code prove to be incompatible with what follows, and particularly with the requirements of sub-paragraph 21.3, they will override the provisions of this paragraph with immediate effect.]

21.1 1. So that vigorous competition may not be hindered and that public information may be furthered, comparisons, whether between products themselves or between the prices of products, are regarded as in conformity with this Code provided that such comparisons do not conflict with the requirements of this paragraph and of the following three paragraphs (B.22 to B.24). This is so even in circumstances in which the comparison identifies a competitor of the advertiser or that competitor's product.

2. The requirements of this paragraph and of paragraphs B.22 to B.24 apply also, where relevant, to comparisons made by an advertiser between two or more of his own products, or between the price at which one of his products is sold, and the price at which it was sold, or is to be sold.

21.2 Advertisements containing comparisons should deal fairly with any competitors involved and should be so designed that there is no likelihood of a consumer being misled. In particular:

— it should be clear with what the advertised product is being compared, and upon what basis;

— the subject matter of the comparison and the terms in which it is expressed should not be such as to confer any artificial advantage upon one product as against another (this is of especial importance in comparisons between branded and unbranded products and between natural products and substitutes for them);

— claims to objectively superior or superlative status should be expressed in terms which accurately reflect the extent and the nature of the evidence available to substantiate them; and

— no claim that a competitive product is generally unsatisfactory should be based on the highlighting of selected advantages only of the advertised product.

21.3 1. When a price for a product is quoted in a way which may suggest that the product concerned is a bargain, and particularly when one price is compared directly with another, there should be no exaggeration of the extent to which a purchaser may benefit by buying at that price.

2. Specifically, comparisons may be regarded as unfair when one (or both) of the elements in the comparison have been artificially selected or manipulated so as to maximise any apparent saving.

On the quotation of prices generally, see B.7 above.

Denigration

22.1 Advertisers should not seek to discredit the products of their competitors by any unfair means.

22.2 In particular, no advertisement should contain inaccurate or irrelevant comments on the person, character or actions of a competitor.

22.3 Nor should an advertisement describe or show the products of a competitor as broken or defaced, inoperative or ineffective. The only exception to this rule is where the description or depiction is based upon the outcome of fair comparative tests to which the advertiser's product also has been subjected and the results of such tests are stated.

Exploitation of goodwill

23. Advertisements should not exploit the goodwill attached to the trade name or mark of another, or his advertising campaign, in any fashion which may unfairly prejudice his interests.

Imitation

24. No advertisement should so closely resemble another advertisement as to be likely to mislead or confuse.

Section C.VII

Advertising of financial services and products

1.1 The rules in this section of the Code (C.VII) apply to advertisements for the following:

— financial services and products;

— investment opportunities;

— credit facilities; and

— financial information.

Such advertisements are required to conform also, wherever appropriate, to the other provisions of this Code. It is not to be assumed that such conformity will necessarily be achieved by conformity with the various legal requirements referred to in paragraph 2 below.

1.2 All advertisements within the scope of this section should be prepared with care and with the conscious aim of ensuring that members of the public fully grasp the nature of any commitment into which they may enter as a result of responding to an advertisement. Advertisers should take into account that the complexities of finance may well be beyond many of those to whom the opportunity they offer will appeal and that therefore they bear a direct responsibility to ensure that in no sense do their advertisements take advantage of inexperience or credulity.

1.3 Advertisers inviting an immediate commitment (e.g. by coupon), whether or not this involves the sending of money, should take particular care to ensure thorough comprehensibility, and should clearly state, in the body of the advertisement and not only in the coupon, if one is included, their full postal address....

2.1 Advertisements for **credit** are subject to stringent requirements under the legislation referred to below. These requirements are described in booklets available from the Office of Fair Trading but advertisers are advised that it may be necessary also to seek professional advice on the interpretation of the Consumer Credit Act and the relevant regulations.

2.2 Attention is drawn to the Consumer Credit Act 1974 (sections 43 to 47) and Regs 151 (1) and (2) of the Consumer Credit (Advertisements) Regulations 1980 (SI 1980 No. 54). Written quotations of terms for credit and hire business are subject to the Consumer Credit (Quotations) Regulations 1980 (SI 1980 No. 55). As this edition of BCAP goes to press, the Regulations referred to above are under revision with the object, in particular, of providing that where any loan is secured upon property this fact shall be adequately disclosed.

2.3 Many investment advertisements are affected by stringent legislative provisions, notably under the regime established by the Financial Services Act 1986 and administered by the Securities and Investments Board (SIB).

The rules in this section, which apply to a wider range of advertisements than does the Act, enshrine the same principles of fair dealing. Conformity with these rules, however, must not be assumed to guarantee conformity with any other provisions, whether made in or under the Act or imposed by SIB, or by any of the financial self-regulating organisations, whether SROs or professional bodies, which exercise responsibilities under SIB.

3.1 Any advertisement which may lead to the employment of consumers' money for the purchase of any **financial product or service from which profit, interest or benefit is expected** should comply with the conditions below.

3.2 Advertisements which are limited to indicating in general terms the availability of financial opportunities are acceptable as long as full explanatory material concerning the facilities or opportunities available is provided to the consumer, free of charge, before any contract entered into becomes finally binding.

3.3   Advertisements which go beyond a general indication of the availability of an opportunity, and especially those which invite immediate investment or commitment, should clearly indicate, in particular:

— any limitations on eligibility;

— the type of contract forming the basis of the product or service offered; and

— any charges, expenses or penalties attached: and in particular the terms upon which withdrawal, if permitted, may be arranged.

Whenever the nature of the investments underlying the contract, or to which it is linked, may be material to the consumer's choice, a fair description of investment objectives and of such investments should be given.

3.4   When an advertisement contains any **forecast or projection,** whether of a specific growth rate, or of a specific return or rate of return, it should make clear the basis upon which that forecast or projection is made, explaining, for instance:

— whether reinvestment of income is assumed;

— whether account has been taken of the incidence of any taxes or duties (and if so, how); and

— whether the forecast or projected rate of return will be subject to any deductions, either upon premature realisation or otherwise.

Likewise, if reference is made to any rate of interest other than the rate actually payable on the sum invested (the contractual rate), the basis upon which that other rate has been calculated should be explained and that rate should be given no greater prominence than the contractual rate.

3.5   Advertisements which may lead to the **employment of money in anything the value of which is not guaranteed** should clearly indicate that the value of the investment can go down as well as up and that the return upon the investment will therefore necessarily be variable. Where values are guaranteed, sufficient detail should be included to give the reader a fair view of the nature of the guarantee.

3.6   All advertisements which make reference to past performance or experience should do so in a manner which gives a fair and representative picture and should include a warning, given due prominence, that neither is necessarily a guide to the future. Nothing in the rest of the copy should have the effect of undermining or removing the impact of such warning.

3.7   When an advertiser reserves the right, in certain circumstances, to **defer requests for repayment** of any sum invested (and for which, in normal circumstances, immediate repayments might be expected by the investor), the maximum period during which repayment may thus be withheld should be stated in the advertisement.

3.8   When investors are offered the facility of **planned withdrawal from capital** as an income equivalent (e.g. by cashing in units of unit trusts) the advertiser should ensure that the effect of such withdrawals upon the investment is clearly explained.

3.9   When **claims to investment skill** are based upon an asserted increase in the value of particular items purchased (or recommended for purchase) by the advertiser in the past, he should be able adequately to substantiate that the purchase or recommendation upon which his assertion is based was made at the time claimed, and that the present value asserted for the investment corresponds to the price actually obtained for identical items when sold in the open market in the period immediately preceding the appearance of the advertisement. No claim to increase in the value of investments or collectibles should be based upon the performance within a given market of selected items only, unless substantiation for the claim can be provided in the form set out above...

3.10 Phrases such as **tax-free, tax-paid** should not be used

—   unless it is made clear which particular tax(es) and/or duties are involved, and

—   the advertiser states, as clearly as possible, what liabilities may arise and by whom they will be paid.

3.11 When the achievement or maintenance of the **return** claimed or offered for a given investment is in any way **dependent upon the assumed effects of tax or duty,** this should be clearly explained; and the advertisement should make it clear that no undertaking can be given that the fiscal system may not be revised, with consequent effect upon the return offered.

(Attention is drawn to the requirements of the Code in relation to comparative advertisements and in particular the need to make clear the basis on which any comparison is made. (See B.21-24 above.)...

Section C.VIII

Advertisements offering employment and business opportunities

1.   Advertisements for **situations vacant**

—   should correspond to genuine vacancies the existence of which can be fully substantiated;

—   should not require those interested to send money for further details; and

—   should not misrepresent either working or living conditions, or net remuneration i.e. remuneration after mandatory deductions...

3.   Advertisements offering **vocational training** or other instructional courses should

—   make no unconditional promises of further employment (whether or not by the advertiser) or of future remuneration for those taking the course; and

—   if appropriate, make clear the actual duration of the course and the level of prior attainment needed to derive benefit from it...

Annex 11D

Guidance — claims to specialisation and particular expertise

Following the Council's decision in July 1990 to amend aspects of the Publicity Code dealing with claims to specialisation and particular expertise, the Standards and Guidance Committee, having consulted with the Specialisation Committee, have prepared the following statement, which gives guidance to the profession on the factors which should be considered by solicitors wishing to take advantage of the new provision.

Para. 2(b) of the Solicitors' Publicity Code 1990, which came into force on 1st September 1990, states that it is not improper for a claim to be made that a solicitor is a specialist, or an expert, in a particular field provided that such a claim can be justified. It is clear, therefore, that there has not been complete deregulation in this aspect of solicitors' publicity. A claim to specialisation or expertise in a particular field will imply that the solicitor making the claim has skills, knowledge or expertise in that field over and above that of other solicitors who could not make such a claim.

The onus of deciding whether a particular claim can be justified is on the solicitor or the firm making the claim. The Professional Ethics Division can only give guidance as to the factors you may wish to consider before making that decision. Ultimately, it would be for the Adjudication Committee or the Solicitors' Disciplinary Tribunal to determine whether a particular claim was justified, should a complaint reach that stage. As this is a new provision of the code we do not as yet have any committee or tribunal decisions to use as indicators.

The factors you may wish to consider are, for example, in the case of individual solicitors, the experience, competence and level of knowledge of the solicitor concerned, membership of a Law Society panel, and any additional qualifications the solicitor holds. You may also wish to consider the amount of time he or she spends on the particular type of work, but you should not base a claim to specialisation solely on the amount of time spent — because members of the public interpret a claim to specialisation as a claim to additional expertise.

In the case of a department or the firm as a whole you may wish to consider the number of solicitors within the firm or department dealing with a particular type of work, and whether the standard of service which you are able to offer is high enough to meet the expectations of clients who may instruct you on the basis that you are specialists or experts.

It is likely that a complaint by a client that a solicitor or firm had wrongly claimed to be a specialist or an expert could be coupled with an allegation of inadequate professional services and it may be that the adequacy of the service provided will be measured against any claims made. Further, there are *dicta* in some cases which suggest that if a solicitor holds himself or herself out as a specialist or expert in a particular field, the client can expect a higher standard than that of a reasonably competent solicitor.

You should therefore carefully consider whether, if you choose to describe yourself as an expert or a specialist in a particular field, this could lead to complaints that the claim is unjustified and whether, if a complaint should be made, you would be able to justify your claim on the basis of the factors set out above or on any other basis which you feel entitles you to make such a claim.

[1990] Gazette, 12 December, 45

Annex 11E

Guidance — advertisements for mortgages — Consumer Credit (Advertisements) Regulations 1989

Solicitors who advertise that they are able to arrange mortgages will be carrying on credit brokerage within the meaning of the Consumer Credit Act 1974. While the Society has a group licence covering, *inter alia*, credit brokerage by solicitors, albeit limited to activities arising in the course of practice as solicitors, any such advertisement must comply with the Consumer Credit (Advertisements) Regulations 1989. These came into force on 1st February 1990 and consolidated, with amendments, the Consumer Credit (Advertisements) Regulations 1980 (as amended).

* Such an advertisement, provided it contains no details of amounts due in repayment of the mortgage, will be an intermediate credit advertisement for the purpose of the regulations which provide that the following information must be contained in the advertisement:

  (a)   the name of the solicitors and a postal address or telephone number;

  (b)   a statement in the following form:

  'Your home is at risk if you do not keep up repayments on a mortgage or other loan secured on it.'

  This statement must be in capital letters and afforded no less prominence than the statement relating to the ability to arrange mortgages.

  (c)   The amount of any arrangement fee payable or a statement of its methods of calculation.

  (d)   A statement that individuals may obtain on request a quotation in writing about the terms on which the solicitors are prepared to do business, e.g. 'written details on request'.

It should be noted that there is no longer a requirement to include a reference to the fact that the solicitors are licensed as credit brokers. Any solicitors wishing to do more than merely advertise their ability to arrange mortgages should themselves consult the regulations.

* Since the introduction of the new Publicity Code it may be possible for some solicitors to use a designation such as 'solicitors and mortgage brokers'. However, this designation implies specialism or expertise in the field of mortgage broking and may not be used where the claim to such specialism or expertise cannot be justified. If the designation is justified, then it will be possible to issue a simple credit advertisement (as defined in the regulations) containing no more information

than: the name of the solicitors; a logo; a postal address and telephone number; and the designation 'solicitors and mortgage brokers'. Again, any solicitors wishing to say more than this should themselves consult the regulations.

In the event of any doubt concerning the interpretation of the regulations, solicitors should consult their local trading standards office.

7th November 1990

Chapter 12

Retainer

Acceptance of instructions

12.01 Freedom to accept instructions

Principle

A solicitor is generally free to decide whether to accept instructions from any particular client.

Commentary

1. Although this Principle applies to legal aid work, there is a duty, on both the court and the Legal Aid Area Director when granting legal aid, to specify a named practising solicitor. A solicitor can only act if the certificate has been granted in his or her name.

2. Any refusal to act must not be based upon the race, colour, ethnic or national origins, sex or creed of the prospective client (see Chapter 7).

3. A solicitor who is instructed to bring an action against his or her client's former solicitor should, provided he or she is competent and able, accept those instructions. It is undesirable that a solicitor should accept instructions to sue a colleague with whom or with any of whose partners he or she is on friendly terms. In these circumstances the client should be advised to seek advice elsewhere, preferably outside the solicitor's area, and should assist the client, if necessary, to obtain proper representation.

4. A solicitor cannot be retained by a client who does not have mental capacity. There is a legal presumption of capacity unless the contrary is shown. Whether a client does have capacity is a matter of law and it should be borne in mind that different levels of capacity are required for different activities. If there is doubt about a client's mental capacity it may be advisable, where possible, to seek an opinion from the client's doctor having explained to the doctor the relevant test of capacity. It is important

to note that the donor of an enduring power of attorney remains the client after becoming incapable.

5. For further exceptions to this Principle, see Principles 12.02-12.10.

12.02   When instructions must be refused

Principle

A solicitor must not act or, where relevant, must cease acting further where the instructions would involve the solicitor in a breach of the law or a breach of the principles of professional conduct, unless the client is prepared to change his or her instructions appropriately.

Commentary

A solicitor who has accepted instructions to act is under a duty to observe the rules of professional conduct and a client must accept the limitations imposed by such rules.

12.03   Competence to act

Principle

A solicitor must not act or continue to act in circumstances where the client cannot be represented with competence or diligence.

Commentary

1. This would apply where a solicitor has insufficient time to devote to the matter, or insufficient experience or skill to deal with the instructions.

2. This Principle will not prevent a solicitor from acting if he or she is able to do so competently by, for example, instructing suitable counsel.

12.04   Duress or undue influence

Principle

A solicitor must not accept instructions where he or she suspects that those instructions have been given by a client under duress or undue influence.

Commentary

If a solicitor suspects that the client's instructions infringe this Principle, either the client must be seen alone in order that the solicitor can be satisfied that the instructions were freely given, or the solicitor must refuse to act. Particular care may need to be taken where clients are elderly or otherwise vulnerable to pressure from others.

12.05   Third party instructions

Principle

Where instructions are received not from a client but from a third party purporting to represent that client, a solicitor should obtain written instructions from the client that he or she wishes the solicitor to act. In any case of doubt the solicitor should see the client or take other appropriate steps to confirm instructions.

Commentary

1. In such circumstances a solicitor must advise the client without regard to the interests of the source from which he or she was introduced. See also Principle 11.03 and the Solicitors' Introduction and Referral Code 1990.

2. In relation to the preparation of wills, especially where the client may be elderly, it is important to obtain enough information about the client's circumstances to be able properly to act for the client. When asked to prepare a will on the basis of written instructions alone, a solicitor should always consider carefully whether these are sufficient or whether the solicitor should see the client to discuss the instructions.

12.06   Conflict

Principle

A solicitor must not act, or must decline to act further, where there is a conflict of interests between:

    (a)   the solicitor and the client or prospective client;

    (b)   the solicitor's firm and the client or prospective client;

    (c)   two existing clients; or

    (d)   an existing client or former client and a prospective client.

Commentary

1. Where it becomes apparent that there is a potential conflict of interests within this Principle, a solicitor should consider carefully whether he or she can act or continue to act.

2. This Principle precludes a solicitor, or a member of his or her family or his or her firm, from making or being a party to an arrangement for making a secret profit out of the relationship with the client and ensures that, where such a conflict exists, the client is independently represented.

3. Disclosure of the conflicting interest to the client or potential client does not permit the instructions to be accepted by the solicitor, even where the client consents.

4. Chapter 15 deals with conflicts of interest generally.

12.07 Appointment leading to conflict

Principle

A solicitor must decline to act where either he or she, his or her partner, employer, employee or relative holds some office or appointment which may lead to a conflict of interests or which might give the impression to the public that the solicitor is able to make use of such appointment for the advantage of the client.

Commentary

1. The expression 'relative' includes spouse, parent, child, brother, sister, or spouse of any of them.

2. Examples of such offices and appointments to which this Principle relates appear in Annex 15B.

12.08 Solicitor as witness

Principle

A solicitor must not accept instructions to act as an advocate for a client if it is clear that he or she or a member of his or her firm will be called as a witness on behalf of the client, unless his or her evidence is purely formal.

Commentary

See Commentary to Principle 22.07.

12.09 Client's malice

Principle

A solicitor must refuse to take action which he or she believes is solely intended to gratify a client's malice or vindictiveness.

12.10 Other solicitor instructed

Principle

A solicitor must not accept instructions to act in a matter where another solicitor is acting for the client in respect of the same matter until the first retainer has been determined.

Commentary

1. Where the first retainer has been determined, there is no duty on the second solicitor to inform the first solicitor that he or she has been instructed, except in litigation where the first solicitor is on the record.

2. This Principle does not preclude a solicitor from giving a second opinion without the first solicitor's knowledge. However, the solicitor from whom a second opinion is sought must carefully consider whether he or she is in possession of sufficient facts to give such an opinion. In no circumstances should the second solicitor improperly seek to influence the client to determine the first solicitor's retainer.

3. A solicitor is not precluded from advising another party on the subject matter of the first solicitor's advice if the other party has a separate or distinct interest.

4. Executors appointed under a will are free to choose any solicitor to act in the administration, notwithstanding that the testator may have expressed a wish in the will that a particular firm be used. There is no duty imposed on the solicitor instructed to act to notify the firm named in the will.

5. For details on contacting another solicitor's client see Principle 20.02.

Duties owed by a solicitor during retainer

12.11   Care and skill

Principle

A solicitor who has accepted instructions on behalf of a client is bound to carry out those instructions with diligence and must exercise reasonable care and skill.

Commentary

1.   This Principle is stated in *Groom* v. *Crocker* [1939] 1 K.B. 194 at p. 222. For the statutory duty, see section 13 of the Supply of Goods and Services Act 1982.

2.   A solicitor must act within his or her client's express or implied authority. It is therefore essential at the outset for a solicitor to agree clearly with the client the scope of the retainer and subsequently to refer any matter of doubt to the client. If a solicitor limits the scope of the retainer it is good practice for the limits of the retainer to be precisely defined and communicated in writing to the client.

3.   Rule 15 of the Solicitors' Practice Rules 1990 and the written professional standards set out the information with which a solicitor must normally provide the client at the outset of the retainer and as the client's matter progresses (see Chapters 13 and 17).

4.   The Council have issued a statement on 'Limitation of Liability by Contract' (see Annex 12A).

12.12   Confidentiality

Principle

A solicitor must keep his or her client's business and affairs confidential.

Commentary

1.   This duty extends to the solicitor's staff, whether admitted or unadmitted, and it is the responsibility of the solicitor to ensure compliance.

2.   Chapter 16 deals with the topic of confidentiality generally.

12.13 Observation of principles of conduct

Principle

It is an implied term of the retainer that a solicitor is under a duty, at all times, to observe the principles of professional conduct.

Commentary

1. This means that there will be limitations upon the freedom of a solicitor to do what the client wants him or her to do. A solicitor must not breach the principles of professional conduct in order to benefit the client.

2. A solicitor owes a duty to the court (see Chapter 22) which must be reconciled with the duty owed to the client.

3. With regard to the stopping of a client account cheque see Principle 18.02.

12.14 Not taking advantage of the client

Principle

A solicitor must not take advantage of the age, inexperience, want of education or business experience or ill health of the client.

Commentary

A solicitor must not induce a client to pay a sum of money on account of costs to be incurred which is out of proportion to what could be justified by the work which the solicitor has been instructed to do.

12.15 Client to be kept informed

Principle

A solicitor is under a duty to keep the client properly informed and to comply with reasonable requests from the client for information concerning his or her affairs.

Commentary

1. The information referred to in this Principle includes recent changes of law

where those changes affect the subject matter of the retainer (see also Chapter 17).

2. The extent and frequency of the information supplied and the degree of consultation will depend on the circumstances and upon the type and urgency of the matter and upon the extent of the experience of the client in that type of matter (see Chapter 13).

3. There may be exceptional circumstances in which a solicitor would be justified in withholding information from a client (see Commentary 3 to Principle 16.07).

4. A solicitor in carrying out the retainer has implied authority to bind the client in certain circumstances; however, as a matter of good practice, it would not be appropriate for a solicitor to rely upon implied authority for non-routine matters other than in exceptional circumstances, e.g. where it was impossible to obtain express authority.

12.16   Advice on legal aid

Principle

A solicitor is under a duty to consider and advise a client on the availability of legal aid where the client might be entitled to assistance under the Legal Aid Act 1988.

Commentary

A failure to advise a client promptly of his or her rights under the Legal Aid Act can amount to unbefitting conduct and may also lead to a claim in negligence against a solicitor for breach of duty owed to the client (see Principle 5.01).

12.17   Termination of retainer

Principle

A solicitor must not terminate his or her retainer with the client except for good reason and upon reasonable notice.

Commentary

1. Whilst it is open to a client to terminate a solicitor's retainer for whatever

reason, a solicitor must complete the retainer unless he or she has a good reason for terminating it.

2. Examples of good reasons include where a solicitor cannot continue to act without being in breach of the rules or principles of conduct, or where a solicitor is unable to obtain clear instructions from a client or where there is a serious breakdown in the confidence between them (see also Commentary 2 to Principle 14.01).

3. The retainer may be determined by operation of law, e.g. the client's or solicitor's bankruptcy or mental incapacity. Where the client suffers mental incapacity the solicitor should take reasonable steps to ensure that the client's interests are protected. This may involve contact with the relatives. The solicitor may also contact the Court of Protection or the Official Solicitor.

4. As to remuneration generally, see Chapter 14.

12.18 Lien

Principle

On termination a solicitor should, subject to any lien, deliver to the client all papers and property to which the client is entitled or hold them to his or her order and account for all funds of the client then held by the solicitor.

Commentary

1. Where a lien arises over a client's papers and documents delivered to a solicitor in his or her professional capacity for costs due and work done, they can be retained until those costs are paid. The lien is passive in nature and does not entitle the solicitor to sell or dispose of the client's property. For the effect of the general law see *Cordery on Solicitors*.

2. Despite the lien referred to above, the Law Society has certain powers to gain possession of a solicitor's documents and assets under Schedule 1 to the Solicitors Act 1974 (see Annex 30A).

3. The court has power to order a solicitor to deliver up a client's papers notwithstanding the existence of the solicitor's lien (see section 68 of the Solicitors Act 1974).

4. Where a solicitor is properly exercising a lien in respect of unpaid costs, following his or her discharge by the client during the course of proceedings, the Law Society recommends that the solicitor's papers should be released to the successor solicitor subject to a satisfactory undertaking as to the outstanding costs being given in lieu of the lien.

There is, however, no duty on the original solicitor to accept an undertaking. See Chapter 19 on the subject of undertakings generally.

5.   Where the client is legally aided, the Law Society takes the view that a solicitor's costs are secured by a legal aid order or certificate and it follows that it would be inappropriate to call for a professional undertaking from the successor solicitor to pay the costs except in respect of any outstanding pre-certificate costs. A solicitor should not part with the papers on a legally aided matter until the certificate is transferred to the successor solicitor, although the papers should be made available for inspection in the meantime or copies provided. In respect of legal aid costs it is permissible to ask for an undertaking requiring the successor solicitor to:

(a)   return the papers on completion; or

(b)   have the first solicitor's costs included in the successor solicitor's bill.

6.   Details of which papers are to be handed over on the termination of a solicitor's retainer are contained in Annex 12B.

7.   When a client requires his or her file, a solicitor should not charge for removing the file from storage for collection but a reasonable amount may be charged for the cost of delivery. A reasonable charge could be made for retrieving documents from a client's file at the request of the client as this is fee-earner's work for which a charge is normally made.

8.   Details of how documents may be stored and for how long documents should be retained are contained in Annex 12C.

Annex 12A

Council statement on limitation of liability by contract

---

1.   The Council has decided that although it is not acceptable for solicitors to attempt to exclude by contract all liability to their clients, there is no objection as a matter of conduct to solicitors seeking to limit their liability provided that such limitation is not below the minimum level of cover required from time to time by the Solicitors' Indemnity Rules made under section 37 of the Solicitors Act 1974 (as from 1st September 1989 this minimum is £1,000,000 per firm per claim).

2.   This statement is subject to the position in law. The following points should be noted:

(a)   Liability for fraud or reckless disregard of professional obligations may not be limited.

(b)   Existing legal restraints on solicitors cannot be overridden. In particular the courts will not enforce in the solicitor's favour an unfair agreement with his or her client.

(c)   Moreover, under section 60(5) of the Solicitors Act 1974 a provision in a contentious business agreement that the solicitor shall not be liable for negligence or that he or she shall be relieved from any responsibility to which he or she would otherwise be subject as a solicitor shall be void.

(d)   Solicitors must also take into account the provisions of the Unfair Contract Terms Act 1977. Section 2(2) of that Act provides that a contract term is of no effect except in so far as it satisfies the requirement of reasonableness set out in section 11, namely that the contract term must be a fair and reasonable one having regard to the circumstances which were or ought reasonably to have been known to or in the contemplation of the parties when the contract was made.

(e)   Section 11(4) of the Unfair Contract Terms Act 1977 provides that where a contractual term seeks to restrict liability to a specified sum of money, the question of whether the requirement of reasonableness has been satisfied must take into account the resources which the person seeking to impose it could expect to be available to him or her for the purpose of meeting the liability should it arise, and how far it was open to him or her to cover himself or herself by insurance.

When the retainer may be affected by a foreign law, matters such as the foregoing may need to be considered according to the law applicable.

3.   In any case the limitation must be brought clearly to the attention of the client and

be understood and accepted by him or her. The action necessary in this regard will vary from client to client.

4.   It is preferable that the client's acceptance of the limitation should be evidenced in or confirmed by writing.

5.   Practitioners are reminded that:

(a)   top-up indemnity insurance cover is not necessarily available on an each and every claim basis. It may only be available on an aggregate basis so that there would be no guarantee that the amount of top-up cover maintained by the solicitor would be sufficient to meet any particular claim affected by a prospective limitation of liability;

(b)   the insurance cover available to meet any particular claim is usually ascertained by reference to the claims year, i.e. the year in which the claim itself or notice of circumstances which may give rise to a claim, is brought to the attention of insurers. This may mean that the top-up cover available when the contract is made may not be the same as the top-up cover available when the claim is actually brought (or notice of circumstances given).

6.   As to the solicitor's liability to persons who are not his or her clients, the Council continue to take the view that it may be reasonable in some circumstances for a solicitor to seek to limit or exclude altogether the liability he or she might otherwise incur to such persons under the principle in *Hedley Byrne & Co. Ltd.* v *Heller & Partners Ltd* [1964] A.C. 465 (H.L.).

27th May 1987 (revised February 1990)

Annex 12B

Guidance — papers to be handed over on termination of retainer

---

Documents in existence before the retainer held by the solicitor as agent for and on behalf of his or her client or a third party must be dealt with in accordance with the instructions of the client or third party (subject to the solicitor's lien). Documents coming into existence during the retainer and for the purpose of the business transacted during that retainer must be dealt with as follows:

(a) Documents prepared by the solicitor for the benefit of the client belong to the client once the solicitor has been paid

Examples of this category are:

> cases, instructions and briefs, drafts and copies made by the solicitor of letters received by him or her, if paid for by the client; copies made by the solicitor of letters written by him or her to third parties, if contained in the client's case file and used for the purpose of the client's business. There would appear to be a distinction between copies of letters written to the client (which may be retained by the solicitor) and copies of letters written to third parties.

(b) Documents prepared by the solicitor for his or her own benefit for which the solicitor does not charge the client belong to the solicitor

Examples of this category are:

> copies made by the solicitor of letters received by him or her and not paid for by the client, copies made by the solicitor or letters written by the solicitor to third parties if contained only in a filing system of all letters written in the solicitor's office, inter office memoranda, diary entries, attendance entries, entries in journals and books of account.

(c) Documents sent by the client to the solicitor, the property in which is intended to pass from the client to the solicitor, such as letters, belong to the solicitor; but the copyright remains with the client unless expressly released

Examples of this category are:

> letters written by the client, authorities and instructions written or given by the client to the solicitor.

(d) Documents prepared by a third party during the retainer and sent to the solicitor other than at the solicitor's expense belong to the client

Examples of this category are:

letters received by the solicitor from third parties and vouchers for disbursements made by the solicitor on behalf of his or her client.

Annex 12C

Matters for consideration before old files are destroyed — practice information

Before old files are destroyed, the following factors should be considered.

1. Ownership of documents

It is unlikely that all documents (here used in the sense of all papers in the file, including letters and copies thereof) will belong to the solicitor. No documents should be destroyed without the prior consent of the person to whom they belong.

The subject of authority over documents on termination of retainer is discussed in detail in *Cordery on Solicitors* (8th edition, Butterworths, 1988), starting at p.89. In general, file documents fall into four broad categories. The examples given under each category are taken from *Cordery*.

(i) Documents prepared by the solicitor for the benefit of the client and which may be said to have been paid for by the client, belong to the client.

Examples: Draft and copy documents and letters, in addition to cases, instructions and briefs in contentious, and deeds and documents in non-contentious matters.

(ii) Documents prepared by the solicitor for the solicitor's own benefit or protection, the preparation of which is not regarded as an item chargeable against the client, belong to the solicitor.

Examples: Copies of letters written to the client, entries of attendances, tape recordings and conversations, proofs of evidence, inter-office memoranda, entries in diaries, time sheets, computerised records, office journals and books of account.

(iii) Documents sent by the client to the solicitor during the course of the retainer, the property in which was intended at the date of despatch to pass from the client to the solicitor, belong to the solicitor.

Examples: Letters, authorities and instructions written or given by the client to the solicitor.

(iv) Documents prepared by a third party during the course of the retainer and sent to the solicitor (other than at the solicitor's expense) belong to the client.

Examples: Letters, receipts and vouchers for disbursements made by the solicitor on behalf of the client, medical and witness reports and counsel's advice and opinion.

For further guidance into which of the above categories particular documents are likely to fall, reference should be made to *Cordery* as above. It is essential to decide who owns which papers before old files are destroyed. For example, a client for whom a solicitor has acted on the purchase of a property may not address his or her mind to papers in the solicitor's file until the client comes to sell, which may be many years later, and if the client then asks for documents that belong to him or her and the file has been destroyed in the meantime without the client's authority, liability may fall on the solicitor.

2.   Statutory provisions that make it necessary or desirable to retain documents for stated periods

Such provisions need to be taken into account and some examples are given:

(i)   Under Value Added Tax Act 1983, Sched. 7, para. 7(2), as amended, records and papers relevant to VAT liability have to be kept for six years; this obligation could in any case cover all the papers in a solicitor's file and subject to Customs and Excise agreeing the contrary in any particular case, the whole file should therefore be kept for this period. This obligation may be discharged by keeping the papers on microfilm or microfiche, but Customs and Excise's detailed requirements in connection with these alternatives should first be checked with the local VAT office.

(ii)   The Latent Damage Act 1986, which came into force on 18th September 1986, makes certain important amendments to the Limitation Act 1980. New sections 14A and 14B have been inserted into the 1980 Act. Section 14A provides a special time limit for negligence actions where facts relevant to the cause of action are not known at the date of accrual. It prevents bringing such actions after six years from the date on which the cause of action accrued or three years from the date on which the plaintiff knew or ought to have known the facts, whichever is later. Section 14B provides an overriding time limit (or 'long stop') for negligence actions involving latent damage in order to prevent the bringing of such actions after 15 years from the defendant's breach of duty.

For additional details reference should be made to these and other statutes that may be relevant. A note on the Latent Damage Act 1986 appeared in [1986] *Gazette,* 3 September, 2543, and a more detailed article by Margaret Rutherford, a senior lecturer at the College of Law, was published in [1986] *Gazette,* 10 September, 2620-3.

3.   The microfilm alternative

A number of requests have been made by solicitors in private practice for guidance as to the evidential value of microfilm in cases where the originals have been destroyed after the taking of microfilms. The Law Society sought the opinion of Mr Robert Gatehouse QC in 1978. There is a dearth of judicial authority on this topic and, until such times as the law and practice on the subject of microfilming are clarified by legislation or otherwise, it is only possible to provide general guidelines. The Law Society is aware of the finanical and physical problems involved in storing old documents. Attention is drawn to *Cordery on Solicitors* (8th edition), p.89. The Society cannot lay down any precise period of time after which specific types of papers can be destroyed.

Microfilming gives rise to two principal questions. First, what are the legal consequences of destroying the originals? Secondly, what documents can be safely destroyed?

As regards the first, the Society has been advised that:

(i)   A microfilm of any document in a solicitor's file will be admissible evidence to the same extent, no more and no less, as the document itself, provided that there is admissible evidence of the destruction of the document and identification of the copy.

(ii)   The only difference between criminal and civil proceedings in which microfilm is to be used lies in the proviso. Written evidence of destruction and identification of the copy must always by preserved in case oral evidence is no longer available when needed. Such evidence will enable the microfilm to be adduced in any subsequent civil proceedings under the provisions of the Civil Evidence Act 1968 and the rules made thereunder. The evidence will be admissible in criminal proceedings under the provisions of the Police and Criminal Evidence Act 1984.

As regards the second question, namely what documents can be safely destroyed, it is possible to give only the following guidelines:

(iii)   Original documents, as for example deeds, guarantees or certificates, which are not the solicitor's own property should not be destroyed without the express written permission of their owner.

(iv)   In the case of other documents, including a solicitors's file of papers where the work has been completed and the bill paid, it is reasonable to accept that current practice warrants the microfilming and destruction of such documents after a reasonable time. In cases of doubt the owner's written permission should always be sought. If it is not possible to obtain such permission the solicitor will have to form a view and evaluate the risk.

(v)   When seeking owners' permission to microfilm, and destroy documents the opportunity should be taken, if such is the intention, to make it clear that the right is reserved to make a reasonable charge for retrieval and copies if they are asked for thereafter. The Society ventures to remind solicitors that it is always open to them to invite clients to take possession of their own papers, balancing the potential saving of space and expense against a possible loss of goodwill.

(vi)   As indicated in section 2 above, 'Statutory Provisions', where it is intended to microfilm file documents within a period of six years the solicitor should also first ensure that the method and procedure to be used is acceptable to Customs and Excise.

As regards the procedure to be followed in cases where original documents are microfilmed and then destroyed, the following guidelines are offered:

(vii) There must be admissible evidence of the destruction of the original and of the identification of the copy.

(viii) The precise procedure will vary depending on whether a member of the firm of solicitors or another party undertakes the microfilming.

(ix)   There should be a proper system:

    (a)   identifying each file or document destroyed;

    (b)   recording that the complete file or document has been photographed as the case may be;

    (c)   recording identification by the camera operator of the negatives as copies of the documents photographed;

    (d)   for preservation and indexing of the negatives.

In the event that a particular microfilm record is required to be produced in evidence, a responsible member of the practice (meaning a partner or senior member of staff) should be able to certify that:

    (a)   the document has been destroyed;

(b) the microfilm is a true record of that document; and

(c) the enlargement is an enlargement of that microfilm recording.

It should, of course, always be remembered that the microfilm copies of some documents (e.g. coloured plans) can be unsatisfactory, however carefully the operation is carried out, in which case the originals should be preserved.

4. The position under the Indemnity Rules

The Solicitors' Indemnity Fund provides cover for each firm in respect of any description of civil liability whatsoever incurred in connection with the practice carried on by the firm (including the acceptance of obligations as trustee), provided always that any fees or income accruing ensure to the benefits of the practice, subject always to the limited exceptions and exclusions set out in the Indemnity Rules.

It follows, therefore, that cover is given where a solicitor incurs liability either to the client or to a third party by the destruction of documents. Practically speaking, this may, in certain circumstances, be of little financial benefit to the solicitor, as the contribution payable by way of self-insured deductible may well exceed the amount of the client's or third party's loss and the solicitor's liability.

It has been suggested, on occasion, that the Fund could argue that cover would not be available when a solicitor had destroyed documents relating to a matter the subject of a claim, which if they had not been destroyed could have provided grounds for defeating a claim.

In so far as cover under the Indemnity Rules is concerned, the Fund would be unable to argue such a position. The Rules provide that the Fund will not seek to avoid, repudiate or rescind the cover upon any ground whatsover, including in particular non-disclosure or misrepresentation.

There are provisions which permit the Fund if it can show that it has been prejudiced to proceed against the firm to recover the difference between the sum payable by the Fund in respect of a claim and the sum that would have been payable in the absence of any breach or non-compliance with any condition of the Rules. However, such prejudice is likely to occur in the instance of destruction of documents only if they were destroyed after a claim had been made or after knowledge of circumstances likely to give rise to a claim came to the knowledge of the firm. In such a case, the firm would clearly be in breach of its obligation to allow the Fund to take over and to conduct the defence or settlement of the claim. It therefore follows that extra care should be taken of any papers that related to a claim or possible claim.

In most instances, top-up insurance (additional voluntary insurance to a higher level of cover than that provided by the Fund) will follow the terms and conditions of the Fund, but before assuming that this is so, solicitors should take care to check the terms of such policies.

It may, of course, be worthwhile for solicitors who wish to do so to explore with their own insurers the prospect of obtaining block cover against all claims arising out of loss or destruction of documents: this could possibly be extended to cover loss of documents. Any such insurance would clearly be subject to conditions governing procedures leading to destruction of papers and might well extend to any claims for loss of confidentiality, due to the faulty carrying out of such destruction. Where a solicitor arranges for documents to be destroyed, he or she is responsible for ensuring that such destruction is confidentially carried out whether this is done by the solicitor, the local authority or by an independent contractor.

5.   How long should old files be retained?

The Society is not able to specify particular periods of years for which individual old files should be retained. Solicitors should exercise their own judgement in this respect, having regard to such factors as the subject matter of the contents and their own circumstances, including the availability of storage space and the cost thereof. Subject to that, it may well be considered advisable, with particular reference to the section on statutory provisions above, to retain all files for a minimum period of six years from when the subject matter was wholly completed. At the end of the six-year period, solicitors should review the files again according to the nature of the particular transactions to which they refer, and the likelihood of any claims arising therefrom within the appropriate limitation period. In cases where a party was under a disability at the time of the action or where judgement for provisional damages has been obtained, files should be retained for a minimum period of six years from the date on which the client would have a cause of action or final judgement has been obtained, as the case may be.

6.   Preservation of documents of archival quality

After taking all the matters referred to above into account and before deciding that certain old files can be destroyed, solicitors should consider whether there are any documents among them that ought nevertheless, to be preserved for their archival or historical value. If there is any possibility of this, it is suggested that contact should be made with the county archivist in order to arrange for a confidential inspection of the documents in the old files. If it is necessary to preserve the confidentiality of archival material due, for example, to the true ownership being in doubt, appropriate arrangements should be made with the county archivist for it to be deposited on that basis, so that if at some time in the future the ownership is established, it can be returned. Alternatively, if the owner of relevant documents is known and consents to their being deposited in an archive, there should be no difficulty. For further details on this subject, it may help to contact the British Records Association, Records Preservation Section, at 18 Padbury Court, London E2 7EH (tel: 071-729 1415).

7.   Files sent for destruction

Finally, when it is decided, after taking everything into account including owners' authorities where necessary, that certain old files can be destroyed, it should be borne in mind that solicitors remain responsible for ensuring that there is no breach of confidentiality. The best way to ensure this is to arrange for the old files to be shredded in the office sufficiently finely to avoid any risk. If, however, that is not possible for any reason, and while this responsibility remains with the solicitor, it should be possible to contract either with the local council or a member firm of the British Waste Paper Association for their confidential destruction in sealed bags. The Association's address is Alexander House, Station Road, Aldershot, Hants. GU11 1BQ (0252 344454).

17th December 1986 (revised February 1990)

Chapter 13

Client care

13.01 Complaints procedure

Principle

'Every principal in private practice shall operate a complaints handling procedure which shall, *inter alia,* ensure that clients are informed whom to approach in the event of any problem with the service provided.'

Solicitors' Practice Rules 1990, Rule 15(1)

'Every solicitor in private practice shall, unless it is inappropriate in the circumstances ... ensure that clients know whom to approach in the event of any problem with the service provided....'

Solicitors' Practice Rules 1990, Rule 15(2)(b)

Commentary

1. Rule 15(1) requires that a firm must operate a complaints handling procedure. Rule 15(2)(b) requires that all solicitors in the firm, whether assistant solicitors or partners, must ensure that their clients know whom to approach in the event of any problem. The firm's complaints handling procedure should assist in showing how and when this should be done. A booklet *Client care, a guide for solicitors* published by the Society contains additional good practice advice on Rule 15, including specimen terms of business letters.

2. The rule does not require that the complaints handling procedure be set out in writing, but this is preferable. All staff should be aware of the procedure. If a complaint is made to the Solicitors Complaints Bureau a firm may have to explain its procedure and whether it had been followed. A helpsheet from the SCB on setting up a complaints procedure is contained in Annex 13A. Further advice on how to avoid complaints is also available from the SCB.

3. The following are considered to be the basic elements of a complaints handling procedure:

THE GUIDE TO THE PROFESSIONAL CONDUCT OF SOLICITORS 1993

(a) Clients should be told that if they have any problem with the service provided, they should make it known.

(b) Clients should be told whom to inform in the event of such a problem. This may be the fee-earner handling the case. It may be the senior partner, sole practitioner, principal with overall responsibility for the matter or another person within the practice nominated for the purpose. However, it could be someone outside the firm altogether.

(c) The procedure should ensure that any complaint is investigated promptly and thoroughly, that an explanation of the investigation is given to the client and any appropriate action taken.

(d) If the client is not satisfied (or if there is any doubt) the client should be told that he or she can seek further help from the SCB. It is helpful to give the client details of the firm's response to the complaint in writing.

4.   It is possible to comply with the rule by having a simple procedure, although something more elaborate may be considered desirable. This could involve third parties such as local law societies or fellow practitioners in other local firms. Whatever system is used the response should be quick and effective and any client who remains dissatisfied should be told about the SCB. The SCB publishes a leaflet — *How and When* — describing in detail the procedures for clients when contacting the SCB. The recommendation of the SCB is that this leaflet should be given to all clients who are informed of the SCB's role when internal remedies to resolve a problem have been exhausted. Copies of the leaflet are available from the SCB.

5.   The client may be informed about the whole complaints procedure at the start of the matter — for example, as part of any general information about the firm given to new clients. However, this is not essential and the rule simply requires that the client must be told at the outset the name of the person with whom any problems should be raised. This should preferably be confirmed in writing. Only in the event of a problem arising which cannot be solved at that level, need the whole procedure be explained, again preferably in writing.

6.   Rule 15(2) provides that the duty in Rule 15(2)(b) does not apply where it is 'inappropriate in the circumstances'. It is for each solicitor to judge whether it is or is not appropriate. For example, it is not necessary to tell established clients each time they confirm new instructions provided that they know whom to contact. If a complaint is subsequently investigated by the SCB the solicitor will need to show that the client has been informed. See also Commentary 3 to Principle 13.02.

13.02   Responsibility for client's case or matter

Principle

'Every solicitor in private practice shall, unless it is inappropriate in the circumstances, ensure that clients know the name and status of the person responsible for the day to day conduct of the matter and the principal responsible for its overall supervision.'

Solicitors' Practice Rules 1990, Rule 15(2)(a)

Commentary

1.   The rule requires that the client be informed not only of the name, but also of the status of the person responsible for conduct of the matter. Status refers to qualification as well as partnership status, e.g. whether the person is a solicitor or a legal executive.

2.   If the conduct or the overall supervision of the whole or part of the client's matter is transferred to another person in the firm the client should be informed and the reasons must be explained.

3.   Rule 15(2) provides that the duty to give information does not apply where it is 'inappropriate in the circumstances'. Solicitors must judge whether the provision of information is or is not appropriate. Solicitors will have to justify a decision should the client feel aggrieved. The following are examples of instances where solicitors may consider it inappropriate to provide the full information required by the rule:

   (a)   for the regular client for whom repetitive work is done — but it will certainly be appropriate to inform such a client if there is a change to the way in which the work is handled, e.g. if a new member of staff becomes involved;

   (b)   for major commercial clients sufficiently familiar with the conduct of their business and in a position to require the provision of further information if they want it;

   (c)   where particular sensitivity is required in handling the matter, for example when preparing a death-bed will, in a domestic violence emergency, or when seeing a person very recently bereaved, although in the latter case it will be possible to give the information at a more appropriate time;

   (d)   in case of urgency where it is not practical to provide full information, e.g. where emergency injunctive or similar relief is sought.

13.03 General information for clients

Principle

'Every solicitor in private practice shall, unless it is inappropriate in the circumstances, ensure that clients are at all relevant times given any appropriate information as to the issues raised and the progress of the matter.'

Solicitors' Practice Rules 1990, Rule 15(2)(c)

Commentary

1. One of the objects of this rule is to ensure that clients who are unfamiliar with the law and lawyers receive the information they need to make the legal process more comprehensible. This will reduce areas of potential conflict and complaint. Different levels of information may be appropriate for different clients.

2. Clients should normally be told in appropriate language at the outset of a matter or as soon as possible thereafter the issues in the case and how they will be dealt with. In particular, the immediate steps to be taken must be clearly explained. It may be helpful to give an explanatory leaflet to the client.

3. Solicitors should keep clients informed both of the progress of matters and of the reason for any serious delay which occurs. This may often be assisted by sending to clients copies of letters. Requests for information should be answered promptly.

4. The solicitor should advise the client when it is appropriate to instruct counsel. Whenever clients are to attend hearings at which they are to be represented, they must be told the name of the advocate who it is intended will represent them.

5. Solicitors should normally explain to clients the effect of any important and relevant documents. At the end of the matter solicitors should normally write to clients confirming that it has been completed and summarising any future action to be taken by the client or the solicitor.

6. Solicitors should consider whether it is appropriate to confirm the advice given and instructions received in writing. Confirmation in writing of key points will both reduce the risk of misunderstanding by clients and assist colleagues who may have to deal with the matter.

7. Rule 15(2) provides that the duty to give information does not apply where

it is 'inappropriate in the circumstances'. Commentary 3 to Principle 13.02 gives examples of when it may be inappropriate.

13.04   Written professional standards — information on costs for clients

In February 1991 the Council revised the written professional standards following the introduction of Rule 15 of the Solicitors' Practice Rules 1990. The remaining standards deal with giving clients advance information on costs as follows:

The standards are of general application although one of their particular objects is to ensure that clients who are unfamiliar with the law and lawyers receive the information they need to make what is happening more comprehensible and thus to reduce areas of potential conflict and complaint. Failure to give adequate information on costs frequently gives rise to complaints about solicitors.

Some of the standards may not be appropriate in every case — e.g. for regular clients for whom repetitive work is done or for those clients whose knowledge and experience in instructing and dealing with solicitors is such that they can reasonably be expected to ask for or be aware of the information on costs that would otherwise be required by the standards to be given. Where a solicitor decides in a particular case that a given standard is inapplicable, it will be for the solicitor to justify the decision should a client make a complaint.

A material breach of the standards could lead to a finding that the solicitor has provided inadequate professional services or, in a serious or persistent case, a finding of professional misconduct. Unreasonable failure to advise a client properly on some matters, particularly on the risks as to costs in litigation or the availability of legal aid, may well give rise to a claim in negligence.

The Council is concerned that solicitors have not been sufficiently aware of the standards and may not have appreciated how important they are. As well as arranging for further publicity for the standards in the *Gazette* and the *Professional Standards Bulletin,* the Council has promoted a good practice guide on client care. This gives practical advice to solicitors on compliance both with Rule 15 and the written professional standards.

Information on costs for clients

(a)   On taking instructions

On taking instructions the solicitor should:

(i)   give clients the best information possible about the likely cost of the matter. If no fee has been agreed or estimate given, the solicitor should tell clients how the fee will be calculated, e.g. whether on the basis of an hourly rate plus mark-up, a percentage of the value of the transaction, or a combination of both, or any other proposed basis;

(ii) discuss with clients how the legal charges and disbursements are to be met and must consider whether they may be eligible and should apply for legal aid (including legal advice and assistance); and

(iii) consider whether the client's liability for the costs may be covered by insurance.

(b) On confirming instructions

When confirming clients' instructions in writing the solicitor should :

(i) record whether a fee has been agreed and, if so, what it is and what it covers and whether it includes VAT and disbursements;

(ii) tell clients what other reasonably foreseeable payments they may have to make either to the solicitor or to a third party and the stages at which they are likely to be required; and

(iii) confirm oral estimates — the final amount payable should not vary substantially from the estimate unless clients have been informed of the changed circumstances in writing.

(c) Further information for privately paying clients — generally

Where clients are personally liable for the costs, in appropriate cases the solicitor should:

(i) inform them that they may set a limit on the costs which may be incurred without further reference;

(ii) explain that it is often not possible to estimate the costs in advance;

(iii) inform them every six months of the approximate amount of the costs to date, whether or not they have set a limit — in appropriate cases an interim bill should be delivered.

(d) Further information for privately paying clients — contentious matters

Where clients are not legally aided but the matter is contentious they should be informed at the outset of a case and at appropriate stages thereafter:

(i) that in any event they will be personally responsible for payment of their own solicitor's bill of costs in full regardless of any order for costs made against opponents;

(ii) of the probability that if they lose they will have to pay their opponent's costs as well as their own;

(iii) that even if they win their opponent may not be ordered to pay the full amount of the clients' own costs and may not be capable of paying what they have been ordered to pay; and

(iv) that if their opponent is legally aided they may not recover their costs even if successful in civil proceedings.

(e) Further information for legally aided clients

Where clients are legally aided they should be informed at the outset of any case and at appropriate stages thereafter:

(i) of the effect of the statutory charge on the case;

(ii) that if they lose the case they may still be ordered by the court to contribute to their opponent's costs even though their own costs are covered by legal aid;

(iii) that even if they win their opponent may not be ordered to pay the full amount of their costs and may not be capable of paying what they have been ordered to pay;

(iv) of their obligations to pay any contribution assessed and of the consequences of any failure to do so.

(f) Generally

In all matters a solicitor should consider with clients whether the likely outcome will justify the expense or risk involved.

13.05 Initial information on costs

Standard (a)(i) states

'On taking instructions the solicitor should ... give clients the best information possible about the likely cost of the matter.'

Commentary

1. It is an implied term in law that solicitors when instructed in their professional capacity will be paid reasonable remuneration for their services (see section 15 of the Supply of Goods and Services Act 1982).

2. A solicitor should not, however, rely solely upon this implied term but should explain to the client, so far as is possible, the work which is likely to be involved in carrying out the instructions and the time which may be taken, both of which will have direct relevance to the likely amount of fees.

3. Wherever possible, a solicitor should give an estimate of the likely cost of acting in a particular matter. If, because of the nature of the work, a solicitor cannot give even an approximate estimate of the fees and

disbursements, the client should be informed accordingly and in that case should be given as general a forecast as possible, and be kept informed about the costs as the matter proceeds. When giving such an estimate or forecast, regard should be had to Part III of the Consumer Protection Act 1987 which deals with misleading price indications.

4. When giving estimates, solicitors should take care to ensure that they are not binding themselves to an agreed fee unless this is their intention. Clear and appropriate words should be used to indicate the nature of the estimate. To give an estimate which has been pitched at an unrealistically low level solely to attract the work and subsequently to charge a higher fee for that work is improper because it misleads the client as to the true or likely cost. Regard should also be had to Principle 13.09 and Commentary.

5. It may not be appropriate to give the same information on costs to all clients. There may be occasions when it would be inappropriate to give costs information at the outset, for example in the case of an emergency injunction application where time may not allow for a full discussion, or in the case of a brief interview not leading to further work, where a fee is simply agreed and paid.

6. Solicitors may advertise their fees but any publicity concerning charges or a basis of charging must comply generally with the Solicitors' Publicity Code 1990, and in particular paragraph 5 (see Annex 11A).

13.06 Basis of charging

Standard (a)(i) also states:

'...If no fee has been agreed or estimate given, the solicitor should tell clients how the fee will be calculated, e.g. whether on the basis of an hourly rate plus mark-up, a percentage of the value of the transaction or a combination of both, or any other proposed basis.'

Commentary

1. A client should be informed of the charging rate of the person doing the work, or alternatively, if charges are based on an expense rate, the expense rate of the person doing the work and the range of the possible mark-up. A client should also be informed if such rates are to be subject to periodic review. Where applicable, the client should be told that factors other than time will be taken into account when settling the actual fee.

2. In non-contentious matters, regard must be had to the Solicitors' Remuneration Order 1972 (see Annex 14A).

13.07 Method of payment

Standards (a)(ii) and (iii) state:

'On taking instructions the solicitor should .... discuss with clients how the
legal charges and disbursements are to be met and must consider whether
they may be eligible and should apply for legal aid (including legal advice
and assistance).... [The solicitor should] consider whether the client's
liability for costs may be covered by insurance.'

Commentary

1.   With regard to a solicitor's duty to a client where the client is legally aided,
     either in civil or criminal proceedings see Principle 13.13. For the duty to
     advise a client on the availability of legal aid see Principle 5.01.

2.   Where a solicitor considers that legal aid is likely to be available to the
     client, the availability of an emergency certificate or the green form scheme
     should be borne in mind. A solicitor who commences work without legal
     aid cover runs the risk of being unable to recover pre-certificate costs.

3.   The duty to advise as to legal aid does not only apply at the outset of the
     retainer but, as the matter proceeds, it is the duty of solicitors to ensure that
     any material change of which they are aware in a client's means is at once
     taken into consideration in the context of eligibility for legal aid.

4.   For the position where a solicitor requires a client to make a payment on
     account of costs see Principle 14.01.

5.   There is no objection to solicitors accepting payment of their fees by the
     use of a credit card facility. For the position regarding payment by Access
     see Annex 14B.

13.08 Confirmation

Standards (b)(i) and (ii) state:

'When confirming the clients' instructions in writing the solicitor should ...
record whether a fee has been agreed and, if so, what it is and what it
covers and whether it includes VAT and disbursements ... [and] tell clients
what other reasonably foreseeable payments they may have to make either
to the solicitor or to a third party and the stages at which they are likely to
be required...'

Commentary

1. If there is an agreement between a solicitor and client that the solicitor is to be remunerated by an agreed fee, the solicitor is bound to do the work covered by the agreement for that fee, even though circumstances arise which make the work unremunerative for the solicitor.

2. Section 57(3) of the Solicitors Act 1974, requires a non-contentious business agreement to be in writing and signed by the person to be bound by it. Under section 59(1) an agreement as to costs in contentious matters must also be in writing.

3. A solicitor providing property selling services must, when accepting instructions to act in the sale of a property, give the client a written statement setting out their agreement as to the amount of the solicitor's remuneration or the method of its calculation, the circumstances in which it is to become payable, the amount of any disbursements to be charged separately (or the basis on which they will be calculated) and the circumstances in which they may be incurred, and as to the incidence of VAT. The statement should also deal with whether or not the solicitor is to be the sole agent and the consequence of subsequently instructing other agents where the solicitor has been so instructed. See Chapter 25 on property selling by solicitors.

4. Under Rule 9 of the Solicitors' Accounts Rules 1991, money received for or on account of an agreed fee which is paid by the client to the solicitor must not be paid into client account (see Chapter 27, paragraph 27.35).

13.09   Confirmation of estimates

Standard (b)(iii) states:

'When confirming clients' instructions in writing the solicitor should ... confirm oral estimates — the final amount payable should not vary substantially from the estimate unless clients have been informed of the changed circumstances in writing.'

Commentary

Solicitors should inform clients immediately it appears that an estimate will be or is likely to be exceeded. They should not wait until submitting the bill of costs.

13.10   Limit on costs

Standard (c)(i) states:

'Where clients are personally liable for the costs, in appropriate cases the solicitor should ... inform them that they may set a limit on the costs which may be incurred without further reference...'

Commentary

1.   Before instructions are accepted by a solicitor in the circumstances envisaged by this standard, the client should be warned of the consequences. A solicitor must not exceed any limit without the authority of the client. Further, a solicitor must, as soon as possible, inform the client where the limit imposed on the expenditure is insufficient and obtain the client's instructions as to whether the solicitor should continue with the matter.

2.   Where a solicitor continues to act in such circumstances regardless of the limit which the client has fixed and then presents a bill for a sum which exceeds that limit, he or she may be guilty of professional misconduct as well as having the excess disallowed on an application for a remuneration certificate and/or taxation.

13.11   Further information for privately paying clients

Standards (c)(ii) and (iii) state:

'Where clients are personally liable for the costs, in appropriate cases the solicitor should ... explain that it is often not possible to estimate the costs in advance... [and should] inform clients every six months of the approximate amount of the costs to date, whether or not they have set a limit — in appropriate cases an interim bill should be delivered.'

Commentary

1.   The solicitor should monitor the position regularly regarding costs which have accrued to date. The keeping of adequate time records will assist.

2.   Failure to keep the client informed, so far as possible, regarding the costs incurred, could prejudice a solicitor's ability to recover a fair and reasonable fee for the work done.

3. In non-contentious matters, a solicitor may render an interim bill if the client has agreed or acquiesced, or if the transaction or proceedings have reached a natural break.

4. In contentious matters, the question of an interim bill in respect of costs incurred is dealt with by reference to section 65(2) of the Solicitors Act 1974.

13.12 Privately paying clients — contentious matters

Standard (d) states:

'Where clients are not legally aided but the matter is contentious they should be informed at the outset of the case and at appropriate stages thereafter:

(i) that in any event they will be personally responsible for payment of their own solicitor's bill of costs in full regardless of any order for costs made against opponents;

(ii) of the probability that if they lose they will have to pay their opponent's costs as well as their own;

(iii) that even if they win their opponent may not be ordered to pay the full amount of the clients' own costs and may not be capable of paying what they have been ordered to pay; and

(iv) that if their opponent is legally aided they may not recover their costs even if successful in civil proceedings.'

13.13 Further information for legally aided clients

Standard (e) states:

'Where clients are legally aided they should be informed at the outset of a case and at appropriate stages thereafter:

(i) of the effect of the statutory charge on the case;

(ii) that if they lose the case they may still be ordered by the court to contribute to their opponent's costs even though their own costs are covered by legal aid;

(iii) that even if they win their opponent may not be ordered to pay the full amount of their costs and may not be capable of paying what they have been ordered to pay;

(iv) **of their obligations to pay any contribution assessed and of the consequences of any failure to do so.'**

13.14   Discussing the risk

Standard (f) states:

'In all matters a solicitor should consider with clients whether the likely outcome will justify the expense or risk involved.'

Commentary

It is in the interests of both the solicitor and the client that this advice should be in writing.

Annex 13A

Setting up a complaints procedure — SCB help sheet — practice information

---

What complaints handling procedures are needed?

All firms (small and large) need procedures. Sole practitioners can investigate complaints about their staff, but for a complaint about the sole practitioner the Bureau is likely to be the next stage. Firms can make other arrangements if they wish, e.g. with another firm/local Law Society, but this is not necessary.

The simpler and more direct the better. A two-tier approach can be:

— Someone with whom a client can raise problems (such as the fee-earner dealing with the matter), and

— A high-ranking person with whom a client can raise a complaint not resolved by the fee-earner.

— Respond to problems promptly (by building time targets into the procedure).

— Look at the problems objectively and thoroughly.

— If remedial action is necessary be speedy.

— Keep a note of your investigation with written confirmation to a client of your final response (this saves you lost fee-earning time if the Bureau gets involved).

— If clients remain dissatisfied after all your efforts tell them about the Bureau, give them our complaints leaflet and 'helpform'.

Remember

The Rule expects you to keep clients informed on the issues and progress throughout a matter.

(Suggested checklists/leaflets with standards information/costs information are included with this Information Pack.)

Making things easier

The Bureau is pleased to offer help/advice about complaints handling procedures. Contact The Professional and Public Relations Department on 0926 822042.

If you are having problems with a client you can suggest they ring the Bureau's Helpline: 0926 822007/008 — for advice to callers whether they have grounds for complaint and how best to go about it. If Helpline think the caller's best action is to resolve problems direct with the firm they will say so.

Why not have a direct liaison arrangement with the Bureau? We make immediate contact with a nominated link person in your firm with complaints of poor service. This is a quick informal way of giving your firm the first opportunity of resolving a problem. Ask us for more details.

Resolving complaints: responding

— Should it be the fee-earner? (For 'problems' probably yes, but formal complaints need senior-level response.)

— Quick response — speedy resolution.

— Telephone/meet the client. Letter to confirm the solution.

— Be understanding (expressing irritation to a client won't help!).

— Be thorough. (If there are several problems resolve them all — big and small.)

— Confirm the solution in writing (saves time if SCB gets involved).

The options

— Apology (very effective — not the same as accepting liability).

— Explanation/update (clients need reassurance).

— Immediate action (essential for complaints of delay/lack of progress).

— A change of fee-earner (may help retain the client).

— Costs concession (the right remedy for poor service).

— Compensation (where recompense is obvious and fair).

— Remuneration Certificate (useful, even if time limits have run out, where costs are the problem).

— Terminate the retainer (this should only be for good reason/on reasonable notice. Be clear about handing over/retaining papers. Do not use a justified complaint to cast the client adrift).

— Refer them to the Bureau (give them our complaints leaflet, and 'helpform'. If they need advice they can phone Helpline: 0926 822007/008).

Should you offer a costs concession and/or compensation?

* Is there poor service? (S.93 Courts and Legal Services Act 1990.)

* Checklist. Was the transaction:

— Started with objectives agreed with the client.

— Achieving these objectives.

— In accordance with the client's instructions.

— Without delay.

— Within a reasonable time/the agreed time.

— With adequate/the promised expertise/legal skills.

— Keeping the client informed as to progress throughout.

— Without unnecessary input/chasing/inconvenience by/to the client.

— With competent solicitor/client and office management.

— Using properly supervised staff.

— In accordance with promises made by the firm.

— Keeping the client informed about costs throughout.

— For the agreed/estimated costs (where applicable)?

— Have you resolved client problems/complaints about the service?

— Have problems been caused by events out of your control?

— Has the firm followed all Guide Principles/Law Society 'best practice' recommendations?

— How is the balance sheet? Measure your service and make the right response.

* Should you reduce/waive your charges for poor service?

* Should you also recompense the client? (S.93 Courts and and Legal Services Act — SCB can require you to compensate a client up to £1,000 for an inadequate professional service.)

* A small/soon-remedied shortcoming without loss/significant inconvenience to the client may be resolved short of a costs concession.

* For recompense issues and/or where a complaint 'scores' poorly on the checklist consider concessions/compensation.

* Where your firm has promised a quality service shortcomings should be reflected by costs concessions.

Cutting out problems — avoiding complaints

* Communication is the key.

* Do not take on too much work.

* Do not undertake work without the right expertise.

* Do supervise staff adequately.

* Do not leave the client in the dark about progress.

* Do tackle the client 'problem' before it becomes a 'complaint'.

Complaints procedure — check list

Have you:

— Worked out your firm's complaints handling procedures.

— Written them up.

— Nominated a senior person to co-ordinate complaints.

— Required staff to record problems/complaints so you will know how the firm has handled them. A centralised list of formal complaints held by the nominated person would save time if you have to respond to the Bureau.

— Made sure that all staff know and operate the procedures.

— Established what costs information you will give clients.

— Agreed what other standard information each client will receive.

— Obtained a supply of the Bureau's complaints leaflet *How and When* to give to clients where your attempts to resolve the problem have failed.

— Decided how you will tell a client of your procedures and costs information (a standard format ensures consistency).

There are suggestions for these with this information pack.

They can be amended at will.

Chapter 14

Professional fees

14.01 Payments on account

Principle

A solicitor may, at the outset of the retainer, require the client to make a payment or payments on account of costs and disbursements to be incurred.

Commentary

1. In non-contentious matters, a solicitor must make any requirement for a payment on account of charges, as distinct from disbursements, to be incurred a condition of accepting instructions. Without this condition (or the client's subsequent agreement), a solicitor cannot justifiably terminate the retainer if a client refuses to make such a payment. For the position with regard to termination generally see Principle 12.17.

2. In contentious matters, on the other hand, section 65(2) of the Solicitors Act 1974 provides that where a solicitor who has been retained by a client requests the client to make a payment of a sum of money, being a reasonable sum on account of the costs incurred or to be incurred, and the client refuses or fails within a reasonable time to make that payment, then the refusal or failure will be good cause for the solicitor to terminate the retainer upon giving reasonable notice. See also Annex 14E for further details.

3. In either case, where a solicitor receives such a payment on account of costs or disbursements to be incurred, it should be made clear to the client that the costs may be greater than the sum paid in advance, since such sums may not represent the fee for the whole work. Any sum requested must be reasonable (see Principle 14.10).

4. Where no bill or written intimation of the amount of costs has been delivered, monies paid on account of costs (as opposed to an agreed fee) must be paid into client account pending delivery of the bill or interim bill or written intimation of the amount of costs incurred (see Chapter 27, paragraph 27.35).

5.   Payment on account and payment of interim or final bills may be made by credit card (see Annex 14B).

14.02 Fee-sharing

Principle

'A solicitor shall not share or agree to share his or her professional fees with any person except:

    (a)   **a practising solicitor;**

    (b)   **a practising foreign lawyer (other than a foreign lawyer whose registration in the register of foreign lawyers is suspended or whose name has been struck off the register);**

    (c)   **the solicitor's *bona fide* employee, which provision shall not permit under the cloak of employment a partnership prohibited by paragraph (6) of this rule; or**

    (d)   **a retired partner or predecessor of the solicitor or the dependants or personal representatives of a deceased partner or predecessor'.**

Solicitors' Practice Rules 1990, Rule 7(1)

Commentary

1.   The term 'professional fees' does not include commissions received by a solicitor from any third party, but it does include negotiation fees. Note also Rule 10 of the Solicitors' Practice Rules 1990 and Principle 15.06 which deal with the solicitor's duty to account to clients for commissions and secret profits.

2.   The purpose of Practice Rules 7 (Fee-sharing), 8 (Contingency fees) and 9 (Claims assessors) is to safeguard the solicitor's independence and ability to give impartial advice to clients. See Annex 1A and Principle 14.03. The CCBE code of conduct also restricts fee-sharing with non-lawyers (see article 3.6 in Annex 10B).

3.   As an exception to this Principle, Rule 7(2) permits a solicitor who instructs an estate agent as sub-agent for the sale of a property to remunerate the sub-agent on the basis of a proportion of the solicitor's professional fee.

4.   Rule 7(3), (4) and (5) also allows exceptions for solicitors employed by non-solicitors in certain circumstances (see Annexes 1A and 4A).

14.03 Contingency fees

Principle

'(1) A solicitor who is retained or employed to prosecute any action, suit or other contentious proceeding shall not enter into any arrangement to receive a contingency fee in respect of that proceeding.

(2) Paragraph (1) of this rule shall not apply to an arrangement in respect of an action, suit or other contentious proceeding in any country other than England and Wales to the extent that a local lawyer would be permitted to receive a contingency fee in respect of that proceeding.'

Solicitors' Practice Rules 1990, Rule 8

Commentary

1. A contingency is any sum (whether fixed, or calculated either as a percentage of the proceeds or otherwise howsoever) payable only in the event of success in the prosecution of any action, suit or other contentious proceeding. The fact that an agreement further stipulates a minimum fee in any case, win or lose, will not prevent it from being an arrangement for a contingency fee. Section 58 of the Courts and Legal Services Act will permit conditional fee agreements between solicitors and clients subject to regulations to be made by the Lord Chancellor and subject to the necessary change in Rule 8.

2. A solicitor should not enter into any arrangement or understanding with a client or prospective client prior to the conclusion of the matter giving rise to the retainer by which the solicitor acquires an interest in the publication rights with respect to that matter. This applies equally to non-contentious business.

3. Rule 8 only extends to agreements which involve the institution of proceedings. Consequently, it would not be unlawful for a solicitor to enter into an agreement on a commission basis to recover debts due to a client, provided that the agreement is limited strictly to debts which are recovered without the institution of legal proceedings.

4. Section 59(2) of the Solicitors Act 1974 (contentious business agreements) provides expressly that nothing in the Act shall give validity to either:

   (a) any purchase by a solicitor of the interest or any part of the interest of his clients in any action, suit or other contentious proceeding, or

   (b) any agreement by which a solicitor retained or employed to prosecute any action, suit or other contentious proceeding, stipulates for payment only in the event of success in that action, suit or proceeding.

14.04   When to bill

Principle

A solicitor is under a duty to render a bill of costs to a client within a reasonable time of concluding the matter to which the bill relates.

Commentary

1.   In a contentious matter, where the court has made an order for costs or there is a legal aid taxation the bill must be lodged for taxation or assessment within three months of the end of the proceedings (Rules of the Supreme Court, County Court Rules and Legal Aid Regulations).

2.   In any event, it is good practice to submit a bill of costs as soon as possible. This is particularly important where a solicitor is holding sums of money on behalf of a client and awaits approval of the costs before accounting to the client or where the client has asked for the papers and the solicitor claims a lien.

14.05   Content of bill

Principle

A solicitor's bill of costs should contain sufficient information to identify the matter to which it relates and the period covered.

Commentary

1.   A solicitor should ensure that the form of the bill complies with the requirement of section 69 of the Solicitors Act 1974. This section provides that where a solicitor wishes to sue on the bill, it must be signed by the solicitor if a sole practitioner or, if the costs are due to a firm by one of the partners of that firm, (either in the partner's name or in the name of the firm). Alternatively, the bill should be accompanied by a letter which is so signed and which refers to the bill.

2.   The bill should show disbursements separately from professional fees. If the disbursements included in a bill have not been paid before the delivery of the bill, the solicitor should comply with section 67 of the Solicitors Act 1974, which requires the disbursements to be described in the bill as not then paid and, if the bill is to be taxed, requires the disbursements to be paid before the taxation is completed.

3.   If a non-contentious bill is challenged, the solicitor is under a duty to satisfy the Law Society or the taxing officer, as the case may be, as to the

fairness and reasonableness of the sum charged. For remuneration certificates and taxation, see Principle 14.06. See further the Solicitors' Remuneration Order 1972 (Annex 14A).

4. If a contentious bill is disputed, the client has the right to require the solicitor to deliver, in lieu of a gross sum bill, a bill containing detailed items, providing the client makes the request before being served with any originating process for the recovery of costs included in the bill and before the expiration of three months from delivery of the bill (see section 64 of the Solicitors Act 1974). Once such a request has been made the original gross sum bill is of no effect. Consequently, the solicitor must render a detailed bill within a reasonable time.

5. Sections 57 and 59-63 of the Solicitors Act 1974 make provision respectively for non-contentious and contentious business agreements. Such agreements restrict the client's right to challenge the bill, subject to safeguards. These sections were amended by the Courts and Legal Services Act 1990 to permit solicitors to make non-contentious and contentious business agreements based on an hourly rate.

14.06   Recovery of fees — non-contentious

Principle

In a non-contentious matter, a solicitor may not sue the client until the expiration of one month from the delivery of the bill, unless the solicitor has been given leave to do so on the grounds set out in section 69 of the Solicitors Act 1974. Further, a solicitor must not sue or threaten to sue unless he or she has first informed the client in writing of the right to require a remuneration certificate and of the right to seek taxation of the bill.

Commentary

1. This Principle is contained in section 69 of the Solicitors Act 1974 and article 3(2) of the Solicitors' Remuneration Order 1972, and applies as a matter of law as well as conduct. Consequently, any judgment obtained against a client is unenforceable unless this Principle has been complied with. For suing on a dishonoured cheque, see *Boston (Martin) & Co. (a firm)* v. *Levy and another* [1982] 3 All E.R. 193. The case of *Re Laceward Ltd.* [1981] 1 All E.R. 254 involved the dismissal of a solicitor's petition to wind up a client company on an alleged debt for non-contentious business, because the company had not been informed of its rights to have the bill taxed or to require a remuneration certificate. A statutory demand is not a proceeding and can be served prior to service of the notice upon the client (*Re a debtor; Marshalls (a firm)* v. *a debtor* [1992] 4 All E.R. 301).

2. A form of notice to the client under article 3(2) is contained in Annex 14D.

3. The Solicitors' Remuneration Order 1972 (Annex 14A) was made under a provision of the Solicitors Act 1957 (now section 56(2) of the Solicitors Act 1974) and regulates a solicitor's remuneration for non-contentious business. Solicitors who fail to comply with the terms of the Remuneration Order may be guilty of unprofessional conduct and liable to disciplinary proceedings. Annex 14F contains examples of contentious and non-contentious business.

4. The right of the client to a remuneration certificate from the Law Society arises under article 3 of the 1972 Order. The failure of a solicitor to apply for a remuneration certificate on the request of a client is a disciplinary matter. The certificate will either state that in the opinion of the Society the sum charged is fair and reasonable or, as the case may be, what lesser sum would be fair and reasonable. If the sum stated in the certificate is less than that charged, then that lesser sum shall be payable by the client.

5. The client is not entitled to require the solicitor to obtain a remuneration certificate after the expiry of one month from the date on which the client was notified of the right to such a certificate or after a bill has been delivered and paid (otherwise than by deduction without authority), or after the High Court has ordered the bill to be taxed.

6. Costs may be taken by deduction only after a bill or other written intimation of the amount of costs incurred has been delivered to the client. Payment of costs in this way is considered to be without prejudice to the client's right of recourse to a remuneration certificate from the Law Society if the client objects to the quantum of the charge within a reasonable time (usually one month) after delivery of the bill.

7. As an alternative, or in addition to seeking a remuneration certificate, a client who is dissatisfied with the amount of a solicitor's bill in respect of a non-contentious matter may apply to have the bill taxed by the High Court. Although a solicitor may, either of his or her volition or at the request of the client or a third party liable to pay the bill, apply for taxation, a solicitor is under no duty to do so. The solicitor may consider suggesting that the client or third party should seek advice from another solicitor on the bill.

14.07 Recovery of fees — contentious

Principle

In a contentious matter, under section 69 of the Solicitors Act 1974, the solicitor may not, without leave of the court, sue the client until the expiration of one month from the delivery of the bill, save in specified circumstances.

Commentary

1. Where there has been an agreement regarding costs in a contentious matter, a solicitor may not bring an action to recover under it. However, any person who is a party to the agreement (including the solicitor) may apply to the court who shall decide whether to enforce the agreement or to set it aside. (See section 61 of the Solicitors Act 1974, and Principle 14.05.)

2. In other cases, a client who is dissatisfied with the amount of a solicitor's bill may apply to the appropriate court within the period set out in section 70 of the Solicitors Act for a statutory taxation of the bill. A client is not entitled to obtain a remuneration certificate in respect of a contentious bill and there is no duty upon a solicitor to inform clients of their rights to apply for taxation. It is, however, prudent when a solicitor sues on a contentious bill to inform the client in the letter before action of the right to apply for a taxation. The same considerations will apply as are referred to in Commentary 5 to Principle 14.05.

3. The topic of bills and bills on account is discussed in Annex 14E (Cashflow in litigation).

14.08 Interest — non-contentious

Principle

In a non-contentious matter, a solicitor may charge interest on the whole or outstanding part of an unpaid bill with effect from one month after delivery of the bill, provided that notice as mentioned in Principle 14.06 has been given to the client.

Commentary

The right to charge interest is governed by article 5 of the Solicitors' Remuneration Order 1972, which also equates the rate of interest to that payable from time to time in respect of judgment debts. Terms of business may provide for a different rate of interest. Interest runs one month from the date of the delivery of the bill irrespective of when the notice was given (*Walton* v. *Egan* [1982] Q.B. 1232). If a bill is reduced, whether as a result of a remuneration certificate or of taxation, the rate of interest may only be applied by reference to the bill as so reduced.

14.09 Interest — contentious

Principle

In a contentious matter, a solicitor may charge interest on an unpaid bill:

   (a) if the right to charge interest has been expressly reserved in the original retainer agreement, or

   (b) if a client has later agreed to pay it for a contractual consideration, or

   (c) where the solicitor has sued the client and claimed interest under section 35A of the Supreme Court Act 1981.

14.10 Overcharging

Principle

A solicitor must not take unfair advantage of the client by overcharging for work done or to be done.

Commentary

1.   It is a question of fact in each case whether the charge is so excessive as to amount to culpable overcharging.

2.   If an agreement has been made between a solicitor and client which is found to be wholly unreasonable as to the amount of the fees charged or to be charged, disciplinary action could be taken against the solicitor on the grounds that he or she had taken unfair advantage of the client.

3.   Under article 4(2) of the Solicitors' Remuneration Order 1972, if a taxing officer allows less than one-half of the sum charged in a non-contentious bill, the officer is under a duty to bring the facts of the case to the attention of the Law Society.

4.   Where a solicitor has a bill of costs prepared by a costs draftsman, the bill is nonetheless the responsibility of the solicitor who must decide how much to charge the client.

5.   If a solicitor requires the client to pay a sum on account of costs to be incurred, that sum must be a reasonable amount by reference to the subject matter of the retainer.

14.11　Commissions

Principle

'Solicitors shall account to their clients for any commission received of more than £20 unless, having disclosed to the client in writing the amount or basis of calculation of the commission or (if the precise amount or basis cannot be ascertained) an approximation thereof, they have the client's agreement to retain it.'

Solicitors' Practice Rules 1990, Rule 10(1)

Commentary

This rule derives from the fiduciary relationship between solicitor and client. Detailed guidance on the application of the rule is contained in Annex 14C.

Annex 14A

Solicitors' Remuneration Order 1972 (S.I. 1972 no.1139)

1.   (1) This Order may be cited as the Solicitors' Remuneration Order 1972.

    (2) The Interpretation Act 1889 shall apply to the interpretation of this Order as it applies to the interpretation of an Act of Parliament.

    (3) This Order shall come into operation on 1st January 1973 and shall apply to all business for which instructions are accepted on or after that date.

2.   A solicitor's remuneration for non-contentious business (including business under the Land Registration Act 1925) shall be such sum as may be fair and reasonable having regard to all the circumstances of the case and in particular to:

    (i)   The complexity of the matter or the difficulty or novelty of the questions raised;

    (ii)   the skill, labour, specialised knowledge and responsibility involved;

    (iii)   the time spent on the business;

    (iv)   the number and importance of the documents prepared or perused, without regard to length;

    (v)   the place where and the circumstances in which the business or any part thereof is transacted;

    (vi)   the amount or value of any money or property involved;

    (vii)   whether any land involved is registered land within the meaning of the Land Registration Act 1925; and

    (viii)   the importance of the matter to the client.

3.   (1) Without prejudice to the provisions of sections 69, 70 and 71 of the Solicitors Act 1957[a] (which relate to taxation of costs) the client may require the solicitor to obtain a certificate from The Law Society stating that in their opinion the sum charged is fair and reasonable or, as the case may be, what other sum would be fair and reasonable, and in the absence of taxation the sum stated in the certificate, if less than that charged, shall be the sum payable by the client.

    (2) Before the solicitor brings proceedings to recover costs on a bill for non-contentious business he must, unless the costs have been taxed, have informed the client in writing:

---

[a] See now sections 70, 71 and 72, Solicitors Act 1974.

    THE GUIDE TO THE PROFESSIONAL CONDUCT OF SOLICITORS 1993

    (i)   of his right under paragraph (1) of this article to require the solicitor to obtain a certificate from The Law Society, and

    (ii)   of the provisions of the Solicitors Act 1957[b] relating to taxation of costs.

(3) The client shall not be entitled to require the solicitor to obtain a certificate from The Law Society under paragraph (1) of this article:

    (i)   after the expiry of one month from the date on which the client was given the information required by paragraph (2) of this article;

    (ii)   after a bill has been delivered and paid; or

    (iii)   after the High Court has ordered the bill to be taxed.

4.   (1) On the taxation of any bill delivered under this Order it shall be the duty of the solicitor to satisfy the taxing officer as to the fairness and reasonableness of the sum charged.

    (2) If the taxing officer allows less than one half of the sum charged, he shall bring the facts of the case to the attention of The Law Society.

5.   (1) After the expiry of one month from the delivery of any bill for non-contentious business a solicitor may charge interest on the amount of the bill (including any disbursements) at a rate not exceeding the rate for the time being payable on judgment debts, so, however, that before interest may be charged the client must have been given the information required by article 3(2) of this Order.

    (2) If an application is made for the bill to be taxed or the solicitor is required to obtain a certificate from The Law Society, interest shall be calculated by reference to the amount finally ascertained.

6.   A solicitor may take from his client security for the payment of any remuneration, including the amount of any interest to which the solicitor may become entitled under article 5 of this Order.

7.   The Orders specified in the schedule[c] hereto are hereby revoked except in their application to business for which instructions are accepted before this Order comes into operation.

Dated 27th July 1972.

Hailsham of St. Marylebone, C.

Widgery, C.J.

Denning, M.R.

Desmond Heap

G.P. Akinson

Theodore B.F. Ruoff

---

[b] See now Solicitors Act 1974.
[c] Not printed.

Annex 14B

Council statement on credit cards

A retailer agreement designed for use by the profession was negotiated by the Council with Access. It is an agreement which addresses the problems of confidentiality, the resolution of disputes and the acceptance of profit costs and VAT only. Access have agreed that solicitors need not accept the payment of disbursements by credit card and Access have prepared showcards indicating that the facility is restricted for this purpose.

There is no professional inhibition upon solicitors using the facility. It is for a solicitor to decide whether or not the terms of the agreement offered by Access are acceptable. The Council are not parties to any such arrangements.

These agreements were previously dealt with by the Joint Credit Card Co. Ltd. (Access). However, the individual banks now deal with the agreements themselves and solicitors wishing to avail themselves of the arrangements made with Access should contact the bank of their choice.

Note

The Council have agreed a facility to suit the requirements of the profession with Access only. Practitioners considering an agreement with other credit card companies are advised to seek terms as favourable as those offered by Access.

Revised February 1990

Annex 14C

Guidance — commissions

Rule 10 of the Solicitors' Practice Rules 1990

Why has the Law Society made a rule to prevent solicitors keeping commission unless their clients consent?

To what sort of commissions does the rule apply?

What exactly is meant by 'account to' the client?

These are some of the most commonly asked questions relating to commissions and Rule 10. This article aims to answer these and other questions which are put to the Professional Ethics Division.

Q.1: Why has the Law Society made a rule to prevent solicitors keeping commission unless their clients consent?

A: Many solicitors believe that the Law Society suddenly decided in 1987, when Rule 10 was first introduced, that solicitors could only keep commission if they had their client's consent to do so. In fact, the new rule simply put into practice rule form what had long been required of solicitors both as a matter of law and of professional conduct. The position at law results from the fiduciary and agency relationships which exist between the solicitor and the client. One of the consequences of these relationships is that a solicitor cannot unless otherwise authorised by law, contract or a trust deed, keep a secret remuneration or financial benefit arising from the use of client's property. There are many authorities which support this proposition, a number of which are set out on page 26 of *Cordery on Solicitors,* 8th edition, including the landmark case of *Brown* v. *I.R.C.* [1965] A.C. 244.

Q.2: To what sort of commissions does the rule apply?

A: The rule applies to any type of commission you receive in respect of a client, the most common types being commissions in respect of financial services (such as in relation to life policies, stocks and shares and pensions) and other general insurances such as household contents and fire policies. The rule applies equally to commissions paid on the renewal of any such policies. Also subject to the rule would be a payment made to you for introducing a client to a third party, unless the introduction was unconnected with any particular matter which you were currently or had been handling for the client. Commissions on opening a building society account for a client are covered by the rule. In fact, any financial benefit which you obtain by reason of and in the course of the relationship of solicitor and client is caught by the rule.

Q.3:   What exactly is meant by 'account to' the client?

A: 'Account to' does not mean simply telling the client that you will receive
         commission. It means that unless the client agrees to you keeping the
         commission it belongs to and must be paid to the client. In this respect, the rule
         goes further than many of the statutory rules governing, for example, the
         financial services industry in general, but that is because the general law
         relating to solicitors requires a higher duty from solicitors.

**Q.4:   The 1990 Rule imposes the further requirement that disclosure
         must be in writing. Why is this?**

A: The requirement that disclosure be in writing is new to the 1990 rule and is
         intended to protect the interests of both the solicitor and the client. The new rule
         reflects the advice which the Society has always given. The rule does not
         require the client's *consent* to be in writing, but this would be advisable (see
         next question).

**Q.5:   Can I write to clients setting out details of the commission I will
         receive and saying that if I do not hear from them within seven
         days I will assume that they agree to me keeping the commission?**

A: It would be unwise to rely on this as it would be an attempt to impose an
         agreement on the client unilaterally. Even if the client did consent verbally, the
         case of *Jordy* v. *Vanderpump* (1920) S.J. 324 made it clear that the onus is on
         the solicitor to show the client's consent. In that case the solicitor lost his claim
         to retain the commission as he could not prove that he had the client's consent.
         The court believed the client in the absence of proof by the solicitor. Therefore,
         although it is not a requirement of the rule, the Society would always advise
         solicitors to obtain the client's written consent.

Q.6:   Exactly what has to be disclosed to the client?

A: The rule requires that the client be told the amount or basis of calculation of the
         commission or (if the precise amount or basis cannot be ascertained) an
         approximation thereof. The 1990 rule is more flexible than previous rules in
         that where the solicitor is unable to tell the client the precise amount of the
         commission or the precise basis on which it will be calculated, an
         approximation may be given. The previous rule, strictly interpreted, meant that
         if the precise amount or basis of calculation was not known to the solicitor, the
         client's consent could not properly be given.

         Although the new rule gives the solicitor a choice of disclosing the actual
         amount *or* the basis of calculation, the Society considers that if the actual
         amount is known then it should be disclosed to the client when the solicitor is
         seeking consent, bearing in mind the solicitor's duty to act in the best interests
         of the client. This is particularly so where the basis of calculation of the
         commission is very complicated and may not mean much to the client, for
         example a percentage of the former LAUTRO maximum commission scales. If
         the exact amount is not known then the calculation should be explained to the
         client and in some cases, it may be that an approximation would be more
         helpful than the basis of the calculation, or should be given as well as the basis

of calculation. This may depend on the level of understanding of the client. It is also acceptable for a range to be given into which the amount of the commission is likely to fall provided that the range is not unreasonably wide.

Q.7:   What if the estimate I give turns out to have been too low?

A: If the commission actually received by the solicitor is *materially* in excess of the estimate given by the solicitor, or indeed the amount or basis originally disclosed to the client, the rule provides that the solicitor must account to the client for the excess. Whether the commission is 'materially in excess' of the original figure will depend on the circumstances of each case and consideration should be given to the amount of any excess both on its own and as a proportion of the amount which the client has agreed to the solicitor keeping, and the client's financial circumstances. The main reason for the use of the word 'material' in the rule is to avoid situations where the cost to the solicitor of accounting to the client for the excess would be greater than the actual amount of the excess. Solicitors may prefer simply to have a policy of accounting for all excesses rather than having to worry about whether the sums involved are materially in excess of the original figure or it may be possible to use the £20 *de minimis* figure as a guideline (see next question).

Q.8:   What is the significance of the £20 figure in the rule?

A: The £20 figure set out in the rule attempts to define for practical purposes what would be acceptable in law as being *de minimis*.

Q.9:   What if I receive a number of commissions of less than £20 in the course of acting for one client?

A: Whether such commissions can be treated separately for the purposes of the rule will depend on the facts of the particular case. Where the commissions are received in respect of separate transactions they can generally be treated separately. It would be wrong, however, to attempt to split up a transaction for the purpose of creating several commissions of £20 or less as this would not be acting in the best interests of the client. Also the commission would probably not, as a matter of law, be retainable on the basis of the *de minimis* principle. Similarly, a solicitor may carry out for a client a number of small transactions as part of a single retainer each of which results in the solicitor receiving a commission of less than £20. It may be difficult to argue that the total of the commission is retainable by the solicitor on the *de minimis* principle. Such difficulties could, of course, be avoided by the solicitor obtaining the client's consent to retain the commission at the outset of the retainer. Often it is these small amounts of commission which cause the most difficulties and yet it is in these circumstances that clients are most likely to consent to the solicitor keeping the commission.

Q.10:   When should the client's consent be obtained?

A: Although the rule does not contain any specific requirements on timing, as a matter of law the best time to obtain the client's consent is at the outset of the retainer or at least before you do the work which results in the commission being payable. Under the law of contract it is likely to be your agreement to do the work which amounts to the consideration for the client's agreement. Therefore, if the client has not consented when you receive the commission arguably it belongs to the client. Further, it cannot be in keeping with a duty to act in the best interests of the client for a solicitor, having received a commission to then seek the client's consent to keep it, when the client is entitled in law to receive it.

Q.11: **When commissions are received should they be placed on office or client account?**

A: If the client has consented to the solicitor retaining the commission then the money belongs to you and can be placed on office account. When no such agreement has been obtained the money is the property of the client and should be placed on client account. However, if you have any outstanding costs against the client in respect of this or any other matter, you may, provided a bill or some other written intimation of costs has been submitted to the client, withdraw from client account the sum of money owed in accordance with Rule 7 of the Solicitors' Accounts Rules 1991.

Q.12: **If the client does not consent to me keeping the commission can I still charge him or her for the work which leads to the commission being payable?**

A: Yes. The fact that you may have to account to the client for commission does not mean that you cannot charge for the work which results in the commission being payable, e.g. the arrangement of a policy. When the client is charged on a fee basis the fee must be calculated in accordance with the Solicitors' Remuneration Order 1972, i.e. it must be fair and reasonable having regard to all the circumstances of the case, and in particular to the factors set out in the Order (see *The Guide to the Professional Conduct of Solicitors*). If a bill is submitted for an amount equal to the amount of commission received and this cannot be justified by the factors set out in the Remuneration Order, such as the amount of work done by the solicitor and the value element, the bill may be reduced under the remuneration certifying procedure or on taxation. However, the Order would not apply if you and the client entered into a non-contentious business agreement under section 57 of the Solicitors Act 1974 — although the agreement could be set aside if the court considered it to be unfair or unreasonable.

Q.13: **If I am charging the client on a fee basis can I take my fee out of the commission?**

A: Yes. Providing that you have not agreed with the client to utilise any commission received for some other specific purpose, you have a lien on the commission in respect of any costs due to you in this or any other matter. The amount of the commission can be offset against any costs due to you, providing the client has been sent a bill or some other written intimation of costs. In this situation there is no requirement for prior disclosure of the amount of commission or for the client's agreement, as you are, in effect, accounting to the client for the commission and the offsetting is merely a convenient accounting arrangement. So, for example, if in connection with a conveyance, you arrange an endowment mortgage you could make a charge for the work involved in arranging the mortgage and then submit a bill to the client for the conveyancing and for arranging the mortgage, showing a reduction in the amount actually payable by the client.

In some situations the amount of the commission will exceed the amount of the bill, in which case you should submit a bill to the client showing the way in which part of the commission has been offset against your costs and account to the client for the balance.

The *Client Care Guide,* which was sent to all solicitors in connection with the new Practice Rule 15, contains various standard letters which can be used or adapted when confirming the nature of the retainer at the outset of a matter. One of these deals with conveyancing transactions involving financial services and contains a section on commissions, explaining to the client how the commission may be offset against the solicitor's costs (see page 35 of the *Client Care Guide*).

Q.14: **Can I advertise 'free conveyancing' where I propose to offset commission against my fees ?**

A: No. This is prohibited by paragraph 5 of the Solicitors' Publicity Code 1991. Any fee quoted in such circumstances must be the gross fee. However, there is no objection to mentioning that the availability of commission may reduce the cost of the transaction, provided that in relation to mortgages there is no implication that endowment policies are appropriate in all circumstances and that there is an indication of your willingness to advise as to the appropriate type of mortgage for the client's circumstances.

Q.15: **What is the position regarding VAT if I offset commission against costs ?**

A: Until recently, Customs and Excise took the view that where a bill was reduced to a net figure by the offsetting of commission, VAT was only payable on the net figure. However, Customs and Excise have changed their view and are expected to issue practice guidance saying that VAT must be calculated on the full, unreduced fee and the commission offset after that. As at January 1993 the new guidance has not been issued and the position is unchanged — but you should look out for further details of the new position in future editions of the *Gazette.*

Q.16: **If the client signs a section 57 agreement will this also meet the requirements of Rule 10?**

A: Provided the agreement contains disclosure of the amount or basis of calculation of commission and a clause that the client consents to you retaining the commission, there will normally have been compliance with Rule 10.

Q.17: **Could I choose to offer financial services on a commission only basis?**

A: There is nothing to prevent you stating at the outset of a transaction that you are only prepared to act on the basis that you retain any or part of any commission received, provided this does not conflict with your duty to act in the best interests of the client. There may be circumstances, for example in respect of endowment policies, in which some of the products available to the client are not commission-paying products. In such circumstances you would be wise to leave open the option of charging a fee. Simply obtaining the client's agreement to you acting on a commission only basis will not satisfy the requirements of Rule 10 where the amount or basis of calculation of the commission is not known or an approximation cannot be given. The client's informed consent is still required. A possible drawback in working on a commission only basis may be that you could spend time and effort advising the client on various types of policy or getting numerous quotes only to find the client has been using you as a sounding board for quotes received from another party. In such a situation you could only charge a fee for the work done if you had made clear at the outset your intention to do so.

Q.18: **What if the client defaults on a life policy and I become liable to repay some of the commission ?**

A: This can cause difficulties where you have accounted to the client for the commission. One option might be to agree with the client that the client will be liable for the amount which you have to repay, although the prospects of recovering from the client may not be very good. Other options would be to come to an agreement with the client for the late payment of the commission to the client (in which case the money should be kept on client account) or for you to elect to receive the commission from the insurer on a non-indemnity basis, in which case the commission is paid to you in instalments and if the client defaults no refund is necessary.

Q.19: **What if the insurance company prohibits me from passing the commission on to the client ?**

A: Some insurance companies have been known to state in their agreements with solicitors that the solicitors must not pass any commission on to their clients. In this case if you cannot obtain the client's agreement to retain the commission, which in these circumstances is probably unlikely, you will normally have to decline to accept the commission, and to charge the client a fee instead. It may be possible for you to offset the commission against your fee, but this will depend on the exact nature of the agreement with the insurance company.

Q.20: **Surely if I am acting in the renewal of an insurance policy I am acting as the agent of the insurance company and therefore I am entitled to the commission ?**

A: This is an argument often put forward by solicitors in respect of insurance commissions, and in particular renewal commissions, i.e. that they are not acting as the client's solicitor but as agent for the insurance company. This argument was rejected in the case of *Copp* v. *Lynch and Law Life Assurance Co.* (1882) 26 S.J. 348. This case involved renewal commission on a life policy. It was argued on behalf of the solicitor that he was not acting as the client's solicitor but as the agent of the insurance company and that as such he was entitled to the commission. (Interestingly the case was brought by the solicitor for the return of commission which had been paid directly to the client.) It was held that the plaintiff was acting as the defendant's solicitor and not as agent for the insurance company.

Even though it might be argued in the case of renewals, i.e. where solicitors are instructed by insurance companies to send out renewal notices and collect premiums, that solicitors might be effectively acting as agent for the insurance company they are still the client's solicitor and therefore Rule 10 applies.

Q.21: **What if the insurance company sends me one cheque in respect of various clients and I cannot attribute the commission to individual clients ?**

A: An argument commonly put forward is that it is often impossible (or certainly not worth the administrative headache) to attribute commissions to particular clients. A similar argument was rejected by the House of Lords in *Brown* v. *I.R.C.* [1965] A.C. 244. In the words of Lord Reid, 'I do not see how the difficulty in discovering who is the owner can make the money the property of the solicitor'. (This case dealt with interest rather than commission, but the legal requirement in relation to each was the same before what is now section 33 of the Solicitors Act 1974 changed the legal position in relation to interest.) Having regard to the interests of clients, it might be possible for you to make a reasonable estimate as to how much is attributable to each individual client. If this cannot be done without disproportionate expense, you may have to decline to accept the commission.

The same principles will apply in relation to general client accounts held with building societies. Some building societies offer to pay to the solicitor a commission based on the average amount held in the account at a particular time and it is often difficult to attribute this to individual clients. (Any additional *interest* payable on such an account should be dealt with in accordance with the Solicitors' Accounts Rules 1991.)

Q.22: **If I am the sole executor of a will can I consent to myself retaining any commission earned in dealing with the estate ?**

A: As a matter of law trustees cannot profit from their trust and Rule 10 does not permit a solicitor to retain a commission where this would not be permitted at law. Therefore any commission earned in dealing with the estate should be accounted for to the estate. The same principle would apply to a solicitor who was the donee of a power of attorney.

March 1992 (updated January 1993)

Annex 14D

Guidance — notice of rights under Solicitors' Remuneration Order 1972 and on taxation

(see article 3(2) of the Order — Annex 14A)

The following is a specimen of the notice which must be given to a client before a solicitor can charge interest or bring proceedings on an unpaid bill relating to non-contentious business.

Solicitors frequently endorse the back of a bill with notice of the client's rights. It would be inappropriate to advise a client of a right which he or she does not have, and hence contentious bills should not contain any notice of the client's rights under the Solicitors' Remuneration Order 1972.

NOTICE TO CLIENT

1. You have the right to ask us to obtain a certificate from the Law Society, stating *either*

    (a) that the sum charged is fair and reasonable, or

    (b) what lesser sum would be fair and reasonable.

    The details of this right are set out in the Solicitors' Remuneration Order 1972.

    If you wish us to obtain a certificate, you must ask us to do so within one month of receiving this notice.

    Interest may be charged on unpaid bills[, and we intend to charge interest at the rate payable on High Court judgment debts from one calendar month from the date of our bill].

2. You may also have the additional right to apply to the High Court to review the sum charged, (the procedure is called taxation) but this is subject to certain limitations.

    The details of this right are set out in sections 70, 71 and 72 of the Solicitors Act 1974.

Annex 14E

Cash flow in litigation — practice information

The Council of the Law Society is acutely aware of the cash-flow problems of solicitors in an era of high interest rates and ever-increasing overheads. The Contentious Business Committee (now replaced by the Remuneration and Practice Development Committee) considered the matter and the following paragraphs set out the Committee's advice which is based on the state of the law at the time (September 1980). The advice does not apply to work which is done under a legal aid order, legal aid certificate, or under the green form scheme.

Obtaining payments on account

A solicitor may agree with a client either at the outset or during the course of the retainer that the client shall make payments on account and/or provide security for the costs payable by him to the solicitor. Further, section 65(2) of the Solicitors Act 1974 states:

'If a solicitor who has been retained by a client to conduct contentious business requests the client to make a payment of a sum of money, being a reasonable sum on account of the costs incurred or to be incurred in the conduct of that business, and the client refuses or fails within a reasonable time to make that payment, the refusal or failure shall be deemed to be a good cause whereby the solicitor may, upon giving reasonable notice to the client, withdraw from the retainer'.

It will be seen that this section (i) gives a solicitor a right to make reasonable demands for payments on account from the client, even if there is no agreement between the solicitor and the client that the client shall make such payments, and (ii) enables a solicitor, despite the fact that his retainer may constitute an entire contract, e.g. a contract to prosecute a suit to its conclusion, to determine the retainer on failure by the client to pay a reasonable sum on account.

Security for costs and/or lien

Section 65(1) states: 'A solicitor may take security from his client for his costs, to be ascertained by taxation or otherwise, in respect of any contentious business to be done by him'. This section is self-explanatory. It is most important to remember that a solicitor who takes security may lose his lien unless it is expressly reserved.

Practitioners are reminded that they have a lien on money belonging to the client which properly comes into their possession, unless the money is paid to the solicitor for a particular purpose so that the solicitor becomes, in effect, a trustee of that money. The lien extends to all costs incurred in the matter in connection with which the money was received and applies to unbilled costs as well as unpaid bills.

In addition, solicitors have a common law lien on property recovered or preserved through their instrumentality in litigation for their costs in relation to that litigation, which lien, if the property or money is in the possession of the client or a third party, can be enforced under section 73 of the Solicitors Act 1974 or by other appropriate proceedings.

For well over a century the law has been that, if the solicitor discharges himself in the course of an action, however justified the discharge may be, the court will normally order him to hand over the client's papers to a new solicitor against undertakings by the new solicitor, *inter alia,* to preserve the previous solicitor's lien. If, however, the client discharges the solicitor, the solicitor is entitled to rely on the lien and retain the client's papers until the costs are paid. The case of *Gamlen Chemical Co. (U.K.) Ltd.* v. *Rochem Ltd.* in the Court of Appeal reported at [1980] 1 All E.R. 1049 has re-affirmed the law on this point. The report should be referred to for full details of the undertakings which the new solicitors are required to give.

Agreed fees

A solicitor may agree a fee with a client, either at the outset or during the course of the business or after its conclusion. However, if it is necessary to enforce payment of an agreed fee, attention is drawn to sections 59-63 of the Solicitors Act 1974 which deal, *inter alia,* with the procedure to be followed on enforcement.

Bills rendered during the course of litigation

The judgment of the Court of Appeal in *Davidsons* v. *Jones-Fenleigh* (1980) 124 S.J. 204, highlighted the point that there are two classes of bills and it is very important to distinguish between them. First, there is a bill which is delivered during the course of litigation, but is intended by the solicitor to be a final bill for the work included in it. Second, there is a bill which is not intended to be a final bill for the work covered by it, but merely a bill on account. The first class of bill is referred to hereafter as a 'statute bill' and the second class is referred to as a 'bill on account'. Each class of bill has its advantages and disadvantages which are explained hereafter.

'Statute bill'

If a bill is to be a 'statute bill' the following conditions must be observed. First, it must be made quite clear to the client either in the bill or otherwise that it is intended to be a complete bill in respect of the specified work. Second, the circumstances must be such that the solicitor has the right to render the bill, or the client has accepted it without objecting to its validity.

A right to render a 'statute bill' arises in the following circumstances: (a) at the conclusion of the matter; (b) when the client has agreed to or required the delivery of a bill; (c) when the client has withdrawn instructions in the matter; (d) when the solicitor has determined the retainer by reason of the client's failure to comply with a reasonable demand under section 65(2) or for other good cause — and (e) at a 'natural break', in protracted, complicated, or lingering litigation. A 'natural break' can arise either at a specified point in the litigation or by reference to a specified point in time. In either case, whether a 'natural break' has occurred is a question of fact. The cases do not give much help in determining this. Whilst there may be circumstances in which it will be necessary for a solicitor to decide whether there has been a 'natural break', in the opinion of the committee it is wiser in general not to rely on the 'natural break' as a ground for delivering a bill, except in the clearest cases. It is better to take advantage of section 65(2) and make a reasonable demand for payment on account. If the client complies with the demand an amount to cover costs incurred can be paid into or transferred to office account provided the conditions set out hereafter are observed.

'Bill on account'

A 'bill on account' can be rendered to the client at any time because such a bill is not intended to be a bill which can be sued on under the Solicitors Act 1974 and is really nothing more than a demand for a payment on account of the 'statute bill' which will be delivered later. It should be made clear to the client that the bill is not intended to be a 'statute bill'. A 'bill on account' cannot be sued upon by the solicitor nor can a client apply for it to be taxed under the statute. However, in such a case the client can request the solicitor to render a 'statute bill' and, if the solicitor refuses, can apply to the court for an order for delivery thereof. When the 'statute bill' is later delivered by the solicitor the client can have it taxed. The provisions of the Solicitors Act 1974 limiting the time within which a client may apply to tax a 'statute bill' will not cause time to run against a client after delivery of a 'bill on account'. Time will not commence running until a 'statute bill' is delivered.

Transfer to or payment into office account

The basic principle is that every solicitor who holds or receives clients' money must without delay pay it in to a client account. There are various exceptions to the basic principle. So far as cash flow is concerned, the important question is in what circumstances can money held for or received from a client be transferred to or paid into office account? The position under the Solicitors' Accounts Rules 1986* is as follows:

(a) money expressly received as or on account of an agreed fee must be paid directly into office account;

(b) money expressly received in payment or on account of a 'statute bill' or 'bill on account' must be paid directly into office account;

(c) money received for or towards payment of a debt due to the solicitor from the client or in reimbursement of money expended by the solicitor on behalf of the client must be paid directly into office account;

(d) money which is expressly paid on account of costs incurred in respect of which a written intimation of the amount of the costs incurred has been delivered to the client for payment must be paid directly into office account;

(e) there may be drawn from a client account, clients' money properly required for a payment to or on behalf of the client;

(f) there may be drawn from a client account, money properly required for or towards payment of a debt due to the solicitor from the client or in reimbursement of money expended by the solicitor on behalf of the client; and

(g) there may be drawn from a client account, clients' money properly required for or towards payment of the solicitor's costs where there has been delivered to the client a bill (whether a 'statute bill' or 'bill on account') or other written intimation of the amount of the costs incurred.

---

* Now see the Solicitors' Accounts Rules 1991.

In the last case, the transfer of money from client account to office account cannot take place until the client has been clearly informed in writing that the money held is being or will be applied towards or in satisfaction of such costs.

Money received or held by a solicitor on account of costs should not be paid into or transferred to office account unless a bill has been delivered or a written intimation sent in accordance with the above paragraphs. The mere deposit of a sum on account of costs without a bill or written intimation does not entitle a solicitor to pay or transfer money into office account.

Written intimation of costs incurred

It will be seen from the above that money received from a client can be paid into or transferred to office account even if no 'statute bill' or 'bill on account' has been delivered, provided a written intimation of the amount of the costs incurred has been sent to the client. The purpose of requiring such intimation is to inform the clients how their money is being applied so that they may take appropriate steps if they do not agree.

If the money has been sent to the solicitor in response to a written intimation of costs incurred, and the communication from the client has made it clear in express terms that it is paid on account of or in satisfaction thereof, the money must be paid into office account.

Where the money is not paid expressly on account of or in satisfaction of the written intimation, or the money was paid into client account before the written intimation was sent, money can be transferred from client account to office account providing (a) a written intimation of the amount of the costs incurred has been delivered and (b) it has been made clear to the client in writing that the money will be applied towards or in satisfaction of such costs.

It cannot be emphasised too strongly that the sums which can be paid into or transferred to office account on giving a written intimation are restricted to the amount of costs already incurred and must not cover anticipated future costs. It is the responsibility of the practitioner to ensure that such payments and transfers are so restricted.

As it will be necessary to provide for the appropriate amount of VAT and it may be necessary to send the client a tax invoice for any sum paid or transferred into office account, practitioners may take the view that it would be more convenient to render a 'bill on account'. However, a 'bill on account' must also be restricted to costs incurred.

VAT

When a solicitor renders a bill to a client, he or she must, unless the matter is zero-rated, add VAT to the bill. If the bill relates to business matters in respect of which the client is registered for VAT purposes, the solicitor must send the client a tax invoice. When a solicitor receives a deposit of a sum on account of costs no liability to VAT arises unless and until a bill is rendered or money in respect of costs incurred is transferred to or directly paid into office account. Therefore, if money is transferred to or paid into office account consequent on a written intimation rather than a bill, VAT must be accounted for and, where appropriate, a tax invoice must be sent to the client.

Conclusion

It will be seen from the above that a solicitor acting for a client in connection with contentious work is, provided he or she takes advantage of the relevant statutory and other provisions, able to obtain reasonable sums on account of costs incurred or to be incurred and to transfer to or pay into office account sums to cover disbursements paid by the solicitor and costs incurred by the solicitor on behalf of the client. Therefore, if the client is able and willing to finance the litigation, the solicitor acting will be able to ameliorate cash flow problems. If the client is unable or unwilling to finance the litigation, the solicitor can cease acting for the client providing there is compliance with the provisions of section 65(2).

It will also be seen that both 'statute bills' and 'bills on account' have their advantages and disadvantages. One important point of difference which has not been alluded to are the constraints on charging which arise from delivery of a 'statute bill'.

If a 'bill on account' has been delivered the solicitor can, when preparing a later 'statute bill', assess a fair overall charge for all work done since the delivery of any earlier 'statute bill' and, if none, since the inception of the matter. This is so provided it is made clear to the client that the 'bill on account' is not intended to be a 'statute bill' and is merely a demand for a payment on account. On the other hand, if a 'statute bill' is delivered during the course of the litigation, it is not possible to deliver another bill covering the work specified in it.

Revised August 1989

Examples of contentious and non-contentious business — practice information

Contentious

1. Proceedings actually begun in the county courts, High Court, magistrates' courts (including licensing), Crown Court, and the Court of Protection.

2. Proceedings actually begun before the Lands Tribunal and the Employment Appeals Tribunal.

3. Contentious probate proceedings actually begun.

4. Proceedings on appeal to the Court of Appeal, Privy Council and House of Lords

5. Proceedings in an arbitration.

6. Work done preliminary to proceedings covered by 1-5 above including advice, preparation and negotiations provided the proceedings are subsequently begun.

Non-contentious

1. Proceedings before all tribunals (including industrial tribunals) other than the Lands Tribunal and the Employment Appeals Tribunal.

2. Planning and other public inquiries.

3. Non-contentious or common form probate business.

4. Conveyancing, company acquisitions and mergers, the administration of estates and trusts out of court, the preparation of wills, statements and contracts, and any other work not included in the 'contentious' list.

5. Work done preliminary to the proceedings included in the 'contentious' list if such proceedings are not subsequently begun.

6. Criminal Injuries Compensation Board.

Chapter 15

Conflict of interests

15.01 When instructions must be refused

Principle

A solicitor or firm of solicitors should not accept instructions to act for two or more clients where there is a conflict or a significant risk of a conflict between the interests of those clients.

Commentary

1. Where a solicitor already acts for one client and is asked to act for another client whose interests conflict or appear likely to conflict with those of the first client, the solicitor must refuse to act for the second client.

2. There is no objection to a solicitor acting as a conciliator or mediator between parties in a domestic dispute. Once a solicitor has acted as a conciliator or mediator the solicitor may not subsequently act for either party as a solicitor in respect of that dispute. See Principles 22.17 to 22.22 for further guidance.

15.02 Relevant knowledge

Principle

If a solicitor or firm of solicitors has acquired relevant knowledge concerning a former client during the course of acting for that client, the solicitor or the firm must not accept instructions to act against the client.

Commentary

1. Any knowledge acquired by a solicitor whilst acting for the former client is confidential and cannot be disclosed without that client's consent (see

Principle 16.01). However, a solicitor is under a duty to the present client to inform the client of all matters which are material to the retainer (see Principle 16.07). Consequently, a solicitor in possession of knowledge concerning a former client which is or might be relevant, is put in an impossible position and cannot act against that client. Moreover, if a solicitor would feel embarrassed in acting against a former client, the solicitor should not act.

2.   As a result of this Principle, a solicitor who has acted jointly for both husband and wife in matters of common interest, must not act for one of them in matrimonial or other proceedings where he or she is in possession of confidential relevant information concerning the other, which was received in the course of the joint retainer and which information is not known by the party for whom he or she now proposes to act.

3.   Where a solicitor has acted for members of a family and is then asked to act against one or more of those former clients, this Principle will apply. If, however, the solicitor is obliged by the Principle to refuse to act for a particular member of the family who is under a legal disability (e.g. not of full legal age), then the solicitor should make every effort to ensure that that person is separately advised; it is not sufficient for the solicitor merely to cease to act.

4.   Another example of the operation of this Principle is where a solicitor has acted for both lender and borrower in the making of a loan. The solicitor should not subsequently act for the lender against the borrower to enforce repayment if the solicitor has obtained confidential relevant knowledge, e.g. of the borrower's financial position, when acting for the borrower in connection with the original loan. See also Principle 24.01.

5.   This Principle also applies to partnerships. If a solicitor has either acted for a partnership or has acted in the formation of that partnership, the solicitor may only accept instructions to act against an individual partner or former partner provided no relevant knowledge has been obtained about that individual whilst acting for the partnership, or in its formation.

6.   A solicitor who has acted for a company in a particular matter and has also separately acted for directors or shareholders in their personal capacity in the same matter may not act for either the company or the other parties if litigation ensues between them in respect of that matter.

15.03 Conflict arising between two or more current clients

Principle

A solicitor or firm of solicitors must not continue to act for two or more clients where a conflict of interest arises between those clients.

Commentary

1. If a solicitor has already accepted instructions from two clients in a matter or related matters and a conflict subsequently arises between the interests of those clients, the solicitor must cease to act for both clients, unless he or she can without embarrassment (see Commentary 1 to Principle 15.02) and with propriety, continue to represent one client with the other's consent. A solicitor may only continue to represent one client if not in possession of relevant confidential knowledge concerning the other obtained whilst acting for the other. Even in such a case the consent should be sought of the other client (usually through his or her new solicitors) and the solicitor should proceed in the absence of such consent only if there is no good cause for its refusal.

2. Where a solicitor acts for two or more co-defendants in criminal proceedings, and one or more of them changes his or her plea, the solicitor must consider carefully whether it is proper to continue to represent any of them. In reaching a decision, the solicitor must bear in mind that if his or her duty of disclosure to the retained client or clients conflicts with his or her duty of confidentiality to the other client or clients, the solicitor must cease to act for all of them. Before agreeing to continue to represent one client the solicitor must, therefore, examine carefully whether there is any information in his or her possession relating to the other clients which may be relevant to the retained client (see *R. v. Ataou* [1988] Q.B. 798).

3. Following the amalgamation of two or more firms, the clients of the individual firms will, as a result of an express or implied change of retainer, become clients of the new firm; care must be taken to ensure that the interests of the clients of the new firm do not conflict. If they do, the firm must cease to act for both clients unless they are able, within the terms of Commentary 1, to continue to act for one. In certain exceptional circumstances the amalgamated firm may continue to act for one client after erecting a 'Chinese wall'. Further guidance can be found at Annex 15A.

4. It is doubtful whether, in circumstances other than where there has been an amalgamation of two or more firms, a 'Chinese wall' can be erected so that a firm can continue to represent the interests of two clients whose interests conflict. The courts have expressed doubts on whether an impregnable wall can ever be created because of the practical difficulties of ensuring the absolute confidentiality of each client's affairs (see *Re a firm of solicitors* [1992] 1 All E.R. 353).

15.04   Acting for seller and buyer

Principle

A solicitor must not act for both seller and buyer on a transfer of land or of an interest in land or for a lender and borrower in a private mortgage unless he or she is able to do so in compliance with Rule 6 of the Solicitors' Practice Rules 1990.

Commentary

See Annex 1A and Principle 24.01 for details.

15.05   Solicitor's interests conflicting with client's

Principle

A solicitor must not act where his or her own interests conflict with the interests of a client or a potential client.

Commentary

1. Because of the fiduciary relationship which exists between solicitor and client, a solicitor must not take advantage of the client nor act where there is a conflict of interest or potential conflict of interest between the client and the solicitor. In conduct there is a conflict of interest where a solicitor in his or her personal capacity sells to, or purchases from or lends to or borrows from his or her own client. The solicitor should in these cases ensure that the client takes independent legal advice. If the client should refuse to do so, the solicitor must not proceed with the transaction. It is generally proper for a solicitor to provide short term bridging finance for a client in a conveyancing transaction (see Principle 24.02).

2. A solicitor must at all times disclose with complete frankness whenever the solicitor has or might obtain any personal interest or benefit in a transaction in which he or she is acting for the client. In such circumstances, it is incumbent upon a solicitor to insist that the client receives independent advice. Failure to do so may lead to civil action by the client for account.

3. It should be understood that by independent advice is meant not only legal advice, but where appropriate, competent advice from a member of another profession, e.g. a chartered surveyor.

4. The interests of the solicitor referred to in the Principle may be direct (for

example, where a solicitor seeks to sell or buy property from the client or lends to, or borrows from, the client), or indirect (for example, where the solicitor's business interests lead the solicitor to recommend the client to invest in a concern in which the solicitor is interested).

5. This Principle applies not only where a solicitor is personally interested in a transaction, but equally where a partner or a member of the solicitor's staff is so interested.

6. A solicitor must also consider whether any family relationship, office or appointment inhibits his or her ability to advise the client properly and impartially (see Principle 12.07 and Annex 15B).

7. The interests envisaged by this Principle are not restricted to those of a primarily economic nature only. For example, a solicitor who becomes involved in a sexual relationship with a client should consider whether this may place his or her interests in conflict with those of the client or otherwise impair the solicitor's ability to act in the best interests of the client.

8. A solicitor who is a director or shareholder of a company for which the solicitor also acts must consider whether he or she is in a position of conflict when asked to advise the company upon steps it has taken or should take. It may be necessary for the solicitor to resign from the board or for another solicitor to advise the company in that particular matter. A solicitor acting for a company in which he or she has a personal interest should always ensure that his or her ability to give independent and impartial advice is not thereby impaired.

9. A solicitor who is in breach of this Principle may be subject to disciplinary action; in some circumstances failure to comply with the Principle may also lead to legal difficulties. For the legal position in respect of sales to, and purchases from, clients and loans by the solicitor to, and borrowing from, the client see, e.g. *Cordery on Solicitors* (8th edition, Butterworths).

10. Chapter 23 deals with the conflict issues arising where a solicitor is acting as an insolvency practitioner.

15.06 Commissions

Principle

'(1) **Solicitors shall account to their clients for any commission received of more than £20 unless, having disclosed to the client in writing the amount or basis of calculation of the commission or (if the precise amount or basis cannot be ascertained) an approximation thereof, they have the client's agreement to retain it.**

(2) **Where the commission actually received is materially in excess of the amount or basis or approximation disclosed to the client the solicitor shall account to the client for the excess.**

(3) **This rule does not apply where a member of the public deposits money with a solicitor who is acting as agent for a building society or other financial institution and the solicitor has not advised that person as a client as to the disposition of the money.'**

Solicitors' Practice Rules 1990, Rule 10

Commentary

1. Rule 10 follows the position at law from which it is clear that a solicitor may not make a secret profit but must disclose to the client fully the receipt of any such profit. It may only be retained provided the client agrees. See *Brown* v. *I.R.C.* [1965] A.C. 244, *Copp* v. *Lynch and Law Life Assurance Co.* (1882) 26 S.J. 348 and *Jordy* v. *Vanderpump* (1920) 64 S.J. 324.

2. This Principle also applies to the receipt by solicitors of, for example, commissions on insurances and from the Stock Exchange. Further guidance on commissions is contained in Annex 14C.

15.07   Solicitor holding power of attorney

Principle

A solicitor who holds a power of attorney from a client must not use that power to gain a benefit which, if acting as a professional adviser to that client, he or she would not be prepared to allow to an independent third party.

Commentary

The Principle applies regardless of the legal position, e.g. as to whether a solicitor acting under a power of attorney can properly lend the donor's money to himself or herself.

15.08 Gifts to solicitor

Principle

Where a client intends to make a gift *inter vivos* or by will to his or her solicitor, or to the solicitor's partner, or a member of staff or to the families of any of them and the gift is of a significant amount, either in itself or having regard to the size of the client's estate and the reasonable expectations of prospective beneficiaries, the solicitor must advise the client to be independently advised as to that gift and if the client declines, must refuse to act.

Commentary

1. If the client declines to be independently advised, the solicitor must refuse to act for the client in drawing the will or any other document by which the gift is to be made. It is not sufficient merely to have the will or other document witnessed by an independent solicitor.

2. A solicitor must also ensure that members of staff do not embody in any will or document a gift to themselves without the approval of the solicitor. If the member of staff seeks the solicitor's approval, the same rule as to independent advice applies.

3. Where a client wishes to leave a legacy to the solicitor which is not of a significant amount, there is no need for independent advice. However, the solicitor should be satisfied that the client does not feel obliged to make such a gift.

4. Occasionally, a testator may wish to leave all or a substantial part of his or her estate to a solicitor to be dealt with in accordance with the testator's wishes as communicated to the solicitor either orally or in a document, or as a secret trust. The Council consider that where a solicitor in such circumstances will not benefit personally and financially, there is no need to ensure the testator receives independent advice. However, solicitors should preserve the instructions from which the will was drawn and should also see that the terms of such secret trust are embodied in a written document signed or initialled by the testator.

5. Where the donor or testator is a relative of the solicitor and wishes to make a gift or leave a legacy to the solicitor, the solicitor must consider whether in these circumstances independent advice is essential. The same principle will apply if the intended recipient is a partner of the solicitor, or a member of staff and the donor or testator is a relative of the intended recipient.

Annex 15A

Guidance — conflict arising on the amalgamation of two firms of solicitors

1. Solicitors should be aware that where as the result of an amalgamation, a conflict of interest arises, the general rule remains that the new firm must cease acting for both clients. In certain exceptional circumstances however — and it is to be emphasised that the circumstances will indeed be rare — the best interests of the client(s) may permit the amalgamated firm to continue acting for one or, just possibly, both clients.

2. In order to act in those exceptional circumstances the firm has to be able to erect an effective 'Chinese wall' and in any event the following circumstances must apply:

   (a)   there must be no embarrassment to the solicitors involved;

   (b)   both clients must have consented;

   (c)   both clients must have obtained full and frank independent advice, prior to the giving of consent; and

   (d)   despite the possession of knowledge concerning a client obtained whilst acting for them, the overriding duty to act in the best interests of the client must demand, as an exception to the general rule, that the amalgamated firm continue acting despite the conflict of interest.

3. The erection of a 'Chinese wall' does not eliminate the conflict of interests. It provides a method of dealing with the conflict where, in exceptional circumstances, it is in the best interests of the client or clients for the solicitor(s) to continue acting. An overriding and compelling case needs to be made for it being in the client(s) best interests.

4. Prior to amalgamation, the solicitors representing each client must consider the possibility that their personal interest in the amalgamation may conflict with their duty to provide the client with best advice. The client must be independently advised where there is or might be a conflict.

5. Where an amalgamation has been agreed but not effected and the proposed new firm is in the position of having two clients with conflicting interests, each of whom may wish to instruct it, the new firm — and the individual solicitors concerned — must treat each of those two clients equally in ascertaining whether either or both of them wish to instruct the new firm. Thus, something akin to a standard letter should be sent to each which must emphasise that while each may wish to instruct the new firm, each must seek independent advice in relation to that decision. The letter should also emphasise that lack of consent of one is an absolute bar to acting for either or both.

6.   If one or both clients, having received independent advice, wish to instruct the new firm, steps must be taken actually to 'erect the wall'. The solicitors acting for each client will owe a duty of confidence to their client. But they will also owe a duty to pass on to their client all information relevant to the retainer from whatever source. The 'wall' must deal with this otherwise impossible situation by ensuring separation — both geographical and otherwise — of the affairs of the client(s) and the personnel dealing with them.

7.   For the 'wall' to be effective strict conditions must be imposed to keep separate and confidential the affairs of each client. These conditions will include, *inter alia*, appropriate undertakings from relevant personnel. Ideally, there will also be a geographical separation between those members of staff dealing with one client's matter and those who have dealt with the other. It should be borne in mind that the risk of breaching confidence does not merely apply to qualified staff, but extends to other personnel as well. Arrangements would have to be made so that opening of mail and other day-to-day administrative matters did not infringe the intra-firm confidentiality.

8.   The governing principle being the client(s) best interests, it is — in principle — possible for a 'Chinese wall' to allow an amalgamated firm to act for both clients of the previous firms. However, in practice, the difficulties in maintaining the requisite separation, and the risk of embarrassment and impropriety, must be so great as to mean that the new firm can virtually never act for both and invariably not in litigation. A heavy onus would be on the amalgamated firm to displace the *prima facie* pragmatic prohibition.

9.   Solicitors should always have in mind the likelihood of an actual conflict arising at a later stage, despite the erection of a wall; and the greater detriment to the client of a resulting later withdrawal must be borne in mind.

10.   The court, under its inherent jurisdiction to supervise the conduct of its officers, can order a solicitor to cease acting and (R.S.C., Order 62, Rule 8) can order a solicitor to pay to his or her client or another party any costs unreasonably incurred as a result of acting improperly.

May 1987

Annex 15B

Guidance — examples of offices and appointments where solicitors should decline to act

1. Solicitors exercising judicial functions in the Crown Court or County Court

The Lord Chancellor has directed that a solicitor who is a recorder or an assistant recorder shall not appear personally as an advocate in any criminal court within seven days of the end of any period in which he or she has sat there as a recorder or an assistant recorder. Further a solicitor must not sit as a recorder or an assistant recorder in a court before which he or she or a partner or an employee regularly practises. The same direction applies to a solicitor sitting as a deputy judge or deputy registrar in a County Court. 'Court' in this context refers to the Crown Court or County Court for the geographical area in which the solicitor concerned or his or her partner or firm regularly practises, and not to the Crown or County Court in a national sense.

2. Justices and Clerks to Justices

Section 38 of the Solicitors Act 1974 governs the position of solicitors who are Justices of the Peace. Section 38 provides that a solicitor who is a JP in a particular area, or (where the area is divided into petty sessional divisions) a particular petty sessional division, cannot act in connection with proceedings before Justices in that particular area or petty sessional division. The restrictions on acting also apply to the solicitor JP's partners.

This restriction only applies where the solicitor JP exercises his or her functions as a Justice; consequently where the solicitor's name appears in the supplemental list (kept under section 8 of the Justices of the Peace Act 1979), the restriction on acting will not apply to the solicitor or any partner.

The Council take the view that section 38 should be deemed to apply not only to a solicitor who is a Justice of the Peace but also to a solicitor who is a Clerk to the Justices or his or her Deputy Clerk and to any partner, assistant solicitor or other employee in the firm.

3. Industrial tribunals

A solicitor who is a part-time chairman of an industrial tribunal must not appear as an advocate before a tribunal in the region in which the solicitor sits as a chairman. Further, he or she should not appear as an advocate on an appeal from an industrial tribunal in the region in which the solicitor sits as chairman, to the Employment Appeals Tribunal or to a court.

4.   Gaming Board

Following discussions with the Home Office in 1971, the Law Society reached an understanding whereby a solicitor who is a member of the Gaming Board or any partner or employee shall not act in connection with any application made to the Board, nor should the solicitor or any partner or employee act in any subsequent or consequential licensing applications in which the Board has an interest.

5.   Coroners

A solicitor who is a coroner or deputy or assistant deputy coroner must not appear on behalf of a client before a coroner's court for the area or district for which he or she is appointed.

A solicitor who is a coroner or deputy or assistant deputy coroner or any partner or employee of the solicitor must not act professionally in any civil or criminal proceedings resulting from a death where such a solicitor has held an inquest into the circumstances of such death. Further, since the coroner acts in a judicial capacity, a solicitor who is a coroner, deputy or assistant deputy coroner must make arrangements for another person to carry out an inquest into the death of a person where it might be thought that some bias could arise out of his or her personal or professional connection with the deceased or with a near relative of the deceased.

6.   Police authority

A solicitor who is a member of a police authority should not appear as an advocate in police prosecutions in that authority's area.

7.   Legal Aid Committees

A solicitor member of an Area Legal Aid Committee may act (or continue to act) for the applicant in a case coming before that Committee, provided he or she declares an interest in the case and withdraws from the adjudication.

Where a solicitor has adjudicated on an application submitted to a Legal Aid Committee, he or she must not act or continue to act for the opponent of the applicant. Even if the solicitor does not remember details of the case, it would be undesirable for him or her to act. Adjudication by a member of a Legal Aid Committee should not inhibit the solicitor's partners or other members of the firm dealing with the matter.

8.   Criminal Injuries Compensation Board

Firms in which a member of the Criminal Injuries Compensation Board is a partner or employee should not accept instructions to act before the Board.

Chapter 16

Confidentiality

16.01 General duty

Principle

A solicitor is under a duty to keep confidential to his or her firm the affairs of clients and to ensure that the staff do the same.

Commentary

1. In any discussion of the solicitor's duty to keep clients' affairs confidential, it is important to bear in mind the distinction between such duty in conduct and the concept of law known as client's legal privilege. The duty in conduct extends to all matters communicated to a solicitor by the client, save as mentioned in the Commentaries to Principles 16.03 and 16.04. Legal privilege protects communication between a client and solicitor from being disclosed, even in a court of law. There are, however, certain communications which are not protected by legal privilege and reference should be made to an appropriate authority on the law of evidence. Such non-privileged communications remain subject to the solicitor's duty to keep the client's affairs confidential until a court orders disclosure.

2. Unauthorised disclosure of a client's confidences could lead to disciplinary proceedings against a solicitor and could also render a solicitor liable, in certain circumstances, to a civil action by the client arising out of the misuse of confidential information.

3. The duty extends to the disclosure of the contents of a will after the death of the testator. Where a solicitor has acted in drawing up the will, information about its contents should not, before probate is granted, be disclosed except to, or with the consent of, the executors.

4. Whether a solicitor should disclose the contents of a will during the testator's lifetime to the donee of a power of attorney granted by the testator, will depend upon the extent to which the power of attorney enables the donee to stand in the place of the testator. Where there is an ordinary power of attorney in force it should be possible to obtain the

donor's consent as he or she will have mental capacity. An enduring power of attorney will not be effective following incapacity until it is registered. Once registered, if the power is silent on the subject of disclosure, it is necessary to obtain a decision from the Court of Protection as to whether the will can be disclosed.

5.   When acting for two or more clients jointly, information communicated to a solicitor in the capacity of solicitor acting for only one of the clients in a separate matter must not be disclosed to the other clients without the consent of that one client.

6.   Where two or more firms amalgamate, information which each firm has obtained when acting for its clients will pass to the new firm as a result of any express or implied retainer of the new firm. In this situation conflicts of interest could arise from the competing duties of confidentiality and disclosure. For conflicts of interest see Chapter 15; for Chinese walls see Annex 15A.

7.   Problems with confidentiality can arise where more than one solicitor or firm share office services, computers or other equipment or use a common typing agency. Solicitors should only make use of these where strict confidentiality of client matters can be ensured.

8.   A solicitor should not sell book debts to a factoring company because of the special confidential nature of a solicitor's bill and the danger of breaches of confidence which might occur. Such factoring might also lead to a breach of Rule 7 of the Solicitors' Practice Rules 1990 (see Annex 1A).

9.   Where a solicitor sends postcards to acknowledge receipt of communications, care must be taken to ensure that no confidential information of any kind appears on them. The use of open postcards should be discouraged since it is preferable to use cards which can be folded and sealed, or secured in some other way.

16.02   Source of information

Principle

The duty to keep confidential information about a client and his or her affairs applies irrespective of the source of the information.

16.03   Confidentiality lasts forever

Principle

The duty to keep confidential a client's business continues until the client permits disclosure or waives the confidentiality.

Commentary

1. The duty is not determined by the end of the retainer, nor by the conclusion of the particular matter on which the solicitor or the firm were engaged nor by the death of the client.

2. Following the death of the client the right to confidentiality passes to the personal representatives of the client and can only be waived by them.

3. Where a solicitor is in possession of information received from joint clients, the consent of both clients is required to waive the duty of confidentiality.

16.04   Circumstances which override confidentiality

Principle

The duty to keep a client's confidences can be overridden in certain exceptional circumstances.

Commentary

1. Communications made by a client to the solicitor before the commission of a crime for the purpose of being guided or helped in the commission of it are not confidential since such communications do not come within the ordinary scope of the professional retainer.

2. Express consent by a client to disclosure of information relating to his or her affairs overrides any duty of confidentiality, as does consent by the personal representatives of a deceased client.

3. There may be certain exceptional circumstances involving children where a solicitor should consider revealing confidential information to an appropriate authority. This may be in situations where the child is the client and the child reveals information which indicates continuing sexual or other physical abuse but is refusing to allow disclosure of such information. Similarly, there may be situations where an adult discloses abuse either by himself or herself or by another adult against a child but is

refusing to allow any disclosure. The solicitor must consider carefully whether the threat to the child's life or health, both mental and physical, is sufficiently serious to justify a breach of the duty of confidentiality. For additional guidance see Annex 16B.

4. A solicitor should reveal matters which are otherwise subject to the duty to preserve confidentiality where a court orders that such matters are to be disclosed or where a warrant permits a police officer or other authority to seize confidential documents. If a solicitor is of the opinion that the documents are subject to legal privilege or that for some other reason the order or warrant ought not to have been made or issued, he or she should discuss with the client the possibility of making an application to have the order or warrant set aside without unlawfully obstructing its execution. The solicitor may also seek the advice of the Professional Adviser.

5. Occasionally, a solicitor is asked by the police to give information or to show them documents which the solicitor has obtained when acting for a client. Unless the client is prepared to waive confidentiality, or where the solicitor has been used by the client to perpetrate fraud or other criminal purpose and the duty of confidence does not arise, the solicitor should insist upon receiving a witness summons or subpoena so that, where appropriate, privilege may be claimed and the court asked to decide the issue. If the request is made by the police under the terms of the Police and Criminal Evidence Act 1984 then, again, the solicitor should, where appropriate, leave the question of privilege to the court to decide on the particular circumstances. Advice may be obtained from the Professional Adviser.

6. Certain communciations from a client are not confidential if they are a matter of public record. For example, the fact that a solicitor has been instructed by a named client in connection with contentious business for which that client's name is on the public record is not confidential, but the type of business involved will usually be subject to the duty of confidentiality.

7. In the case of a legally aided client, a solicitor may, in certain circumstances, be under a duty to report to the Legal Aid Board information concerning the client which is confidential and privileged. See regulations 67 and 70 of the Civil Legal Aid (General) Regulations 1989 and Principle 5.04.

8. A solicitor may reveal confidential information concerning the client to the extent that it is reasonably necessary to establish a defence to a criminal charge or civil claim against the solicitor or where the solicitor's conduct is under investigation by the Solicitors Complaints Bureau or the Solicitors' Disciplinary Tribunal.

9. Under section 24 of the Drug Trafficking Offences Act 1986 and section 12 of the Prevention of Terrorism (Temporary Provisions) Act 1989 a solicitor may in certain circumstances, notwithstanding the duty of

confidentiality, disclose to the police a suspicion or belief that certain monies are derived from or used in connection with drug trafficking or that certain money or property is or is derived from terrorist funds and, in certain circumstances, such disclosure may prevent the solicitor from committing an offence under these provisions. Advice may be obtained from the Professional Adviser.

10. Under section 18 of the Prevention of Terrorism (Temporary Provisions) Act 1989 it is an offence for a person who has certain information about acts of terrorism to fail without reasonable excuse to disclose that information. The Law Society takes the view that, in the light of the reasonable excuse defence, a solicitor is not obliged to disclose confidential or privileged information under this provision other than in wholly exceptional circumstances.

11. Difficulties often arise in relation to a solicitor's duties when a client becomes insolvent. Upon the liquidation or receivership of a company client, authority is vested in the liquidator or administrative receiver who is entitled to information and documents relating to the company and can authorise disclosures to others. If the solicitor has also acted for directors or shareholders in their personal matters, care must be taken to ensure that confidentiality in respect of such personal matters is maintained.

12. The position is more difficult in relation to a client against whom a bankruptcy order has been made. The Insolvency Act 1986 has made considerable changes in the law but most of the Act has not yet been the subject of judicial interpretation. In the absence of such judicial guidance the Professional Adviser offers the following advice. Section 312(3) of the Insolvency Act 1986 places a solicitor under an obligation to deliver up to the trustee papers belonging to the bankrupt and, under section 311, this includes privileged communications. It is a contempt of court for any person without reasonable excuse to decline to hand over papers (section 312(4)). Solicitors should draw their clients' attention to the series of sections starting from section 351 which create bankruptcy offences. For example, under section 353 a bankrupt is guilty of an offence if he or she does not, to the best of his or her knowledge and belief, disclose all the property comprised in his or her estate to the Official Receiver or trustee. Aiding and abetting any of these offences would equally be an offence. A solicitor is not obliged by any of these sections to hand over to the Official Receiver or trustee those papers on the solicitor's file which belong to the solicitor and not to the client. However, the Official Receiver or trustee can, under section 366, apply to the court for an order that any person appearing to the court to be able to give information concerning the bankrupt or his or her affairs should give an account of his or her dealings with the bankrupt or produce any documents in his or her possession. A solicitor who, without good reason, obliges the Official Receiver or trustee to resort to section 366 might be ordered to pay costs.

16.05 Client's address

Principle

A solicitor must not disclose a client's address without the client's consent.

Commentary

Where a solicitor is asked for the client's address, the solicitor may, as a matter of courtesy, offer to send on to the client a letter from the enquirer addressed to the client, care of the solicitor.

16.06 Duty not to profit

Principle

A solicitor must not make any profit by the use of confidential information for his or her own purposes.

Commentary

In such circumstances a solicitor may be liable to civil action by the client in an action for account and could also be liable to disciplinary proceedings or, in some cases, criminal proceedings. See also Principle 15.06.

16.07 Duty to disclose all relevant information to client

Principle

A solicitor is usually under a duty to pass on to the client and use all information which is material to the client's business regardless of the source of that information. There are, however, exceptional circumstances where such duty does not apply.

Commentary

1. A breach of this duty may well be actionable in law in certain circumstances and might involve the solicitor in disciplinary action.

2. In general terms, since the solicitor is the agent of the client, all information coming into his or her possession relating to the client's affairs

must be disclosed to the client. Consequently, it is undesirable that a solicitor should seek to pass on to the solicitor on the other side information which is not to be disclosed to the other side's client. Equally, the recipient should decline to accept or receive confidential information on the basis that it will not be disclosed. If such a confidential letter is written to the solicitor on the other side, the writer cannot insist on such letter not being shown to the client. When offered information from another solicitor or any other source, which the solicitor is asked to treat as confidential and not to disclose to the client, the solicitor should consider carefully before accepting such confidential information.

3. There might, however, be certain circumstances where the imparting to the client of information received by the solicitor could be harmful to the client because it will affect the client's mental or physical condition. Consequently, it will be necessary for a solicitor to decide whether to disclose such information to the client, e.g. a medical report disclosing a terminal illness.

4. A solicitor should not seek to obtain access to or information from private correspondence or documents belonging to or intended for the other side. This includes not opening or reading letters addressed to someone other than himself or herself or the firm. If, however, the contents of such documents otherwise come to the solicitor's knowledge (and other than in circumstances described in Commentaries 5 and 6 below), the solicitor is entitled and may have a duty to use the information for the benefit of the client. The intention to do so should, however, be disclosed to the other side.

5. Where it is obvious that privileged documents have been mistakenly disclosed to a solicitor on discovery or otherwise, the solicitor should immediately cease to read the documents, inform the other side and return the documents. Before informing the other side the solicitor should consider whether to obtain instructions from the client, and if deciding to do so should advise the client that the court will probably grant an injunction to prevent the overt use of any information gleaned from the documents and that both the client and the solicitor might find costs awarded against them in respect of such an injunction (see *English and American Insurance Company Ltd* v. *Herbert Smith* [1988] F.S.R. 232).

6. Where a solicitor comes into possession of information relating to state security or intelligence matters to which the Official Secrets Act 1989 applies, and which is pertinent to a client's affairs, the solicitor should not disclose such information to the client without lawful authority unless satisfied that the information was itself disclosed by someone with lawful authority to do so. Section 5 of the Official Secrets Act 1989 makes such disclosure a criminal offence where the disclosure will be 'damaging' within the terms of the Act. It is unclear as yet what is meant by lawful authority, although that term obviously includes the authority of the

appropriate government department. Advice may be obtained from the Professional Adviser.

7. Where, in relation to a drug trafficking or terrorist investigation, certain orders or warrants have been applied for, made or issued, it is an offence for a person to make any disclosure which is likely to prejudice the investigation (see section 31 of the Drug Trafficking Offences Act 1986 and section 17 of the Prevention of Terrorism (Temporary Provisions) Act 1989). These statutes provide a defence of reasonable excuse. There are doubts as to whether the solicitor-client relationship provides a 'reasonable excuse' for a solicitor, in order to obtain instructions, to inform the client of an order or warrant and, until there is clear authority on this point it would be prudent for a solicitor not to disclose to the client that an order or warrant has been applied for, made or issued unless the solicitor has ascertained that the investigating authorities have no serious objection. Advice may be obtained from the Professional Adviser. It should be noted that at the time of going to print new guidance in relation to drug trafficking and terrorist investigation is anticipated shortly in the light of the EC Directive on money laundering and the Criminal Justice Bill.

8. A solicitor who acts for borrower and lender in the same transaction should bear in mind that two separate retainers are involved and that if the borrower does not consent to relevant facts being brought to the attention of the lender, the solicitor must honour the duty of confidentiality to the borrower. Should that situation arise, however, the solicitor will be faced with a conflict of interests and must cease to act for the lender and probably also the borrower (see Principle 15.03). For cases where there is, or may be, mortgage fraud see Commentaries 1 and 5; Annex 24M contains the Society's 'Green Card' warning on mortgage fraud and Annex 24L contains guidance on a solicitor's duty in conduct when acting for a lender and borrower when there is some variation in the purchase price.

Annex 16A

Guidance — Police and Criminal Evidence Act 1984 — production orders and client confidentiality

It is usually solicitors concerned in non-contentious matters who find themselves a party to an application by the police under section 9 of and Schedule 1 to the Police and Criminal Evidence Act 1984 for a production order. Such solicitors are not at ease with criminal matters and will frequently telephone the Law Society for advice. Most criminal law practitioners have already got to grips with this part of the Act, but just in case there are any of you out there who have been fortunate enough not to be involved in such an application, here is some advice on the professional conduct issues to be considered when an application is received.

The Guide at Chapter 16 deals with the solicitor's duty to keep confidential to his or her firm the affairs of clients. But what exactly should a solicitor do when served with a notice of application for a production order?

The solicitor should remember that he/she is the party to the application, the client is not a party and has no locus in the matter. However, the solicitor must inform the client of the existence of the notice of application; a solicitor is under a professional duty to keep the client properly informed of matters affecting the client's affairs (Principle 12.15 of the Guide). The solicitor should seek instructions from the client as to whether or not the client would like the application to be opposed. However, as the client is not a party to the proceedings, the solicitor is not under any obligation to oppose the application unless and until he/she is put in funds by the client to do so.

Once the production order is made and served upon a solicitor, the solicitor must comply with the order, unless there is a clear error on the face of the order or the solicitor has instructions and funds to appeal against the terms of the order. (In *Barclays Bank Plc* v. *Taylor; Trustee Savings Bank of Wales and Border Counties* v. *Taylor* [1989] 1 W.L.R. 1066, the Court of Appeal reminded the banks in these cases relating to production orders under PACE, that the banks must comply with the terms of a production order because a court order which is valid on its face is fully effective and demands compliance, unless or until it is set aside by due process of law.)

However, the solicitor should scrutinise the terms of the order very carefully. If the order contains words which exclude from production items subject to legal professional privilege, the solicitor must consider what items he or she has on the file which would come within that definition. There is a difference between items which are subject to legal professional privilege on a contentious file and those which are subject to legal professional privilege on a non-contentious file. If, however, the order is silent as to the exclusion of items subject to legal privilege, the whole of the file and other documents listed in the production order must be disclosed. This is because the judge hearing the application is under a duty to consider whether all of the access conditions in Schedule 1 to PACE have been fulfilled. Amongst other matters, the judge must consider whether or not there are items or materials subject to legal professional privilege. To assist in those deliberations, the judge will have considered section 10 of PACE where at sub-section 2 it is clear that 'items held with the intention of furthering a criminal purpose are not items subject to legal privilege'. (See also *R*. v. *Central Criminal Court ex p. Francis & Francis* [1988] 3 All E.R. 775.)

If in doubt at any time, you can always telephone the Professional Adviser for further advice (tel: 071-242 1222).

May 1991 (revised January 1993)

Annex 16B

Guidance — confidentiality and privilege — child abuse and abduction

The following guidance has been produced by the Standards and Guidance Committee and the Family Law Committee and is a revised version of the guidance on confidentiality and privilege in cases of child abuse and abduction originally produced by the Family Law Committee in September 1987.

The guidance has been revised in the light of problems encountered by practitioners. Typically, the solicitor has either received information from a client, or is about to receive information from a client, which he or she considers privileged, but which, if given to the court, police or social services, might protect the child or children at risk.

This guidance attempts to set out some general principles to which a practitioner should have regard and considers how these are affected depending on who is the client. The guidance gives examples of how certain situations might be dealt with as well as giving suggestions of bodies which may be able to give further help.

(A) General principles

1. The Committees take the view that child abduction is merely one example of child abuse and therefore any guidance given applies equally to cases of abuse and abduction.

2. A solicitor has two basic duties to a client whether parent or child:

   (a) the duty to act in the best interests of his or her client; and

   (b) the duty of confidentiality.

(a) The duty to act in the client's best interests

Clearly the nature of this duty depends on who is the client. In considering the duty to act in the client's best interests the solicitor will need to draw a distinction between those children who are competent to give instructions and those who are not. A child who is competent to give instructions should be represented in accordance with those instructions. If a child is not competent to give instructions the solicitor should act in the child's best interests.

(b)   The duty of confidentiality

A number of preliminary points can be made *before* considering how the situation is affected by the question of who is the client:

(i)   Is the information confidential?

It has been held at common law that when communications are made by a client to his or her solicitor before the commission of a crime, for the purpose of being guided or helped in the commission of it, this constitutes a move outside the solicitor/client relationship and any communications made are not confidential and the solicitor is free to pass them on to a third party. The solicitor will therefore need to consider whether or not the proposed action is in fact a crime and reference should be made to the appropriate provisions, e.g. the common law offence of kidnapping or the provisions of the Child Abduction Act 1984 and the Child Abduction and Custody Act 1985 and provisions relating to child abuse.

(ii)   Assuming that the information received is confidential, which will usually be the case, a solicitor also has a duty to the *court* (as opposed to the client). As a result the solicitor may still be ordered by the court to disclose the information — for instance in a wardship case — see *Ramsbotham* v. *Senior (*1869) L.R. 8 Eq. 575 (*Rayden and Jackson on Divorce and Family Matters,* 16th edition, Butterworths, para. 44.47). In all cases it is the solicitor's duty not to mislead the court. (See Chapter 22 of the Guide.)

(iii)   In circumstances other than those outlined above the Committees are in favour of the principle of absolute confidentiality being maintained save in truly exceptional circumstances. Any solicitor considering the disclosure of confidential information should bear in mind that he or she is bound by a *duty* of confidentiality and may only be entitled to depart from this duty in exceptional circumstances.

In considering what might constitute exceptional circumstances a solicitor must consider what would be in the public interest. There is a public interest in maintaining the duty of confidentiality. Without this the public interest in being able to confide in professional advisers would be harmed and the duty of confidentiality would be brought into disrepute. There is also a public interest in protecting children at risk from serious harm. Only in cases where the solicitor believes that the public interest in protecting children at risk outweighs the public interest in maintaining the duty of confidentiality does the solicitor have a discretion to disclose confidential information.

It may be that a parallel can be drawn with the case of *W.* v. *Egdell* [1990] 1 All E.R. 835. In this case a consultant psychologist felt obliged to reveal his report showing that W, if released from a secure hospital, was likely to commit further murders. It was held that although the duty of confidentiality should rarely be breached it is sometimes essential for a balancing act to be carried out to determine whether greater public interest lies in revealing the information or in maintaining the duty of confidentiality. A similar test was applied in *Re M.* [1990] 20 Fam. Law 259.

(iv)   If a solicitor, having considered the arguments set out above, feels that he or she may be entitled to disclose confidential information he or she should, in addition, consider the following points:

(a)   Is there any other way of remedying the situation other than revealing the information? If so, thought should be given as to whether this course would have the desired effect of protecting the child and if so whether it should be taken.

(b)   If the information is or is not disclosed will the solicitor involved be able to justify his or her actions if called upon to do so by the court or Solicitors Complaints Bureau? Before revealing any information a junior solicitor or member of the solicitor's staff should always consult with his or her principal on the appropriate course of action to take.

(B)   Who is the client?

Five different situations have been considered.

(i)   An adult

(a)   An adult (parent or otherwise) who is not an abuser but is asserting that a third party is abusing a child.

In this situation a solicitor's duty to act in the best interests of his or her client might entail suggesting that the client alerts a relevant agency, e.g. police or Social Services Department, himself or herself or accepting instructions to do so. If the client does not wish to alert a relevant agency or does not give the solicitor instructions to do so the solicitor must accept the client's decision and may remain bound by the duty of confidentiality. A solicitor in this position should explain the legal position and can seek to persuade the client to disclose the abuse or allow the solicitor to do so. If the client refuses to follow either of these courses of action the solicitor may still exercise his or her discretion and reveal the information. This will only be the case if the public interest in revealing the information outweighs that of keeping it confidential.

(b)   An adult who is abusing or the solicitor believes will abuse a child.

Where the client is an abuser or potential abuser it becomes necessary to consider not only the duty to act in the client's best interests and the duty of confidentiality but also whether or not any distinction should be made between continuing and future abuse and how and when a solicitor should explain his duty of confidentiality and any possible limitations to it.

Where a client is continuing to commit an offence or is proposing to commit an offence, the duty to act in the client's best interests means that a solicitor should explain the legal implications of what a client has done, is doing or is proposing to do. For example, a client who tells a solicitor that he or she has or is proposing to abduct a child should be told about the common law offence of kidnapping, the provisions of the Child Abduction Act 1984, the Child Abduction and Custody Act 1985 and the client's duty to obey orders of the court, if there are any which are relevant. Similar steps should be taken in relation to cases of child abuse.

In the case of future abuse if, after receiving the solicitor's advice on the legal position, the client is dissuaded from his or her criminal course of action the solicitor's duty of confidentiality is absolute. In the case of a continuing offence, which as a result of the advice then ceases, this is equally the case.

In the case of a continuing crime which does not cease as a result of the advice given, or a future crime which the solicitor understands from the client may or will take place, the solicitor must then go on to consider whether or not it is justifiable to breach his or her duty of confidentiality bearing in mind the guidance set out above (see (A)2(b)(i) and (iii)). In addition, it may be appropriate for the solicitor to point out that he or she has a discretion to inform a third party of the offence that is being, may be, or will be committed.

(c) An adult who has been abused or is being abused.

As above, where the client is an adult who has been or is being abused, the duty to act in the client's best interests would entail outlining the legal position and suggesting where the client, or the solicitor on the client's behalf, could go for help. A solicitor in these circumstances is absolutely bound by the duty of confidentiality to the client but it is always permissible to try to persuade the client to reveal the abuse.

(ii) A child who is being abused

The extent of a solicitor's potential entitlement to breach the duty of confidentiality will depend on whether the child is mature or immature. It will often be difficult for a solicitor to judge the maturity of a child and the solicitor will need to make a judgment on the basis of the child's understanding. Reference should be made to the principles in *Gillick* v. *West Norfolk and Wisbech Area Health Authority and the DHSS* [1986] A.C. 112, subsequent case law and the Children Act 1989. In difficult cases it may be appropriate for a solicitor to approach a third party with knowledge of the child and expertise in this area, for instance, the guardian ad litem involved in the case (if any). A solicitor should never breach the duty of confidentiality unless he or she strongly suspects or knows that abuse has taken, is taking, or will take place.

(d) A mature child who is being abused.

Where a mature child is the client the guidance in (c) above applies except that a solicitor may have a discretion to breach the duty of confidentiality where he or she knows or strongly suspects that younger siblings are being abused or where the child is in fear of his or her life or of serious injury.

(e) An immature child who is being abused.

Where an immature child is the client the solicitor's duty is as in (c) above in relation to doing the best for the client. A solicitor can try to persuade the client to reveal the abuse. If the client refuses the solicitor is not absolutely bound by the duty of confidentiality and may feel, bearing the above arguments in mind, that he or she is entitled to disclose what the child has told him or her to a third party. This should only be done if it is in the public interest and there is no other less oppressive method of dealing with the situation (such as a guardian ad litem disclosing the abuse — see example 3 below).

Where the client is an immature child the solicitor may need to consider whether or not he or she should reveal any disclosures to the child's parents. It may be that a disclosure of information to another third party such as the police or social services would best serve the interests of the client.

(C) The decision to disclose and possible consequences

Any client whether child or adult has a right to be made aware of when and in what circumstances the solicitor's duty of confidentiality may be breached. The decision of when and how to tell the client of the solicitor's decision will clearly be a difficult one although it is thought to be preferable to make the position clear during the first interview. This will present the solicitor with a dilemma — if he or she fails to disclose the abuse he or she will not be in a position to help protect the child from further abuse. On the other hand, if the solicitor tells the child he or she may breach the duty of confidentiality there is a risk that further disclosures will not be forthcoming from the child. Despite this if a solicitor is about to breach his or her duty of confidentiality there is a high expectation that the solicitor will tell the client of his or her decision and explore with the client how this should be done. However, in the end it is for the solicitor to exercise his or her professional judgement about when and how to explain the duty of confidentiality to any client; it is impossible to formulate a rule that can be applied in all circumstances.

Any solicitor who tells the client that the solicitor will breach the duty of confidentiality should inform the client that the client is entitled to terminate the solicitor's retainer if such disclosure is contrary to the client's wishes. However, it is almost inevitable that the breaching of the duty of confidentiality by the solicitor will cause the client to terminate the solicitor's retainer whether or not the client is informed by the solicitor of his or her intentions. Upon the termination of the retainer the duty of confidentiality still remains, subject to the solicitor being able to justify a breach of the duty in the exceptional circumstances referred to in section (A)2(b)(iii) above.

(D) Working examples

The illustrative examples given below set out four situations in which a solicitor needs to consider whether or not her duty of confidentiality should be breached. These examples have been drafted on the basis of the law before the implementation of the Children Act 1989. Nevertheless, it is hoped that they will be of assistance to solicitors.

Jane Potter is a solicitor in private practice. She does general family work and some criminal law work. She has four matters where she is concerned that the children involved may be at risk of harm. She does not know who to tell, or whether indeed she can tell anyone of her concerns. These are her problems and the advice that was given her by the Professional Ethics Division and Professional Adviser.

1.   Jane is acting for the mother of a child who has recently been made a ward of court. After becoming a ward of court the child continued to reside with the mother. Accommodation for the mother and child is in itself a cause for concern, being a hostel for homeless persons. The rest of the accommodation is shared with a number of other adults. The mother has come to see Jane and tells her that the child is subject to abuse by another adult in the house. The mother does not want this information to be made known to anyone else as she is fearful that the child will be taken away, particularly as the child is already a ward of court.

    Jane is under a duty of confidentiality to her client which means that any information given to her cannot be passed on to another without the consent of the client. Jane should strongly advise the client to reveal the abuse and discuss with the client the options that are open to her of expressing her concerns to social services and seeking alternative accommodation; of social services encouraging the local authority to remove the alleged abuser from the hostel; and of reporting her suspicions to the police.

Jane is in the very difficult position of having to decide whether her duty of confidentiality towards the mother is outweighed by the public interest in the reporting of the abuse. Jane must explore very carefully the basis of the mother's allegations to be satisfied that they are true. She must also explore the nature of the abuse to the child. Jane should look at the terms of any order made in the wardship proceedings to see if there are any matters which must by order be reported to the court. It is for Jane to decide on all the evidence whether there is a strong case for believing that the child will suffer serious abuse such as will outweigh her duty of confidentiality towards her client.

2.   Jane is acting for a young man who is charged in the local magistrates' court of an offence of indecent assault upon a young child. The client has admitted the offence to Jane, and in the course of interview has indicated to Jane that he has committed more offences than the police know about. The client, however, is on bail, one condition being that he should not contact the child in question. One evening after working late Jane popped into the local McDonalds and saw her client seated at a table with the child. There was no other adult present. Jane did not know what to do and left the building.

Jane is not under any duty to inform the police of the breach of the bail conditions. No one is under any duty to report a suspicion of an offence. However, Jane must advise her client of the effect of his breaching his conditions of bail. She should seek to persuade her client not to repeat this breach. If there is no real evidence that the client was abusing the child, Jane should take no further action. If the client indicates to her that a further offence has taken place, Jane must try to assess whether there is a substantial risk of the child suffering significant harm in future from the client. If so, Jane may inform a third party and cease to act for her client if she is satisfied there is no other less oppressive way of dealing with the situation. If Jane believes that there is no serious risk of harm to the child, but the client indicates that he will continue to see the child, she is not under any duty to inform a third party of the breach. This case is difficult as the solicitor has the very onerous task of trying to establish whether the client is telling the truth or not. If the solicitor had evidence to suggest that the client was positively misleading her then it may be that she would have to cease acting because the solicitor–client relationship had broken down.

3.   Jane is also acting in care proceedings for a boy aged 12. The child has not been attending school and has been involved in solvent abuse. No guardian ad litem has been appointed to date. The child is living at home with his mother and his mother's boyfriend. Jane has seen the child on his own in order to ascertain if the child is old enough to give proper instructions and has decided that he is. In the course of the interview the child stated that the mother's boyfriend has sexually abused him on a number of occasions. The child is adamant that Jane should not reveal this allegation to anyone as he does not wish his mother to know.

Jane's discussions with the local authority reveal that the local authority intend that the child remain at home after a care order is made, as the local authority wish to 'work with the family'.

Jane should urge the court to appoint a guardian ad litem as soon as possible. With the help of the guardian ad litem Jane must try to assess the truth of the allegations made by the child. If the allegations are well founded the guardian ad litem would be able to reveal them as a guardian ad litem is an officer of the court and is not bound by a duty of confidentiality to the boy in the same way that Jane is. If the court refuses to appoint a guardian ad litem, Jane must decide what to do by reference to the principles set out earlier in this guidance. This is equally the case where a guardian ad litem is appointed but the child does not reveal the abuse to him or her — indeed the fact that the child does not reveal the abuse to the guardian ad litem may be a factor for Jane to consider in deciding how serious the abuse is and whether or not it should be revealed.

4.　　Jane's final problem is in a matrimonial case where she acts for the mother. The father has obtained a residence order in respect of the child. Jane has advised her client fully on the effect of the order in relation to removing the child from the U.K. Nevertheless her client has disappeared with the child and both are assumed to be out of the jurisdiction. Jane has received a telephone call from her client indicating that she wishes Jane to continue to act for her. Jane should of course advise her client to return to the jurisdiction and to return the child. Jane is not under any obligation to reveal the client's whereabouts, if she knows them, unless or until she is ordered to do so by the court. If there is no prospect of Jane being paid for continuing to act for the client, she can end the retainer. She is certainly under a duty to inform the legal aid authorities of her client's action; though not of her whereabouts, if her client is in receipt of a legal aid certificate.

Two weeks later Jane receives news that her client and the child are destitute, living on the proceeds of begging in the streets and sleeping rough. Jane is concerned that the child, who is three years old, could be in danger.

Jane is under no obligation to reveal the client's whereabouts. She must strongly advise her client to return to the jurisdiction for the sake of the child. If Jane is satisfied that the child is in serious danger she may breach her normal duty of confidentiality towards her client by making disclosure to the court of her client's whereabouts.

(E)　Bodies to contact

Child abduction

Official Solicitor's Department, 4th Floor, 81 Chancery Lane, London WC2A 1DD, telephone 071-911 7045/7047.

Foreign and Commonwealth Office, Consular Department, Clive House, Petty France, London SW1H 9HD, telephone 071-270 3000.

Passport Department, Home Office, Clive House, Petty France, London SW1H 9HD, telephone 071-271 8629.

'Reunite' National Council for Abducted Children, P.O. Box 158, London N4 1AU, telephone 071-404 8356.

The Police.

Child abuse

The Police.

Local authority Social Services Department.

The Children's Legal Centre, 20 Compton Terrace, London N1 2NU, telephone 071-359 9392.

NSPCC, 67 Saffron Hill, London EC1, telephone 071-242 1626.

Criminal Injuries Compensation Board, 19 Alfred Place, London WC1, telephone 071-636 9501.

September 1987 (revised September 1991 and updated January 1993)

Chapter 17

Proper standard of work

17.01 Care and skill

Principle

A solicitor is under a duty to carry out the terms of a retainer with care and skill, proper diligence and promptness and to keep the client properly informed.

Commentary

1. Rule 15 of the Solicitors' Practice Rules 1990 deals with certain aspects of client care, including the obligation to keep a client informed. See Chapter 13 for detailed commentary on the rule.

2. A solicitor should not accept instructions if he or she has insufficient time to devote to a matter, or insufficient experience or skill to deal with it competently. A solicitor may act if he or she is able to do so competently by, for example, instructing suitable counsel.

3. A solicitor who is in breach of a duty of care and who has caused loss to a client, or to some other person to whom that duty of care is owed, may be liable in damages.

4. A solicitor may limit the scope of the retainer before accepting instructions (see Principle 12.11).

5. However, under section 60(5) of the Solicitors Act 1974 a provision in a contentious business agreement that the solicitor shall not be liable for negligence or that he or she shall be relieved from any responsibility to which he or she would otherwise be subject as a solicitor, is void. For limitation of liability by contract in other cases, see Annex 12A.

6. Similarly a solicitor's duties in conduct cannot be excluded or limited by contract. A solicitor cannot exclude or restrict the right of the client or of any other person to make a complaint in respect of professional misconduct.

7. For details of a solicitor's obligations to notify claims to Solicitors

THE GUIDE TO THE PROFESSIONAL CONDUCT OF SOLICITORS 1993

Indemnity Fund Limited and to advise the client to seek independent
advice, see Principles 28.07 and 28.08.

Delay

8. The Society has statutory power, under section 35 of and Schedule 1 to the
    Solicitors Act 1974, to take over from the solicitor who is guilty of undue
    delay all the papers and money affected by a client's complaint and to
    deliver them to the client or to the client's new solicitor.

9. Where a solicitor is guilty of avoidable delay in either criminal or civil
    litigation, the court may exercise the powers which are available under
    section 19A of the Prosecution of Offences Act 1985, section 145A of the
    Magistrates' Courts Act 1980 and section 51(6) of the Supreme Court Act
    1981 to award 'wasted costs' against legal representatives. Further, where
    the solicitor is guilty of gross misconduct or gross negligence, he or she
    risks being penalised by the court under its inherent jurisdiction; if the
    action is struck out for want of prosecution, the solicitor may be ordered to
    pay costs and may also be involved in an action for damages.

Inadequate professional services (IPS)

10. The Solicitors Complaints Bureau has powers under section 37A of and
    Schedule 1A to the Solicitors Act 1974, to direct a solicitor to afford the
    client redress for IPS where the solicitor has provided services which are
    not of the quality which it is reasonable to expect. IPS covers a wider field
    than professional incompetence and includes organisational incompetence.
    An example of professional incompetence might be a case where a
    solicitor takes on work knowing that he or she is insufficiently experienced
    in that particular field to provide services of a satisfactory standard. An
    example of organisational incompetence would be where the solicitor is
    fully experienced to undertake the work but completes it in an
    unacceptably long period of time. While the solicitor's behaviour may fall
    short of negligence it may nevertheless be incompetent. For full details of
    the SCB's powers, see Chapter 30.

Misconduct

11. If a solicitor's acts or omissions are such as would reasonably be regarded
    as 'dishonourable' or 'deplorable' by other members of the profession, it
    would be open to the Solicitors' Disciplinary Tribunal to reach a finding of
    professional misconduct in respect of which disciplinary action may be
    taken. This is so even if the client suffers no loss and is thus unable to sue
    for damages.

17.02 Correspondence

Principle

A solicitor should deal promptly with correspondence relating to the matter of a client or a former client.

Commentary

1. A solicitor who fails to answer and deal with the issues raised in letters from a client or former client on that client's business, may be subject to disciplinary action.

2. Where a solicitor receives letters from third parties relating to the business of a client or former client, instructions should be sought from the client. Unless instructed to provide a substantive reply, failure to do so would not normally amount to professional misconduct. However, as a matter of courtesy the solicitor should acknowledge such letters and may add that he or she will not entertain any further correspondence.

3. For a solicitor's obligation to deal with other correspondence received from a third party, see Principle 18.01. The obligation to deal with letters received from the SCB is dealt with in paragraph 30.36 of Chapter 30.

PART IV — OBLIGATIONS TO OTHERS

Chapter 18

Relations with third parties

18.01 Fairness

Principle

Solicitors must not act, whether in their professional capacity or otherwise, towards anyone in a way which is fraudulent, deceitful or otherwise contrary to their position as solicitors. Nor must solicitors use their position as solicitors to take unfair advantage either for themselves or another person.

Commentary

1. When dealing and corresponding with an unrepresented third party a solicitor must take particular care to ensure that no retainer arises by implication between the solicitor and the third party.

2. In non-contentious matters, a solicitor may be instructed by a client and be aware of the name and address of the other party, but not of the other party's solicitor. The normal practice is for the solicitor to write to the other party asking to be put in touch with his or her solicitor.

3. Where a solicitor is dealing with an unrepresented third party, any draft document sent to the solicitor should be amended if it contains errors which could be put right by a reasonable amount of correction, provided that it is in his or her own client's interests to do so. If it is so badly drawn as to be inappropriate, there is no objection to returning it to the lay party and advising that a solicitor should be consulted on its preparation.

4. When giving a reference as to character and financial standing, a solicitor must take care to give one that is true. A solicitor may be guilty of unbefitting conduct and may incur a potential liability where a false or

misleading reference is given. The same principle applies where a solicitor makes or corroborates a statement on an application by another person for a passport.

5.   It is unbefitting conduct for a solicitor to write offensive letters to third parties. The same principle applies to offensive behaviour, and advocating breaking the law. Such conduct is likely to be in breach of Rule 1 of the Solicitors' Practice Rules 1990 and could bring the profession into disrepute. (With regard to offensive letters written to other solicitors see Principle 20.01.)

6.   Where a solicitor receives a letter which asks for a reply from persons who are not clients and to whom no professional duty is owed or a letter which does not relate to the business of a client or former client, failure to reply does not normally amount to professional misconduct. As a matter of courtesy the solicitor should acknowledge such letters.

7.   As to a solicitor's duty to pay professional, non-lawyer or other agents' fees or witness expenses, see Principles 21.01 and 21.02.

18.02   Stopping client account cheques

Principle

To stop a client account cheque is not inevitably professional misconduct, but may be if notice of intention to stop the cheque is not given promptly and effectively to the recipient.

Commentary

1.   For the purpose of this Principle notice will be 'prompt and effective' if it is received before the recipient has committed himself or herself to an action which was reasonably foreseeable by the giver as likely to follow the receipt of the cheque, e.g. effecting exchange of contracts.

2.   Where the recipient of the cheque is another solicitor who has paid it into his or her client account it is open to the giver to place a stop even where the solicitor has not awaited clearance before accounting to the client.

3.   This Principle does not affect any action in law which the recipient may have if the cheque is stopped.

18.03   Agreeing costs with another party

Principle

When stipulating, as a term of any settlement or agreement between a client and another party, that costs should be paid by the other party, a solicitor should give the other party sufficient opportunity to agree those costs on an informed basis, or to apply for taxation.

Commentary

1.   This Principle addresses a practice, now considered improper, whereby in litigation a settlement would be negotiated on the basis that the defendant would pay the plaintiff's costs but the plaintiff declined to give any indication as to the breakdown of the figure sought and stipulated that there should be no taxation of the costs.

2.   A solicitor should not use a client's bargaining position to prevent agreement on costs being reached on a reasonably informed basis, nor must unfair advantage be taken of another party for the solicitor's own benefit by overcharging for work done or to be done. The solicitor should, if requested, be prepared to offer the other party a sufficient breakdown of how the costs are calculated.

3.   This Principle also applies in relation to non-contentious matters. For example, in the practice of a landlord or lender demanding an undertaking in respect of costs at the outset of a transaction. Solicitors who are requested to give undertakings are reminded of their professional obligations (see Chapter 19) and the need to consider carefully whether it is possible to comply with any undertaking given. A solicitor who requests an undertaking should give sufficient indication as to the basis of charging or an estimate of the amount, together in any case with a cap on the amount to be covered by the undertaking. This cap will not affect any right to charge the full amount of costs. As it relates only to the amount to be covered by the undertaking, a further undertaking may be sought if it subsequently appears that the cap will be exceeded.

18.04   Dealing with unqualified persons

Principle

If a solicitor discovers another party is represented by an unqualified person who is carrying out prohibited and unqualfied acts then, subject to the interests of the solicitor's own client, the proper course is to decline to communicate with the unqualified person.

Commentary

1. The provision of advocacy, litigation, probate and conveyancing services is limited to certain categories of persons by the Solicitors Act 1974, the Administration of Justice Act 1985 and the Courts and Legal Services Act 1990. (For guidance on dealing with unqualified conveyancers see Annex 24F.)

2. Solicitors are asked to report to the Law Society, Professional Adviser, any cases where it appears that an unqualified person has acted in breach of the law.

18.05   Letters before action

Principle

When writing a letter before action, a solicitor must not demand anything other than that recoverable under the due process of law.

Commentary

1. For example, where a solicitor is retained to collect a simple debt, he or she must not demand from the debtor the cost of the letter before action, since it cannot be said at the stage when the first letter is written, that such costs are legally recoverable.

2. Where a solicitor is instructed by a creditor to collect a debt, there is nothing improper in the solicitor communicating with the employer of the debtor in order to obtain information as to the debtor's status or means. A solicitor should not, however, use the threat of contacting the employer or the media as a means of obtaining payment. (As to a solicitor instructing an enquiry agent to enquire into the means of a debtor, see Principle 20.02.)

3. A solicitor must not seek to enforce a gaming debt, except in cases permitted by the Gaming Act.

18.06   Administering oaths

Principle

When administering oaths and affirmations or taking declarations, a solicitor is under a duty to ascertain:

(a) that the deponent is in the solicitor's presence, by enquiring whether the signature to the document before the solicitor is the name and in the handwriting of the deponent;

(b) that the deponent is apparently competent to depose to the affidavit or declaration;

(c) that the deponent knows he or she is about to be sworn or declared by the solicitor to the truth of the statement; and

(d) that the exhibits, if any, are the documents referred to.

Commentary

1. Only if the answers to the questions set out in the Principle are satisfactory may the oath be administered.

2. The Solicitors Act 1974, section 81 enables every solicitor holding a practising certificate to exercise the powers of a Commissioner for Oaths.

3. Section 113(10) of the Courts and Legal Services Act 1990, provides that every solicitor who holds a practising certificate (and certain other persons) has the right to use the title 'Commissioner for Oaths'.

4. The responsibility for the contents of the affidavit or declaration rests with the deponent and the solicitor who prepared it. There is a duty on the solicitor administering the oath to be satisfied that the oath is in a proper form and, upon the face of it, an oath which the solicitor is authorised to administer. If it comes to the solicitor's notice that the affidavit or declaration is incomplete, for example, because it contains blanks, the solicitor should refuse to administer it.

5. Although a solicitor is under no duty to read through the oath or declaration, if for some extraneous reason a solicitor has good reason to believe that the oath or declaration is false (even if that was unknown to the deponent), the solicitor must refuse to administer it.

6. It is improper for a solicitor to share any part of the fees received for administering the oath with any person, since the administration of oaths is a discharge of a public office.

18.07 Circumstances where an oath should not be administered

Principle

A solicitor should not administer oaths and affirmations nor take declarations in a proceeding in which the solicitor or the solicitor's firm is acting for any of the parties, or is otherwise interested.

Commentary

1. This Principle is contained in the Solicitors Act 1974, section 81(2) and a similar provision applies to Commissioners for Oaths by the Commissioners for Oaths Act 1889, section 1(3). It applies to both contentious and non-contentious matters.

2. Because the administering of oaths and affirmations and the taking of declarations involve the discharge of a public office, the Principle would, for example, prevent a solicitor from administering oaths and affirmations or taking declarations in the following circumstances :

    (a) a solicitor should not take affidavits and declarations relating to a local authority's business where the solicitor is a member or employee of that local authority;

    (b) a solicitor should not take affidavits regarding proofs in bankruptcy when acting for that proving creditor or regarding the winding-up of an estate when acting for the personal representative of the testator;

    (c) a solicitor who is employed part-time by another solicitor must not administer oaths for a client of his or her employer;

    (d) a solicitor who is in the full or part-time employment of a company ought not to administer oaths in matters in which the company is concerned.

3. It is not necessarily improper for a solicitor to administer an oath to his or her spouse, who is also a solicitor, arising out of a matter connected with that spouse's practice or employment as a solicitor. It should nevertheless be borne in mind that, whilst there is nothing inherently unprofessional in this, doubts may arise as to the impartiality of the solicitor administering the oath and this may lead to a challenge to the admissibility of the affidavit.

    On the other hand, section 81(2) of the Solicitors Act 1974 prevents a solicitor from administering an oath to his or her spouse (who may or may not be a solicitor) arising out of a matter personal to that spouse (for example, a claim for damages for personal injury suffered by that spouse) if, by reason of their personal relationship, it could be said that the solicitor administering the oath had an interest in the proceedings.

Chapter 19

Professional undertakings

19.01   Definition of undertaking

Principle

An undertaking is any unequivocal declaration of intention addressed to someone who reasonably places reliance on it and made by:

    (a)   a solicitor or a member of staff in the course of practice; or

    (b)   a solicitor as 'solicitor', but not in the course of practice

whereby the solicitor becomes personally bound.

Commentary

1.   A professional undertaking may be given orally or in writing and need not necessarily include the word 'undertake'.

2.   Although an oral undertaking has the same effect as a written one, there may be evidential problems as to its existence unless there is available a contemporaneous note, transcript or written confirmation of its terms. If the recipient confirms the terms of the oral undertaking and the giver does not promptly repudiate those terms, this is likely to be accepted by the Council as sufficient evidence of the existence and terms of the undertaking.

3.   A promise to give an undertaking at some future date will be treated by the Council as an undertaking, provided the promise sufficiently identifies the terms of the undertaking and provided any conditions precedent have been satisfied. If the promise refers to the 'usual undertaking', current practice will be taken into account, but the giving of such vague undertakings is discouraged.

4.   The Society's formulae for exchanging contracts and its code for completion by post embody undertakings (see Principle 24.09 and Annexes 24I and 24J). For forms of undertakings used in conveyancing, see Annexes 24G and 24H.

19.02   No obligation to give or accept

Principle

There is no obligation on a solicitor either to give or accept an undertaking.

Commentary

Although there is a duty to act in a client's best interests this does not imply a duty to assume or underwrite a client's financial or other obligations.

19.03   Performance outside solicitor's control

Principle

An undertaking is still binding even if it is to do something outside the solicitor's control.

Commentary

1. Solicitors must consider carefully whether they will be able to implement an undertaking before they give it. If there is a complaint of professional misconduct, it is no defence that the undertaking was to do something outside the solicitor's control (e.g. that it was dependent upon action being taken by a third party and that the action has not been taken) unless the undertaking was suitably qualified.

2. If an undertaking involves the payment of money, solicitors must decide whether they are able to give such an undertaking, since they can be required in conduct to discharge this out of their own and their partners' resources. If asked to give such an undertaking, a solicitor must consider all eventualities including the possibility of the client terminating the retainer or being made bankrupt; a client's bankruptcy will not discharge such an undertaking. Further, the client's trustee in bankruptcy may have a prior claim over the fund from which the solicitor has agreed to remit monies, as may a garnishee.

19.04 Indemnity

Principle

A solicitor who incurs loss which arises directly from a claim based on an undertaking given by the solicitor (or by a partner or member of staff) in the course of private practice may be entitled to an indemnity out of the Solicitors' Indemnity Fund.

Commentary

1. Although it is the solicitor giving the undertaking (or his or her firm) who is entitled to any indemnity which may be available under the Solicitors' Indemnity Rules, in practice Solicitors Indemnity Fund Limited would usually make payment to the person to whom money was due pursuant to the undertaking.

2. Even if cover is provided by the Indemnity Fund, this does not remove the possibility of disciplinary action for failure to honour the undertaking.

3. No cover is provided for a trading debt incurred by a practice or by any of its members, nor (in general) for an undertaking given in connection with the provision of finance, property, assistance or other advantage for the benefit of the solicitor or certain connected persons or organisations (see Rule 31.2(v) of the Solicitors' Indemnity Rules 1992 in Annex 28B). For these reasons:

   (a) where a solicitor borrows money on the basis of an undertaking to repay it, and the solicitor then re-lends the money to a client who subsequently defaults, the solicitor would have no cover from the Indemnity Fund;

   (b) there could likewise be circumstances where a solicitor would be without cover from the Indemnity Fund if an undertaking was given which amounted to a bare guarantee of the financial obligations of a client or third party.

19.05 Breach and misconduct

Principle

A solicitor who fails to honour a professional undertaking is *prima facie* guilty of professional misconduct. Consequently, the Council will expect its implementation as a matter of conduct.

Commentary

1. Neither the Council nor the Solicitors' Disciplinary Tribunal have power to order payment of compensation or to procure the specific performance of an undertaking if a solicitor declines to implement it. The only step open to the Council is to take disciplinary action for failure to honour the undertaking. See Chapters 30 and 31 for details of the disciplinary process.

2. The Council will expect undertakings to be honoured by solicitors for so long as their names remain on the roll and regardless of whether or not they hold practising certificates. It should be noted that the Tribunal has power to consider allegations against a former solicitor relating to a time when he or she was a solicitor.

3. The Council have no power to order the release of a solicitor from the terms of an undertaking. This is a matter for the Court, or the person entitled to the benefit of the undertaking.

4. In certain circumstances, the Council can give notice, on receipt of a request from the giver of an undertaking, that unless steps are taken within a specified time by the recipient of the undertaking, the Council will not thereafter entertain a complaint in respect of it. Such a request should be made in writing to the Solicitors Complaints Bureau. This would apply where the recipient of the undertaking is required to take some action, but has not done so.

5. Subject to Commentary 4, a solicitor cannot claim to be released from an undertaking on the basis that the recipient has been slow in drawing attention to the breach, although this is a matter to which the Council may have regard if a complaint is made.

6. The Council will not intervene where:

    (a) the undertaking has been procured by fraud, deceit or, in certain circumstances, by innocent misrepresentation; or

    (b) the performance of the undertaking turns on a disputed point of law.

19.06   Who is bound? — Who may complain?

Principle

Normally only the giver of an undertaking will be expected to honour it and only the recipient of an undertaking may complain of a breach.

Commentary

1. The Council will normally consider a complaint of breach of an undertaking only at the instance of a recipient.

2. Where a solicitor has received an undertaking for the benefit of a client and that client instructs another solicitor in his or her place then, unless for good reason the former solicitor objects, the benefit of the undertaking will remain vested in the client and any complaint can be made at the client's request by the new solicitor.

3. A solicitor cannot assign the burden of an undertaking (and thus claim to be released from its terms) without the express approval of the recipient.

4. Where a solicitor acquires a practice from another and consequently takes over the conduct of a matter in which there is an undertaking outstanding, the acquiring solicitor is not liable on the undertaking unless it is expressly or impliedly adopted. If the solicitor adopts the undertaking, the giver of the original undertaking nevertheless remains liable under it until the giver expressly obtains a release from the recipient.

19.07   Ambiguous undertakings

Principle

An ambiguous undertaking is generally construed in favour of the recipient.

Commentary

1. This Principle is particularly applicable if the undertaking is given to a lay person. Only in limited circumstances will the Council consider extraneous evidence to clarify an ambiguity (see also Principle 19.16 on implied terms).

2. Care should be taken when giving or accepting an undertaking which includes the words 'to use best endeavours'. What constitutes 'best endeavours' is arguable and each case must be construed on its own facts.

19.08   Consideration

Principle

An undertaking does not have to constitute a legal contract for disciplinary action to be taken in respect of a breach.

Commentary

1. Breach of an undertaking can give rise to disciplinary action even if no consideration was given for the undertaking.

2. If the undertaking is expressed to be given for consideration but, through no fault of the solicitor giving the undertaking, that consideration has failed, the solicitor will not be bound by the undertaking. Consequently, where there is consideration, it should be expressly stated in the undertaking itself.

19.09   Undertakings 'on behalf of' clients

Principle

A solicitor will be held personally liable to honour an undertaking given 'on behalf of' anyone unless such liability is expressly and clearly disclaimed in the undertaking itself.

Commentary

1. This is an example of the professional conduct obligation being more onerous than the legal requirement.

2. It is, however, necessary to distinguish between a professional undertaking (including one given 'on behalf of' a client) and a mere statement of a client's intentions or an agreement between solicitors as agents for their clients which is manifestly without the assumption of any personal liability.

19.10   Liability for undertakings of staff

Principle

A solicitor employer is responsible for honouring an undertaking given by any member of staff, including unadmitted staff.

Commentary

1. Where an assistant solicitor gives an undertaking, his or her own conduct in giving it may also be called into question by the Council.

2. In view of their own liability, principals should limit those members of staff who are permitted to give undertakings and should prescribe the manner in which any undertaking is given. It is strongly recommended that all undertakings should be confirmed in writing.

19.11 Employed solicitors

Principle

A solicitor in employment outside private practice will be held personally liable as a matter of conduct on a professional undertaking, whether or not given in the course of employment.

Commentary

1. A solicitor in employment outside private practice must consider carefully the personal implications of an undertaking given in the course of employment, particularly in commerce or industry, because of the possibility that the employer might become insolvent. Such insolvency will not affect the personal responsibility of the solicitor for an undertaking.

2. Where the head of a legal department in commerce, industry or local government is a solicitor, that person has the primary liability for an undertaking given by the department. This applies whether the undertaking is given over the signature of an admitted or unadmitted staff member.

3. Solicitors who accept an undertaking from legal departments in commerce, industry or local government should take particular care where the head of the department is an unadmitted person. The Council can entertain a complaint only where an undertaking is given by a solicitor or a member of his or her staff.

19.12 Liability of partners

Principle

Where a solicitor in partnership gives an undertaking in the course of his or her practice, all partners are responsible for its performance.

Commentary

1. A partner will remain responsible for the firm's undertakings even after he or she leaves the firm or the partnership is dissolved.

2. As a matter of conduct no liability will normally attach to a solicitor who becomes a partner after an undertaking was given.

19.13   Client's instructions

Principle

A solicitor cannot avoid liability on an undertaking by pleading that to honour it would be a breach of the duty owed to a client.

Commentary

1. Since a solicitor will be personally bound to honour undertakings, it is vital that before giving an undertaking he or she has the client's express or implied authority.

2. Where a solicitor gives an undertaking without such authority and as a result, the client suffers loss, the client's remedies may include, where appropriate, a claim in negligence against the solicitor.

3. If a solicitor has received written instructions from a client which are expressed to be irrevocable, those instructions are nonetheless revocable unless the solicitor has acted on them in such a way as to change the solicitor's personal position. Accordingly, any such instructions may be revoked before the solicitor has given the undertaking but not thereafter.

4. The Council will not allow a solicitor to avoid the obligations on an undertaking by claiming set-off or lien.

19.14   Conditional undertakings

Principle

A solicitor who gives an undertaking which is dependent upon the happening of a future event must notify the recipient immediately if it becomes clear that the event will not occur.

19.15 Demanding payment for not complaining

Principle

A solicitor must not demand compensation in consideration of refraining from reporting an alleged breach of undertaking to the Solicitors Complaints Bureau.

Commentary

See also Principle 2.15.

19.16 Implied terms and extraneous evidence

Principle

In general, no terms will be implied into a professional undertaking and extraneous evidence will not normally be considered.

Commentary

There are some specific exceptions to this Principle as follows:

1. In an undertaking as to the payment of costs:

    (a) When a solicitor gives an undertaking to pay another solicitor's costs in connection with a matter, the undertaking will be discharged if the matter does not proceed unless, in the body of the undertaking, or in a separate agreement, there is an express provision that the costs are payable whether or not the matter proceeds to completion.

    (b) An undertaking to pay another solicitor's costs is an undertaking to pay 'proper costs' whether expressed to be so or not, unless otherwise stated; for this reason it is always open to the giver of the undertaking to require the bill to be taxed, provided that this requirement is communicated promptly and the undertaking then takes effect on the bill as taxed (see also Principle 21.01).

    (c) An undertaking to pay the costs of a professional agent other than a solicitor is similarly an undertaking to pay 'proper costs'. However, unless the agent's professional body has means whereby it can determine whether the costs are proper, the Council may be unwilling to take disciplinary action in respect of such an undertaking and a *bona fide* dispute as to quantum will have to be resolved through the court (see also Principle 21.01).

2.   In an undertaking given in conveyancing matters:

(a)   An undertaking to redeem a mortgage means that the mortgage must be redeemed in the normal course of business. To delay doing so in order, e.g. to arrange refinancing for a client, would constitute a breach of the undertaking.

(b)   A reply to a requisition on title in the course of a conveyancing transaction can and often does amount to an undertaking. For example, if the reply to the standard requisition concerning the discharge of mortgages before completion or the giving of an undertaking in lieu is 'noted', 'confirmed', 'yes' or 'this will be done', the seller's solicitor will have undertaken to do one or the other if the matter proceeds to completion; if the solicitor opts to give an undertaking, it is advisable to use the form recommended by the Society (see Annex 24G). Following completion, it is no valid reason for non-compliance that, at the particular time, the seller's solicitor was unaware of the existence of any charge on the property, even though the buyer's solicitor may have had that knowledge. Accordingly, it is recommended that when replying to this requisition, the seller's solicitor should make quite clear which mortgage or mortgages will be discharged on completion.

(c)   In an undertaking to pay money out of the proceeds of sale of a property, a term is not implied that the undertaking is intended to take effect only if the proceeds of sale actually come into the hands of the solicitor giving the undertaking. Accordingly, if this restriction is intended, it is crucial that a term to that effect is incorporated in the body of the undertaking itself, otherwise the solicitor giving the undertaking may have to satisfy the payment out of his or her own resources.

3.   Generally:

(a)   If an undertaking is given to pay money out of a fund at some specified time, there is an implied warranty that the fund will be sufficient for that purpose. Accordingly, if so desired, it is crucial that this warranty is negatived in the body of the undertaking itself.

(b)   Where a solicitor asks another solicitor to supply copies of documents, there is a professional obligation to pay a proper charge for them.

(c)   If a person sends documents or money to a solicitor subject to an express condition, the recipient is deemed to be subject to a professional obligation to return the documents or money if the recipient is unwilling or unable to comply with the condition upon which they were sent. Further, if documents or money are sent to a solicitor subject to the condition that they should be held to the sender's order, the recipient is subject to a professional obligation to return the documents or money to the sender on demand. In these circumstances, cheques or drafts must not be presented for payment without the consent of the sender.

(d) A solicitor who has undertaken to accept service of a writ should, as far as practicable, on the day of receipt of the writ, endorse upon the writ that service is accepted and return to the plaintiff.

(e) Where an undertaking is given to pay a sum of money out of the proceeds of sale of an asset, there is no implied term that the sum is payable out of the net proceeds. Consequently, it is essential that any undertaking of this nature should stipulate what deductions have been agreed.

(f) There is no implied term in an undertaking that a solicitor is deemed to be released should he or she subsequently cease to act for the particular client. If this term is desired, it should be incorporated in the undertaking.

(g) In the absence of an express term, there is an implied term in a professional undertaking that it is to be performed within a reasonable time having regard to its nature. If there is any delay, the giver is under an obligation in professional conduct to keep the recipient of the undertaking informed.

(h) An undertaking will not be affected by events which occur subsequently, unless these events are provided for in the undertaking itself.

(i) Although, in the case of a written undertaking, all of the terms are normally contained in one document, some terms may be contained in other documents (see *Goldman* v. *Abbott* (1989) 139 S.J. 828).

19.17 Enforcement by the Court

Principle

The Court, by virtue of its inherent jurisdiction over its own officers, has power of enforcement in respect of undertakings.

Commentary

1. If court proceedings to enforce an undertaking are pending, the Council will not contemporaneously take disciplinary steps in relation to any breach.

2. Where undertakings are given by solicitors to the Court, the Council take the view that enforcement is a matter for the Court; for this reason the Council will not normally intervene.

3.   The Council have no power to enforce compliance with an undertaking but
     may take disciplinary proceedings against a solicitor in respect of a breach.

Chapter 20

Relations with other solicitors

20.01 Duty to act with good faith

Principle

A solicitor must act towards other solicitors with frankness and good faith consistent with his or her overriding duty to the client.

Commentary

1. Any fraudulent or deceitful conduct by one solicitor towards another will render the offending solicitor liable to disciplinary action, in addition to the possibility of civil or criminal proceedings.

2. This Principle also requires that a solicitor must honour his or her word given either personally, or by partners or by any other member of the solicitor's firm, and whether or not in writing. Solicitors' undertakings are dealt with in Chapter 19.

3. A solicitor must at all times maintain his or her personal integrity and observe the requirements of good manners and courtesy towards other members of the profession or their staff, no matter how bitter the feelings between clients. A solicitor must not behave in a manner which is acrimonious or offensive or otherwise inconsistent with his or her position as a solicitor.

4. This Principle also applies to correspondence. A solicitor must not write offensive letters to other members of the profession, whatever the degree of bad feeling existing between the respective clients.

5. A solicitor will normally warn the other party to a telephone conversation if it is going to be recorded. This warning may, however, be dispensed with in cases where the solicitor believes that considerations of courtesy are outweighed by other factors.

6.   In the absence of an agreement, a solicitor is personally responsible for paying the proper costs of solicitor agents instructed on behalf of his or her client (see Principle 21.01).

7.   For the duty of a solicitor involved in a 'contract race', see Principle 24.04 and Annex 24A.

8.   With regard to the stopping of a client account cheque see Principle 18.02.

20.02   Interviewing other party to a matter

Principle

A solicitor should not interview or otherwise communicate with any party who to the solicitor's knowledge has retained a solicitor to act in the matter except with that other solicitor's consent.

Commentary

1.   A solicitor who has been instructed by a client should not write directly to the client of another solicitor where the solicitor has reason to believe that the other solicitor's retainer still exists.

2.   Despite this Principle, a solicitor may be justified in writing direct to the client of another solicitor if that solicitor fails to reply to a letter, or where the solicitor has refused for no adequate reason to pass on any messages to his or her client. However, this step should only be taken after warning the other solicitor of the intention to write direct to his or her client. It is also courteous to copy such correspondence to the other solicitor.

3.   This Principle does not prevent a solicitor suggesting to a client that the client should communicate directly with the solicitor's client on the other side.

4.   Where a solicitor considers it appropriate, and the client agrees, this Principle does not prevent a solicitor from instructing an enquiry agent in an endeavour to ascertain for example the whereabouts or means of the other side or to serve documents. However, where the third party is already represented, a solicitor should not instruct an enquiry agent to approach the other party to obtain a statement, until notice of the intention to do so has been given to the other party's solicitor.

5.   This Principle extends to employed solicitors. Thus, for example, a solicitor acting for a client in a matter concerning a local authority who has express or implied notice that the authority's solicitor has been instructed to act in the matter, must not discuss that matter directly with the appropriate committee chairman, any individual councillor or any political

group on the authority. However, this Principle does not prevent political lobbying of individual councillors or a political group on the authority by a solicitor on behalf of a client, even where the solicitor knows that the authority's solicitor has been instructed to deal with the legal issues.

6. In the context of this Principle, only those employees or officers of a corporation who are responsible for the giving of instructions are to be regarded as the client (see also Principle 22.05).

7. Save as stated in Commentary 6, it is not a breach of this Principle to interview employees of an organisation on the other side in a matter. When contemplating interviewing such an employee, the solicitor should have regard to the employee's position *qua* employee and in appropriate circumstances should advise the employer or its solicitor of the intention to interview the employee. This would enable the employee to be advised as to his or her position. Before making the decision to interview an employee the interviewing solicitor should have regard to:

   (a) the liability of the employee;

   (b) the fact that the information sought may be confidential to the employer which, if disclosed, may place the employee in breach of his or her contract or the common law, similarly, the position as to privileged information may be relevant.

8. Solicitors may write, on behalf of a client, direct to the Legal Aid Board complaining about the grant of legal aid to another party, as the Legal Aid Board is not a client of the solicitor, merely the funding agent of the other solicitor's client.

9. For details on giving a second opinion to another solicitor's client see Principle 12.10.

20.03 Supplying information to other solicitors

Principle

A solicitor should supply information concerning documents in his or her possession to another solicitor upon satisfactory provision being made for the payment of proper costs, provided that there is no breach of the solicitor's duty of confidentiality towards the client.

Commentary

A solicitor's duty of confidentiality is dealt with in detail in Chapter 16.

20.04   Duty to report another solicitor

Principle

A solicitor is under a duty to report to the Solicitors Complaints Bureau any serious breach of conduct on the part of another solicitor which the solicitor believes falls short of the proper standard of conduct of the profession. Where necessary the solicitor must obtain the client's consent.

Commentary

1. Where a solicitor has reason to believe that another solicitor may be in financial difficulty or where the solicitor's integrity is in question, the solicitor should report those suspicions to the SCB.

2. The principle that every solicitor must maintain the highest standards of professional conduct and ensure that those in his or her employment do likewise, extends to a duty to inform the SCB of misconduct in the solicitor's own firm, e.g. theft by members of his or her staff whether solicitors or not. Unadmitted staff can have orders made against them under section 43 of the Solicitors Act 1974 restricting their employment in solicitors' offices.

3. The SCB should be informed where a solicitor is charged with an offence involving dishonesty or deception or a serious arrestable offence as defined by section 116 of the Police and Criminal Evidence Act 1984.

20.05   Signing certificates

Principle

Where a solicitor is asked to sign a certificate or otherwise give information concerning another solicitor, he or she must give a full and frank assessment of that other solicitor and must not mislead.

Commentary

1. This Principle applies particularly where a solicitor agrees to sign a certificate to the effect that an individual is a proper person:

    (a)   to be admitted as a solicitor;

    (b)   to hold a practising certificate;

    (c)   to be restored to the roll; or

    (d)   to be employed as a solicitor.

2.   This Principle also applies to solicitors who are asked to give information
     to the Society, or to give evidence before the Solicitors' Disciplinary
     Tribunal, where a former solicitor seeks to have his or her name restored to
     the roll.

Chapter 21

Relations with the Bar, other lawyers and professional agents

___

21.01 Duty to pay agents' fees

Principle

Unless there is an agreement to the contrary, a solicitor is personally responsible for paying the proper costs of any professional agent or other person whom he or she instructs on behalf of a client, whether or not the solicitor receives payment from the client.

Commentary

1. This Principle covers the proper costs of experts as well as professional and ordinary witnesses and enquiry agents.

2. Where there is a dispute as to what are the proper fees of the agent, it is not normally possible for the Law Society to determine the correct amount. Reference to the professional association of the agent in question may be made by the Solicitors Complaints Bureau, but this will not always assist.

3. If the solicitor and the agent have agreed a fee in advance, this will be the sum which will be payable.

4. Where the solicitor wishes to restrict liability to an agent to whatever sums are allowed on taxation, this should be made clear to the agent before instructions are given. This may be particularly relevant in a legal aid case.

5. A solicitor is not personally responsible for payment of the fees of witnesses who have declined an invitation to give evidence and have had to be subpoenaed (see also Principle 22.06).

6. For the position as to counsel's fees see Principle 21.08.

21.02   Fees of foreign lawyers

Principle

A solicitor who instructs a lawyer of a jurisdiction other than England and Wales is liable personally to pay that lawyer's proper fees, unless there has been an express agreement to the contrary.

Commentary

1. The Law Society accepts Rule 19 of the International Code of Ethics of the International Bar Association (see Annex 9B) which provides that:

   'Lawyers who engage a foreign colleague to advise on a case or to co-operate in handling it, are responsible for the payment of the latter's charges except where there is express agreement to the contrary.'

   Corresponding provisions are in article 5.7 of the CCBE Code of Conduct for Lawyers in the European Community (see Annex 10B).

2. Difficulties may sometimes arise in ascertaining what are the proper fees of a foreign lawyer. In some circumstances, such fees will be regulated by a scale approved by the relevant bar association or law society and in these cases the scale fees will be payable. In other circumstances, reference may be made to Legal Practice (International) who may contact the appropriate bar association or foreign law society in an endeavour to ascertain what would be a proper fee in the case in question. It should be noted that there are sometimes time limits within which fees must be challenged, so that prompt notification of the difficulty to Legal Practice (International) is desirable.

3. The CCBE Code of Conduct provides that where a lawyer considers that a colleague in another member state has acted in breach of a rule of professional conduct or any personal dispute of a professional nature has arisen between them, he or she must not commence any form of proceedings against the colleague without first informing the bars or law societies to which they both belong, so as to afford an opportunity for those bodies to assist in reaching a settlement (see articles 5.9.1-5.9.3). The entire code with explanatory memorandum and commentary is set out in Annex 10B.

21.03   Instructing a barrister

Principle

When instructing a barrister, it is the solicitor's responsibility to ensure so

far as practicable that adequate instructions, supporting statements and documents are sent to counsel in good time.

Commentary

For a statement of the rules of conduct affecting barristers, reference should be made to the *Code of Conduct of The Bar of England and Wales 1990* published by the General Council of the Bar. Extracts from the code appear in Annex 21B and include the following topics:

  —relationships with solicitors (see paragraphs 203, 207, 601 and 605);

  —acceptance of instructions and the 'cab-rank' rule (see paragraphs 208, 209, 501, 502, 503, 503A.1, 503A.2 and 503A.3);

  —withdrawal from a case (see paragraphs 504, 505 and 506);

  —drafting pleadings and other documents (see paragraph 606);

  —contact with witnesses (see paragraphs 607.1, 607.2 and 607.3);

  —conduct at Court (see paragraphs 608, 609 and 610);

  —fees and remuneration (see paragraphs 211, 308, 309.1 and 309.2).

21.04 Conferences

Principle

Where necessary and practicable, solicitors should arrange conferences with counsel to enable the barrister to clarify the instructions by direct discussion with the solicitor and/or the lay client, to discuss the facts, evidence and law with the solicitor; and to give advice more directly than is possible in writing.

21.05 Attending counsel at court

Principle

Where counsel has been instructed, the instructing solicitor is under a duty to attend or arrange for the attendance of a responsible representative throughout the proceedings, save that attendance may be dispensed with in the magistrates' court or in certain categories of Crown court proceeding where, in either case, the solicitor is satisfied that it is reasonable in the particular circumstances of the case that counsel be unattended and, in

particular, that the interests of the client and the interests of justice will not be prejudiced.

Commentary

For further details of this duty, see Principle 22.03.

21.06   Solicitors' responsibility to clients

Principle

Solicitors may not abrogate their responsibility to clients by instructing counsel.

Commentary

1. A solicitor should take care in the selection of suitable counsel and must, when considering counsel's advice, ensure that it contains no obvious errors. If counsel's advice conflicts with previous advice it may be necessary to seek clarification.

2. Solicitors must use their best endeavours to ensure that the barrister carries out instructions within a reasonable time and that the claim does not become statute barred or liable to be struck out for want of prosecution. Where appropriate a solicitor must ask for the return of the papers in order to instruct another barrister.

3. The Bar's code (see Annex 21B) requires that where a barrister has received instructions and it is or becomes apparent that the work cannot be done within a reasonable time, the barrister should inform the instructing solicitor forthwith. Where a brief has been delivered, immediately that there is an appreciable risk that the barrister may not be able to undertake the case, the brief should be returned in sufficient time to allow another barrister to be engaged and to master the brief.

21.07   Employment of barristers

Principle

A solicitor may employ a barrister full time in the solicitor's office.

Commentary

1. Where a solicitor employs a barrister, the solicitor's duty of supervision is the same as that which must be exercised over other employees.

2. It should be noted that this Principle applies only where the barrister is in employment and is not practising at the Bar. Paragraph 207 of the Bar's code (see Annex 21B) provides that a practising barrister may not be employed in a solicitor's office.

21.08   Solicitors' liability for counsel's fees

Principle

Except in legal aid cases, solicitors are personally liable as a matter of professional conduct for the payment of counsel's proper fees, whether or not they have been placed in funds by the client.

Commentary

1. A barrister does not have a contractual relationship with the instructing solicitor or the client and therefore cannot sue for the fees. The barrister is, however, entitled to demand payment of the fee with the brief except in legal aid cases.

2. In non-legal aid cases, where there is no special agreement, counsel's fees must be paid or challenged within three months of the delivery of the fee note at the conclusion of the case, whether or not the solicitor has been put in funds by the client or has taxed the costs. The non-payment of such fees may be raised as a matter of professional conduct and result in disciplinary action against the solicitor.

3. In legal aid cases, a delay on the part of a solicitor in submitting the bill and papers for taxation, which results in counsel not receiving fees within a reasonable time after submission of the fee note, can amount to unbefitting conduct and result in disciplinary action against the solicitor.

4. If a solicitor wishes to challenge counsel's fees, this must be done promptly upon receipt of the fee note. For details of the procedure for resolving disputes as to fees, see Principle 21.09.

5. The Law Society and the General Council of the Bar have published an agreed statement concerning the liability of solicitors for the payment of counsel's fees following a transfer of practice or the disappearance, death or bankruptcy of a solicitor (see Annex 21A).

6. This Principle applies equally to solicitors employed by lay-employers.

However, a solicitor in salaried employment should ensure that counsel and counsel's clerk are made aware at the outset of the matter that the solicitor is employed.

7. The Bar keep a list of solicitors whom they consider to be in default. Solicitors should note that the Bar may consider that a default has occurred in circumstances which would not necessarily constitute professional misconduct. Further, it is understood that the list may be operated against future partners or employers of a listed solicitor.

21.09   Counsel's fees: dispute resolution

Principle

Disputes as to counsel's fees may be referred to a Joint Tribunal consisting of a member of the Council and a Queen's Counsel nominated respectively by the President of the Law Society and the Chairman of the Bar.

Commentary

1. Where a dispute as to fees is referred to it, the Joint Tribunal's task is to look at all the circumstances in dispute. Where matters touching counsel's competence amounting to professional misconduct are in issue, such matters are first considered by the Professional Conduct Committee of the General Council of the Bar.

2. The Joint Tribunal is an informal body, fixing its own procedure which may or may not involve a hearing of the parties. Both parties are asked to agree the documentation to be submitted to the Joint Tribunal and, where possible, the Tribunal will reach a decision on that documentation. The parties to an adjudication bear their own expenses, unless these are otherwise awarded. The parties are required to undertake to abide by the decision of the Tribunal. Failure on the part of a solicitor to comply with the award of a Tribunal is regarded by the Council as unbefitting conduct and can lead to disciplinary proceedings. Solicitors wishing to invoke the procedure should inform counsel within three months of the delivery of the fee note and make application to the Solicitors Complaints Bureau.

21.10 Counsel's fees: appearances outside the jurisdiction

Principle

In certain circumstances, solicitors are exonerated from liability for payment of counsel's fees where counsel is instructed to appear outside England and Wales.

Commentary

This Principle will apply only where counsel is instructed to appear before a court or tribunal outside England and Wales and:

(a) the solicitor is acting, whether as agent or not, for a client who is normally resident outside the jurisdiction; and

(b) the solicitor informs counsel in writing a reasonable time before the date planned for counsel's departure abroad that the solicitor has not been put in funds.

Annex 21A

Guidance — liability of solicitors for counsel's fees following a transfer of practice or the disappearance, death or bankruptcy of a solicitor

The following is an agreed statement between the General Council of the Bar and the Law Society:

'The Bar Council has expressed concern to the Council of the Law Society about cases where an outstanding liability to pay counsel is overtaken by one of the events mentioned above [a transfer of practice or the disappearance, death or bankruptcy of a solicitor].

The general principle to be recognised in all cases is as follows:

A solicitor is personally liable for payment of counsel's proper fees whether or not the solicitor has received the money from the client with which to pay the fees. Where instructions have been given in the name of a firm all partners at that date incur personal liability.

The liability of a sole practitioner and of partners for the liabilities of their co-partners is a continuing one and is not cancelled or superseded by any transfer of the practice, without counsel's express consent. Equally, a partner or partners in a firm remain liable for the payment of counsel's fees incurred on behalf of the firm by a deceased, bankrupt or otherwise defaulting former partner of the firm.

If a transfer of a practice is contemplated, consideration should be given to outstanding counsel's fees on files taken over.'

23rd March 1988

Annex 21B

Code of Conduct of the Bar* — practice information

(relevant extracts)

---

203 A practising barrister:

(a)   must promote and protect fearlessly and by all proper and lawful means his lay client's best interests and do so without regard to his own interests or to any consequences to himself or to any other person (including his professional client or fellow members of the legal profession);

(b)   subject only to compliance with the specific provisions of Legal Aid Regulations owes his primary duty:

(i)   as between his lay client and his professional client; and

(ii)   as between the Legal Aid Fund and his lay client;

to his lay client and must not permit the Legal Aid Fund or his professional client to limit his discretion as to how the interests of his lay client can best be served;

(c)   must act towards his lay client and his professional client at all times in good faith.

207 A practising barrister must not:

(a)   enter into a professional partnership with another barrister or enter into a professional partnership or any other form of unincorporated association with any person other than a barrister;

(b)   be a member of a firm or be employed or engaged by any person firm or company which is either wholly or in part a device whereby the barrister himself (with or without others) is intended directly or indirectly to supply legal services to the public or a section of the public;

(c)   have a seat in the office of any person (other than his employer in the case of an employed barrister) entitled to instruct him;

(d)   give a commission or present or lend any money for any professional purpose to or save as a fee in accordance with the provisions of this Code accept any money by way of loan or otherwise from any person (other than his employer in the case of an employed barrister) entitled to instruct him.

---

*   Reproduced from the *Code of Conduct of the Bar of England and Wales,* 5th Edition 1990 (as subsequently amended) by kind permission of the General Council of the Bar.

THE GUIDE TO THE PROFESSIONAL CONDUCT OF SOLICITORS 1993

208 A barrister in independent practice must make his practice in England and Wales or in the Courts of the European Community his primary occupation and must hold himself out as being and must be willing at all times in return for the payment of fees to render legal services to the public generally in England and Wales.

209 A barrister in independent practice must comply with the 'Cab-rank rule' and accordingly except only as otherwise provided in paragraphs 501 502 and 503 he must in any field in which he professes to practise in relation to work appropriate to his experience and seniority and irrespective of whether his client is paying privately or is legally aided or otherwise publicly funded:

(a)   accept any brief to appear before a court in which he professes to practise;

(b)   accept any instructions;

(c)   act for any person on whose behalf he is briefed or instructed;

and do so irrespective of (i) the party on whose behalf he is briefed or instructed (ii) the nature of the case and (iii) any belief or opinion which he may have formed as to the character reputation cause conduct guilt or innocence of that person.

211 Except as permitted by the Act [The Courts and Legal Services Act 1990] a barrister in independent practice must not accept a brief or instruction on terms that payment of fees shall depend upon or be related to or postponed on account of the outcome of the case or of any hearing.

308 A barrister in independent practice may charge for any work undertaken by him (whether or not it involves an appearance in court) on any basis or by any method he thinks fit which does not infringe paragraph 211 but must not represent any person authority or organisation for a fixed salary or at a fixed fee for advising or otherwise acting over a fixed period irrespective of the amount of work he does provided that a barrister may accept a brief to conduct a list of cases in any Court on the basis of a single agreed fee for a session or half session.

(a)   pay proper financial remuneration for the work done;

309.1 A barrister in independent practice who receives fees in respect of work done by another barrister must himself and without delegating the responsibility to anyone else forthwith pay the whole of the fee in respect of that work to that other barrister.

309.2 A barrister in independent practice who arranges for another barrister to undertake work on his behalf (other than a person who has asked to do the work in order to increase his own skill or experience) must himself and without delegating the responsibility to anyone else:

(b)   make payment within a reasonable time and if possible within three months after the work has been done unless othewise agreed in advance with the other barrister.

501 A practising barrister must not accept any brief or instructions if to do so would cause him to be professionally embarrassed and for this purpose a barrister will be professionally embarrassed:

(a)   if he lacks sufficient experience or competence to handle the matter;

(b)   if having regard to his other professional commitments he will be unable to do or will not have adequate time and opportunity to prepare that which he is required to do;

(c)   if the brief or instructions seek to limit the ordinary authority or discretion of a barrister in the conduct of proceedings in Court or to impose on a barrister an obligation to do any excepted work (except as permitted by the Overseas Practice Rules or in the case of an employed barrister by paragraph 405) or to act otherwise than in conformity with the provisions of this Code;

(d)   if the matter is one in which he has reason to believe that he is likely to be a witness or in which whether by reason of any connection of his with the client or with the Court or a member of it or otherwise it will be difficult for him to maintain professional independence or the administration of justice might be or appear to be prejudiced;

(e)   if there is or appears to be some conflict or a significant risk of some conflict either between the interest of the barrister and some other person or between the interest of any one or more of his clients;

(f)   if the matter is one in which there is a risk of a breach of confidences entrusted to him by another client or where the knowledge which he possesses of the affairs of another client would give an undue advantage to the new client;

(g)   if he is a barrister in independent practice in a privately funded matter if the brief or instructions are delivered by a solicitor or firm of solicitors in respect of whom a Withdrawal of Credit Direction has been issued by the Chairman of the Bar pursuant to the Terms of Work on which Barristers Offer their Services to Solicitors and the Withdrawal of Credit Scheme 1988 (reproduced in Annex D) unless the brief or instructions are accompanied by payment of an agreed fee or the barrister agrees in advance to accept no fee for such work or has obtained the consent of the Chairman of the Bar;

(h)   if he is a barrister in independent practice in a Direct Professional Access matter or an Overseas matter unless he has previously informed BMIF that he intends to accept Direct Professional Access work or Overseas work (as the case may be) and has paid the appropriate insurance premium.

502   A barrister in independent practice is not obliged to accept a brief or instructions:

(a)   requiring him to do anything other than during the course of his ordinary working year;

(b)   other than at a fee which is proper having regard to the complexity length and difficulty of the case and to his ability experience and seniority and any brief or instructions in a legally aided matter shall for this purpose unless the Bar Council or the Bar in general meeting otherwise determines (either in a particular case or in any class or classes of case or generally) be deemed to be at a proper professional fee;

(c)   if the expenses which will be incurred are likely to be unreasonably high in relation to the fee likely to be paid and are not to be paid additionally to such fee;

(d)   save in the case of legal aid work:

(i)   unless and until his fees are agreed;

(ii)   if having required his fees to be paid before he accepts the brief or instructions to which the fees relate those fees are not paid;

(e)   in a Direct Professional Access matter unless he has previously notified BMIF that he intends to accept Direct Professional Access work and has paid the appropriate insurance premium;

(f)   in an Overseas matter.

503 A Queen's Counsel in independent practice is not obliged to accept a brief or instructions:

(a)   to settle alone any document of a kind generally settled only by or in conjunction with a junior;

(b)   to act without a junior if he considers that the interests of the lay client require that a junior should also be instructed.

503A.1 A practising barrister (whether he is instructed on his own or with another advocate) must in the case of each brief and if he is a barrister in independent practice also in the case of all instructions consider whether consistently with the proper and efficient administration of justice and having regard to:

(i)   the circumstances (including in particular the gravity complexity and likely cost) of the case;

(ii)   the nature of his practice;

(iii)   his ability experience and seniority; and

(iv)   his relationship with his client;

the best interests of the client would be served by instructing or continuing to instruct him in that matter.

503A.2 Where more than one advocate is instructed in any matter each barrister must in particular consider whether the best interests of the client would be served by:

(a)   his representing the client together with the other advocate or advocates; or

(b)   his representing the client without the other advocate or advocates; or

(c)   the client instructing only the other advocate or advocates; or

(d)   the client instructing some other advocate.

503A.3 Unless he considers that the best interests of the client would be served by his continuing to represent the client (together with any other advocate instructed with him) a barrister must immediately advise the client accordingly.

504 A practising barrister must cease to act and if he is a barrister in independent practice must return any brief or instructions:

(a)   if continuing to act would cause him to be professionally embarrassed within the meaning of paragraph 501 provided that if he would be professionally embarrassed only because it appears to him that he is likely to be a witness on a material question of fact he may retire or withdraw only if he can do so without jeopardising his client's interests;

(b)   if having accepted a brief or instructions on behalf of more than one client there is or appears to be:

(i)   a conflict or a significant risk of a conflict between the interests of any one or more of such clients; or

(ii)   a risk of a breach of confidence;

and the clients do not all consent to him continuing to act;

(c)   in any legally aided case (whether civil or criminal) it has become apparent to him that legal aid has been wrongly obtained by false or inaccurate information and action to remedy the situation is not immediately taken by his client;

(d)   if the circumstances set out in Regulation 67 of the Civil Legal Aid (General) Regulations 1989 arise at a time when it is impracticable for the Area Commmittee to meet in time to prevent an abuse of the Legal Aid Fund;

(e)   if the client refuses to authorise him to make some disclosure to the court which his duty to the court requires him to make;

(f)   if having become aware during the course of a case of the existence of a document which should have been but has not been disclosed on discovery the client fails forthwith to disclose it;

(g)   if having come into possession of a document belonging to another party by some means other than the normal and proper channels and having read it before he realises that it ought to have been returned unread to the person entitled to possession of it he would thereby be embarrassed in the discharge of his duties by his knowledge of the contents of the document provided that he may retire or withdraw only if he can do so without jeopardising his client's interests.

505   Subject to paragraph 506 a practising barrister may withdraw from a case where he is satisfied that:

(a)   his brief or instructions have been withdrawn;

(b)   his professional conduct is being impugned; or

(c)   there is some other substantial reason for so doing.

506   A practising barrister must not:

(a)   cease to act or return a brief or instructions without having first explained to his professional client his reasons for doing so;

(b)   return a brief or instructions to another barrister without the consent of his professional client or his representative;

(c)   if he is a barrister in independent practice return a brief which he has accepted and for which a fixed date has been obtained or (except with the consent of his lay client and where appropriate the Court) break any other professional engagement so as to enable him to attend a social or non-professional engagement;

(d)   except as provided in paragraph 504 return any brief or instructions or withdraw from a case in such a way or in such circumstances that his client may be unable to find other legal assistance in time to prevent prejudice being suffered by the client.

601   A practising barrister:

(a)   must in all his professional activities be courteous and act promptly conscientiously diligently and with reasonable competence and take all reasonable and practicable steps to avoid unnecessary expense or waste of the Court's time and to ensure that professional engagements are fulfilled;

(b)   must not undertake any task which:

(i)   he knows or ought to know he is not competent to handle;

(ii)   he does not have adequate time and opportunity to prepare for or perform; or

(iii)   he cannot discharge within a reasonable time having regard to the pressure of other work;

(c)   must read all briefs and instructions delivered to him expeditiously;

(d)   must have regard to the relevant Written Standards for the conduct of Professional Work (reproduced in Annex H);

(e)   must inform his professional client forthwith;

    (i)   if it becomes apparent to him that he will not be able to do the work within a reasonable time after receipt of instructions;

    (ii)   if there is an appreciable risk that he may not be able to undertake a brief or fulfil any other professional engagement which he has accepted.

605 If a barrister in independent practice forms the view that there is a conflict of interest between his lay client and his professional client he must advise that it would be in the lay client's interest to instruct another professional adviser and such advice must be given either in writing or at a conference at which both the professional client and the lay client are present.

606 A practising barrister must not devise facts which will assist in advancing his lay client's case and must not draft any originating process pleading affidavit witness statement or notice of appeal containing:

(a)   any statement of fact or contention (as the case may be) which is not supported by his lay client or by his brief or instructions;

(b)   any contention which he does not consider to be properly arguable;

(c)   any allegation of fraud unless he has clear instructions to make such allegation and has before him reasonably credible material which as it stands establishes a prima facie case of fraud;

(d)   in the case of an affidavit or witness statement any statement of fact other than the evidence which in substance according to his instructions the barrister reasonably believes the witness would give if the evidence contained in the affidavit or witness statement were being given viva voce;

provided that nothing in this paragraph shall prevent a barrister drafting a pleading affidavit or witness statement containing specific facts matters or contentions included by the barrister subject to the lay client's confirmation as to their accuracy.

607.1 Save in exceptional circumstances and subject to paragraphs 607.2 and 609 a barrister in independent practice must not discuss a case in which he may expect to examine any witness:

(a)   with or in the presence of potential witnesses other than the lay client character witnesses or expert witnesses;

(b)   with the lay client character witnesses or expert witnesses in the absence of his professional client or his representative.

607.2 In a civil case a practising barrister may in the presence of his professional client or his representative discuss the case with a potential witness if he considers that the interests of his lay client so require and after he has been supplied with a proper proof of evidence of that potential witness prepared by the witness himself or by his professional client or by a third party.

607.3 A practising barrister must not when interviewing a witness out of Court:

(a)   place a witness who is being interviewed under any pressure to provide other than a truthful account of his evidence;

(b)   rehearse practise or coach a witness in relation to his evidence or the way in which he should give it.

608 Provided that he is satisfied that the interests of the lay client and the interests of justice will not be prejudiced a practising barrister to whom a brief has been delivered may agree with his professional client that attendance by the professional client and his representative may be dispensed with for all or part of any hearing

(a)   in a Magistrates' Court or a County Court;

(b)   provided that he has been supplied with any necessary proofs of evidence in any other Court.

609 Notwithstanding that neither his professional client nor his representative is present a practising barrister who has been briefed in a case may:

(a)   if the attendance of his professional client has been dispensed with pursuant to paragraph 608; or

(b)   if he arrives at Court and neither the professional client nor his representative is in attendance and there are no other grounds on which to request an adjournment and no practicable alternative

conduct the case on behalf of the lay client and if necessary interview witnesses and take proofs of evidence.

610 A practising barrister when conducting proceedings at Court:

(a)   is personally responsible for the conduct and presentation of his case and must exercise personal judgement upon the substance and purpose of statements made and questions asked;

(b)   must not unless invited to do so by the Court or when appearing before a tribunal where it is his duty to do so assert a personal opinion of the facts or the law;

(c)   must ensure that the Court is informed of all relevant decisions and legislative provisions of which he is aware whether the effect is favourable or unfavourable towards the contention for which he argues and must bring any procedural irregularity to the attention of the Court during the hearing and not reserve such matter to be raised on appeal;

(d)   must not adduce evidence obtained otherwise than from or through his professional client or devise facts which will assist in advancing his lay client's case;

(e)   must not make statements or ask questions which are merely scandalous or intended or calculated only to vilify insult or annoy either a witness or some other person;

(f)   must if possible avoid the naming in open Court of third parties whose character would thereby be impugned;

(g)   must not by assertion in a speech impugn a witness whom he has had an opportunity to cross-examine unless in cross-examination he has given the witness an opportunity to answer the allegation;

(h)   must not suggest that a witness or other person is guilty of crime fraud or misconduct or attribute to another person the crime or conduct of which his lay client is accused unless such allegations go to a matter in issue (including the credibility of the witness) which is material to his lay client's case and which appear to him to be supported by reasonable grounds.

PART V — PARTICULAR AREAS OF PRACTICE

Chapter 22

Litigation, advocacy and alternative dispute resolution

Litigation and advocacy

22.01 Duty to court

Principle

Solicitors who act in litigation, whilst under a duty to do their best for their client, must never deceive or mislead the court.

Commentary

1. Although a solicitor is entitled to take every point, technical or otherwise, that is fairly arguable on behalf of the client, the court must be advised of relevant cases and statutory provisions by the advocates on both sides; if one of them omits a case or provision or makes an incorrect reference to a case or provision, it is the duty of the other to draw attention to it even if it assists the opponent's case.

2. Except when acting or appearing for the prosecution, a solicitor who knows of facts which, or of a witness who, would assist the adversary is not under any duty to inform the adversary or the court of this to the prejudice of his or her own client. But if the solicitor knows that a relevant affidavit has been filed in the proceedings and is therefore notionally within the knowledge of the court, then there is a duty to inform the judge of its existence.

THE GUIDE TO THE PROFESSIONAL CONDUCT OF SOLICITORS 1993

3. A solicitor would be guilty of unbefitting conduct if he or she called a witness whose evidence is untrue to the solicitor's knowledge, as opposed to his or her belief. For further guidance see Annex 22C.

4. This Principle applies equally to proceedings before tribunals and inquiries as well as to proceedings before the courts.

5. For the court's power to penalise a solicitor in costs, see Commentary 9 to Principle 17.01.

22.02 Improper allegations

Principle

A solicitor must not make or instruct counsel to make an allegation which is intended only to insult, degrade or annoy the other side, the witness or any other person.

Commentary

1. This Principle would also preclude a solicitor from making or instructing counsel to make an allegation which is merely scandalous.

2. In any litigation, a solicitor should, if possible, avoid the naming in open court of persons who are neither parties nor witnesses if their characters would thereby be impugned. The court should be invited to receive in writing the names, addresses and other details of such third parties.

3. A solicitor should not, in a plea in mitigation, make or instruct counsel to make an allegation which is likely to vilify or insult any person, without first being satisfied that there are reasonable grounds for making the statement.

22.03 Attending counsel

Principle

Where counsel has been instructed, the instructing solicitor is under a duty to attend or arrange for the attendance of a responsible representative throughout the proceedings save that attendance may be dispensed with in the magistrates' court or in certain categories of Crown court proceedings where, in either case, the solicitor is satisfied that it is reasonable in the particular circumstances of the case that counsel be unattended and, in particular, that the interests of the client and the interests of justice will not be prejudiced.

Commentary

1. Attendance on counsel may be dispensed with in the Crown court only in the following categories of case:

    (a) committals for sentence,

    (b) appeals against sentence, and

    (c) guilty pleas, where the solicitor was so instructed at the time when the brief to counsel was prepared.

2. Solicitors should exercise careful judgement in considering whether non-attendance is reasonable in a particular case. A solicitor should normally attend in the Crown court or send a representative where:

    (a) the client is a person at risk which expression includes, for example, juveniles, persons with inadequate knowledge of English, persons subject to mental illness or mental handicap, or with sight, speech or hearing impediments; this list does not purport to be exhaustive and whether someone is a person at risk is a matter as to which a solicitor must exercise judgement; or

    (b) the client is of such a difficult character that it is desirable that counsel be attended; or

    (c) there is a probability that the client will receive a substantial sentence of imprisonment or will receive an immediate sentence of imprisonment for the first time; or

    (d) witnesses as to fact or opinion (i.e. not character witnesses) are required to be present, whether or not they are actually called; or

    (e) counsel actually appearing in the particular case is not the counsel instructed unless the solicitor is satisfied that the change of counsel is unlikely to be prejudicial to the interests of the client; or

    (f) there are any other circumstances in which the solicitor considers attendance on counsel is reasonable.

3. In any case where a solicitor proposes that counsel should appear unattended he or she must:

    (a) so inform counsel and deliver a full and detailed brief sufficiently early before the hearing to enable counsel to consider the papers and to decide whether it would be appropriate for counsel to attend alone (guidelines issued by the Criminal Law Committee as to the contents and handling of such briefs and remuneration are to be found in Annex 22D); and

(b)   inform the client that counsel will be unattended and tell the client the name of counsel instructed; and

(c)   attend on counsel or send a representative where counsel originally instructed or subsequently substituted informs the solicitor that he or she does not believe that it is appropriate for counsel to be unattended.

4.   The Council, when considering any complaint that this Principle has not been observed, will take into account all the practical difficulties.

22.04   Private communications with judge

Principle

Except when making an application to the court, a solicitor must not discuss the merits of the case with a judge, magistrate or other adjudicator before whom a case is pending or may be heard, unless invited to do so in the presence of the solicitor or counsel for the other side or party.

Commentary

1.   If a written communication is to be made to the judge, magistrate or other adjudicator at any time, the solicitor should at the same time deliver a copy of it to his or her professional adversary or to the opposing party if not legally represented. Where oral communication is proper, prior notice to the other party or that party's solicitor or counsel should be given.

2.   Where, after a hearing, judgment is reserved and a relevant point of law is subsequently discovered, a solicitor who intends to bring it to the judge's attention should inform the advocate on the other side, who should not oppose this course of action, though that advocate knows that the point of law is against him or her.

22.05   Interviewing witnesses

Principle

It is permissible for a solicitor acting for any party to interview and take statements from any witness or prospective witness at any stage in the proceedings, whether or not that witness has been interviewed or called as a witness by another party.

Commentary

1. This Principle stems from the fact that there is no property in a witness and applies both before and after the witness has given evidence at the hearing.

2. A solicitor must not, of course, tamper with the evidence of a witness or attempt to suborn the witness into changing evidence. Once a witness has given evidence, the case must be very unusual in which a solicitor acting for the other side needs to interview that witness without seeking to persuade the witness to change evidence.

3. A solicitor should be aware that in seeking to exercise the right to interview a witness who has already been called by the other side or who to the solicitor's knowledge is likely to be called by them, the solicitor may well be exposed to the suggestion that he or she has improperly tampered with the evidence. This may be so particularly where the witness subsequently changes his or her evidence. It is wise in these circumstances for such solicitor to offer to interview the witness in the presence of a representative of the other side.

4. In interviewing an expert witness or professional agent instructed by the other side there should be no attempt to induce the witness to disclose privileged information. In these circumstances also it would be wise to offer to interview the witness in the presence of the other solicitor's representative.

5. As a general rule, it is not improper for a solicitor to advise a witness from whom a statement is being sought that he or she need not make such a statement. The advice that the solicitor should give must depend upon the client's interests and the circumstances of the case.

6. A solicitor must not, without leave of the court, or without the consent of counsel or solicitor for the other party, discuss the case with a witness, whether or not the witness is the client, whilst the witness is in the course of giving evidence. This prohibition covers the whole of the relevant time including adjournments and weekends.

22.06 Payments to witnesses

Principle

A solicitor must not make or offer to make payments to a witness contingent upon the nature of the evidence given or upon the outcome of a case.

Commentary

1. There is no objection to the payment of reasonable expenses to witnesses and reasonable compensation for loss of time attending court. In the case of an expert witness, there is an implied obligation to pay a reasonable fee (see also Principle 21.01).

2. A solicitor is professionally responsible for payment of the reasonable agreed fees and expenses of expert, professional and other witnesses whom the solicitor calls to give evidence on behalf of the client, unless a specific disclaimer is first conveyed to the witness. This obligation includes witnesses who have been subpoenaed where they have been invited to give evidence and have agreed to do so. Therefore, a solicitor who does not wish to accept such responsibility should make this clear to the witness in advance. In criminal cases in the Crown court all witnesses other than expert witnesses, can obtain payment of their fees and expenses, within the limits of the statutory scale, from the Court Office. It is good practice to inform such witnesses of this and to agree in advance whether the solicitor will accept responsibility for any sum in excess of such scale.

3. In legal aid cases, whether civil or criminal, a solicitor should draw the attention of the witnesses to the fact of legal aid and that the witnesses' fees and disbursements will have to be taxed or assessed and that only such amounts can be paid to the witness. A solicitor should expressly disclaim personal responsibility for payment of fees beyond those allowed on taxation or assessment. It should be noted that:

    (a) prior authority is not mandatory;

    (b) Area Committees do not have the power to grant prior authority for the costs of tendering expert evidence in criminal cases;

    (c) witness expenses are not payable under a criminal legal aid order unless the court directs that they may not be paid from Central Funds (see Practice Direction on Costs in Criminal Proceedings, 3 May 1991 [1991] 2 All E.R. 924).

4. A solicitor, on the client's instructions, may insert advertisements for witnesses to come forward as to a particular occurrence. However, care must be taken to draft the advertisement so that, so far as practicable, it does not suggest the detailed testimony sought.

22.07 Advocate called as witness

Principle

A solicitor must not accept instructions to act as an advocate for a client if

it is clear that he or she or a member of the firm will be called as a witness on behalf of the client, unless the evidence is purely formal.

Commentary

1.   A solicitor must exercise judgement as to whether to cease acting where he or she:

     (a)   has already accepted instructions as an advocate and then becomes aware that he or she or a member of the firm will be called as a witness on behalf of the client; or

     (b)   is instructed to act, but not as an advocate, and knows that he or she must give evidence.

2.   The circumstances in which a solicitor should continue to act as an advocate, or at all, must be extremely rare where it is likely that he or she will be called to give evidence other than that which is purely formal.

3.   It may be possible for a solicitor to continue to act as an advocate if a member of the firm will be called to give evidence as to events witnessed whilst advising or assisting a client, for example at a police station or at an identification parade. In exercising judgment, the solicitor should consider the nature of evidence to be given, its importance to the case overall and the difficulties faced by the client if the solicitor were to cease to act. The decision should be taken in the interests of justice as a whole and not solely in the interests of the client.

22.08   Client's perjury

Principle

Where a client, prior to or in the course of any proceedings, admits to his or her solicitor that the client has committed perjury or misled the court in any material matter in continuing proceedings in relation to those proceedings, the solicitor must decline to act further in the proceedings, unless the client agrees fully to disclose his or her conduct to the court.

22.09   Duty to obey court

Principle

A solicitor must comply with any order of the court which the court can properly make requiring the solicitor or the firm to take or refrain from taking some particular course of action; equally, a solicitor is bound to honour an undertaking given to any court or tribunal.

Commentary

1. A breach of this Principle may amount to contempt of court (see also Principle 19.17).

2. A solicitor must not aid and abet a client where the client refuses to obey a lawful court order.

3. The Society has issued guidance as to the steps a solicitor should take to secure the attendance of his client at the Crown court for trial (see Annex 22B).

22.10 Solicitor standing bail

Principle

It is undesirable for a solicitor to offer to stand bail for a person for whom the solicitor or any partner is acting as solicitor or agent.

Commentary

It should also be noted that it is unlawful for any person, including a solicitor, to be a party to a bargain to indemnify a surety for bail.

22.11 Dealing with recorded evidence

Principle

When solicitors act in the defence or prosecution of an accused and have in their possession a copy of an audio or video recording of a child witness which has been identified as having been prepared to be admitted in evidence at a criminal trial in accordance with section 54 of the Criminal Justice Act 1991 they must comply with the Council statement on access to recordings of a child witness's evidence dated 25th November 1992.

Commentary

The Council statement and recommended form of undertaking, together with practice notes, are set out in Annex 22A.

22.12   Court dress

Principle

A solicitor appearing in court as an advocate should appear duly robed where this is customary and must always wear suitable clothing.

Commentary

1.   Whilst it is proper for a solicitor or firm of solicitors to act as solicitors in a matter where the solicitor or the firm have an interest, they must, when engaged in such litigation, sue or appear as litigants in person. If they appear before the court in such a capacity they should not be robed, so that it is clear that they are not acting as professional advocates.

2.   Where a solicitor, an employee or the firm is one of a number of plaintiffs or defendants, the firm is permitted to go on the record as the solicitors, but a solicitor or employee who is a party to the litigation should not appear as a professional advocate on behalf of the parties either in chambers or in open court. If the solicitor does appear he or she must not be robed; the alternative being for the litigants to be represented by some other person who can act as a professional advocate.

3.   It is customary for a solicitor to appear robed before a court martial.

22.13   Statements to the press

Principle

A solicitor who on the client's instructions gives a statement to the press must not become in contempt of court by publishing any statement which is calculated to interfere with the fair trial of a case which has not been concluded.

22.14 Solicitor as advocate for the prosecution

Principle

Whilst a solicitor prosecuting a criminal case must ensure that every material point is made which supports the prosecution, the evidence must be presented dispassionately and with scrupulous fairness.

Commentary

1. The prosecutor should state all relevant facts and should limit expressions of opinion to those fairly required to present the case. He or she should reveal any mitigating circumstances and should inform the court of its sentencing powers if invited to do so and whenever it appears to be under a misapprehension about those powers.

2. If a prosecutor obtains evidence which he or she does not intend to use but which may assist the defence, the prosecutor must supply particulars of witnesses to the defence, but is not obliged to supply copies of the statements made by those witnesses. If, however, the prosecutor knows of a credible witness who can speak to material facts which tend to show the accused to be innocent, he or she must either call that witness or make the statement available to the defence. Further, if the prosecutor knows, not of a credible witness, but a witness whom he or she does not accept as credible, the prosecutor should tell the defence about the witness so that they can call that person if they wish. The prosecutor must reveal to the defence factual evidence of which he or she has knowledge and which is inconsistent with that which he, as prosecutor, has presented or proposes to present to the court.

3. The prosecutor must reveal all relevant cases and statutory provisions known to him or her whether it be for or against the prosecution's case. This is so whether or not the prosecutor has been called upon to argue the point in question (see Principle 22.01).

22.15 Solicitor as advocate for the defence

Principle

A solicitor who appears in court for the defence in a criminal case is under a duty to say on behalf of the client what the client should properly say for himself or herself if the client possessed the requisite skill and knowledge. The solicitor has a concurrent duty to ensure that the prosecution discharges the onus placed upon it to prove the guilt of the accused.

Commentary

1. Unlike the advocate for the prosecution, a solicitor who appears for the defendant is under no duty of disclosure to the prosecution or the court, save that he or she is bound to reveal all relevant cases and statutory provisions. Moreover, save in exceptional and specific circumstances, the client's privilege precludes the solicitor from making a disclosure of privileged material without the client's consent. Consequently, the solicitor must not, without instructions, disclose facts known to him or her regarding the client's character or antecedents nor must the solicitor correct any information which may be given to the court by the prosecution if the correction would be to the client's detriment. The solicitor must not, however, knowingly put forward or let the client put forward false information with intent to mislead the court. Similarly, the solicitor must not indicate agreement with information that the prosecution puts forward which the solicitor knows to be false. For further guidance see Annex 22C.

2. It is an implied term of the retainer that the advocate is free to present the client's case at the trial or hearing in such a way as he or she considers appropriate. If the client's express instructions do not permit the solicitor to present the case in a manner which the solicitor considers to be the most appropriate, then unless the instructions are varied, the solicitor may withdraw from the case after seeking the approval of the court to that course, but without disclosing matters which are protected by the client's privilege.

3. If the client instructs the solicitor that he or she is not guilty, the solicitor must put before the court the client's defence, even if the client decides not to give evidence and must, in any event, put the prosecution to proof. Whilst a solicitor may present a technical defence which is available to the client, he or she must never fabricate a defence on the facts.

4. In general, there is no duty upon a solicitor to enquire in every case as to whether the client is telling the truth. However, where instructions or other information are such as should put the solicitor upon enquiry, he or she must, where practicable, check the truth of what the client says to the extent that such statements will be relied upon before the court or in pleadings or affidavits.

5. Where, prior to the commencement or during the course of the proceedings, a client admits to the solicitor that he or she is guilty of the charge, the solicitor must decline to act in the proceedings if the client insists on giving evidence in the witness box in denial of guilt or requires the making of a statement asserting his or her innocence. The advocate who acts for a client who has admitted guilt but has pleaded not guilty (as the client is entitled), is under a duty to put the prosecution to proof of its case and may submit that there is insufficient evidence to justify a conviction. Further, the advocate may advance any defence open to the client, other

than protesting the client's innocence or suggesting, expressly or by implication, that someone other than the client committed the offence.

6.   If, either before or during the course of proceedings, the client makes statements to the solicitor which are inconsistent, this is not of itself a ground for the solicitor to refuse to act further on behalf of the client. Only where it is clear that the client is attempting to put forward false evidence to the court should the solicitor cease to act. In other circumstances, it would be for the court, and not the solicitor, to assess the truth or otherwise of the client's statement.

7.   If the client wishes to plead guilty, but at the same time asserts the truth of facts which, if true, would or could lead to an acquittal, the solicitor should use his or her best endeavours to persuade the client to plead not guilty. However, if the client insists on pleading guilty, despite being advised that such a plea may or will restrict the ambit of any plea in mitigation or appeal, then the solicitor is not prevented from continuing to act in accordance with the client's instructions, doing the best he or she can. The solicitor will not, in mitigation, be entitled to suggest that the facts are such that the ingredients of the offence have not been established.

22.16   Solicitor acting as advocate in civil proceedings

Principle

A solicitor who appears in court or in chambers in civil proceedings is under a duty to say on behalf of the client what the client should properly say for himself or herself if the client possessed the requisite skill and knowledge.

Commentary

1.   A solicitor who appears as advocate for the plaintiff, the defendant or any other party in civil proceedings is under no duty of disclosure to the other parties or the court, save that he or she is bound to reveal all relevant cases and statutory provisions. Moreover, save in exceptional and specific circumstances, the client's privilege precludes the solicitor from making a disclosure of privileged material without the client's consent. However, the advocate should not act in such a way that, in the context of the language used, failure to disclose amounts to a positive deception of the court.

2.   It is an implied term of the advocate's retainer that he or she is free to present the client's case at the trial or hearing in such a way as the advocate considers appropriate. If the client's express instructions do not permit the solicitor to present the case in what the solicitor considers to be the most appropriate manner, then unless the instructions are varied, the solicitor

may withdraw from the case after seeking the approval of the court to that course, but without disclosing matters which are protected by the client's privilege.

3. Whilst a solicitor may present any technical argument which is available to the client, he or she must never fabricate an argument on the facts for the client.

4. In general, there is no duty upon a solicitor to enquire in every case where he or she is instructed as to whether the client is telling the truth. However, where the solicitor's instructions or other information are such as should put him or her upon enquiry, a solicitor must, where practicable, check the truth of what the client says to the extent that such statements will be relied on before the court or in pleadings or affidavits.

5. If, either before or during the course of proceedings, the client makes statements to the solicitor which are inconsistent, this is not of itself a ground for the solicitor to refuse to act further on behalf of the client. Only where it is clear that the client is attempting to put forward false evidence to the court should the solicitor cease to act. In other circumstances, it would be for the court, and not the solicitor, to assess the truth or otherwise of the client's statement.

Alternative dispute resolution (ADR)

22.17 Provision of ADR services

Principle

Solicitors may offer ADR services either as part of their practices or as a separate business.

Commentary

'ADR services' means a service where a solicitor acts as an independent neutral, e.g. mediator, conciliator or arbitrator.

22.18 Information to parties

Principle

A solicitor who provides ADR services must inform the parties to the dispute in writing, and the parties must agree, that the solicitor will be independent, neutral and impartial and will not advise either party.

22.19   Restrictions on acting for parties

Principle

A solicitor must not provide an ADR service in connection with a dispute in which he or she or a member of his or her firm, has acted as a professional adviser to any party; nor, having provided an ADR service, may a solicitor or member of his or her firm act for any participant individually in relation to the dispute.

22.20   Indemnity

Principle

A solicitor who offers ADR services as a separate business should obtain indemnity cover.

Commentary

Solicitors offering ADR services as part of their practices will be covered by the Solicitors' Indemnity Fund up to the current limit of indemnity.

22.21   Training

Principle

It is recommended that solicitors wishing to offer ADR services should undertake appropriate training and work with one of the bodies which provide training and a regulatory framework.

22.22   Specimen code of practice

Principle

It is recommended that solicitors who offer ADR services comply with a code of practice.

Commentary

A specimen code of practice is at Annex 22E. Although not prescribed, it is recommended as it sets out valuable guidance about ethical issues which can arise.

Annex 22A

Council statement on access to recordings of a child witness's evidence

Council statement

When solicitors act in the defence or prosecution of an accused and have in their possession a copy of an audio or video recording of a child witness which has been identified as having been prepared to be admitted in evidence at a criminal trial in accordance with section 54 of the Criminal Justice Act 1991, they must:

(a) not make or permit any person to make a copy of the recording;

(b) not release the recording to the accused;

(c) not make or permit any disclosure of the recording or its contents to any person except when in the opinion of the solicitor it is necessary in the course of preparing the prosecution, defence or appeal against conviction and/or sentence;

(d) ensure that the recording is always kept in a locked, secure container when not in use;

(e) return the recording when they are no longer instructed in the matter.

Undertaking

Form of undertaking recommended by the Law Society for use by solicitors when receiving recorded evidence of child witnesses prepared to be admitted in evidence at criminal trials in accordance with section 54 of the Criminal Justice Act 1991.

I/We acknowledge receipt of the recording marked 'evidence of ....'.

I/We undertake that whilst the recording is in my/our possession I/we shall:

(a) not make or permit any other person to make a copy of the recording;

(b) not release the recording to [name of the accused];

(c) not make or permit any disclosure of the recording or its contents to any person except when in my/our opinion it is necessary in the course of preparing the prosecution, defence, or appeal against conviction and/or sentence;

(d) ensure that the recording is always kept in a locked, secure container when not in use;

(e) return the recording to you when I am/we are no longer instructed in the matter.

Practice notes

1. Recordings should preferably be delivered to third parties by hand but where this is not possible (e.g. because a solicitor may practise a long distance away from the barrister or expert instructed) the recording may be sent by document exchange or by recorded delivery post. To avoid the risk of theft, the contents of the package should not be apparent from the outside. If a solicitor or staff member personally collects a recording, he or she should be able to produce a proper form of identification.

2. 'Locked, secure container' — no special type of container is defined. Because of the ease and prevalence of theft from and of cars, a locked car cannot be considered as being a 'locked, secure container' and a recording should not be left unattended in a car.

3. The Home Office has published a memorandum of good practice to help those making such recordings. The memorandum contains a form of undertaking which it recommends be required of anyone who receives a copy of a recording (e.g. a barrister or expert who receives a recording from a solicitor). The terms are broadly similar to those of the Law Society's recommended undertaking. It is possible that solicitors may be asked to provide an undertaking in the form of that recommended by the Home Office. As with the giving of any undertaking, solicitors should first ensure that they can comply with its terms.

25th November 1992

Guidance — client's failure to attend court — a solicitor's duties

---

Since guidance was last published at [1987] *Gazette,* 22 July, 2201, on a solicitor's duties in regard to the attendance of clients at the Crown court for trial, there have been a number of developments. The guidance published in July 1987 was in response to requests where solicitors have been placed in a dilemma arising out of their competing duties owed to the court and to their clients in circumstances where their clients have failed to present themselves at court for trial. The problem stemmed from the solicitor's duty as an officer of the court, the duty of confidentiality to the client, and the protection of legal professional privilege.

The Lord Chancellor's Department in September 1987 requested the Law Society to alter the guidance because it limited too far the role or duty of the solicitor to notify clients of the date for attendance at court. The Law Society has, on behalf of the profession, taken up with the Lord Chancellor's Department the concern of the profession as to payment for items of work done in attempting to inform clients of the requirement to appear in the Crown court on a particular date.

The Standards and Guidance Committee and the Criminal Law Committee have reviewed the guidance issued last year. The guidance resulting from this review is set out below.

The Lord Chancellor's Department has, in response to the Law Society's concern as to costs, issued guidance to circuit taxing co-ordinators and determining officers, and that too is reproduced below.

The Law Society's guidance

It is accepted that there is a duty to provide reasonable assistance in the smooth running of the court lists, but the duty of confidentiality and right of privilege override the duty to the court and, therefore, the solicitor should provide only such assistance to the court as is consistent with the duty to the client.

The Society has received enquiries from solicitors as to the lengths to which they should go to ensure that clients receive notification of listing arrangements of matters to be tried in the Crown court. The Society's view is that, while a solicitor ought to take reasonable steps to ensure that the client is aware of the date for attendance at the Crown court and of the client's duty to attend, the solicitor is not under an obligation to take all possible steps to secure attendance.

Should a client fail to attend for trial, a solicitor should, as mentioned above, consider the limitations imposed upon him or her by the duty of confidentiality and the client's privilege when deciding what information might be revealed to the court. There would be no objection to a solicitor stating that he or she had written to the client about the hearing and that the letter had not been returned undelivered. Where a solicitor believes that a client is unlikely to attend court it is reasonable for the solicitor to advise the court accordingly although he or she might not be able to state the grounds for this belief. If the client has failed to respond to requests to attend the solicitor's office, it might be reasonable, depending on the facts, for the solicitor to advise the court that he or she is without instructions and/or that it would be desirable to list the case.'

With reference to the above guidance, the Criminal Law Committee take the view that different circumstances will make different steps reasonable. The following are some examples.

Notification by post will be reasonable if the client can read English or such other language as the solicitor might reasonably be expected to use; and only if there are sufficient days between the date of posting and date of hearing for the client to be warned in time (bearing in mind postal conditions at the time) and to advise the solicitor that he or she has received the notice.

A request to clients to telephone daily after a case appears in the warned list should be used with great caution. It will only be appropriate for clients with ready access to a private telephone and for offices where a responsible fee-earner will be readily available to take the calls.

If it is not reasonable to expect the client to telephone the solicitor's office daily to check the position of the case in the warned list, then some other method may be reasonable, such as delivery of a letter by taxi or courier or the 'lexigram' service in London. These should also be considered if there has been no acknowledgement of a written notice.

In cases where personal service is reasonable the solicitor may need to consider who should or can effect such service. It may need to be done by a person who knows the client; the time of day or type of area in which the client lives or some other factor, may make it unreasonable to expect a junior or female employee or colleague, or perhaps any person alone, to undertake the task.

The Criminal Law Committee are continuing to press for an end to short-notice listing of cases for hearing in the Crown court. Although there have been some improvements in some places, the position remains far from satisfactory. The Criminal Law Committee remain concerned at the incidence of judicial criticism of defendants' solicitors in public, particularly where such criticism is unjustified, and are asking the Lord Chancellor's Department (LCD) to remind members of the judiciary that these issues should be dealt with in chambers.

Practitioners are reminded that the Law Society's support is available to solicitors who are unjustly criticised or penalised by the court; or who, after taxation, wish to take further a claim against unjustified disallowance or reduction of costs. In appropriate cases, financial assistance from the Society will be given if the Council should so agree.

Lord Chancellor's Department guidance to court taxing co-ordinators

Notification of defendant for court hearings

The Law Society has written to the department expressing the concern of many practitioners about the seeming lack of consistency between Crown courts when considering claims by solicitors for notifying defendants of court hearings.

This subject was discussed at the recent circuit taxing co-ordinators meeting. Those present were surprised by the letter, being under the impression that in cases where it was reasonable to make payment for warning the defendant, determining officers were doing so.

I would ask you to bring this matter to the attention of all determining officers reminding them of the tests to be applied when considering such a claim.

Where a case is included in a fixed list which is published far enough in advance for the defendant to be warned by correspondence then a letter (allowed at unit cost) should usually suffice. But it might also be reasonable to allow an occasional telephone call in from the defendant to the solicitor to check that the position is unchanged.

Where a case is brought into a list at shorter notice and assuming the defendant is not on the telephone the determining officer should consider:

(a)   was there reasonably sufficient time for the solicitor to warn the defendant by letter;

(b)   if not, was the method of warning chosen reasonable.

As to (b), if the notice of listing is several days in advance it might be considered:

(a)   that notification should have reasonably been covered by adequate arrangements made by the solicitor for the defendant to telephone or call in at the office;

(b)   that a form of notice other than personal service would have been reasonable (e.g. a letter sent by taxi);

(c)   that in the circumstances of the particular case personal service was reasonable.

If a case is brought into a list at very short notice then personal service would normally be reasonable and should be allowed. Personal service should generally be regarded as fee-earner work and in normal circumstances would be appropriate to a grade C fee-earner. It is, as always, for the solicitor to provide the determining officer with full details in support of his claim.

With reference to the LCD guidance, the Criminal Law Committee take the view that 'several days' normally means four to six days and 'very short notice' normally means three days or less; and that Sundays cannot count for this purpose.

In regard to criminal legal aid costs generally, practitioners are reminded of the need to record every telephone call to ensure that none is forgotten when drawing the bill. Dealing with a telephone call from the client or from witnesses, for example, is normally done by a fee-earner and if reasonable, is normally paid for.

The Legal Practice Directorate wish to be kept informed, please, of any disallowances thought to be unfair, of items of cost claimed in Crown court cases; in particular, please inform the directorate team of any difficulties encountered concerning items of cost or disbursement claimed for informing or attempting to inform the client of the date for attendance at court.

26th October 1988 (updated January 1993)

Guidance — misleading the court — conflict between a solicitor's duty to the client and to the court

---

Much concern has been expressed by the profession as a result of disciplinary proceedings against solicitor John Francis Bridgwood, reported in [1988] *Gazette,* 9 November, 53. The Criminal Law Committee of the Law Society realises that those solicitors who practise regularly in the magistrates' court are constantly making decisions relating to their duty to their client and their duty to the court. Often decisions need to be made almost instantly, as solicitors are informed of new facts or given information as they go into court as their client's case is called on.

Bridgwood's dilemma

Mr Bridgwood was contacted by a client for whom he had acted on many previous occasions. The client was facing criminal charges at Manchester City Magistrates' Court. The client told Mr Bridgwood that she had given the police a false name and address and date of birth and Mr Bridgwood advised her to reveal her true identity to the police as it would be established in any event through fingerprint evidence. Some two weeks later Mr Bridgwood attended court where he was contacted again by his client. He discovered that the prosectuion had not established his client's true identity. He was able to spend only a very short period of time with his client prior to the case being called into the court and his client's instructions to him were that she intended to appear before the court using the false name. Mr Bridgwood went into court with his client who pleaded guilty in her false name and Mr Bridgwood spoke in mitigation. He considered that he could act properly on her behalf provided he did not refer to her assumed name and provided that he made no reference to her character.

In November 1987 Mr Bridgwood was tried and convicted in the Crown court on a charge of acting in a manner tending and intending to pervert the course of public justice. He was sentenced to nine months' imprisonment, suspended for two years. He was subsequently fined £2000 by the Solicitors' Disciplinary Tribunal.

Deception?

The question arises as to what is meant by a 'false' name. Whilst it is true that a person can call him/herself by whatever name they choose, the solicitor (in the context of court proceedings) must be satisfied that the client is not adopting a name other than that with which he or she was born with the intention of deceiving the court, (as in *Bridgwood*) so that the client could avoid previous convictions and thereby obtain a lighter sentence than would otherwise be the case. A name changed legally, for example, by marriage or by deed poll, could never be a false name. Likewise a client's address is not necessarily false, even though it may not be his or her place of residence, provided it is an address at which correspondence can reach the client or at which contact with the client can be made.

Principle 22.01 is the principle which most criminal law practitioners know by heart; it clearly states that solicitors, whilst owing a duty to do their best for the client, must never deceive or positively mislead the court. A solicitor has many duties which must be balanced with each other. These can be set out briefly as:

(a)   to say on a client's behalf all that a client would properly say for himself or herself;

(b)   to keep confidential information about a client and his or her affairs;

(c)   to ensure that the prosecution discharges the onus placed upon it to prove the guilt of the accused;

(d)   to disclose to the prosecution and the court all relevant cases and statutory provisions relating to the client's case but not evidence for the defence; and

(e)   not to participate in a positive deception of the court.

A solicitor takes part in a positive deception of the court when he or she puts forward to the court or lets the client put forward, information which the solicitor knows to be false, with the intent of misleading the court. The defence solicitor need not correct information given to the court by the prosecution or any other party which the solicitor knows will have the effect of allowing the court to make incorrect assumptions about the client or the case, provided the solicitor does not indicate in any way his or her agreement with that information. The solicitor can, as it were, sit back and do nothing about it, as opposed to participating actively in misleading the court by adopting that false information.

Law Society advice

The Criminal Law Committee have considered the specific problems raised by *Bridgwood* and tenders the following advice to practitioners.

—   Where, to the knowledge of the solicitor, the client seeks to give to the court a false name and address and date of birth, the solicitor's first duty is to discuss the matter with the client to try to persuade the client to change his or her mind. The solicitor should explain that unless the client changes his or her mind the solicitor will have to withdraw from acting. The client should be advised further that if the solicitor withdraws from acting there could be problems with the client's legal aid order, if one is in existence. If, having explained this to the client, it is clear that the client does not accept this, then the solicitor should cease to act. The solicitor's duty to say on the client's behalf all that the client would wish the solicitor to say is in clear conflict with the solicitor's duty not to participate in a positive deception of the court.

—   Sometimes the client will give his or her correct name to the court, but will put forward a false address or false date of birth. The solicitor should cease to act in these circumstances. It is arguable that the client is not attempting to conceal his or her identity, but the solicitor must be aware of the importance of the correct date of birth and correct address to the course of the administration of justice. The date of birth is the key to the record of previous convictions. The correct address is essential to the proper administration of justice as it is required for the purposes of consideration of bail, and it is the point of contact between the court, the solicitor, the police and the client.

— There are special difficulties for a solicitor who feels obliged to withdraw from the case where the client is in receipt of legal aid. The solicitor must apply to the court to be released from the legal aid order. The duty of confidentiality prevents the solicitor from revealing the reason for this request. The Committee considered that solicitors in these circumstances must be firm. The court must be advised that because of the solicitor's duty of confidentiality he or she cannot give the court reasons for the request to be released from the legal aid order, but the court must accept that a matter has arisen making it impossible for him or her to continue to act. The solicitor should explain the situation to the client so that the client is not taken unawares.

— Solicitors should endeavour to obtain a list of their client's previous convictions in good time to take the client's instructions upon them before going into court. Solicitors are frequently asked by magistrates' clerks to confirm the accuracy of previous convictions, or to accept previous convictions on the client's behalf, or to confirm that the previous convictions are a full list of previous convictions. Whilst these are perfectly proper questions to ask, serious problems arise for solicitors where they know that the list does not accurately reflect the number or type of convictions recorded against the client, or the sentences previously imposed. To confirm such an inaccurate list as 'accurate', or as a 'full list' could amount to a positive deception of the court. As a matter of professional conduct the solicitor must not disclose facts known to him or her regarding the client's character or previous convictions without the client's express consent. Therefore it is advised that in the future solicitors and their clients should decline to comment on the accuracy of such lists. It can be seen that if solicitors do obtain a list of previous convictions in good time before going into court, these problems can be discussed with the client and it can be pointed out to the client the difficulties which could arise if the client were to mislead the court by confirming the accuracy of a list known by both solicitor and client to be inaccurate. If the client insists that, if asked, the client will contribute to a positive deception of the court by pretending that the list is accurate, the solicitor must cease to act.

5th July 1989 (updated January 1993)

Annex 22D

Preparation of cases where counsel is unattended — practice information

ATTENDANCE AT THE CROWN COURT WITH COUNSEL

The Council have, in certain circumstances, relaxed the requirement that an instructing solicitor or a responsible representative attend on counsel in the Crown court. The circumstances in which attendance may be dispensed with are set out in Principle 22.03.

Content and handling of briefs

The Society's Criminal Law Committee have considered the content and handling of briefs where a solicitor proposes that counsel be unattended and believe that the following guidelines will be of assistance to the profession.

The Commentary to Principle 22.03 provides that where a solicitor proposes that counsel be unattended the solicitor must so inform counsel and deliver a full and detailed brief sufficiently early before the hearing to enable counsel to consider the papers and to decide whether it would be appropriate for counsel to attend alone. The Criminal Law Committee take the view that whenever possible such briefs should be delivered not later than seven days in advance of the case. In order to alert counsel and their clerks, briefs should be clearly marked with a red star where solicitors propose that counsel should be unattended.

The brief will need to contain more than it would if the solicitor or a representative was in attendance as counsel will have to undertake those duties normally carried out by the solicitor or the representative in attending court. Solicitors should insert clear instructions in the brief so that counsel is aware of precisely what duties will have to be fulfilled in the absence of the solicitor or a representative. Broadly, such instructions should cover actions required and details needed in respect of dealings with the client and witnesses, and recording and reporting what takes place in court. Thus the instructions should, where appropriate:

(a) deal with counsel's early arrival at court in order to see the client;

(b) include sufficient details about the defendant and any witnesses to enable counsel to contact them if they do not appear;

(c) require the judge's comments on sentence to be fully recorded;

(d) require notes to be provided of the headings of counsel's speech in mitigation;

(e) require a telephone report to the solicitor after the case ends;

(f) require counsel to deal with witnesses' expenses;

(g)   require counsel to deal with the client and any relatives who may be present after the case has been concluded;

(h)   require counsel to find out where the client has been taken, if in custody, and pass that information to the solicitor; and

(i)   require counsel to endorse on the brief within two days what oral advice on appeal has been given to the client.

Remuneration

Solicitors will be remunerated for the extra work involved where counsel is unattended. The Legal Aid in Criminal and Care Proceedings (Costs) Regulations 1989 provide for additional fees in standard fee cases for solicitors (and counsel) where counsel is unattended in the Crown Court. This additional fee is (at 1992/93 rates) £28.00 for outside London and £30 in London and is to remunerate the solicitor for any additional preparation involved.

In non-standard fee cases the assessment of what additional preparation should reasonably be allowed will be subject to *ex post facto* determination in the normal way. The Directions to Determining Officers issued by the Lord Chancellor's Department state: 'The assessment of what additional preparation should reasonably be allowed will depend upon the circumstances of individual cases. For example, a solicitor may need to spend more time with the defendant both before the hearing to discuss non-attendance and afterwards to discuss sentence and in some cases to take instructions on appeal. In addition, the brief to counsel will need to reflect the fact that the solicitor will not be present at the hearing.' The Directions then give as examples matters similar to those set out at (a) to (i) above.

The Directions to Determining Officers state that where a solicitor prepares on the basis that he or she will not attend on counsel but subsequently does attend the solicitor must justify a claim for additional preparation. The Directions continue that this is likely to arise most commonly (but not exclusively) where counsel does not consent to appear alone and state that where counsel has not so consented, that should be sufficient justification of the solicitor's claim.

Solicitors should note that the Directions state that where a solicitor has elected to attend on counsel in an apparently straightforward case involving one defendant and which is within the categories of case in which attendance on counsel is not required, it may be reasonable for a determining officer to disallow the attendance unless it can be justified by the solicitor. The Directions state, however, that a solicitor would be justified in attending court in circumstances akin to those set out in Commentary 2 to Principle 22.03.

11th January 1989 (updated January 1993)

Annex 22E

Mediation — specimen code of practice — practice information

I   Principles of mediation

1.   Mediation is an informal process in which a neutral mediator (or in some cases, two mediators) will help parties in dispute to try to work out their own principles and terms for the resolution of the issues between them. Mediators do not arbitrate and have no authority to impose decisions.

2.   Mediation is voluntary, and any party or the mediator may terminate it at any time.

3.   Notwithstanding that a mediator may be a solicitor, barrister, accountant or other professional, when acting as a mediator he or she acts as a neutral facilitator of negotiations and does not give professional advice to the parties, individually or collectively, nor does he or she represent any party, and mediation is not a substitute for each party obtaining independent legal, accounting, tax or other professional advice.

4.   The mediator tries to assist the parties to reach a conclusion of the dispute which is appropriate to their particular circumstances, and not necessarily the same conclusion that might be arrived at in the event of adjudication by the court. That allows the parties to explore and agree upon a wider range of options for settlement than might othewise be the case.

5.   The mediator may meet the parties individually and/or together and may assist the parties, for example, by identifying areas of agreement, narrowing and clarifying areas of disagreement, and defining the issues; establishing and examining alternative options for resolving any disagreement; considering the applicability of specialised management, legal, accounting or other assistance; examining the basis for continuing any existing relationship, or helping the parties to agree how and on what terms to end that relationship and generally facilitating discussion and negotiation and helping them to try to resolve their differences.

6.   A mediator will not act as such in a dispute in which he or she has at any time acted as a professional adviser for any party, nor in respect of which he or she is in possession of any information which was obtained by the mediator (or any member of his or her firm) as a result of having so acted or advised; nor having once acted as a mediator will he or she act for any party individually in relation to the subject matter of the mediation.

II   Confidentiality and privilege

1.   The mediator will conduct the mediation on a confidential basis, and will not

voluntarily disclose information obtained through the mediation process except to the extent that such matters are already public or with the consent of the parties. The only exception to this is that if the mediator considers from information received in the mediation that the life or safety of any person is or may be at serious risk, the duty of confidentiality shall not apply; and in such event the mediator shall try to agree with the person furnishing such information as to how disclosure shall be made.

2. Where the mediator meets the parties separately and obtains information from any party which is confidential to that party and which is not already public, the mediator shall maintain the confidentiality of that information from all other parties except to the extent that the mediator has been authorised to disclose any such information.

3. All discussions and negotiations during the mediation will be on a privileged 'without prejudice' basis, unless such privilege is waived by the parties by agreement, either generally or in relation to any specific aspect. No party is to refer in any proceedings that may subsequently take place to any such privileged discussions and negotiations, or require the mediator to do so, nor may any party have access to any of the mediator's notes or call any mediator as a witness in any proceedings.

III Duty of impartiality

1. The duty of impartiality of the mediator is inherent in the mediation process.

2. If a mediator believes that any party is abusing the mediation process, or that power imbalances are so substantial that the mediation is unlikely to result in a mutually acceptable resolution, or that the parties are proposing a result which appears to be so unfair that it would be a manifest miscarriage of justice, then the mediator will inform the parties accordingly, and may terminate the mediation.

IV Information and documents

1. The mediator will assist the parties, so far as appropriate and practicable, to identify what information and documents would help the resolution of any issue, and how best such information and documents may be obtained.

2. Mediation does not provide for the disclosure and discovery of documents in the same way or to the same extent as required by court rules. The parties may voluntarily agree to provide such documentation, or any lesser form of disclosure considered by them to be sufficient. This may be considered and discussed in the mediation.

3. The mediator has no power and does not purport to make or require independent enquiries or verification to be made in relation to any information or documentation sought or provided in the mediation. If this may be material to the resolution of any issues, consideration will need to be given in the mediation to the ways in which the parties may obtain any such information, documents or verification.

V Relationship with professional advisers

1. Solicitors or other professional advisers acting for the individual parties may, but need not necessarily, participate in the mediation process. Such solicitors and/or

advisers may take part in discussions and meetings, with or without the parties, and in any other communications and representations, in such manner as the mediator may consider useful and appropriate.

2. Professional advisers representing all the parties collectively, such as the accountants of a partnership whose partners are mediating their differences, may be asked to assist in the mediation in such manner as may be agreed.

3. Parties are free to consult with their individual professional advisers as the mediation progresses. On some occasions the mediator may make recommendations to the parties as to the desirability of seeking further assistance from professional advisers such as lawyers, accountants, expert valuers or others.

VI Recording of proposed agreement

1. At the end of the mediation, or at any interim stage if required, the mediator will prepare a written memorandum or summary of any agreement reached by the parties, which may, where considered by the mediator to be appropriate, comprise draft heads of such agreement for formalisation by the legal advisers acting for the parties.

2. If the participants wish to consult their respective individual legal advisers before entering into any binding agreement, then any terms which they may provisionally propose as the basis for resolution will not be binding on them until they have each had an opportunity of taking advice from such legal advisers and have thereafter agreed to be bound.

Chapter 23

Insolvency practice

General

23.01   Solicitor insolvency practitioners are bound by the Solicitors' Practice Rules 1990 and the Guide, but in their capacity as office holder must also comply with the Insolvency Act 1986, Rules and Regulations.

Close relationship with insolvent

23.02   Solicitor insolvency practitioners (SIPs) should not accept any appointment as an office holder, whether solely or jointly with any other authorised insolvency practitioner (whether a solicitor or not), where they have at any time had a close personal relationship or a close business, financial or working relationship with:

(i)   the person, firm or company over which it is contemplated the appointment be made; or

(ii)   any person connected with the same (within the Insolvency Act 1986, sections 249 and 435);

except that they may accept appointment:

(a)   as liquidator in a members' voluntary liquidation where it is beyond all reasonable doubt at the time of acceptance of such an appointment that the company is solvent and that all its liabilities can be satisfied in full; or

(b)   by the court, provided the relevant circumstances have been disclosed to the court.

A relationship is 'close' for this purpose if it is such as to impair or appear to impair the SIP's independence or objectivity in relation to the proposed appointment. Not all professional relationships are of such a nature particularly if they are with other members of the SIP's firm. If in the three years prior to such an appointment, the SIP's firm or a partner, consultant or senior employee of the firm had such a relationship, the propriety of accepting appointment will depend on whether this could influence the SIP or be thought to be of influence in the performance of the SIP's duties. The SIP may only properly act if satisfied that his or her independence and objectivity will not be or appear to be compromised. In particular, the SIP will usually be free to accept appointment if the relationship with the insolvent arose from investigations undertaken at the instigation of a creditor.

'Office holder' for the above purpose means holding office as:

(1) supervisor of a voluntary arrangement whether for a company or an individual or a nominee;

(2) administrator;

(3) administrative receiver;

(4) receiver;

(5) liquidator, including a provisional liquidator or interim receiver;

(6) trustee in bankruptcy;

(7) trustee under the Deeds of Arrangement Act 1914; or

(8) administrator of the estate of a deceased person, in respect of which an insolvency administration order has been made.

Where one such office follows another, SIPs are referred to paragraphs 23.09-23.14.

Joint appointments with non-solicitors

23.03   An SIP may accept a joint appointment with a non-solicitor insolvency practitioner. They may jointly negotiate for a combined fee and many agree between themselves the appropriate apportionment of that fee. The solicitor could receive the joint fee in the first instance and then pass on the non-solicitor's fee without being in breach of Rule 7 of the Solicitors' Practice Rules 1990.

Conflict of interest

23.04   An SIP should not accept appointment if to the SIP's knowledge this would result in a conflict of interest with clients of the firm unless acceptance is at the request of such clients or unless they are independently advised and consent. The fact that the SIP or the firm acts for creditors of the insolvent is not in itself a conflict of interest for this purpose unless there is likely to be a material dispute about the amount provable in the insolvency. If, having accepted appointment, a conflict is subsequently discovered, the SIP must instruct another firm of solicitors to act for him or her in relation to such conflict and ensure that the client with whom the conflict arises is independently advised. The SIP should resign his appointment on the ground of conflict of interest only if actual personal knowledge prevents the SIP fulfilling the duties of office holder without breach of confidence. Imputed knowledge of other partners may be disregarded for this purpose in view of the public duties of an office holder to creditors.

Gifts

23.05   SIPs should decline any gift, benefit or favour which might influence, or be seen by others as likely to influence, them in the performance of their duties. In particular, SIPs holding any insolvency office must not themselves directly or indirectly acquire any assets of the insolvent nor knowingly permit any partner or employee of their firm or any close relative of any of the same directly or indirectly to do so.

Legal services

23.06   SIPs may act as solicitors, employ their own firms or any of their partners, give legal and other advice, instruct counsel, and generally act in any capacity in relation to an insolvency, notwithstanding that they are office holders acting either alone or jointly with one or more other office holders. However, under the Insolvency Rules 1986, Rules 4.128(3), 2.47(7) and 6.139(3), they and their firms will only be entitled to costs for the provision of legal services if such costs are authorised by the creditors' committee, the creditors or the court. An SIP should obtain appropriate authority from the creditors' committee or from the court authorising the SIP or the firm to undertake specific legal services and agreeing that services be remunerated in accordance with the Solicitors' Remuneration Order 1972 or court order before the services are rendered except in an emergency where the services are clearly necessary and beneficial to creditors.

Solicitor creditors

23.07   If an SIP, or the SIP's firm, or a client of the firm, is a creditor of the person in relation to whom or which the SIP is an office holder, the SIP shall not vote for or in relation to, or act as proxy for, or act as a solicitor in relation to, any such claim. If the SIP is a sole office holder, the directions of the creditors' committee or the court shall be sought in relation to such claim. If acting jointly, the joint office holder shall take all decisions regarding the claim and the SIP shall not permit or allow the firm to act in relation to such a claim in whatever capacity, and shall instruct other advisers if the creditors' meeting and/or creditors' committee so decides.

Commission

23.08   The offer or payment of commission for, or the furnishing of any valuable consideration for the introduction of an insolvency appointment is prohibited. By section 164 of the Insolvency Act 1986, it is an offence punishable by a fine to offer a member or creditor of a company any valuable consideration with a view to securing nomination as a liquidator.

Conversion of members' voluntary winding up into creditors' voluntary winding up

23.09   Where an SIP has accepted appointment as liquidator in a members' voluntary winding up and is obliged to summon a creditors' meeting under section 95 of the Insolvency Act 1986 because it appears that the company will be unable to pay its debts in full within the period stated in the directors' declaration of solvency, the SIP's continuance as liquidator will depend on whether the SIP is satisfied beyond all reasonable doubt that the company will eventually be able to meet all its liabilities in full.

(a) If the SIP is not so satisfied and has previously had a close personal relationship or a close business, financial or working relationship such as is set out in paragraph 23.02, nomination under the creditors' winding up should not be accepted.

(b) If the company will not be able to meet all its liabilities in full but the SIP has had no such relationship, the SIP may accept nomination by the creditors and continue as liquidator with the creditors' approval.

(c) If the SIP has a close personal relationship or a close business, financial or working relationship such as is set out in paragraph 23.02 but is satisfied beyond reasonable doubt that the company will eventually be able to meet all its liabilities in full, the SIP may accept nomination by the creditors and continue as liquidator, but if it should subsequently appear that the SIP's assessment was mistaken, the SIP must then offer his or her resignation, and may not accept re-appointment.

Administration or insolvent liquidation following appointment as administrative or other receiver

23.10 Where a partner, consultant or senior employee of a practice is, or in the previous three years has been, administrative receiver of a company, or a receiver under the Law of Property Act 1925 or otherwise of any of its assets, no partner, consultant or employee of the practice should accept appointment as liquidator of the company. This restriction does not apply where the previous appointment was made by the court. However, before a court appointed receiver accepts subsequent appointment as liquidator, he or she should give careful consideration as to whether the SIP's objectivity could be open to question.

Liquidation following appointment as supervisor of a voluntary arrangement or administrator

23.11 Where an SIP, or any partner, consultant or senior employee of the practice, has been supervisor of a voluntary arrangement or administrator of a company, the SIP may accept appointment as liquidator if so nominated by the creditors provided the criteria in paragraphs 23.02 and 23.04 are satisfied.

However where the relevant previous role is that of administrator, the SIP should not accept nomination or appointment as liquidator unless either:

(a) the SIP has the support of a creditors' committee appointed under section 26 of the Insolvency Act 1986; or

(b) the SIP has the support of a meeting of creditors called either under the Act or informally, of which all known creditors have been given notice.

Bankruptcy following appointment as supervisor of individual voluntary arrangement

23.12 Where an SIP, or any partner, consultant or senior employee of the practice, has been supervisor of a voluntary arrangement in relation to a debtor, the SIP may, provided the criteria in paragraphs 23.02 and 23.04 are satisfied, accept appointment as trustee in bankruptcy of that debtor provided that the appointment is effected by a general meeting of the creditors under section 292(1)(a) of the Insolvency Act 1986 or the SIP has been appointed by the court under section 297(5) of the Act.

Group companies

23.13 Difficulties are likely to arise from the existence of inter-company transactions or guarantees in group or associated companies. Acceptance of an insolvency appointment in relation to more than one company in the group or association may cause a conflict of interest but it may be impracticable for a series of different insolvency practitioners to act. An SIP should not accept multiple appointments in such situations unless satisfied that effective steps can be taken to minimise problems of conflict and that the SIP's overall integrity and objectivity are, and are seen to be, maintained.

Relationships between insolvent individuals and insolvent companies

23.14 Difficulties also arise where an SIP who has been appointed as trustee in bankruptcy of a debtor becomes liquidator, or where any partner, consultant or senior employee of the practice becomes liquidator, of a company of which the debtor is a major shareholder or creditor, or where the company is a creditor of the debtor. It is essential, if the SIP or the practice is to continue in both roles, that effective steps can be taken to minimise problems of conflict and that overall integrity and objectivity are, and are seen to be, maintained.

Practice mergers and transfers

23.15 When two practices merge, partners, consultants and senior employees of the merged practice become subject to common ethical constraints in relation to insolvency appointments. The situation must be reviewed and paragraph 23.04 applied.

Where a partner, consultant or senior employee of a practice has, in any former practice, undertaken work upon the affairs of a company or debtor in a capacity which is incompatible with an insolvency appointment of the new practice, he or she should not personally work on or be involved in that assignment.

Chapter 24

Conveyancing

24.01 Acting for seller and buyer

Principle

'(1) Without prejudice to the general principle of professional conduct that a solicitor shall not accept instructions to act for two or more clients where there is a conflict between the interests of those clients, a solicitor or two or more solicitors practising in partnership or association shall not act for both seller and buyer on a transfer of land for value at arm's length, or for both lessor and lessee on the grant of a lease for value at arm's length, or for both lender and borrower in a private mortgage at arm's length.

(2) Provided no conflict of interest appears, and provided the seller or lessor is not a builder or developer selling or leasing as such, and provided the solicitor or any solicitor practising in partnership or association with that solicitor is not instructed to negotiate the sale of the property concerned, the rule set out in paragraph (1) of this rule shall not apply if:

    (a) the parties are associated companies; or

    (b) the parties are related by blood, adoption or marriage; or

    (c) both parties are established clients (which expression shall include persons related by blood, adoption or marriage to established clients); or

    (d) on a transfer of land, the consideration is less than £5,000; or

    (e) there is no other solicitor or other qualified conveyancer in the vicinity whom either party can reasonably be expected to consult; or

    (f) two associated firms or two offices of the same firm are respectively acting for the parties, provided that:

        (i) the respective firms or offices are in different localities; and

(ii) neither party was referred to the firm or office acting for him or her from an associated firm or from another office of the same firm; and

(iii) the transaction is dealt with or supervised by a different solicitor in regular attendance at each firm or office.

(3) **In this rule:**

(a) "association" refers to a situation where two or more firms of solicitors have at least one common principal; and where either firm is a recognised body 'principal' means a director or member of that body, or the beneficial owner of any share in the body held by a member as nominee, or the body itself; and

(aa) "firm of solicitors" includes a multi-national partnership; and

(b) "private mortgage" means any mortgage other than one provided by an institution which provides mortgages in the normal course of its activities.'

Solicitors' Practice Rules 1990, Rule 6

Commentary

1. Rule 6(1) is mandatory and unless a particular transaction either falls outside the rule or is covered by one of the exceptions to it, failure to observe it raises an issue of conduct.

2. The exceptions contained in Rule 6(2) are not available in all circumstances. In particular they do not apply where there is a conflict of interest (see Principles 15.01 and 15.02). If a conflict arises during the course of a transaction falling within one of the exceptions, the solicitor must comply with Principle 15.03.

3. The test of whether a person is an 'established client' is an objective one, that is, whether a reasonable and fair-minded solicitor would regard the person as an established client. An existing client is not the same as an established client. Thus, for example, if a seller instructs a solicitor for the first time and, after those instructions are received, it is discovered that the buyer is an established client, the exception in Rule 6(2)(c) would not apply and the solicitor could not act for both parties.

4. The fact that a transaction is at market value does not necessarily mean that it is 'at arm's length' for the purpose of the rule. A transaction which for other reasons is stated to be on arm's length terms (i.e. at market value) may not, for the purposes of Rule 6, be at arm's length, e.g. where trustees are conveying land to a beneficiary. Whether a transaction is 'at arm's length' must be determined by reference to the proximity and relationship between the parties. Examples of situations where a transaction may not necessarily be at arm's length are:

    (a) where there exists between the parties a fiduciary relationship. It would therefore be possible, subject to there being no conflict of interest, for a solicitor to act for both:

        — the settlor of a trust and the trustees;

        — the trustees of a trust and its beneficiary or the beneficiary's relative;

        — personal representatives and a beneficiary;

        — the trustees of separate trusts for the same family;

    (b) where an unincorporated business is to be incorporated. Subject to there being no conflict of interest, a solicitor would be permitted to act for both the sole trader or partners and the limited company set up to enable the incorporation of the business;

    (c) where the transaction is between a local authority and a related body within the meaning of paragraph 6(b) of the Employed Solicitors' Code 1990.

5. Even in cases which would fall within Rule 6(2), a solicitor should not, save in exceptional circumstances, act for both the seller and a buyer where the seller is dealing with two or more prospective buyers (see the Council direction on submitting draft contracts to more than one prospective buyer contained in Annex 24A).

6. In those circumstances where a solicitor may properly act for both parties he or she must ensure that both clients consent to the arrangement.

24.02 Conflict — solicitor providing bridging loan

Principle

A solicitor must not act where his or her own interests conflict with the interests of a client.

Commentary

1. There is a conflict of interest where a solicitor in his or her personal capacity sells to, or buys from, or lends to or borrows from a client (see Principle 15.05).

2. In order to enable a conveyancing completion to take place a solicitor may wish to provide bridging finance to a client to cover the amount of any shortfall on completion. A solicitor considering making such a bridging loan to a client should consider whether the basis upon which the loan is made raises any particular professional obligations to the client. Generally,

where the solicitor stands to make no personal gain from the transaction and where the terms of the facility are not unusually onerous, the client will not need to be separately represented in relation to the terms of the loan.

3.   However, there may be circumstances where independent advice is required. For example, where the solicitor is lending from personal resources or from the firm's resources and charges a commercial rate for the loan, he or she may be receiving a personal benefit if the rate which the money would otherwise have been earning would be less than the rate being charged to the client.

4.   A solicitor may seek to secure the bridging loan by taking an equitable charge from the client. Provided the terms of the charge are usual this would not normally raise any issue of conflict. It is advisable that the solicitor explains to the client the ramifications of granting this type of security. In circumstances where the charge contains unusual terms, the client should be advised to obtain separate independent advice on the terms.

5.   A solicitor extending bridging finance should consider whether the provisions of the Consumer Credit Act 1974 apply where the loan does not exceed £15,000.

24.03   Preparing contracts for signature

Principle

A solicitor acting for the seller of property should not prepare a form of contract which he or she knows or ought to know will be placed before a prospective buyer for signature before that party has obtained or has had a proper opportunity to obtain legal advice.

Commentary

Even if the contract allows the buyer to rescind without penalty during a stated period, this Principle will still apply. This is because although the buyer may consult a solicitor during that period, it could then be too late to negotiate any amendments to the contract if the buyer wished to proceed and, in practice, it may be impossible to make the necessary searches and enquiries of local authorities within that period.

24.04 Contract races

Principle

A solicitor acting for a seller must comply with the Council direction of 6th October 1977 when instructed to deal with more than one prospective buyer at the same time.

Commentary

1. The full text of the Council direction (together with guidance notes) appears in Annex 24A.

2. The requirements of the Council direction are mandatory. Failure to observe its provisions raises issues of conduct.

3. What must be notified to the solicitor or other qualified conveyancer acting for each prospective buyer or (where no solicitor or other qualified conveyancer is acting) to the prospective buyer in person, is the seller's decision to deal with more than one prospective buyer. The seller's solicitor must not wait until the contracts are actually submitted to notify the appropriate parties. Notification must be given immediately the instructions to deal with a prospective buyer (other than the first) are received. Such disclosure, if made by telephone or fax, should be confirmed by letter.

4. When a prospective buyer has been notified of the seller's decision to deal with more than one prospective buyer, it is not necessary to notify that prospective buyer each time a decision is taken to deal with a further prospective buyer.

5. Since the requirements apply to all sales and purchases of freehold or leasehold property, the direction will also affect, for example, vending agreements where part of the assets to be sold consist of freehold or leasehold property.

6. The direction will apply where the contracts contain non-identical terms or relate to different interests in the same property, e.g. where one party is negotiating for a lease of premises whilst another party is interested in purchasing the freehold.

7. The direction does not apply to a property which is being or has been offered for sale by auction or tender unless and until the auction or return date has passed and the property, remaining unsold, is subsequently offered for sale by private treaty.

8. Solicitors should take particular care where a contract has been submitted but nothing has been heard from the prospective buyer's solicitors for some considerable time. If the seller decides to deal with another buyer, the

direction must still be complied with unless the seller's solicitor has already withdrawn the first contract.

9. If the seller refuses to authorise disclosure in accordance with the provisions of the direction, the solicitor must immediately cease to act for the seller.

24.05   Unqualified conveyancers

Principle

If a solicitor discovers that the party on the other side is represented by an unqualified conveyancer then, subject to the interests of his or her own client, the solicitor's proper course is to decline to communicate with the unqualified conveyancer.

Commentary

1. Although this Principle does not prohibit a solicitor from dealing with an unqualified person, reference should be made to the Council guidance published on 16th March 1988 on dealing with unqualified conveyancers, which is contained in Annex 24F. This guidance sets out the steps which solicitors ought to take in order to ensure that neither they nor their clients are involved in procuring breaches of section 22 of the Solicitors Act 1974 by the unqualified person; it also contains guidance on the practical difficulties in dealing with unqualified conveyancers.

2. Solicitors are asked to report to the Professional Adviser any cases where it appears that an unqualified conveyancer has acted in breach of the law.

3. For guidance on dealing with licensed conveyancers see Annex 24E.

24.06   General insurance business

Principle

A solicitor who conducts general insurance business should do so only as independent intermediary and not as tied agent.

Commentary

The Association of British Insurers Code of Practice for Intermediaries, together with the Council requirement summarised in this Principle, are contained in Annex 24B.

24.07 Mortgages and life policies

Principle

Solicitors must comply with the Council statement on the Financial Services Act 1986: life policies and tied agents.

Commentary

1. The Council statement is to be found at Annex 24C. It concerns introductions and referrals in relation to endowment policies or similar life insurance with an investment element. See also section 4 of the Solicitors' Introduction and Referral Code 1990 (Annex 11B).

2. Although a mortgage of land is not an investment under the Financial Services Act 1986, solicitors who advise on or make arrangements in respect of mortgages where an endowment policy or pension policy is to be used as additional security may well find themselves caught by the Act. However, it should be noted that a mere referral of a client to an independent intermediary will not be caught by the Act.

3. It is important for solicitors to be aware of the status under the Financial Services Act of persons to whom clients are referred as many banks, building societies, estate agents and insurance agents are appointed representatives of particular insurance companies and are not able to offer independent advice.

4. The Council statement also deals with the duty of a solicitor where a conveyancing client is referred to the solicitor by a life office, bank, building society or an appointed representative and the client is proposing to take out a company life policy without having received independent advice. If the client appears to be taking out an unsuitable policy, it may be the solicitor's duty to provide independent advice or to refer the client to an independent intermediary.

5. Rule 12 of the Solicitors' Practice Rules 1990 provides that solicitors shall not, in connection with investment business, be appointed representatives or operate any separate business which is an appointed representative.

6. Guidance on home income and equity release schemes — mortgages and remortgages — is contained in Annex 24K. A product warning on home income plans is to be found at Annex 26H.

7. Solicitors who advertise that they are able to arrange mortgages must

comply with the Consumer Credit (Advertisement) Regulations 1989 (see Annex 11E).

8.   Solicitors who arrange mortgages will be carrying on credit brokerage within the meaning of the Consumer Credit Act 1974 and should take care to comply with the Consumer Credit (Quotations) Regulations 1989 when giving quotations.

24.08   Contractual referrals for conveyancing

Principle

A solicitor must comply with section 3A of the Solicitors' Introduction and Referral Code 1990 when making an agreement for the introduction of clients under which the solicitor agrees with an introducer to be paid by the introducer to provide conveyancing services for the introducer's customers.

Commentary

1.   The full text of the Solicitors' Introduction and Referral Code 1990 is to be found in Annex 11B.

2.   The normal solicitor/client relationship is unaffected by the fact that the introducer pays the solicitor for the conveyancing services. The work remains the professional responsibility of the solicitor.

3.   An agreement under section 3A of the code is not permitted with an introducer who is a seller (including a builder or developer) or a sellers' agent if the conveyancing services are to be provided to the buyer.

4.   At paragraph (8) of section 3A, the code requires that the introducer give the client written details of the conveyancing service to be provided by the solicitor and of the charge payable by the customer. Where the introducer is a lending institution, it must be made clear to the customer whether or not the solicitor will also be doing the conveyancing work for the lender, and if so the charge quoted must include that work.

5.   Although normally the instructions from the introducer will be limited to conveyancing services, this does not mean that the solicitor can disregard or exclude the general duty to act in the best interest of the client. While it is not part of a solicitor's general duty in a conveyancing matter to re-advise the client on financial matters, it is a solicitor's responsibility to point out to the client any aspects of the transaction that are manifestly disadvantageous to the client.

6.   At paragraph (9) of section 3A, the code requires the solicitor to provide the client with written terms of business which must include certain

specified matters. The paragraph does not set out everything that should be included in the solicitor's terms of business and reference should be made to Practice Rule 15 and the written professional standards (see Chapter 13).

7.   If the client instructs the solicitor to carry out supplementary work not covered by the agreement, the solicitor should make it clear that the client and not the introducer will be liable for the solicitor's costs for those services.

24.09   Honouring professional undertakings

Principle

A solicitor who fails to honour the terms of a professional undertaking is *prima facie* **guilty of professional misconduct.**

Commentary

1.   For detailed discussion on professional undertakings, see Chapter 19.

2.   An undertaking to redeem a mortgage means that the mortgage must be redeemed in the normal course of business. To delay doing so in order, for example, to arrange refinancing for a client would constitute a breach of the undertaking.

3.   A reply to a requisition on title in the course of a conveyancing transaction can and often does amount to an undertaking. For example, if the reply to the standard requisition concerning the discharge of mortgages before completion or the giving of an undertaking in lieu is 'noted', 'confirmed', 'yes' or 'this will be done' the seller's solicitor will have undertaken to do one or the other if the matter proceeds to completion; if the solicitor opts to give an undertaking, it is advisable to use the form recommended by the Society (see Annex 24G). Following completion, it is no valid reason for non-compliance that, at the particular time, the seller's solicitor was unaware of the existence of any charge on the property, even though the buyer's solicitor may have had that knowledge. Accordingly, it is recommended that when replying to this requisition, the seller's solicitor should make quite clear which mortgage or mortgages will be discharged on completion.

4.   Forms of undertakings agreed with banks are contained in Annex 24H.

5.   In an undertaking to pay money out of the proceeds of sale of a property, a term is not implied that the undertaking is intended to take effect only if the proceeds of sale actually come into the hands of the solicitor giving the undertaking. Accordingly, if this restriction is intended, it is crucial that a term to that effect is incorporated in the body of the undertaking itself,

otherwise the solicitor giving the undertaking may have to satisfy the payment out of his or her own resources.

6. The Council of Mortgage Lenders (CML) have produced advice on mortgage redemption statements. This deals with the situation when a seller's solicitor is faced with the possibility of having insufficient funds to comply with an undertaking to discharge a mortgage on completion because the bank or building society supplied an incorrect redemption statement. CML take the view that where an incorrect redemption figure has been provided which is clearly due to an error by the lender or to lack of clarification, it is unreasonable that a solicitor should be put in breach of undertaking. Lenders are therefore advised to seal the discharge (see Annex 24N).

7. The Society's formulae for exchanging contracts are contained in Annex 24I. Because professional undertakings form the basis of the formulae, solicitors should carefully consider who is to be authorised to effect exchange of contracts in accordance with the formulae and ensure that the use of the procedure is restricted to those authorised. The formulae are recommended for use only between firms of solicitors and licensed conveyancers.

8. On exchange of contracts under formula B solicitors must comply with the undertaking which forms part of the formula that the contract (and if appropriate the deposit) will be sent to the other party's solicitor that day. If a solicitor knows that this will not be possible, the undertaking should be varied at the time of exchange. If it is not possible to send the deposit cheque, this should be made quite clear on exchange. Arrangements could be made for the deposit cheque to be sent direct to the seller's solicitor from another firm in the chain. This would mean either varying formula B or making use of formula C.

9. The Society's code for completion by post is contained in Annex 24J. Again, as the code embodies professional undertakings it is recommended for adoption only between solicitors and licensed conveyancers.

10. Although the adoption of the National Conveyancing Protocol for domestic freehold or leasehold property does have certain conduct implications, it is essentially a form of 'preferred practice' and its requirements should not be construed as undertakings. For the Council statement on the protocol see Annex 24D. For detailed guidance on the procedures to be adopted under the protocol reference should be made to *The National Conveyancing Protocol (Second Edition)* which may be obtained from the Law Society Shop.

11. For detailed guidance on conveyancing practice, reference may be made to *The Law Society's Conveyancing Handbook* which may be obtained from the Law Society Shop.

24.10   Mortgage fraud

Principle

A solicitor must not act or, where relevant, must cease to act further where the instructions would involve the solicitor in a breach of the law or a breach of the principles of professional conduct unless the client is prepared to change his or her instructions accordingly.

Commentary

Annex 24M contains the Society's 'Green Card' warning on mortgage fraud and Annex 24L contains guidance on a solicitor's duty in conduct when acting for a lender and borrower when there is some variation in the purchase price.

24.11   Lien over title deeds

Principle

It is not unprofessional for a solicitor to retain title deeds belonging to his or her client pending payment of professional costs owed by that client where the retention is a proper exercise of a solicitor's lien.

Commentary

1.   Care should be taken to distinguish between a solicitor's lien and an unpaid seller's lien. For detailed commentary on the nature and effect of a solicitor's lien see *Cordery on Solicitors* and Principle 12.18.

2.   In relation to the unpaid seller's lien, reference should be made to an appropriate authority on the law of lien. It should be noted that use of the Standard Conditions of Sale and the Society's code for completion by post will affect the seller's right to exercise a lien — see *The Law Society's Conveyancing Handbook*.

24.12   Deposit interest on stakeholder money

Principle

A solicitor must pay deposit interest on money held in his or her capacity as stakeholder in accordance with Part III of the Solicitors' Accounts Rules 1991, to the person to whom the stake is paid.

Commentary

1.   For detailed commentary on the application of Part III see Chapter 27.

2.   The operation of the deposit interest provisions may be excluded by
      written agreement between the parties. It is not, however, normal practice
      for a stakeholder in conveyancing transactions to retain interest instead of
      paying it to the recipient of the stake (see Annex 27G).

24.13   Stamp duty and Land Registry fees

Principle

**Money paid to a solicitor for stamp duty or Land Registry fees must be
paid into client account and must remain there until paid out.**

24.14   Refusal to complete for non-payment of costs

Principle

**Unless a solicitor has, at the outset of the retainer, required the client to
make a payment or payments on account of costs, the solicitor should not
refuse to complete a transaction for the client if the sole reason for that
refusal is that the client has not made such a payment.**

Commentary

1.   It will be noted that this Principle does not apply in relation to
      non-payment of disbursements. A solicitor may refuse to complete where
      disbursements which are necessary to enable completion to take place
      remain outstanding. If completion does take place the solicitor should
      consider his or her duty to act in the best interests of any mortgagee client
      in relation to registration and stamping.

2.   See Principle 14.01 for further guidance.

Annex 24A

Council direction on submitting draft contracts to more than one prospective purchaser

1. The Council is concerned that the volume of complaints about breaches of the above Direction has not diminished since the Direction was first published in the Society's *Gazette* on 6th October 1977.

2. The Council have therefore decided to republish the Direction and this is set out below.

3. For the avoidance of doubt the Council wish to emphasise that the Direction applies to all sales and purchases of freehold and leasehold property.

4. The Council also wish to emphasise to the profession that the Direction is mandatory upon all solicitors and that any solicitor who is found to be in breach of the Direction in future is liable to face proceedings before the Solicitors' Disciplinary Tribunal.

Council Direction — Vendor's solicitor submitting draft contracts to more than one prospective purchaser

The Council recognise that a solicitor acting for a vendor may sometimes be instructed by his client to deal with more than one prospective purchaser at the same time.

The Council have accordingly directed that where a vendor instructs his solicitor to submit (whether simultaneously or otherwise) forms of contract to more than one prospective purchaser, the following steps by the solicitor are obligatory:

(A) Where solicitor is acting for vendor

The solicitor (with his client's authority) must at once disclose the vendor's decision direct to the solicitor acting for each prospective purchaser or (where no solicitor is acting) to the prospective purchaser(s) in person and such disclosure, if made orally, must at once be confirmed in writing. If the vendor refuses to authorise disclosure, the solicitor must cease acting for the vendor forthwith.

(B) Where solicitor is entitled to act for both vendor and purchaser

Notwithstanding the exceptions contained in paragraph (2) of Rule 6 of the Solicitors' Practice Rules 1990, a solicitor cannot act for both vendor and purchaser if a conflict of interest arises. Where there is more than one prospective purchaser, the Council consider that the danger of a conflict of interest is greatly increased. The Council are reluctant to issue a general prohibition against acting in such cases and they therefore warn all solicitors concerned to consider most carefully whether, and if so to what extent, they can properly act in these cases. If, in an exceptional case, a solicitor decides that he can properly act for both vendor and one of the prospective purchasers, then (in addition to the steps he must take under paragraph (A) above) the solicitor must at once disclose his decision direct to those two clients and also to the solicitor acting for every other prospective purchaser or (where no solicitor is acting) to the prospective purchaser(s) in person and such disclosure, if made orally, must at once be confirmed in writing.

(C) Where solicitor is asked to act for more than one purchaser

Where forms of contract are submitted to more than one prospective purchaser, a solicitor must not accept instructions to act for more than one prospective purchaser.

28th November 1979 (updated January 1993)

Annex 24B

Council requirement on the ABI Code of Practice for Intermediaries — general insurance business

The Association of British Insurers, with the approval of the Minister of State for Trade and Industry, has promulgated a revised code of practice for all intermediaries conducting general insurance business. Preliminary notice of the code and of the attitude of the Law Society to it appeared in [1989] *Gazette*, 26 April, 14.

First, the code introduces requirements for professional indemnity cover for intermediaries. Following discussion between the Law Society, Solicitors Indemnity Fund Limited (SIF) and the ABI it has now been agreed that the cover provided to solicitors by SIF will satisfy the professional indemnity requirements of the ABI code.

Secondly, the code of practice provides that an intermediary shall make it known to a prospective policyholder that he or she is:

* an employee of an insurance company, for whose conduct the company accepts responsibility; or

* an agent of one company, for whose conduct the company accepts responsibility; or

* an agent of two or up to six companies for whose conduct the companies accept responsibility; or

* an independent intermediary seeking to act on behalf of the prospective policyholder for whose conduct the company/companies do not accept responsibility.

The Council is of the view that solicitors conducting general insurance business should do so only as independent intermediaries. It considers it incompatible with the independence of the solicitor and the primacy of the solicitor's duty to the client to accept an accountability to an insurance company that could conflict with his or her duty to the client. Any tied agency would be inconsistent with the status of solicitors as independent intermediaries in the provision of financial services.

Having the status of an independent intermediary does not prevent a solicitor having agency arrangements with whatever number of insurance companies the solicitor considers appropriate. Insurance companies are making available to their intermediaries for signature declarations of status as either independent intermediary or company agent. A requirement that solicitors must act as independent intermediaries does not prevent agency arrangements continuing but it will ensure that within such arrangements the primacy of the interest of the client is upheld.

At its meeting on 8th June 1989 the Council resolved to require solicitors who act as intermediaries for general insurance business to do so only as independent intermediaries within the meaning of the ABI code of practice.

12th July 1989 (updated January 1993)

General Insurance Business
— Code of Practice for all Intermediaries
(Including Employees of Insurance Companies)
other than Registered Insurance Brokers
(Introduced January 1989)*

This Code applies to general business as defined in the Insurance Companies Act 1982, but does not apply to reinsurance business. As a condition of membership of the Association of British Insurers, members undertake to enforce this Code and to use their best endeavours to ensure that all those involved in selling their policies observe its provisions.

It shall be an overriding obligation of an intermediary at all times to conduct business with the utmost good faith and integrity.

In the case of complaints from policyholders (either direct or indirect, for example through a trading standards officer or citizens' advice bureau), the insurance company concerned shall require an intermediary to co-operate so that the facts can be established. An intermediary shall inform the policyholder complaining that he can take his problem direct to the insurance company concerned.

A.   General sales principles

1.   The intermediary shall:

(i)   where appropriate, make a prior appointment to call. Unsolicited or unarranged calls shall be made at an hour likely to be suitable to the prospective policyholder;

(ii)   when he makes contact with the prospective policyholder, identify himself and explain as soon as possible that the arrangements he wishes to discuss could include insurance. He shall make it known that he is:

(a)   an employee of an insurance company, for whose conduct the company accepts responsibility; or

(b)   an agent of one company, for whose conduct the company accepts responsibility; or

(c)   an agent of two or up to six companies, for whose conduct the companies accept responsibility; or

(d)   an independent intermediary seeking to act on behalf of the prospective policyholder, for whose conduct the company/companies do not accept responsibility;

(iii)   ensure as far as possible that the policy proposed is suitable to the needs and resources of the prospective policyholder;

---

* Reproduced with the kind permission of the Association of British Insurers.

(iv) give advice only on those insurance matters in which he is knowledgeable and seek or recommend other specialist advice when necessary; and

(v) treat all information supplied by the prospective policyholder as completely confidential to himself and to the company or companies to which the business is being offered.

2. The intermediary shall not:

(i) inform the prospective policyholder that his name has been given by another person, unless he is prepared to disclose that person's name if requested to do so by the prospective policyholder and has that person's consent to make that disclosure;

(ii) make inaccurate or unfair criticisms of any insurer; or

(iii) make comparisons with other types of policy unless he makes clear the differing characteristics of each policy.

B.   Explanation of the contract

The intermediary shall:

(i) identify the insurance company;

(ii) explain all the essential provisions of the cover afforded by the policy, or policies, which he is recommending, so as to ensure as far as possible that the prospective policyholder understands what he is buying;

(iii) draw attention to any restrictions and exclusions applying to the policy;

(iv) if necessary, obtain from the insurance company specialist advice in relation to items (ii) and (iii) above;

(v) not impose any charge in addition to the premium required by the insurance company without disclosing the amount and purpose of such charge; and

(vi) if he is an independent intermediary, disclose his commission on request.

C.   Disclosure of underwriting information

The intermediary shall, in obtaining the completion of the proposal form or any other material:

(i) avoid influencing the prospective policyholder and make it clear that all the answers or statements are the latter's own responsibility; and

(ii) ensure that the consequences of non-disclosure and inaccuracies are pointed out to the prospective policyholder by drawing his attention to the relevant statement in the proposal form and by explaining them himself to the prospective policyholder.

D.   Accounts and financial aspects

The intermediary shall, if authorised to collect monies in accordance with the terms of his agency appointment:

(i) keep a proper account of all financial transactions with a prospective policyholder which involve the transmission of money in respect of insurance;

(ii) acknowledge receipt (which, unless the intermediary has been otherwise authorised by the insurance company, shall be on his own behalf) of all money received in connection with an insurance policy and shall distinguish the premium from any other payment included in the money; and

(iii) remit any such monies so collected in strict conformity with his agency appointment.

E.   Documentation

The intermediary shall not withhold from the policyholder any written evidence or documentation relating to the contract of insurance.

F.   Existing policyholders

The intermediary shall abide by the principles set out in this Code to the extent that they are relevant to his dealings with existing policyholders.

G.   Claims

If the policyholder advises the intermediary of an incident which might give rise to a claim, the intermediary shall inform the company without delay, and in any event within three working days, and thereafter give prompt advice to the policyholder of the company's requirements concerning the claim, including the provision as soon as possible of information required to establish the nature and extent of the loss. Information received from the policyholder shall be passed to the company without delay.

H.   Professional indemnity cover for independent intermediaries

The intermediary shall obtain, and maintain in force, professional indemnity insurance in accordance with the requirements of the Association of British Insurers as set out [below], which may be updated from time to time.

I.   Letters of appointment

This Code of Practice shall be incorporated verbatim or by reference in all Letters of Appointment of non-registered intermediaries and no policy of the company shall be sold by such intermediaries except within the terms of such a Letter of Appointment.

**Professional Indemnity Cover
for Non-Registered Independent Intermediaries**

As from 1st January 1989 (new agents) and by 1st July 1989 (existing agents) all non-registered independent intermediaries must take out and maintain in force professional indemnity cover in accordance with the requirements set out below.

The insurance may be taken out with any authorised UK or EEC insurer who has agreed to:

(a)   issue cover in accordance with the requirements set out below;

(b)   provide the intermediary with an annual certificate as evidence that the cover meets the ABI requirements, this certificate to contain the name and address including postcode of the intermediary, the policy number, the period of the policy, the limit of indemnity, the self-insured excess and the name of the insurer;

(c)   send a duplicate certificate to ABI at the time the certificate is issued to the intermediary;

(d)   inform ABI, by means of monthly lists, of any cases of non-renewal, cancellation of the cover mid-term or of the cover becoming inadequate.

The requirements are as follows:

A.   Limits of indemnity

The policy shall at inception and at each renewal date, which shall not be more than 12 months from inception or the last renewal date, provide a minimum limit of indemnity of either:

(a)   a sum equal to three times the annual general business commission of the business for the last accounting period ending prior to inception or renewal of the policy, or a sum of £250,000, whichever sum is the greater.

       In no case shall the minimum limit of indemnity be required to exceed £5m, and a minimum sum of £250,000 shall apply at all times to each and every claim or series of claims arising out of the same occurrence.

       or

(b)   a sum equal to three times the annual general business commission of the business for the last accounting period ending prior to inception or renewal of the policy, or a sum of £500,000 whichever sum shall be the greater.

In no case shall the minimum limit of indemnity be required to exceed £5m.

B.   Maximum self-insured excess

The maximum self-insured excess permitted in normal circumstances shall be 1% of the minimum limit of indemnity required by paragraph A(a) or A(b) above as the case may be. Subject to the agreement of the professional indemnity insurer, the self-insured excess may be increased to a maximum of 2% of such minimum limit of indemnity.

C.   Scope of policy cover

The policy shall indemnify the insured:

(a)   against losses arising from claims made against the insured:

      (i)   for breach of duty in connection with the business by reason of any negligent act, error or omission; and

      (ii)   in respect of libel or slander or in Scotland defamation, committed in the conduct of the business by the insured, any employee or former employee of the insured, and where the business is or was carried on in partnership any partner or former partner of the insured; and

      (iii)   by reason of any dishonest or fraudulent act or omission committed or made in the conduct of the business by any employee (other than a director of a body corporate) or former employee (other than a director of a body corporate) of the insured;

and

(b)   against claims arising in connection with the business in respect of:

(i)   any loss of money or other property whatsoever belonging to the insured or for which the insured is legally liable in consequence of any dishonest or fraudulent act or omission of any employee or former employee (other than a director of a body corporate) or former employee (other than a director of a body corporate) of the insured; and

(ii)   legal liability incurred by reason of loss of documents and costs and expenses incurred in replacing or restoring such documents.

D.   General business only

The above requirements relate only to the intermediary's general insurance business.

Association of British Insurers
November 1988

Annex 24C

Council statement on the Financial Services Act 1986 — life policies and tied agents

It is the Council's view that it is in the best interests of anyone who is likely to need an endowment policy, or similar life insurance with an investment element, that he or she should receive advice from an independent intermediary authorised to give investment advice. Neither the Financial Services Act 1986 nor the rules of the SIB bring about that situation. Sales representatives of insurance companies will be able to sell to the public direct or through intermediaries. In addition many estate agency and building society offices will be tied agents of life companies and members of the public who either approach them direct or are referred to them will be offered policies issued by the company to which they are tied. Many banks will apparently offer both independent intermediary services and also act as company representatives selling their own products.

The Financial Services Act 1986 is not clear as to whether introducing clients to life offices or their tied agents' outlets is 'investment business'. There is certainly a fine line btween introducing and 'arranging' (defined as 'making, or offering or agreeing to make, arrangements with a view to another person buying ... a particular investment'). The latter is investment business requiring authorisation. Mere referrals are not regulated, and in the light of the polarisation between independents and tied agents, solicitors need to set their own standards in this field against the background of our clear duty expressed in Rule 1 of the Solicitors' Practice Rules 1990, to act in the best interests of the client.

Client needing advice on life insurance

A solicitor's independence, and thus his or her ability to give impartial and disinterested advice, is a fundamental element of the solicitor's relationship with clients. In relation therefore to clients who need, or are likely to need, life insurance, solicitors should either act as independent intermediaries themselves and assess the client's requirements, survey the market, recommend the best policy available, and arrange for the transaction, or they should introduce the client to another independent intermediary who will do the same. The solicitor's duty to give the client independent advice would not be discharged by referring such a client to an adviser who is not an independent intermediary, for example, a bank, building society or estate agent or insurance agent which is an appointed representative, i.e. a tied agent. If, however, a solicitor has assessed a client's need for life assurance, identified the client's requirements, surveyed the market and selected a life office on appropriate criteria, then the solicitor may either arrange the taking out of the policy or may introduce the client to the life office or its representative so that can be done. This work would need authorisation and would be 'discrete investment business' under the Solicitors' Investment Business Rules 1990. Alternatively the solicitor who does not profess expertise in life insurance can always refer the client to an independent intermediary.

Client seeking mortgage advice

As many as 80% of those who take out mortgages do so on an endowment basis. Accordingly the need for independent advice referred to above will also be important for the client who merely knows that he or she needs a mortgage and is unaware of the precise relationship between the obtaining of mortgage finance and his or her likely need for a life policy. Although no statutory framework governs 'mortgage advice' solicitors will normally assess a client's needs and bear in mind a variety of considerations including speed and reliability of administration, availability, interest rates and terms of mortgage finance in deciding where to refer clients. They should also bear in mind that some mortgage providers are tied agents and that referral of a mortgage-seeking client to a tied agent may result in that client not receiving independent investment advice. If the particular client's interests dictate that he or she should be referred to a tied agent's office, the client should be informed that the office only has investment products from a single company to offer, though it may in turn refer the client to an independent intermediary if this proves to be necessary or desirable.

(Solicitors may note that the Building Societies Association has issued a code of practice with regard to the linking of services. This prohibits a member society from making the arrangement of an insurance policy (or other services) by the society a condition of the offer of a class 1 (first) mortgage. Society staff must not suggest to customers that such mortgages are conditional in this way, and will, if asked, explain that a mortgage may be obtained without using the society's insurance arrangements.)

Clients referred to solicitors

What is a solicitor's duty when a conveyancing client is referred by a life office, bank, building society or estate agent which is itself a tied agent, and the client is proposing, not having received independent advice, to take out a company life policy?

There is no universal answer applicable to all circumstances. It is not and cannot be a solicitor's obligation to force a client to receive independent advice on a life policy unless he or she wishes to receive it. Tied agents are required to draw customers' attention to the fact that they are not independent, and the client ought thus to have entered the transaction with open eyes. That may not, however, always be the case and solicitors should always be prepared to make further enquiries of clients who appear to be proposing to take out policies which are not suitable for their requirements. It may then be the solicitor's duty either to provide independent 'best advice', or to refer the client to an independent intermediary who can do so. The solicitor should indicate whether there will be a cost or delay involved and should also consider whether the proposed purchase transaction is likely to be prejudiced.

For all these purposes it will be necessary for solicitors to be aware which banks, building societies and estate agents are acting as independent intermediaries and which are tied agents. Solicitors should also note the other authorised financial advisers who could also act as independent intermediaries.

Building society agencies

Rule 12 of the Solicitors' Practice Rules 1990 prohibits solicitors from being 'appointed representatives' or tied agents for investment business, and the agency arrangements solicitors may have with building societies which are tied agents clearly must be confined to non-investment business otherwise the solicitor-agent might be in breach of the rule. Where a solicitor has a building society agency, his or her function is usually confined to paying and receiving sums of money on behalf of the building society. However there may be occasions when he or she is asked about mortgages and in such event the solicitor should bear in mind the need for independent advice referred to above. This applies equally whether the agency is conducted from the solicitor's general office or from an adjoining office which is used solely for the building society agency work. It is important that there should be no possible confusion to clients as to the nature and status of the office in relation to the sale of investment products. This will present no problem if the building society is itself an independent intermediary. If the society is a tied agent the business transacted at the solicitor's agency office must be confined to non-investment business.

These principles apply equally where the solicitor is agent for a financial institution other than a building society.

Insurance company agencies

So far as investment business is concerned, insurance companies have cancelled their existing agency agreements and arranged for those solicitors who will themselves be giving independent advice to register with the companies for the purpose of the payment of commissions. However, it is still possible for solicitors to have agencies with insurance companies for business other than investment business, e.g. buildings insurance (although a solicitor must not enter into any arrangement under which he or she will be constrained to refer business to a particular company).

23rd March 1988 (updated January 1993)

Annex 24D

Council statement on the National Protocol for domestic freehold and leasehold property

The National Protocol for domestic freehold and leasehold property was launched on 21st March 1990. All solicitors engaged in domestic conveyancing should be aware of the Council statement which forms part of the Protocol. The following extract from the Council statement sets out those aspects relevant to professional conduct:

'4. The Protocol is a form of "preferred practice" and its requirements should not be construed as undertakings. Nor are they intended to widen a solicitor's duty save as set out in the next paragraph. The Protocol must always be considered in the context of a solicitor's overriding duty to his or her own client's interests and where compliance with the Protocol would conflict with that duty, the client's wishes must always be paramount.

5. A solicitor acting in domestic conveyancing transactions should inform the solicitor acting for the other party at the outset of a transaction, whether or not he or she is proposing to act in accordance with the Protocol in full or in part. If the solicitor is using the Protocol he or she should give notice to the solicitor acting for the other party if during the course of the transaction it becomes necessary to depart from Protocol procedures.

6. A solicitor is, as a matter of professional conduct, under a duty to keep confidential client's business. The confidentiality continues until the client permits disclosure or waives the confidentiality (Principle 16.03 of the Guide). With reference to paragraphs 4.5 and 5.3 of the Protocol [supplying information to the other party], the disclosure of information about a client's position is strictly subject to obtaining that client's authority to disclose. In the absence of such authority, a solicitor is not deemed to be departing from the terms of the Protocol and, as such, is not required to give notice as set out in paragraph 5 of this statement.'

(updated January 1993)

THE GUIDE TO THE PROFESSIONAL CONDUCT OF SOLICITORS 1993

Annex 24E

Council statement on dealing with licensed conveyancers

The first licences were granted by the Council for Licensed Conveyancers on 1st May 1987, and solicitors will therefore be likely to encounter licensed conveyancers in practice from time to time.

Licensed conveyancers will be permitted to practise in partnership with each other, or in partnership or association with non-licensed conveyancers (but not of course with solicitors). In addition to this, licensed conveyancers may practise through the medium of a 'recognised body', which in this context means a body corporate recognised by the Council for Licensed Conveyancers.

The identity of firms of licensed conveyancers can be checked by looking them up in the current *Directory of Solicitors and Barristers*. In all cases of doubt you are advised to contact the Council for Licensed Conveyancers at Suite 3, Cairngorm House, 203 Marsh Wall, Docklands, London E14 9YT (071-537 2953).

Rules on conduct and discipline, including accounts rules, have been made by the Council for Licensed Conveyancers, which are in many respects similar to those which apply to solicitors, although there are differences. Licensed conveyancers will be covered by compulsory indemnity insurance and will have to contribute to a compensation fund. In so far as dealings with licensed conveyancers are concerned, it should normally be possible to proceed as if the conveyancer was a solicitor and was bound by the same professional obligations as a solicitor. For example, if it is agreed to use the Law Society's code for exchange of contracts by telephone, it is understood that any failure to respect the code would expose the licensed conveyancer to disciplinary proceedings of the same kind to which a solicitor would be exposed in similar circumstances: the same comment applies to the Society's code for completion by post, the use of client account cheques at completion and reliance on undertakings. In view of the fact that licensed conveyancers may practise in partnership or association with others, subject to approval by the Council for Licensed Conveyancers, it is however important to make sure that the person you are dealing with is a licensed conveyancer, or a person working immediately under his or her supervision.

In dealings with licensed conveyancers the overriding concern will always be for the interests of the client for whom you are acting. As with dealings with another solicitor, wherever there is a good reason to suspect that some unethical or unlawful practice is being undertaken in which your client's collaboration is sought, the right thing is to err on the side of caution and, if it is practicable, to take advice from Professional Ethics.

29th April 1987 (updated January 1993)

Council guidance — dealing with unqualified conveyancers

Unqualified conveyancers

1.   The following guidance relates to unqualified conveyancers and *not* to licensed conveyancers.

Criminal offences

2.   Under section 22 of the Solicitors Act 1974 (as amended by the Administration of Justice Act 1985) it is an offence for an unqualified person to draw or prepare, *inter alia,* a contract for sale or a transfer, conveyance, lease or mortgage relating to land, unless that person can prove that the act was not done in expectation of fee, gain or reward. The persons qualified under this section are solicitors, barristers, notaries public, licensed conveyancers, Scottish solicitors and some public officers.

3.   It follows that when an unqualified person undertakes a conveyancing transaction, in the course of a conveyancing business, on behalf of a client, it is inevitable that the unqualified conveyancer will commit an offence under section 22 unless the drawing or preparation of the relevant documents is undertaken by a qualified person. In such circumstances, the unqualified conveyancer's client is likely, albeit unwittingly, to be guilty of aiding and abetting the offence. It is also possible that a solicitor acting for the other party could be guilty of procuring the commission of an offence under section 22 by inviting or urging the unqualified person to provide a draft contract or transfer or to progress the transaction.

Council's decisions

4.   The Council's view is that on these grounds solicitors should refuse to have any dealings with any unqualified person carrying on a conveyancing business unless the solicitor has clear evidence that offences under section 22 will not be committed.

5.   It is recommended that, at the outset of any transaction, the solicitor should write to the unqualified conveyancer drawing attention to the Council's guidance and informing him or her that the solicitor cannot enter into any dealings with him or her unless the solicitor has clear evidence that no offences will be committed. An example of satisfactory evidence will be a letter from a qualified person confirming that he or she will prepare the relevant documents. It is also recommended that the solicitor should immediately report the matter to his or her own client and explain why he or she cannot enter into any dealings with the unqualified conveyancer unless clear evidence is forthcoming.

Proposed letter to unqualified conveyancer

Dear Sir/Madam

Re: Sale and purchase

We have been instructed to act for the seller/buyer in connection with the above transaction and have been informed that you have been instructed by the buyer/seller. We will be grateful if you will confirm that you are a solicitor or licensed conveyancer. If not, please state who will be preparing the contract/conveyance/transfer for you; please arrange for us to receive written confirmation from the qualified person as soon as possible that he or she will personally be settling the contract/conveyance/transfer.

As you know, it is an offence for an unqualified person to prepare a contract for sale or transfer, conveyance, or mortgage relating to land unless that person can prove that the act was not done in expectation of fee, gain or reward. We have been advised by the Law Society that we should not deal with an unqualified person carrying on a conveyancing business unless clear evidence is provided to us that offences under section 22 will not be committed. The letter referred to above, if it is explicit and unequivocal, could provide such evidence.

Therefore, unless you are a solicitor or licensed conveyancer, we cannot deal with you unless you can provide the evidence required above.

Yours faithfully,

Letter to client of solicitor

Dear

Re: Sale and purchase

I thank you for your instructions relating to the above transactions but unfortunately there is a hitch. The seller/buyer appears to have instructed an unqualified conveyancer to act for him/her and this could lead to the conveyancer, his/her client and even me being involved in the commission of criminal offences under the Solicitors Act 1974. In addition, the Law Society, my professional body, has advised solicitors that they should not deal with unqualified conveyancers because of the possibility of committing criminal offences.

In the circumstances, I have written to the firm acting for the seller/buyer and have asked them to confirm whether or not they are unqualified conveyancers and if they are whether they can satisfy me that they will be making arrangements which will prevent the commission of such offences. If they cannot satisfy me about this, the seller/buyer will have to make arrangements to instruct a solicitor or licensed conveyancer, or I will only be able to deal with him/her direct.

Yours sincerely,

Law Society's Legal Practice Directorate

6.   The directorate can offer help and guidance to practitioners dealing with unqualified conveyancers if the above guidance and the practice notes below do not cover the situation:

(a)   Telephone calls should be made to the Legal Practice Directorate Practice Advice Service with whom a check can also be made as to whether a person is a licensed conveyancer or not. If he or she is a licensed conveyancer then he or she can be dealt with in a similar way to a solicitor.

(b)   The Professional Adviser has responsibility for investigating and if necessary prosecuting persons who appear to be in breach of the relevant provisions of the Solicitors Act 1974. Solicitors are asked to report (without submitting their files) any case with which they deal where an unqualified person is involved.

(c)   For dealing with licensed conveyancers see Annex 24E in the Guide.

(d)   Written guidance on specific points of procedure can be obtained from the Secretary of the Land Law and Succession Committee.

Practice notes

7.   For assistance in those cases where the solicitor has clear evidence that no offences under section 22 will be committed, there is set out below a series of practice notes relating to the problems which might arise in a transaction in which the other party is represented by an unqualified conveyancer. These practice notes are given by way of advice only and it is for solicitors to decide for themselves what steps should properly be taken in any particular situation.

PRACTICE NOTES

(applicable only where evidence is provided of compliance with section 22)

Undertakings

1.   Any undertaking which unqualified agents may offer in the course of a transaction is not enforceable in the same way as an undertaking given by a solicitor or licensed conveyancer. Solicitors should therefore never accept such undertakings.

Completions by post

2.   Solicitors are under no duty to undertake agency work by way of completions by post on behalf of unqualified persons, or to attend to other formalities on behalf of third parties who are not clients, even where such third parties offer to pay the agent's charges.

3.   The Council also suggests that in cases where a solicitor is dealing with an unqualified conveyancer, the solicitor should bear in mind the line of decisions starting with *Hedley Byrne* v. *Heller* [1964] A.C. 465, which extends the duty of care owed by a solicitor so as to include persons who are not clients, but who rely and act on his or her advice to the solicitor's knowledge.

Draft contracts

4.   Solicitors must decide in each case whether special provisions should be incorporated in the draft contract to take account of the problems which arise by reason of the other party having no solicitor or licensed conveyancer, e.g. that the seller should attend personally at completion if represented by an unqualified agent. All such matters

must be considered prior to exchange of contracts since contractual conditions cannot, of course, be imposed subsequently.

5.   The protection provided by section 69 of the Law of Property Act 1925 only applies when a document containing a receipt for purchase money is handed over by a solicitor or licensed conveyancer or the seller himself or herself. Thus it should be considered whether a condition be incorporated in the contract providing either for the seller to attend personally at completion or for an authority signed by the seller, for the purchase money to be paid to his or her agent, to be handed over on completion.

Acting for seller: buyer not represented by a solicitor or licensed conveyancer

6.   Attention is drawn to paragraph 4 above.

Completion

7.   It is important to ensure that the deeds, and keys in cases where these are also handed over, are passed to the person entitled to receive them, i.e the buyer. If an authority on behalf of the buyer is offered to the seller's solicitor, it is for that solicitor to decide whether or not to accept it, bearing in mind that no authority, however expressed, can be irrevocable. Again it is worth considering at the outset whether the point should be covered by express condition in the contract.

Acting for the buyer: seller not represented by a solicitor or licensed conveyancer

Preliminary enquiries and requisitions on title

8.   It may be prudent to require and ensure that replies to preliminary enquiries and requisitions are signed by the seller.

Payment of deposit

9.   Difficulties may arise in connection with the payment of the usual 10% deposit where there is no estate agent involved who is a member of one of the recognised professional bodies and to whom the deposit may be paid as stakeholder in the ordinary way. It is, of course, possible for the deposit to be paid direct to the seller, but this course of action cannot be recommended since it is equivalent to parting with a portion of the purchase money in advance of investigation of the title and other matters.

10.   Some unqualified agents are now insisting that the deposit be paid to them. The Council does not recommend that this be done. If a solicitor is obliged to pay the deposit to unqualified agents, incorporated or otherwise, he or she should make certain to inform the client of the considerable dangers involved, and obtain the client's specific instructions before proceeding.

11.   An alternative method is for the deposit to be paid to the buyer's solicitor as stakeholder. The buyer's solicitor should insist that where possible the deposit is paid to him or her as stakeholder. If the seller will not agree to this course, then it may be possible to agree that the deposit be placed in a deposit account in the joint names of the buyer's solicitor and the seller, or for such an account to be in the seller's name, with the deposit receipt to be retained by the buyer's solicitor.

Payment of purchase money

12.   As referred to in practice note 5 above, the buyer's solicitor should ensure that all the purchase money, including any deposit, is paid either to the seller or to the seller's properly authorised agent.

Matters unresolved at completion

13.   Whilst it is unusual to leave any issues revealed by searches and other enquiries outstanding at completion, undertakings relating to their discharge or resolution may on occasions be given between solicitors or licensed conveyancers. Such undertakings must not be accepted from unqualified agents for the reason mentioned in practice note 1 above.

Power of attorney

14.   Unqualified agents sometimes obtain a power of attorney to enable themselves or their employees to conduct certain aspects of the transaction. It is clearly important to ensure that such powers are valid, properly granted, and effective for all relevant purposes.

Acting for the mortgagee: borrower not represented by a solicitor or licensed conveyancer

15.   The mortgagee's solicitor often finds himself or herself undertaking much of the work which a buyer's solicitor would do. Whilst the solicitor must hold the client's interests paramount, the solicitor must ensure that he or she does not render the unqualified agent additional assistance, nor establish any kind of arrangement with such an agent which could present difficulties under Rule 7 of the Solicitors' Practice Rules 1990 or by virtue of the *Hedley Byrne* line of cases.

Advances

16.   As regards the drafting and preparation of the instrument of transfer by the buyer/borrower's representatives there is no obligation on the mortgagee's solicitors to undertake work which would normally be done by the buyer's solicitor. Solicitors are reminded, however, that it is of paramount importance to their mortgagee client that good title is conveyed to the buyer.

17.   Payment of mortgage advances — the importance of paying advances only to those properly entitled to receive them — is an additional reason for insisting either that the borrower attends personally on completion or that a signed authority from the borrower in favour of his or her agent be received on completion. Section 69 of the Law of Property Act 1925 as amended is a relevant consideration in this context.

Redemptions

18.   On completion, cheques or drafts should be drawn in favour of solicitors or licensed conveyancers or their clients, and not endorsed over to some intermediate party. The deeds should normally be handed over to the borrower personally, unless he or she provides a valid authority for them to be handed to a third party.

19.   Any issues of doubt or difficulty must be referred to the mortgagees so as to obtain detailed instructions. Where the mortgagee is a building society and its solicitor considers that the totality of the work involved justifies a charge in excess of the building society's guideline fee, he or she should seek the approval of the client/mortgagee thereto, supported if necessary by a bill of costs containing sufficient detail of the work and the time spent on it.

16th March 1988 (updated January 1993)

Annex 24G

Guidance — discharge of building society mortgages — form of undertaking recommended by the Law Society

'In consideration of your today completing the purchase of ....
WE HEREBY UNDERTAKE forthwith to pay over to the ....
Building Society the money required to redeem the mortgage/legal charge dated ....
.........................and to forward the receipted mortgage/legal charge to you as soon as it is
received by us from the ....Building Society.'

Annex 24H

Guidance — forms of undertaking agreed with banks

FORM No. 1

Undertaking by Solicitor — Deeds/Land Certificate loaned to the Solicitor for purpose of inspection only and return.

..........................19...

To .... Bank Limited

I/We hereby acknowledge to have received on loan from you the Title Deeds and/or Land Certificate and documents relating to................................in accordance with the schedule hereto.

I/We undertake to hold them on your behalf and to return them to you on demand in the same condition in which they now are and without the property to which they relate or any interest therein being, to our knowledge, in any way charged, conveyed, assigned, leased, encumbered, disposed of or dealt with.

Signature ....

SCHEDULE

FORM No. 2

Undertaking by Solicitor — Deeds/Land Certificate handed to the Solicitor re Sale or Mortgage of property, or part of it, and to account to the Bank for net proceeds.

..........................19...

To .... Bank Limited

I/We hereby acknowledge to have received from you the Title Deeds and/or Land Certificate and documents *together with a charge to the Bank* relating to.........................
in accordance with the schedule hereto for the purpose of the sale/mortgage of this property.

I/We undertake to hold them on your behalf and to return them to you on demand in the same condition in which they now are, pending completion of such transaction. If the transaction is completed I/we undertake:

(a) to pay to you the amount of the purchase/mortgage money, not being less than £.....
gross subject only to the deduction therefrom of the deposit (if held by the estate
agent(s)), the estate agents' commission and the legal costs and disbursements
relating to the transaction, and

(b) if the Title Deeds and/or Land Certificate and documents also relate to other
property in addition to that referred to above, to return same to you suitably
endorsed or noted.

Signature ....

NOTE: *If there are likely to be any deductions from the purchase price other than those
shown above, these must be specifically mentioned.*

SCHEDULE

* Delete if no charge form has been taken

FORM No. 3

*Undertaking by Solicitor — to send Deeds/Land Certificate to Bank on completion of a
purchase, the Bank and/or its customer having provided the purchase monies.*

...........................19 ...

To .... Bank Limited

If you provide facilities to my/our client .... for the purchase of the
Freehold/Leasehold property *[Description of Property]*

I/We undertake:

(a) that any sums received from you or your customer for the purpose of this
transaction will be applied solely for acquiring a good marketable title to such
property and in paying any necessary deposit legal costs and disbursements in
connection with such purchase. The purchase price contemplated is £ .... gross
and with apportionments and any necessary disbursements is not expected to
exceed £.......

and

(b) after the property has been acquired by ....and all necessary stamping and
registration has been completed to send the Title Deeds and/or Land Certificate and
documents to you and in the meantime to hold them to your order.

Signature ....

FORM No. 4 (BRIDGING FINANCE)

Undertaking by Solicitors (with form of authority from client) to account to the Bank for net proceeds of sale of the existing property, the Bank having provided funds in connection with the purchase of the new property.

Authority from client(s)

........................19...

To ....

....

(name and address of solicitors)

I/We hereby irrevocably authorise and request you to give an undertaking in the form set out below and accordingly to pay the net proceeds of sale after deduction of your costs to ....Bank Limited......................Branch.

Signature of client(s)...........................

Undertaking

........................19...

To .... Bank Limited

If you provide facilities to our client...

....

for the purchase of the Freehold/Leasehold property (the new property)

....

(description of property)

pending the sale by our client of the Freehold/Leasehold property (the existing property)

....

(description of property)

We undertake:

1. That any sums received from you or your customer will be applied solely for the following purposes

*   (a) *in discharging the present mortgage(s) on the existing property*

(b) in acquiring a good marketable title to the new property **subject to the mortgage mentioned below*

(c) in paying any necessary deposit legal fees costs and disbursements in connection with the purchase.

The purchase price contemplated is £........gross.

*We are informed that a sum of £.........is being advanced on mortgage by.................The amount required from our client for the transaction including the deposit and together with costs disbursements and apportionments is not expected to exceed £....................

2. To hold to your order when received by us the documents of title of the existing property pending completion of the sale (unless subject to any prior mortgage(s)) and of the new property (unless subject to any prior mortgage(s)).

3. To pay to you the net proceeds of sale of the existing property when received by us. The sale price contemplated is £........ and the only deductions which will have to be made at present known to us are:

  (i)   the deposit (if not held by us)

  (ii)   the estate agents' commission

  (iii) the amount required to redeem any mortgages and charges which so far as known to us at present do not exceed £........

  (iv)   the legal fees costs and disbursements relating to the transaction.

4. To advise you immediately of any subsequent claim by a third party upon the net proceeds of sale of which we have knowledge.

NOTE

(1)   *If any deductions will have to be made from the net proceeds of sale other than those shown above, these must be specifically mentioned.*

(2)   *It would be convenient if this form of undertaking were presented in duplicate so that a carbon copy could be retained by the solicitor.*

---

* Delete if not applicable.

Annex 24I

Guidance — the Law Society's formulae for exchanging contracts by telephone or telex

---

FORMULAE A & B (1986)

Introduction

These formulae, which solicitors are free to adopt, were first published in 1980 ([1980] *Gazette,* 13th February, 144), shortly after *Domb* v. *Isoz* [1980] Ch. 548, which had suggested their creation. They have been republished twice: first in January 1984 unchanged ([1984] *Gazette*, 18th January, 82), and again in July 1984 when they were extended to include document exchanges as a standard alternative means of communication ([1984] *Gazette,* 4th July, 1891). Although there is only minimal change in the wording of the formulae themselves from July 1984, this guidance has been revised to reflect some of the points that have come to light through experience of the use of the formulae. The one change in the wording of the formulae themselves is the reference to 'clients(s)' to emphasise that the solicitor warrants that all necessary parties have signed. **These formulae replace the earlier versions with effect from 31st July 1986.**

Experience has shown that to avoid the risk of misunderstandings, it is essential that an agreed memorandum of the details and, in particular, of any variations of the formula should be made at the time and retained in the file. This will be very important if any question on the exchange is raised subsequently. Moreover, agreed variations should be confirmed in the subsequent correspondence. The serious risks of effecting exchange of contracts without a deposit were demonstrated in the case of *Morris* v. *Duke-Cohan & Co.* (1975) 119 S.J. 826.

As the persons involved in the exchange will bind their firms to the undertakings in the formula used, solicitors should carefully consider who is to be authorised to effect exchange of contracts by telephone or telex and should ensure that the use of the procedure is restricted to them. Because professional undertakings form the basis of the formulae, they are only recommended for use between firms of solicitors.

Law Society Telephone/Telex Exchange — Formula A (1986)

(for use where one solicitor holds both signed parts of the contract):

A.   A completion date of   19   is agreed. The solicitor holding both parts of the contract confirms that he holds the part signed by his client(s), which is identical to the part he is also holding signed by the other solicitor's client(s) and will forthwith insert the agreed completion date in each part.

Solicitors mutually agree that exchange shall take place from that moment and the solicitor holding both parts confirms that, as of that moment, he holds the part signed by his client(s) to the order of the other. He undertakes that day by first class post, or where the other solicitor is a member of a document exchange (as to which the inclusion of a reference thereto in the solicitor's letterhead shall be conclusive evidence) by delivery to that or any other affiliated exchange or by hand delivery direct to that solicitor's office, to send his signed part of the contract to the other solicitor, together, where he is the purchaser's solicitor, with a banker's draft or a solicitor's client account cheque for the deposit amounting to £.....

Law Society Telephone/Telex Exchange — Formula B (1986)

(for use where each solicitor holds his own client's signed part of the contract):

B.   A completion date of   19   is agreed. Each solicitor confirms to the other that he holds a part contract in the agreed form signed by the client(s) and will forthwith insert the agreed completion date.

Each solicitor undertakes to the other thenceforth to hold the signed part of the contract to the other's order, so that contracts are exchanged at that moment. Each solicitor further undertakes that day by first class post, or, where the other solicitor is a member of a document exchange (as to which the inclusion of a reference thereto in the solicitor's letterhead shall be conclusive evidence) by delivery to that or any other affiliated exchange or by hand delivery direct to that solicitor's office, to send his signed part of the contract to the other together, in the case of a purchaser's solicitor, with a banker's draft or a solicitor's client account cheque for the deposit amounting to £....

Notes

1.   A memorandum should be prepared, after use of a formula, recording:

    (a)   date and time of exchange;

    (b)   the formula used and exact wording of agreed variations;

    (c)   the completion date;

    (d)   the (balance) deposit to be paid;

    (e)   the identities of those involved in any conversation.

2.   In formula B cases, those who are going to effect the exchange must first confirm the details in order to ensure that both parts are identical. This means in particular, that if either part of the contract has been amended since it was originally prepared, the solicitor who holds a part contract with the amendments must disclose them, so that it can be confirmed that the other part is similarly amended.

9th July 1986 (updated January 1993)

FORMULA C

Introduction

Experience has shown the need for a further procedure in domestic conveyancing to cover cases where there is a chain of transactions when formulae A and B are not intended to be used. The Law Society's formula C for exchange of contract by telephone or telex has been drafted for use in this type of case.

Experience has shown that to avoid risk or misunderstanding, it is essential that an agreed memorandum of the details and, in particular, of any variations of the formula should be made at the time and retained in the file. This would be very important if any question on the exchange were raised subsequently. Moreover, agreed variation should be confirmed in writing. The serious risks of effecting exchange of contracts without a deposit, unless the full implications are explained to and accepted by the seller client, are demonstrated in *Morris* v. *Duke-Cohan Co.* (1975) 119 S.J. 826.

As the persons involved in the exchange will bind their firms to the undertakings in the formula used, solicitors should carefully consider who is to be authorised to exchange contracts by telephone or telex and should ensure that the use of the procedure is restricted to them. Professional undertakings form the basis of the formulae so the undertakings are only recommended for use between firms of solicitors and licensed conveyancers.

The Council for Licensed Conveyancers have confirmed that they would regard any undertaking given by a licensed conveyancer under formula C as a professional undertaking. Accordingly, formula C and the accompanying introduction and notes may be read as substituting 'licensed conveyancer' for 'solicitor' where appropriate.

Formula C for exchange of contracts by telephone or telex is designed for cases of linked chains of transactions. It is in two stages: first, the solicitors confirm that they hold their own client's part of the contract duly signed, and the buyer's solicitor undertakes to exchange if — by an agreed time later that day (the time agreed should take account of the circumstances of the chain) — the seller's solicitor so requests; secondly, the seller's solicitor requests exchange, and the contract is binding. Both stages need to be recorded in the memoranda made by both solicitors. Special provisions apply to deposits (see below).

Formula C works like this. Assume a short chain: W sells to X, who sells to Y, who sells to Z.

10am: Z's solicitor telephones Y's solicitor: formula C, part I is agreed.

10.10am: Y's solicitor telephones X's solicitor: formula C, part I is agreed.

10.20am: X's solicitor telephones W's solicitor: formula B agreed — at the top of the chain, with part I of formula C in place further down the chain, an immediate exchange is possible.

10.30am: X's solicitor telephones Y's solicitor: formula C, part II activated — the X-Y contract is now binding.

10.40am: Y's solicitor telephones Z's solicitor: formula C, part II activated — the Y-Z contract is now binding.

Deposits

Formula C assumes that all the contracts in the chain require payment of a deposit on exchange. It allows for the case where some or all of the same money is used for all the deposits, because each seller uses the deposit received on the sale to pay the deposit on the purchase. To avoid delay on exchange of contract, formula C requires the deposit to be paid direct to the person who will ultimately hold it. The formula requires that the deposit under each contract is paid to the seller's solicitors as agents so that the deposit may be used to pay another deposit. The deposit must ultimately be held by a solicitor as stakeholder.

Arrangements for holding the deposit have to be made when the formula is used. To illustrate what happens, assume that the three-link chain used in the example above provides for 10% deposits, and W is selling to X for £60,000, X to Y for £50,000 and Y to Z for £40,000.

10am: when agreeing formula C part I, Y's solicitor requests Z's solicitor to pay the £4000 deposit to X's solicitor.

10.10am: when agreeing formula C part I, X's solicitor requests Y's solicitor to pay, or arrange payment, of the £5000 deposit to W's solicitor.

10.20am: when agreeing formula B, X's solicitor stipulates (as a variation to formula B) that to make up the deposit of £6000, he or she will send £1000 to W's solicitor and will procure that £5000 is sent by solicitors further down the chain.

10.30am: nothing further is required when X's solicitors and Y's solicitor activate formula C part II. (The result of the 10.10am agreement is that Y's solicitor must remit £1000 to W's solicitor.)

10.40am: When activating formula C part II, Y's solicitor amends the request to Z's solicitor, asking him or her to send the £4000 deposit to W's solicitor. W's solicitor will therefore receive the deposit of £6000 made up from: £4000 sent by Z's solicitor, £1000 sent by Y's solicitor and £1000 sent by X's solicitor.

Five points should be noted:

1.   Formula C assumes the payment of a full contractual deposit (normally 10%). It is open to the parties to vary this but it is essential that negotiations to reduce the amount of the deposit should be undertaken at an early stage (for example when raising enquiries before contract) and *not* when exchange of contracts is imminent as this can be extremely inconvenient and likely, at least temporarily, to cause the chain to break.

2.   Obviously, when requesting all or part of a deposit to be paid to other solicitors, it is necessary to supply full details (name, address or DX number, reference and that solicitor's client's name). If particulars are given early in the transaction, it will be easier to guarantee a smooth exchange.

3.   The contract term relating to the deposit must allow it to be passed on, with payment direct from payer to ultimate recipient, in the way in which the formula contemplates. The deposit must ultimately be held by a solicitor as stakeholder. Whilst some variation in the formula can be agreed this is a term of the formula which must *not* be varied, unless all the solicitors involved in the chain have agreed.

4.   If a buyer proposes to use a deposit guarantee policy formula C will need substantial adaptation. It is essential that agreement on this, not only between the parties to the contract in question but also, so far as relevant, from the parties to the other contracts in the chain, is reached at an early stage in the transaction.

5.   It is essential prior to agreeing part I of formula C that those who are going to effect the exchange must ensure that both parts of the contract are identical.

Solicitors' authority

Solicitors do not, automatically and as a matter of general law, have authority to exchange contracts on a formula C basis. To ensure that the formula works satisfactorily, and that solicitors do not become liable to their clients for a breach of professional duty, the solicitor should always ensure that he or she has the client's express authority to use formula C, preferably in writing. A suggested form of authority is set out below. It should be adapted to cover any special circumstances of the case.

Return calls

When part I of formula C is agreed, to avoid confusion and delay the buyer's solicitor should give the seller's solicitor the names of at least two people to whom the call to activate part II can be made. It is essential that there is somebody available in the buyer's solicitor's office up to the 'final time for exchange' to activate part II immediately the telephone call is received from the seller's solicitor and part I of the formula contains an undertaking to this effect.

Time for exchange

The contracts in a chain must be exchanged in the appropriate order. The 'final time for exchange' agreed in the case of each contract should be fixed with that in mind, i.e. the times should be staggered to allow, before the end of the day, time to exchange the later contracts. Formula C assumes that contracts will be exchanged during the day on which it is initiated. Where part I has been agreed, but part II is not activated on the same day, the process must be started again, by agreeing part I on another day.

Solicitors' responsibility

Using formula C involves a solicitor in giving a number of professional undertakings. These must be performed precisely. Any failure will be a serious breach of professional discipline.

One of the undertakings may be to arrange that someone over whom the solicitor has no control will do something (i.e. to arrange for someone else to despatch the cheque or banker's draft in payment of the deposit). An undertaking is still binding even if it is to do something outside the solicitor's control (see Principle 19.03 in the Guide).

The Law Society accepts that solicitors can offer professional undertakings to, and accept professional undertakings from, licensed conveyancers in the same way as when dealing with solicitors.

Law Society Telephone/Telex Exchange — Forumla C (1989)

(Incorporating amendments to include a reference to fax as stated in [1991] Gazette 11 December.)

Part I

The following is agreed:

Final time for exchange: pm

Completion date: 19

Deposit to be paid to:

Each solicitor confirms that he or she holds a part of the contract in the agreed form signed by his or her client, or, if there is more than one client, by all of them. Each solicitor undertakes to the other that:

(a)   he or she will continue to hold that part of the contract until the final time for exchange on the date the formula is used, and

(b)   if the vendor's solicitor so notifies the purchaser's solicitor by fax, telephone or telex (whichever was previously agreed) by that time, they will both comply with part II of the formula.

The purchaser's solicitor further undertakes that either he or some other named person in his office will be available up to the final time for exchange to activate part II of the formula on receipt of the telephone call, fax or telex from the vendor's solicitors.

Part II

Each solicitor undertakes to the other henceforth to hold the part of the contract in his possession to the other's order, so that contracts are exchanged at that moment, and to despatch it to the other on that day. The purchaser's solicitor further undertakes to the vendor's solicitor to despatch on that day, or to arrange for the despatch on that day of, a banker's draft or a solicitor's client account cheque for the full deposit specified in the agreed form of contract (divided as the vendor's solicitor may have specified) to the vendor's solicitor and/or to some other solicitor whom the vendor's solicitor nominates, to be held on formula C terms.

'To despatch' means to send by first class post, or, where the other solicitor is a member of a document exchange (as to which the inclusion of a reference thereto in the solicitor's letterhead is to be conclusive evidence) by delivery to that or any other affiliated exchange, or by hand delivery direct to the recipient solicitor's office. 'Formula C terms' means that the deposit is held as stakeholder, or as agent for the vendor with authority to part with it only for the purpose of passing it to another solicitor as deposit in a related property purchase transaction on these terms.

Notes

1.   Two memoranda will be required when using formula C. One needs to record the use of part I, and a second needs to record the request of the vendor's solicitor to the purchaser's solicitor to activate part II.

2.   The first memorandum should record:

(a)   the date and time when it was agreed to use formula C;

(b)   the exact wording of any agreed variations;

(c)   the final time, later that day, for exchange;

(d)   the completion date;

(e)   the name of the solicitor to whom the deposit was to be paid, or details of amounts and names if it was to be split; and

(f)   the identities of those involved in any conversation.

Authority from client to client's solicitor

I/We..................understand that my/our sale and purchase of.................are both part of a chain of linked property transactions, in which all parties want the security of contracts which become binding on the same day.

I/We agree that you should make arrangements with the other solicitors or licensed conveyancers involved to achieve this.

I/We understand that this involves each property-buyer offering, early on one day, to exchange contracts whenever, later that day, the seller so requests, and that the buyer's offer is on the basis that it cannot be withdrawn or varied during that day.

I/We agree that when I/we authorise you to exchange contracts, you may agree to exchange contracts on the above basis and give any necessary undertakings to the other parties involved in the chain and that my/our authority to you cannot be revoked throughout the day on which the offer to exchange contracts is made.

15th March 1989 (updated January 1993)

Guidance — The Law Society's code for completion by post

The Law Society's code for completion by post ('the code') was approved for publication by the Council's Non-Contentious Business Committee and is set out below. The attention of practitioners is drawn, in particular, to the notes that are published with it.

The Law Society's code for completion by post (1984 edition)

Preamble

The code provides a procedure for postal completion which practising solicitors may adopt by reference.

First, each solicitor must satisfy himself that no circumstances exist that are likely to give rise to a conflict between this code and the interest of his own client (including where applicable a mortgagee client).

The code, where adopted, will apply without variation except so far as recorded in writing beforehand.

The Code

1.   Adoption hereof must be specifically agreed by all the solicitors concerned and preferably in writing.

2.   On completion the vendor's solicitor will act as agent for the purchaser's solicitor without fee or disbursements.

3.   The vendor's solicitor undertakes that on completion he:

   (1)   will have the vendor's authority to receive the purchase money; and

   (2)   will be the duly authorised agent of the proprietor of any charge upon the property to receive the part of the money paid to him which is needed to discharge such charge.

4.   The purchaser's solicitor shall send to the vendor's solicitor instructions as to:

   (1)   documents to be examined and marked;

   (2)   memoranda to be endorsed;

   (3)   deeds, documents, undertakings and authorities relating to rents, deposits, keys, etc; and

   (4)   any other relevant matters.

In default of instructions, the vendor's solicitor shall not be under any duty to examine, mark or endorse any documents.

5.   The purchaser's solicitor shall remit to the vendor's solicitor the balance due on completion specified in the vendor's solicitor's completion statement or with written notification; in default of either, the balance shown due by the contract. If the funds are remitted by transfer between banks, the vendor's solicitor shall instruct his bank to advise him by telephone immediately the funds are received. The vendor's solicitor shall hold such funds to the purchaser's solicitor's order pending completion.

6.   The vendor's solicitor, having received the items specified in paras 4 and 5, shall forthwith, or at such later times as may have been agreed, complete. Thereupon he shall hold all documents and other items to be sent to the purchaser's solicitor as agent for such solicitor.

7.   Once completion has taken place, the vendor's solicitor shall as soon as possible thereafter on the same day confirm the fact to the purchaser's solicitor by telephone or telex and shall also as soon as possible send by first class post or document exchange written confirmation to the purchaser's solicitor, together with the enclosures referred to in para 4 hereof. The vendor's solicitor shall ensure that such title deeds and any other items are correctly committed to the post or document exchange. Thereafter, they are at the risk of the purchaser's solicitor.

8.   If either the authorities specified in para 3 or the instructions specified in para 4 or the funds specified in para 5 have not been received by the vendor's solicitor by the agreed completion date and time, he shall forthwith notify the purchaser's solicitor and request further instructions.

9.   Nothing herein shall override any rights and obligations of parties under the contract or otherwise.

10.   Any dispute or difference which may arise between solicitors that is directly referable to a completion agreed to be carried out in accordance herewith, whether or not amended or supplemented in any way, shall be referred to an arbitrator to be agreed, within one month of any such dispute or difference arising between the solicitors who are party thereto, and, in the default of such agreement, on the application of any such solicitor, to an arbitrator to be appointed by the President of the Law Society.

11.   Reference herein to vendor's solicitor and purchaser's solicitor shall, where appropriate, be deemed to include solicitors acting for parties other than vendor and purchaser.

Notes:

1.   The object of the code is to provide solicitors with a convenient means for completion, on an agency basis, that can be adopted for use, where they so agree beforehand, in completions where a representative of the purchaser's solicitors is not attending at the office of the vendor's solicitors for the purpose.

2.   As with the Law Society's formulae for exchange of contract by telephone/telex [see Annex 24I in the Guide], the code embodies professional undertakings and is, in consequence, only recommended for adoption between solicitors.

3.   Cl 2 of the code expressly provides that the vendor's solicitor will act as agent for the purchaser's solicitor without fee or disbursements. It is envisaged that, in the usual case, the convenience of not having to make a specific appointment on the day of

completion for the purchaser's solicitor to attend for the purpose will offset the agency work that the vendor's solicitor has to do and any postage he has to pay in completing under the code, and on the basis that most solicitors will from time to time act both for the vendors and purchasers. If, nevertheless, a vendor's solicitor does consider that charges and/or disbursements are necessary in a particular case, as such an arrangement represents a variation in the code, it should be agreed in writing beforehand.

4.   Having regard to the decision in *Edward Wong Finance Co. Ltd.* v. *Johnson, Stokes & Master* [1984] A.C. 1296, cl 3(2) of the code requires the vendor's solicitor to confirm, before he agrees to use the code, that he will be the duly authorised agent of the proprietor of any charge upon the property (typically but not exclusively the vendor's building society) to receive that part of the money paid to him which is needed to discharge such charge.

5.   Cl 9 of the code expressly provides that nothing therein shall override any rights and obligations of parties under the contract or otherwise.

The above notes refer only to some of the points in the code that practitioners may wish to consider before agreeing to adopt it. It is emphasised that it is a matter for the solicitors concerned to read the code in full, so that they can decide beforehand whether they will make use of it as it stands or with any variations agreed in writing beforehand, whether or not they are referred to in the above notes, as the case may be.

Annex 24K

Guidance — home income and equity release schemes — mortgages and remortgages

I   Home income and equity release schemes

1. On 3rd July 1991 the Society published a 'product warning' on home income or equity release schemes (see Annex 26H in the Guide). All such schemes now on the market carry an element of risk, but the two types described in the product warning have a much higher risk factor. The schemes are targeted at the elderly and have lately given rise to a number of potential claims being notified against advisers, including solicitors. So far as they can, solicitors should dissuade clients from entering into any scheme of this kind without expert and independent advice.

2. *Outline of the two schemes*

    The 'investment bond scheme' is one under which a capital sum is raised by the mortgage and put into an investment bond.

    The 'roll-up loan scheme' is one under which interest payable under a mortgage is rolled up for repayment when the house is eventually sold.

3. *The problems*

    Under the investment bond scheme, if the bond appreciates each year it will provide an extra income as well as paying the interest on the loan. If it does not do so — and over the past two or three years this has usually been the case — it will become necessary to take money from the original capital, leading to a continuous reduction in this capital.

    Under the roll-up loan scheme, the amount of the mortgage debt increases at a very high rate as accrued interest is added. There is no guarantee that the value of the property will increase sufficiently to preserve the borrower's remaining equity.

    Both schemes look attractive in a rising market, but can be disastrous for those who have risked not just their capital but their home on what is essentially a speculation. A point may be reached where the home-owners have to sell their homes during their lifetime in order to repay the mortgage.

II   Mortgages and remortgages generally

1. *Referral by tied agents*

    Where a financial product related to a conveyance has serious and obvious defects, a question arises as to the extent of the solicitor's duty of care to the borrower client, where the solicitor is instructed in the conveyancing.

Section 2(6) of the Solicitors' Introduction and Referral Code 1990 states that where a tied agent refers a client who is proposing to take out a company life policy, the solicitor should, where necessary, have regard to the suitability of that policy in each particular case.

The Council statement on the Financial Services Act 1986 : life policies and tied agents (see Annex 24C in the Guide) refers to circumstances where it may be the solicitor's duty either to provide independent 'best advice' or to refer the client to an independent intermediary who can do so. The guidance in the Council statement will also apply to financial products other than life policies.

2. *Referral by independent advisers*

The same question arises where a client is referred by an independent financial adviser who has persuaded the client to enter into an obviously inappropriate scheme. Whilst a solicitor cannot be held to be under a duty to readvise, or to offer investment business advice as part of a conveyancing retainer, there is a general duty in relation to the conveyancing retainer to give legal advice on the implications of the particular scheme chosen, including pointing out the dangers to the client.

3. *Instructions from lenders*

A solicitor might be instructed only by a lender or receive instructions initially from a lender on behalf of both lender and borrower. Where the solicitor is acting only for the lender he or she should ensure that no retainer arises by implication with the borrower. Where the solicitor is acting for both borrower and lender he or she should be alert to the possibility of a conflict of interests arising.

III Practice Rule 6 and conflicts generally

1. Rule 6 of the Solicitors' Practice Rules 1990 does not prohibit solicitors from acting for lender and borrower in an institutional mortgage, and for some years it has been standard practice to do so.

2. There would normally be no conflict between the lender and borrower but under the general rules and law on conflict, if a duty to one client prevents a solicitor fulfilling a duty to another, the solicitor must cease acting for both.

3. Where a solicitor's duties require him or her to advise a borrower client of the dangers of a lender's scheme, there would be a conflict of interests preventing the solicitor accepting instructions from the lender until that duty was discharged.

4. The general duty of a solicitor may require him or her to try to ensure the borrower obtains independent financial advice — sometimes a second opinion. Much will depend on the level of sophistication, the vulnerability and the general understanding of the client as well as the complexity of the scheme.

18th December 1991 (updated January 1993)

Annex 24L

Guidance — mortgage fraud

This guidance deals with the solicitor's duty in conduct when acting for lender and borrower when there is some variation in the purchase price.

The Professional Ethics Division is frequently asked to advise on a solicitor's duty to the lender in conduct when there is some variation in the purchase price of a property of which the lender may be unaware. Therefore the Council's Standards and Guidance Committee considers it is appropriate to publish the following guidance (which is supported by the Council of Mortgage Lenders) on the professional conduct issues involved.

Solicitors acting contemporaneously for a buyer and a lender should consider their position very carefully if there is any change in the purchase price, or if the solicitors become aware of any other information which they would reasonably expect the lender to consider important in deciding whether, or on what terms, it would make the mortgage advance available. In such circumstances the solicitor's duty to act in the best interests of the lender would require them to pass on such information to the lender.

Solicitors have a duty of confidentiality to clients, but this does not affect their duty to act in the best interests of each client. Therefore any such information concerning variations to the purchase price should be forwarded to the lender with the consent of the buyer. If the buyer will not agree to the information being given to the lender, then there will be a conflict between the solicitor's duty of confidentiality to the buyer and the duty to act in the best interests of the lender. Solicitors must therefore cease acting for the lender and must consider carefully whether they are able to continue acting for the buyer, bearing in mind Principle 12.02 referred to below.

Solicitors must not withhold information relevant to a transaction from any client and for a lender this includes not only straightforward price reductions but may also include other allowances (e.g. for repairs, payment of costs, the inclusion of chattels in the price and incentives of the kind offered by builders such as free holidays and part-subsidisation or mortgage payments) which amount to a price reduction and which would affect the lender's decision to make the advance. Solicitors should not attempt to arbitrate on whether the price change is material but should notify the lender. It is recommended that solicitors advise their clients as soon as practicable that it would be regarded as fraud to misrepresent the purchase price and that a solicitor is under a duty to inform the lender of the true price being paid for a property.

Solicitors who are party to an attempt to deceive a lender may be exposing both the buyer and themselves to criminal prosecution and/or civil action and will be liable to be disciplined for having breached the principles of professional conduct (see Principle 12.02 in the Guide). If a solicitor is aware that his or her client is attempting to perpetrate fraud in any form he or she must immediately cease acting for that client.

12th December 1990 (updated January 1993)

Annex 24M

'Green card' warning on mortgage fraud — practice information

Could you be involved?

Could you be being unwittingly assisting in a fraud? The general assumption is that if there has been a mortgage fraud a solicitor *must* have been involved. Solicitors should therefore be vigilant both to protect their mortgagee clients and themselves. Steps can be taken to minimise the risk of being involved in a fraud (see below).

Could you spot a mortgage fraud?

The signs to watch for:

(1) **Fictitious buyer** — especially if the buyer is introduced to your practice by a third party (for example a broker or estate agent) who is not well known to you. Beware of invented clients who you never meet.

(2) **Unusual instructions** — for example a solicitor being instructed by the seller to remit the net proceeds of sale to the estate agent who was instructed.

(3) **Misrepresentation of the purchase price** — ensure that the true cash price to be actually paid is stated as the consideration in the contract and transfer and is identical to the price shown in the mortgage instructions.

(4) **A deposit paid direct** — a deposit, perhaps exceeding a normal deposit, paid direct or said to be paid direct, to the seller.

(5) **Incomplete contract documentation** — contract documents not fully completed by the seller's representative, i.e. dates missing or the identity of the parties not fully described.

(6) **Changes in the purchase price** — adjustments to the purchase price, particularly in high percentage mortgage cases or allowances off the purchase price, for example, for works to be carried out.

(7) **Unusual transactions** — transactions which do not follow their normal course or the usual pattern of events.

What steps can I take to minimise the risk of fraud?

Be vigilant, if you have any doubts about a transaction, consider whether any of the following steps could be taken to minimise the risk of fraud:

(1) **Verify the identity and bona fides of your client** — meet the clients where possible and get to know them a little.

(2) **Question unusual instructions** — if you receive unusual instructions from your client discuss them with your client fully.

(3) **Discuss any aspects of the transaction which worry you with your client** — if for example you have any suspicion that your client may have submitted a false mortgage application or references, discuss this with your clients and if you believe they intend to proceed with a fraudulent application you must refuse to continue to act for the buyer and the mortgagee.

(4) **Check that the true price is shown in all documentation** — check that the actual price paid is stated in the contract, transfer and mortgage instructions. Ensure that your client understands that, where you are also acting for the lender, you will have to report all allowances and incentives to the mortgagee before exchange of contracts. See also the guidance printed in [1990] *Gazette,* 12 December, 16 [see Annex 24L].

(5) **Do not witness pre-signed documentation** — no deed should be witnessed by a solicitor or his or her staff unless the person signing does so in the presence of the witness. If the deed is pre-signed ensure that it is re-signed in the presence of a witness.

(6) **Verify signatures** — consider whether signatures on all documents connected with a transaction should be examined and compared with signatures on any other available documentation.

(7) **Make a company search** — where a private company is the seller or the seller has purchased from a private company in the recent past and you suspect that there may be a connection between the company and the seller or the buyer, which is being used for improper purposes, then consideration should be given to making a search in the company's register to ascertain the names and addresses of the officers and shareholders which can then be compared with the names of those connected with the transaction and the seller and buyer.

Remember, that even where investigations result in a solicitor ceasing to act for a client the solicitor will still owe a duty of confidentiality which would prevent the solicitor passing on information to the lender. It is only where the solicitor is satisfied that there is a strong *prima facie* case that the client was using him to further a criminal purpose or fraud that the duty of confidentiality would not apply.

March 1991

Mortgage redemption statements — advice from the Council of Mortgage Lenders — practice information

Problems relating to mortgage redemption statements have caused difficulties for lenders and solicitors (this expression to include licensed conveyancers) for a number of years. In 1985 the Building Societies Association and the Law Society issued detailed advice to their respective members on this subject because of the difficulties which were apparent at that time.

The advice comprised paragraphs 9 to 13 of BSA circular No. 3155. Those paragraphs are now replaced by the new guidance set out hereunder. In recent months, the Council of Mortgage Lenders (CML) has received a number of enquiries in respect of redemption statements provided by lenders to solicitors acting for the lender (who will often also act for the seller). This guidance refers to some of the circumstances which can produce errors and problems, and the consequences which this can have for the solicitor in the conveyancing transaction. It also suggests certain practical measures designed to reduce problems in this area. Accordingly, it is of importance to all lenders and covers:

(a)   the function and importance of solicitors' undertakings;

(b)   the general principle that lenders should seal a discharge where a redemption statement was incorrect;

(c)   ways in which lenders might overcome the difficulty caused when the borrower prematurely stops payments;

(d)   similar proposals as to the problem of dishonoured cheques;

(e)   suggestions for overcoming difficulties sometimes presented by multiple mortgage accounts;

(f)   information to be provided to banks for inclusion in telegraphic transfers; and

(g)   the importance of returning the sealed discharge promptly.

Terms of reference

This guidance applies to England and Wales; separate guidance for Scotland and Northern Ireland will follow, if necessary.

Redemption on sale

This guidance applies primarily to redemption of a mortgage on sale of the security and, consequently, the lender's/seller's solicitor is required to give an undertaking to the buyer's solicitor that the charge will be discharged.

Remortgages

It is appreciated than an undertaking will also be given on a remortgage and that, accordingly, the guidance should be interpreted as including this situation.

Simple redemption

Much of the guidance is inapplicable to a straightforward redemption (without sale or mortgage) as no undertaking is given. However, even in redemptions *per se,* solicitors and lenders will no doubt wish to provide accurate information and deal promptly with their respective responsibilities.

Solicitors' undertakings

The solicitor acting for the seller will need, on completion, to satisfy the buyer's solicitor that the mortgage on the property being sold has been or will be discharged. In theory the buyer's solicitor will wish to see the mortgage discharged before the purchase money is paid. However, where the monies to repay the mortgage are being provided wholly or partly by the proceeds of sale, then the mortgage cannot be paid off until after completion.

Most lenders will not seal the discharge (this expression to include sealing the vacating receipt on a mortgage deed or sealing of form 53) until they receive the redemption money. This leaves the buyer's solicitor with a problem in that he or she has to be satisfied that the mortgage will be discharged and that he or she will obtain the receipted mortgage or Land Registry form 53. This problem is solved by the use of the solicitor's undertaking.

On completion, the seller's/lender's solicitor will provide the buyer's solicitor with a written undertaking to redeem the mortgage(s) in a form recommended by the Law Society similar to that set out below:

'In consideration of your today completing the purchase of .... we hereby undertake forthwith to pay over to .... [the lender] the money required to redeem the mortgage/legal charge dated .... and to forward the receipted mortgage/legal charge [form 53] to you as soon as it is received by us from... [the lender].'

Incorrect redemption statements

Before completion of sale, the lender's/seller's solicitor will obtain a redemption statement calculated to the date of redemption. He or she will sometimes request the daily figure for interest which will be added if completion is delayed. If the lender supplies an incorrect redemption statement, the solicitor is likely to forward insufficient money to redeem the mortgage. The lender might be unwilling to discharge the mortgage and, if the solicitor is not holding more funds on behalf of the borrower, the solicitor would be in breach of his or her undertaking.

Problem areas

Problems with redemption statements can arise for a number of reasons:

(a)   a lender might simply make a mistake in calculating the redemption figure;

(b)   difficulties could be caused by the cancellation of standing orders or direct debit payments or by borrowers' cheques being dishonoured; and

(c)   there might be misunderstanding between a lender and the solicitor.

Some of the more common practical problems are outlined below.

Cancellation

A difficulty arises if the mortgage payments are made by standing order and, shortly before completion, the borrower stops the payments without notice to the lender. There will be a shortfall if the lender assumed, without making this assumption clear, that the next payment would be paid and made the redemption figure calculation accordingly. If this is the case, and the solicitor has acted in good faith and with no knowledge that a payment has been or is likely to be cancelled, the view of the CML is that the lender should seal the discharge. This is to avoid the solicitor being in breach of his or her undertaking to the buyer's solicitor. (The lender would then have to recoup the money from the borrower.)

This difficulty is less likely to arise where payments are made by direct debit because the lender is the originator of the debit and therefore has control over the raising of any future direct debits from the borrower's bank account. However, there is no guarantee that direct debits will be honoured and they may be returned on the ground of insufficient funds or that the customer has closed his or her account or instructed his or her bank to cancel the direct debit.

Some lenders overcome this problem by excluding any future payments due when calculating the redemption figure. In other words, they "freeze" the account balance at the day of the redemption calculation. The disadvantages of this are that (if the payment has not been cancelled) the borrower has to pay a higher redemption figure and the lender has to make a refund to the borrower after redemption.

An alternative is for the lender on the redemption statement to make it clear to the solicitor that it is assumed that the next payment will be made and that, if it is not paid, the mortgage will not be discharged until the balance is received. This gives the solicitor an early chance to address his or her and his or her borrower client's mind to the situation and to ensure that sufficient monies will be available to redeem the mortgage. Indeed, this would also serve as a reminder to the solicitor to warn the borrower client of the importance of continuing the payments in the normal way up to completion.

Uncleared cheques

This is a very similar situation to that of standing orders and direct debits. The CML's view is that if the lender does not notify the solicitor that it is assumed that the borrower's cheque will clear then, provided that the solicitor acts in good faith and without knowledge that the cheque would be or is likely to be dishonoured, the lender should seal the discharge. Exceptions to this are if the lender:

(a) prepares the redemption statement on the assumption that the cheque will not clear and informs the solicitor of this, probably, in a note on the statement. This has the disadvantages described above; or

(b) notifies the solicitor that a cheque has been received and that, if it does not clear by the date of redemption, the mortgage will not be discharged until the balance is received.

Separate loan account

The lender may have more than one loan secured on the property. For example, in addition to the principal mortgage, there could be a secured personal loan which is a regulated agreement under the Consumer Credit Act 1974 and/or a further advance conducted on a separate account basis. In such cases, there will be more than one account number.

On a sale, as all mortgage accounts will be repaid, multiplicity of accounts should not present a problem unless the solicitor does not know and is unable to specify every account and has no notice or cause to query the matter and the lender fails to cross-check the matter internally.

However, it is possible, for example, on certain remortgages, that it is the intention of the borrower and the lender that not all mortgages will be discharged and replaced. If so, when requesting the redemption statement, the solicitor should make it clear to the lender which mortgages the borrower wishes to redeem. The solicitor should inform the lender of any mortgages of which he or she is aware which are outstanding with the lender but which are not being redeemed. The solicitor should also quote all relevant account numbers if known as far as possible and ensure that the redemption statement received from the lender includes all the mortgages which are intended to be redeemed.

The lender should have its own internal cross-checking system but it is vital that the solicitor (who will, after all, be acting for the lender in most cases) is as clear as possible about the mortgage account(s) being redeemed. It is suggested that the solicitor should if possible, and time permits, send a copy of that redemption statement to the borrower to check agreement on the amount shown as due to the lender. Solicitors should be encouraged to ask for a statement at the earliest possible date.

Telegraphic transfers

Lenders could request that solicitors adopt procedures to assist in the identification of telegraphic transfers. When mortgages are being redeemed the telegraphic transfer which a lender receives is often difficult to identify and to match to a particular account.

The administrative difficulties which are caused by the inability to identify the money would be overcome if solicitors provided to the bank the information to be included in the telegraphic transfer, i.e. the borrower's mortgage account number and the firm's name and address.

Delay

Lenders are sometimes criticised for delay in providing a form of discharge after redemption of the mortgage. It is recognised that most lenders can and do return the receipted mortgage or form 53 promptly and that solicitors can apply for registration to protect priority. However, unless there is good reason for the delay, e.g. a solicitor sending the form to the wrong office of the lender, lenders will no doubt deal promptly with this important procedure.

It is suggested that lenders should aim to return the receipted mortgage or form 53 within seven days, and if there is likely to be a delay beyond that period they should notify the seller's solicitor. This would enable the buyer's solicitor to lodge an application with the Land Registry pending receipt of receipted mortgage or sealed form 53, although it is hoped that this would only be necessary in exceptional circumstances.

The CML view

Many of the difficulties described above would be reduced if, as a matter of course, solicitors gave lenders correct information about the borrower, the property, the account number(s), etc., and lenders, in turn, operated internal cross-checking systems and provided accurate and complete redemption statements showing clearly the last payment to be taken into account and, systems permitting, details of all the borrower's accounts relating to the property which represent mortgages to be discharged.

If the solicitor, relying on an incorrrect redemption statement provided by the lender, sends insufficient money to redeem a mortgage, the lender should discharge the mortgage. (However, the lender might wish to make it clear that the release was not intended to discharge the borrower from his or her outstanding personal liability. This might prevent the borrower from successfully claiming estoppel against the lender.)

Such cases do not occur frequently; when they do, it is generally because of a clerical or administrative error on the part of the lender, such as by omitting one month's interest or an insurance premium, and the amount is usually small. Nevertheless, where it appears that there has been an error, the solicitor should immediately draw this to the lender's notice and should pursue his or her borrower client actively for any shortfall.

Very rare cases could arise where general guidance of this kind is inapplicable, for example, if there is such a major discrepancy in the redemption figure that the borrower, and, perhaps, his or her solicitor, could not reasonably have believed in the accuracy of the statement.

Conclusion

Where there is an incorrect redemption statement, which is clearly due to an error by the lender or lack of clarification, it is unreasonable that a solicitor should be put in breach of his or her undertaking. The undertaking given to the buyer's solicitor is a vital part of the conveyancing process. It is the CML's view, in such cases, that the lender should seal the discharge.

The Law Society and the Council for Licensed Conveyancers agree with the views expressed in these paragraphs. It is hoped that some of the practical measures referred to above will be implemented to avoid difficulties on redemption.

March 1992

Chapter 25

Property selling

Solicitors selling property

25.01 Property selling is work which a solicitor may properly carry on in the course of his or her professional practice.

25.02 A solicitor who carries on such work is acting as a solicitor and is therefore subject to the Solicitors Act 1974, the Solicitors' Practice Rules, the Solicitors' Accounts Rules and the Solicitors' Indemnity Rules and all other rules, regulations and principles of conduct affecting solicitors in practice. (The only exception to this would be where a solicitor was selling property by way of a separate business already legitimately providing services before 11th December 1986 and was not held out as doing so as a solicitor — see paragraph 25.52.) For questions and answers on property selling see Annex 25A.

25.03 A solicitor may sell property either as an activity of his or her existing practice or through a separate practice formed for that purpose and either alone or together with other firms of solicitors (but see paragraphs 25.40 and 25.41).

25.04 Rule 7(6) of the Solicitors' Practice Rules 1990 (SPR 1990) prohibits solicitors from entering into partnership with non-solicitors, other than registered foreign lawyers and recognised bodies (see paragraph 25.05). Rule 7(1) of the SPR 1990 prohibits solicitors from otherwise sharing their fees with non-solicitors (other than registered foreign lawyers and recognised bodies), although there are exceptions; for instance, fees can be shared with the solicitor's bona fide employee. Rule 7(2) permits a solicitor who instructs an estate agent as his or her sub-agent for the sale of a property to remunerate the sub-agent on the basis of a proportion of the solicitor's professional fee.

25.05 Under the Solicitors' Incorporated Practice Rules 1988, made pursuant to section 9 of the Administration of Justice Act 1985, solicitors may practise through a company (a recognised body). The guidance in this chapter applies equally to an incorporated practice and its directors, employees and shareholders. It also applies to a multi-national partnership.

25.06 Rule 3 of the SPR 1990 permits arrangements for the introduction of clients. Such arrangements are subject to the Solicitors' Introduction and Referral Code 1990 (see paragraphs 25.29 – 25.31).

Description of property selling work

25.07 A designation may be used in addition to the name of a solicitor's practice but the word 'solicitor' or 'solicitors' must be included and the designation must not be misleading. It would be possible to designate a practice 'solicitor and estate agent', provided that the firm could justify a claim to specialism or expertise in the field of estate agency (see paragraphs 6 and 2(b) of the Solicitors' Publicity Code 1990).

25.08 A solicitor may advertise that he or she undertakes property selling work. Provided that any such description is not misleading or inaccurate the solicitor may describe the relevant part of his or her practice (e.g. the property selling department or a branch office where he or she conducts only or mainly property selling) as an estate agency or a property centre or as his or her property selling department or by any other suitable description. As to appearance under the classification 'Estate Agents' in a directory, see paragraph 25.28.

25.09 Rule 11 of the SPR 1990 provides that the name of a firm of solicitors must be in traditional form. However, paragraph 9 of the Solicitors' Publicity Code 1990 permits the use of a subsidiary practising style of a type other than that used as the name of a firm of solicitors in relation to a firm or a part of a firm, provided that it is used in conjunction with the firm's name and provided that the word 'solicitor' or 'solicitors' is also used.

Staff

25.10 In property selling, a solicitor may employ staff experienced in estate agency. Rule 7(1) of the SPR 1990 allows a solicitor to share fees with his or her bona fide employee, whether or not a solicitor.

25.11 Paragraph 7 of the Solicitors' Publicity Code 1990 allows all members of staff (including a partner or director) to be named in publicity (including on stationery), but where the staff member is not a solicitor holding a current practising certificate his or her status must be unambiguously stated.

Supervision rules

25.12 An application for a waiver of Rule 13 of the SPR 1990 (relating to the management and supervision of offices) will be considered in the case of an office at which the only work carried out is the selling of property. See also paragraphs 25.45 and 25.46 as regards a property display centre; only limited activities can take place at such a centre.

Conflict of interests

25.13 Reference in paragraphs 25.14, 25.18 and 25.20 to a connected person includes:

(a) any of the solicitor's family; 'family', here and throughout the remainder of this paragraph meaning a spouse, former spouse, reputed spouse, brother, sister, uncle, aunt, nephew, niece, direct descendant, parent or other direct ancestor;

(b) any employee of the solicitor and any family of an employee;

(c) any partner in an associated firm as defined in Rule 6 of the SPR 1990 (i.e. where two or more firms have at least one common principal), any employee of that firm and any family of an employee;

(d) any company of which the solicitor is a director or employee or in which the solicitor, either alone or with any other connected person or persons as herein defined, is entitled to exercise, or control the exercise of, one-third or more of the voting power at any general meeting;

(e) any company of which any of the persons mentioned in (a), (b) and (c) above is a director or employee or in which any of them, either alone or with any other connected person or persons as herein defined, is entitled to exercise, or control the exercise of, one-third or more of the voting power at any general meeting;

(f) any other associate of the solicitor as defined in section 32 of the Estate Agents Act 1979.

The requirements in paragraphs 25.14 and 25.18 – 25.21 are similar to requirements imposed on estate agents by the Estate Agents (Provision of Information) Regulations 1991 and the Estate Agents (Undesirable Practices) Order 1991.

25.14 A solicitor must always place the client's interests before the solicitor's own. In addition to the requirements of Principle 11.05, the solicitor should promptly and in writing inform the client whenever the solicitor or, to his or her knowledge, any connected person has, or is seeking to acquire, a beneficial interest in the property or in the proceeds of sale of any interest in the property.

25.15 A solicitor and his or her partners who act in the sale of a property may be faced with difficult questions of conflict of interests which may be insuperable. In accordance with the general principles of professional conduct, a solicitor must not act (or continue to act) if such conflict of interests arises or is likely to arise. Reference in paragraphs 25.13 – 25.22 to a solicitor's partners includes those with whom he or she carries on a joint property selling practice and also partners in an associated firm; Rule 6 of the SPR 1990 provides that two or more firms are associated where they have at least one common principal.

25.16   In particular, because of the likelihood of conflicting interests, the solicitor who or whose partners act in the sale, even if not acting for the seller in the conveyancing, must not act also for the buyer, either in the negotiations or in respect of a mortgage (but see paragraphs 25.22 – 25.24) or in the subsequent conveyancing. Rule 6 of the SPR 1990 provides that none of its exceptions can apply where a solicitor or a solicitor practising in partnership or association with him or her is instructed to negotiate the sale of the property concerned.

25.17   Even where a solicitor acting for the seller in the conveyancing has not acted in the sale of the property, Rule 6 of the SPR 1990 would, subject to its exceptions, prevent any firm with whom that solicitor practises in partnership or association (including one with whom he or she has a joint property selling practice) from acting for the buyer in the conveyancing of the property.

25.18   Quite apart from cases governed by Rule 6, difficult questions of conflict may arise where the solicitor and his or her partners act also for parties in related transactions. Where a prospective buyer has made an offer for a client's property, the solicitor must promptly and in writing inform the client if, to the solicitor's knowledge, he or she or any connected person has also been instructed by the buyer to sell an interest in land, and that sale is necessary to enable the buyer to buy from the solicitor's client or results from that prospective purchase.

25.19   A solicitor must promptly and in writing forward to the client accurate details (other than those of a description which the client has indicated in writing he or she does not wish to receive) of any offer the solicitor has received from a prospective buyer in respect of an interest in the property.

Duties to buyers

25.20   In addition to the general requirements of Principle 18.01 which provides *inter alia* that a solicitor must not use his or her position as a solicitor to take unfair advantage either for the solicitor or another person, a solicitor must promptly and in writing inform any person negotiating to acquire or dispose of any interest in the property whenever the solicitor or, to his or her knowledge, any connected person has a beneficial interest in the property or in the proceeds of sale of any interest in it. The solicitor should not enter into negotiations with any such person until such disclosure has been made.

25.21   A solicitor must not discriminate against a prospective buyer because he or she has not or is unlikely to instruct the solicitor to sell an interest in land, which sale is necessary to enable the buyer to buy from the solicitor's client or results from that prospective purchase.

Mortgages

25.22   In order to facilitate the sale of properties, solicitors providing a property selling service sometimes wish to assist buyers to obtain mortgage finance. A solicitor who or whose partners (for 'partners' see paragraph 25.15) act in the sale of a property may not also act for the buyer in respect of a mortgage. An example of what a solicitor may do to facilitate a sale is set out in paragraph 25.23.

25.23   A solicitor may, acting as solicitor for the seller, arrange (either in a particular case or as part of a scheme) with a building society or other financial institution that a mortgage will be made available on a property (subject to the status of the buyer). The solicitor may inform a prospective buyer of the availability of such mortgage but may not act (which includes giving advice) for him or her in respect of the mortgage. The solicitor must make it clear in writing to the prospective buyer that the solicitor cannot advise or act for him or her in respect of the mortgage, that the mortgage may not be the only one available and that he or she should consult his or her own solicitor.

25.24   Where a solicitor wishes to give advice on mortgages linked with a particular life policy the solicitor will have to exercise care to ensure compliance with the Financial Services Act 1986. It is likely that in order to give such advice the solicitor would require authorisation under the above Act. This would normally be by way of an investment business certificate from the Law Society in which case the solicitor would also need to comply with the Solicitors' Investment Business Rules 1990.

Publicity

25.25   A solicitor may publicise his or her property selling service or properties for sale subject to the provisions of the Solicitors' Publicity Code 1990.

25.26   Most provisions in the Publicity Code apply to all aspects of a solicitor's practice. However, two provisions refer specifically to property selling:

   (a) paragraph 3 prohibits unsolicited visits or unsolicited telephone calls. However, one of the exceptions provided by that paragraph is where such visit or call is made to publicise a specific commercial property or properties the solicitor has for sale or to let;

   (b) paragraph 4 permits the naming or identification of a client in advertisements with the client's written consent and where such naming or identification is not likely to prejudice the client's interests. A solicitor may thus name a client with the client's written consent in advertising property for sale or to let on that client's behalf.

25.27 Where a solicitor publicises a composite fee for a package of property selling and conveyancing (and/or some other service) paragraph 5(d) of the Solicitors' Publicity Code 1990 provides that he or she must be willing if required:

(a) to quote separate fees for the individual services (which separate fees may not total more than the composite fee), and

(b) to carry out any one only of those services on the basis of such separate fee.

A solicitor is 'required' for this purpose if he or she has a clear indication that a prospective client may wish to instruct him or her in respect of only one service in the package.

25.28 An entry or advertisement of a solicitor who provides a property selling service may appear in a directory, such as the Yellow Pages, under the classification 'Estate Agents' provided that the word 'solicitor(s)' appears *either* in the heading of the directory or listing *or* in a designation of the practice appearing in the entry or advertisement itself. See paragraph 8 of the Solicitors' Publicity Code 1990 as to that and as to the special provision for a directory referring wholly or mainly to practice outside England and Wales.

Introductions and referrals

25.29 Rule 3 of the SPR 1990 allows solicitors to enter into arrangements for the introduction and referral of clients to and from the solicitor's practice, provided there is compliance with the Solicitors' Introduction and Referral Code 1990. The code provides *inter alia* that a solicitor may not reward an introducer by the payment of commission or otherwise (see section 2(3) of the code). Also a solicitor should not enter into any agreement or association which would restrict his or her freedom to recommend any particular firm, agency or business to his or her clients as all recommendations must be made on the basis that they are in the best interests of the client (see section 4 of the code).

25.30 Rule 12 of the SPR 1990 places conditions on the ability of a solicitor to enter into arrangements in respect of introductions and referrals in the field of investment business. In particular the rule prevents a solicitor from acting as an appointed representative as defined in the Financial Services Act 1986.

25.31 In accepting or making referrals in the field of mortgages or investment business, solicitors must comply with the Council statement on the Financial Services Act 1986: life policies and tied agents (see Annex 24C). The basic principle underlying the Council statement, which is of particular relevance to solicitors selling property, is that it is in the best interests of anyone who is likely to need an endowment policy, or similar life insurance with an investment element, that he or she should receive advice from an independent intermediary authorised to give investment advice. Therefore, when referring clients or accepting referrals in relation to investment business, a solicitor should make enquiries as to the status of the intermediary under the Financial Services Act 1986.

Statement as to remuneration

25.32 When accepting instructions to act in the sale of a property, a solicitor must give the client a written statement setting out their agreement as to the amount of the solicitor's fee or the method of its calculation, the circumstances in which it is to become payable, the amount of any disbursements to be charged separately (or the basis on which they will be calculated) and the circumstances in which they may be incurred, and as to the incidence of VAT. It should state the identity of the property, the interest to be sold and the price to be sought. The requirement for a written statement as to remuneration is similar to that imposed on estate agents by the Estate Agents Act 1979.

25.33 The statement should also deal with whether or not the solicitor is to have 'sole agency' or 'sole selling rights' and, if so, explain the intention and effect of those terms (or any similar terms used) in the following manner:

(a) *Sole selling rights*

'You will be liable to pay a fee to us, in addition to any other costs or charges agreed, in each of the following circumstances —

— if unconditional contracts for the sale of the property are exchanged in the period during which we have sole selling rights, even if the buyer was not found by us but by another agent or by any other person, including yourself;

— if unconditional contracts for the sale of the property are exchanged after the expiry of the period during which we have sole selling rights but to a buyer who was introduced to you during that period or with whom we had negotiations about the property during that period.'

(b) *Sole agency*

'You will be liable to pay a fee to us, in addition to any other costs or charges agreed, if unconditional contracts for the sale of the property are exchanged at any time —

— with a buyer introduced by us with whom we had negotiations about the property in the period during which we have sole agency; or

> — with a buyer introduced by another agent during the period of our sole agency.'

The requirements in this paragraph and those in paragraphs 25.34 – 25.36 are similar to the obligations imposed on estate agents by the Estate Agents (Provision of Information) Regulations 1991.

25.34 If reference is made to a 'ready, willing and able' buyer (or similar term), the statement should contain the following explanation:

> 'A buyer is a "ready, willing and able" buyer if he or she is prepared and is able to exchange unconditional contracts for the purchase of your property. You will be liable to pay a fee to us, in addition to any other costs or charges agreed, if such a buyer is introduced by us in accordance with your instructions and this must be paid even if you subsequently withdraw and unconditional contracts for sale are not exchanged, irrespective of your reasons.'

25.35 If, by reason of the provisions of the statement in which any of the terms referred to in paragraphs 25.33 and 25.34 appear, any of the prescribed explanations is in any way misleading, the content of the explanation shall be altered so as accurately to describe the liability of the client to pay a fee in accordance with those provisions. Subject to this requirement, the explanations prescribed in paragraphs 25.33 and 25.34 should be reproduced prominently, clearly and legibly without any material alterations or additions and should be given no less prominence than that given to any other information in the statement apart from the heading, practice names, names of the parties, numbers or lettering subsequently inserted.

25.36 Any statement incorporating an explanation of any of the terms referred to in paragraphs 25.33 and 25.34 must be given at the time when communication commences between the solicitor and the client or as soon as is reasonably practicable thereafter, provided that this is before the client is committed to any liability towards the solicitor.

Interest earned on preliminary deposits

25.37 A solicitor will normally hold a pre-contract deposit on behalf of the buyer, although the solicitor will have received it in his or her role as the seller's agent. A preliminary deposit is usually fully refundable to the buyer. Part III of the Solicitors' Accounts Rules 1991 (deposit interest) applies only to interest arising on client's money and stakeholder money. It is recommended however, as a matter of good practice, that solicitors should always consider, when refunding a preliminary deposit, whether it is appropriate to pay interest to the buyer.

25.38 The effect of paragraph 7 of the Estate Agents (Accounts) Regulations 1981 is that estate agents must account to the buyer in any case where the amount of the preliminary deposit exceeds £500, and the interest actually earned on it, or which could have been earned if it had been kept in a separate deposit account, is at least £10. If that is the case, the estate agent has to account for all interest earned on the preliminary deposit in a separate deposit account, or for the interest which could have been earned on it had it been kept in a separate deposit account. Solicitors could use these Regulations as guidelines as to when it might be appropriate to pay interest. Alternatively, they might wish to consult the table contained in Part III of the Solicitors' Accounts Rules 1991. Another approach might be to operate a system of accounting for interest of over £20 (the aim of Part III of the rules being to produce an overall *de minimis* figure of £20).

Surveys and valuations

25.39 A solicitor may carry out structural surveys and formal valuations of property as part of his or her practice provided that such work is undertaken by appropriately qualified persons. Rule 14 of the SPR 1990 provides that a solicitor may not provide structural surveys or formal valuations of property unless the work is carried out by a principal or employee who is a chartered surveyor or who holds another professional qualification approved by the Council and the appropriate contribution has been paid to the Solicitors' Indemnity Fund. Rule 17.5 of the Solicitors' Indemnity Rules 1992 details the additional contribution payable and provides that any practice intending to undertake this work must immediately notify Solicitors Indemnity Fund Limited with details.

Joint property selling practice

25.40 Where a number of firms of solicitors undertake property selling jointly, for example at jointly run premises, those firms will be carrying on a joint property selling practice. The professional rules applicable to such joint practices are the same as those applicable to individual firms.

25.41 Severe constraints for firms in such a joint property selling practice are presented by the principles on conflict of interests and Rule 6 of the SPR 1990 (see paragraphs 25.14 – 25.18).

Property display centre

25.42 Rather than carrying on a joint property selling practice with the resultant constraints referred to in paragraph 25.41, a number of independent firms of solicitors ('the participating firms') may join together to carry on a joint property display centre (PDC) to publicise properties in the sale of which an individual participating firm is instructed.

25.43   A PDC which accords with the guidance set out in paragraph 25.44 (which guidance is based on the application of the rules and principles of conduct) is regarded as an administrative extension of the practices of the participating firms. It is not regarded either as a department, branch office or practising address of all or any of the participating firms or as a joint property selling practice (as referred to in paragraphs 25.40 and 25.41). Although it may involve a partnership for certain administrative purposes between participating firms, it is not a partnership for the purposes of carrying on a solicitor's practice.

25.44   (a)   A PDC can have no clients; it may merely carry out certain activities on behalf of the participating firms. Only individual participating firms may be instructed in the sale of a property.

(b)   A PDC is a place where the principal activity carried on is the display and dissemination of information about properties which the individual participating firms have for sale.

(c)   No solicitor's professional practice may be carried on at a PDC. In particular no negotiations may be carried on there; prospective buyers must be referred to the individual participating firm instructed in the sale of the property in question. Instructions to sell a property may only be accepted at offices of participating firms. To avoid problems with conflict of interests (see paragraphs 25.14 – 25.18 and 25.41) the participating firms must operate totally independently so far as their professional business, including property selling, is concerned.

(d)   A PDC must not be set up as a separate legal entity, as a PDC is inherently an administrative extension of the practices of the participating firms. As a separate business it would involve a breach of Rule 5 of the SPR 1990.

(e)   The participating firms may wish to establish a joint service company to carry out necessary support functions concerned with the running of the PDC, e.g. hiring premises and equipment. The service company (as with a service company established by an individual firm of solicitors) cannot carry on any legal practice or have any dealings with the property selling or property buying public, otherwise there would be a breach of Rule 5 of the SPR 1990 and the Solicitors Act 1974.

(f)   Having regard to Rule 1(b) and (c) of the SPR 1990 a participating firm may not make it a condition that a prospective buyer instructs another participating firm in his or her conveyancing or any other matter.

25.45   As no part of a solicitor's practice is carried on at a PDC, Rule 13 of the SPR 1990 (supervision and management of offices) does not apply. Note that the participating firms are nevertheless responsible for the activities of the PDC staff and have a duty to supervise them.

25.46 A single firm of solicitors could establish its own PDC (see paragraphs 25.42 – 25.44) where no negotiations or any other part of the firm's practice was conducted. Rule 13 of the SPR 1990 would not apply to such a PDC. The firm would nevertheless be responsible for the activities of its PDC staff and would have a duty to supervise them. Note that Rule 13 applies to a branch office (as opposed to a PDC) but an application for a waiver of this rule will be considered in the case of an office at which the only work carried out is the selling of property — see paragraph 25.12.

Joint property display centres — publicity

25.47 Paragraph 10 of the Solicitors' Publicity Code 1990 contains detailed provisions regarding 'flag advertising'. This term includes any advertising by a joint PDC which does not name the firm or firms whose services are being advertised and any advertising by an individual participating firm which includes reference to the PDC.

25.48 Any advertising under the logo of or in the name of a joint PDC, if it does not name the firm or firms whose services are being advertised, must include the word 'solicitor(s)' (or, as an additional option in the case of publicity conducted outside England and Wales, the word 'lawyer(s)') and the PDC's address (or some other address at which the names of all the participating firms are available). A name such as 'Solicitors' Property Centre' or 'Solicitors' Property Centre, Craxenford' (provided it is not misleading or inaccurate) may appear on the PDC premises, advertisements or stationery. On the PDC premises the PDC name must be accompanied by the names of the participating firms (either outside or visible from outside the premises) and the word 'solicitor' or 'solicitors'. The PDC stationery must be used only in connection with activities which a PDC may properly undertake in accordance with paragraph 25.44. In particular it must not be used in connection with negotiations. For the reasons stated in paragraph 25.44(e), the name of a service company (e.g. 'Solicitors' Property Centre Ltd') should not appear on the PDC itself or in its advertisements or on its stationery.

25.49 An individual participating firm advertising in its own name may refer to its membership of the PDC or include the PDC logo in its advertisements.The firm's stationery may include the PDC logo or refer to the firm's membership of the PDC. Notepaper used for a solicitor's professional business, including notepaper used in negotiating a sale of property, must include the name of the firm and not merely the name of a PDC.

25.50 'For Sale' boards and particulars of properties for sale may, at the discretion of the participating firms, either be the boards and particulars of an individual participating firm or the boards and particulars of the PDC. Boards and particulars of the PDC must comply with paragraph 25.48. An individual participating firm may use the PDC name and/or logo on its boards or particulars in addition to the firm's own name.

Joint property display centres — referrals

25.51   In practice a prospective client may either first approach an individual participating firm or the PDC itself. A joint PDC must not accept instructions on behalf of participating firms. However, Rule 3 of the SPR 1990 allows a PDC to refer prospective clients to the participating firms. In the light of Rule 1(b) of the SPR 1990 a prospective client should be asked to make his or her own choice from amongst the participating firms. If, however, he or she decides not to make a choice the method whereby a participating firm is selected for a referral is a matter for the participating firms. Note, however, that if a member of staff at the PDC is asked for a recommendation (rather than being asked merely for a referral to a participating firm), such recommendation must only be given on the basis of a genuine belief that the firm concerned should indeed be recommended.

Selling property as a separate business

25.52   Rule 5 of the SPR 1990 prohibits a solicitor from engaging in property selling by way of a separate business; he or she may only do so as part of a solicitor's practice or the practice of a multi-national partnership or a recognised body. However, the rule provides an exception for a separate business already providing services before 11th December 1986 without infringing the Solicitors' Practice Rules 1936/72 (as amended). As regards such a business it should be noted that:

(a)   Such exception to Rule 5 applies only until 1st September 1993.

(b)   The Estate Agents Act 1979 applies to such a separate business.

(c)   Claims incurred in connection with such a separate business would not be covered by the Solicitors' Indemnity Fund.

(d)   Rule 3 of the SPR 1990 allows such a separate property selling business to refer clients for conveyancing to the solicitor's practice, subject to the Solicitors' Introduction and Referral Code 1990.

(e)   If a solicitor recommends the separate business to a client, he or she must fully disclose his or her interest in that business to the client and must ensure that the recommendation is in the best interests of the client (see Rule 1(c) of the SPR 1990 and section 4 of the Solicitors' Introduction and Referral Code 1990).

(f)   Such a separate business is not covered by the group licence issued to the Law Society under the Consumer Credit Act 1974.

Annex 25A

Guidance — questions and answers on property selling

General

Q.1. Is property selling in effect to be regarded in the same light, as say, conveyancing or probate work?

A.   Yes. If a solicitor undertakes to sell a property for a seller, the seller will be his or her client; the solicitor's relationship with and the work he or she does for the client will be subject to the law and professional rules binding on solicitors in relation to their other work.

Premises

Q.2. Are solicitors able to conduct their property selling practice in the same office that they use for the rest of their practice?

A.   Yes.

Q.3. Is there any objection to solicitors opening a branch office with, for example, a street-level window purely for the purpose of their property selling business?

A.   No.

Supervision rules

Q.4. Does this office have to comply with the rules relating to the management and supervision of solicitors' offices (Rule 13 of the Solicitors' Practice Rules 1990)?

A.   Yes, because it will indeed be a branch of a solicitor's practice and must therefore be staffed and supervised in accordance with the rules, unless a waiver is granted — see Chapter 25 of the Guide, paragraph 25.12. See paragraphs 25.45 and 25.46 as regards supervision of a property display centre, but note that only restricted activities can be carried out at such a centre — see paragraphs 25.42 and 25.44.

Publicity

Q.5. Can a solicitor's office with a street-level window be used for the display of particulars of property for sale in the same way as an estate agent's office?

A.   Yes, but the solicitor must comply with the Solicitors' Publicity Code 1990.

Q.6. Can a solicitor put a 'For Sale' notice on a property he or she is selling and send particulars to prospective buyers?

A.   Yes, but the solicitor must comply with the Solicitors' Publicity Code 1990.

Description

Q.7.   Can a solicitor undertaking property selling describe himself or herself as 'Solicitor and Estate Agent'?

A.   Yes. See paragraph 25.07 in the Guide; see also paragraph 25.28 for directory entries.

Q.8.   In advertising can a solicitor include a reference to the fact that he or she is a member of any particular organisation or association of solicitors?

A.   Yes. If, however, the advertising does not name the solicitor's firm, it must comply with paragraph 10 of the Solicitors' Publicity Code 1990 (flag advertising).

Estate Agents Act

Q.9.   Does the Estate Agents Act 1979 apply to solicitors?

A.   Section 1(2)(a) exempts from the Act 'things done in the course of his profession by a practising solicitor or a person employed by him'.

Remuneration

Q.10.   What is the purpose of the statement as to remuneration as mentioned in paragraphs 25.32 – 25.36 of the Guide?

A.   To enable the client to be clear as to the basis on which it is proposed that he or she should be charged.

Q.11.   Will commission charged on property sales be subject to the Law Society's remuneration certificate procedure and to taxation by the Court?

A.   Yes. However, if an agreement is signed by the client which accords with section 57 of the Solicitors Act 1974, the Law Society's remuneration certificate procedure becomes inappropriate. Section 57(5) further provides that if on any taxation the agreement is objected to by the client as unfair or unreasonable, the taxing officer may enquire into the facts and certify them to the Court which may, if it thinks fit, order the agreement to be set aside or the amount payable under it to be reduced.

Q.12.   What matters should be covered in the written statement relating to property selling?

A.   See paragraphs 25.32 — 25.36 of the Guide.

Q.13.   Does the Law Society make any recommendation about property selling commissions?

A.   No; it is a matter for agreement between the solicitor and the client, subject to what is said in reply to Question 11.

Commission from a third party

Q.14.   What is the position with regard to commission paid to a solicitor by an insurance company, for example, where the solicitor's client takes out an endowment policy as security for a loan?

A.   Such commission is quite distinct from the remuneration paid by the client to the solicitor in relation to the property transaction. Rule 10 of the Solicitors' Practice Rules 1990 (SPR 1990) requires a solicitor to account to the client for any commission received of more than £20 unless, having disclosed to the client in writing the amount or basis of calculation of the commission or, if the precise amount or basis cannot be ascertained, an approximation thereof, he or she has the client's agreement to retain it. It should be remembered that a solicitor who acts in the sale of a property for a seller cannot arrange a mortgage for the buyer — see paragraphs 25.22 – 25.24.

Composite fees

Q.15. Is there any objection to a solicitor quoting a composite fee for property selling and conveyancing?

A.   No, but he or she should be prepared to quote separate fees if so required, and where the solicitor publicises a package at a composite fee he or she must comply with paragraph 5(d) of the Solicitors' Publicity Code 1990 (see paragraph 25.27).

Payment of staff

Q.16. Can a solicitor pay his or her property selling negotiators on a commission basis?

A.   Yes (see Rule 7(1) of the SPR 1990), provided they are *bona fide* employees. This provision does not permit, under the cloak of employment, a partnership with anyone other than a solicitor, registered foreign lawyer or a recognised body.

Insurance

Q.17. Will a solicitor who undertakes property selling work be covered by the Solicitors' Indemnity Rules?

A.   Yes. The position will be just the same as for any other part of his or her practice, as is his or her liability in negligence and contract. See also paragraph 25.39 on surveys and valuations.

Q.18. Will the solicitor's earnings from property selling work have to be included in his or her gross fees returns?

A.   Yes.

Type of property not usually handled by the solicitor

Q.19. What is the duty of a solicitor who is asked to sell property of a value or character not usually handled by him or her or by the property centre in which he or she is involved?

A.   As in the case of any work the solicitor does not feel he or she can properly handle, the solicitor must decline instructions and advise the client to consult another property seller, possibly a specialist agent. Furthermore, the solicitor should be aware that he or she could be negligent should this course not be taken in appropriate circumstances.

Partnerships and incorporated practices

Q.20. Can a solicitor undertake property selling business in conjunction with someone else?

A.   He or she may do so in partnership with other solicitors, registered foreign lawyers or recognised bodies. If two or more solicitors choose to form a new partnership for the purpose of property selling, the new partnership will be a new practice for all purposes including the Indemnity Rules, the Accounts Rules, the SPR 1990 and conflict of interests (see paragraphs 25.40 and 25.41 in the Guide). Solicitors can incorporate their practices, or any part of a practice, through a recognised body. All share owners must be solicitors, registered foreign lawyers, or recognised bodies. All directors must be solicitors or registered foreign lawyers. Recognised bodies can practise in partnership with other recognised bodies or solicitors. See also paragraphs 25.42 – 25.51 as regards a property display centre, but note that only restricted activities can be carried out at such a centre.

Relations with estate agents

Q.21. Is there any objection to a solicitor handling the sale where a non-solicitor is also acting?

A.   No. A solicitor may instruct an estate agent as sub-agent (see Rule 7(2) of the SPR 1990), and may be instructed as the sub-agent of an estate agent.

Q.22. Is it a breach of the rules for a solicitor to agree to be on an estate agent's panel on a composite fee (or any other) basis?

A.   No, provided there is compliance with the Solicitors' Introduction and Referral Code 1990 (see Rule 3 of the SPR 1990).

Conveyancing instructions

Q.23. If a client instructs a solicitor to undertake the sale of a property, is there any objection if the solicitor accepts instructions for the conveyancing as well?

A.   No.

Q.24. If a seller instructs one solicitor to undertake the conveyancing, is there any objection to another solicitor accepting instructions to undertake the sale of the property?

A.   No.

30th January 1985 (updated January 1993)

Chapter 26

Investment business

Introduction

Financial Services Act 1986

26.01   The Financial Services Act 1986 ('the Act') introduced a regime which controls persons carrying on investment business by means of a system of self regulation under the supervision of the Securities and Investments Board (SIB), the body to which virtually all of the powers of the Secretary of State under the Act have been delegated. The definition of investment business contained in the Act is so wide that it applies not only to persons involved in mainstream investment business but also to those who, in the course of their profession, provide financial services of a more general nature. In view of this wide definition of investment business it is likely that most firms of solicitors fall within the ambit of the Act.

26.02   Section 3 of the Act provides that no person shall carry on investment business unless he or she is authorised to do so or is an exempted person. The category of exempted persons includes appointed representatives (tied agents), but Rule 12 of the Solicitors' Practice Rules 1990 prohibits solicitors from being appointed representatives of, for example, life offices or independent networks/brokers. Other exempted persons include the Bank of England and recognised investment exchanges.

As solicitors are not exempted persons under the Act it is necessary for them to become authorised if they wish to carry on any investment business as part of a business, as opposed to in a purely personal capacity without remuneration.

26.03   There are two elements to investment business, firstly, whether an 'investment' is involved and secondly, whether there is an 'activity constituting investment business' involved. It should be noted that the Act came into force on 29th April 1988 and that any work done before that date is not 'investment business'.

Investments

26.04 Investments are defined in Part I of Schedule 1 to the Act (see Annex 26A) and are as follows:

(a)   company stocks and shares (though not most building society shares);

(b)   debentures, loan stock and bonds;

(c)   government and public securities;

(d)   warrants or other instruments entitling the holder to subscribe to (a)-(c) above;

(e)   certificates or other instruments representing securities;

(f)   units in collective investment schemes;

(g)   options;

(h)   futures;

(i)   contracts for differences;

(j)   long-term insurance contracts, e.g. life policies with an investment element and pensions;

(k)   rights and interests in any investment.

26.05 Shares in building societies, industrial and provident societies or credit unions are generally not caught by the Act. Thus most building society share accounts are not investments as defined in the Act, although deferred building society shares are now caught by the Act. Bank or building society deposit or savings accounts are also excluded from the definition of investments. National savings products such as National Savings Certificates, Income Bonds and Premium Bonds are no longer caught by the Act although gilt-edged stocks remain investments. Insurance policies which are taken out for pure protection, e.g. buildings insurance and most policies which limit benefits to death or incapacity are excluded from the definition of 'investments'.

Activities constituting investment business

26.06 The activities which may constitute investment business are set out in Part II of Schedule 1 to the Act. The activities which are caught are as follows:

(a)   dealing in investments — this includes buying or selling shares as agent for a client, i.e. where the solicitor gives the instructions to the stockbroker;

(b)   arranging deals in investments — this includes making arrangements for a client to take out a life policy in connection with a house purchase, or for a client to buy or sell unit trusts;

(c)   managing investments — this includes, for example, acting as trustee where the trust funds include or may include investments, or acting as a donee under certain powers of attorney, or as receiver appointed by the Court of Protection;

(d)   investment advice — this includes giving advice on a particular investment, but not generic advice; therefore advice that a repayment mortgage is more appropriate than an endowment mortgage would not be caught;

(e)   establishing, operating or winding up collective investment schemes.

Authorisation

26.07   Authorisation under the Act may be obtained in three ways:

(a)   through a recognised self-regulating organisation (SRO);

(b)   through a recognised professional body (RPB); or

(c)   directly from SIB.

The Law Society is an RPB and as such is able to authorise solicitors to conduct investment business, which is done by issuing investment business certificates. Solicitors who are authorised by the Society are governed by the Solicitors' Investment Business Rules 1990 (SIBR) — see paragraph 26.17 and Annex 26B. The majority of solicitors will obtain authorisation from the Society but in certain cases, where a large proportion of a solicitor's work is investment business (in excess of the 20% limit set by SIB — see paragraph 26.11), it may be necessary for a firm to obtain authorisation through an SRO such as the Financial Intermediaries Managers and Brokers Regulatory Association (FIMBRA).

26.08   There are now four SROs, the Securities and Futures Authority (SFA), the Investment Management Regulatory Organisation (IMRO), FIMBRA and the Life Assurance and Unit Trust Regulatory Organisation (LAUTRO).

The nine RPBs are the Law Societies of England and Wales, Scotland and Northern Ireland, the Institutes of Chartered Accountants of England and Wales, Scotland and Ireland, the Insurance Brokers Registration Council, the Institute of Actuaries and the Chartered Institute of Certified Accountants.

26.09   A new SRO, the Personal Investment Authority (PIA), is currently proposed and is likely to come into existence in 1993. PIA, which will cover investment business for private investors, is likely to include FIMBRA, LAUTRO and some IMRO members.

Application for investment business certificate

26.10   Firms wishing to be authorised by the Society are required to apply for an investment business certificate. Initial application for such certificates must be made on the appropriate form:

(a)   FSA1 — for a solicitor or partnership of solicitors;

(b)   FSA3 — for a multi-national partnership;

(c)   FSA5 — for a recognised body;

(d)   FSA7 — for a partnership including at least one recognised body.

These forms are available from the Financial Services Section. The Society may at its discretion refuse to issue an investment business certificate or may issue one subject to conditions. The application form requires general information about the firm, and an indication as to whether the firm carries on or intends to carry on discrete investment business (DIB). It is therefore necessary, when completing the application form, for firms to understand the definition of DIB (see paragraph 26.18). However, it should be noted that there is only one type of authorisation from the Society. Therefore, any firm that has been issued with an investment business certificate may undertake any type of investment business (subject to paragraph 26.12). It will not be restricted to the areas of work which it has indicated on the form that it will undertake.

Scope of authorisation

26.11   It has been agreed between the Society and SIB that the Society will not normally continue to authorise firms whose commission from investment business (excluding any amount paid or credited to the client) together with fee income from DIB exceeds 20% of the firm's total gross income from both investment business and non-investment business. This calculation is required in the annual renewal form FSA2, FSA4, FSA6 or FSA8 (see paragraph 26.16). It should be noted that for the purpose of this calculation the reference to fee income from DIB does not include fee income from:

(a)   DIB where that activity is incidental to other services provided by the firm which are not themselves DIB (see annual renewal form); or

(b)   DIB undertaken by a partner or employee of the firm in his or her capacity as a trustee or donee of an enduring power of attorney or trustee power of attorney or as receiver appointed by the Court of Protection (see Rule 3(2)(c)(ii));

(c)   DIB undertaken where the firm makes arrangements to effect a transaction as a result of a decision taken by an individual referred to in (b) above (see Rule 3(2)(c)(iii) of SIBR).

Firms which exceed the 20% limit will usually be required to seek authorisation elsewhere, although an exception may be made where a firm is normally under the 20% limit, but rises above it in an exceptional year.

26.12 Solicitors authorised by the Society are prohibited from carrying out certain activities constituting investment business and these are set out in Rule 3(1) of the SIBR:

(a) market making in investments;

(b) buying, selling, subscribing for or underwriting investments as principal where the firm holds itself out as engaging in the business of buying such investments with a view to selling them;

(c) entering into margined transactions as agent for a client. This prohibition does not apply to any such transaction effected with or through a permitted third party (see paragraph 26.18);

(d) acting as a stabilising manager within Part 10 of the Financial Services (Conduct of Business) Rules 1987 in relation to any issue of relevant securities (as there defined);

(e) acting as the trustee or manager of a regulated collective investment scheme; and

(f) entering into a broker funds arrangement.

26.13 Authorisation from the Society is given to the firm and covers the activities of all partners, employees and consultants of the firm. The certificate which is issued to a firm will only cover one partnership. Thus, if a firm has more than one office with different partnerships at each office, even though the practices have a common name, separate investment business certificates will be needed for each partnership. However, if one partnership has several offices which practise under different names, the certificate issued to the partnership will cover all the offices of that partnership if the appropriate information is given on the notepaper. Further guidance on this matter may be sought from Professional Ethics.

Authorisation for non-U.K. offices

26.14 Guidance on the need for authorisation for non-U.K. offices is in Annex 26G. A firm's authorisation will extend to any overseas office provided that it is the same partnership. If, for example, the Hong Kong office has a foreign lawyer as a partner who is not a partner in the London office, the Hong Kong office will not be authorised.

Fees

26.15 The fee for the investment business certificate is based partly on the number of partners (salaried or equity) within a firm and shown as such on the notepaper. No refund will be made if a partner leaves the firm during the certification year (which runs from April to March); nor will any additional fee be levied for a new partner joining a firm during the year. Where two or more firms merge and the new firm applies for a certificate during the year, a fee will be calculated in the usual way.

However, in calculating that fee, no further fee will be payable in respect of partners who have already been taken into account as partners of one or other of the merging firms. The position is similar where a certified firm splits during the year and any of the resultant firms apply for a certificate. No further fee will be payable in respect of any partners in the new firms who have already been taken into account as partners in the former firm.

In the case of a multi-national partnership fees will be calculated partly by reference to the number of partners whether solicitors or registered foreign lawyers. However, no account will be taken of any partner who is a registered foreign lawyer practising mainly from an office or offices outside England and Wales, provided no investment business is conducted from that office in or into any part of the United Kingdom.

In calculating the fee for a recognised body, the solicitors or registered foreign lawyers who are directors or share-owners are treated as if they were partners. Similar principles apply in calculating the fee for a recognised body which has other recognised bodies as share-owners, or for a partnership which has one or more recognised bodies as partners.

Renewal of certificates

26.16   Applications for a new certificate should be made before 1st April each year. Applications must be made on the appropriate renewal form:

(a)   FSA 2 — for a solicitor or a partnership of solicitors;

(b)   FSA 4 — for a multi-national partnership;

(c)   FSA 6 — for a recognised body;

(d)   FSA 8 — for a partnership including at least one recognised body.

A renewal form will be sent automatically to all firms holding a current investment business certificate. Where there has been a change in the make-up of the firm which means that it is no longer in the same category (see (a)-(d) above) the firm should ensure that it completes the appropriate form. It should be noted that the renewal form requires detailed information concerning the amount of commission which has been received in respect of investment business and the amount of fee income derived from DIB (see paragraph 26.11). This information is required in order to establish whether firms are still within the 20% limit. Firms should therefore maintain appropriate records throughout the year to enable them to complete the renewal form as required by Rule 13 of the SIBR.

The firm is asked whether it has conducted DIB and if so, to give details. The form also asks whether a firm employs a specialist non-solicitor financial adviser. The Society has issued good practice guidelines relating to the recruitment, supervision and training of non-solicitor financial advisers (see Annex 26I).

Solicitors' Investment Business Rules 1990

26.17 Under the Act, the Society is obliged to have rules governing the conduct of investment business. By virtue of Schedule 3, paragraph 3(1) of the Act those rules must afford adequate investor protection. The SIBR apply to all firms which hold an investment business certificate issued by the Society but do not apply to firms which have sought authorisation elsewhere. The SIBR are arranged as follows:

(a) Chapter 1 — Citation and Interpretation and Application;

(b) Chapter 2 — Certification;

(c) Chapter 3 — Notification of certain matters to the Society;

(d) Chapter 4 — Conduct rules;

(e) Chapter 5 — Monitoring by the Society;

(f) Chapter 6 — Waivers and service of documents.

The text of the SIBR appears in Annex 26B. Solicitors must also comply with SIB's Ten Principles which together with guidance from the Society are at Annex 26C.

Discrete investment business and non-discrete investment business

26.18 The SIBR distinguish between investment business which is discrete investment business (DIB) and that which (by way of exception) is non-discrete. DIB is, in effect, mainstream investment business and most of the detailed rules of the SIBR will apply only to DIB. There are two main categories of exceptions which make investment business non-discrete:

(a) Incidental exception

Where the investment business carried on is incidental to the main purpose of the retainer, for example, investment business which is incidental to the legal work involved in the takeover of a company or the sale of shares which is incidental to the winding up of the estate of a deceased person. Guidance on corporate finance activities appears at Annex 26F. However, the incidental exception is not available in relation to life policies and unit trusts except for sales during probate work. Thus, even though advice on an endowment policy may be incidental to a conveyancing transaction, the advice remains DIB.

(b) Permitted third party exception

Where a permitted third party (PTP) is used by a solicitor to carry out investment business. The PTP may be an insurance broker, or a stockbroker, who is independent and authorised to conduct investment business. In such circumstances, the PTP will be responsible for complying with the rules of his or her own SRO or RPB in respect of the particular client. The PTP exception will be available only where the firm of solicitors acts as disclosed agent for a named client; if the PTP is a member of SFA or IMRO, the PTP must have agreed with or confirmed to the firm that the client is or will be treated by such member as its customer and additionally in the case of a member of the SFA, that all the conduct of business rules of the SFA will apply. Such agreement or confirmation may be in the form or substantially in the form set out in Appendix 9 to the SIBR.

Investment advertisements

26.19   Solicitors may issue their own investment advertisements or approve clients' investment advertisements for the purposes of section 57 of the Act. Rule 8(2) of the SIBR sets out the requirements for such issue or approval. Where solicitors issue investment advertisements, the British Code of Advertising Practice (Annex 11C) and Part III of Appendix 5 of the SIBR will apply. Where solicitors are approving investment advertisements, Part 7 of the Financial Services (Conduct of Business) Rules 1990 (Annex 26D) will apply.

Rules applying to investment business generally

26.20   The majority of the conduct rules (see Chapter 4) of the SIBR apply to DIB only. The exceptions are the following rules which apply to both DIB and non-discrete investment business:

(a)   Rule 8(2) — advertisements,

(b)   Rule 8(3) — published recommendations,

(c)   Rule 8(4) — unsolicited calls,

(d)   Rule 8(5) — records and central register,

(e)   Rule 8(6) — complaints,

(f)   Rule 8(7) — *force majeure*,

(g)   Rule 12(5) — records of transactions.

However, Rules 8(5), 8(6) and 12(5) do not apply where the incidental exception is used.

Rules applying to DIB only

26.21   The main rules which apply to DIB are:

(a)   **Rule 9(1) — know your client**

Before performing any investment service, as defined, for the client, the solicitor must usually obtain information concerning the client's personal and financial circumstances.

(b) Rule 9(2) — suitability

Care must be taken to ensure that the particular transaction is suitable for the client.

(c) Rule 10 — client documentation

There must be either a client agreement or, where appropriate, a private client letter (see Annex 26E) which sets out the terms on which a solicitor will conduct investment business. Such an agreement or letter is not required in relation to life policies, unit trusts or a PEP containing these items ('type C PEP') provided that the firm reasonably believes that the investment service which the client requires from the firm at that time relates solely to such investments and, in the case of type C PEPs, the firm does not advise on investments (other than unit trusts) to be included in the PEP. However, a 'buyer's guide' (see Appendix 7 of the SIBR) will normally be required for these investments.

(d) Rule 11 and Appendix 7 — best advice

The solicitor must not recommend a transaction involving a life policy, unit trust or type C PEP unless, after making reasonable enquiries, the solicitor neither is, nor ought to be, aware of another policy or other unit trusts which would be better for the client and, usually, the client has been given a buyer's guide. Details of these and other requirements relating to such investments are set out in Appendix 7 to the SIBR.

Record keeping

26.22 There are various provisions in the SIBR regarding record keeping, so it is important for solicitors to establish systems within their offices which will enable them to satisfy the record keeping requirements. In particular, it will usually be necessary for firms to maintain a central register (Rule 8(5)). This must be separate from client files, in which most of the records would be kept. Records are required in order to demonstrate compliance with the rules and may be referred to by the client or the Solicitors Complaints Bureau if any complaint is made in relation to investment business. They must also be available for inspection by the Society's Monitoring Unit. Forms IB1, IB2 and IB3, which have been designed for the purpose of keeping some of these records, are available from the Law Society Shop.

Notification

26.23 Chapter 3 of the SIBR contains the notification rules which require firms to notify the Society of certain events. Such notification should be sent to the Financial Services Section.

Monitoring

26.24 Under the Act, all SROs and RPBs are obliged to have adequate monitoring arrangements. The Society maintains a monitoring unit which carries out periodic visits to firms to ensure compliance with the SIBR, other rules governing the conduct of investment business by solicitors, and SIB's Ten Principles.

Further help

26.25 A step-by-step guide to the SIBR can be found in *Solicitors and Financial Services: a compliance handbook* by Peter Camp which is available from the Law Society Shop. Solicitors requiring advice on any aspect of the SIBR may wish to contact Professional Ethics.

Practice rules and other conduct requirements

Solicitors' Practice Rules 1990

26.26 Whilst the SIBR apply only to firms which are authorised by the Society to conduct investment business, the Solicitors' Practice Rules 1990 (SPR) apply to all practising solicitors. All firms which are authorised to conduct investment business whether by the Law Society or another regulatory body will need to ensure that they comply with the SPR (see Annex 1A).

Paragraphs 26.27–26.33 highlight certain of the SPR which are particularly relevant to investment business.

Basic principles

26.27 Rule 1 of the SPR sets out the basic principles governing a solicitors' practice. In particular it sets out the duties of a solicitor to remain independent and to act in the best interests of the client.

Publicity

26.28 Rule 2 of the SPR provides that solicitors must comply with the Solicitors' Publicity Code 1990 (see Annex 11A). Solicitors authorised by the Society must ensure that any publicity relating to investment business also complies with Rule 8 of the SIBR. Solicitors who are FIMBRA members will need to have regard to the rules of FIMBRA. Solicitors will need to comply with the Consumer Credit (Advertisements) Regulations 1989 if they are arranging mortgages and advertising this service (see Annex 11E).

Introductions and referrals

26.29 Rule 3 of the SPR concerns making and accepting referrals of business to or from other persons. The Solicitors' Introduction and Referral Code 1990 contains principles to be observed in relation to the introduction of clients by third parties to solicitors or by solicitors to third parties (see Annex 11B). Sections 2(6) and 4(2) and (3) relate to accepting and making referrals in the field of mortgages or investment business. It should also be noted that a solicitor must not reward an introducer by the payment of commission or otherwise (section 2(3)).

Separate businesses

26.30 Rule 5 of the SPR prohibits a solicitor, either alone or with any other person, from setting up, operating, actively participating in or controlling a separate business, other than a solicitor's practice, which offers any of the services set out in Rule 5(2). One such service is investment business as defined in the Act. Therefore, it would not be possible for a solicitor to set up a company other than a solicitor's incorporated practice (see Chapter 3) which provides financial services, or to become involved in an existing company which offers such services. A transitional period exists for any business already providing services before 11th December 1986 without putting the solicitor in breach of the Solicitors' Practice Rules 1936/72 (as amended). This transitional period expires 1st September 1993 — see Annex 3E.

Commissions

26.31 Rule 10 of the SPR provides that solicitors shall account to their clients for any commission received of more than £20 unless, having disclosed to the client in writing the amount or basis of calculation of the commission or (if the precise amount or basis cannot be ascertained) an approximation thereof, they have the client's agreement to retain it. This is particularly relevant to investment business in view of the substantial commissions which are often received in relation to such business. A further provision covers the position where the commission received is materially in excess of the amount disclosed. Further guidance may be found in Annex 14C.

Arrangements relating to investment business

26.32 Rule 12 of the SPR applies specifically to investment business. The rule prohibits a solicitor from being an appointed representative (more commonly known as a tied agent) or from setting up, operating, actively participating in or controlling any separate business which is an appointed representative. The rule also prohibits solicitors from entering into any arrangement with other persons under which the solicitor could be constrained to recommend to clients or effect for them (or refrain from doing so) transactions in some investments but not others, with some persons but not others, or through the agency of some persons but not others, or to introduce or refer clients, or other persons with whom the solicitor deals, to some persons but not others. This rule would not prevent a solicitor from regularly introducing clients to a particular broker, provided that the solicitor had not entered into any arrangement which could constrain him or her to use that broker.

Buyer's guide — solicitors regulated by FIMBRA

26.33   Rule 12(3) of the SPR requires firms authorised by other regulatory bodies to use a buyer's guide in a form which has been approved by the Law Society. The buyer's guide approved for firms regulated by FIMBRA reproduces the normal FIMBRA buyer's guide but substitutes the following wording in paragraph 3:

> 3.   Your adviser is independent. He will act on your behalf in recommending a product picked from the ranges of all the companies that make up the market place. As [solicitors] [solicitors and registered foreign lawyers] [registered foreign lawyers and solicitors], your adviser's firm is also subject to rules made by the Law Society. These rules require your adviser to pay you or credit you with any commission which he receives unless, after he has told you the amount of the commission or, if the amount cannot be worked out, the basis of calculation of the commission, you agree that he can keep it. You will in any event be given details of this commission by the company paying it.

Building societies and other agencies

26.34   Where solicitors have agency arrangements with building societies or other financial institutions which are tied agents, the agency must be confined to non-investment business. Otherwise the solicitor-agent might be in breach of Rule 12 of the SPR. This would apply equally whether the agency is conducted from the solicitor's general office or from an adjoining office which is used solely for the building society agency work. See also Annex 24C.

Council statement on the Financial Services Act 1986: life policies and tied agents

26.35   The Council statement on the Financial Services Act 1986: life policies and tied agents is set out in Annex 24C. The Council statement is discussed in Chapter 24. Solicitors should ensure either that they refer clients needing investment advice to independent intermediaries or conduct DIB themselves. Accordingly, it is important for solicitors to be aware of the status of persons to whom clients are referred, as many banks, building societies, estate agents and insurance agents are tied to particular insurance companies or unit trust operators and would not be able to offer independent advice.

Where clients are referred by tied agents, solicitors should consider the Council statement and, where appropriate, provide independent advice or refer the client to an independent intermediary.

General insurance

26.36 Solicitors involved in general insurance must also be independent intermediaries and are referred to the Council requirement on the ABI Code of Practice for intermediaries (see Annex 24B).

Home income plans

26.37 The Society has issued a product warning on home income plans which is attached at Annex 26H. Further guidance on solicitors' duties in relation to such plans may be found in Annex 24K.

Accounts Rules

26.38 Solicitors conducting investment business must also comply with the Solicitors Accounts Rules 1991 (see Chapter 27).

Annex 26A

Financial Services Act 1986

Schedule 1 — investments and investment business
(incorporating amendments to 1st June 1992)

PART I — INVESTMENTS

Shares etc.

1.   Shares and stock in the share capital of a company.

Note

In this paragraph "company" includes any body corporate and also any unincorporated
body constituted under the law of a country or territory outside the United Kingdom but
does not, except in relation to any shares of a class defined as deferred shares for the
purposes of section 119 of the Building Societies Act 1986, include a building society
incorporated under the law of, or of any part of, the United Kingdom, nor does it include
an open-ended investment company or any body incorporated under the law of, or of any
part of, the United Kingdom relating to industrial and provident societies or credit
unions.

Debentures

2.   Debentures, including debenture stock, loan stock, bonds, certificates of deposit
and other instruments creating or acknowledging indebtedness, not being instruments
falling within paragraph 3 below.

Note

This paragraph shall not be construed as applying -

(a)   to any instrument acknowledging or creating indebtedness for, or for money
borrowed to defray, the consideration payable under a contract for the supply of
goods or services;

(b)   to a cheque or other bill of exchange, a banker's draft or a letter of credit; or

(c)   to a banknote, a statement showing a balance in a current, deposit or savings
account or (by reason of any financial obligation contained in it) to a lease or other
disposition of property, a heritable security or an insurance policy.

Government and public securities

3.   Loan stock, bonds and other instruments creating or acknowledging indebtedness issued by or on behalf of a government, local authority or public authority.

Notes

(1)   In this paragraph "government, local authority or public authority" means -

(a)   the government of the United Kingdom, of Northern Ireland, or of any country or territory outside the United Kingdom;

(b)   a local authority in the United Kingdom or elsewhere;

(c)   any international organisation the members of which include the United Kingdom or another member State.

(2)   The note to paragraph 2 above shall, so far as applicable, apply also to this paragraph.

(3)   This paragraph does not apply to any instrument creating or acknowledging indebtedness in respect of money received by the Director of Savings as deposits or otherwise in connection with the business of the National Savings Bank or in respect of money raised under the National Loans Act 1968 under the auspices of the Director of Savings or in respect of money treated as having been so raised by virtue of section 11(3) of the National Debt Act 1972.

Instruments entitling to shares or securities

4.   Warrants or other instruments entitling the holder to subscribe for investments falling within paragraph 1, 2 or 3 above.

Notes

(1)   It is immaterial whether the investments are for the time being in existence or identifiable.

(2)   An investment falling within this paragraph shall not be regarded as falling within paragraph 7, 8 or 9 below.

Certificates representing securities

5.   Certificates or other instruments which confer -

(a)   property rights in respect of any investment falling within paragraph 1, 2, 3 or 4 above;

(b)   any right to acquire, dispose of, underwrite or convert an investment, being a right to which the holder would be entitled if he held any such investment to which the certificate or instrument relates; or

(c)   a contractual right (other than an option) to acquire any such investment otherwise than by subscription.

Note

This paragraph does not apply to any instrument which confers rights in respect of two or more investments issued by different persons or in respect of two or more different investments falling within paragraph 3 above and issued by the same person.

Units in collective investment scheme

6.   Units in a collective investment scheme, including shares in or securities of an open-ended investment company.

Options

7.   Options to acquire or dispose of -

(a)   an investment falling within any other paragraph of this Part of this Schedule;

(b)   currency of the United Kingdom or of any other country or territory;

(c)   gold, palladium, platinum or silver; or

(d)   an option to acquire or dispose of an investment falling within this paragraph by virtue of (a), (b) or (c) above.

Futures

8.   Rights under a contract for the sale of a commodity or property of any other description under which delivery is to be made at a future date and at a price agreed upon when the contract is made.

Notes

(1)   This paragraph does not apply if the contract is made for commercial and not investment purposes.

(2)   A contract shall be regarded as made for investment purposes if it is made or traded on a recognised investment exchange or made otherwise than on a recognised investment exchange but expressed to be as traded on such an exchange or on the same terms as those on which an equivalent contract would be made on such an exchange.

(3)   A contract not falling within Note (2) above shall be regarded as made for commercial purposes if under the terms of the contract delivery is to be made within seven days.

(4)   The following are indications that any other contract is made for a commercial purpose and the absence of any of them is an indication that it is made for investment purposes-

(a)   either or each of the parties is a producer of the commodity or other property or uses it in his business;

(b)   the seller delivers or intends to deliver the property or the purchaser takes or intends to take delivery of it.

(5)   It is an indication that a contract is made for commercial purposes that the price, the lot, the delivery date or the other terms are determined by the parties for the purposes of the particular contract and not by reference to regularly published prices, to standard lots or delivery dates or to standard terms.

(6)   The following are also indications that a contract is made for investment purposes-

(a)   it is expressed to be as traded on a market or on an exchange;

(b)   performance of the contract is ensured by an investment exchange or a clearing house;

(c)   there are arrangements for the payment or provision of margin.

(7)   A price shall be taken to have been agreed upon when a contract is made -

(a)   notwithstanding that it is left to be determined by reference to the price at which a contract is to be entered into on a market or exchange or could be entered into at a time and place specified in the contract; or

(b)   in a case where the contract is expressed to be by reference to a standard lot and quality, notwithstanding that provision is made for a variation in the price to take account of any variation in quantity or quality on delivery.

Contracts for differences etc.

9.   Rights under a contract for differences or under any other contract the purpose or pretended purpose of which is to secure a profit or avoid a loss by reference to fluctuations in the value or price of property of any description or in an index or other factor designated for that purpose in the contract.

Notes

(1)   This paragraph does not apply where the parties intended that the profit is to be obtained or the loss avoided by taking delivery of any property to which the contract relates.

(2)   This paragraph does not apply to rights under any contract under which money is received by the Director of Savings as deposits or otherwise in connection with the business of the National Savings Bank or raised under the National Loans Act 1968 under the auspices of the Director of Savings or under which money raised is treated as having been so raised by virtue of section 11(3) of the National Debt Act 1972.

Long term insurance contracts

10.   Rights under a contract the effecting and carrying out of which constitutes long term business within the meaning of the Insurance Companies Act 1982.

Notes

(1)   This paragraph does not apply to rights under a contract of insurance if -

(a)   the benefits under the contract are payable only on death or in respect of incapacity due to injury, sickness or infirmity;

(b)   no benefits are payable under the contract on a death (other than a death due to accident) unless it occurs within ten years of the date on which the life of the person in question was first insured under the contract or before that person attains a specified age not exceeding seventy years;

(c)   the contract has no surrender value or the consideration consists of a single premium and the surrender value does not exceed that premium; and

(d)   the contract does not make provision for its conversion or extension in a manner that would result in its ceasing to comply with paragraphs (a), (b) and (c) above.

(2)   Where the provisions of a contract of insurance are such that the effecting and carrying out of the contract -

(a)   constitutes both long term business within the meaning of the Insurance Companies Act 1982 and general business within the meaning of that Act; or

(b)   by virtue of section 1(3) of that Act constitutes long term business notwithstanding the inclusion of subsidiary general business provisions,

references in this paragraph to rights and benefits under the contract are references only to such rights and benefits as are attributable to the provisions of the contract relating to long term business.

(3)   This paragraph does not apply to rights under a re-insurance contract.

(4)   Rights falling within this paragraph shall not be regarded as falling within paragraph 9 above.

Rights and interests in investments

11.   Rights to and interests in anything which is an investment falling within any other paragraph of this Part of this Schedule.

Notes

(1)   This paragraph does not apply to interests under the trusts of an occupational pension scheme.

(2)   This paragraph does not apply to rights or interests which are investments by virtue of any other paragraph of this Part of this Schedule.

PART II — ACTIVITIES CONSTITUTING INVESTMENT BUSINESS

Dealing in investments

12.   Buying, selling, subscribing for or underwriting investments or offering or agreeing to do so, either as principal or as an agent.

Notes

(1)   This paragraph does not apply to a person by reason of his accepting, or offering or agreeing to accept, whether as principal or as agent, an instrument creating or acknowledging indebtedness in respect of any loan, credit, guarantee or other similar financial accommodation or assurance which he or his principal has made, granted or provided or which he or his principal has offered or agreed to make, grant or provide.

(2)   The references in (1) above to a person accepting, or offering or agreeing to accept, an instrument include references to a person becoming, or offering or agreeing to become, a party to an instrument otherwise than as a debtor or a surety.

Arranging deals in investments

13.   Making, or offering or agreeing to make-

(a)   arrangements with a view to another person buying, selling, subscribing for or underwriting a particular investment; or

(b)   arrangements with a view to a person who participates in the arrangements buying, selling, subscribing for or underwriting investments.

Notes

(1)   This paragraph does not apply to a person by reason of his making, or offering or agreeing to make, arrangements with a view to a transaction to which he will himself be a party as principal or which will be entered into by him as agent for one of the parties.

(2)   The arrangements in (a) above are arrangements which bring about or would bring about the transaction in question.

(3)   This paragraph does not apply to a person ("the relevant person") who is either a money-lending company within the meaning of section 338 of the Companies Act 1985 or a body corporate incorporated under the law of, or of any part of, the United Kingdom relating to building societies or a person whose ordinary business includes the making of loans or the giving of guarantees in connection with loans by reason of the relevant person making, or offering or agreeing to make, arrangements with a view to a person ("the authorised person") who is either authorised under section 22 or 23 of this Act or who is authorised under section 31 of this Act and carries on insurance business which is investment business selling an investment which falls within paragraph 10 above or, so far as relevant to that paragraph, paragraph 11 above if the arrangements are either -

(a)   that the authorised person or a person on his behalf will introduce persons to whom the authorised person has sold or proposes to sell an investment of the kind described above, or will advise such persons to approach, the relevant person with a view to the relevant person lending money on the security of that investment; or

(b)   that the authorised person gives an assurance to the relevant person as to the amount which will or may be received by the relevant person, should that person lend money to a person to whom the authorised person has sold or proposes to sell an investment of the kind described above, on the surrender or maturity of that investment if it is taken as security for the loan.

(4)   This paragraph does not apply to a person by reason of his making, or offering or agreeing to make, arrangements with a view to a person accepting, whether as principal or as agent, an instrument creating or acknowledging indebtedness in respect of any loan, credit, guarantee or other similar financial accommodation or assurance which he or his principal has made, granted or provided or which he or his principal has offered or agreed to make, grant or provide.

(5)   Arrangements do not fall within (b) above by reason of their having as their purpose the provision of finance to enable a person to buy, sell, subscribe for or underwrite investments.

(6)   This paragraph does not apply to arrangements for the introduction of persons to another person if -

(a)   the person to whom the introduction is made is an authorised or exempted person or is a person whose ordinary business involves him in engaging in activities which fall within this Part of this Schedule or would do apart from the provisions of Part III or Part IV and who is not unlawfully carrying on investment business in the United Kingdom; and

(b)   the introduction is made with a view to the provision of independent advice or the independent exercise of discretion either -

(i)   in relation to investments generally; or

(ii)   in relation to any class of investments if the transaction or advice is or is to be with respect to an investment within that class.

(7)   The references in (4) above to a person accepting an instrument include references to a person becoming a party to an instrument otherwise than as a debtor or a surety.

Managing investments

14.   Managing, or offering or agreeing to manage, assets belonging to another person if

(a)   those assets consist of or include investments; or

(b)   the arrangements for their management are such that those assets may consist of or include investments at the discretion of the person managing or offering or agreeing to manage them and either they have at any time since the date of the coming into force of section 3 of this Act done so or the arrangements have at any time (whether before or after that date) been held out as arrangements under which they would do so.

Investment advice

15.   Giving, or offering or agreeing to give, to persons in their capacity as investors or potential investors advice on the merits of their purchasing, selling, subscribing for or underwriting an investment, or exercising any right conferred by an investment to acquire, dispose of, underwrite or convert an investment.

Establishing etc. collective investment schemes

16.   Establishing, operating or winding up a collective investment scheme, including acting as trustee of an authorised unit trust scheme.

PART III — EXCLUDED ACTIVITIES

Dealings as principal

17.(1) Paragraph 12 above applies to a transaction which is or is to be entered into by a person as principal only if -

(a)   he holds himself out as willing to enter into transactions of that kind at prices determined by him generally and continuously rather than in respect of each particular transaction; or

(b)   he holds himself out as engaging in the business of buying investments with a view to selling them and those investments are or include investments of the kind to which the transaction relates; or

(c)   he regularly solicits members of the public for the purpose of inducing them to enter as principals or agents into transactions to which that paragraph applies and the transaction is or is to be entered into as a result of his having solicited members of the public in that manner.

(2)   In sub-paragraph (1) above "buying" and "selling" means buying and selling by transactions to which paragraph 12 above applies and "members of the public", in relation to the person soliciting them ("the relevant person"), means any other persons except -

(a)   authorised persons, exempted persons, or persons holding a permission under paragraph 23 below;

(b)   members of the same group as the relevant person;

(c)   persons who are, or propose to become, participators with the relevant person in a joint enterprise;

(d)   any person who is solicited by the relevant person with a view to -

(i)   the acquisition by the relevant person of 20 per cent. or more of the voting shares in a body corporate (that is to say, shares carrying not less than that percentage of the voting rights attributable to share capital which are exercisable in all circumstances at any general meeting of the body); or

(ii)   if the relevant person (either alone or with other members of the same group as himself) holds 20 per cent. or more of the voting shares in a body corporate, the acquisition by him of further shares in the body or the disposal by him of shares in that body to the person solicited or to a member of the same group as that person; or

(iii)   if the person solicited (either alone or with other members of the same group as himself) holds 20 per cent. or more of the voting shares in a body corporate, the disposal by the relevant person of further shares in that body to the person solicited or to a member of the same group as that person;

(e)   any person whose head office is outside the United Kingdom, who is solicited by an approach made or directed to him at a place outside the United Kingdom and whose ordinary business involves him in engaging in activities which fall within Part II of this Schedule or would do so apart from this Part or Part IV.

(3)   Sub-paragraph (1) above applies only -

(a)   if the investment to which the transaction relates or will relate falls within any of paragraphs 1 to 6 above or, so far as relevant to any of those paragraphs, paragraph 11 above; or

(b)   if the transaction is the assignment (or, in Scotland, the assignation) of an investment falling within paragraph 10 above or is the assignment (or, in Scotland, the assignation) of an investment falling within paragaph 11 above which confers rights to or interests in an investment falling within paragaph 10 above.

(4)   Paragraph 12 above does not apply to any transaction which relates or is to relate to an investment which falls within paragaph 10 above or, so far as relevant to that paragraph, paragraph 11 above nor does it apply to a transaction which relates or is to relate to an investment which falls within any of paragraphs 7 to 9 above or, so far as relevant to any of those paragraphs, paragraph 11 above being a transaction which, in either case, is or is to be entered into by a person as principal if he is not an authorised person and the transaction is or is to be entered into by him -

(a)   with or through an authorised person, an exempted person or a person holding a permission under paragraph 23 below; or

(b)   through an office outside the United Kingdom, maintained by a party to the transaction, and with or through a person whose head office is situated outside the United Kingdom and whose ordinary business is such as is mentioned in sub-paragraph (2)(e) above.

Groups and joint enterprises

18.(1) Paragraph 12 above does not apply to any transaction which is or is to be entered into by a person as principal with another person if -

(a)   they are bodies corporate in the same group; or

(b)   they are, or propose to become, participators in a joint enterprise and the transaction is or is to be entered into for the purposes of, or in connection with, that enterprise.

(2)   Paragraph 12 above does not apply to any transaction which is or is to be entered into by any person as agent for another person in the circumstances mentioned in sub-paragraph (1)(a) or (b) above if -

(a)   where the investment falls within any of paragraphs 1 to 6 above or, so far as relevant to any of those paragraphs, paragraph 11 above, the agent does not -

(i)   hold himself out (otherwise than to other bodies corporate in the same group or persons who are or propose to become participators with him in a joint enterprise) as engaging in the business of buying investments with a view to selling them and those investments are or include investments of the kind to which the transaction relates; or

(ii)   regularly solicit members of the public for the purpose of inducing them to enter as principals or agents into transactions to which paragraph 12 above applies;

and the transaction is not or is not to be entered into as a result of his having solicited members of the public in that manner;

(b)   where the investment is not as mentioned in paragraph (a) above -

(i)   the agent enters into the transaction with or through an authorised person, an exempted person or a person holding a permission under paragraph 23 below; or

(ii)   the transaction is effected through an office outside the United Kingdom, maintained by a party to the transaction, and with or through a person whose head office is situated outside the United Kingdom and whose ordinary business involves him in engaging in activities which fall within Part II of this Schedule or would do so apart from this Part or Part IV.

(3)   Paragraph 13 above does not apply to arrangements which a person makes or offers or agrees to make if -

(a)   that person is a body corporate and the arrangements are with a view to another body corporate in the same group entering into a transaction of the kind mentioned in that paragraph; or

(b)   that person is or proposes to become a participator in a joint enterprise and the arrangements are with a view to another person who is or proposes to become a participator in the enterprise entering into such a transaction for the purposes of or in connection with that enterprise.

(4)   Paragraph 14 above does not apply to a person by reason of his managing or offering or agreeing to manage the investments of another person if -

(a)   they are bodies corporate in the same group; or

(b)   they are, or propose to become, participators in a joint enterprise and the investments are or are to be managed for the purposes of, or in connection with, that enterprise.

(5)   Paragraph 15 above does not apply to advice given by a person to another person if

(a)   they are bodies corporate in the same group; or

(b)   they are, or propose to become, participators in a joint enterprise and the advice is given for the purposes of, or in connection with, that enterprise.

(6)   The definitions in paragraph 17(2) above shall apply also for the purposes of sub-paragraph (2)(a) above except that the relevant person referred to in paragraph 17(2)(d) shall be the person for whom the agent is acting.

Sale of goods and supply of services

19.(1) Subject to sub-paragraph (9) below, this paragraph has effect where a person ("the supplier") sells or offers or agrees to sell goods to another person ("the customer") or supplies or offers or agrees to supply him with services and the supplier's main business is to supply goods or services and not to engage in activities falling within Part II of this Schedule.

(2)   Paragraph 12 above does not apply to any transaction which is or is to be entered into by the supplier as principal if it is or is to be entered into by him with the customer for the purposes of or in connection with the sale or supply or a related sale or supply (that is to say, a sale or supply to the customer otherwise than by the supplier but for or in connection with the same purpose as the first-mentioned sale or supply).

(3)   Paragraph 12 above does not apply to any transaction which is or is to be entered into by the supplier as agent for the customer if it is or is to be entered into for the purposes of or in connection with the sale or supply or a related sale or supply and —

(a)   where the investment falls within any of paragraphs 1 to 5 above or, so far as relevant to any of those paragraphs, paragraph 11 above, the supplier does not -

(i)   hold himself out (otherwise than to the customer) as engaging in the business of buying investments with a view to selling them and those investments are or include investments of the kind to which the transaction relates; or

(ii)   regularly solicit members of the public for the purpose of inducing them to enter as principals or agents into transactions to which paragraph 12 above applies;

and the transaction is not or is not to be entered into as a result of his having solicited members of the public in that manner;

(b)   where the investment is not as mentioned in paragraph (a) above, the supplier enters into the transaction -

(i)   with or through an authorised person, an exempted person or a person holding a permission under paragraph 23 below; or

(ii)   through an office outside the United Kingdom, maintained by a party to the transaction, and with or through a person whose head office is situated outside the United Kingdom and whose ordinary business involves him in engaging in activities which fall within Part II of this Schedule or would do so apart from this Part or Part IV.

(4)   Paragraph 13 above does not apply to arrangements which the supplier makes or offers or agrees to make with a view to the customer entering into a transaction for the purposes of or in connection with the sale or supply or a related sale or supply.

(5)   Paragraph 14 above does not apply to the supplier by reason of his managing or offering or agreeing to manage the investments of the customer if they are or are to be managed for the purposes of or in connection with the sale or supply or a related sale or supply.

(6)   Paragraph 15 above does not apply to advice given by the supplier to the customer for the purposes of or in connection with the sale or supply or a related sale or supply or to a person with whom the customer proposes to enter into a transaction for the purposes of or in connection with the sale or supply or a related sale or supply.

(7)   Where the supplier is a body corporate and a member of a group sub-paragraphs (2) to (6) above shall apply to any other member of the group as they apply to the supplier; and where the customer is a body corporate and a member of a group references in those sub-paragraphs to the customer include references to any other member of the group.

(8)   The definitions in paragraphs 17(2) above shall apply also for the purposes of sub-paragraph (3)(a) above.

(9)   This paragraph does not have effect where either -

(a)   the customer is an individual; or

(b)   the transaction in question is the purchase or sale of an investment which falls within paragraph 6 or 10 above or, so far as relevant to either of those paragraphs, paragraph 11 above; or

(c)   the investments which the supplier manages or offers or agrees to manage consist of investments falling within paragraph 6 or 10 above or, so far as relevant to either of those paragraphs, paragraph 11 above; or

(d)   the advice which the supplier gives is advice on an investment falling within the paragraph 6 or 10 above or, so far as relevant to either of those paragraphs, paragraph 11 above.

Employees' share schemes

20.(1) Paragraphs 12 and 13 above do not apply to anything done by a body corporate, a body corporate connected with it or a relevant trustee for the purpose of enabling or facilitating transactions in shares in or debentures of the first-mentioned body between or for the benefit of any of the persons mentioned in sub-paragraph (2) below or the holding of such shares or debentures by or for the benefit of any such persons.

(2)   The persons referred to in sub-paragraph (1) above are -

(a)   the bona fide employees or former employees of the body corporate or of another body corporate in the same group; or

(b)   the wives, husbands, widows, widowers, or children or step-children under the age of eighteeen of such employees or former employees.

(3)   In this paragraph "a relevant trustee" means a person holding shares in or debentures of a body corporate as trustee in pursuance of arrangements made for the purpose mentioned in sub-paragraph (1) above by, or by a body corporate connected with, that body corporate.

(4)   In this paragraph "shares" and "debentures" include any investment falling within paragraph 1 or 2 above and also include any investment falling within paragraph 4 or 5 above so far as relating to those paragraphs or any investment falling within paragraph 11 above so far as relating to paragraph 1, 2, 4 or 5.

(5)   For the purposes of this paragraph a body corporate is connected with another body corporate if -

(a)   they are in the same group; or

(b)   one is entitled, either alone or with any other body corporate in the same group, to exercise or control the exercise of a majority of the voting rights attributable to the share capital which are exercisable in all circumstances at any general meeting of the other body corporate or of its holding company.

Sale of body corporate

21.(1) Paragraphs 12 and 13 above do not apply to the acquisition or disposal of, or to anything done for the purposes of the acquisition or disposal of, shares in a body corporate other than an open-ended investment company, and paragraph 15 above does not apply to advice given in connection with the acquisition or disposal of such shares, if

(a)   the shares consist of or include shares carrying 75 per cent. or more of the voting rights attributable to share capital which are exercisable in all circumstances at any general meeting of the body corporate; or

(b)   the shares, together with any already held by the person acquiring them, carry not less than that percentage of those voting rights; and

(c)   in either case, the acquisition and disposal is, or is to be, between parties each of whom is a body corporate, a partnership, a single individual or a group of connected individuals.

(2)   For the purposes of subsection (1)(c) above "a group of connected individuals", in relation to the party disposing of the shares, means persons each of whom is, or is a close relative of, a director or manager of the body corporate and, in relation to the party acquiring the shares, means persons each of whom is, or is a close relative of, a person who is to be a director or manager of the body corporate.

(3)   In this paragraph "close relative" means a person's spouse, his children and step-children, his parents and step-parents, his brothers and sisters and his step-brothers and step-sisters.

Trustees and personal representatives

22.(1) Paragraph 12 above does not apply to a person by reason of his buying, selling or subscribing for an investment or offering or agreeing to do so if -

(a)   the investment is or, as the case may be, is to be held by him as bare trustee or, in Scotland, as nominee for another person;

(b)   he is acting on that person's instructions; and

(c)   he does not hold himself out as providing a service of buying and selling investments.

(2)   Paragraph 13 above does not apply to anything done by a person as trustee or personal representative with a view to -

(a)   a fellow trustee or personal representative and himself engaging in their capacity as such in an activity falling within paragraph 12 above; or

(b)   a beneficiary under the trust, will or intestacy engaging in any such activity,

unless that person is remunerated for what he does in addition to any remuneration he receives for discharging his duties as trustee or personal representative.

(3)   Paragraph 14 above does not apply to anything done by a person as trustee or personal representative unless he holds himself out as offering investment management services or is remunerated for providing such services in addition to any remuneration he receives for discharging his duties as trustee or personal representative.

(4)   Paragraph 15 above does not apply to advice given by a person as trustee or personal representative to -

(a)   a fellow trustee or personal representative for the purposes of the trust or estate; or

(b)   a beneficiary under the trust, will or intestacy concerning his interest in the trust fund or estate, unless that person is remunerated for doing so in addition to any remuneration he receives for discharging his duties as trustee or personal representative.

(5)   Sub-paragraph (1) above has effect to the exclusion of paragraph 17 above as respects any transaction in respect of which the conditions in sub-paragraph (1)(a) and (b) are satisfied.

Dealings in course of non-investment business

23.(1) Paragraph 12 above does not apply to anything done by a person -

(a)   as principal;

(b)   if that person is a body corporate in a group, as agent for another member of the group; or

(c)   as agent for a person who is or proposes to become a participator with him in a joint enterprise and for the purposes of or in connection with that enterprise,

if it is done in accordance with the terms and conditions of a permission granted to him by the Secretary of State under this paragraph.

(2)   Any application for permission under this paragraph shall be accompanied or supported by such information as the Secretary of State may require and shall not be regarded as duly made unless accompanied by the prescribed fee.

(3)   The Secretary of State may grant a permission under this paragraph if it appears to him -

(a)   that the applicant's main business, or if he is a member of a group the main business of the group, does not consist of activities for which a person is required to be authorised under this Act;

(b)   that the applicant's business is likely to involve such activities which fall within paragraph 12 above; and

(c)   that, having regard to the nature of the applicant's main business and, if he is a member of a group, the main business of the group taken as a whole, the manner in which, the persons with whom and the purposes for which the applicant proposes to engage in activities that would require him to be an authorised person and to any other relevant matters, it is inappropriate to require him to be subject to regulation as an authorised person.

(4)   Any permission under this paragraph shall be granted by a notice in writing; and the Secretary of State may by a further notice in writing withdraw any such permission if for any reason it appears to him that it is not appropriate for it to continue in force.

(5)   The Secretary of State may make regulations requiring persons holding permissions under the paragraph to furnish him with information for the purpose of enabling him to determine whether those permissions should continue in force; and such regulations may, in particular, require such persons -

(a)   to give him notice forthwith of the occurrence of such events as are specified in the regulations and such information in respect of those events as is so specified;

(b)   to furnish him at such times or in respect of such periods as are specified in the regulations with such information as is so specified.

(6)   Section 61 of this Act shall have effect in relation to a contravention of any condition imposed by a permission under this paragraph as it has effect in relation to any such contravention as is mentioned in subsection (1)(a) of that section.

(7)   Section 104 of this Act shall apply to a person holding a permission under this paragraph as if he were authorised to carry on investment business as there mentioned; and sections 105 and 106 of this Act shall have effect as if anything done by him in accordance with such permission constituted the carrying on of investment business.

Advice given or arrangements made in course of profession or non-investment business

24.(1) Paragraph 15 above does not apply to advice -

(a)   which is given in the course of the carrying on of any profession or of a business not otherwise constituting investment business; and

(b)   the giving of which is a necessary part of other advice or services given in the course of carrying on that profession or business.

(2)   Paragraph 13 above does not apply to arrangements -

(a)   which are made in the course of the carrying on of any profession or of a business not otherwise constituting investment business; and

(b)   the making of which is a necessary part of other services provided in the course of carrying on that profession or business.

(3)   Advice shall not be regarded as falling within sub-paragraph (1)(b) above and the making of arrangements shall not be regarded as falling within sub-paragraph (2)(b) above if the giving of the advice or the making of the arrangements is remunerated separately from the other advice or services.

Newspapers

25.(1) Paragraph 15 above does not apply to advice given in a newspaper, journal, magazine or other periodical publication if the principal purpose of the publication, taken as a whole and including any advertisements contained in it, is not to lead persons to invest in any particular investment.

(2)   The Secretary of State may, on the application of the proprietor of any periodical publication, certify that it is of the nature described in sub-paragraph (1) above and revoke any such certificate if he considers that it is no longer justified.

(3)   A certificate given under sub-paragraph (2) above and not revoked shall be conclusive evidence of the matters certified.

Advice given in television, sound or teletext services

25A.(1) Paragraph 15 above does not apply to any advice given in any programme included, or made for inclusion, in -

   (a)   any television broadcasting service or other television programme service (within the meaning of Part I of the Broadcasting Act 1990); or

   (b)   any sound broadcasting service or licensable sound programme service (within the meaning of Part III of the Act); or

   (c)   any teletext service.

(2)   For the purposes of this paragraph, "programme", in relation to a service mentioned in sub-paragraph (1) above, includes an advertisement and any other item included in the service.

International securities self-regulating organisations

25B.(1) An activity within paragraph 13 above engaged in for the purposes of carrying out the functions of a body or association which is approved under this paragraph as an international securities self-regulating organisation, whether by the organisation or by any person acting on its behalf, shall not constitute the carrying on of investment business in the United Kingdom for the purposes of Chapter II of Part I of this Act.

(2)   In this paragraph -

"international securities business" means the business of buying, selling, subscribing for or underwriting investments (or offering or agreeing to do so, either as principal or agent) which fall within any of the paragraphs in Part I above other than paragraph 10 and, so far as relevant to paragraph 10, paragraph 11 and which, by their nature, and the manner in which the business is conducted, may be expected normally to be bought or dealt in by persons sufficiently expert to understand any risks involved, where either the transaction is international or each of the parties may be expected to be indifferent to the location of the other, and, for the purposes of this definition, the fact that the investments may ultimately be bought otherwise than in the course of international securities business by persons not so expert shall be disregarded; and

"international securities self-regulating organisation" means a body corporate or unincorporated association which

   (a)   does not have its head office in the United Kingdom;

   (b)   is not eligible for recognition under section 37 or section 39 of this Act on the ground that (whether or not it has applied, and whether or not it would be eligible on other grounds) it is unable to satisfy the requirements of section 40(2)(a) or (c) of this Act;

(c)   has a membership composed of persons falling within any of the following categories, that is to say, authorised persons, exempted persons, persons holding a permission under paragraph 23 above and persons whose head offices are outside the United Kingdom and whose ordinary business is such as is mentioned in paragraph 17(2)(e) above; and

(d)   which facilitates and regulates the activity of its members in the conduct of international securities business.

(3)   The Secretary of State may approve as an international securities self-regulating organisation any body or association appearing to him to fall within sub-paragraph (2) above if, having regard to such matters affecting international trade, overseas earnings and the balance of payments or otherwise as he considers relevant, it appears to him that to do so would be desirable and not result in any undue risk to investors.

(4)   Any approval under this paragraph shall be given by notice in writing; and the Secretary of State may by a further notice in writing withdraw any such approval if for any reason it appears to him that it is not appropriate for it to continue in force.

PART IV — ADDITIONAL EXCLUSIONS FOR PERSONS WITHOUT PERMANENT PLACE OF BUSINESS IN UNITED KINGDOM

Transactions with or through authorised or exempted persons

26.(1) Paragraph 12 above does not apply to any transaction by a person not falling within section 1(3)(a) of this Act ("an overseas person") with or through -

(a)   an authorised person; or

(b)   an exempted person acting in the course of business in respect of which he is exempt.

(2)   Paragraph 13 above does not apply if -

(a)   the arrangements are made by an overseas person with, or the offer or agreement to make them is made by him to or with, an authorised person or an exempted person and, in the case of an exempted person, the arrangements are with a view to his entering into a transaction in respect of which he is exempt; or

(b)   the transactions with a view to which the arangements are made are, as respects transactions in the United Kingdom, confined to transactions by authorised persons and transactions by exempted persons in respect of which they are exempt.

Unsolicited or legitimately solicited transactions etc. with or for other persons

27.(1) Paragraph 12 above does not apply to any transaction entered into by an overseas person as principal with, or as agent for, a person in the United Kingdom, paragraphs 13, 14 and 15 above do not apply to any offer made by an overseas person to or agreement made by him with a person in the United Kingdom and paragraph 15 above does not apply to any advice given by an overseas person to a person in the United Kingdom if the transaction, offer, agreement or advice is the result of -

(a)   an approach made to the overseas person by or on behalf of the person in the United Kingdom which either has not been in any way solicited by the overseas person or has been solicited by him in a way which has not contravened section 56 or 57 of this Act; or

(b)   an approach made by the overseas person which has not contravened either of those sections.

(2)   Where the transaction is entered into by the overseas person as agent for a person in the United Kingdom, sub-paragraph (1) above applies only if -

(a)   the other party is outside the United Kingdom; or

(b)   the other party is in the United Kingdom and the transaction is the result of such an approach by the other party as is mentioned in sub-paragraph (1)(a) above or of such an approach as is mentioned in sub-paragraph (1)(b) above.

PART V — INTERPRETATION

28.(1) In this Schedule -

(a)   "property" includes currency of the United Kingdom or any other country or territory;

(b)   references to an instrument include references to any record whether or not in the form of a document;

(c)   references to an offer include references to an invitation to treat;

(d)   references to buying and selling include references to any acquisition or disposal for valuable consideration.

(2)   In sub-paragraph (1)(d) above "disposal" includes -

(a)   in the case of an investment consisting of rights under a contract or other arrangements, assuming the corresponding liabilities under the contract or arrangements;

(b)   in the case of any other investment, issuing or creating the investment or granting the rights or interests of which it consists;

(c)   in the case of an investment consisting of rights under a contract, surrendering, assigning or converting those rights.

(3)   A company shall not by reason of issuing its own shares or share warrants, and a person shall not by reason of issuing his own debentures or debenture warrants, be regarded for the purposes of this Schedule as disposing of them or, by reason of anything done for the purpose of issuing them, be regarded as making arrangements with a view to a person subscribing for or otherwise acquiring them or underwriting them.

(4)   In sub-paragraph (3) above "company" has the same meaning as in paragraph 1 above, "shares" and "debentures" include any investments falling within paragraph 1 or 2 above and "share warrants" and "debenture warrants" means any investment which falls within paragraph 4 above and relates to shares in the company concerned or, as the case may be, to debentures issued by the person concerned.

29.   For the purposes of this Schedule a transaction is entered into through a person if he enters into it as agent or arranges for it to be entered into by another person as principal or agent.

30.(1) For the purposes of this Schedule a group shall be treated as including any body corporate in which a member of the group holds a qualifying capital interest.

(2) A qualifying capital interest means an interest in relevant shares of the body corporate which the member holds on a long-term basis for the purpose of securing a contribution to its own activities by the exercise of control or influence arising from that interest.

(3) Relevant shares means shares comprised in the equity share capital of the body corporate of a class carrying rights to vote in all circumstances at general meetings of the body.

(4) A holding of 20 per cent. or more of the nominal value of the relevant shares of a body corporate shall be presumed to be a qualifying capital interest unless the contrary is shown.

(5) In this paragraph "equity share capital" has the same meaning as in the Companies Act 1985 and the Companies (Northern Ireland) Order 1986.

31. In this Schedule "a joint enterprise" means an enterprise into which two or more persons ("the participators") enter for commercial reasons related to a business or businesses (other than investment business) carried on by them; and where a participator is a body corporate and a member of a group each other member of the group shall also be regarded as a participator in the enterprise.

32. Where a person is an exempted person as respects only part of the investment business carried on by him anything done by him in carrying on that part shall be disregarded in determining whether any paragraph of Part III or IV of this Schedule applies to anything done by him in the course of business in respect of which he is not exempt.

33. In determining for the purposes of this Schedule whether anything constitutes an investment or the carrying on of investment business section 18 of the Gaming Act 1845, section 1 of the Gaming Act 1892, any corresponding provision in force in Northern Ireland and any rule of the law of Scotland whereby a contract by way of gaming or wagering is not legally enforceable shall be disregarded.

34.(1) For the purpose of this Schedule arrangements are not a collective investment scheme if -

(a) the property to which the arrangements relate (other than cash awaiting investment) consists of shares;

(b) they constitute a complying fund;

(c) each participant is the owner of a part of the property to which the arrangements relate and, to the extent that his part of that property -

(i) comprises relevant shares of a class which are admitted to the Official List of any member State or to dealings on a recognised investment exchange, he is entitled to withdraw it at any time after the end of the period of five years beginning with the date on which the shares in question were issued;

(ii) comprises relevant shares which do not fall within sub-paragraph (i) above, he is entitled to withdraw it at any time after the end of the period of two years beginning with the date upon which the period referred to in sub-paragraph (i) above expired;

(iii) comprises any other shares, he is entitled to withdraw it at any time after the end of the period of six months beginning with the date upon which the shares in question ceased to be relevant shares; and

(iv)   comprises cash which the operator has not agreed (conditionally or unconditionally) to apply in subscribing for shares, he is entitled to withdraw it at any time; and

(d)   the arrangements would meet the conditions described in section 75(5)(c) of this Act were it not for the fact that the operator is entitled to exercise all or any of the rights conferred by shares included in the property to which the arrangements relate.

(2)   For the purposes of this paragraph -

(a)   "shares" means investments falling within paragraph 1 of this Schedule;

(b)   shares shall be regarded as being relevant shares if and so long as they are shares in respect of which neither-

(i)   a claim for relief made in accordance with section 306 of the Income and Corporation Taxes Act 1988 has been disallowed; nor

(ii)   an assessment has been made pursuant to section 307 of that Act withdrawing or refusing relief by reason of the body corporate in which the shares are held having ceased to be a body corporate which is a qualifying company for the purposes of section 293 of that Act; and

(c)   arrangements shall be regarded as constituting a complying fund if they provide that -

(i)   the operator will, so far as practicable, make investments each of which, subject to each participant's individual circumstances, qualify for relief by virtue of Chapter III of Part VII of the Income and Corporation Taxes Act 1988; and

(ii)   the minimum subscription to the arrangements made by each participant must be not less than £2,000.

35.   For the purposes of this Schedule the following are not collective investment schemes -

(a)   arrangements where the entire contribution of each participant is a deposit within the meaning of section 5 of the Banking Act 1987 or a sum of a kind described in subsection (3) of that section;

(b)   arrangements under which the rights or interests of the participants are represented by the following -

(i)   investments falling within paragraph 2 of this Schedule which are issued by a single body corporate which is not an open-ended investment company or which are issued by a single issuer which is not a body corporate and are guaranteed by the government of the United Kingdom, of Northern Ireland, or of any country or territory outside the United Kingdom; or

(ii)   investments falling within sub-paragraph (i) above which are convertible into or exchangeable for investments falling within paragraph 1 of this Schedule provided that those latter investments are issued by the same person as issued the investments falling within sub-paragraph (i) above or are issued by a single other issuer; or

(iii)   investments falling within paragraph 3 of this Schedule issued by the same government, local authority or public authority; or

(iv)   investments falling within paragraph 4 of this Schedule which are issued otherwise than by an open-ended investment company and which confer rights in respect of investments, issued by the same issuer, falling within paragraph 1 of this Schedule or within sub-paragraph (i), (ii) or (iii) above;

(c)   arrangements which would fall within paragraph (b) above were it not for the fact that the rights or interests of a participant ("the counterparty") whose ordinary business involves him in engaging in activities which fall within Part II of this Schedule or would do so apart from Part III or IV are or include rights or interests under a swap arrangement, that is to say, an arrangement the purpose of which is to facilitate the making of payments to participants whether in a particular amount or currency or at a particular time or rate of interest or all or any combination of those things, being an arrangement under which -

(i)   the counterparty is entitled to receive amounts (whether representing principal or interest) payable in respect of any property subject to the scheme or sums determined by reference to such amounts; and

(ii)   the counterparty makes payments (whether or not of the same amount and whether or not in the same currency as those referred to in sub-paragraph (i) above) which are calculated in accordance with an agreed formula by reference to the amounts or sums referred to in sub-paragraph (i) above;

(d)   arrangements under which the rights or interests of participants are rights to or interests in money held in a common account in circumstances in which the money so held is held on the understanding that an amount representing the contribution of each participant is to be applied either in making payments to him or in satisfaction of sums owed by him or in the acquisition of property or the provision of services for him;

(e)   arrangements under which the rights and interests of participants are rights and interests in a fund which is a trust fund within the meaning of section 42(1) of the Landlord and Tenant Act 1987;

(f)   arrangements where -

(i)   each of the participants is a bona fide employee or former employee (or the wife, husband, widow, widower, or child (including, in Northern Ireland, adopted child) or step-child under the age of eighteen of such an employee or former employee) of any of the following bodies corporate, that is to say, The National Grid Company plc, Electricity Association Services Limited or any other body corporate in the same group as either of them being arrangements which are operated by any of those bodies corporate; and

(ii)   the property to which the arrangements relate consists of shares or debentures (as defined in paragraph 20(4) above) in or of a body corporate which is an electricity successor company for the purposes of Part II of the Electricity Act 1989 or a body corporate which would be regarded as connected with such an electricity successor company for the purposes of paragraph 20 above,

and for the purposes of this paragraph references to former employees shall have the same meaning as in the Financial Services Act 1986 (Electricity Industry Exemptions) Order 1990.

Annex 26B

Solicitors' Investment Business Rules 1990

(with consolidated amendments to 1st April 1992)

Rules dated 6th February 1990 made by the Council of the Law Society with the concurrence of the Master of the Rolls under sections 31 and 32 of the Solicitors Act 1974, schedule 15 paragraph 6 of the Financial Services Act 1986 and section 9 of the Administration of Justice Act 1985 regulating the English and Welsh practices of those firms of solicitors, multi-national partnerships and recognised bodies authorised by the Law Society in the conduct of investment business, and regulating the overseas practices of such persons in the conduct of investment business in or into any part of the United Kingdom.

Chapter 1 —Citation, interpretation and application

1. CITATION AND COMMENCEMENT

These Rules may be cited as the Solicitors' Investment Business Rules 1990 and shall come into operation on 15th March 1990, whereupon the Solicitors' Investment Business Rules 1988 shall cease to have effect.

2. INTERPRETATION

(1) In these Rules unless the context otherwise requires:

'the Act' means the Financial Services Act 1986 as amended from time to time;

'advisory client' means a client who is not an execution-only client;

'advisory portfolio' means such a fund as is referred to in the definition of 'portfolio adviser';

'approved fund' means a Business Expansion Scheme fund approved by the Board of Inland Revenue for the purposes of section 311 of the Income and Corporation Taxes Act 1988;

'authorised insolvency practitioner' means an individual who is qualified to act as an insolvency practitioner pursuant to the Insolvency Act 1986;

'BES advisory portfolio' means an advisory portfolio which is to be invested wholly or mainly in BES shares;

'BES fund' means an arrangement which would be a collective investment scheme but for the fact that it is regarded as constituting a complying fund for the purposes of section 75(5A) of the Act;

'BES scheme' means a BES advisory portfolio or a BES fund;

'BES share' means a share in a company in relation to which the beneficial owner may qualify for relief by virtue of Chapter III of Part VII of the Income and Corporation Taxes Act 1988;

'broker funds arrangement' means an arrangement whereby a life office issues policies or an authorised unit trust manager issues units to the clients of a firm and the firm is authorised to determine any matters affecting the performance of the fund or funds of the life office to which the policies are linked or the composition of the property of the unit trust scheme, as the case may be;

'defined benefits pension scheme' means a pension policy or a personal pension contract under which the only money purchase benefits are benefits ancillary to other benefits which are not money purchase benefits;

'designated investment exchange' means an exchange for the time being designated as such by the Financial Services (Conduct of Business) Rules 1987;

'discrete investment business' has the meaning set out in sub-rule (2);

'discretionary managed portfolio' means such a fund as is referred to in the definition of 'discretionary portfolio manager';

'discretionary portfolio manager' means a firm which has general authority over an advisory portfolio to effect transactions at its discretion but, in the case of any such authority arising by reason of the firm or a partner or employee of the firm being:

(i)   a personal representative of any deceased's estate, such authority is excluded; and

(ii)   a trustee of any trust or a donee of any enduring power of attorney or trustee power of attorney or a receiver appointed by the Court of Protection, such authority is excluded except for the purpose of the definition of discrete investment business;

'employee' means an individual who is employed in connection with the firm's investment business under a contract of service or under a contract for services such that he is held out as an employee or consultant of the firm;

'enduring power of attorney' means a power of attorney which is registered by the Court under section 6 of the Enduring Powers of Attorney Act 1985;

'execution-only client', in relation to the effecting of a transaction by a firm, means a person for whom that transaction is effected in circumstances in which the firm can reasonably assume that he is not relying upon the firm to advise him on or to exercise any judgment on his behalf as to the merits of or the suitability for him of that transaction;

'firm' means such a solicitor, partnership of solicitors and/or recognised bodies, multi-national partnership or recognised body as is referred to in Rule 3(2)(a) of these Rules;

'independent approval', in relation to a decision or recommendation as to the investment of subscriptions to a BES scheme, means approval of that decision or recommendation given:

(a)   by a person:

(i)   who does not have a material interest in that decision or recommendation, and

(ii)   who is fully aware of all material interests of all persons concerned in the making of that decision or recommendation, and

(iii)   has appropriate professional experience of the subject matter of the decision or recommendation, and

(b)   in the course of a business carried on by that person which relates to the subject matter of the decision or recommendation in question;

'investment service' means any activity referred to in the definition of 'discrete investment business' carried out for a client;

'life office' means a person who carries on long term business within the meaning of section 1 of the Insurance Companies Act 1982;

'life policy' means an investment within paragraph 10 of Schedule 1 to the Act (long term insurance contracts);

'margined transaction' means a transaction effected by a firm for a client relating to an investment within paragraphs 7, 8 and 9 of Schedule 1 to the Act (options, futures or contracts for differences) under the terms of which the client will or may be liable to make deposits in cash or collateral to secure payment of what will or may be due to be paid by him when the transaction falls to be completed or upon the earlier closing out of his position;

'material interest', in relation to a decision or recommendation as to the investment of subscriptions to a BES scheme and any person, means any direct or indirect pecuniary interest, whether present or expected, of that person or of his associate which might reasonably be expected to influence that person's judgment in making that decision or recommendation;

'multi-national partnership' means a partnership whose members consist of one or more registered foreign lawyers and one or more solicitors;

'officer' means a director or secretary of a recognised body;

'Overseas Investments' means investments issued by a person incorporated or established outside the United Kingdom which, in respect of the particular transaction, are not traded on a recognised investment exchange in the United Kingdom;

'Overseas Professional' means a person:

(a)   whose ordinary business is carried on from a permanent place of business outside the United Kingdom and involves him in engaging in activities which fall within Part II of Schedule 1 to the Act (dealing in investments, arranging deals in investments, managing investments, giving investment advice and/or establishing, operating or winding-up collective investment schemes) or would do so apart from Parts III or IV of such Schedule; and

(b)   who the firm reasonably believes is suitable for performing the investment transaction in question;

'pension fund management policy' means a life policy the effecting or carrying out of which constitutes life insurance business by reason only that it is business falling within class VII of Schedule 1 to the Insurance Companies Act 1982;

'Permitted Third Party' means:

(a)   a person authorised under the Act; or

(b)   an exempted person who, in engaging in the activity in question, is acting in the course of a business in respect of which he is exempt; or

(c)   in relation to Overseas Investments, an Overseas Professional,

but in relation to Specified Investments (other than in relation to Rule 12) does not include the life office or operator of the regulated collective investment scheme in question, or an appointed representative of either;

'PEP' means a personal equity plan within the Personal Equity Plan Regulations 1989;

'portfolio adviser' means a firm which undertakes to keep under review the particular investments into which a fund belonging to a client should for the time being be invested and what those investments should be, excluding any undertaking arising by reason of the firm or a partner, employee or officer of the firm being a personal representative of any deceased's estate or (except for the purpose of the definition of discretionary portfolio manager) a trustee of any trust or a donee of any enduring power of attorney or trustee power of attorney or a receiver appointed by the Court of Protection;

'private offer', in relation to shares in a company, means an offer or invitation in relation to those shares which falls not to be treated as made to the public by virtue of section 60 of the Companies Act 1985;

'prospectus' is to be construed in accordance with sub-rule (5)(vi);

'recognised body' means a body corporate for the time being recognised by the Council under the Solicitors' Incorporated Practice Rules 1988 as being a suitable body to undertake the provision of professional services such as are provided by individuals practising as solicitors or by multi-national partnerships;

'registered foreign lawyer' means a person whose name is on the register of foreign lawyers;

'the register of foreign lawyers' means the register maintained by the Society under section 89 of the Courts and Legal Services Act 1990;

'regulated collective investment scheme' means an authorised unit trust scheme or an overseas collective investment scheme recognised under sections 86, 87 or 88 of the Act;

'scheme particulars' is to be construed in accordance with sub-rule (5)(iv);

'sophisticated investor' means a client whose knowledge and experience is such that he can reasonably be expected to understand the risks involved in a particular transaction (including, in particular, risks as to marketability);

'Specified Investments' means type C PEPs or investments which are life policies or units in a regulated collective investment scheme;

'statement of prescribed information', in relation to an advertisement of BES shares, means all such information as a person such as the person or persons to whom the advertisement is addressed and their professional advisers would reasonably require and reasonably expect to find in the advertisement for the purpose of making an informed assessment of the assets and liabilities, financial position, profits and losses and prospects of the company whose shares they are or will be and the rights attaching to those shares;

'trailer advertisement' has the meaning set out in sub-rule (4);

'transaction' means the purchase, sale, subscription or underwriting of an investment;

'trustee power of attorney' means a power of attorney entered into pursuant to section 25 of the Trustee Act 1925;

a 'type A PEP' means a PEP which provides that investment will be made only in sterling deposits or units of authorised unit trust schemes;

a 'type B PEP' means a PEP which provides that investment will be made only in:

(a)   sterling deposits,

(b)   investments listed on The Stock Exchange which:

    (i)   are constituents of the FT-A All Share Index, or

    (ii)   were, on 13th January 1991, classified by The Stock Exchange as alpha or beta stocks,

(c)   units of authorised unit trust schemes, or

(d)   specified categories of such investments or units;

a 'type C PEP' means a PEP, which may also be a type A PEP or a type B PEP, under the terms of which some or all of the cash subscriptions of the plan investor which are not invested in sterling deposits will in any event be invested in the units of regulated collective investment schemes or which is marketed in such a way as necessarily to create an expectation that that will be so;

'these Rules' means The Solicitors' Investment Business Rules 1990 as amended from time to time.

(2)   'Discrete investment business' means the business of engaging in one or more of the following activities so far as they fall within Part II of Schedule 1 to the Act and are not excluded by Part III thereof:

(1)   Dealing

Buying, selling, subscribing for or underwriting investments or offering or agreeing to do so either as principal or as an agent except where:

(a)   the firm acts as disclosed agent for a named client and the transaction is carried out with or through a Permitted Third Party; or

(b)   the activity is incidental; or

(c)   the dealing occurs pursuant to an activity of management which is within one of the exceptions contained in (3)(a) or (b) or (5)(b) below;

(2) Arranging

Making arrangements for a client to buy, sell, subscribe for or underwrite one or more particular investments being arrangements which bring about the transaction in question except where:

(a)   the firm acts as disclosed agent for a named client and the arrangements are carried out with or through a Permitted Third Party;

(b)   in the case of Specified Investments,

(i)   the arrangements are made in consequence of advice given in relation thereto by a Permitted Third Party which, if obtained by the firm, has been obtained by it acting as disclosed agent for a named client; or

(ii)   the client is an execution-only client; or

(c)   in the case of,

(i)   investments other than Specified Investments; or

(ii)   the disposal of Specified Investments by or for a personal representative

the activity is incidental;

(d)   the arranging occurs pursuant to an activity of management which is within one of the exceptions contained in (3)(a) or (b) or (5)(b) below;

(e)   the transaction involves the acquisition or disposal of an investment by accepting an offer or responding to an invitation made to the public or to the holders of securities of any body corporate or any class thereof or by exercising any right conferred by an investment to acquire, dispose of or convert an investment;

(3) Discretionary management

Acting or offering or agreeing to act as a discretionary portfolio manager except where:

(a)   in the case where the firm or a partner, employee or officer of the firm is a trustee or donee of a power of attorney or receiver appointed by the Court of Protection:

(i)   neither he nor the firm receives remuneration for acting as discretionary portfolio manager in addition to the remuneration which he or the firm may receive in connection with his or its acting as trustee or attorney or receiver as the case may be;

(ii)   the activity is incidental;

(iii)   any decisions to buy, sell, subscribe for or underwrite a particular investment for the trust or the donor of the power of attorney or estate are taken substantially in accordance with the advice of a Permitted Third Party which, if obtained by such partner, employee, officer or firm, has been obtained by him or it having disclosed the basis on which he or it is acting; or

(iv)   all day to day decisions in the carrying on of that activity so far as relating to assets of the trust or donor of the power of attorney or estate which are investments are or are to be taken by a Permitted Third Party pursuant to a customer agreement; or

(b)   in any other case all decisions in the carrying on of that activity so far as relating to assets which are investments are or are to be taken on behalf of the person concerned pursuant to a customer agreement between that person and the Permitted Third Party;

(4) Advising

Recommending the entry into of a transaction in a particular investment or the exercise of a right conferred by such an investment to acquire, dispose of, underwrite or convert such an investment except where:

(a)   such recommendation is in substance the advice of a Permitted Third Party and, if obtained by the firm, has been obtained by it acting as disclosed agent for a named client; or

(b)   in the case of

    (i)   investments other than Specified Investments; or

    (ii)   the disposal of Specified Investments by or for a personal representative

the activity is incidental;

(5)   Establishing etc. collective investment schemes

(a)   Establishing, operating or winding-up a collective investment scheme which is marketed pursuant to regulations made under section 76(3) of the Act, including acting as a trustee of any such scheme; or

(b)   establishing, operating or winding-up any collective investment scheme, other than one referred to in sub-paragraph (a) above or a regulated collective investment scheme, except where such activity is incidental.

(3)   For the purposes of sub-rule (2) and Rule 3(1):

(a)   no activity carried out by the firm or a partner, employee or officer of the firm as a personal representative of any deceased's estate shall be discrete investment business;

(b)   a transaction is entered into through a person if that person enters into it as agent or arranges for it to be entered into as principal or agent by another person and the arrangements are such that they bring about the transaction in question;

(c)   an activity is incidental if it is carried out in the course of providing other services provided by the firm in the course of carrying on the profession of a solicitor (being services which do not themselves constitute discrete investment business) and is subordinate to the main purpose for which those services are provided; and

(d)   in the case of any reference to the firm acting as disclosed agent for a named client where the Permitted Third Party is:

    (i)   a member of IMRO, the member must have agreed with or confirmed to the firm that the client is or will be treated by the member as its customer, or

    (ii)   a member of the Securities and Futures Authority, the member must have agreed with or confirmed to the firm that the client is or will be treated by the member as its customer for the purposes of all the conduct of business rules of the Securities and Futures Authority.

(4)   'trailer advertisement' means an advertisement of a BES scheme or of BES shares which:

(a)   sets out with particular prominence the following statements:

(i)   a statement to the effect that investment in unquoted companies carries higher risks than investment in quoted companies, and

(ii)   a statement that the advertiser or the firm which has approved the advertisement, as the case may be, is regulated in the conduct of its investment business by the Society, or authorised by the Society to conduct investment business, and

(iii)   a statement that expert advice should be sought by an investor before investing in BES schemes or shares, and

(iv)   a statement that applications to subscribe will be accepted only on the terms and conditions set out in the scheme particulars, the prospectus or the statement of prescribed information, as the case may be, and

(b)   contains only such of the following matters as are consistent with the advertisement's not being a prospectus within the meaning of section 744 of the Companies Act 1985:

(i)   a symbol or logogram representing the advertiser;

(ii)   the name and business address of:

(A)   the firm issuing or approving the advertisement, and

(B)   in the case of a BES scheme, the scheme manager;

(iii)   the name of the BES scheme or of the company whose shares are advertised and, in the case of a BES scheme which is an approved fund, that fact;

(iv)   in the case of a BES scheme, the investment objectives of the scheme and the nature of the businesses of the companies in which the assets of the scheme will or may be invested;

(v)   in the case of BES shares, the nature of the company's business;

(vi)   if the advertisement is of BES shares, the fact that those shares may qualify as BES shares and, if the advertisement is of a BES scheme, the fact that the purpose of the scheme is investment in BES shares;

(vii)   an indication of where and how a copy of the scheme particulars, the prospectus or the statement of prescribed information, as the case may be, may be obtained;

(viii)   if a minimum aggregate subscription is sought by means of the advertisement, that minimum amount;

(ix)   if there is a minimum amount to the subscriptions of any one person, that minimum amount;

(x)   the dates when subscriptions open and close and any extension of a previously published closing date:

and also falls to be construed in accordance with sub-rule 5(v).

(5)   In these Rules references to:

(i)   effecting a transaction for a client include references to the firm making arrangements for the client to effect the transaction where the arrangements bring about the transaction in question;

(ii)   rules or regulations other than these Rules include any modification or amendment thereof;

(iii)   a firm 'carrying on the profession of a solicitor' shall include references to:

(a)   a recognised body providing professional services such as are provided by individuals practising as solicitors or by multi-national partnerships; and

(b)   a multi-national partnership providing professional services as such;

(iv)   scheme particulars are references to a document containing all the matters, so far as applicable, set out in Part IV of Appendix 5, but in the application of any Rule containing references to scheme particulars to a firm which is not the scheme manager or an associate of the scheme manager, those references are to a document which that firm has reason to believe contains all those matters;

(v)   a trailer advertisement include references to an advertisement of the services provided by a firm generally which contains no matter other than any of the following:

(a)   the name, business address and telephone number of the advertiser, and

(b)   a statement that the business of the advertiser includes advising on and arranging investments in BES shares or BES schemes, and

(c)   a symbol or logogram representing the advertiser, and

(d)   a statement that the advertiser is regulated in the conduct of its investment business by the Society, or authorised by the Society to conduct investment business;

(vi)   a prospectus are, unless the context otherwise requires, references to a prospectus in relation to which the requirements of the Act and of the Companies Act 1985 which apply to prospectuses have been complied with but, in the application of any Rule containing references to a prospectus to a firm which has no interest (whether direct or indirect) in the company the subject of the prospectus, those references are to a prospectus in relation to which that firm has reason to believe that those requirements have been complied with.

(6)   As the context requires, other words and expressions shall have the meanings assigned to them by the Interpretation Act 1978, the Act and the Solicitors Act 1974.

(7)   The headings to these Rules do not form part of them.

3.   APPLICATION

(1)   Scope of authorisation

A firm may carry on any activity constituting investment business except:

(a)   market making in investments;

(b)   buying, selling, subscribing for or underwriting investments as principal where the firm holds itself out as engaging in the business of buying such investments with a view to selling them;

(c)   entering into margined transactions as agent for a client. This prohibition does not apply to any such transaction effected with or through a Permitted Third Party;

(d)   acting as a stabilising manager within Part 10 of the Financial Services (Conduct of Business) Rules 1987 in relation to any issue of relevant securities (as there defined);

(e)   acting as the trustee or manager of a regulated collective investment scheme; and

(f)   entering into a broker funds arrangement.

A firm's authorisation shall extend to any activity constituting investment business (except as provided above) carried out by any individual in his capacity as a partner, employee or officer of the firm.

(2)   Application of rules

(a)   These Rules shall apply only to a solicitor, partnership of solicitors and/or recognised bodies, multi-national partnership or recognised body, whether practising in England and Wales or elsewhere, in respect of which the Society has issued a certificate pursuant to section 15 of the Act which is currently in force.

(b)   Chapter 4 of these Rules (Conduct of Investment Business Rules) shall apply as follows:

(i)   Subject as otherwise provided in Rules 8(6)(a) and 12(5)(e), Chapter 4 shall apply only to the conduct of discrete investment business, save that Rules 8(2)-(5) and (7) shall apply to all investment business;

(ii)   Chapter 4 shall apply only to the conduct of such business within or into the United Kingdom, but not to such business conducted wholly outside the United Kingdom; and

(iii)   In the conduct of discrete investment business with or on behalf of a client who is a sophisticated investor only the following Rules in Chapter 4 shall apply:

8(4) to (7), 9(6), 10(7) (and, to the extent that the investment service provided is that of a portfolio adviser, 9(2)(c) and the remaining provisions of 10, 11(a) and Appendix 6), 11(b) and (c), 12, 13, Appendix 7 and Appendix 8.

(c)   (i)   In relation to any investment services carried out by a firm for a trust or the estate of a deceased person all references in these Rules to 'client' shall be deemed to be references to the trustees or personal representatives in their capacity as such and not to any person who is a beneficiary under the trust or interested in the estate.

(ii)   Where the firm or a partner, employee or officer of the firm is a trustee of such trust or is acting as the donee of any enduring power of attorney or trustee power of attorney or is a receiver appointed by the Court of Protection, only the following Rules in Chapter 4 shall apply to the conduct of discrete investment business by him or, in the case where the firm is the trustee, attorney or receiver, by it:

8(5), (6) and (7), 9(1), (2), (4) and (5), 10(7) and 12(5).

(iii)   For the purposes of sub-paragraph (ii), where pursuant to a decision made by such a partner, employee or officer to buy, sell, subscribe for or underwrite an investment the consequent arrangements are made by another member of the firm, these Rules shall apply to those arrangements as if the partner, employee or officer had made them himself.

(d)   These Rules shall not apply to a firm of which an authorised insolvency practitioner is a principal, employee or officer to the extent that the firm is carrying on investment business as a result of the authorised insolvency practitioner acting in his capacity as such.

(3)   Other practice rules

Where a solicitor, a registered foreign lawyer or recognised body being a partner in a firm is subject to any rule of the Society relating to his or its professional practice, in so far as that rule regulates the conduct of investment business by the partner, that rule shall be deemed to apply to the firm and not only to the partner.

Chapter 2 — Certification Rules

4.   ISSUE OF CERTIFICATES

(1)   Form of application and fee

Every application for a certificate shall be:

(i)   in form FSA.1 set out in Part I of Appendix 1 for a solicitor or a partnership of solicitors;

(ii)   in form FSA.3 set out in Part III of Appendix 1 for a multi-national partnership;

(iii)   in form FSA.5 set out in Part V of Appendix 1 for a recognised body; or

(iv)   in form FSA.7 set out in Part VII of Appendix 1 for a partnership including at least one recognised body;

(or in such other form as the Council may from time to time decide), and shall be accompanied by such fee as may be determined by the Council from time to time and such other information as the Council may request.

(2)   Issue of certificate

The Council may, on an application duly made under sub-rule (1) above, issue or refuse to issue a certificate or issue it subject to conditions as provided in Rule 5(1). Without prejudice to its discretion in any other case, the Council may refuse to issue a certificate if it considers that circumstances exist such that, if the certificate were issued, it could be withdrawn under Rule 5(1).

(3)   Form of certificate

(a)   The certificate issued to a sole practitioner shall be in the name in which he carries on his practice and shall authorise the carrying on by him of investment business.

(b)   The certificate issued to a partnership:

(i)   shall be issued in the partnership name; and

(ii)   shall authorise the carrying on of investment business in that name:

(1)   by the partnership to which the certificate is issued; and

(2)   by any partnership which succeeds to that business; and

(3)   by any person who succeeds to that business having previously carried it on in partnership.

(c)   If there is a dissolution of a partnership to which a certificate has been issued and more than one firm subsequently claims to be the successor to the business of the partnership, the certificate shall be deemed to be withdrawn at the expiration of 28 days from the date of the dissolution.

(d)   The certificate issued to a recognised body shall be in its name and shall authorise the carrying on by it of investment business.

(e)   Every certificate shall:

(i)   have effect from the beginning of the day of which it bears the date and that date shall be entered by the Society in a Register;

(ii)   be deemed to be issued subject to these Rules.

(4)   Annual form and fee

Every firm wishing to continue to conduct investment business shall, by 1st April in each year, apply to the Society for the issue of a new certificate:

(i)   in form FSA.2 set out in Part II of Appendix 1 for a solicitor or a partnership of solicitors;

(ii)   in form FSA.4 set out in Part IV of Appendix 1 for a multi-national partnership;

(iii)   in form FSA.6 set out in Part VI of Appendix 1 for a recognised body; or

(iv)   in form FSA.8 set out in Part VIII of Appendix 1 for a partnership including at least one recognised body;

(or in such other form as the Council may from time to time determine) accompanied by such fee as may be determined by the Council from time to time.

(5) Liability

It shall be a condition of any certificate that neither the Society nor any of its officers or servants or agents nor any members of the Council shall be liable in damages or otherwise for anything done or omitted to be done in the discharge or purported discharge of its functions under these Rules unless the act or omission is shown to have been in bad faith.

5. CONTROL OF CERTIFICATES BY THE COUNCIL

(1) Discretionary power to suspend, withdraw or impose conditions

The Council shall have power to suspend, withdraw or impose such conditions on a firm's certificate or to issue such a certificate with such conditions as it thinks fit in the following circumstances:

(a) if the firm requests it; or

(b) if it appears to the Council that the firm or any partner, employee or officer has committed a breach of any of these Rules or any other rules applicable to the conduct of solicitors, registered foreign lawyers or recognised bodies or any provision of the Act or statements of principle issued under S.47A(1) of the Act, or has furnished the Society with any false, inaccurate or misleading information; or

(c) if it appears to the Council that the firm or any partner, employee or officer is not fit and proper to carry on the investment business which the firm is carrying on; or

(d) if a partner in the firm, not being a sole principal, has been struck off the Roll of Solicitors or suspended from practice as a solicitor or has had his name struck off the register of foreign lawyers or has had his registration in that register suspended; or

(e) if the recognition of an officer of the firm, being a recognised body, has expired under Rule 9 of the Solicitors' Incorporated Practice Rules 1988 or been revoked; or

(f) if a partner or officer of the firm has been the subject of an Order made against him under the Insolvency Act 1986 or a like order in any other jurisdiction; or

(g) if a solicitor who is a partner or director of the firm does not hold a practising certificate; or

(h) if a partner or officer of the firm has had a condition imposed on his practising certificate under the provisions of section 12 of the Solicitors Act 1974 (as amended) or has had his registration in the register of foreign lawyers made subject to a condition under Schedule 14 paragraphs 2(3), 12(2) or 13 of the Courts and Legal Services Act 1990; or

(i) if there has been a change in the nature of the firm's practice so that it consists wholly or mainly of investment business; or

(j) if there has been a failure to comply with any condition imposed by the Society under this Rule; or

(k) if the firm has failed to submit a properly completed form FSA.2, FSA.4, FSA.6 or FSA.8 as required by Rule 4(4); or

(l)   if a principal, partner, employee or officer of the firm was previously a principal, partner, employee or officer of a firm whose certificate was or might have been suspended or withdrawn, or on whose certificate a condition was or might have been imposed, as a result of the activities of such principal, partner, employee or officer.

(2)   Suspension of a certificate

The suspension of a certificate shall be for a specified period or until the occurrence of a specified event or until specified conditions are complied with and while the certificate is suspended the holder shall not be a certified firm.

(3)   Imposition of conditions

Conditions may be imposed for so long as the Council consider it necessary.

(4)   Notice of intention to suspend, withdraw or impose conditions

The Council may suspend or withdraw or impose conditions on a certificate under these Rules by giving written notice to the firm stating the reasons therefor, the date on which the notice is to take effect and, in the case of suspension, its duration or the circumstances in which it will terminate. The firm may make representations to the Council with a view to the suspension or imposition being lifted or the withdrawal revoked or, where it is to take effect from a future date, to it not being brought into effect.

(5)   Automatic withdrawal of a certificate

(a)   When a sole principal or all the solicitors who are partners or directors of a firm have their names removed from or struck off the Roll of Solicitors, and the recognition of all recognised bodies which are partners is revoked or expires, the firm shall immediately cease to be authorised under these Rules.

(b)   When the practising certificate of a sole principal or the practising certificates of all solicitors who are partners or directors of a firm is or are suspended under section 15 of the Solicitors Act 1974 (as amended) as a result of the making of an Order by the Solicitors Disciplinary Tribunal or by the Court suspending the solicitor or solicitors from practice or by reason of adjudication in bankruptcy or under section 13(4)(d) of that Act by the Master of the Rolls, and the recognition of all recognised bodies which are partners is revoked or expires, the firm shall immediately cease to be authorised under these Rules.

(c)   When the Society has exercised its powers of intervention in a firm under section 35 and paragraph 1, Schedule 1 of the Solicitors Act 1974 (as amended), or section 9 and paragraph 32(i), Schedule 2 of the Administration of Justice Act 1985, or section 89 and paragraph 5(3), Schedule 14 of the Courts and Legal Services Act 1990, the firm shall immediately cease to be authorised under these Rules unless and until the Court makes an order under paragraph 6(4) of Schedule 1 of the Solicitors Act 1974 directing the Society to withdraw its notice and paragraph 9(8) of the same Schedule directing the Society to return all documents to the firm or the Society takes such steps of its own volition.

(d)   (i)   If a firm fails to pay any fee which is payable by it under these Rules, the Council may serve written notice on the firm requiring it to pay the fee within 28 days of service of the notice; and if the fee is not paid within that period, unless the Council otherwise directs, the firm's certificate shall be withdrawn forthwith whereupon the firm shall cease to be authorised under these Rules.

(ii)   This paragraph (d) shall have effect without prejudice to the recovery by the Society of any fees as a debt due to the Society.

(e)   When there has been a dissolution of a partnership without succession the firm shall on dissolution cease to be authorised under these Rules.

(f)   When a firm holding a certificate applies for a new certificate under Rule 4(4), the old certificate shall be deemed to be withdrawn on the issue of the new certificate.

(g)   When the recognition of a firm being a recognised body under the Solicitors' Incorporated Practice Rules 1988 is revoked or expires, the firm shall immediately cease to be authorised under these Rules.

(6)   Public notice

The Society may in respect of any certificate give public notice of any suspension, withdrawal or imposition of conditions.

6.   APPEAL

(1)   Right to appeal

(a)   Where a certificate has been suspended or withdrawn or conditions have been imposed on it under these Rules or where the Council has refused to grant or renew a certificate, any firm aggrieved by that decision may within seven days of being notified of the decision appeal to the Master of the Rolls or to a Lord Justice of Appeal nominated by the Master of the Rolls.

(b)   If the office of the Master of the Rolls is vacant, appeal shall lie to the Senior Lord Justice of Appeal.

(c)   The Master of the Rolls or Lord Justice of Appeal who will hear the Appeal is hereinafter referred to as 'the Judge'.

(2)   Procedure on appeal

(a)   An appeal under these Rules shall be made by the applicant lodging with the Secretary to the Judge:

(i)   a petition under the hand of the applicant praying an Order may be made directing the issue of a certificate, the continuance of a certificate, removal of conditions or suspension, reinstatement of any certificate that has been withdrawn or annulment of any decision relating to certification that has been deferred pending appeal, and shall set out the circumstances in which the application is made and the matters of fact upon which the applicant relies in support of his application; and

(ii)   a statutory declaration verifying the facts stated in the petition and copies of any notices served on him under these Rules.

(b)   The appellant shall within two days after lodging the said documents with the Secretary to the Judge, lodge copies at the Society's offices.

(c)   The Judge shall appoint a time for hearing the appeal allowing normally six weeks from the date of the petition before the appeal is heard, but an earlier date may be appointed on request.

(d)   The Secretary to the Judge shall notify the Society and the appellant of the time appointed under the foregoing.

(e)   At the hearing of the appeal the appellant and the Society may appear in person or by solicitor or counsel.

(f)   The Judge may make such order as he sees fit in respect of the appeal including the costs of the appeal.

(g)   Any such order shall be signed by the Judge and shall be filed with the Society by the Secretary to the Judge. The Society shall forthwith on the filing of the said Order take all such steps as may be necessary to give effect to the said order.

(3)   Power to suspend operation of decision pending appeal

(a)   The Council or Judge in its or his absolute discretion shall have the power to defer the operation of any decision made under these Rules pending the hearing and determination of any appeal.

(b)   Where the operation of a decision of the Council is deferred pending appeal then where that decision is confirmed on appeal, it shall take effect on the making of the order on the appeal.

Chapter 3 — Notification Rules

7.   NOTIFICATION

(1)   Notification 28 days in advance

(a)   A firm shall notify the Society in writing of the following changes not less than 28 days before the change is implemented:

   (i)   a change in the name of the firm; and

   (ii)   a change in the address of the principal office of the firm.

(b)   Notification of a change in the name of a firm shall be accompanied by a request for an amendment to its certificate from a stated date to enable it to carry on investment business in the new name together with such fee as may be determined by the Council from time to time.

(1A)   Prior notification

A firm shall notify the Society on form MNP in Appendix 11 before any investment business is conducted by, or under the supervision of, a partner or director who is a registered foreign lawyer.

(2)   Immediate notification

A firm shall give written notice forthwith to the Society of the occurrence of any of the following:

(a)   a solicitor has become or ceased to be a sole practitioner, a partner or a director in the firm;

(aa)   a registered foreign lawyer has become or ceased to be a partner or director in the firm;

(ab)   a recognised body which has become or ceased to be a partner in the firm;

(b)   the appointment of a receiver, administrator, trustee or sequestrator of the assets of the firm;

(c)   the making of a composition or arrangement with creditors of the firm;

(d)   where the firm is a partnership, an application or notice to dissolve the partnership;

(e)   the granting or refusal of any application for, or revocation of, authorisation to carry on investment, banking or insurance business in any country or territory outside the United Kingdom;

(f)   the granting, withdrawal or refusal of an application for, or revocation of, membership of any recognised self-regulating organisation or other recognised professional body under the Act;

(g)   the appointment of inspectors by a statutory or other regulatory authority to investigate the affairs of the firm;

(h)   the imposition of disciplinary measures or sanctions on the firm in relation to its investment business by any other regulatory authority;

(i)   the bringing of any action against the firm under section 61 or 62 of the Act; or

(j)   in relation to any partner, assistant solicitor, clerk or officer:

—   a conviction for any offence involving fraud or other dishonesty;

—   a conviction for any offence under legislation relating to investment, banking, building societies, companies, consumer credit, credit unions, friendly societies, industrial and provident societies, insolvency, insurance or other financial services;

—   in the case of a partner or officer, the presentation of a petition for a bankruptcy order or an award of sequestration;

—   the making of an order by a court disqualifying that individual from serving as director of a company or from being concerned with the management of a company;

(k)   in relation to any officer which is a recognised body, the presentation of a petition for a winding-up order;

(l)   the presentation of a petition for its winding up or the winding up of any other recognised body which is a subsidiary or holding company of the firm.

(3)   Notification within seven days

A firm shall notify the Society within seven days of the happening of any event likely to give rise to suspension or withdrawal of the certificate or the imposition of conditions under these Rules.

Chapter 4 — Conduct of Investment Business Rules

8. GENERAL

(1) Description of business

A firm shall in all its business letters, notices and other publications which relate to its discrete investment business (other than that referred to in Rule 3(2)(c)(ii)) state that it is regulated by the Society in the conduct of investment business, or that it is authorised by the Society to conduct investment business.

(2) Advertisements

(a) A firm shall not, pursuant to section 57(1) of the Act, approve the contents of an investment advertisement issued by another person unless the firm has taken reasonable steps to ensure that, on the basis of the facts known to it, the advertisement could have been approved by the firm if the firm were subject to Part 7 of The Financial Services (Conduct of Business) Rules 1987; provided that:

    (i) Rule 7.23 thereof shall not apply to any advertisement insofar as it contains any general offer or invitation to the holder of securities of any body corporate or any class thereof; and

    (ii) Rule 7.23 thereof shall apply as if the advertisements which may be issued by virtue of paragraph (2) of that Rule included:

        (A) an advertisement of a BES scheme which sets out the full scheme particulars, and

        (B) an advertisement which contains a private offer of BES shares and sets out a statement of prescribed information.

(b) If a firm issues or causes to be issued any advertisement to which the British Code of Advertising Practice applies (other than advertising material provided to the firm by another authorised or exempted person) relating to investment business it shall, in addition to the requirements of that Code, comply with Part I of Appendix 5.

(c) Any advertisement which the firm issues or causes to be issued in respect of a PEP operated by the firm shall comply with Part II of Appendix 5, in addition to any other requirements of this sub-rule.

(d) Any advertisement which the firm issues, causes to be issued or approves for issue by another person pursuant to section 57(1) of the Act and which relates to BES shares, including an advertisement which relates to a BES scheme, shall comply with Part III of Appendix 5, in addition to any other requirements of this sub-rule.

(e) For the purposes of paragraphs (a) and (d), an advertisement may be approved only by a partner or officer designated for the purpose and a copy of the advertisement shall be kept for three years from the date of approval.

(f) Any advertisement to which this sub-rule applies which the firm issues or causes to be issued shall be approved prior to its issue by a partner or officer designated for the purpose and a copy shall be kept for three years from the date of its issue.

(g)   Nothing in this sub-rule shall apply to any advertisement issued by or on behalf of any body corporate for the purpose of giving financial or other information relating to it and/or the group of companies of which it forms part where the advertisement does not relate to an investment agreement to be entered into with that company or a member of that group and does not invite or advise those to whom the advertisement is directed to buy investments issued by that company from a person named in the advertisement.

(3)   Published recommendations

(a)   This sub-rule applies to any journal, tip-sheet or other publication (including a publication by sound broadcasting or television) which is issued at regular intervals or from time to time and will or may contain recommendations as to the purchase, retention or sale of investments of any description.

(b)   No matter shall be included in such a publication which states or implies that any recommendation is based on the evidence of research or analysis unless such research or analysis has been carried out and the firm is in possession of that evidence and it is adequate to support the recommendation.

(c)   Any recommendation contained in such a publication shall include a risk warning statement as required by Rule 7.22 of Part 7 of the Financial Services (Conduct of Business) Rules 1987 unless the publication is distributed in such a way that it is unlikely to be received by anyone other than clients whose client agreements contain such a risk warning.

(d)   Any such publication and any such evidence as is referred to in paragraph (b) above shall be kept for one year from the date of issue of the publication.

(4)   Unsolicited calls

By way of exception to the prohibition in section 56 of the Act, a firm may (except to the extent restricted by any client agreement required under Rule 10) enter into an investment agreement in the course of or in consequence of an unsolicited call on any client or otherwise as permitted by the Solicitors' Practice Rules 1988 or the Solicitors' Publicity Code 1988, or any modification or amendment thereof.

(5)   Records

(a)   Any matter required to be recorded by these Rules may be recorded in any form so long as the record can be reproduced in hard printed form within a reasonable time.

(b)   The matters required to be recorded or retained by Rules 8(6)(c) and (d), 9(5), 10(6), 10(7)(d) and 12(5) shall be kept in a central register separate from the firm's client files, but those required by Rules 9(5), 10(6), 10(7)(d) and 12(5) may be kept at a branch office of the firm, if the discrete investment business for the relevant client has been or will be carried out principally from that office.

(c)   A firm shall (subject to any duty of confidentiality or professional privilege) allow a client on request during normal business hours either personally or by his agent to inspect any entry in a record kept by the firm of matters relating to him and shall do so as soon as reasonably practicable after the request is made but in any event not later than seven days thereafter.

(6) Complaints

(a)   A firm shall ensure in relation to each complaint made to it by a client relating to the conduct of its discrete investment business or to transactions effected with or through, or advice obtained from, a Permitted Third Party so that the investment business concerned is not discrete investment business solely by reason of it being so effected:

(i)   that the complaint is investigated promptly and thoroughly; and

(ii)   that appropriate action is taken; and

(iii) if the complaint is not disposed of to the apparent satisfaction of the client, that he is reminded that it is open to him to report the matter to the Solicitors Complaints Bureau and to ask the Bureau to investigate the complaint, but the requirements of this sub-rule are without prejudice to any duty of the firm to inform the client that he should seek separate advice if the client makes a claim against the firm or notifies his intention of doing so or the firm discovers an act or omission which would justify such a claim.

(b)   The investigation referred to in paragraph (a)(i) above shall, if practicable, be made by a partner or officer or (if it relates to an employee) by a partner, officer or employee of the firm who was not concerned in the particular act or omission complained of (otherwise than in a general supervisory capacity) being a person who is sufficiently experienced, competent and senior to investigate the complaint adequately or, if this is not possible, by the most senior partner, officer or employee of the firm available.

(c)   A firm shall keep for at least three years from the date when the complaint was received copies of each complaint in relation to which this sub-rule applies together with a record of the action taken in response to the complaint.

(d)   If a firm takes any steps to discipline any employee permitted by the firm to carry on discrete investment business, it shall make a record identifying the employee, the particulars of the conduct in question and the steps taken. The record shall be kept for a period of six years from the time the steps were taken.

(7) Force majeure

(a)   If any event happens or any circumstances arise which make it impossible, impracticable or unreasonable for a firm to comply with any obligation imposed upon it by these Rules, the firm shall forthwith inform the Society of what has happened and the steps (if any can be taken) which the firm proposes to take to deal with it.

(b)   If the event or circumstances were outside the control of the firm, it shall not, so long as it or they subsist and the firm is expeditiously taking all practicable steps available to it to relieve the situation, be regarded as in breach of any of these Rules to the extent that in consequence thereof it has become impossible, impracticable or unreasonable to comply with that Rule.

9.   KNOW YOUR CLIENT AND INVESTMENT ADVICE

(1)   Investigation of facts

A firm shall not perform any investment service for a client unless it has taken reasonable steps to ascertain from the client such facts about his personal and financial situation as may reasonably be expected to be relevant to the proper performance of those services in accordance with these Rules.

(2)   Suitability of investments and transactions in them

(a)   A firm shall not make a recommendation to, or exercise a discretion on behalf of, an advisory client in relation to an investment unless it reasonably believes that the transaction is suitable for the client having regard to the facts known, or which ought reasonably to be known, to the firm about the investment and the client's other investments and his personal and financial situation.

(b)   If an advisory client instructs the firm to effect a transaction which the firm believes to be unsuitable for the client, the firm shall not effect the transaction unless it has advised the client not to proceed and, following the giving of that advice, he has repeated his instructions.

(c)   A firm shall not make recommendations to, or exercise discretions for, an advisory client likely to lead to it effecting transactions for him with unnecessary frequency or in excessive size.

(d)   A firm shall not make a recommendation to nor effect a transaction for an advisory client in investments which it knows or ought reasonably to know are or have recently been the subject of stabilising bids or stabilising transactions made or effected in accordance with Part 10 of the Financial Services (Conduct of Business) Rules 1987 unless:

(i)   the client agreement permits the client's funds to be invested in investments which are so subject;

(ii)   the client has been given at some time before the recommendation is made or transaction effected a notice in the form set out in Appendix E to Part 4 of such Rules; and

(iii)   except in the case of a transaction effected by the firm as a discretionary portfolio manager, the client has consented.

(3)   Client's understanding of risk

Except in the case of a discretionary managed portfolio (as to which paragraph 1 of Part I of Appendix 6 applies), a firm shall not recommend or effect a transaction to or for an advisory client unless the firm has taken reasonable steps to explain to the client the extent to which he will be exposed to risk (including risk resulting from unmarketability) or further liability by entering into the transaction.

(4) Exclusions

(a)   Sub-rules (1), (2)(a) and (b) and (3) above do not apply to an investment service performed for a partner or officer of the firm in his personal capacity or contemplated by and performed in accordance with Rule 8(3).

(b)   For the purposes of sub-rules (2)(a) and (b) and (3) above a firm is not required to take into account or to disclose facts known to it about the relevant investment if to do so would be a breach of any duty to another person.

(5) Records

A firm shall maintain a record in relation to each advisory client of the facts ascertained pursuant to sub-rule (1) and, if sub-rule 2(b) applies, of the relevant sequence of events. Such records shall be kept for at least three years from the performance of the investment service to which the records relate.

(6) Sophisticated investors

A firm shall not provide investment services for a client on the basis that he is a sophisticated investor unless:

(a)   the firm has taken such steps (if any) as it has reason to believe are appropriate in order to establish that the client is such a person;

(b)   the firm has notified the client in writing that it regards him as such a person and, subject to paragraph (c) below, will provide investment services for him on that basis and has explained to him the consequences of his being so treated; and

(c)   the client did not, immediately following receipt of such notice or, if later, by the time investment services are first provided by the firm to the client, object to his being so treated.

10. CLIENT DOCUMENTATION

(1) Application

(a)   This Rule (other than sub-rule (7)) applies in relation to any investment service performed by a firm for an advisory client other than:

(i)   by means of a publication to which Rule 8(3) applies;

(ii)   subject to sub-rule (1)(b), the giving of advice about, or arranging the entry into or variation of, a type C PEP or the giving of advice about, or the arranging of transactions in, life policies or units in regulated collective investment schemes for a client if the firm reasonably believes that the investment service which the client requires from the firm at that time relates solely to such investments;

(iii)   a partner or officer of the firm in his personal capacity.

(b)   Sub-rule (1)(a)(ii) shall not exclude from the provisions of this Rule a service which consists of:

(i)   giving advice on the investments to be included in a PEP other than units in regulated collective investment schemes, or

(ii)   exercising discretion as to the investments to be included in a PEP.

(2)   Requirement for client agreement

A firm shall not provide an investment service to an advisory client otherwise than in pursuance of and in accordance with the terms of a client agreement complying with this Rule, except as provided in sub-rule (5).

(3)   Form of client agreement

(a)   A client agreement which is not for an advisory portfolio shall include such provisions as are required by Part I of Appendix 2.

(b)   A firm may rephrase in a client agreement any provision of Appendix 2 provided that the meaning is substantially the same or may include any additional provision which is not inconsistent therewith.

(c)   A client agreement may not provide for any additional payment to be made to the firm upon the termination of the agreement in respect of that termination, but this does not apply where the client agreement is a PEP.

(4)   Notification of client agreement

A firm shall not provide an investment service to an advisory client unless:

(a)   it has sent to the client a copy of the client agreement signed by or on behalf of the firm; and

(b)   either:

> (i)   the client has returned a copy signed by him or on his behalf; or

> (ii)   if the client is not resident in the United Kingdom and has declined the opportunity to sign a copy of the agreement, the firm reasonably believes that he has consented to its terms

but, in any case where the delay occasioned by compliance with this Rule would, in the view of the firm, disadvantage the client or expose him to loss, it shall be sufficient if the agreement has been signed by both the client and the firm no later than the time when the firm provides or starts to provide the relevant investment service.

(5)   Private client letter

A firm may provide an investment service to an advisory client where there is a Private Client Letter which;

(a)   is in the form specified by the Council in guidance settled in February 1990 or as subsequently amended, and

(b)   contains no matter other than matter set out in that form, and

(c)   does not confer any discretion on the firm to buy or sell investments without reference to the client, and

(d)   does not relate to and does not permit the purchase of any investment which is difficult to realise,

and a copy of the Private Client Letter has been given or sent to the client.

(6)   Record of client agreements

A firm shall keep a copy of each client agreement or Private Client Letter and of each amendment for at least three years from the last performance of an investment service by the firm for the client pursuant to such agreement or amended agreement, or Private Client Letter or amended letter.

(7)   Safekeeping of documents of title

(a)   This sub-rule applies to documents of, or evidencing, title to investments falling within paragraphs 1 to 6 of Schedule 1 to the Act which belong to any client and which are in the possession or control of the firm in connection with or for the purposes of its discrete investment business.

(b)   A firm shall be responsible for exercising reasonable care in the safekeeping of such documents until they are delivered to the client or, on his instructions, to another person.

(c)   A firm may, without the client's instructions, deliver such documents to another person for safekeeping only if that person is an authorised institution within the meaning of the Banking Act 1987 or a building society within the meaning of the Building Societies Act 1986.

(d)   A firm shall keep a separate record for each client of documents held by the firm under this Rule and the investments to which they relate and shall periodically check that such documents continue to be held. Such record shall be kept for at least three years from the date when the firm ceases to hold such documents.

(e)   A firm shall send the client a statement at least once a year made up to a date not more than one month previously specifying the documents for which the firm is responsible under this sub-rule and the investments to which they relate.

11.   SPECIAL CATEGORIES: ADVISORY PORTFOLIOS, LIFE POLICIES AND UNITS AND MARGINED TRANSACTIONS

A firm shall comply with the following Appendices in respect of the following categories:

	Appendix	Category
(a)	6	Advisory portfolios
(b)	7	Life policies, units in regulated collective investment schemes and type C PEPs
(c)	8	Margined transactions
(d)	10	BES investments

12. DEALING AND ARRANGING DEALS

(1) Best execution

(a)   This sub-rule applies to any transaction other than one which:

(i)   relates to a life policy or units in a collective investment scheme;

(ii)   is effected by the firm with or through a Permitted Third Party on the basis that the Permitted Third Party is instructed to obtain best execution. Such instruction may be in the form or substantially in the form of Part I of Appendix 4; or

(iii)   is effected by the firm for an execution-only client introduced to the firm through a third person and it is reasonable for the firm to assume that the third person is responsible for securing best execution for the client.

(b)   In effecting a transaction in an investment for a client, a firm shall have a best execution obligation in accordance with Part II of Appendix 4.

(2) Clients' orders

Where a firm is instructed by a client to effect a transaction for him on terms which do not give the firm a discretion as to when to do so, it shall effect the transaction as soon as is reasonably practicable. Where the firm is instructed by a client to effect a transaction for him on terms which do give the firm such a discretion, or where it has made a decision as discretionary portfolio manager to effect a transaction for a client, it shall enter into the transaction when it considers it best for the client concerned or as soon as may be practicable thereafter.

(3) Allocation of bargains between clients

Where a firm has acted in a transaction collectively for more than one client and all cannot be satisfied, the transaction shall as soon as reasonably practicable thereafter be allocated between the clients for whom the firm has acted:

(a)   in a manner which the firm in good faith believes does not unfairly benefit one client at the expense of another;

(b)   so as to be reasonable in the interests of each client;

(c)   so as not to conflict with any instructions a client may have given the firm; and

(d)   so as not to conflict with any limitations which may have been placed by a client agreement on the firm's discretion to act for a discretionary managed portfolio.

(4) Contract notes

(a)   After a firm has effected a transaction (other than relating to a life policy) on behalf of a client it shall deliver or send to the client (or to a person nominated by the client) either:

(i)   such contract note or statement as is received by the firm from any Permitted Third Party involved in the transaction (or a copy or relevant part thereof) together with (if relevant) a statement of the commission payable to the firm for its own account; or

(ii)   a contract note or statement which includes such provisions as are required by Appendix 3.

The person nominated by the client for such purpose may not include the firm or a partner, officer or employee of the firm unless the nomination is necessary for the convenience of the client and has been given by the client in writing.

(b)   The contract note or statement shall be despatched:

(i)   promptly after receipt of the same from any Permitted Third Party involved in the transaction; or

(ii)   if a Permitted Third Party is not involved in the transaction or such person is not to supply a contract note to the firm:

— where the transaction falls to be allocated in accordance with sub-rule (3) above, before the close of business on the business day after that on which such allocation was made; or

— in any other case, before the close of business on the business day after that on which the transaction was effected.

(c)   In the case of a type A PEP or type B PEP of which the firm is plan manager, the firm need not despatch contract notes in accordance with paragraphs (a) and (b) above if it despatches to the client at least once every six months a statement containing the information referred to in paragraphs 1, 2, 4 and 5 of Appendix 3.

(5)   Records of transactions

(a)   As soon as reasonably practicable after:

(i)   the receipt by a firm of instructions from a client to effect a transaction for the client; or

(ii)   the making of a decision by the firm to effect a transaction for a discretionary managed portfolio,

the firm shall make a record of:

(A)   the investment and the number of units thereof the subject of the instructions or the decision;

(B)   the nature of the proposed transaction; and

(C)   in the case of instructions, the date and (except in the case of a life policy) time when they were received; and

(D)   the name of the client.

(b)   Where a firm gives instructions to another person to effect such a transaction as is referred to in paragraph (a) above, the firm shall as soon as reasonably practicable thereafter make a record of:

(i)   the name of the other person so instructed;

(ii)   the terms of the instructions;

(iii)   the date and (except in the case of a life policy) time when the instructions were so given; and

(iv)   the name of the client.

(c)   Where a firm has effected such a transaction as is referred to in paragraph (a) above on behalf of more than one client, it shall, as soon as reasonably practicable after any such allocation as is referred to in sub-rule (3) above, make a record of:

(i)   the date and time of the allocation;

(ii)   the investments allocated; and

(iii)   the relevant clients.

(d)   Each record made in pursuance of this sub-rule shall be kept for at least three years from the date when it is made.

(e)   This sub-rule shall apply to the conduct of discrete investment business and also where a transaction is effected with or through a Permitted Third Party so that the investment business concerned is not discrete investment business solely by reason of it being so effected.

13. BILLS OF COST AND RELATED MATTERS

(1)   All bills of costs shall record the amount of costs attributable to discrete investment business (except where the activity is incidental or is as referred to in Rule 3(2)(c)(ii)) separately from the amount of costs attributable to other work.

(2)   All bills of costs containing an item attributable to discrete investment business (except where the activity is incidental or is as referred to in Rule 3(2)(c)(ii)) shall be:

(a)   identified separately from other bills in the bills delivered book or file of copies of bills, or

(b)   recorded in a separate bills delivered book or file of copies of bills maintained solely for such bills.

(3)   A firm shall maintain such records as are necessary to enable it to complete paragraph 2 of form FSA.2 set out in Part II of Appendix 1 or form FSA.4 set out in Part IV of Appendix 1 for a recognised body.

Chapter 5 — Monitoring Rules

14. INSPECTION

(1)   In order to ascertain whether these Rules or any other Rule of the Society, in so far as it regulates the conduct of investment business by solicitors, registered foreign lawyers or recognised bodies, or statements of principle issued under S.47A(1) of the Act, have been complied with, the Secretary of the Society, or such person as he may appoint, may require any firm to produce, at a time and place notified, the accounting and other records of the firm relating to investment business and any other necessary documents for the inspection of any person appointed by the Secretary and to supply to such person any necessary information and explanations and such person shall prepare for the information of the Council a report on the result of such inspection, if so requested by the Council or if he otherwise thinks fit.

(2)   Upon being required so to do a firm shall produce such accounting and other records of the firm relating to investment business and any other necessary documents, at the time and place fixed.

(3) Every requirement made by the Council under this Rule shall be made in writing and sent or delivered to the firm at the place specified as the firm's principal practising address or registered office in its latest application for a certificate or in any subsequent notice under Rule 7(1).

(4) For the purposes of sub-rule (3), if the requirement is sent by registered post or the recorded delivery service, it shall be deemed to have been received by the firm within 48 hours (excluding Saturdays, Sundays and Bank Holidays) after the time of posting.

Chapter 6 — Miscellaneous

15. WAIVERS

The Council shall have power to waive in writing any of the provisions of these Rules in any particular case or cases, but shall not do so unless it appears that:

(1) compliance with the requirements in question would be unduly burdensome for the applicant having regard to the benefit which compliance would confer on investors; and

(2) the exercise of the power would not result in any undue risk to investors.

16. SERVICE

(1) Except as otherwise expressly provided in these Rules, any notice or other document required or authorised by these Rules to be served on any firm may be served by leaving it at or sending it by post to the firm's principal practising address or registered office.

(2) Any such notice or document may be served on a firm, without prejudice to any other method of service, by sending it in a pre-paid envelope by ordinary first class post addressed to the firm at the place specified as the firm's principal practising address or registered office, in its latest application for a certificate or in any subsequent notice under Rule 7(1).

APPENDIX 1: APPLICATION FORMS

[These forms are sent out by the Law Society and are not reproduced here.]

APPENDIX 2: CLIENT AGREEMENTS

PART I

Form of general client agreement

To: [Client]

This agreement is being entered into pursuant and subject to the Solicitors' Investment Business Rules.

Regulation of investment business

1.   We are regulated in the conduct of our investment business by the Law Society.

Services to be provided

2.   The services to be provided to you are:-

*(a)   the *acquisition/disposal *(and/or arranging for the acquisition/ disposal) of investments *generally/the following investments:-

    * ....

*(b)   acting as *portfolio adviser/discretionary portfolio manager

*(c)   giving investment advice *generally/in relation to the following investments:-

    * ....

*3.   The services to be provided by us to you are to include advising on or effecting transactions in *foreign exchange/futures/options contracts for differences.

*[Such transactions will be carried out through * ....under a customer agreement between you and that person which authorises us to give instructions on your behalf.]

*[As regards such transactions:-

*(a)   they may be effected otherwise than under the rules of a recognised or designated investment exchange;

(b)   margin will be payable by you on demand and in such form as we may specify and, if you fail to make any such payment, we may close out all or any open position and sell all or any other investments held for you;

(c)   your existing positions may be closed out without reference to you otherwise than upon your default in payment or supplementing any margin or deposit *[only in the following events:-

    * ....];

*(d)   any collateral received from you will cease to be your property once such transactions are undertaken and may be passed on to an intermediate broker through whom the transaction is effected.]

[Note: the provisions in square brackets are alternative. The second set should be included only where the client is not to enter into a customer agreement direct with a Permitted Third Party.]

*4.   The services to be provided to you relate to investments which are single premium life policies issued by regulated life offices or units in regulated collective investment schemes. You will not have any right under the Financial Services (Cancellation) Regulations 1989 to cancel any such transaction so effected.

[Note: this should not be included for discretionary clients.]

Investment objectives and parameters

5.   Your investment objectives are:-

    * ....

[Note: objectives such as 'capital growth', 'income' or 'mixed portfolio' may be inserted. These are generally only appropriate to advisory portfolios.]

6.   There are *no/the following restrictions on the types of investment into which you wish your available funds to be invested [:- *...]

7.   There are *no/the following restrictions as to the markets on which transactions are to be effected on your behalf [:- * ....]

*8.   Your funds may be invested in investments:-

(i)   which may be difficult to realise;

(ii)   in which there can be no certainty that market makers will be prepared to deal;

(iii)   proper information for determining the current value of which may not be available; or

(iv)   in relation to which stabilising bids may be made or stabilising transactions occur.

*9.   You agree that transactions for you may be aggregated with those of other clients.

Accounting for transactions, custody and client money

10.   We shall account to you in respect of transactions arranged on your behalf *on demand/as follows:-

* ....

11.   (a) *Nobody/.......... is to be the *nominal holder of your registered investments/the custodian of your documents of title or certificates evidencing title to your investments. We *do/do not accept liability for default by such person(s).

(b) Such documents *may/may not be lent to a third party and money *may/may not be borrowed on your behalf against the security of those documents.

*12.   We may hold your money in a client bank account outside the United Kingdom.

Unsolicited calls

*13.   We may call upon you otherwise than at your express invitation, in the following circumstances:-

*   in relation to any investment or investment activity

*   in relation to the following investments:-

*   ....

In relation to any investment agreement entered into in the course of or in consequence of such a call you will forfeit the right conferred upon you by Section 56 of the Financial Services Act to treat the investment agreement as unenforceable.

Fees

14.   You will pay us fees for our services under this agreement [*in accordance with the Solicitors' Remuneration Order 1972] [*on the following basis: — ....]

Amendments and termination

15.   These terms may be amended by notification to you which is either delivered or despatched by post *or telex or other form of instantaneous communication at least *... days before such amendment is to take effect.

[Note: the period of days to be inserted may be less than 10]

*16.   (i) We may terminate the agreement between us as follows:-

*   ....

(ii)   You may, without prejudice to the completion of transactions already initiated, terminate the agreement between us on immediate written notice given by you to us.

*On termination of this Personal Equity Plan or transfer to another plan manager the following will be payable by you: * ....

[Note: this sentence should be included only for PEPs of which the firm is plan manager.]

*Note: delete or complete as appropriate.

PART II

Additional requirements in relation to client agreement for an advisory portfolio

17.   The initial value of the portfolio is: *......

[Note: 'initial value' means the value on the date of transfer to the firm.]

18.   The initial composition of the portfolio is as follows:-

    * ....

19.   The periods of acount for which statements of the portfolio are to be provided to you are *quarterly/monthly/ ....

*Note: Delete or complete as appropriate

20.   The scheme particulars of this BES advisory portfolio are attached to this agreement.

[Note: only include in the case of BES advisory portfolio.]

21.   The scheme particulars of the BES fund to which this agreement relates are attached.

[Note: only include in the case of a BES fund.]

PART III

Additional requirements in relation to client agreement for a discretionary managed portfolio

22.   There is *no/the following restrictions on the amount or on the proportion of the fund comprised in the portfolio which may be invested in any category of investment or in any one investment [:- * ....].

23. We may, delegate to .... the function or any part of the function of deciding how our discretion on your behalf is to be exercised.

*24. We may commit you to a financial obligation to supplement the funds in the portfolio by borrowing on your behalf *and/or by committing you to a contract the performance of which may not be possible without such a supplement.

This authority is *unlimited generally/unlimited in respect of the following transactions:-
....

*In respect of the following transactions it is limited in the following respects: -

Types of *transactions*	*Limit*	*Circumstances* *in which limits* *may be exceeded*

*25. Your available funds may be invested in transactions in futures/options/contracts for differences and margin for such transactions may not be taken out of your portfolio beyond the following amounts:

* ....

26. The fund comprised in the portfolio may be committed to an obligation as an underwriter of any issue or offer for sale of securities. *There are *no/the following restrictions on the categories of security which may be so underwritten

[:- ....].

*There are *no/the following financial limits on the extent of such underwriting [:- ....].

27. You will be supplied with a statement of the money and investments comprised in the portfolio and a valuation thereof each *year/quarter/month/.................. . The basis of such valuation will be [*..........].

[Note: the period inserted must not be greater than a year. If paragraph 11(b) provides for lending, or paragraphs 24 or 25 are included, the statement must be at least monthly.]

These statements *will/will not include a measure of portfolio performance. *The basis on which that performance is to be measured will be:.............

*We may deduct our fees from cash comprising any part of the portfolio.

*28. We have a commercial arrangement with *................ under which we will receive investment advice from that third party as to how your funds ought or might be invested.

APPENDIX 3: FORM OF CONTRACT NOTE

[On firm's notepaper]

To: [Client]

1. At ....a.m./p.m. on .... 19.... we *placed an order with .... for the *purchase/sale of the following investments:-

*bought/sold for you the following investments:-

    Number ....

    Description ....

    Price per *share/unit ....

Total consideration *payable/receivable is £ ....

Settlement date: *................. 19 ......

*2. The transaction is *ex div./cum div.

*3. Foreign exchange was converted from *........... into *........... at the rate of *.............

4.   Our commission is *£ ....

*5.   You will have to pay the following *taxes/duties/fees:-

Nature: ....

Amount: £ ....

[Notes: *Delete or complete as appropriate.

Where the transaction concerned is an option, futures contract, contract for differences or the exercise of an option by or against the client, the above should be amended as appropriate to disclose to the client the relevant details, including client's profit or loss and fees payable.]

APPENDIX 4: BEST EXECUTION

PART I

Instructions to Permitted Third Party to obtain best execution

To: [Permitted Third Party]   [Date]

All instructions to effect transactions which we may give to you are (until you receive from us written notification to the contrary) on terms that you will obtain 'best execution of the transaction' [in accordance with the rules of the *self-regulatory organisation/*recognised professional body/*relevant investment exchange of which you are a member] *[in accordance with the Code of Conduct of the Bank of England].

[Firm]

*[Note: delete as appropriate]

PART II

The best execution obligation

A firm shall take reasonable steps to ensure that the terms of the transaction are such that it is effected on the best terms reasonably available, at the time the transaction is effected, on the market generally for transactions with reliable counterparties of the same size and nature as the transaction in question. For this purpose:-

(i)   any fees payable by the client to the firm shall be disregarded;

(ii)   regard may be had, in comparing one possible manner of effecting the transaction with another, not only to the price to be paid or received but also to such of the following factors as are relevant:-

(a)   the charges which would be incurred by the firm for the client's account in addition to its own fees;

(b)   the other terms of the transaction;

(c)   the likelihood of the counterparty expeditiously and satisfactorily performing his obligations; and

(d)   any other advantages which would be likely to enure directly or indirectly to the client in connection with the transaction or in connection with other transactions likely to be effected by the firm for the client on other occasions.

APPENDIX 5: ADVERTISING

PART I

General Rules

1.   If the advertisement contains any matter based on an assumed rate of taxation it shall state what that rate is.

2.   The advertisement shall not describe any investment as being free of tax unless no tax is payable either by the investor in respect of the investment or by any fund of which the investment forms part or to which its value is linked.

3.   If the advertisement relates to an investment where deductions for charges and expenses are loaded disproportionately onto the early years, the advertisement shall draw attention to that fact and state that, if the investor withdraws from the investment in the early years, he may not get back the amount he has invested.

4.   If the advertisement relates to a with profits life policy, the statement shall draw attention to the fact that the return on the investment depends on what profits are made and on what decisions are made by the life office as to their distribution.

5.   Where the advertisement relates to an investment denominated in a foreign currency, the advertisement shall draw attention to the fact that changes in rates of exchange between currencies may cause the value of the investments to diminish or to increase.

6.   If the advertisement contemplates the recipient entering into a transaction as a result of which he may not only lose what he pays at the outset but may incur a liability to pay unspecified additional amounts later, it shall draw attention to both those facts.

7.   If the advertisement relates to a margined transaction which is not a limited liability transaction and which will or may be effected otherwise than on a recognised or designated investment exchange and in a contract of a type traded theron, it shall draw attention to the fact that the transaction is suitable only for a person who has experience in transactions of that description.

PART II

Rules regarding PEPs operated by firm

1.   Advertisement not to imply Government approval

The advertisement shall not contain any matter that states or implies that the PEP has the approval of any Government department. However, it may refer to any reliefs from taxation which may be available from time to time in respect of investment in personal equity plans.

2.   Taxation

Any reference to reliefs from taxation:-

   (a)   shall state that the reliefs are those which currently apply; and

   (b)   shall contain a statement that the value of a relief from taxation depends upon the circumstances of the taxpayer.

3.   Off the page advertisements

A firm shall not issue an advertisement for a PEP which would permit a client to enter into such a PEP by responding in the manner specified in the advertisement and without further correspondence or discussion with the firm unless the firm has already complied with its obligations (if any) to that client under Rule 9(1) in respect of the PEP.

PART III

Rules regarding BES investments

1.   A firm shall not issue or cause to be issued an advertisement relating to a BES fund unless the terms of the fund provide that the amount which may be invested in any one company may not exceed 27.5 per cent. of the subscriptions.

2.   A firm may:-

(i)   issue, cause to be issued or approve for issue:-

(a)   a trailer advertisement relating to BES shares, including an advertisement relating to a BES scheme; and

(b)   an advertisement relating to a private offer of BES shares provided that the advertisement includes a statement of prescribed information;

(ii)   provide to a client a prospectus relating to BES shares, or scheme particulars relating to a BES scheme, where the client has requested this without having been solicited by the firm (other than by means of a trailer advertisement) to subscribe for those BES shares or to a BES scheme.

3.   Save as provided in paragraph 2 above, a firm shall not issue or cause to be issued any advertisement relating to BES shares, including an advertisement relating to a BES scheme, or distribute a prospectus relating to BES shares, other than to clients who are:-

(i)   sophisticated investors;

(ii)   reasonably believed by the firm to be clients for whom investments which may be difficult to realise are suitable;

(iii)   reasonably believed already to have invested directly or indirectly in BES shares; or

(iv)   authorised or exempted persons.

4.   Save as provided in paragraph 2 above, a firm shall not issue or cause to be issued an advertisement relating to a BES scheme unless:-

(i)   the advertisement sets out or is accompanied by the scheme particulars;

(ii)   where the firm is aware that the manager of the BES scheme intends to invest subscriptions in BES shares in a company in which he has a material interest, a copy of the prospectus or, if there is no prospectus, a statement of prescribed information relating to each such company is included in or accompanies the advertisement; and

(iii)   if the advertisement contains or is accompanied by a form of application to subscribe to the scheme, the form of application contains:-

(a)   a statement that applications may only be made and accepted subject to the terms and conditions of the scheme particulars, and

(b)   a statement, placed above the space provided for the signature of the applicant, to the effect that he has been advised not to subscribe unless he:-

(A) has read and understood the terms and conditions of the scheme particulars,

(B) has taken appropriate expert advice before submitting his application, and

(C) is aware of the risks involved in investing in BES shares and BES schemes.

5.   In the case of an advertisement which a firm is permitted to approve by virtue of Rule 8(2)(a)(ii), the firm shall (in addition to complying with Rule 8(2)) take reasonable steps to ensure that:-

(i)   the terms of the advertisement are such that:-

(a)   any offer invited to be made cannot be accepted until seven days after the day on which the offer is received by the offeror, and

(b)   any acceptance by an investor of an offer contained in the advertisement may be withdrawn at any time within the period of seven days beginning with the day next following the day on which the acceptance is received by the offeror, and

(c)   they do not give any authority to make unsolicited calls upon the investor, and

(ii)   the advertisement contains at its head a notice advising that any investor who responds to the advertisement may withdraw that response within the period of seven days beginning with the day after the day on which that response is received by the offeror, and

(iii)   the advertisement contains a tear-off slip with a form of notice to be used by the investor as a means of communicating his wish to withdraw.

PART IV

Scheme particulars

1.   The following statements with particular prominence:-

(a)   a statement that investment in unquoted shares carries higher risks than investment in quoted shares, and

(b)   a statement to the effect that investments in unquoted shares may be difficult to realise, that there can be no certainty that market makers will be prepared to deal in them and, where the investment objectives of the scheme include investment in private companies, that restrictions may apply to the transfer of shares in such companies, and

(c)   a statement that proper information for determining the current value of investments may not be available, and

(d)   a statement to the effect that the recipient should before proceeding seek expert advice, and

(e)   a statement that the scheme manager is regulated in the conduct of his investment business by the Society, or that he is authorised by the Society to conduct investment business.

2.   The following statement:-

'The [firm] [fund manager] [scheme manager] [and its directors] [has] [have] taken all reasonable care to ensure that all facts stated in this document are true and accurate in all material respects and there are no other material facts the omission of which would make misleading any statement herein whether of fact or opinion. The [firm] [fund manager] [scheme manager] [and its directors] accept[s] responsibility accordingly.'

3.   The name and business address of:-

(a)   the scheme manager, and

(b)   the promoter of the scheme (if any), and

(c)   every person acting in a professional capacity in relation to the scheme, and

(d)   every person likely to take part in any decision or recommendation relating to investment of moneys subscribed to the scheme.

4.   The opening and closing dates for receipt of subscriptions.

5.   The maximum and minimum sizes, if any, proposed for the scheme.

6.   The maximum and minimum permitted individual subscription to the scheme.

7.   A statement of the arrangements for the holding of subscription moneys pending investment.

8.   The arrangements for the return of subscription moneys should the scheme be over-subscribed or the moneys not accepted for other reasons.

9.   The arrangements for the return of subscription moneys remaining uninvested at the time when the final investment of the scheme has been made or the final date for investment has passed.

10.   Any arrangements by virtue of which any preferential treatment will or may be given in relation to subscription to the scheme to particular persons or class of persons subscribing to the scheme.

11.   The circumstances in which persons or particular classes of person are excluded from participation in the scheme or in any particular investment of scheme moneys.

12.   The manner in which shares in companies in which scheme moneys are to be invested are to be held on behalf of participants in the scheme and the manner in which, according to their subscriptions, interests in such shares are to be allocated to each participant.

13.   Any arrangements for registering shares in the names of participants in the scheme at or after the end of the period during which shares must be held in order to obtain tax relief.

14.   Any arrangements for the payment of dividends, if any, to participants in the scheme.

15.   The circumstances in which a person's participation in the scheme may be terminated.

16.   Any arrangements for dealing with scheme moneys which become available as a result of a sale of scheme investments by the scheme manager.

17.   The scheme manager's powers and discretion in relation to the scheme, including, for example, the exercise of voting rights, the selection and the disposal of investments and syndication of the scheme with other sources of investment.

18.   The following information concerning charges and costs to be stated together in a part of the document dealing solely with that information:-

(a)   the amount or rate of the scheme manager's remuneration currently charged, whether that may be varied in any way in the future and, if so the maximum to which it may be increased, and

(b)   the same information as under sub-paragraph (a) but in relation to any other charges or costs made or arising in connection with the scheme.

19.   The commission rate payable to any intermediary in return for his introducing participants to the scheme.

20.   Whether the scheme manager remains free to subscribe for shares, or to hold options to do so, in companies in which the scheme is invested and, if so, an indication of the price or the formula by which a price is determined at which he may subscribe and the maximum proportion of the ordinary share capital of those companies for which he may subscribe or which may be the subject of options in his favour.

21.   Whether the scheme manager proposes to establish another BES scheme and, if so, whether or not arrangements exist to ensure that the scheme manager does not discriminate between one BES scheme and another and, if such arrangements exist, what they are.

22.   A summary of the fiscal provisions concerning the Business Expansion Scheme.

23.   A description of any arrangements there may be:-

(a)   for securing that any person who knowingly has a material interest in any decision or recommendation concerning the investment of subscriptions which is not subject to independent approval is excluded from participation in the making of that decision or recommendation, and

(b)   for securing independent approval of decisions and recommendations concerning the investment of subscriptions which may be made by persons who have a material interest in them, and, if no arrangements exist relating to any of the above matters, a statement to that effect.

24.   If the arrangements described in accordance with paragraph 23 do not cover any of the following interests:-

(a)   an interest of the scheme manager or of an associate of his arising by way of remuneration in connection with the management or operation of the scheme or any other BES scheme,

(b)   an interest arising from investment of subscriptions of the scheme or of any other BES scheme of which the scheme manager of the scheme in question or his associate is also the scheme manager,

(c)   an interest of an authorised institution within the meaning of the Banking Act 1987 resulting from a loan made by such an institution,

(d)   an interest arising from the formation by the scheme manager or his associate of a company with a view to interests in that company being acquired on behalf of BES schemes of which he or his associate is the scheme manager, the fact that they do not cover that interest need not be disclosed if there be disclosed the fact that investment may be made despite the existence of such an interest and, in the case of (c), details of any arrangements made to avoid conflicts of interest or, if there be no such arrangements, that fact.

25.   If the scheme manager has any interest (whether direct or indirect) or duty the nature of which may place him in conflict with the interests of participants in the scheme or his duty to those participants, particulars of that interest or duty.

26.   A statement at the head of any summary contained in the scheme particulars that the summary must be read subject to the full terms and conditions of the scheme as set out in the scheme particulars.

27.   A statement of any arrangements to enable participants in the scheme to notify the scheme manager of companies with which they are connected within the meaning of section 291 of the Income and Corporation Taxes Act 1988.

28.   A statement of the investment policies and objectives of the scheme including, for example, details of the status, nature, location and types of business activities of the companies in which it is intended the scheme should be invested.

29.   A statement of what periodic reports will be made to participants and how frequently those reports will be made in compliance with the requirements of the principal rules.

APPENDIX 6: ADVISORY PORTFOLIOS

PART I

General

1.   Discretionary portfolios: client's understanding of risk

A firm shall not act as a discretionary portfolio manager on behalf of a client unless it has taken such steps (if any) as are reasonable to explain to the client the risks (including risks resulting from unmarketability) to which he will be exposed in connection with the management of the portfolio having regard to:-

(a)   the investment objectives set out in the client agreement;

(b)   the extent of the discretion conferred on the firm; and

(c)   the extent to which the client is relying on the firm to supply expertise which he does not possess.

2.   Form of client agreement

(a)   A client agreement for an advisory portfolio shall include such provisions as are required by Parts I and II of Appendix 2.

(b)   A client agreement for a discretionary managed portfolio shall include such provisions as are required by Parts I, II and III of Appendix 2.

(c)   For the purposes of this paragraph, the exception provided by Rule 10(1)(a)(ii) shall not apply.

3.   Statements and records

In relation to each advisory portfolio a firm shall:-

(a)   prepare and send to the client in accordance with the client agreement a statement of the client's portfolio for each period of account identified in the client agreement. Such statement shall provide at least the information set out in Part II of this Appendix; and

(b)   keep a separate record for such client of the investments included in his portfolio. Such record shall be kept for at least three years from the date when it is made.

PART II

Form of periodic statement for advisory portfolios

[On firm's notepaper]

To: [Client]   Date:......19..

1.   Assets: *[Insert list]

2.   Aggregate acquisition cost of assets or value at date of transfer to the firm: * £......

3.   Aggregate value of assets at the date of this statement: * £......

4.   The basis of valuation is * ....

*Basis of conversion of currency: * ....

5.   Assets lent to third party at date of this statement: *[Insert list]

6.   Income received in each investment period, except if mandated to client:

Investment   *Income received*

*[Insert list]

7.   Interest payments made on borrowings for portfolio during period totalled: * £......

8.   During the period the following transactions occurred:

Investment   *Number*   *Buy/Sell Price*   *Other remarks*

*[Insert list]

9.   *We/............ hold for you in safekeeping the following documents of or evidencing title to the following investments:

Document   *Investment*   *Number*   *Other remarks*

*[Insert list]

[Note: This section need only be included in the annual statement: see Rule 10(7)(e)]

10.   Our fees in the period amounted to: * £.....

11.   Period covered by this statement is *............ 19...... to .... 19......

[*Note: delete or complete as appropriate.

Where options, futures or contracts for differences are entered into, the above should be amended as appropriate to disclose to the client the relevant details, including client's profit or loss.]

APPENDIX 7: LIFE POLICIES, UNITS IN REGULATED

COLLECTIVE INVESTMENT SCHEMES AND PEPS

PART I

General

1.   Best advice

(a)   A firm shall not:-

(i)   recommend to a client the acquisition of a life policy, units in a regulated collective investment scheme or a type C PEP; or

(ii) effect on behalf of an advisory client a transaction under which any person makes such an acquisition,

unless the firm, after making reasonable enquiries, neither is nor ought to be aware that the same or another life office, operator of a regulated collective investment scheme or plan manager of a type C PEP would be willing to offer the client another life policy, other units in a regulated collective investment scheme or another type C PEP which would be likely to secure his investment objectives more advantageously than the life policy, units in a regulated collective investment scheme or type C PEP in question.

(b)   A firm shall not recommend to an advisory client the realisation of units in a regulated collective investment scheme or a life policy unless it has reason to believe that to do so would be for his advantage.

(c)   A firm shall keep a record of the results of the enquiries made in pursuance of paragraph (a) above for at least three years after they have been made.

2.   Published forecasts

A firm shall not provide to a client:-

(a)   any forecast of the amount of benefits under a life policy, except for a defined benefits pension scheme or pension fund management policy;

(b)   any forecast of the realisable value of an investment in units in a regulated collective investment scheme or their acquisition as the plan investments of a type A PEP; or

(c)   any illustration of what such a benefit or realisable value might be on any particular assumption,

other than the entire contents (without any additions or amendments) of a written statement supplied by, as the case may be, the life office, operator of the scheme or plan manager for distribution to members of the public.

3.   Buyer's guide

(a)   In this paragraph, 'buyer's guide' means a document in the form set out in Part II of this Appendix on plain paper.

(b)   A firm shall not recommend to a client a transaction relating to the issue to him of a life policy, the purchase by him of units in a regulated collective investment scheme or a type C PEP unless:-

(i)   the firm gave or sent to the client a buyer's guide within the previous six months, or

(ii)   the firm gives or sends to the client a buyer's guide at the same time or, if that is not practicable, immediately thereafter.

(c)   Sub-paragraph (b) does not apply where the recommendation is made:-

(i)   in pursuance of a client agreement, or

(ii)   to an established client.

4.   Recommendations

(a)   A firm shall not recommend to a client a transaction relating to the issue to him of a life policy (which is not a defined benefits pension scheme or a pension fund management policy) or the purchase by him of units in a regulated collective investment scheme unless the firm at the time it makes the recommendation gives him, or immediately thereafter sends to him, a written statement of product particulars in the form supplied by the life office or operator of the scheme.

(b)   A firm shall not recommend to a client a transaction relating to the issue to him of a life policy (which is not a defined benefits pension scheme or a pension fund management policy), the purchase by him of units in a regulated collective investment scheme or his entering into a type C PEP unless the firm at the time it makes the recommendation gives him:-

(i)   (A) a written statement as referred to in sub-paragraph (a), or

(B) such information about that policy, those units or that PEP and the financial implications of the transaction as the firm reasonably considers it necessary for him to know to enable him to make an informed decision as to whether to proceed with the transaction; and

(ii)   notice of any rights he may have to change his mind about entering into the transaction.

[*Note: Rule 10 of the Solicitors' Practice Rules 1988 must also be complied with. It provides that 'A solicitor shall account to his client for any commission received of more than £10 unless, having disclosed to the client the amount of the commission or, if the amount cannot be ascertained, the basis of calculation of the commission, he has the client's agreement to retain it.']

PART II

The Law Society

Buyer's guide: Life assurance, personal pensions and unit trust products

1.   Advisers on life assurance, personal pensions and/or unit trust products are of two types:-

either representatives of a particular company; or

independent.

Both types of adviser may only recommend life assurance, personal pensions, or unit trust products if they consider such a product suitable to your needs.

2.   A representative of a particular company acts on *its* behalf and will recommend a product picked *only* from the range of those offered by that particular company.

3.   [We] [name of firm] as [solicitors] [solicitors and registered foreign lawyers] [registered foreign lawyers and solicitors] are independent. We will act on *your* behalf in recommending a product picked from the ranges of *all* the companies that make up the market place. The Law Society's rules require us to account to you for any commission which we receive unless, after we have told you the amount of the commission or, if the amount cannot be worked out, the basis of calculation of the commission, you agree that we can keep it. After the life policy has been arranged or unit trusts purchased, you will, in any event, be given details of this commission.

[Firm to delete/complete as appropriate.]

4.   The Law Society's rules also require that:-

    *   We must explain the main features of the product we are recommending to you; we will help you to understand the risks there may be and the possible costs as well as the potential future benefits you could gain from it.

    *   We must tell you whether you have a right to change your mind about your decision to purchase a product. If you do change your mind, in some cases you may not get back all that you paid if investment values have fallen. Be sure to ask us about any right to change your mind and any cost you might incur by doing so.

5.   The company whose product you buy will give you the following in writing:-

    *   Full details of the product, including how you pay, how much and for how long; its benefits to you and, for certain types of product, an indication of the company's expenses or charges that will be taken out of the money you pay. These expenses or charges may arise both at the time you first buy the product and also in the future.

    *   Details of the commission. This commission will form part of the company's expenses or charges.

    *   An indication, where your investment is a life policy, of how much money, if any, you would receive if you surrender the policy within five years of taking it out.

6.   *   Note carefully: If you want more information now about any of these matters, or if anything else is not clear to you, ask us. It is our job to help you understand everything you want to know.

7.   Issuing this guide is a requirement of the Law Society, Ipsley Court, Berrington Close, Redditch, Worcestershire B98 0TD, 071-242 1222.

APPENDIX 8: MARGINED TRANSACTIONS

PART I

General

1.   A firm shall not effect for a client or advise a client to enter into a margined transaction or any option which, if exercised, would give rise to a margined transaction:

    (a)   otherwise than on a recognised or designated investment exchange unless permitted by the client agreement; and

(b)   otherwise than with or through a Permitted Third Party and:-

(i)   after instructing the Permitted Third Party to obtain best execution and that any money or investments deposited is or are to be treated by the Permitted Third Party as client money. Such instruction may be in the form or substantially in the form of Part II of this Appendix;

(ii)   if the transaction is effected by the firm in the capacity of discretionary portfolio manager, the firm shall enter into (as agent for the client) any customer agreement required by the Permitted Third Party; and

(iii)   if the client is to receive advice, the firm shall obtain that advice from or confirm that advice with the Permitted Third Party and, unless there is a customer agreement directly between the client and the Permitted Third Party under which advice is to be given to the client, shall enter into (as agent for the client) any customer agreement required by the Permitted Third Party.

The firm shall forward to the client, within one business day of receipt, any written risk disclosure or warning statement received from the Permitted Third Party.

The firm shall not effect any such transaction for a client unless it has first given or sent to the client such disclosure or statement or a statement in the form set out in Appendix C or D (as appropriate) to the Financial Services (Conduct of Business) Rules 1987.

2.   A firm which undertakes margined transactions for a client shall ensure that the client's initial margin and equity balance is calculated and relevant sums and/or collateral held by the firm in accordance with Part III of this Appendix.

3.   A firm which has acquired an option contract for a client which is subsequently exercised by or against the client shall deliver or send to the client a contract note or statement in accordance with Rule 12(4).

PART II

Instruction to permitted third party to obtain best execution with regard to transactions in futures, options and contracts for differences

To: [Permitted Third Party]

[Date]

All instructions to effect transactions which we may give to you are (until you receive from us written notification to the contrary) on terms that you will obtain best execution of the transaction* [in accordance with the rules of the *self-regulatory organisation/*recognised professional body/*relevant investment exchange of which you are a member] *[in accordance with the Code of Conduct of the Bank of England].

In addition, all money and/or collateral which we lodge with you by way of margin or otherwise will be money and/or collateral of our clients and is to be treated by you accordingly.

[Firm]

*[*Note: delete as appropriate]*

PART III

Initial margin and equity balance

1. Interpretation

(1)   For the purpose of this Part:-

(a)   the following terms have the following meanings:-

'approved collateral', in relation to a margined transaction undertaken under the rules of an Exchange, means such collateral as, under the rules of that Exchange, is acceptable as an alternative to a deposit in cash;

'collateral' means any form of security guarantee or indemnity provided by way of security for the discharge of any liability arising from margined transactions;

'clients account', in relation to a firm and an Exchange or an intermediate broker, means an account maintained by the Exchange or the intermediate broker, as the case may be, in respect of margined transactions undertaken by the firm for its clients;

'Exchange' means a recognised or designated investment exchange under the rules of which margined transactions are effected together with any clearing house through which transactions effected under the rules of that investment exchange may be cleared;

'intermediate broker', in relation to a margined transaction, means any person with or through whom the firm undertakes that transaction;

'limited liability transaction' means a margined transaction effected by a firm for a client the terms of which provide that the maximum liability of the client in respect of the transaction shall be limited to an amount which has been determined before the effecting of the transaction;

'margined client money', in relation to a firm, means client money which is received or held by that firm in respect of margined transactions effected by the firm for a client;

'relevant margined transaction' means a margined transaction undertaken by a firm with or through an intermediate broker under the rules of an Exchange and in a type of contract traded thereon with or for a client;

'value', in relation to approved collateral, means its value as calculated in accordance with the rules of the Exchange on which the margined transaction to which the approved collateral relates is or will be effected;

(b)   client's equity balance at any time is the amount which that client would be liable to pay to a firm or which the firm would be liable to pay to the client in respect of his relevant margined transactions if each of his open positions was liquidated at the closing or settlement prices published by the relevant Exchange and his account closed; and the amount of an equity balance is a positive amount where the balance is payable to the client and it is a negative amount where the balance is payable by the client;

(c)   a firm's equity balance at any time with an intermediate broker is the amount which that firm would be liable to pay to the intermediate broker or which the intermediate broker would be liable to pay to the firm in respect of the firm's relevant margined transactions if each of the open positions of the firm's clients was liquidated at the closing or settlement prices published by the relevant Exchange and the firm's clients account with the intermediate broker closed; and the amount of an equity balance is a positive amount where the balance is payable to the firm and it is a negative amount where the balance is payable by the firm;

(d)   a client's initial margin requirement at any time is the total amount which under the rules of the relevant Exchange or Exchanges an intermediate broker would be required to deposit in cash or (when permitted) approved collateral as a fidelity deposit in respect of all that client's open positions in relevant margined transactions at that time, irrespective of any unrealised profit or loss on such positions, on the assumption that those transactions were the only transactions undertaken under the rules of that Exchange or those Exchanges by the intermediate broker at that time.

2.   Notification to intermediate broker

A firm undertaking any margined transaction for the account of a client with or through an intermediate broker shall instruct the intermediate broker that:-

(a)   any money paid or the value of any collateral passed to him in respect of that transaction is to be credited to the firm's client account with him, and

(b)   any money paid to him in respect of that transaction is to be paid into his segregated bank account opened for the purpose of holding money received in respect of transactions of the type in question, that is to say:-

(i)   if the transaction is undertaken under the rules of an Exchange and in a type of contract traded thereon, transactions so undertaken, or

(ii)   if the transaction is not so undertaken, transactions not so undertaken.

3.   Initial margins

(1)   A firm shall not undertake any relevant margined transaction except after requiring the client to deposit with the firm in cash or approved collateral an amount not less than the initial margin requirement and, except where the firm is acting for a client under a limited liability contract, shall require the client to deposit additional cash or approved collateral on any increase in his initial margin requirement in relation to his relevant margined transactions.

(2)   The amount required under paragraph (1) above to be deposited shall be required to be deposited in cash unless, and to the extent that, approved collateral is permitted by the Exchange under the rules of which the transaction is to be undertaken.

4.   Segregation

(1)   This rule applies only in relation to relevant margined transactions.

(2)   A firm shall ensure that, on each business day, the aggregate of the amounts described in paragraph (3) below as at the close of business on the immediately preceding business day (a negative balance in sub-paragraph (b) being deducted), is not less than the aggregate of all the firm's clients' required contributions (as defined in paragraph (4) below) as at the close of business on the immediately preceding business day; and the firm shall, if need be, comply with the requirements of this paragraph by utilising its own money or approved collateral.

(3)   The amounts referred to in paragraph (2) above are:-

(a)   the balance on the firm's client account in which is held margined client money in respect of relevant margined transactions or, if the firm maintains more than one client account, on all client accounts,

(b)   the net aggregate of the firm's equity balances with intermediate brokers (negative balances being deducted from positive balances),

(c)   the value of approved collateral deposited with the firm, whether held by it or by an intermediate broker for the firm's client account.

(4)   For the purposes of paragraph (2) above a 'client's required contribution' at any time is the greater of the following amounts:-

(a)   the amount of the client's initial margin requirement at that time, and

(b)   the aggregate of the client's equity balance at that time and the amount of the value of the approved collateral which the client deposited with the firm.

5.   Client's liabilities

(1)   This Rule applies only in relation to any relevant margined transactions unless it is a limited liability transaction.

(2)   If at the close of business on any day the amount of a client's initial margin requirement at that time exceeds the aggregate of that client's equity balance at that time and the amount of the value of that client's approved collateral at that time held by the firm or by an intermediate broker, the firm shall require the client to deposit with the firm, not later than the close of business on the next following business day, an amount in cash or approved collateral to a value not less than the amount of that excess.

(3)   Failure by any client to comply with a requirement made of him by the firm under paragraph (2) does not excuse the firm from complying with the requirements of Rule 3 above but, on failure by a client to comply with any such requirement made of him by the firm, the firm may close out that client's positions acquired under relevant margined transactions and shall do so if the client fails to comply with requirements made of him on five consecutive business days unless the firm is satisfied on reasonable grounds that the failure is due to temporary circumstances beyond the client's control and that action has been taken by him or on his behalf which will ensure that the requirement is met in full without further delay.

APPENDIX 9: INSTRUCTIONS TO PERMITTED THIRD PARTY WHERE MEMBER OF THE SECURITIES AND FUTURES AUTHORITY OR THE INVESTMENT MANAGEMENT REGULATORY ORGANISATION LIMITED

To: [Permitted Third Party]   [Date]

We [propose to give you instructions] [refer to our instructions given to you [   ]] on behalf of   ('the client') to [effect certain transactions in investments] [give investment advice] to the client.

Please confirm that in carrying out such instructions [and, until you receive from us written notification to the contrary, any subsequent instructions given by us on behalf of the client] [you will treat the client as your customer for the purposes of (the rules of IMRO) (all the conduct of business rules of the Securities and Futures Authority)].

[Firm]

[on copy]

To: [Firm] [Date]

We confirm that we will treat the customer as stated above.

[Permitted Third Party]

APPENDIX 10: BES INVESTMENTS

1. A firm shall not recommend any client to subscribe to a BES scheme or to subscribe for BES shares, otherwise than by means of an advertisement in accordance with Rule 8, except: -

(i) where the client:-

(a) is a sophisticated investor;

(b) is reasonably believed by the firm to be a client for whom investments which may be difficult to realise are suitable;

(c) is reasonably believed by the firm to have already invested directly or indirectly in BES shares; or

(d) without any solicitation by the firm, other than by means of a trailer advertisement, has sought advice from the firm about BES schemes and BES shares; and

(ii) where the firm has available for distribution (in the case of a BES scheme) copies of the scheme particulars or (in the case of an offer of BES shares other than a private offer) copies of the prospectus, together with an application form which will enable section 56 of the Companies Act 1985 to be complied with.

2. A firm shall not, whether in an advertisement or otherwise, publish or cause to be published to any person any forecast of the realisable value of an investment either directly or indirectly in BES shares or an illustration of what such realisable value might be on any particular assumption.

3. (a) A firm shall not lend money or extend credit to any person with a view to facilitating that person's subscribing to a BES scheme or subscribing for BES shares unless that person has, without solicitation, invited the firm to do so.

(b) A firm shall not enter into or procure any arrangements under which any person other than the firm will or may directly or indirectly facilitate any third person's subscribing to a BES scheme or subscribing for BES shares by the lending of money or the extending of credit except in relation to such third persons as have, without solicitation, sought to borrow money or obtain credit for that purpose.

APPENDIX 11: FORM MNP

Form MNP

Firm name ....

Address ....

....

We hereby give notice that investment business will be conducted by, or under the supervision of, ... [insert name of partner or director who is a registered foreign lawyer 'RFL']

Tick as appropriate

1.   The only such work to be undertaken
      will be company and commercial work.   [   ]

2.   Such work may involve advising
      clients on their personal finances,
      or trustees on appropriate investments.   [   ]

3.   Such work may involve discrete
      investment business.   [   ]

[If either box 2 or box 3 is ticked, please provide details of the basis on which the expertise of the RFL's involvement in that business is deemed to exist, and of the supervision arrangements, where appropriate, which will apply when that RFL is conducting or supervising that business. Please use a separate sheet.]

Date ....   Signature ....

Partner/Officer

Annex 26C

Securities and Investments Board — the Ten Principles

Additional guidance issued by the Law Society 2nd May 1990 (updated January 1993)

Under the Financial Services Act 1986 SIB are empowered to issue 'statements of principle with respect to the conduct and financial standing expected of persons authorised to carry on investment business'.

The first of these statements of principle is set out below. The principles came into force on 30th April 1990 and apply to all firms of solicitors which hold investment business certificates.

The following points should be noted:

* As solicitors are already subject to the stringent requirements of Rule 1 of the Solicitors' Practice Rules 1990 and the general principles of professional conduct set out in the Guide, it seems unlikely that the new principles promulgated by SIB impose any greater duty on solicitors than that which already exists.

* Where the requirements of a particular principle are less onerous than the existing standard of conduct expected of solicitors (e.g. in relation to principle 6 — conflicts of interest) then the higher standard of conduct will prevail.

* Principle 3 (market practice) is unlikely to be of significance to most solicitors. The reference to a 'code' is intended to relate to, e.g. the Takeover Code. The endorsement of the Takeover Code is presently under consideration by SIB.

* The combined effect of compliance with the Solicitors' Accounts Rules and the existence of the Solicitors Indemnity Fund and the Compensation Fund will be sufficient to ensure compliance with principle 8 (financial resources).

Statements of principle

This statement of principle was issued by SIB on 15th March 1990 under section 47A of (and, in relation to friendly societies, paragraph 13A of Schedule 11 to) the Financial Services Act 1986.

Introduction

1. These principles are intended to form a universal statement of the standards expected. They apply directly to the conduct of investment business and financial standing of all authorised persons ('firms'), including members of recognised

self-regulating organisations and firms certified by recognised professional bodies.

2.   The principles are not exhaustive of the standards expected. Conformity with the principles does not absolve a failure to observe other requirements, while the observance of other requirements does not necessarily amount to conformity with the principles.

3.   The principles do not give rise to actions for damages, but will be available for purposes of discipline and intervention.

4.   Where the principles refer to customers, they should be taken to refer also to clients and to potential customers, and where they refer to a firm's regulator, they mean SIB, or a self-regulating organisation or professional body which regulates the firm.

5.   Although the principles may be taken as expressing existing standards, they came into force formally, with additional sanctions resulting, on 30th April 1990.

The Principles

Integrity

1.   A firm should observe high standards of integrity and fair dealing.

Skill, care and diligence

2.   A firm should act with due skill, care and diligence.

Market practice

3.   A firm should observe high standards of market conduct. It should also, to the extent endorsed for the purpose of this principle, comply with any code or standard as in force from time to time and as it applies to the firm either according to its terms or by rulings made under it.

Information about customers

4.   A firm should seek from customers it advises or for whom it exercises discretion any information about their circumstances and investment objectives which might reasonably be expected to be relevant in enabling it to fulfil its responsibilities to them.

Information for customers

5.   A firm should take reasonable steps to give a customer it advises, in a comprehensible and timely way, any information needed to enable him to make a balanced and informed decision. A firm should similarly be ready to provide a customer with a full and fair account of the fulfilment of its responsibilities to him.

Conflicts of interests

6.   A firm should either avoid any conflict of interest arising or, where conflicts arise, should ensure fair treatment to all its customers by disclosure, internal rules of confidentiality, declining to act, or otherwise. A firm should not unfairly place its

interests above those of its customers and, where a properly informed customer would reasonably expect that the firm would place his interests above its own, the firm should live up to that expectation.

Customer assets

7.   Where a firm has control of, or is otherwise responsible for, assets belonging to a customer which it is required to safeguard, it should arrange proper protection for them, by way of segregation and identification of those assets or otherwise, in accordance with the responsibility it has accepted.

Financial resources

8.   A firm should ensure that it maintains adequate financial resources to meet its investment business commitments and to withstand the risks to which its business is subject.

Internal organisation

9.   A firm should organise and control its internal affairs in a responsible manner, keeping proper records, and where the firm employs staff or is responsible for the conduct of investment business by others, should have adequate arrangements to ensure that they are suitable, adequately trained and properly supervised and that it has well-defined compliance procedures.

Relations with regulators

10.   A firm should deal with its regulator in an open and co-operative manner and keep the regulator promptly informed of anything concerning the firm which might reasonably be expected to be disclosed to it.

Annex 26D

Financial Services (Conduct of Business) Rules 1990*

Part 7 — advertisements
(incorporating amendments to 20th June 1991)

Additional guidance issued by the Law Society

These rules, which were made by the Securities and Investments Board, are referred to in Rule 8(2)(a) of the Solicitors' Investment Business Rules 1990 (see Annex 26B). The 1990 Conduct of Business Rules replace the 1987 Conduct of Business Rules. Changes are of only minor consequence.

Definitions

The definitions found in the 1987 Rules are now in SIB's Glossary and Interpretation Rules and Regulations 1990. The relevant definitions are set out below:

'Image advertisement: means an advertisement which does no more than:

    (a)   promote public awareness of the advertiser;

    (b)   describe the services it provides or the products it markets;

    (c)   commend the advertiser in general, but not any particular service it provides or product it markets or,

    (d)   offer to supply further information on request.'

'Short form advertisement: means an advertisement which contains the advertiser's name and in respect of investment business otherwise does no more than some or all of:

    (a)   display the advertiser's
address
telephone number
symbol or logogram;

    (b)   describe the advertiser's
business
fees charged;

    (c)   contain one or both of a statement that, or a symbol approved by the Board to show that, the advertiser (or the firm approving the advertisement) is regulated in the conduct of investment business by the Board;

---

*   Reproduced by the kind permission of the Securities and Investments Board.

(d)   state, in relation to investments which the advertiser will or may buy or sell (or arrange to buy or sell)

their names

indicative prices

difference of prices from previous prices

their income and yields

their earnings (or price/earnings ratio);

(e)   state, simply as a matter of fact, and not so as to imply any offer to deal, that the advertiser, alone or with other names, arranged the issue of or a transaction in a particular investment.'

Transitional provisions

The following is an extract from Part 17 of SIB's Conduct of Business Rules 1990:

'17.03   Paragraph (3) of Rule 7.12 shall not come into operation until 1 March 1991.

17.04   (1) In relation to an advertisement issued before 1 July 1991 rule 7.23 shall have effect as if the following were added to paragraph (2):

"or

(d) an investment (other than one mentioned in sub-paragraph (a), (b) or (c)) which could lawfully have been the subject of an advertisement of the same description as an advertisement to which this rule applies issued in the United Kingdom before 29 April 1988"

and rules 7.24 to 7.26 shall not apply to an advertisement the issue of which is, by virtue of rule 7.23(2)(d), excluded from the prohibition contained in this rule.

(2) Nothing in this rule applies to an advertisement relating to futures, options, contracts for differences or rights to any of them.'

PART 7

Advertisements

7.01 Application

(1)   This Part of these rules applies to advertisements in respect of investment business other than:

a.   an advertisement which is excluded from paragraph (e) of section 48(2) of the Act by virtue of section 48(5) of the Act, and

b.   an advertisement which contains matter required or permitted to be published:

(i)   by or under any enactment, or

(ia)   by or under any provision of the law of a member State other than the United Kingdom corresponding to section 85 of the Act, or

(ii)   by an exchange which is:

(A) a recognised investment exchange,

(B) a designated investment exchange,

(C) an approved exchange under Part V of the Act,

and contains no other matter, and

c.   an advertisement offering any securities within the meaning of section 159(1) of the Act, an advertisement offering securities which is a primary or secondary offer within the meaning of section 160 of the Act and an advertisement offering securities which is exempted from sections 159 and 160 of the Act by virtue of section 161 of the Act, and

d.   an advertisement issued in such circumstances that it is unlikely that it will be communicated to persons who are neither business investors nor persons who carry on investment business.

Practice Note

The Board considers that a person within sub-paragraph (d) who by way of business passes on an advertisement which he receives as such will be issuing an advertisement and so is subject to section 57 of the Act and, if a firm, this Part of these rules.

(2)   Except where the context otherwise requires references in this Part of these rules to an advertisement are references to an advertisement to which this Part of these rules applies.

7.02 [Not used]

7.03 Issue of advertisements by a firm

A firm shall not issue an advertisement unless the requirements of this Part of these rules are complied with in relation to that advertisement.

7.04 Approval by a firm of advertisements issued by unauthorised persons

(1)   [Not used]

(2)   A firm shall not approve for the purposes of section 57 of the Act the contents of an investment advertisement to be issued or caused to be issued by a person who is not an authorised person unless the requirements of this rule are complied with in relation to that advertisement.

(3)   In the case of an advertisement which relates to a collective investment scheme the requirements of this rule are that:

a.   all the requirements of this Part of these rules are complied with in relation to the advertisement as if the unauthorised person were a firm, and

b.   if the approval is required for the purpose of the advertisement's being issued by an overseas person, that person is the operator of a regulated collective investment scheme and the advertisement relates to units in that scheme.

(4)   In the case of an advertisement which relates to a life policy the requirements of this rule are that:

a.   all the requirements of rule 5.11 (if applicable) and of this Part of these rules are complied with in relation to the advertisement as if the unauthorised person were a firm, and,

b.   if the life policy is to be issued by a life office which is an overseas person:

      (i)   that life office is one referred to in section 130(2)(c) or (d) of the Act, or

      (ii)   that life office is one referred to in section 130(3)(a) of the Act and the requirements of section 130(3) of the Act have been fulfilled.

(5)   In the case of an advertisement which does not relate to a collective investment scheme or to a life policy and is an image advertisement or a short form advertisement, the requirements of this rule are that all the requirements of this Part of these rules are complied with in relation to the advertisement as if the unauthorised person were a firm.

(6)   In the case of an advertisement which does not relate to a collective investment scheme or to a life policy and is not an image advertisement or a short form advertisement and is not an advertisement to which rule 7.23 applies, the requirements of this rule are:

a.   if the approval is required for the purpose of the advertisement's being issued by an overseas person who is an associate of the firm in circumstances in which the advertisement is not likely to be received by anyone other than an established customer with whom the firm or the associate has a continuing relationship governed by a written agreement, that the firm has no reason to believe that any matter in the advertisement is inaccurate, unfair or misleading, or

b.   if the approval is not required for the purpose and in the circumstances mentioned in sub-paragraph a.:

      (i)   that all the requirements of this Part of these rules are complied with in relation to the advertisement as if the unauthorised person were a firm, and

      (ii)   if the approval is required for the purpose of the advertisement's being issued by an overseas person:

           (A)   that the firm carries on in the United Kingdom in compliance with rule 2.01 (business plan) investment business which relates to investments of the same description as the investment the subject of the advertisement, and

           (B)   if the advertisement is a relevant publication within the meaning of Part 8 of these rules which will or may include recommendations to acquire investments which are not readily realisable, that the firm has reasonable grounds for believing that the issuer will not:

               (I)   give or send that publication to any person in the United Kingdom, or

               (II)   enter into any arrangement with any person in the United Kingdom or procure any such person to enter into any arrangement under which that person will be regularly given or sent issues of that publication,

              unless that person is a person whom the issuer believes, on the basis of such facts about his financial situation and competence in financial matters as may be expected to be relevant, to be a person for whom investments which are not readily realisable are suitable, and

(C)   that the firm has no reason to believe that the issuer of the advertisement will not treat responders to the advertisement honestly and fairly, and

(D)   that the advertisement contains warnings that rules and regulations made under the Act for the protection of investors do not apply to the issuer of the advertisement and that the Board's compensation scheme will not apply in relation to the investment the subject of the advertisement, and

(E)   except in the case of a tombstone, that the advertisement contains statements that the advertisement has been approved by the firm and that the firm is regulated in the conduct of its business by the Board.

7.04A Overseas insurers

(1)   This rule applies in the case of an advertisement which relates to life policies which is issued at a time when the insurer who is to issue the life policies is not authorised to carry on long term business in the United Kingdom of the class to which the advertisement relates by or under section 3 or 4 of the Insurance Companies Act 1982 and is not otherwise permitted to carry on long term business of that class in the United Kingdom.

(2)   A firm shall not issue an advertisement to which this rule applies unless the contents of the advertisement and the manner of its presentation are such that the advertisement would have complied with regulations 65 to 65C of the Insurance Companies Regulations 1981 (Statutory Instruments 1981 No.1654) as amended by the Insurance Companies (Advertisements) (Amendment) (No.2) Regulations 1983 (Statutory Instruments 1983 No.396) as those regulations had effect on 20 September 1990 as if they applied to the advertisement but subject to the amendment that, in regulation 65B there be inserted at the beginning of sub-paragraph (f) of paragraph (3) the following:

'except in a case where the insurer is authorised to effect or carry out contracts of insurance to which the advertisement relates in any country or territory which is for the time being designated for the purposes of section 130 of the Financial Services Act 1986 by an order made by the Secretary of State and where any conditions imposed by the order designating the country or territory have been satisfied'.

7.05 Prominence of required statements

The significance of any statement or other matter required by these rules to be included in an advertisement shall not be disguised either through lack of prominence in relation to the other matter in the advertisement or by the inclusion of matter calculated to minimise the significance of the statement.

7.06 Approval

(1)   A firm which issues an advertisement shall ensure that the advertisement is approved prior to its issue by an individual within the firm, or within a group of which the firm is a member, appointed for the purpose of this rule.

(2)   A firm shall not approve the contents of an advertisement in pursuance of rules 7.03 or 7.04 except through the agency of an individual within the firm, or within a group of which the firm is a member, appointed for the purpose of this rule.

Practice Note

In relation to a short form advertisement in the form of a screen price quotation service, the Board considers that an individual empowered by his firm to input its prices to the system might properly also be empowered to approve short form advertisements of that type.

7.07 Advertisements to be clear and not misleading

(1) The content of an advertisement and the manner of its presentation shall be such that the advertisement is not likely to be misunderstood by those to whom it is addressed including, if it be the case, persons who cannot be expected to have any special understanding of the matter in the advertisement.

(2) An advertisement shall not contain any statement, promise or forecast unless the firm issuing or approving the advertisement has taken all reasonable steps to satisfy itself that each such statement, promise or forecast is not misleading in the form or context in which it appears.

(3) An advertisement shall not contain any statement purporting to be a statement of fact which the firm issuing it does not reasonably believe at the time of issue, on the basis of evidence of which it has a record in its possession, to be true.

(4) An advertisement shall not contain any statement of fact which, although true when the advertisement is issued, the firm has reason to believe is likely to become untrue before the advertisement ceases to be current.

(5) An advertisement shall not state that any person is of any particular opinion unless the firm issuing or approving the advertisement has taken all reasonable steps to satisfy itself that the advertiser or other person, as the case may be, is of that opinion when the advertisement is issued.

(6) If the investment or service to which an advertisement relates is available in limited quantities, for a limited period or on special terms for a limited period the advertisement may say so but, if that is not the case, the advertisement shall not contain any statement or matter which implies that it is so.

7.08 Advertisements to be distinguished from other matter

(1) The terms of an advertisement and the manner of its presentation shall be such that it appears to be an advertisement issued with the object of promoting the investment, service or firm to which it relates.

(2) Where the medium in which the advertisement is carried contains or presents other matter, the advertisement shall be distinguished from that other matter so that what is an advertisement does not appear to be or to form part of a news item, report, bulletin, entertainment, instruction, story, drama, performance or other such means of communication.

Practice Note

The Board takes the view that an advertisement on a hoarding at a football ground would not contravene this rule but that an advertisement forming part of a dialogue of a televised drama would do so.

7.09 Advertisements to identify the investments or services to which they relate

Except in the case of a short form advertisement or an image advertisement, the nature of the investment or the services to which an advertisement relates shall be clearly described.

7.10 Promotions to be genuine

An advertisement shall not be issued with the intention not of persuading persons who respond to the advertisement to pursue the subject matter of the advertisement but instead of persuading them to enter into an investment agreement, or use financial services, of a description not mentioned in the advertisement.

7.11 Disclosure of advertiser's capacity

An advertisement which invites those to whom it is addressed to enter into an investment agreement with a named person shall:

a.   disclose, by statement or by necessary implication, whether it is proposed that the named person will enter into the agreement as a principal on his own account or as an agent for another person, and

b.   if the named person is to enter into the agreement as an agent for another person and that person can be identified when the advertisement is issued, state the name of that other person.

7.12 Identity of regulators

(1)   An advertisement which is not a short form advertisement or an image advertisement shall state:

a.   if the advertisement has been issued by a firm, that the person who has issued it is a person regulated by the Board, or

b.   if the advertisement has not been issued by an authorised person but has been approved by a firm, that the advertisement has been approved by a person regulated by the Board.

(2)   Where an advertisement offers the product or the services of a person other than the firm which has issued or approved it, the advertisement shall state:

a.   whether or not that other person is an authorised person, and

b.   if he is an authorised person:

(i)   the name of the body responsible for regulating his conduct of business, and

(ii)   the fact that the body is so responsible or, if it be the case, that that person is a member of that body, and

(iii) if it be the case that that body regulates the conduct of that person on an interim basis only that that person has applied to that body:

And any statement in an advertisement that that person has applied to a body responsible for regulating the conduct of that person's business shall be accompanied by the words "Not covered by The Investors' Compensation Scheme" and may be accompanied by a statement that that person is interim authorised.

(3)   An advertisement which is not an advertisement in respect of investment business shall not contain any matter referring to the Board.

7.13 Advertisements not to imply government approval

(1)   Subject to paragraphs (2) and (3) an advertisement shall not contain any matter which states or implies that the investment the subject of the advertisement or any matter in the advertisement has the approval of any Government department or of the Board.

(2)   This rule does not prohibit the issue of an advertisement which contains or advertises an offer for sale of investments owned by Her Majesty's Government.

(3)   Where the investment the subject of an advertisement is recognised by the Inland Revenue for the purpose of qualifying those who acquire the investment for any reliefs from taxation, the advertisement may refer to that recognition.

7.14 Synopses to be fair

An advertisement which states some only of the rights and obligations attaching to an investment or some only of the terms and conditions of an investment agreement shall:

a.   state sufficient of them to give a fair view of the nature of the investment or of the investment agreement, of the financial commitment undertaken by an investor in acquiring the investment or in entering into the agreement and of the risks involved, and

b.   state how a written statement of all of them can be obtained.

7.15 Commendations

An advertisement may include a quotation from a statement made by any person commending an investment or service if and only if:

a.   where that person is an employee or associate of the firm, that fact is disclosed in the advertisement, and

b.   the quotation is included with that person's consent, and

c.   the statement is relevant to the investment or service which is the subject of the advertisement, and

d.   where the whole of the statement is not quoted, what is quoted represents fairly the message contained in the whole of the statement, and

e.   the statement has not become inaccurate or misleading through the passage of time since it was made.

7.16 Comparison with other investments

(1)   An advertisement shall not compare or contrast:

a.   an investment with an alternative application of an investor's funds, or

b.   a service or a provider of a service or of an investment with an alternative service or provider,

unless the comparisons and contrasts are fair in relation to what is promoted and to the alternative having regard to what is not stated as well as to what is stated.

Practice Note

The Board considers that it would be a breach of this rule:

a.   *to omit a feature of possible comparison or contrast so as to exaggerate the significance of what is included, or*

b.   *to misrepresent or unfairly to criticise the alternative or the person who offers it.*

(1A)   An advertisement of units in a regulated collective scheme shall not compare or contrast the performance or the likely performance of an investment in units of the scheme with an investment in a collective investment scheme which is not a regulated collective investment scheme.

(2)   Without prejudice to the generality of paragraph (1) if, in the case of an advertisement of units in a collective investment scheme or in a unit linked life policy, comparison is made between the performance of an investment in those units over a period of time with the performance of an alternative application of the investor's funds over the same period of time, the comparison shall be on an offer to bid basis, that is to say, on the basis of what it would have cost to acquire an amount of the investment and the alternative at the beginning of the period and what a disposal of that amount of the investment and the alternative would have realised at the end of the period, and the fact that that is the basis of the comparison shall be stated.

(3)   Without prejudice to the generality of paragraph (1) if, in the case of an advertisement of units in a collective investment scheme or in a unit linked life policy, comparison is made between the performance of an investment in those units over a period of time with the performance of an index over the same period of time, the comparison shall be on whatever basis is consistent with the basis on which the index is constructed, and the fact that that is the basis of the comparison shall be stated.

7.17 Life policies

(1)   The requirements of this Part of these rules apply to an advertisement relating to a life policy in addition to the requirements of rule 5.11 which rule applies in the case of an advertisement as it applies in the case of publications generally.

(2)   An advertisement relating to a life policy which gives particulars of any of the benefits payable under the policy shall state:

a.   which of the benefits under the contract (if any) are of fixed amounts and what those amounts are, and

b.   which of them (if any) are not of fixed amounts.

(3)   Such an advertisement may describe a benefit of a fixed amount or a minimum amount of a variable benefit as a 'guaranteed' amount but, if it does so and the advertisement refers to the participation of a third party and that third party will not stand as surety for the life office should the life office not meet its obligations, the advertisement shall not contain any matter which implies that the third party will so stand as surety.

Practice Note   :

An example of a breach of this rule would be the following: an advertisement of a life policy, the benefits under which are linked to the performance of a fund held by a third party as trustee but not as a guarantor, states that certain benefits are 'guaranteed' without also stating that the trustee is not the guarantor of the obligations of the insurance company.

7.18 Taxation

(1) An advertisement which refers to taxation shall contain a warning that the levels and bases of taxation can change.

(2) An advertisement which contains any matter based on an assumed rate of taxation shall state what that rate is.

(3) An advertisement which refers to reliefs from taxation:

    a.   shall state that the reliefs are those which currently apply, and

    b.   shall contain a statement that the value of a relief from taxation depends upon the circumstances of the taxpayer.

(4) An advertisement which relates to an investment the income from which:

    a.   is payable out of a fund the income of which has already been taxed, and

    b.   is not or may not be subject to income tax in the hands of the investor,

shall not describe the investment as one free from liability to income tax unless the fact that the income is payable out of a fund from which income tax has already been paid is stated with equal prominence.

(5) An advertisement which relates to an investment in whose case:-

    a.   an investor will not be liable to taxation on realised capital gains in the investment, and

    b.   any realised capital gains of the assets of a fund to which the value of the investments is linked are subject to taxation,

shall not describe the investment as one free from liability to capital gains taxation unless the fact that the value of the investment is linked to a fund which will be liable to taxation on realised capital gains in the assets of which it is comprised is stated with equal prominence.

(6) An advertisement which refers to reliefs from taxation shall distinguish between reliefs which apply directly to investors and those which apply to the issuer of the investment or to a fund in which the investor participates.

7.19 Cancellation rights

An advertisement may state (if it be the case) that an investor who enters into an investment agreement to which the advertisement relates will be given an opportunity to cancel the agreement but, if it does so, the advertisement shall state:

a.   the period during which the investor will have that right and the time when that period will begin, and

b.   (if it be the case) that the right to cancel is conferred by law, and

c.   if upon cancellation the investor will not recover his investment in full should the market have fallen since the investment was acquired:

    (i)   that fact, and

    (ii)   if the advertisement is an advertisement of a higher volatility investment, notice that the shortfall in what he recovers should the market have fallen could be very high because of the possibility of sudden and large falls in the value of the units.

7.20 Past performance

An advertisement shall not contain information about the past performance of investments of any description unless:

a.   it is relevant to the performance of the investment the subject of the advertisement, and

b.   except where the source of the information is the advertiser itself, the source of the information is stated, and

bb.   in the case of an advertisement of a higher volatility investment, information is given for the period of five years ending with the date on which the advertisement is approved for issue and beginning five years before that date or, if the fund came into existence less than five years before that date, beginning when the fund came into existence, and

c.   if the whole of the information is not set out:

    (i)   what is included is not unrepresentative, unfair or otherwise misleading, and

    (ii)   the exclusion of what is excluded does not have the effect of exaggerating the success of performance over the period to which the information which is included relates, and

d.   if the information is presented in the form of a graph or chart, no part of the information is omitted so as to give a misleading impression of the rate at which variable quantities have changed, and

e.   in the case of an advertisement of units in a collective investment scheme or in a unit linked life policy, any comparison made between the value of an investment in those units at different times is on an offer to bid basis, that is to say, on the basis of what it would have cost to acquire an amount of the units at the earlier time and what a disposal of that amount of those units would have realised at the later time, and the fact that that is the basis of the comparison is stated, and

f.   the advertisement contains a warning that the past is not necessarily a guide to the future.

Practice Note

The Board considers that a unit trust manager could commit a breach of this rule if it were to issue an advertisement which:

a.   advertised all or a number of its funds, and

b.   either:-

    (i)   claimed notable successes for some of those funds without indicating that it was some only of those funds which had attained those levels of success, or

    (ii)   chose to show only an unrepresentative few months of performance.

7.21 Indications of the scale of business activities

An advertisement shall not contain any statement indicating the scale of the activities or the extent of the resources of a person who carries on investment business, or of any group of which such a person is a member, so as to imply that the resources available to support performance of the firm's obligations are greater than they are.

Practice Note

The Board would regard the following as breaches of this rule:

(1) An advertisement which states the amount of the authorised share capital of a company but does not also state the amount of the issued share capital of that company.

(2) An advertisement which states the amount of a company's issued share capital but does not also state how much of that capital has been paid up.

(3) An advertisement which states the amount of a company's total assets but does not also state the amount of the company's liabilities.

(4) An advertisement which states the amount of a company's income or turnover but does not state the period to which that amount relates.

(5) An advertisement which refers to a subsidiary in a group and which mentions the amount of the capital or of the assets of the group as a whole so as to imply that they are resources on which the subsidiary can draw when that is not the case.

(6) An advertisement which states the amount of funds under a firm's management in such a way as to imply that those funds are assets of the firm.

7.22 Risk warnings

(1) This rule applies to any advertisement which is not:

    a.   a short form advertisement, or

    b.   an image advertisement.

(2) An advertisement to which this rule applies shall contain a statement or statements in accordance with this rule warning of the risks involved in acquiring or holding the investment the subject of the advertisement.

(3) Where the advertisement relates to an investment in the case of which deductions for charges and expenses are not made uniformly throughout the life of the investment but are loaded disproportionately onto the early years, the advertisement shall draw attention to that fact and that accordingly, if the investor withdraws from the investment in the early years, he may not get back the amount he has invested.

(4) Where the advertisement relates to an investment which can fluctuate in value in money terms, the statement shall draw attention to that fact and to the fact that the investor may not get back the whole of what he has invested and, where the advertisement is an advertisement of a higher volatility investment, the statement shall draw attention to the possibility of sudden and large falls in the value of the units and to the fact that the investor may lose the whole of his investment.

(5) Where the advertisement offers an investment as likely to yield a high income or as suitable for an investor particularly seeking income from his investment, the

statement shall draw attention to the fact that income from the investment may fluctuate in value in money terms.

(6)   Where the advertisement relates to an investment denominated in a currency other than that of the country in which the advertisement is issued, the advertisement shall draw attention to the fact that changes in rates of exchange between currencies may cause the value of the investment to diminish or to increase.

(7)   Where the advertisement relates to a with profits life policy, that statement shall draw attention to the fact that the return on the investment depends on what profits are made and on what decisions are made by the life office as to their distribution.

(8)   Where the advertisement contemplates the customer entering into a transaction the nature of which is such that the customer may not only lose what he pays at the outset but may incur a liability to pay unspecified additional amounts later, the statement shall draw attention to the fact that the investor may or, as the case may be, will have to pay more money later and that accordingly a transaction in that investment can lose the investor more than his first payment.

(9)   Where the advertisement relates to a margined transaction which is not a limited liability transaction and which will or may be effected otherwise than on a recognised or designated investment exchange and in a contract of a type traded thereon, the advertisement shall draw attention to the fact that the transaction is only suitable for a person who has experience in transactions of that description:

But this does not apply in the case of an advertisement which advertises the services of an execution-only dealer.

Practice Note

This rule should be read in conjunction with rule 9.11(1)b.(iii) below.

(10) Where the advertisement relates to an investment which is not readily realisable:

a.   if the investment is not traded on a recognised or designated investment exchange, the statement shall draw attention to the fact that there is no recognised market for the investment so that it may be difficult for the investor to sell the investment or for him to obtain reliable information about its value or the extent of the risks to which it is exposed, or

b.   if the investment is traded on a recognised or designated investment exchange but is dealt in so irregularly or infrequently:

(i)   that it cannot be certain that a price for that investment will be quoted at all times, or

(ii)   that it may be difficult to effect transactions at any price which may be quoted, and

the statement shall draw attention to that fact or those facts, as the case may be, and, if there are less than three market makers in that investment or the firm which has issued the advertisement is the only market maker in that investment, the statement shall draw attention to that or to those facts, as the case may be.

Practice Note

Examples of investments contemplated by paragraph (10)b. of this rule might be investments which are classified by The Stock Exchange as 'delta' or 'gamma' stocks and 'off-the-run' bonds which have been in issue for a long time.

(11) Where the advertisement relates to units:

    a.   in a property fund, or

    b.   in a constituent part of an umbrella fund which, if that part were a separate fund, would be a property fund, or

    c.   in a fund of funds in the case of which one of the schemes to which it is dedicated is a property fund,

the statement shall draw attention:

    (i)   to the fact that land and buildings may at times be difficult to sell so that there may be periods during which the operator will have the right to refuse to repurchase units offered to him for redemption, and

    (ii)   to the fact that a valuation of land and buildings has to be the judgement of an individual valuer.

(12) Where the advertisement is of a life policy and refers to benefits under the policy which are measured by reference to the value of, to fluctuations in the value of or to income from land or any interest in land, the statement shall draw attention:

    (i)   to the fact that the assets to which the benefits under the policy are linked may at times be difficult to sell so that there may be periods during which the life office will be unable to accept surrenders of the policy, and

    (ii)   to the fact that a valuation of land and buildings has to be the judgement of an individual valuer.

(13) Where the advertisement relates to units in a regulated collective investment scheme, and at the time when the advertisement is prepared for issue, the property of the scheme consists, or there is an expectation that the property of the scheme may consist, as to more than 35% thereof in Government and other public securities issued by one issuer, the statement shall include reference to that fact or, as the case may be, to that expectation and shall identify that issuer.

7.22A   [Revoked]

7.23 General duty of disclosure in 'off-the-page' and 'off-the-screen' advertisements

(1) Subject to paragraph (1A) this rule applies to an advertisement containing:

    a.   an offer to enter into an investment agreement with a person who responds to the advertisement, or

    b.   an invitation to a person to respond to the advertisement by making an offer to enter into an investment agreement, and

in either case, specifying the manner in which that response is invited to be made.

(1A) This rule does not apply to an advertisement if:

    a.   the investment agreement the subject of the advertisement is an agreement for the supply of a publication to which Part 8 of these rules applies, or

    b.   the investment agreement the subject of the advertisement is an agreement for the acquisition or disposal of shares, debentures, warrants, options or other securities of a company or of an interest in the securities of a company and the advertisement contains:

(i)   all such information as investors and their professional advisers would reasonably require, and reasonably expect to find there, for the purpose of making an informed assessment of:

(A)   the assets and liabilities, financial position, profits and losses, and prospects of the issuer of the securities, and

(B)   the rights attaching to those securities, and

(ii)   no other matter.

(2)   An advertisement to which this rule applies may not be issued if the investment agreement the subject of the advertisement is an agreement for the provision of the services of a portfolio manager or investor broker fund adviser or if it relates to an investment other than:

a.   a life policy, or

b.   units in a regulated collective investment scheme, or

c.   a type A or a type B PEP.

(3)   A firm shall not issue an advertisement to which this rule applies if the advertisement contains any matter likely to lead to the supposition that the investment agreement the subject of the advertisement is or is thought to be suitable for a particular individual who is the recipient of the advertisement.

Practice Note

This rule constrains the issuer of personalised circulars to refrain from implying that he knows a recipient sufficiently well to be sure that the investment is suitable. The rule is not intended to constrain the content of letters to individuals whom the firm writing the letter does know.

(4)   A firm shall not issue an advertisement to which this rule applies unless the advertisement is contained in a printed document or is otherwise capable of being examined continuously for a reasonable period of time.

7.24 'Off-the-page' advertisements for life policies

A firm shall not issue an advertisement to which rule 7.23 applies which relates to a life policy unless the advertisement contains statements of the matters specified for the purpose in relation to the investment agreement the subject of the advertisement in Appendix D to Part 5 of these rules and gives information about the following matters:

a.   any minimum to the amount which may be invested or paid regularly, and

b.   if regular amounts are invited to be invested, what those amounts may be, and

c.   how and where full details of the policy may be obtained, and

d.   if any of the benefits under the policy are 'linked benefits' within the meaning of Appendix D to this Part of these rules:-

(i)   where prices of the units to which the benefits are linked and the yields of those units may be obtained, and

(ii)   the most recent difference between the bid and offer prices of the units as a percentage of the maximum offer price and the maximum permitted such differences or, if there is no such maximum, the discretion available to the life office to vary the difference, and

     (iii)   the current price at which units will be allocated to the policy and the basis on which units will be allocated on payment of premiums, and

     (iv)   any arrangements under which the investor may make regular withdrawals from the amount of his investment, and

     (v)   what periodic information will be sent to the investor and at what intervals, and

e.   what rights the investor will have to cancel any agreement he enters into in response to the advertisement and whether those rights derive from rules made by the Board under section 51 of the Act or are granted by the life office voluntarily.

7.25 'Off-the-page' advertisements for regulated collective investment schemes

(1)   A firm shall not issue an advertisement to which rule 7.23 applies which relates to units in a regulated collective investment scheme (including a type C PEP) unless:

   a.   the advertisement contains information about the following matters:

     (i)   any minimum amount below which any one person may not invest in the scheme, and

     (ii)   if regular amounts are invited to be invested in the scheme, what those amounts may be, and

     (iii)   a statement of the investment objectives of the scheme and of any policies which the operator of the scheme proposes to adopt in selecting the investments in which the funds of the scheme will be invested, and

Practice Note

The Board considers that sub-paragraph (iii) requires the advertisement to disclose any sectoral, geographical or other restrictions on the investments which may be made, for example, that the trust will be invested as to X per cent in Japanese high technology small companies.

     (iv)   the most recent difference between the bid and offer prices of the units expressed as a percentage of the maximum offer price and the maximum permitted such difference or, if there is no such maximum, the discretion available to the operator of the scheme to vary the difference, and

     (v)   in the case of a lump sum investment, the price at which units will be issued or, if this price is not fixed at the time of the issue of the advertisement, the basis for determining that price, and

     (vi)   in the case of a series of payments, the basis for determining the price at which units will be issued, and

     (vii)   the nature and amount or rate of the charges which will be made to the customer and what discretion the operator of the scheme has to vary these (including charges which are included in the price at which units are issued), and

     (viii)   what the annual gross yield is expected to be in the future on the basis of the most recent price or the price at which units are to be issued, and

     (ix)   where information about current prices of units and the most recent yield or the anticipated future yields may be seen or obtained, and

(x)   if an investor may authorise the income due to him to be reinvested in the scheme, that fact and how the income will or may be reinvested, and

(xi)   the name of the trustee or custodian (if any), and

(xii)   if an application will not be acknowledged, that fact, and

(xiii) when certificates will be sent to the investor, and

(xiv)   the frequency with which the property of the scheme is valued for the purposes of determining the issue and redemption prices of units and when the operator of the scheme will be available and willing to deal in those units, and

(xv)   how units may be redeemed and when payments on redemption will be made, and

(xvi)   details of any arrangements under which an investor may make regular withdrawals from the amount of his investment in the scheme, and

(xvii) when statements of the value of a person's investment in the scheme will be sent to him, and

(xviii) where and how copies of the scheme particulars may be obtained, and

b.   except where it relates to a type C PEP, the advertisement contains a statement that a person entering into an investment agreement in consequence of a response to the advertisement will not have a right to cancel the agreement under rules made by the Board under section 51 of the Act, and

bb.   if any commission is or will be payable by or on behalf of the operator of the scheme or an associate of the operator (assuming for the purpose of this reference to an associate that the operator, if not a firm, is a firm) in connection with the transaction to any person other than a person who is not independent of the operator:

(i)   the fact that commission will be so paid, and

(ii)   the identity of the person to whom commission will be paid to the extentthat that identity is known when the advertisement is issued, and

(iii)   particulars of the amounts of the commission in accordance with paragraph (2)b. of item 15 (Commissions) in Section 2 of Appendix D to this Part of these rules in the appropriate form referred to in paragraph (3) of that item:

but any of the matter specified above under (iii) may be omitted, and

c.   in the case of a type C PEP, its terms do not give authority to anyone to make unsolicited calls upon the investor:

But the statement required by paragraph b. may be omitted if the firm provides such a right as is referred to therein voluntarily.

(2) The requirements of paragraph (1) in the case of a type C PEP are in addition to the requirements of Part 4 of these rules as to the contents of a customer agreement.

(2A) Paragraph (2B) applies in the case of an advertisement:

    a.   to which rule 7.23 applies, and

    b.   which relates to a type C PEP under the terms of which the plan investor's cash subscriptions will or may be invested in the units of four or more authorised unit trust schemes, and

    c.   which contains no offer which a responder may accept but only an invitation to make an offer.

(2B) An advertisement to which this paragraph applies need comply with sub-sub-paragraphs (iii), (vii) and (viii) of sub-paragraph a. of paragraph (1).

(2C) Before a firm accepts any offer which it receives in response to an advertisement to which paragraph (2B) applies and which complies with sub-sub-paragraphs (iii), (vii) and (viii) only of sub-paragraph a. of paragraph (1), the firm shall carry out the procedures specified in (A) of rule 4.12(2)b.(ii).

(3)   In the case of an advertisement of units in an umbrella fund within the meaning of the Authorised Unit Trust Scheme (Investment and Borrowing Powers) Regulations 1988 (S.I. 1988 No.284) which contains an offer or an invitation to make an offer which is confined to a particular constituent part of the umbrella fund, it shall be a sufficient compliance with the requirements of heads (iii) to (viii) and (xiv) of sub-paragraph a. of paragraph (1) if particulars are given only in relation to that constituent part.

7.26 'Off-the-page' advertisements for type B PEPs

(1)   A firm shall not issue an advertisement to which rule 7.23 applies which relates to a type B PEP unless the terms of the type B PEP the subject of the advertisement do not give any authority to anyone to make unsolicited calls upon the investor.

(2)   The requirements of paragraph (1) are in addition to the requirements of Part 4 of these rules as to the contents of a customer agreement.

7.27 Restrictions on promotion of unregulated collective investment schemes

A firm shall not issue or cause to be issued an advertisement containing any matter which invites any person to become or offer to become a participant in a collective investment scheme which is not a regulated collective investment scheme or contains information calculated to lead directly or indirectly to any person becoming or offering to become a participant in such a scheme unless the issue of the advertisement does not contravene sub-section (1) of section 76 of the Act by virtue of sub-section (2), (3) or (4) of that section.

Practice Note

In relation to an advertisement issued or caused to be issued by a firm, this rule merely restates what is already an obligation under section 76(1) of the Act, but the rule has effect, by virtue of section 58(1)(c) of the Act, in relation to advertisements issued or caused to be issued by a national of a member State other than the United Kingdom in the course of investment business lawfully carried on by him in such a State.

7.28 Advertisements by appointed representatives

(1) A firm which is a collective investment marketing firm shall ensure that an advertisement issued by an appointed representative of the firm (other than an image advertisement or a short form advertisement):

    a. does not contain any statement commending the principal or its services or products in such a way as to suggest or imply that the appointed representative was free to exercise independent judgement in deciding to make the commendation, and

    b. contains a prominent statement, no less prominent than any other statement describing the relationship between the advertiser and the firm which draws attention to:

        (i) the fact that the advertiser is an appointed representative of the firm, and

        (ii) the fact that the advertiser has entered into arrangements with the firm which preclude the advertiser from selling or recommending any products other than those of the firm, and

    c. if the advertisement relates to a product of the firm, is not cast in terms which suggest or imply that the product is that of the appointed representative and not that of the firm.

(2) A firm which is a collective investment marketing firm shall ensure that, in an advertisement issued by an appointed representative of the firm which relates to any activitiy of the appointed representative which is not investment business as well as to an activity of the appointed representative which is investment business, any claim made to independence in respect of the activity which is not investment business does not appear with such prominence relative to the matter in the advertisement which relates to investment business as to create a likelihood that a person reasonably attentive to the advertisement might suppose that the claim to independence applied to the activity of the appointed representative which is investment business.

(3) A firm which is a collective investment marketing firm shall ensure that an advertisement issued by an appointed representative of the firm which is not an advertisement in respect of investment business does not contain any matter referring to the Board or to the fact that the advertiser is connected with a person who is regulated by the Board.

7.29 Advertisements not to disguise lack of independence

(1) A firm which is not a collective investment marketing firm and which has an associate which is:

    a. a collective investment marketing firm, or

    b. an appointed representative of a collective investment marketing firm,

shall not issue an advertisement of the products or services of the firm in such manner or containing such matter as is likely to cause a reader of the advertisement in its context to suppose that the associate has the same independence as that of the firm.

(2)   A firm which is a collective investment marketing firm and which has an appointed representative which is an associate of a person who is not a collective investment marketing firm shall ensure that no advertisement of the products or services of the firm is issued by the appointed representative in such manner or containing such matter as is likely to cause a reader of the advertisement in its context to suppose that the firm has the same independence as that of the said person who is not a collective investment marketing firm.

(3)   A firm which is a collective investment marketing firm and which has an associate which is not a collective investment marketing firm shall not issue an advertisement of the products or services of the firm in such manner or containing such matter as is likely to cause a reader of the advertisement in its context to suppose that the firm has the same independence as that of the associate.

Practice Note

The Board considers the following to be an example of a breach of this rule. The issue of an advertisement of the services of financial adviser X (the appointed representative of life office Y) in a brochure which advertises the services generally of firm Z (an independent financial adviser) without special mention of the status of X and so to give the impression that X has the same independence as Z. This would be particularly so if X and Z, being associates, have similar names.

Annex 26E

Council guidance — private client letter

settled by the Council for the purposes of Rule 10(5) of the Solicitors' Investment Business Rules 1990

[on firm's headed notepaper]

Dear [Client],

This statement is given pursuant and subject to the Solicitors' Investment Business Rules 1990 ('the Rules') and sets out the terms on which we have agreed to provide the services described below. If you have any queries or wish us to amend anything in this statement, please let us know as soon as possible.

1. Our services

The services to be provided to you are [giving investment advice in relation to] [and effecting transactions in]

[(a) shares or debt securities normally traded on reputable exchanges, in the U.K. or overseas, and]

[(b) units in regulated collective investment schemes (such as authorised unit trusts)]

We will not recommend or effect the purchase of shares or debt securities which are difficult to realise or where proper information for determining their current value may not be available.

If you wish to restrict these types of investment further please let us know in writing as soon as possible.

2. Your investment objectives

We understand that your investment objectives are:

*   high income with due consideration to the safety of your capital
*   a balanced return between income and capital growth
*   capital growth combined with a reasonable level of capital safety
*   a high level of capital growth at the possible risk of the safety of your capital
*   other defined investment objectives as follows:

[Firm to delete/complete as appropriate]

THE GUIDE TO THE PROFESSIONAL CONDUCT OF SOLICITORS 1993

3.   Basis of dealing for unit trusts

Once we have bought units in regulated collective investment schemes in accordance with your instructions, you will not have any right under the Financial Services (Cancellation) Rules 1989 to cancel the transaction.

4.   Unsolicited calls

We may call you, without you asking us to do so, in relation to any investments to which this statement applies.

[Firm to delete this paragraph if it does not apply]

5.   Fees

You will pay us fees for our services under this statement

*in accordance with the Solicitors' Remuneration Order 1972

*on the following basis:

[Firm to complete/delete as appropriate]

6.   Your money

[In accordance with your instructions, we may hold your money in a client bank account outside the U.K.]

[This may only be included if, in accordance with R.9(2)(a) of the Solicitors' Accounts Rules 1986, the client's instructions have been given for his own convenience]

7.   Your investments

All registrable investments purchased through us will be registered in your name [at the following address*] and certificates will be [sent to you] [retained by us], unless you give us written instructions to the contrary.

[Firm to complete/delete as appropriate]

[*optional]

8.   Variation and termination

These arrangements may be amended by mutual agreement in writing.

Either of us may terminate these arrangements by written notice at any time. Any such termination will be without prejudice to all rights and obligations accrued prior to such termination.

Yours [faithfully]

Annex 26F

Council guidance — Corporate finance activities

1. Introduction

1.1 The Society has received a number of inquiries as to how the Solicitors' Investment Business Rules (SIBR) apply to so-called 'corporate finance activities'. The commonest inquiry relates to the situation where a firm advises a client who is a principal shareholder and director of a family company which is to be sold to a third party. The first concern is whether the firm can become involved in the negotiation of the deal without engaging in discrete investment business. The second is whether it can express views directly or indirectly to the client about the adequacy of the price or other business or financial aspects of the deal without engaging in discrete investment business.

1.2 The answers to these inquiries depend not only on the terms of the SIBR but upon those of the Financial Services Act. There are three distinct questions:

(1) Is the firm's activity capable of constituting investment business under the Financial Services Act? This depends on whether it falls within Part II of Schedule 1.

(2) If so, is the activity exempted from the statutory definition of investment business as falling within one of the 'Excluded Activities' in Part III of Schedule 1?

(3) If the activity is capable of being investment business under the Act and is not excluded from the definition, then is it discrete investment business for the purposes of the SIBR? In the context of corporate finance activities, this will depend on whether the activity is 'incidental'. If it is 'incidental' then it is not discrete investment business.

1.3 It is the Council's view (which has been confirmed by leading counsel) that firms engaged in this sort of work will frequently be carrying on investment business. However, except in unusual situations, they will not be carrying on discrete investment business. Accordingly Chapter 4 of the SIBR (Conduct of Business) is unlikely to apply to such activities.

2. The position under the Act

2.1 It is not every involvement in a deal or every kind of advice about it which is affected by the Act. The application of the Act depends on the exact nature of the services provided. However, a solicitor who himself negotiates the deal or gives advice not only about its legal aspects but about the business or other financial considerations, will frequently be carrying on an activity within Part II of Schedule 1 to the Act. The relevant headings are 'Arranging deals in Investments' (paragraph 13) and 'Investment Advice' (paragraph 15). In these cases the question whether the Act applies therefore depends upon the ambit of its exceptions.

2.2 The exception for sales of companies

There is an exception in paragraph 21 of Schedule 1 to the Act (as amended) which may be applicable. Under that exception paragraphs 12, 13 and 15 of Schedule 1 do not apply to the sale or purchase of any company (other than an open-ended investment company) where the shares being sold carry 75% or more of the voting rights or where those shares, together with shares already held by the purchaser, carry not less than that percentage. However, it is a condition of the exemption that both the vendors and the purchasers fall into one of the following categories:

— a body corporate

— a partnership

— a single individual or

— a group of connected individuals (as defined)

It is not necessary that the vendors should fall into the same category as the purchasers. However, all the vendors must fall into one category and all the purchasers must fall into one category. Thus the sale of a typical family company to a corporate purchaser will qualify for exemption only if the vendors are 'a group of connected individuals'. This will often not be the case.

2.3 The exception for 'necessary activities'

Paragraph 24 of Schedule 1 (as amended) contains an exemption applicable to arranging deals and investment advice. Like all exemptions in Part III of the Schedule it arises only if the activity in question constitutes 'arranging deals' or giving 'investment advice' as those activities are defined in Part II: see paragraph 2.1 of this note. The activity is exempted if the arranging is done or the advice is given in the course of carrying on a profession not otherwise constituting investment business and is a *necessary* part of the other advice or services given in the course of carrying on that profession. The operation of the exemption will depend upon the particular facts of each case. The variety of possible facts and the uncertain ambit of the exception mean that it would be unwise for any solicitor who engages in corporate finance activities to place undue reliance upon it. It is the view of the Council (and of leading counsel) that 'arranging deals' and giving 'investment advice' in the course of such activities is unlikely to be a 'necessary' part of other advice or services given by a solicitor in the course of his profession. The reason is that in almost every case the solicitor will be instructed because he is a provider of legal services. In very many cases it will be convenient for the firm also to undertake negotiation and investment advice, and instructions to do so will accordingly be given either expressly or by implication. But although convenient, it will not be 'necessary' (in the sense meant by the Act) for the firm to perform these activities even if such instructions are given and accepted. This is because the firm can provide the legal services for which it is primarily retained and which constitute the essence of a solicitor's profession without doing so.

2.4   It is an additional condition of the exemption for necessary activities that the activity in question should not be remunerated separately from other activities. Separate remuneration in such circumstances would be unusual. This condition is therefore unlikely to cause a problem.

3.   The position under the SIBR

3.1   Many firms may find themselves in the position where the arrangements made or advice given by them do not fall within one of the statutory exemptions in all respects, or where it is unclear whether they do. This does not mean that the work which is carried out will necessarily be 'discrete investment business' for the purposes of the SIBR. The reason is that the exclusion of a solicitor's investment business from Chapter 4 (Conduct of Business) of the SIBR depends not upon its being a 'necessary' part of the professional activities for which he is primarily employed, but upon its being 'incidental' to them, which is a wider test.

3.2   The Rules provide that an activity is incidental 'if it is carried out in the course of providing other services provided by the firm in the course of carrying on the profession of a solicitor (being services which do not themselves constitute discrete investment business) and is subordinate to the main purpose for which those services are provided'. To decide what is incidental it is therefore necessary to decide what is the main purpose of the other services provided and whether the other services are themselves discrete investment business.

3.3   In the view of the Council (and of leading counsel) the main purpose for which a solicitor's services are provided is to make available to the client the solicitor's knowledge of the law and his expertise in activities (such as drafting or dealing with regulatory or other quasi legal bodies) for which a specifically legal expertise is required. A client will normally choose a solicitor (as opposed to some other professional person) for that reason. The negotiation of the deal may be particularly important to the client. His choice of a *particular* solicitor may well be influenced by the fact that that solicitor possesses other skills also, such as a special expertise in negotiation. Nevertheless, in the great majority of cases, it is the legal qualification of the solicitor which has led to his employment. His other skills are desirable but subordinate.

3.4   When the SIBR were being drafted some suggested that where a firm was involved in arranging a deal or was instructed, inter alia, to negotiate its terms, the 'incidental' exemption would not apply because, in effect, the main purpose of the services provided by the solicitor was 'arranging deals in investments', his legal advice being incidental to that activity rather than the other way round. As a result, it was suggested, the arranging or advising function could not be regarded as subordinate to an activity which did not constitute discrete investment business. The Council's view (which leading counsel has confirmed) is that for the reasons given above this is not correct.

3.5   As regards advice on the price or other business or financial aspects of the deal, the answer is similar. If the solicitor gives that advice in the course of his services as a solicitor, the exemption should apply.

3.6   It is therefore the Council's view that in most cases the 'incidental' exemption will apply to corporate finance activities where those activities are not exempted by Schedule 1 of the Act. Inevitably, some cases will arise where neither exemption applies or where there is some doubt. However, these are likely to be unusual cases such as, for example, where the firm acts as a merger broker for a fee.

31st January 1990 (updated January 1993)

Annex 26G

Guidance — the need for authorisation for non-U.K. offices

If a firm is certified, the certification will extend to its overseas offices. However, there may be cases where a firm without a permanent place of business in the U.K. will nevertheless need certification. If such a firm carries on investment activities in the U.K., e.g. by giving investment advice to U.K. clients, instructing U.K. stockbrokers to buy or sell investments for clients, or arranging for an overseas client to take out a life policy with a U.K. life office, then it may well be exempted from the need for certification by Part IV of Schedule 1 to the Act. However, the exemption does not apply in all such cases where, in effect, the investment activity results from an oral communication made to the client by the firm without express invitation. This could include the case where, during the course of discussion of a non-investment matter with a U.K. client, a solicitor considers that the client might benefit from a particular investment and the solicitor so advises the client. In such circumstances the solicitor might well need certification. Thus English solicitors practising outside the U.K. who discuss investment matters with clients in the U.K. are in danger of infringing the provisions of the Financial Services Act unless their firms are certified.

27th April 1988

Annex 26H

Product warning — home income plans — practice information

There have recently been a number of cases (not necessarily involving solicitors) where home income plans sold to the elderly have given rise to grave concern. Age Concern have issued a strong warning against such plans following an increasing number of elderly people facing the threat of losing their homes. The essence of a home income plan is that the homeowners mortgage their homes to raise a capital sum which is then available for investment to produce an income. Some schemes of this nature are perfectly satisfactory, but two in particular are very risky. Solicitors should be aware that these schemes are unlikely to be suitable for the vast majority of clients.

The first is an investment bond income scheme. Under this scheme, the capital sum raised by the mortgage is put into an investment bond. The assumption is that the bond will appreciate each year and provide an extra income. If it does not do so (and that has usually been the case over the last two or three years), then it may well be necessary to take money from the bond itself. This could well lead to a continuous reduction in the householder's capital.

The second is a roll-up loan scheme. Under this scheme, the interest payable under the mortgage is rolled up, i.e. the amount of interest due is added to the mortgage debt. The intention is that the mortgage will be repaid when the house is sold. The problem, however, is that the amount of the mortgage increases at a very high rate.

The danger with either of these two schemes is that a point may be reached where the homeowners have to sell their homes during their life time in order to repay the mortgage. It is beyond the scope of this note to deal with the technicalities, but a useful account may be found in *Using Your Home as Capital* by Cecil Hinton — published by Age Concern England.

3rd July 1991

Annex 26I

Law Society good practice guidelines on the recruitment and supervision of employees undertaking investment business — practice information

Introduction

In May 1990 the Securities and Investments Board (SIB) published Consultative Paper No.40 on Training and Competence in the Financial Services Industry. The recommendations made in that paper have been endorsed by the Law Society. After a further study by the Law Society, action is now being taken to progress the recommendations.

Amongst the recommendations made by the SIB were several relating to recruitment and supervision of individuals engaged in financial services work and the incentives and discipline applicable to their work.

These guidelines are issued in response to the SIB's recommendations for the benefit of all firms which are authorised or are likely to be authorised for investment business by the Law Society. They represent a statement of good practice which each firm should interpret and put into action as appropriate to their structure and their investment business policy.

They are particularly relevant to firms which employ non-solicitor financial services specialists as it has been found in practice at some firms that the lack of suitable experience of some staff and the absence of effective supervision has caused compliance problems. In a small number of cases, this non-compliance has resulted in disciplinary action being taken by the Law Society against individual partners or sole principals.

Recruitment

On recruitment practices, the SIB Consultative Paper states 'These must be sufficiently thorough as to enable the firm to have reasonable grounds for being satisfied that an individual is capable of acting, with whatever training and supervision may be appropriate, with the necessary degree of competence and integrity. Proper reference checks, with follow-up enquiries where necessary, especially where there are gaps in employment, are essential. Records of these references and checks should be maintained and made available to the regulatory body both as proof that recruitment procedures were sufficiently diligent, and to be available in the event of difficulties within a firm which may be traceable to a particular individual.'

Firms should put procedures in place which meet these recommendations.

Policy

The firm should seek a candidate with appropriate expertise and, if possible, qualifications and should be acquainted with the various financial services qualifications and their strengths and weaknesses. Care should be taken in respect of applicants who have experienced employment only in the 'tied' sector of the investment industry. This should not, however, be interpreted to mean that all those gaining their experience in this sector are unsuitable. In due course, when all regulatory bodies have agreed their training proposals with the SIB, the Law Society may be in a position to provide guidance on the most suitable financial services qualifications for employees of solicitors' firms.

The firm should make a policy decision on the areas of financial services it wishes to provide to clients and appoint a candidate who has the expertise for this work.

For example if the firm wishes to provide advice on the investment of lump sums, a candidate with experience of life insurance products only is unlikely to be suitable.

Advertising

Firms should normally advertise for financial services employees.

The advertisement (or supporting information for applicants) should:

    (1)   set out the profile of the applicant the firm is seeking (e.g. approach, aptitude and experience),

    (2)   stress the need to provide independent advice,

    (3)   require written references.

References

Firms should obtain written references about a prospective employee before an appointment is made. It is usually essential that the applicant's last employer be contacted.

Firms should also:

    (1)   undertake enquiries about an applicant's previous employment by telephone,

    (2)   make further enquiries where there are indications of poor performance or attitude and where information is insufficient,

    (3)   check an applicant's claim that he/she is or has been authorised by a Financial Services Act regulatory body with that organisation.

Interviews

It is essential for the firm to interview applicants prior to making an appointment. Care should be taken in cases where there has been a direct approach regarding employment by the applicant (i.e. when the post has not been advertised). The firm should seek an employee whose approach is likely to be consistent with the required integrity of a firm of solicitors. In particular the potential employee must be one who will put the clients' interests first and provide independent financial advice in compliance with the ethos of Practice Rule 1.

If the firm is seeking a financial services specialist because it lacks this expertise at present, it may encounter difficulty in interviewing in sufficient depth to determine the extent of the applicants' capabilities. The firm may wish to consider the use of consultants in this situation. Initially this may appear to be expensive but may, in the longer term, prevent greater costs being incurred, both in terms of money and loss of client goodwill, which may arise from making a poor appointment.

Contract of employment

Once appointed, the employee should have a contract of employment which should reflect the job description and the standard of work which is expected.

Thus it will be seen that the recruitment stage is vitally important and, if undertaken effectively, will have a positive bearing on subsequent supervision of the employee.

Supervision arrangements

On supervision arrangements, the SIB Consultative Paper states 'These must be sufficient to ensure that individuals are not acting beyond their competence or without integrity. In some cases, for example, new recruits, supervision should be personal, i.e. acccompanying the recruit and providing on-the-spot training. In other cases, the supervision should include quality checking of the activities of the individual; the track record on persistency of business produced from a particular individual; complaints experienced in respect of an individual and so on.'

Firms should put in place procedures which meet these recommendations.

Supervision

Firms are reminded of the Principle of conduct that 'a solicitor is responsible for exercising proper supervision over both his admitted and unadmitted staff' and Practice Rule 13 regarding the supervision and management of offices.

Financial services employees should have clear lines of reporting and accountability to a partner, who has responsibility for financial services (or the sole principal).

It is a matter of judgement as to how much supervision should be given to an employee, but it is likely that in the initial stages of employment a non-solicitor employee will need a substantial amount of direct supervision. The amount of supervision provided should not be affected by the remoteness of the office location in which the employee is to operate. The firm should have an evaluation process for measuring the competence of the employee.

Ongoing evaluation

Firms must find the means to ensure on-going supervision of the financial services employees. The supervisor should attend on occasions when the employee is advising a client and/or examine the files relating to investment business matters.

When attending whilst the employee is advising, the supervisor should ensure that the client is:

    (1)   addressed in clear English,

    (2)   provided with explanations in terms which can reasonably be expected to be understood.

When examining files the supervisor should ascertain that:

    (1)   compliance systems are being adhered to and that suitable and pertinent information about the client is obtained and recorded (know your client investigation),

    (2)   there is evidence of the considerations leading to the eventual investment decision,

    (3)   if the employee has written to the client, lucid explanations have been provided and clear English has been used,

    (4)   the file is properly structured and maintained to the highest professional standards,

    (5)   the investment decision appears to be suitable for the client.

Whilst solicitors should already be fully aware of the necessity for maintaining adequate files and the method by which this is achieved, some non-solicitors, particularly those from a sales oriented background, may lack the required stewardship and may need appropriate instructions and training.

It is possible that a financial services specialist will have a level of expertise beyond that of the supervisor. Despite this, the supervisor must remain in a position to supervise effectively by routinely pursuing intelligent questioning about a sample of investment recommendations made by the specialist. The employee should be able to communicate clearly his/her rationale behind particular investment decisions.

Training

It is important to recognise the role of training in the supervision arrangements.

Non-solicitors must be made fully aware of the environment in which they are to operate and must understand the ethos and philosphy of the firm. This should involve the firm in:

    (1)   giving tuition on the professional conduct of solicitors, the Practice Rules and Principles of conduct (in particular those which impact directly on investment business), Accounts Rules and the Solicitors' Investment Business Rules,

    (2)   giving tuition on the firm's office systems including compliance and accounting procedures,

    (3)   using induction manuals to provide permanent reference material for the employee and support the tuition provided by the manager.

It follows that those providing the training should have full knowledge of the Law Society's Rules.

The firm should ensure that the employee undertakes continuing education so that his/her experience is at least maintained or preferably improved. The manager should ensure that there is an adequate supply of up-to-date reference material and be aware of suitable courses and seminars.

Remuneration, incentives and disciplinary arrangements

On incentives and disciplinary arrangements, the SIB Consultative Paper states 'Thorough supervision and quality checking will provide their own incentives for individuals to seek to keep within the bounds of competence and integrity. But there needs also to be a certainty that appropriate action will follow where shortcomings are perceived. In many cases that appropriate action may be education or re-training or other assistance to the well-intentioned but misguided. But in other cases, stronger action would be called for and firms must not allow their commercial self interest in the profitability of business to stand in the way of the correct selling of that business, and the regulator must ensure that it does not.'

Firms should put in place procedures which meet these recommendations.

Remuneration

The means of remuneration may have a bearing on the manner in which the employee approaches his/her work. This in turn may impact on the firm's supervision arrangements.

It is recommended that employees are rewarded fully or mainly by salary. Whilst the employee may experience a lack of direct incentives to maximise income for the firm, his/her investment recommendations will not be influenced by rewards such as commissions. It is particularly important that the provisions of Practice Rule 10 are fully understood; in particular the need to obtain the client's informed consent to the retention of commission by the firm. If an incentive element in remuneration is considered to be appropriate the firm should find an alternative to retained commission such as a performance bonus.

Disciplinary procedures

The firm should have established procedures for dealing with disciplinary issues arising from the performance and conduct of all its staff. These procedures should be linked with contracts of employment.

Conclusions

Financial services work can be lucrative. But, if undertaken by the wrong type of employee, without suitable training and supervision, it can be the source of considerable problems for the firm. The employment of a specialist may appear for some firms to be the logical solution for undertaking financial services work when the partners or sole principal have insufficient expertise.

The full benefits from financial services work cannot be realised without the active involvement of the management of the firm to ensure that employees continue to operate with the proper level of expertise and in a manner which is consistent with the expected conduct of solicitors.

July 1992

PART VI — FINANCIAL REGULATIONS

Chapter 27

Accounts

Introduction

27.01 Rules dealing with solicitors' accounts consist of the Solicitors' Accounts Rules 1991, the Solicitors' Accounts (Legal Aid Temporary Provision) Rule 1992, Rule 13 of the Solicitors' Investment Business Rules 1990, the Accountant's Report Rules 1991 and Rules 9(3) and 12-16 of the Solicitors' Overseas Practice Rules 1990. These rules are made under the provisions of the Solicitors Act 1974 (see Annex 27A). They include appropriate references to registered foreign lawyers and recognised bodies, as solicitors have been permitted from the 1st January 1992 to enter into multi-national partnerships and to incorporate (see Chapters 3 and 8).

Object of the rules

27.02 The object of the rules is to ensure the fair treatment of client's money and to maintain adequate book-keeping and recording systems. A further object is to avoid any confusion of client's money with the solicitor's own money.

Responsibility

27.03 In a partnership, the responsibility for maintaining a proper book-keeping system is shared by all partners (including salaried partners). This is so even though the financial control of the firm may be delegated to one partner only. Any misappropriation or error by one partner is therefore the responsibility of all the partners. Moreover, all partners must ensure that any breaches of the Accounts Rules are immediately remedied. The books of account must be kept up to date and Rule 11(1)(c) requires the current balance to be shown on each client's ledger. It is recommended that even in the smallest practice the books should be written up weekly and, in the larger practices, on a daily basis.

The Solicitors' Accounts Rules 1991

27.04   The Solicitors' Accounts Rules 1991 consist of five parts:

Part I -   General

Part II - Controlled Trusts

Part III - Interest

Part IV - Compliance

Part V - Application

The full text of the rules appears in Annex 27B and a summary of the effect of Parts I and II appears in the diagram on page 614.

Definitions (Rule 2)

27.05   Rule 2 of the Solicitors' Accounts Rules 1991 contains a list of definitions which apply to certain words or phrases used throughout the rules.

Client's money

27.06   Client's money is defined as money which is held or received by a solicitor 'on account of a person for whom he or she is acting in relation to the holding or receipt of such money either as a solicitor or, in connection with his or her practice as a solicitor, as agent, bailee, stakeholder or in any other capacity'. However, client's money does not include money held or received where a solicitor is a 'controlled trustee' (see paragraph 27.11), or money to which the only person entitled is the solicitor or one or more partners in a firm of solicitors.

Where a solicitor is acting under a power of attorney, the donor of the power is the solicitor's client (see Commentary 4 to Principle 12.01). Where the solicitor holds or receives the donor's money, this is to be treated as client's money. On the other hand, where the solicitor under the power of attorney operates the donor's own bank account, money in the account has not been held or received by the solicitor and therefore is not to be treated as client's money for the purposes of the Accounts Rules.

27.07   It should be appreciated that specific instructions from a client (in writing or acknowledged by the solicitor in writing) take precedence over the rules in relation to money received on the client's behalf (see Rule 9(2)(a)). For example, a client's instructions that the money should be withheld from a client account, or retained in the solicitor's office in the form of cash, or deposited in any account which is not a client account, e.g. a share account with a building society, must be followed, in spite of the Accounts Rules.

27.08   A solicitor cannot treat himself or herself as a client. In consequence, a principal's personal or office transactions cannot be conducted through

Parts I and II Solicitors' Accounts Rules 1991 — Summary of their effects

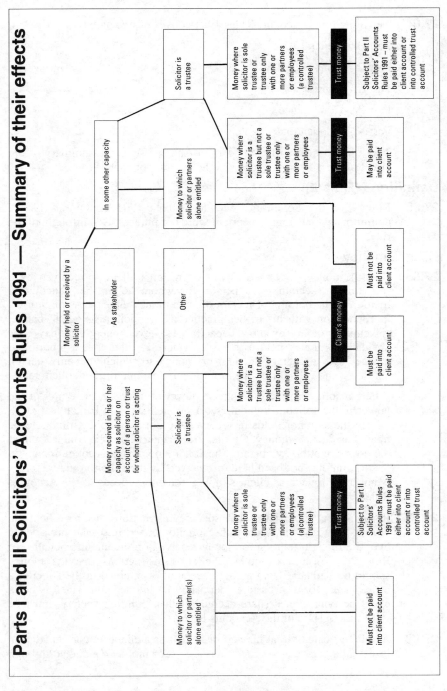

client account and it is a breach of the rules for a principal's personal conveyancing transactions to be conducted through client account. However, if a firm is acting in a conveyancing transaction on behalf of both a principal and his or her spouse (not being a partner in the firm), the firm is acting for both jointly and the matter must be conducted through client account. Further, if the conveyancing matter involves a building society or other lender for whom the firm is also acting, that part of the transaction involving the lender's money must be dealt with through client account. Where a firm conducts a conveyancing transaction on behalf of an assistant solicitor, the assistant solicitor should be treated as a client and any monies kept in client account, even if it is the assistant solicitor who is personally handling the matter.

Monies held by a solicitor in respect of PAYE and VAT are not client's money and therefore should not be paid into or retained in a client account (although see paragraph 27.18(d) and (e)).

27.09 The definition of client's money includes money held by a solicitor, in connection with his or her practice, as a stakeholder. However, if stakeholder money is placed in an account operated jointly by two firms of solicitors, this is not client's money since it is not in the sole control of either firm. This applies equally to any money held jointly by a solicitor with another firm or third party. However, it is preferable for such money to be separately recorded in memorandum form in the books of account of each solicitor.

27.10 Where a solicitor receives commissions paid in respect of a client, then unless the solicitor has the client's prior authority that the commission may be retained, it belongs to the client and should be paid into client account upon receipt (see Rule 10 of the Solicitors' Practice Rules 1990 and Principle 15.06).

Controlled trustee

27.11 'Controlled trustee' is defined as meaning a solicitor who is a sole trustee or a co-trustee only with one or more of his or her partners or employees. A 'controlled trust' is defined as a trust of which a solicitor is a 'controlled trustee'. 'Trustee' includes a personal representative — see Rule 2 of the Solicitors' Accounts Rules 1991 and section 87(1) of the Solicitors Act 1974.

Trust money

27.12 'Trust money' is defined as money held or received by a solicitor which is not client's money and which is subject to a trust of which the solicitor is a trustee, whether or not he or she is a controlled trustee. In most cases 'trust money' will be money which is the subject of a controlled trust, i.e. a trust of which a solicitor is a sole trustee or a co-trustee only with one or more of his or her partners or employees.

Money belonging to any other trust of which a solicitor is trustee will normally be client's money. However, in exceptional circumstances, the solicitor may receive the money in the capacity of trustee, rather than in connection with a trust retainer. In that case, the money will be trust money.

Bank and building society

27.13 'Bank' is defined as the branch, situated in England or Wales, of a bank as defined by section 87(1) of the Solicitors Act 1974 — i.e. 'the Bank of England, the Post Office, in the exercise of its powers to provide banking services, or an institution authorised under the Banking Act 1987'.

The Banking Co-ordination (Second Council Directive) Regulations 1992 state that section 87(1) shall have effect as if the reference to an institution authorised under the Banking Act included a reference to a European authorised institution which has lawfully established a branch in the U.K. for the purpose of accepting deposits.

'Building Society' is defined as the branch, situated in England or Wales, of a building society as defined by paragraph 11(5) of Schedule 18 to the Building Societies Act 1986 — i.e. a building society incorporated (or deemed to be incorporated) under the Act.

27.14 Whichever bank or building society a solicitor uses for the banking of client's money, the Council regard it as essential that money held in client account should be immediately available even though at the sacrifice of interest.

Client account

27.15 Client account is defined as meaning a current or deposit account at a bank or deposit account with a building society in the name of the solicitor and in the title of which the word 'client' appears. It is essential that all client accounts are designated in this way to avoid, in the event of the bankruptcy or death of a sole practitioner, any difficulty which might arise as to the identity of client's money. See also section 85 of the Solicitors Act 1974.

Client's money and client accounts — Solicitors' Accounts Rules Part I

Payments into client account (Rule 3 and the definition of 'costs')

27.16 Rule 3 of the Solicitors' Accounts Rules 1991 provides that subject to certain exceptions (noted in paragraphs 27.33 and 27.34), every solicitor who receives client's money must pay it into a client account without delay, which in normal circumstances means either the day of receipt or on the next working day. There is no objection to a solicitor keeping as many client accounts as he or she thinks fit.

It should be noted that a cheque or draft sent to a solicitor to be held to the sender's order must not be presented for payment without the sender's consent. By contrast, money sent, for example by telegraphic transfer, subject to the condition that it be held to the sender's order, must be held in a client account in accordance with Rule 3. In both cases, the recipient is subject to a professional obligation to return the cheque, draft or money to the sender on demand (see Commentary 3(c) to Principle 19.16).

27.17 The effect of the definition of 'costs' is that money received for payment of unpaid counsel's, agents' and experts' fees ('professional disbursements') must be placed in a client account (earning interest for the client). On the other hand, money received in respect of professional disbursements which the solicitor has already paid must not be paid into client account. There is an exception to each of these requirements (see paragraphs 27.20 and 27.18(e) respectively), provided that an appropriate transfer is made within the specified time. However, solicitors who follow a policy of posting all payments to the correct account in the first instance may well find that this simpler approach carries with it both organisational and financial benefits.

It should also be noted that stamp duty and Land Registry registration fees must be paid into client account. Sums received on account of costs generally must also be paid into client account.

Voluntary and other payments into client account (Rules 4-6)

27.18 The Solicitors' Accounts Rules provide that certain items of non-client money may be paid into client account. These items consist of:

(a)   trust money (Rule 4);

(b)   money belonging to the solicitor placed in the client account in order to open or maintain the account (Rule 4). This obviously refers only to such nominal sums as the bank or building society may require in order to open and maintain the account. In practice, banks will open (and on instructions allow to remain open) accounts with nil balances;

(c)   money paid into client account to replace any sum which has been withdrawn from the account in contravention of the Accounts Rules (Rule 4);

(d)   money received by a solicitor which consists of both client's money and non-client money. A solicitor in these circumstances has a choice. The money may where practicable be split and each part dealt with as if the solicitor had received a separate sum of money in respect of that part. Alternatively, if the solicitor does not split the money, he or she must, if any part consists of client's money, pay the money into client account (Rule 5);

(e)   a payment of an invoice comprising only money to which the solicitor alone is entitled, provided that all such money is transferred out of client account within seven days of receipt (Rule 5A). In effect, Rule 5A allows the prompt banking of any invoice payment in advance of dealing with its constituent parts; for example, where it is not immediately apparent whether the payment includes an *unpaid* professional disbursement and should therefore be dealt with as a mixed payment in accordance with Rule 5 (see (d) above), or whether it includes a *paid* professional disbursement and thus belongs entirely to the solicitor. In such cases, the invoice payment can be placed in client account immediately, provided that all money belonging to the solicitor is transferred out of client account within seven days of receipt.

27.19   No non-client money other than that referred to in paragraph 27.18 can be paid into client account. Money inadvertently paid into client account must therefore be withdrawn without delay on discovery. This extends to interest on a general client account, which belongs to the solicitor and should be credited by the bank or building society to the solicitor's office account. Where the bank or building society, whether or not contrary to instructions, has credited such interest to client account it must be withdrawn without delay (Rule 6).

Payment of client's money into office account

27.20   The Solicitors' Accounts (Legal Aid Temporary Provision) Rule 1992 deals with the specific problems of legal aid practitioners by permitting payments from the Legal Aid Board in respect of costs to be paid *en bloc* into office account (as defined), provided that any professional disbursements which remain unpaid are transferred to client account within fourteen days of receipt. The full text of this rule appears at Annex 27C.

27.21   The following points should be noted:

(a)   where legal aid practitioners elect to pay such payments into office account, unpaid professional disbursements remain client's money and their records must show all dealings with such money;

(b)   unpaid professional disbursements must (subject to the *de minimis* provisions) earn deposit interest for the client. It must also be remembered that deposit interest, if applicable, becomes payable from the date of receipt, even if money is temporarily placed in office account;

(c)   the fees of interpreters and translators are regarded as professional disbursements.

Withdrawal from client account (Rules 7 and 8)

27.22   Rule 7 of the Solicitors' Accounts Rules 1991 deals with the circumstances where a solicitor may withdraw client's money and trust money from client account. Whilst in most circumstances such withdrawals consist of payments to or on behalf of the client, a solicitor may withdraw sums of money properly required for or towards payment of a debt due to him or her from the client, or for or towards payment of his or her costs. A solicitor may only withdraw money from client account for the fees of counsel, an agent or an expert when the solicitor actually pays them. Other disbursements, notably search fees, may be transferred to office account provided the solicitor has incurred a liability to pay those disbursements, e.g. by requesting the search and making arrangements for payment by means of a credit account. An explanation of how to deal with the VAT element of counsel's fees is set out at Annex 27I.

27.23   Money paid to a solicitor in respect of stamp duty and Land Registry registration fees must always be paid into and remain in client account until those fees are paid.

27.24   Rule 7(a)(ii) permits a solicitor to transfer to office account money properly required in full or partial reimbursement of money 'expended' by the solicitor on behalf of the client. A solicitor will be treated as having expended money in these circumstances when the solicitor draws and despatches a cheque in respect of that item, unless the cheque is drawn and despatched on a 'hold to order' basis.

27.25   If money is to be withdrawn from client account for payment of a solicitor's costs, there must have been delivered to the client a bill of costs or other written intimation of the amount of costs incurred. It must further be made clear to the client in writing that the money held for him or her in the client account is to be applied towards or in satisfaction of such costs.

27.26   The withdrawal of costs must be for specific sums which relate to the bill or other written intimation which has been delivered to the client. It will almost inevitably be a breach of the rules to make round sum withdrawals generally on account of costs, as this will result in a shortage on client account if the round sum withdrawals exceed the amount properly available for transfer. The book-keeping entries recording the transfer in respect of costs or disbursements should be made simultaneously with the movement of money between bank or building society accounts or as soon as possible thereafter.

27.27   Costs and disbursements should be transferred out of client account as soon as possible in accordance with these provisions. Undrawn costs should not remain in client account as a 'cushion' against any future errors which could result in a shortage on that account. Notwithstanding delivery to a client of a bill or other written intimation of costs incurred and notwithstanding that a client has been notified that money held for him or her will be used to satisfy such costs, the money held in client account will continue to belong to that client (earning interest) until it is withdrawn in accordance with the rules. Any such credit balances in clients' ledgers cannot therefore be regarded as available to set off against any general shortage on client account or on the account of any one client.

27.28 If a solicitor wishes to make payment on behalf of a client in excess of funds held for that client in client account, the excess payment must be out of his or her office or personal resources. There is no objection to a solicitor lodging sufficient of his or her own funds into client account to enable full payment to be made from that account. However, when the specific amount is lodged in client account and credited to the appropriate client's ledger, it becomes client's money. It can therefore only be withdrawn in accordance with the provisions of Rules 7 or 8.

27.29 Payment to or on behalf of a client should as far as possible always be made by means of a crossed cheque. The Cheques Act 1992 gives statutory effect to the 'account payee' crossing. A cheque crossed with transverse lines and the words 'account payee' or 'A/C payee' on its face, either with or without the word 'only', becomes non-transferable and valid only as between the parties. The advantage of this is that the duty not to collect the proceeds other than for the named payee falls on the collecting bank. It should however be noted that even non-transferability does not provide complete protection as a bank's liability is not absolute.

In order to protect clients' funds against misappropriation where cheques are made payable to banks or building societies, it is strongly recommended that the words 'account of ....' or 'draft payable to ....' be included after the payee's name.

27.30 A solicitor should use discretion in drawing against a cheque received from or on behalf of a client before it has been cleared. If the cheque is not met, other clients' money will have been used to make the payment in breach of the rules. Consequently, on discovery of the breach, a solicitor must at once pay the appropriate amount from his or her own resources into client account. A solicitor can avoid a breach of the rules by instructing the bank or building society, if practicable, to charge all unpaid credits to the solicitor's office or personal account.

27.31 A solicitor who withdraws money from client account simply having been informed that a telegraphic transfer has been authorised, but which then is not received, will be using other clients' money in breach of the rules and in breach of trust.

27.32 Rule 8(1) of the Solicitors' Accounts Rules 1991 provides that where money is to be withdrawn from client account for payment to a solicitor (for example, the proper payment of costs or of a debt owed to the solicitor), such money must be withdrawn either by way of a cheque in favour of the solicitor or by way of a transfer to the solicitor's office or personal account.

Rule 8(2) states that the Council's written authority is necessary for the withdrawal of money from client account, other than as permitted by Rule 7. Applications under Rule 8(2) should be made to Professional Ethics.

Client's money withheld from client account (Rule 9)

27.33 Rule 9 of the Solicitors' Accounts Rules 1991 provides a number of circumstances where a solicitor is under no obligation to pay into client account client's money held or received by the solicitor. The circumstances are:

(a) where money is received in cash and is without delay paid in cash in the ordinary course of business to the client or on the client's behalf; or

(b) where money is received in the form of a cheque which is endorsed over in the ordinary course of business to the client or on the client's behalf; or

(c) where money is paid into a separate bank or building society account in the name of the client or some other person designated by the client in writing or acknowledged by the solicitor in writing to the client.

27.34 Rule 9 also deals with circumstances where a solicitor must not pay money into client account. This includes the circumstances where a client requests the solicitor to withhold his or her money from client account, providing that the request is either in writing or acknowledged by the solicitor to the client in writing. Where funds are withheld from client account under instructions, an adequate accounting record must nevertheless be made.

27.35 Additionally, a solicitor must not (save where an election is made to treat a payment in accordance with Rule 5A) pay into client account sums which are received:

(a) for or towards the payment of a debt owed to the solicitor by the client; or

(b) sums paid on account of costs incurred in respect of which a bill of costs or other written intimation of the amount of costs incurred has been delivered for payment; or

(c) as an agreed fee for business undertaken or to be undertaken.

As explained under paragraphs 27.17 and 27.22, a solicitor must pay into client account client's money paid in respect of the unpaid fees of counsel, an agent or an expert and that money must remain there until those sums are disbursed.

The principle in paragraph 27.23 applies to Rule 9 as well as Rule 7 — money paid to a solicitor in respect of stamp duty and Land Registry registration fees must always be paid into and remain in client account until those fees are disbursed.

Sums received on account of costs generally must be paid into client account and remain there until a bill of costs or written intimation of costs has been delivered.

Client's money held outside a client account

27.36 Rule 3 provides that a solicitor who holds or receives client's money shall pay it into a client account. Rule 9 provides that where a client for his or her convenience requests a solicitor to pay money into an account which is not a client account, the solicitor shall comply with those instructions. Despite the fact that this money is held by the solicitor outside client account, for instance in a Jersey account or a building society share account in the solicitor's name, the money is still client's money and is subject to the record-keeping provisions of the Accounts Rules.

Rule 11 provides that a solicitor shall keep a record of all dealings with client's money. This is not restricted to money in client account. Rule 4 of the Accountant's Report Rules 1991 requires a reporting accountant to satisfy himself or herself that *inter alia* Rule 11 of the Accounts Rules has been complied with. Client's money withdrawn from a non-client account must be paid into client account in accordance with Rule 3 in the absence of the client's instructions. Where money has been wrongly withdrawn and not paid into client account a breach of the Accounts Rules has occurred upon the discovery of which the reporting accountant should report.

Transfers between clients (Rule 10)

27.37 Rule 10 of the Solicitors' Accounts Rules 1991 deals with the transfer of money between clients. Where the book transfer relates to a private loan from one client to another the written authority of the lender must be obtained. This does not apply to loans made by an institutional lender.

Rule 6 of the Solicitors' Practice Rules 1990 prohibits a solicitor from acting for both lender and borrower in a private mortgage at arm's length. Rule 6 defines a private mortgage as 'any mortgage other than one provided by an institution which provides mortgages in the normal course of its activities'.

Books of account (Rule 11)

27.38 Rule 11 of the Solicitors' Accounts Rules 1991 lays down detailed rules as to how the books of account of solicitors must be kept. In particular, the points discussed in paragraphs 27.39-27.48 should be noted.

Current balances

27.39 Rule 11(1)(c) requires a solicitor to maintain accounts at all times so as to show the current balance on each client's ledger. The rule does not impose an obligation on solicitors to keep an historical record of all past balances on each ledger account.

Computerised records

27.40 The records which a solicitor is required to keep under the rules may be kept on a computerised system. In that case there is no obligation to keep a hard copy of those records. However, the information must be capable of being reproduced in hard printed form within a reasonable time. The information must remain capable of being reproduced in hard form for six years (see Rule 11(9)).

Two clients — one ledger

27.41 Where a solicitor is acting for both borrower and lender in a conveyancing transaction and that solicitor receives from the lender a mortgage advance, the solicitor is not required to open two separate ledger accounts, provided that the lender is an institutional lender which provides mortgages in the normal course of its activities and that the funds belonging to each client are 'clearly identifiable' (see Rule 11(3)).

'Clearly identifiable' means that by looking at the ledger account the nature and owner of the mortgage advance are unambiguously stated. For example, where a mortgage advance of £100,000 is received from, say, the Halifax Building Society, the solicitor's duty under this rule is to record the entry as '£100,000, mortgage advance, Halifax Building Society'. Simply to state that the money was received from the Halifax Building Society without specifying the nature of the payment, or *vice versa,* will be insufficient.

Of course, the fact that the solicitor does not open a separate ledger account for the lender does not alter the fact that the mortgage advance credited to that account belongs to the lender, not to the borrower, until completion takes place.

The improper removal of these mortgage funds from client account would be a breach of Rule 7.

Reconciliation statements

27.42 Rule 11(5) requires a solicitor at least once every five weeks (in effect, monthly) to compare the balance on clients' ledgers with the cash book balance and to reconcile the balance on clients' cash book (or clients' column of cash book) with the client account bank and building society pass books or statements. A solicitor must retain a reconciliation statement showing this reconciliation.

Endorsed cheques

27.43   When a cheque or draft is received on behalf of a client and is endorsed over, not passing through a solicitor's client account, it must be recorded in the books of account as a receipt and payment on behalf of a client. Similarly, cash received and not deposited in a client account but paid out on behalf of the client must also be so recorded. A cheque made payable to the client, which is forwarded to the client by the solicitor, is not client's money in the hands of the solicitor and is therefore outside the ambit of the Accounts Rules.

Separate designated accounts

27.44   When clients' funds are placed in separate designated accounts, accounting records must at all times show:

(a)   in a combined cash account the total of clients' funds held in separate designated accounts; and

(b)   on clients' ledger accounts the firm's liability in respect of each individual client.

Bills delivered book

27.45   In addition to the books, ledgers and records which must be kept in accordance with Rule 11, a solicitor must keep a record of all bills of costs and other written intimations of costs delivered to clients. Such record must be contained in a bills delivered book or a file of copies of bills and other written intimations.

Authority for withdrawal from client account

27.46   Rule 11(6) states that a withdrawal from a client bank or building society account may only be made where a specific authority in respect of that withdrawal has been signed by at least one of the following:

(a)   a solicitor who holds a practising certificate; or

(b)   an employee of such a solicitor being either a solicitor or a Fellow of the Institute of Legal Executives who is confirmed by the Institute as being of good standing and who shall have been admitted a Fellow for not less than three years; or

(c)   in the case of an office dealing solely with conveyancing, an employee of such a solicitor being a licensed conveyancer; or

(d)   a registered foreign lawyer who is a partner or director of the practice.

It should be noted that the specific authority in respect of a withdrawal must be signed before that withdrawal is made.

27.47   Instructions to the bank to withdraw money from client account may be given over the telephone, provided that before such instructions are given a specific authority signed in accordance with Rule 11(6) is in existence. If a solicitor decides to take advantage of this arrangement, it is of paramount importance that the operation of the scheme affords the greatest protection possible for clients' funds held at the bank or building society. In order to minimise unauthorised withdrawals, the solicitor should consider very carefully the safeguards which could be built into the system, for example:

(a) in circumstances where the solicitor's cashier is responsible for telephoning instructions to the bank, the bank and the solicitor may, as a safeguard, agree that funds may only be transferred if the instruction is accompanied by a password. The solicitor would communicate the password to the bank and the cashier only and the password would be changed regularly; or

(b) a system whereby the bank agrees that having received an instruction over the telephone it calls back to confirm the instructions with someone other than the person who gave those instructions.

Retention of books of account and records

27.48 A solicitor must retain for at least two years all paid cheques unless there is a written arrangement with the bank or building society that it will retain the cheques on the solicitor's behalf for that period. Other authorities for the withdrawal of money from client account must also be kept for two years. As the bank or building society will wish to keep the original authority, a copy of the authority will suffice for the purpose of Rule 11(9).

All other books of account and supporting records must be kept for at least six years. Bank statements kept must be those as printed and issued by the bank. Statements sent from the bank to its solicitor customer by means of electronic mail, even if they are capable of being printed off as hard copies, will not suffice.

Controlled trusts — Solicitors' Accounts Rules Part II

27.49 Part II of the rules ensures that where a controlled trustee (as defined, see paragraph 27.11) holds or receives trust money subject to a trust of which he or she is a controlled trustee, that money is paid into a separate controlled trust account for the particular trust, unless it is paid into client account (as permitted by Rule 4 of the Solicitors' Accounts Rules, see paragraph 27.18).

27.50 The rules in Part II of the Solicitors' Accounts Rules as to payments into and withdrawals from controlled trust accounts correspond with Part I. The wording of Part I is followed where practicable and notes which are applicable to Part I are equally applicable to Part II (see paragraphs 27.04-27.48).

Record keeping

27.51   The record keeping obligations for controlled trust accounts are set out in Rule 19 of the Solicitors' Accounts Rules 1991. A solicitor is required either to keep together, centrally, the accounts kept under Rule 19 or to maintain a central register of the controlled trusts administered.

Rule 19 requires a solicitor to keep separate accounts for each controlled trust. In many cases this duty will be discharged by simply retaining bank statements and building society passbooks provided that the narrative is sufficient to understand the various movements on the account. However, in the case of a trust which is particularly complex or is likely to be protracted, formal books of account should be kept.

Where controlled trust money is paid into a client account, the record keeping obligations are those set out in Rule 11 of the Solicitors' Accounts Rules 1991 and not those in Rule 19.

Deposit interest — Solicitors' Accounts Rules Part III

General principles

27.52   Section 33 of the Solicitors Act 1974 (see Annex 27A) requires the Council to make rules prescribing the treatment of interest arising on clients' funds held by a solicitor. These rules set out the circumstances in which a client should receive interest on money held by a solicitor on his or her behalf. Except as provided by these rules, a solicitor is entitled to retain personally interest on client's money placed in a general client account (see section 33(3)).

27.53   In cases where solicitors retain interest personally (i.e. on general client accounts), they should instruct their bank or building society to credit such interest direct to an office or personal account. If for any reason such instructions are not complied with, arrangements must be made immediately for such interest to be removed from client account (see Rule 6 of the Solicitors' Accounts Rules and paragraph 27.19). Solicitors may be required to pay sums equivalent to interest to their clients in accordance with Rule 20 (see paragraph 27.54).

Payments of interest on money held by a solicitor

27.54   Rule 20 provides that where a solicitor holds money for or on account of a client, the solicitor must either:

(a)   hold the money on deposit in a separate designated account and account to the client for the interest earned on it, or

(b)   pay the client, in the circumstances set out in Rule 21, a sum equivalent to the interest which would have accrued if the money received had been so kept on deposit, or its gross equivalent if the interest would have been net of tax.

The rule provides that where money is held other than in accordance with (a) above, the solicitor must account to the client for interest if the money is held for a period not less than the number of weeks set out in the left hand column of the table below and the minimum balance held during that period equals or exceeds the corresponding figure in the right hand column of the table.

Table

Number of weeks	Minimum balance
8	£ 1,000
4	£ 2,000
2	£10,000
1	£20,000

As stated in paragraph 27.21, unpaid professional disbursements (subject to the *de minimis* provisions) earn deposit interest for the client.

Clearance times

27.55 For the purpose of calculating interest, the relevant period is that for which cleared funds are held. However, in most cases it should be unnecessary to check on actual clearance dates. Where money is received by cheque and paid out by cheque, the normal clearance periods will usually cancel each other out; it follows that it should usually be satisfactory to treat the relevant period as being that between the dates when the incoming cheque is banked and when the outgoing cheque is drawn.

Different considerations apply where payments in and out are not both made by cheque. So, for example, the relevant periods would normally be:

(a)   from the date when the solicitor receives the incoming money in cash or by telegraphic transfer until the date when the outgoing cheque is or would normally be cleared;

(b)   from the date when an incoming cheque or banker's draft is or would normally be cleared until the date when the outgoing telegraphic transfer is made or banker's draft is obtained.

Sums held for less than one week

27.56 The obligation to pay interest under Rule 20(1)(ii) applies only to sums above £20,000. Provided that the solicitor accounts for such sums with due despatch, it will not normally be necessary for interest to be paid. However, there may be cases where a delay in accounting would justify the payment of interest.

Rate of interest

27.57 The rules state that where solicitors hold money for clients in separate designated accounts, they must account to the clients for any and all interest earned on those accounts. Where client's money is held on general client account solicitors are obliged to pay the equivalent of the amount of interest which *that* money would have earned had it been held on a separate designated account. Solicitors should refer to Annex 27G for guidance on the rate of interest payable under the rules.

Interest payable where solicitor holds more than one sum of money for the same client

27.58 Where a solicitor holds money for a client relating to more than one matter, then for the purposes of ascertaining the amount of interest payable, normally the appropriate course of action would be to treat the money relating to different matters separately. However there may be cases where the matters are so closely related that they ought to be considered together. One such circumstance may be where a solicitor is acting for a client company in connection with numerous debt collection matters.

Relevant bank or building society

27.59 Rule 23 of the Solicitors' Accounts Rules 1991 defines the relevant bank or building society. Rule 23(i) covers the usual situation. Rule 23(ii) is designed to cover the case where a client's money has been placed in a general client account and there is subsequently a transfer of part of the money in that account to a general client account with another bank or building society. In that event, it may no longer be possible to say that the particular client's money remains in the original client account and the position may well be that part of the client's money is with another bank or building society. Accordingly, the rule provides that in such a case the relevant bank or building society shall be whichever of those banks or building societies was offering the highest rate of interest on the day when interest payable under Rule 20 started to accrue. Rule 23(iii) covers the case where there has been a breach of Parts I or II of the Solicitors' Accounts Rules.

Details of the tax treatment of bank or building society interest are set out in Annex 27H.

Stakeholders (Rule 24)

27.60 Money which a solicitor holds as stakeholder is subject to Part III of the Solicitors' Accounts Rules 1991. However, Rule 24 provides that the interest earned on stakeholder money is payable to the person to whom the stake is paid. Any agreement between the parties as to the payment of deposit interest on stakeholder money will override the rules (Rule 26(iii)), but solicitors should refer to the guidance contained in Annex 27G.

Deposit interest certificate (Rule 25)

27.61 Under Rule 25 of the Solicitors' Accounts Rules 1991, any client is entitled to apply to the Solicitors Complaints Bureau for a certificate stating whether interest ought to have been earned under the rules and, if so, the amount of the interest payable. On the issue of such a certificate, such sum as mentioned therein shall be payable by the solicitor to the client. In the case of joint clients, it is sufficient if one client applies for a deposit interest certificate, whether or not the other client(s) agrees. This applies even if the clients are separately represented, e.g. in a matrimonial dispute, but one solicitor acts for both parties on a sale of property.

Contracting out (Rule 26(i))

27.62 Neither section 33 of the Solicitors Act 1974 nor Part III of the Solicitors' Accounts Rules 1991 deprive a solicitor and client of the right, in appropriate circumstances, to come to an arrangement in writing as to the application of the client's money or interest thereon (see Rule 26(i)). Solicitors should refer to Annex 27G for further guidance on contracting out.

If any solicitor contemplates entering into an arrangement whereby interest which has already accrued but does not belong beneficially to him or her is to become the solicitor's property, there is a risk of a double tax charge.

The solicitor who is a trustee (Rule 26(ii))

27.63 A solicitor who is a controlled trustee i.e. sole trustee or trustee only with one or more partners or employees is subject to the general law which precludes a solicitor who is a trustee from obtaining any benefit from the trust. This means that all interest on such money must be accounted for to the trust. Part III of the Solicitors' Accounts Rules 1991 will not apply (see Rule 26(ii)(a)).

Where a solicitor is trustee with others outside the firm and holds money by virtue of a retainer as trust solicitor, Part III of the rules will apply (see Rule 20(2)). This will apply in the majority of situations where the solicitor is trustee of a non-controlled trust. Such money is defined in the rules as client's money.

In exceptional cases, where a solicitor who is trustee with others outside the firm holds money not by virtue of a retainer as trust solicitor but by virtue of the trustee appointment, the general law will apply. Part III of the Rules will not apply (see Rule 26(ii)(b)).

27.64   It is permissible to pay into a general client account any of the following:

(a)   client's money, where the solicitor is not a trustee;

(b)   client's money, where the solicitor is a trustee with others outside the firm and holds the money by virtue of a retainer as trust solicitor;

(c)   trust money, where the solicitor is a controlled trustee;

(d)   trust money, in the exceptional case where the solicitor is a trustee with others outside the firm and holds the money not by virtue of a retainer as trust solicitor but by virtue of the trustee appointment.

In cases (a) and (b) above, the treatment of the interest earned is governed by Part III of the rules. Subject to the rules, the solicitor is permitted to retain the interest.

In cases (c) and (d) above, Part III of the rules does not apply. The solicitor is not entitled to retain the interest earned because the general law does not permit the solicitor to benefit from the trust.

Some solicitors choose, subject to their duty to the trust, to keep monies referred to in (c) and (d) above in a general client account which is separate from their general client account containing monies referred to in (a) and (b) above. This has the advantage of ensuring that the solicitor does not unwittingly make an improper benefit from any of the trusts.

However, if it is possible to calculate the interest on a daily basis on the money held for each trust then solicitors will be able to hold in one general client account both monies which are subject to Part III of the rules and those which are not.

Compliance — Solicitors' Accounts Rules Part IV
Powers of the Law Society to inspect accounts (Rule 27)

27.65   Under Rule 27 of the Solicitors' Accounts Rules, the Council of the Law Society have power to order the inspection of any books of account, statements and any other necessary documents in order to ascertain whether Parts I, II or III of the rules have been observed. An inspection carried out under Rule 27 overrides any confidence or privilege between solicitor and client. It is not the practice of the Council to disclose to the solicitor whose accounts are being inspected any reason for their instituting an inspection. It should be noted that the staff of the Society have been instructed accordingly. Under this power the Council has authorised a programme of regular monitoring visits to check for compliance with the Accounts Rules, similar to those undertaken to monitor compliance with the Solicitors' Investment Business Rules.

The Accountant's Report Rules 1991

General principles

27.66 The Accountant's Report Rules 1991 appear in Annex 27D and section 34 of the Solicitors Act 1974 appears in Annex 27A. Every solicitor who handles client's money or money subject to a controlled trust must produce annually a report by an accountant qualified under Rule 3 of the Accountant's Report Rules to the effect that the solicitor has complied with Parts I and II of the Solicitors' Accounts Rules. The report must be delivered once during each practice year (i.e. between 1st November and the following 31st October, both dates inclusive). When a solicitor retires from practice, he or she is obliged to deliver a report covering the period up to the date on which the solicitor ceased to hold client's money or money subject to a controlled trust.

27.67 The accounting period to which the report relates must normally be the last preceding accounting period and must normally cover not less than twelve months. The accounting period should correspond to the period for which the accounts of the solicitor or firm are ordinarily made up. The report must be delivered within six months of the end of the accounting period to which it relates.

Where a partnership splits up, it is appropriate for the books to be made up as at the date of dissolution, and for an accountant's report to be delivered within six months of that date.

Qualifications of accountant

27.68 Rule 3 of the Accountant's Report Rules 1991 sets out the qualifications required by an accountant competent to give an accountant's report. The accountant must not be a partner or employee of the solicitor, nor must he or she be employed by the same non-solicitor employer as the solicitor for whom the report is to be given. The accountant must not have been disqualified by the Council of the Law Society. There is no objection to a solicitor employing an outside accountant to write up the books of account and instructing the same accountant to prepare the annual report.

27.69 The Council may at their discretion notify an accountant that he or she is not qualified to give an accountant's report where either:

(a) the accountant has been found guilty of professional misconduct or discreditable conduct by the disciplinary tribunal of his or her professional body; or

(b) the Council are satisfied that a solicitor has not complied with the Accounts Rules in respect of matters not specified in the accountant's report and that the accountant was negligent in giving such a report.

27.70 Before coming to their decision, the Council take into consideration any observations or explanation provided by the accountant or his or her professional body. Notice of disqualification is published in the Gazette. The Council may remove the disqualification upon subsequent application by the accountant.

Nature of accountant's examination

27.71   Rule 4 of the Accountant's Report Rules 1991 sets out in detail the nature of the accountant's examination for the purposes of submitting an accountant's report. The rules do not require a complete audit of the solicitor's accounts nor do they require the preparation of a profit and loss account or balance sheet. Provision is made in the rules for a test examination of the solicitor's accounts. If the general examination and detailed tests as required by the rules disclose evidence that the rules have not been complied with, the accountant is required to pursue a more comprehensive investigation. In the case of a solicitor regulated in the conduct of investment business by the Society, the report must also confirm compliance with Rule 13 of the Solicitors' Investment Business Rules 1990. Rule 4(1)(A) of the Accountant's Report Rules sets out the requirements of the accountant's examination in respect of accounts other than controlled trust accounts; Rule 4(1)(B) sets out the requirements for controlled trust accounts.

27.72   Rule 4(1)(A)(f) requires an accountant to extract or check extractions of balances on the client ledger accounts during the accounting period at no fewer than two dates selected by the accountant. At each such date the accountant must compare the total liabilities to clients (including those for whom trust money is held in client account) shown by the ledger accounts with the cash account balance on client account and reconcile that cash account balance with the balances held in client account and elsewhere as confirmed direct to the accountant by the bank or building society.

27.73   The Council have considered the question whether full compliance with Rule 4(1)(A)(f) is essential where a solicitor uses a computerised or mechanised system of accounting and have decided that some relaxation can be permitted. The extent of the relaxation is set out in Rule 4(3). The exception does not relieve the accountant of the obligation to comply with all other requirements of Rule 4(1)(A)(f).

27.74   It has been noted that for the purposes of making the comparisons under Rule 4(1)(A)(f) some accountants improperly use credits of one client against debits of another when checking total client liabilities, thus not disclosing a shortage. A debit balance on a client's account when no funds are held for that client results in a shortage which must be disclosed as a result of the comparison. Liabilities to the clients referred to in Rule 4(1)(A)(f)(i) must include undrawn costs as indicated in the note to Rule 7 of the Solicitors' Accounts Rules (see paragraph 27.27).

27.75 Rule 4(1)(B) requires accountants to select a suitable sample of controlled trust matters and, in relation to those matters only, carry out a limited number of checks for compliance with Part II of the Solicitors' Accounts Rules 1991. The Accountant's Report Rules impose the minimum of requirements. There is no question of the reporting accountant having to look at every controlled trust and the accountant does not have to produce in the report a comparison of the overall liabilities and cash held as he or she would in respect of the solicitor's client accounts. Reference should be made to the accompanying guidance at Annex 27E for further clarification.

Client's confidentiality

27.76 A solicitor may decline to produce to the accountant any document which the accountant may consider it necessary to inspect, on the ground of confidentiality as between the solicitor and client. In these circumstances, the accountant must qualify the report to that effect, setting out the circumstances. When such a qualified report is received by the Society, the solicitor will normally be approached for clarification.

Cases where delivery of an accountant's report is unnecessary

27.77 Rule 7 of the Accountant's Report Rules prescribes certain cases where the delivery of an accountant's report is unnecessary. In the application for a practising certificate a solicitor is required to state whether he or she is or is not obliged to comply with the Solicitors' Accounts Rules.

27.78 However, an accountant's report is required under the rules from a solicitor who has been held out as a partner of another solicitor who has held or received client's money or money subject to a controlled trust, e.g. a salaried partner whose name is included in the list of partners on the letter-heading of the firm, even if the name appears under a separate heading of 'salaried partner' or 'associate partner' (see also Principle 3.10).

Place of examination of solicitor's books

27.79 Unless exceptional circumstances exist, the place of examination of a solicitor's books of account and other relevant documents should be the solicitor's office and not the office of the accountant.

Responsibility for delivery of the accountant's report

27.80 Although a solicitor may agree with the accountant that the accountant may send the report to the Society, the responsibility for delivery is that of the solicitor. The form of the report requires the accountant to confirm that either a copy of the report has been sent to each of the solicitors to whom the report relates or a copy of the report has been sent to a named solicitor on behalf of all the solicitors to whom the report relates. Reports should be sent to Accountants' Reports.

Trivial breaches

27.81 In many practices, clerical and book-keeping errors of one sort or another will arise. In the majority of cases these may be classified by the reporting accountant as trivial breaches and will not call for further comment. However, it should be appreciated that a 'trivial breach' cannot be precisely defined. The amount involved, nature of the breach and the time outstanding before correction are all factors which should be considered by the accountant before deciding whether a breach is trivial. Solicitors may be approached for clarification if a qualified report is received by the Society.

27.82 A reporting accountant is not required to report on trivial breaches of the Accounts Rules due to clerical errors or mistakes in book-keeping, provided that they have been rectified on discovery and the accountant is satisfied that no client suffered any loss as a result.

27.83 A number of accountant's reports are received by the Society which are expressed as being qualified only by reference to trivial breaches but which show a significant difference between liabilities to clients, and clients' money held in client and other accounts. Where such a difference is shown it would be helpful if an explanation for this difference, from either the accountant or the solicitor, could be provided, as this may obviate the need for any further correspondence on the point.

Solicitors' Overseas Practice Rules 1990

27.84 Rules 12-16 of the Solicitors' Overseas Practice Rules 1990 deal with solicitors' accounts, trust accounts, accountant's reports and investigation of accounts in respect of overseas practices (see Annex 9A). These rules embody the general principles of the Solicitors' Accounts Rules, but are less detailed and less onerous in their specific requirements. They do not include any requirement for reporting accountants to make a test check of controlled trust accounts, although this may change.

Where local law or local conditions make it difficult or impossible for a solicitor to comply with the Overseas Practice Rules, application may be made to Professional Ethics for a waiver under Rule 27.

A suggested form of accountant's report for an overseas practice is set out in Annex 27F.

Annex 27A

Solicitors Act 1974

sections 32-34 — accounts
(as amended by the Courts and Legal Services Act 1990)

---

32. *Accounts rules and trust accounts rules*

(1)   The Council shall make rules, with the concurrence of the Master of the Rolls -

(a)   as to the opening and keeping by solicitors of accounts at banks or with building societies for clients' money; and

(b)   as to the keeping by solicitors of accounts containing particulars and information as to money received or held or paid by them for or on account of their clients; and

(c)   empowering the Council to take such action as may be necessary to enable them to ascertain whether or not the rules are being complied with;

and the rules may specify the location of the branches at which the accounts are to be kept.

(2)   The Council shall also make rules, with the concurrence of the Master of the Rolls -

(a)   as to the opening and keeping by solicitors of accounts at banks or with building societies for money comprised in controlled trusts; and

(b)   as to the keeping by solicitors of accounts containing particulars and information as to money received or held or paid by them for or on account of any such trust; and

(c)   empowering the Council to take such action as may be necessary to enable them to ascertain whether or not the rules are being complied with;

and the rules may specify the location of the branches at which the accounts are to be kept.

(3)   If any solicitor fails to comply with rules made under this section, any person may make a complaint in respect of that failure to the Tribunal.

(4)   The Council shall be at liberty to disclose a report on or information about a solicitor's accounts obtained in the exercise of powers conferred by rules made under subsection (1) or (2) to the Director of Public Prosecutions for use in investigating the possible commission of an offence by the solicitor and, if the Director thinks fit, for use in connection with any prosecution of the solicitor consequent on the investigation.

(5)   Rules under this section may specify circumstances in which solicitors or any class

of solicitors are exempt from the rules by virtue of their office or employment.

(6) For the purposes of this section and section 33 references to clients' money and money of a kind mentioned in subsection (1)(b) of this section or (1)(a) of section 33 include references to money held by a solicitor as a stakeholder (whether or not paid by a client of his).

[NOTES

1. By virtue of section 89(3) of the Courts and Legal Services Act 1990 the power to make rules under section 32 is also exercisable in relation to registered foreign lawyers.

2. By virtue of section 9(2)(f) of the Administration of Justice Act 1985 rules made under section 32 may be made to have effect in relation to a recognised body (i.e. an incorporated practice recognised under section 9).

3. For a provision analogous to subsection (4) in the case of the accounts of a recognised body see paragraph 3 of Schedule 2 to the Administration of Justice Act 1985.]

33. *Interest on clients' money*

(1) Rules made under section 32 shall make provision for requiring a solicitor, in such cases as may be prescribed by the rules, either:

(a) to keep on deposit in a separate account at a bank or with a building society for the benefit of the client money received for or on account of a client; or

(b) to make good to the client out of the solicitor's own money a sum equivalent to the interest which would have accrued if the money so received had been so kept on deposit.

(2) The cases in which a solicitor may be required by the rules to act as mentioned in subsection (1) may be defined, among other things, by reference to the amount of any sum received or the period for which it is or is likely to be retained or both; and the rules may include provision for enabling a client (without prejudice to any other remedy) to require that any question arising under the rules in relation to the client's money be referred to and determined by the Society.

(3) Except as provided by the rules, a solicitor shall not be liable by virtue of the relation between solicitor and client to account to any client for interest received by the solicitor on money deposited at a bank or with a building society being money received or held for or on account of his clients generally.

(4) Nothing in this section or in the rules shall affect any arrangement in writing, whenever made, between a solicitor and his client as to the application of the client's money or interest on it.

[NOTE

For provisions analogous to subsections (3) and (4) in the case of a recognised body see paragraph 4 of Schedule 2 to the Administration of Justice Act 1985.]

34. *Accountant's reports*

(1) Every solicitor shall once in each period of twelve months ending with 31st October, unless the Council are satisfied that it is unnecessary for him to do so, deliver to the Society, whether by post or otherwise, a report signed by an accountant (in this

section referred to as an 'accountant's report') and containing such information as may be prescribed by rules made by the Council under this section.

(2)   An accountant's report shall be delivered to the Society not more than six months (or such other period as may be prescribed by rules made under this section) after the end of the accounting period for the purposes of that report.

(3)   Subject to any rules made under this section, the accounting period for the purposes of an accountant's report:

(a)   shall begin at the expiry of the last preceding accounting period for which an accountant's report has been delivered;

(b)   shall cover not less than twelve months; and

(c)   where possible, consistently with the preceding provisions of this section, shall correspond to a period or consecutive periods for which the accounts of the solicitor or his firm are ordinarily made up.

(4)   The Council shall make rules to give effect to the provisions of this section, and those rules shall prescribe -

(a)   the qualification to be held by an accountant by whom an accountant's report is given;

(b)   the information to be contained in an accountant's report;

(c)   the nature and extent of the examination to be made by an accountant of the books and accounts of a solicitor or his firm and of any other relevant documents with a view to the signing of an accountant's report;

(d)   the form of an accountant's report; and

(e)   the evidence, if any, which shall satisfy the Council that the delivery of an accountant's report is unnecessary and the cases in which such evidence is or is not required.

(5)   Rules under this section may include provision -

(a)   permitting in such special circumstances as may be defined by the rules a different accounting period from that specified in subsection (3); and

(b)   regulating any matters of procedure or matters incidental, ancillary or supplemental to the provisions of this section.

(5A) Without prejudice to the generality of subsection (5)(b), rules under this section may make provision requiring a solicitor in advance of delivering an accountant's report to notify the Society of the period which is to be the accounting period for the purposes of that report in accordance with the preceding provisions of this section.

(6)   If any solicitor fails to comply with the provisions of this section or of any rules made under it, a complaint in respect of that failure may be made to the Tribunal by or on behalf of the Society.

(7)   A certificate under the hand of the Secretary of the Society shall, until the contrary is proved, be evidence that a solicitor has or, as the case may be, has not delivered to the Society an accountant's report or supplied any evidence required under this section or any rules made under it.

(8)   Where a solicitor is exempt from rules under section 32:

(a)   nothing in this section shall apply to him unless he takes out a practising certificate;

(b)   an accountant's report shall in no case deal with books, accounts or documents kept by him in the course of employment by virtue of which he is exempt from those rules; and

(c)   no examination shall be made of any such books, accounts and documents under any rules made under this section.

[NOTES

1.   For a similar provision in relation to registered foreign lawyers see paragraph 8 of Schedule 14 to the Courts and Legal Services Act 1990.

2.   By virtue of section 89(3) of the Courts and Legal Services Act 1990 the power to make rules under section 34 is also exercisable in relation to registered foreign lawyers.

3.   For the application of section 34 to a recognised body see paragraph 5 of Schedule 2 to the Administration of Justice Act 1985.

4.   By virtue of section 9(2)(f) of the Administration of Justice Act 1985 rules made under section 34 may be made to have effect in relation to a recognised body.]

Annex 27B

Solicitors' Accounts Rules 1991

(with consolidated amendments to 1st June 1992)

Rules dated 16th July 1991 made by the Council of the Law Society and approved by the Master of the Rolls pursuant to section 32 of the Solicitors Act 1974 and section 9 of the Administration of Justice Act 1985 regulating the keeping of accounts by solicitors, registered foreign lawyers and recognised bodies in respect of their English and Welsh practices.

COMMENCEMENT AND INTERPRETATION

1. These rules may be cited as the Solicitors' Accounts Rules 1991 and shall come into operation on the 1st day of June 1992 whereupon the Solicitors' Accounts Rules 1986, the Solicitors' Trust Accounts Rules 1986 and the Solicitors' Accounts (Deposit Interest) Rules 1988 shall cease to have effect.

2. (1) In these Rules, unless the context otherwise requires -

    the expressions 'accounts', 'books', 'ledgers' and 'records' shall be deemed to include loose-leaf books and such cards or other permanent documents or records as are necessary for the operation of any system of book-keeping, computerised, mechanical or otherwise and where a computerised system is operated, the information recorded on it must be capable of being reproduced in hard printed form within a reasonable time;

    'bank' shall mean the branch, situated in England or Wales, of a bank as defined by section 87(1) of the Solicitors Act 1974, as amended by paragraph 9 of Schedule 6 to the Banking Act 1979 and paragraph 5 of Schedule 6 to the Banking Act 1987;

    'building society' shall mean the branch, situated in England or Wales, of a building society as defined by paragraph 11(5) of Schedule 18 to the Building Societies Act 1986;

    'client', save in Part III of these rules, shall mean any person on whose account a solicitor holds or receives client's money;

    'client account' shall mean a current or deposit account at a bank or deposit account with a building society in the name of the solicitor or his or her firm in the title of which account the word 'client' appears;

    'client's money' shall mean money held or received by a solicitor on account of a person for whom he or she is acting in relation to the holding or receipt of such money either as a solicitor or, in connection with his or her practice as a solicitor, as agent, bailee, stakeholder or in any other capacity; provided that the expression 'client's money' shall not include -

(a) money held or received on account of the trustees of a trust of which the solicitor is a controlled trustee; or

(b) money to which the only person entitled is the solicitor himself or herself or, in the case of a firm of solicitors, one or more of the partners in the firm;

'controlled trust' in relation to a solicitor, shall mean a trust of which he or she is a controlled trustee;

'controlled trust account' shall mean a current or deposit account kept at a bank or deposit account kept with a building society in the title of which the word 'trustee' or 'executor' appears, or which is otherwise clearly designated as a controlled trust account, and kept solely for money subject to a particular trust of which the solicitor is a controlled trustee;

'controlled trustee' shall mean a solicitor who is a sole trustee or co-trustee only with one or more of his or her partners or employees and any reference to a controlled trustee shall be construed as including

(a) a recognised body which is a sole trustee or co-trustee only with one or more of its officers, partners or employees; and

(b) a solicitor or a recognised body who or which is an officer or employee of a recognised body and who or which is a sole trustee or co-trustee only with one or more other officers or employees of that recognised body or the body itself;

'costs' includes fees, charges, disbursements, expenses and remuneration and, for the purpose of rules 7(a)(iv) and 9(2)(c)(i), shall include costs (including VAT) in respect of which a solicitor has incurred a liability but shall exclude the fees of counsel or other lawyer, or of a professional or other agent, or of an expert instructed by the solicitor;

'local authority' shall have the same meaning as is given to this expression by the Local Government Act 1972;

'private loan' shall mean a loan other than one provided by an institution which provides loans in the normal course of its activities;

'public officer' shall mean an officer whose remuneration is defrayed out of moneys provided by Parliament, the revenues of the Duchy of Cornwall or the Duchy of Lancaster, the general fund of the Church Commissioners, the Forestry Fund or the Development Fund;

'recognised body' shall have the meaning assigned to it by the Solicitors' Incorporated Practice Rules 1988 as may be amended, modified or re-enacted from time to time;

'separate designated account' shall mean a deposit account at a bank or building society in the name of the solicitor or his or her firm in the title of which account the word 'client' appears and which is designated by reference to the identity of the client or matter concerned;

'solicitor' shall mean a solicitor of the Supreme Court and shall include a firm of solicitors or a recognised body;

'statutory undertakers' shall mean any person authorised by or under an Act of Parliament, to construct, work, or carry on any railway, canal, inland navigation, dock, harbour, tramway, gas, electricity, water or other public undertaking;

'trust money' shall mean money held or received by a solicitor which is not client's money and which is subject to a trust of which the solicitor is a trustee whether or not he or she is a controlled trustee of such trust;

words in the singular include the plural, words in the plural include the singular and words importing the masculine or feminine shall include the neuter; and

(2) Other expressions in these rules shall except where otherwise stated have the meanings assigned to them by the Solicitors Act 1974.

PART I — GENERAL

3. Subject to the provisions of rule 9 hereof, every solicitor who holds or receives client's money, or money which under rule 4 hereof the solicitor is permitted and elects to pay into a client account, shall without delay pay such money into a client account. Any solicitor may keep one client account or as many such accounts as the solicitor thinks fit.

4. There may be paid into a client account -

   (a) trust money;

   (b) such money belonging to the solicitor as may be necessary for the purpose of opening or maintaining the account;

   (c) money to replace any sum which for any reason may have been drawn from the account in contravention of paragraph (2) of rule 8 of these rules; and

   (d) money received by the solicitor which under paragraph (b) of rule 5 of these rules the solicitor is entitled to split but which the solicitor does not split.

5. Where a solicitor holds or receives money which includes client's money or trust money of one or more trusts -

   (a) he or she may where practicable split such money and, if he or she does so, he or she shall deal with each part thereof as if he or she had received a separate sum of money in respect of that part; or

   (b) if he or she does not split the money he or she shall, if any part thereof consists of client's money, and may, in any other case, pay the money into a client account.

5A. When a solicitor receives, in full or part settlement of a bill of costs, a payment all of which is money to which the solicitor alone is entitled, the solicitor may, as an alternative to treating the money in accordance with rule 9(2), elect to pay it without delay into a client account PROVIDED THAT the money does not remain in a client account longer than seven days from receipt.

6. No money other than money which under the foregoing rules a solicitor is required or permitted to pay into a client account shall be paid into a client account, and it shall be the duty of a solicitor into whose client account any money has been paid in contravention of this rule to withdraw the same without delay on discovery.

7.   There may be drawn from a client account -

    (a)   in the case of client's money -

        (i)   money properly required for a payment to or on behalf of the client;

        (ii)   money properly required in full or partial reimbursement of money expended by the solicitor on behalf of the client;

        (iii)   money drawn on the client's authority;

        (iv)   money properly required for or towards payment of the solicitor's costs where there has been delivered to the client a bill of costs or other written intimation of the amount of the costs incurred and it has thereby or otherwise in writing been made clear to the client that money held for him or her is being or will be applied towards or in satisfaction of such costs; and

        (v)   money which is transferred into another client account;

    (b)   in the case of trust money -

        (i)   money properly required for a payment in the execution of the particular trust, and

        (ii)   money to be transferred to a separate bank or building society account kept solely for the money of the particular trust;

    (c)   money, not being money to which either paragraph (a) or paragraph (b) of this rule applies, as may have been paid into the account under rule 4(b) or rule 5(b) or rule 5A of these rules;

    (d)   money which for any reason may have been paid into the account in contravention of rule 6 of these rules;

provided that in any case under paragraph (a) and paragraph (b) of this rule the money so drawn shall not exceed the total of the money held for the time being in such account on account of such client or trust.

8.   (1)   No money drawn from a client account under sub-paragraph (ii) or sub-paragraph (iv) of paragraph (a) or under paragraph (c) or paragraph (d) of rule 7 of these rules shall be drawn except by -

        (a)   a cheque drawn in favour of the solicitor, or

        (b)   a transfer to a bank or building society account in the name of the solicitor not being a client account.

    (2)   No money other than money permitted by rule 7 to be drawn from a client account shall be so drawn unless the Council upon an application made to them by the solicitor specifically authorise in writing its withdrawal.

9.   (1)   Notwithstanding the provisions of these rules, a solicitor shall not be under an obligation to pay into a client account client's money held or received by him or her -

        (a)   which is received by him or her in the form of cash and is without delay paid in cash in the ordinary course of business to the client or on his or her behalf to a third party; or

        (b)   which is received by him or her in the form of a cheque or draft which is endorsed over in the ordinary course of business to the client or on his or her behalf to a third party and is not passed by the solicitor through a bank or building society account; or

(c)   which he or she pays into a separate bank or building society account opened or to be opened in the name of the client or of some person designated by the client in writing or acknowledged by the solicitor to the client in writing.

(2)   Notwithstanding the provisions of these rules (and except where the solicitor elects to treat a payment in accordance with rule 5A and complies with the requirements of that rule), a solicitor shall not pay into a client account money held or received by him or her-

(a)   which the client for his or her own convenience requests the solicitor to withhold from such account, such request being either in writing from the client or acknowledged by the solicitor to the client in writing; or

(b)   which is received by him or her from the client in full or partial reimbursement of money expended by the solicitor on behalf of the client; or

(c)   which is expressly paid to him or her either -

(i)   for or towards payment of the solicitor's costs in respect of which a bill of costs or other written intimation of the amount of the costs incurred has been delivered for payment; or

(ii)   as an agreed fee (or on account of an agreed fee) for business undertaken or to be undertaken.

(3)   Where money includes client's money as well as money of the nature described in paragraph (2) of this rule such money shall be dealt with in accordance with rule 5 of these rules.

(4)   Notwithstanding the provisions of these rules the Council may upon application made to them by a solicitor specifically authorise such solicitor in writing to withhold any client's money from a client account.

10.   (1)   No sum shall be transferred from the ledger account of one client to that of another except in circumstances in which it would have been permissible under these rules to have withdrawn from client account the sum transferred from the first client and to have paid into client account the sum so transferred to the second client.

(2)   No sum in respect of a private loan shall be paid -

(a)   directly; or

(b)   by means of a transfer from the ledger account of one client to that of another;

out of funds held on account of the lender without the prior written authority of the lender.

11.   (1)   Every solicitor shall at all times keep properly written up such accounts as may be necessary -

(a)   to show the solicitor's dealings with -

      (i)   client's money received, held or paid by him or her; and

      (ii)   any other money dealt with by him or her through a client account; and

  (b) (i)   subject to rule 11 (3) below to show separately in respect of each client all money of the categories specified in sub-paragraph (a) of this paragraph which is received, held or paid by him or her on account of that client; and

      (ii)   to distinguish all money of the said categories received, held or paid by him or her, from any other money received, held or paid by him or her; and

  (c) to show the current balance on each client's ledger.

(2) (a) All dealings referred to in sub-paragraph (a) of paragraph (1) of this rule shall be appropriately recorded -

      (i)   in a clients' cash account; or a clients' column of a cash account or in a record of sums transferred from the ledger account of one client to that of another; and

      (ii)   in a clients' ledger or a clients' column of a ledger; and no other dealings shall be recorded in such clients' cash account, ledger, record of sums transferred or, as the case may be, in such clients' columns.

  (b) All dealings of the solicitor relating to his or her practice as a solicitor other than those referred to in sub-paragraph (a) of paragraph (1) of this rule shall (subject to compliance with Part II of these rules) be recorded in a separate cash account and ledger or such other columns of a cash account and ledger as the solicitor may maintain.

(3) A solicitor acting for both borrower and lender in a conveyancing transaction who receives from the lender a mortgage advance shall not be required to open separate ledger accounts for both borrower and lender in respect of such advance provided that -

  (a) the funds belonging to each client are clearly identifiable; and

  (b) the lender is an institutional lender which provides mortgages in the normal course of its activities.

(4) In addition to the books, ledgers and records referred to in paragraph (2) of this rule, every solicitor shall keep a record of all bills of costs (distinguishing between profit costs and disbursements) and of all written intimations under rule 7(a)(iv) and under rule 9(2)(c) of these rules delivered or made by the solicitor to his or her clients, which record shall be contained in a bills delivered book or a file of copies of such bills and intimations.

(5) Every solicitor shall, at least once every five weeks -

      (i)   compare the total of the balances shown by the clients' ledger accounts of the liabilities to the clients, including those for whom trust money is held in the client account, with the cash account balance; and

      (ii)   prepare a reconciliation statement showing the cause of the difference, if any, shown by the above comparison; and

       (iii)   reconcile that cash account balance with the balances shown on client account bank and building society pass books or statements and money held elsewhere;

and shall preserve the records of all such reconciliations.

(6)   A withdrawal from a bank or building society account, being or forming part of a client account, may only be made where a specific authority in respect of that withdrawal has been signed by one at least of the following (either alone or in conjunction with other persons) namely -

       (i)   a solicitor who holds a current practising certificate; or

       (ii)   an employee of such a solicitor being either a solicitor or a Fellow of the Institute of Legal Executives who is confirmed by the Institute as being of good standing and who shall have been admitted a Fellow for not less than three years;

       (iia)   a registered foreign lawyer who is a partner or director of the practice;

       (iii)   in the case of an office dealing solely with conveyancing, an employee of such a solicitor being a licensed conveyancer.

(7)   Rule 11(6) shall not apply to the transfer of money from one account to another at the same bank or building society where both accounts are client accounts other than separate designated accounts.

(8)   For the purposes of rule 11 (6) of these rules the first and third references to a solicitor shall not be construed as including references to a recognised body and the references to an employee of 'such a solicitor' shall be construed as including a reference to an employee of a recognised body.

(9)   (a)   Every solicitor shall preserve for at least six years -

       (i)   from the date of the last entry therein all accounts, books, ledgers and records; and

       (ii)   all bank statements as printed and issued by the bank.

    (b)   Every solicitor shall retain for at least two years -

       (i)   all paid cheques unless he or she has arranged in writing with the relevant bank(s) and/or building society(ies) that they will retain such paid cheques for that period; and

       (ii)   copies of the authorities (other than cheques) signed pursuant to rule 11(6).

(10) This rule 11 shall apply only to Part I of these rules.

PART II — CONTROLLED TRUSTS

12.   Subject to the provisions of rule 18 of these rules every controlled trustee who holds or receives money subject to a trust of which he or she is a controlled trustee, other than money which is paid into a client account as permitted by Part I of these rules, shall without delay pay such money into a controlled trust account of the particular trust.

13.   There may be paid into a controlled trust account -

(a)   money subject to the particular trust;

(b)   such money belonging to the controlled trustee or to a co-trustee as may be necessary for the purpose of opening or maintaining the account; and

(c)   money to replace any sum which for any reason may have been drawn from the account in contravention of rule 17 of these rules.

14.   Where a solicitor holds or receives money which includes money subject to a trust or trusts of which the solicitor is controlled trustee -

(a)   he or she shall where practicable split such money and, if he or she does so, shall deal with each part thereof as if he or she had received a separate sum of money in respect of that part; or

(b)   if he or she does not split the money, he or she may pay it into a client account as permitted by Part I of these rules.

15.   No money, other than money which under rules 12 to 14 of these rules a solicitor is required or permitted to pay into a controlled trust account, shall be paid into a controlled trust account, and it shall be the duty of a solicitor into whose controlled trust account any money has been paid in contravention of this rule to withdraw the same without delay on discovery.

16.   There may be drawn from a controlled trust account -

(a)   money properly required for a payment in the execution of the particular trust;

(b)   money to be transferred to a client account;

(c)   such money, not being money subject to the particular trust, as may have been paid into the account under paragraph (b) of rule 13 of these rules; or

(d)   money which may for any reason have been paid into the account in contravention of rule 15 of these rules.

17.   No money other than money permitted by rule 16 of these rules to be drawn from a controlled trust account shall be so drawn unless the Council upon an application made to them by the solicitor expressly authorise in writing its withdrawal.

18.   Notwithstanding the provisions of these rules a solicitor shall not be under an obligation to pay into a controlled trust account money held or received by him or her which is subject to a trust of which he or she is controlled trustee -

(a)   if the money is received by him or her in the form of cash and is without delay paid in cash in the execution of the trust to a third party; or

(b)   if the money is received by him or her in the form of a cheque or draft which is without delay endorsed over in the execution of the trust to a third party and is not passed by the solicitor through a bank or building society account.

19.   Except in so far as money is dealt with in accordance with Part I of these rules -

(a)   every controlled trustee shall at all times keep properly written up such accounts as may be necessary -

(i)   to show separately in respect of each trust of which he or she is controlled trustee all his or her dealings with money received, held or paid by him or her on account of that trust; and

(ii)   to distinguish the same from money received held or paid by him or her on any other account;

(b)   every controlled trustee shall preserve for at least six years from the date of the last entry therein all accounts and bank statements;

(c)   every controlled trustee shall either

     (i)   keep together, centrally, the accounts which he or she is required to keep under this rule 19; or

     (ii)   maintain centrally a register of the trusts in respect of which he or she is required to keep accounts under this rule 19.

PART III — INTEREST

20. (1)   Subject to rule 26 of these rules, a solicitor who holds money for or on account of a client shall account to the client for interest or an equivalent sum in the following circumstances:

     (i)   where such money is held on deposit in a separate designated account the solicitor shall account to the client for the interest earned on that money;

     (ii)   where such money is not so held on deposit, the solicitor shall, subject to rule 21 of these rules pay to the client out of the solicitor's own money a sum equivalent to the interest which would have accrued if the money received had been so kept on deposit, or its gross equivalent if the interest would have been net of tax.

   (2)   In paragraph (1) of this rule, for the avoidance of doubt, the reference to a solicitor who holds money for or on account of a client includes the solicitor holding money in his or her capacity as solicitor on account of the trustees of a trust (other than a controlled trust) of which the solicitor is a trustee.

21. A solicitor shall only be required to account in accordance with rule 20(1)(ii) of these rules where:

   (i)   the solicitor holds the money for as long as or longer than the number of weeks set out in the left hand column of the table below and the minimum amount held equals or exceeds the corresponding figure in the right hand column of the table;

TABLE

No. of weeks	Minimum amount
8	£ 1,000
4	£ 2,000
2	£10,000
1	£20,000

or

   (ii)   the solicitor holds a sum of money exceeding £20,000 for less than one week and it is fair and reasonable to so account having regard to all the circumstances; or

   (iii)   the solicitor holds money continuously which varies significantly in amount over the period during which it is held and it is fair and reasonable so to account having regard to any sum payable under paragraph (i) of this rule and to the varying amounts of money and length of time for which these are held; or

(iv) the solicitor holds sums of money intermittently during the course of acting and it is fair and reasonable so to account having regard to all the circumstances including the aggregate of the sums held and the periods for which they are held notwithstanding that no individual sum would have attracted interest under paragraph (i) of this rule; or

(v) rule 22 of these rules applies.

22. Where money is held by a solicitor for or on account of a client for a continuous period and the money is held on deposit in a separate designated account for only part of that period, and no interest would be payable for the rest of the period under rule 21(i) to (iii) of these rules, the solicitor shall:

(i) for the part of the period during which the money was so held on deposit, account for interest in accordance with rule 20(1)(i) of these rules; and

(ii) for the rest of the period, pay interest where it is fair and reasonable to do so having regard to all the circumstances including the interest which would have been payable under rule 21(i) to (iii) if the money had been kept off deposit for the whole of the period.

23. For the purposes of rule 20(1)(ii) of these rules the sum payable to the client shall be calculated by reference to the interest payable on a separate designated account:

(i) at the bank or building society where the money is held; or

(ii) where the money, or part of it, is held in successive and concurrent accounts maintained at different banks or building societies, at whichever of those banks or building societies was offering the highest rate of interest on such account on the day when the sum payable under rule 20(1)(ii) commenced to accrue; or

(iii) where, contrary to the provisions of Parts I and II of these rules, the money is not held in a client account, at any bank or building society nominated by the client.

24. Subject to rule 26(iii) of these rules, where a solicitor holds money as a stakeholder (whether or not such money is paid by a client of the solicitor) the solicitor shall pay interest in accordance with Part III of these rules save that such interest shall be paid to the person to whom the stake is paid.

25. Without prejudice to any other remedy which may be available to him or her, any client who feels aggrieved that interest or a sum equivalent thereto has not been paid to him or her under Part III of these rules shall be entitled to apply to the Law Society for a certificate as to whether or not interest ought to have been earned for him or her and, if so, the amount of such interest: and upon the issue of such a certificate the sum certified to be due shall be payable by the solicitor to the client.

26. Nothing in Part III of these rules shall:

(a) affect any arrangement in writing, whenever made, between a solicitor and his or her client as to the application of the client's money or interest thereon;

(b) apply to money received by a solicitor:

      (i)   being money subject to a controlled trust; or

      (ii)   in his or her capacity as trustee rather than as solicitor, on account of the trustees of any other trust of which the solicitor is a trustee;

  (c)   affect any agreement in writing for payment of interest on stakeholder money held by a solicitor.

PART IV — COMPLIANCE

27. (1)   In order to ascertain whether Parts I, II and III of these rules have been complied with the Council, acting either -

     (a)   on their own motion; or

     (b)   on a written statement and request transmitted to them by or on behalf of the Governing Body of a Local Law Society or a Committee thereof; or

     (c)   on a written complaint lodged with them by a third party,

     may require any solicitor, either in the solicitor's capacity as solicitor or controlled trustee, to produce at a time and place to be fixed by the Council, the solicitor's books of account, bank and building society statements, pass-books, loose-leaf bank and building society statements of account, vouchers and any other necessary documents, including any documents relating to all or any of the trusts of which a solicitor is controlled trustee, for the inspection of any person appointed by the Council and to supply to such person any necessary information and explanations and such person shall be directed to prepare for the information of the Council a report on the result of such inspection. Such report may be used as a basis for proceedings under the Solicitors Act 1974.

  (2)   Upon being required so to do a solicitor shall produce such books of account, bank and building society pass books, loose-leaf bank and building society statements, statements of account, vouchers and documents at the time and place fixed.

  (3)   In any case in which the Governing Body of a Local Law Society or a Committee thereof are of the opinion that an inspection should be made under this rule of the books of account, bank and building society pass books, loose-leaf bank and building society statements, statements of account, vouchers and any other necessary documents of a solicitor, including any documents relating to all or any of the trusts of which a solicitor is controlled trustee, it shall be the duty of such Governing Body or Committee to transmit to the Council a statement containing all relevant information in their possession and a request that such an inspection be made.

  (4)   Before instituting an inspection on a written complaint lodged with them by a third party, the Council shall require *prima facie* evidence that a ground of complaint exists, and may require the payment by such party to the Council of a reasonable sum to be fixed by them to cover the costs of the inspection and the costs of the solicitor against whom the complaint is made. The Council may deal with any sum so paid in such manner as they think fit.

  (5)   Where a requirement is made by the Council of a recognised body under this rule 27, such requirement shall, if so stated in the requirement, be deemed also to be made of any solicitor who is an officer or employee of that recognised

body where, respectively, such solicitor holds or has held client's money or is or has been a controlled trustee.

28. (1) Every requirement to be made by the Council of a solicitor or controlled trustee as the case may be under these rules shall be made in writing, and left at or sent by registered post or the recorded delivery service to the last address of the solicitor appearing in the Roll or in the Register kept by the Society under section 9 of the Solicitors Act 1974. If the requirement is so made and sent, it shall be deemed to have been received by the solicitor within forty-eight hours (excluding Saturdays, Sundays and Bank Holidays) of the time of posting.

(2) For the purposes of rule 28(1) of these rules, the reference to the last address of a solicitor or a controlled trustee appearing in the Roll or in the Register kept by the Society under section 9 of the Solicitors Act 1974 shall be construed, in relation to:

(i) a recognised body or a recognised body which is a controlled trustee, as a reference to the registered office of the recognised body last communicated to the Council or the Society under the Solicitors' Incorporated Practice Rules 1988 (or any rules for the time being replacing those rules); and

(ii) a registered foreign lawyer, or a registered foreign lawyer who is a controlled trustee, as a reference to the address of the registered foreign lawyer appearing in the register kept under section 89 of the Courts and Legal Services Act 1990.

29. Nothing in these rules shall deprive a solicitor of any recourse or right, whether by way of lien, set off, counterclaim, charge or otherwise, against moneys standing to the credit of a client account or controlled trust account.

PART V — APPLICATION

30. These rules shall not apply to a solicitor acting in the course of his or her employment as (a) a public officer, or (b) an officer of statutory undertakers, or (c) an officer of a local authority.

31. (1) These rules shall apply to a recognised body, and to a registered foreign lawyer practising as a member of a multi-national partnership or as the director of a recognised body, as they apply to a solicitor.

(2) In rules 2-30 of these rules, 'solicitor' shall, in addition to the meanings set out in the definition in rule 2(1) of these rules, also include a registered foreign lawyer practising as a member of a multi-national partnership or as the director of a recognised body, and a multi-national partnership.

(3) Notwithstanding paragraph (2) of this rule, the definition of a 'controlled trustee' in rule 2(1) of these rules shall not include a registered foreign lawyer.

(4) In these rules:

(a) 'controlled trustee' shall include:

(i) a registered foreign lawyer who is a member of a multi-national partnership and who is a sole trustee or co-trustee only with one or more of the employees or other partners of that partnership and who is trustee by virtue of being a member of that partnership; and

(ii) a registered foreign lawyer who is the director of a recognised body and who is a sole trustee or co-trustee only with one or more other officers or employees of that recognised body or the body itself and who is trustee by virtue of practising as a director of that body; and

(b) 'multi-national partnership' and 'registered foreign lawyer' shall have the meanings given in section 89 of the Courts and Legal Services Act 1990.

Annex 27C

Solicitors' Accounts (Legal Aid Temporary Provision) Rule 1992

Rule dated 8th May 1992 made by the Council of the Law Society with the concurrence, where requisite, of the Master of the Rolls pursuant to section 32 of the Solicitors Act 1974 and section 9 of the Administration of Justice Act 1985, regulating the keeping of accounts by solicitors, registered foreign lawyers and recognised bodies in respect of their English and Welsh practices.

Receipt of legal aid payments which include unpaid professional disbursements

(1) This rule is supplemental to the Solicitors' Accounts Rules 1991 and may be cited as the Solicitors' Accounts (Legal Aid Temporary Provision) Rule 1992. It shall come into operation on the 1st day of June 1992.

(2) In this rule:

    (a) 'office account' shall mean a bank or building society account in the name of a solicitor which is kept, maintained or operated by the solicitor in connection with his or her practice, not being a client account or controlled trust account;

    (b) all other expressions shall, unless the context otherwise requires, have the meanings assigned to them by rule 2 of the Solicitors' Accounts Rules 1991.

(3) When a solicitor receives from the Legal Aid Board a payment in respect of costs, all or part of which relates to the unpaid fees of another lawyer, professional or other agent, or expert instructed by the solicitor, the solicitor may, notwithstanding rules 3 and 5 of the Solicitors' Accounts Rules 1991, elect to pay the whole of the payment without delay into an office account PROVIDED THAT within fourteen days of receipt the solicitor transfers to a client account any part of the payment which relates to such fees still remaining unpaid.

(4) This rule shall, for the purposes of the Accountant's Report Rules 1991, be deemed to form part of Part I of the Solicitors' Accounts Rules 1991.

Annex 27D

Accountant's Report Rules 1991

(with consolidated amendments to 1st June 1992)

Rules dated 11th July 1991 made by the Council of the Law Society pursuant to section 34 of the Solicitors Act 1974, section 9 of the Administration of Justice Act 1985 and schedule 15 paragraph 6 of the Financial Services Act 1986 with respect to the delivery of accountants' reports by solicitors, registered foreign lawyers and recognised bodies in respect of their English and Welsh practices.

1. These rules may be cited as the Accountant's Report Rules 1991, and shall come into operation on the 1st day of June, 1992, whereupon the Accountant's Report Rules 1986 shall cease to have effect save in relation to reports covering periods prior to 1st June 1992.

2. In these rules:

    (1) the expressions 'client's money', 'client', 'trust money', 'controlled trust', 'controlled trust account', 'recognised body', 'separate designated account' and 'client account' shall have the meanings respectively assigned to them by the Solicitors' Accounts Rules 1991, but in the case of a solicitor holding one of the offices to which rule 30 of the Solicitors' Accounts Rules 1991, or subsection (2) of section 88 of the Solicitors Act 1974 applies, 'client's money' shall not extend to money held or received by the solicitor in the course of his or her employment in such office;

    (2) 'solicitor' means a solicitor of the Supreme Court and shall include a recognised body;

    (3) words in the singular include the plural, words in the plural include the singular and words importing the masculine or feminine shall include the neuter;

    (4) (i) a reference to the Solicitors' Accounts Rules 1991 includes any modification or amendment or re-enactment thereof;

        (ii) a reference to the Solicitors' Investment Business Rules 1990 includes any modification or amendment or re-enactment thereof;

    (5) other expressions shall except where otherwise stated have the meanings assigned to them by the Solicitors Act 1974.

3. (1) An accountant shall be qualified to give an accountant's report on behalf of a solicitor if -

    (a) he or she is a member of -

        (i) The Institute of Chartered Accountants in England and Wales; or

            (ii)   The Institute of Chartered Accountants of Scotland; or

            (iii)   The Chartered Association of Certified Accountants; or

            (iv)   The Institute of Chartered Accountants in Ireland; and

    (b)   he or she has neither been at any time during the accounting period to which the report relates, nor subsequently, before giving the report, become a partner or employee of such solicitor or any partner of the solicitor; and

    (c)   he or she is not employed by the same non-solicitor employer as such solicitor; and

    (d)   he or she is not subject to notice of disqualification under paragraph (2) of this rule.

(2)   In either of the following cases, that is to say, where -

    (a)   the accountant has been found guilty by the Disciplinary Tribunal of his or her professional body of professional misconduct or discreditable conduct; or

    (b)   the Council are satisfied that a solicitor has not complied with the provisions of Part I or Part II of the Solicitors' Accounts Rules 1991, in respect of matters not specified in an accountant's report and that the accountant was negligent in giving such report, whether or not an application be made for a grant out of the Compensation Fund;

the Council may at their discretion, at any time notify the accountant concerned that he or she is not qualified to give an accountant's report, and they may give notice of such fact to any solicitor on whose behalf he or she may have given an accountant's report, or who may appear to the Council to be likely to employ such accountant for the purpose of giving an accountant's report and cause notice of such fact to be publicised in the Law Society's *Gazette* or similar publication. After such accountant shall have been so notified, unless and until such notice of disqualification shall have been withdrawn by the Council, he or she shall not be qualified to give an accountant's report. Before coming to their decision the Council shall take into consideration any observations or explanation made or given by such accountant or on his or her behalf by the professional body of which he or she is a member.

(3)   Rule 3(1)(b) of this rule shall have effect in relation to the qualification of an accountant to give an accountant's report on behalf of a recognised body as if for 'of such solicitor or any partner of the solicitor' were substituted 'or officer (i) of such recognised body or any partner of its or (ii) of any person who or which is an officer, member or employee of such recognised body or of which such recognised body is an officer or member'.

4. (1)   For the purpose of giving an accountant's report, an accountant shall ascertain from the solicitor particulars of all bank and building society accounts (including controlled trust accounts and other accounts which are not client accounts) kept, maintained or operated by the solicitor in connection with his or her practice at any time during the accounting period to which the report relates and subject to paragraph (2) of this rule make the following examination of the books, accounts and other relevant documents of the solicitor:

(A)　relating to accounts other than controlled trust accounts -

(a)　so examine the book-keeping system in every office of the solicitor as to enable the accountant to verify that such system complies with rule 11 of the Solicitors' Accounts Rules 1991, and in respect of those solicitors authorised in the conduct of investment business by the Law Society, rule 13 of the Solicitors' Investment Business Rules 1990, and is so designed that -

　　(i)　an appropriate ledger account is kept for each client;

　　(ii)　such ledger accounts show separately from other information particulars of all clients' money received, held or paid on account of each client;

　　(iii)　transactions relating to clients' money and any other money dealt with through a client account are recorded in the solicitor's books so as to distinguish such transactions from transactions relating to any other money received, held or paid by the solicitor;

(b)　make test checks of postings to clients' ledger accounts from records of receipts and payments of clients' money and make test checks of the casts of such accounts and records;

(c)　compare a sample of lodgments into and payments from the client account as shown in bank and building society statements with the solicitor's records of receipts and payments of clients' money;

(d)　enquire into and test check the system of recording costs and of making transfers in respect of costs from the client account;

(e)　make a test examination of such documents as he or she shall request the solicitor to produce to him or her with the object of ascertaining and confirming -

　　(i)　that the financial transactions, (including those giving rise to transfers from one ledger account to another) evidenced by such documents, are in accordance with Part I of the Solicitors' Accounts Rules 1991 and

　　(ii)　that the entries in the books of account reflect those transactions in a manner complying with Part I of the Solicitors' Accounts Rules 1991;

(f)　subject to paragraph (3) of this rule extract (or check extractions of) balances on the clients' ledger accounts during the accounting period under review at not fewer than two dates selected by the accountant (one of which may be the last day of the accounting period), and at each such date -

　　(i)　compare the total as shown by such ledger accounts of the liabilities to the clients, including those for whom trust money is held in the client account, with the cash account balance; and

　　(ii)　reconcile that cash account balance with the balances held in client account and elsewhere as confirmed direct to the accountant by the relevant banks and building societies or other institutions;

(g) satisfy himself or herself that reconciliation statements have been kept in accordance with rule 11(5) of the Solicitors' Accounts Rules 1991;

(h) make a test examination of the clients' ledger accounts in order to ascertain whether payments from the client account have been made on any individual account in excess of money held on behalf of that client;

(i) check such office ledger and cash accounts and bank and building society statements as the solicitor maintains with a view to ascertaining whether any client's money has not been paid into a client account;

(j) check the books of account which contain details of client's money which, with the client's consent, is not held in a client account, to ascertain what transactions have been effected in respect of such account;

(k) make a test examination of the clients' ledger accounts in order to ascertain whether rule 11(3) of the Solicitors' Accounts Rules 1991 has been complied with;

(l) ask for such information and explanations as he or she may require arising out of sub-paragraphs (a) to (k) of this paragraph;

(B) relating to controlled trust accounts -

(a) ascertain from the solicitor details of the record-keeping system(s);

(b) select a limited number of controlled trust matters and in relation to those:

(i) make test checks of postings to the accounts kept pursuant to rule 19 of the Solicitors' Accounts Rules 1991 from records of receipts and payments of money and test checks of the casts of such accounts and records;

(ii) make a test examination of such documents as he or she shall request the solicitor to produce with the object of ascertaining and confirming that both the financial transactions evidenced by those documents and the entries in the accounting records reflecting those transactions are in accordance with Part II of the Solicitors' Accounts Rules 1991;

(iii) enquire into and test check the system of recording costs and of making transfers in respect of costs;

(iv) compare the balance at the last day of the accounting period under review as shown by the records kept under rule 19 of the Solicitors' Accounts Rules 1991 with the balance on each controlled trust account as confirmed direct to the accountant by the bank(s) and building society(ies);

(v) request such information and explanations as the accountant may require arising out of sub-paragraphs (i)-(iv).

(2) Nothing in paragraph (1) of this rule shall require the accountant -

(a) to extend his or her enquiries beyond the information contained in the relevant documents relating to any client's matter produced to him or her supplemented by such information and explanations as he or she may obtain from the solicitor;

(b)   to enquire into the stocks, shares, other securities or documents of title held by the solicitor on behalf of the solicitor's clients;

(c)   to consider whether the books of account of the solicitor have been properly written up in accordance with rules 11 and 19 of the Solicitors' Accounts Rules 1991, at any time other than the time as at which his or her examination of those books and accounts takes place.

(3)   In so far as rule 4(1)(A)(f) of these rules requires an accountant to extract, or check extractions of, balances on the clients' ledger accounts then, where a solicitor uses a computerised or mechanised system of accounting which automatically produces an extraction of all client ledger balances, in so far as such work merely amounts to a check on the accuracy of the computer or machine, the accountant shall not be required to check all client ledger balances extracted on the list produced by the computer or machine against the individual records of ledger accounts, provided the accountant:

(a)   is satisfied that a satisfactory system of control is in operation and the books are in balance;

(b)   carries out a test check of the extraction against the individual records; and

(c)   specifies in his or her report that he or she has relied on the exception set out in this rule 4(3).

(4)   If after making an examination in accordance with paragraphs (1),(2) and (3) of this rule it appears to the accountant that there is evidence that Part I or Part II of the Solicitors' Accounts Rules 1991 has not been complied with the accountant shall make such further examination as he or she considers necessary in order to complete the report with or without qualification.

(5)   Except where a client's money has been deposited in a separate designated account, nothing in these rules shall apply to any matter arising under section 33 of the Solicitors Act 1974 or Part III of the Solicitors' Accounts Rules 1991, notwithstanding any payment into client account of a sum in lieu of interest.

5.   Nothing in these rules shall deprive a solicitor of the right on the grounds of privilege as between solicitor and client to decline to produce to the accountant any document which the accountant may consider it necessary for him to inspect for the purposes of his or her examination in accordance with rule 4 of these rules and where the solicitor so declines, the accountant shall qualify the report to that effect setting out the circumstances.

6.   An accountant's report delivered by a solicitor under these rules shall be in the form set out in the Schedule to these rules or in a form to the like effect approved by the Council.

7. (1)   A solicitor need not deliver an accountant's report during a practice year if:

(a)   the solicitor did not hold or receive client's money or money subject to a controlled trust at any time during the previous practice year; or

(b)   having held or received client's money or money subject to a controlled trust during the previous practice year, the solicitor has ceased so to do and has delivered an accountant's report which confirms this; or

(c)   the solicitor is exempt from complying with the Solicitors' Accounts

Rules 1991 by virtue of rule 30 of those rules or section 88 (2) of the Solicitors Act 1974.

(2)   If a solicitor has been held out as a partner of another solicitor who has held or received client's money or money subject to a controlled trust that solicitor shall be deemed also to have held or received such money.

(3)   (a)   Rule 7(1) shall not have effect in respect of the delivery of an accountant's report by a recognised body.

        (b)   The Council will in each practice year be satisfied that the delivery of an accountant's report is unnecessary in the case of any recognised body which:

            (i)   did not hold or receive client's money or money subject to a controlled trust during the preceding practice year and which within three months of the end of such year delivers to the Council a declaration to that effect signed by a director of the body; or

            (ii)   having held or received client's money or money subject to a controlled trust during the preceding practice year, has ceased so to do and has delivered an accountant's report which confirms this; or

            (iii)   is exempt from complying with the Solicitors' Accounts Rules 1991 by virtue of rule 30 of those rules or section 88 (2) of the Solicitors Act 1974.

8.(1)   In the case of a solicitor who -

        (a)   becomes under an obligation to deliver his or her first accountant's report; or

        (b)   having been exempt under rule 7 of these rules from delivering an accountant's report in the preceding practice year, becomes under an obligation to deliver an accountant's report;

the accounting period shall begin on the date upon which he or she first held or received client's money or money subject to a controlled trust or, after such exemption, began again to hold or receive client's money or money subject to a controlled trust, and may cover less than twelve months, and shall in all other respects comply with the requirements of subsection (3) of section 34 of the Solicitors Act 1974.

(2)   In the case of a solicitor retiring from practice who, having ceased to hold or receive client's money or money subject to a controlled trust, is under an obligation to deliver his or her final accountant's report, the accounting period shall end on the date upon which the solicitor ceased to hold or receive client's money or money subject to a controlled trust, and may cover less than twelve months, and shall in all other respects comply with the requirements of subsection (3) of section 34 of the Solicitors Act 1974.

(3)   The reference in rule 8 (2) to a solicitor retiring from practice shall be construed as including a reference to a recognised body ceasing to practise.

9. (1)   In the case of a solicitor who -

        (a)   was not exempt under rule 7 of these rules from delivering an accountant's report in the preceding practice year; and

(b)   since the expiry of the accounting period covered by such accountant's report has become, or ceased to be, a member of a firm of solicitors,

the accounting period may cover less than twelve months and shall in all other respects comply with the requirements of subsection (3) of section 34 of the Solicitors Act 1974.

(2)   In the case of a solicitor who has two or more places of business -

(a)   separate accounting periods covered by separate accountant's reports may be adopted in respect of each such place of business, provided that the accounting periods comply with the requirements of subsection (3) of section 34 of the Solicitors Act 1974; and

(b)   the accountant's report or the accountant's reports delivered by the solicitor to the Society in each practice year shall cover all client's money or money subject to a controlled trust held or received by him or her.

10. (1)   Every notice to be given by the Council under these rules to a solicitor shall be in writing and left at or sent by registered post or the recorded delivery service to the last address of the solicitor appearing on the Roll or in the Register kept by the Society under section 9 of the Solicitors Act 1974. If the notice is so given and sent, it shall be deemed to have been received by the solicitor within forty-eight hours (excluding Saturdays, Sundays and Bank Holidays) of the time of posting.

(2)   For the purpose of rule 10 (1) of these rules, the reference to the last address of a solicitor appearing on the Roll or in the Register kept by the Society under section 9 of the Solicitors Act 1974 shall be construed, in relation to:

(i)   a recognised body, as a reference to the registered office of the recognised body last communicated to the Council or the Society under the Solicitors' Incorporated Practice Rules 1988 (or any rules for the time being replacing those rules); and

(ii)   a registered foreign lawyer, as a reference to the address of the registered foreign lawyer appearing in the register kept under section 89 of the Courts and Legal Services Act 1990.

11.   Every notice to be given by the Council under these rules to an accountant shall be in writing and left at or sent by registered post or the recorded delivery service to the address of the accountant as shown on an accountant's report or appearing in the records of the professional body of which the accountant is a member, and, when so given and delivered or sent, shall be deemed to have been received by the accountant within forty-eight hours (excluding Saturdays, Sundays and Bank Holidays) of the time of delivery or posting.

11A.(1)   These rules shall apply to a recognised body, and to a registered foreign lawyer practising as a member of a multi-national partnership or as the director of a recognised body, as they apply to a solicitor.

(2)   There shall be no requirement for a registered foreign lawyer to deliver an accountant's report in respect of any period in which he or she was not practising as set out in paragraph (1) of this rule.

(3)   In rules 2-10 of these rules, 'solicitor' shall, in addition to the meanings given in rule 2(2) of these rules, also include a registered foreign lawyer practising as set out in paragraph (1) of this rule.

(4) In these rules, 'multi-national partnership' and 'registered foreign lawyer' shall have the meanings given in section 89 of the Courts and Legal Services Act 1990.

12. The Council shall have power to waive in writing in any particular case any of the provisions of these rules.

THE SCHEDULE

ACCOUNTANT'S REPORT

Section 34 Solicitors Act 1974,
section 9 Administration of Justice Act 1985
and schedule 15 paragraph 6 of the Financial Services Act 1986

ACCOUNTANT'S REPORT RULES 1991

NOTE — This form may be used for a report in respect of:

1.   a solicitor;

1a.   a registered foreign lawyer ('RFL');

2.   a firm of solicitors, provided the names of all the partners in the firm appear in section A1 below;

2a.   a multi-national partnership, provided the names of all the partners appear in section A1 below;

3.   a recognised body.

SECTION A — DO NOT COMPLETE IF REPORT IS SUBMITTED ON BEHALF OF A RECOGNISED BODY

PLEASE INDICATE WHETHER THIS REPORT COVERS ALL THE PARTNERS WITHIN THE FIRM WHO HAVE HELD CLIENTS' MONIES (OR MONEY SUBJECT TO A CONTROLLED TRUST) DURING THE PERIOD UNDER REVIEW OR WHETHER INDIVIDUAL REPORTS ARE BEING SUBMITTED

*Tick box as appropriate.	*covers all partners/ sole principal	*individual reports submitted
	☐	☐

NOTE — Please complete in block capitals; the letters '(RFL)' must be entered against the surname of any RFL

1. Full name of solicitor(s) and/or RFL(s)
   FORENAMES   SURNAME

(Continue on a separate sheet as necessary)

NOTE — All addresses at which the solicitor(s)/RFL(s) practise(s) must be covered by an Accountant's Report or Reports. If an address is not so covered the reason must be stated.

[In the case of an RFL, this Report only refers to his or her practice(s) as partner of a solicitor(s) or as director of a recognised body].

2. Firm(s) name(s) and address(es)

(Continue on a separate sheet as necessary)

NOTE — The period must comply with section 34(3) of the Solicitors Act 1974, and the Accountant's Report Rules 1991

3. Accounting period

Beginning.................Ending...................

NOTE — Delete (a) or (b) as appropriate

4(a) I/we confirm that a copy of this Report has been sent to each of the solicitors and/or RFLs to whom this Report relates

or

(b)I/we confirm that one copy of this Report has been sent to the following partner of the firm, on behalf of all the partners of the firm:

....

SECTION B — **TO BE COMPLETED ONLY IF REPORT IS SUBMITTED ON BEHALF OF A RECOGNISED BODY**

NOTE: This name must comply with rule 22 of the Solicitors' Incorporated Practice Rules 1988

1. Name of recognised body

....
....

NOTE: The
registered
office must
comply with rule 8
of the Solicitors'
Incorporated
Practice Rules
1988

2. Registered office

....

....

....

3. Principal office, if different from registered office

....

....

4. Places of business other than those specified in
2. and 3.

....

....

NOTE: Please
complete in
block capitals;
the letters
'(RFL)' must be
entered against
the surname of
any RFL

5. Name of officers of recognised body

SURNAME   FORENAMES   OFFICE HELD

(Continue on a separate sheet as necessary)

NOTE — The
period must
comply with section
34(3) of the
Solicitors Act 1974,
and the Accountant's
Report Rules 1991

6. Accounting period

Beginning.................Ending...................

NOTE: Delete (a)
or (b) as
appropriate

7. (a) I/we confirm that a copy of this Report has
been sent to each of the directors of the recognised
body to which this Report relates

or

(b) I/we confirm that one copy of this Report has
been sent to the following officer of the recognised body, on
behalf of all the officers of the recognised body:

....

SECTION C

1.   In compliance with section 34 of the Solicitors Act 1974, and the Accountant's
      Report Rules 1991 made thereunder and under section 9 of the Administration of
      Justice Act 1985 and schedule 15 paragraph 6 of the Financial Services Act 1986,

I/we have examined to the extent required by rule 4 of the said rules the books, accounts and documents produced to me/us in respect of the above practice(s) of the above-named solicitor(s)/ RFL(s) named in section A1/the recognised body named in section B1.

2. In so far as an opinion can be based on this limited examination I am/we are satisfied that during the above-mentioned period he/she/it has/they have complied with the provisions of Parts I and II of the Solicitors' Accounts Rules 1991 and, where he/she/it is/they are authorised in the conduct of investment business by the Law Society, rule 13 of the Solicitors' Investment Business Rules 1990 except so far as concerns:

   (a) certain trivial breaches due to clerical errors or mistakes in book-keeping, all of which were rectified on discovery and none of which, I am/we are satisfied, resulted in any loss to any client;

   (b) the matters set out in Section E, in respect of which I/we have not been able to satisfy myself/ourselves for the reasons therein stated;

   (c) the matters set out in Section F, in respect of which it appears to me/us that the solicitor(s)/RFL(s)/recognised body has/have not complied with the provisions of Parts I and II of the Solicitors' Accounts Rules 1991 and, where he/she/it is /they are authorised in the conduct of investment business by the Law Society, rule 13 of the Solicitors' Investment Business Rules 1990.

3. The results of the comparisons required under rule 4 (1) (A) (f) of the Accountant's Report Rules 1991, at the dates selected by me/us were as follows:

   (i) at..

   £

   (a) Liabilities to clients as shown by clients' ledger accounts

   (b) Cash held in client account and client's money held elsewhere than in a client account after allowances for outstanding cheques and lodgments cleared after date

   (c) Difference between 3(i)(a) and 3(i)(b)(if any)   £

   (ii) at..

   £

   (a) Liabilities to clients as shown by clients' ledger accounts

   (b) Cash held in client account and client's money held elsewhere than in a client account after allowances for outstanding cheques and lodgments cleared after date

   (c) Difference between 3(ii)(a) and 3(ii)(b)(if any)   £

NOTE: The figure to be shown in 3(i)(a) and 3(ii)(a) above is the total of credit balances, without adjustment for debit balances (unless capable of proper set off i.e. being in respect of the same client) or receipts and payments not capable of allocation to individual ledger accounts.

SECTION D — DO NOT COMPLETE IF REPORT IS SUBMITTED ON BEHALF OF A RECOGNISED BODY

1. The following solicitor(s) [RFL(s)] having retired from active practice as solicitor(s) [practice in partnership with solicitor(s) or as director(s) of a recognised body] ceased to hold clients' money (or money subject to a controlled trust) on the date indicated and in respect of this solicitor/these solicitors [this RFL/these RFLs] the report covers the period up to the date of cessation:

    FULL NAME   DATE CEASED TO HOLD CLIENTS' MONEY (OR MONEY SUBJECT TO A CONTROLLED TRUST)

2. The following solicitor(s) [RFL(s)] having left the firm and ceased to practise under this style, ceased to hold clients' money under this style (or money subject to a controlled trust in connection with this practice) on the date indicated and in respect of this solicitor/these solicitors [this RFL/these RFLs] the report covers the period up to the date of cessation:

    FULL NAME   DATE CEASED TO HOLD CLIENTS' MONEY UNDER THIS STYLE (OR MONEY SUBJECT TO A CONTROLLED TRUST IN CONNECTION WITH THIS PRACTICE)

3. The following solicitor(s) [RFL(s)] has/have joined the firm during the period under review on the date indicated and in respect of this solicitor/these solicitors [this RFL/these RFL(s)] the report covers the period from the date on which clients' money was held under this style (or money subject to a controlled trust was held in connection with this practice):

    FULL NAME   DATE FROM WHICH CLIENTS' MONEY HELD UNDER THIS STYLE (OR MONEY SUBJECT TO A CONTROLLED TRUST HELD IN CONNECTION WITH THIS PRACTICE)

SECTION E

Matters in respect of which the accountant has been unable to satisfy himself or herself and the reasons for that inability:

. . . .

SECTION F

Matters (other than trivial breaches) in respect of which it appears to the accountant that the solicitor(s)/RFL(s)/recognised body has/have not complied with the provisions of Parts I and II of the Solicitors' Accounts Rules 1991 and, where he/she/it is/they are authorised in the conduct of investment business, rule 13 of the Solicitors' Investment Business Rules 1990:

. . . .

SECTION G

Particulars of the accountant -

NOTE: Please complete in block capitals	Full name..
	Qualifications...
	Firm name..
	Address..
	....
	Date...
This Report	Signature ....

This Report
may be signed in
the name of the
firm of account-
ants of which the
accountant is a
partner or
employee
provided
that the
particulars
of the
accountant
signing the
Report are
also specified.

To   The Law Society,
     Accountants' Reports,
     Ipsley Court,
     Redditch,
     Worcs. B98 0TD.
     (DX 19114 Redditch)

Annex 27E

Guidance — the Accountant's Report Rules 1991

(see also Annex 27D)

The Accountant's Report Rules 1991, as amended by the Accountant's Report (Controlled Trust Accounts) Amendment Rules 1992, have now extended some of the reporting requirements to *controlled trusts*; i.e. trusts where the solicitor is the sole trustee or co-trustee only with one or more of his or her partners or employees.

1. The accountant is required to make a test check of a limited number of accounts and files relating to controlled trusts.

2. There is no obligation to check every controlled trust account. The number and selection of controlled trust accounts included in the examination is left to the discretion of the reporting accountant. The fact that an accountant (not necessarily the reporting accountant) is already engaged in the management of a particular trust may well be relevant to the reporting accountant's decision whether or not to do test checks in respect of that particular trust, especially if annual accounts are prepared by the trust's accountant.

3. Once details of the record-keeping system have been ascertained from the solicitor, the remaining requirements are simply to make a number of test checks on selected controlled trusts along the lines of those required for other matters. There is no question of the reporting accountant having to check, for instance, that the investments made in respect of the trust are appropriate.

4. The new requirements are not intended materially to increase the workload of the accountant. The reporting accountant will select what he or she considers to be a suitable sample of controlled trust accounts and it may be appropriate to make a correspondingly reduced number of checks in respect of the client and other accounts. For instance, if the reporting accountant currently test checks, say 20 files, he or she might include in those 20 files a couple of controlled trusts.

5. Accountants are reminded that the solicitor's duty to keep separate accounts for each controlled trust will in many cases be discharged by simply retaining bank statements and building society passbooks, provided that the narrative is sufficient to understand the various movements on the account. However, in the case of a trust which is particularly complex or is likely to be protracted, formal books of account should be kept.

1st June 1992

Annex 27F

Guidance — model form of accountant's report for overseas practices

Section 34 Solicitors Act 1974
Rule 16 Solicitors' Overseas Practice Rules 1990
Accountant's report for solicitor(s) practising outside England and Wales

Notes:

1.   In the case of a firm with more than one solicitor partner, one copy of the report may be delivered provided Section B below is completed with the names of all the solicitor partners in the firm.

2.   The obligation to deliver a report extends to all solicitor shareowners and directors of a corporate practice operating entirely overseas in which solicitors own a controlling majority of the shares. The form should be completed as if such solicitor shareowners and directors and any other shareowners and directors were practising in partnership, e.g. if only one copy of the report is being delivered for all such solicitors, a tick should be entered against 'COVERS ALL SOLICITOR PARTNERS' in Section A below.

A.   PLEASE INDICATE WHETHER THIS REPORT COVERS ALL THE SOLICITOR PARTNERS WITHIN THE FIRM WHO HAVE HELD CLIENTS' MONIES DURING THE PERIOD UNDER REVIEW OR WHETHER INDIVIDUAL REPORTS ARE BEING SUBMITTED.

TICK AS APPROPRIATE:

COVERS ALL SOLICITOR PARTNERS   . . . .

INDIVIDUAL REPORTS BEING SUBMITTED   . . . .

NOT PRACTISING IN PARTNERSHIP   . . . .

B.   Solicitor(s) full name(s) (block capitals).

. . . .
. . . .
. . . .

(continue on separate sheet as necessary)

C.   Firm(s) name(s) and address(es) outside England and Wales (Note: All addresses at which the solicitor(s) practise(s) must be covered by an accountant's report or reports. If an address is not so covered, the reason must be stated).

....

....

....

D.   Other practising styles (where applicable).

....

....

....

E.   Where practising in partnership with persons not included in Section B above, give the names of all such partners, indicating whether or not they are solicitors.

....

....

....

F.   Accounting period(s) (Note: The period(s) must comply with section 34(3) of the Solicitors Act 1974 and rule 16 of the Solicitors' Overseas Practice Rules 1990).

beginning: ....   ending: ....

beginning: ....   ending: ....

ACCOUNTANT'S REPORT

In compliance with section 34 of the Solicitors Act 1974 and the Solicitors' Overseas Practice Rules 1990 made thereunder, I have examined to the extent required by rule 16 of the said rules the books, accounts and documents produced to me in respect of the above practice(s) of the above-named solicitor(s).

1.   In so far as an opinion can be based on this limited examination I am satisfied that during the above-mentioned period(s) he/she has/they have complied with the provisions of rule 12(1) to (4) of the Solicitors' Overseas Practice Rules 1990, except so far as concerns (delete sub-paragraphs not applicable): -

(a)   certain trivial breaches due to clerical errors or mistakes in book-keeping, all of which were rectified on discovery and none of which, I am satisfied, resulted in any loss to any client;

(b)   the matters set out in the First Schedule on the back hereof, in respect of which I have not been able to satisfy myself for the reasons therein stated;

(c)   the matters set out in the Second Schedule on the back hereof, in respect of which it appears to me that the solicitor(s) has/have not complied with the provisions of rule 12(1) to (4) of the Solicitors' Overseas Practice Rules 1990.

2.   The statements (and explanation where applicable) required under rule 16(3)(e) of the Solicitors' Overseas Practice Rules 1990 are as follows:

at ....

(last day of the period to which this report relates)

(a)   total amount of money held at banks or similar institutions on behalf of clients   ....

(b)   total liabilities to clients   . . . .

(c)   the explanation for the difference between (a) and (b) (if any) is as follows:

. . . .

. . . .

. . . .

. . . .

3.   The following solicitor(s) having retired from active practice as (a) solicitor(s) ceased to hold client's money on the date(s) indicated and in respect of this solicitor/these solicitors the report covers the period up to the date(s) of cessation:

FULL NAME(S)   DATE(S) CEASED TO HOLD
                                      CLIENT'S MONEY

. . . .

. . . .

. . . .

. . . .

4.   The following solicitor(s) having left the firm and ceased to practise under this style, ceased to hold client's money under this style on the date(s) indicated and in respect of this solicitor/these solicitors the report covers the period up to the date(s) of cessation:

FULL NAME(S)   DATE(S) CEASED TO HOLD
                                      CLIENT'S MONEY UNDER THIS
                                      STYLE

. . . .

. . . .

. . . .

. . . .

5.   The following solicitor(s) has/have joined the firm during the period under review on the date(s) indicated and in respect of this solicitor/these solicitors the report covers the period from the date(s) on which client's money was held under this style:

FULL NAME(S)   DATE(S) FROM WHICH CLIENT'S
                                      MONEY HELD UNDER THIS
                                      STYLE

. . . .

. . . .

. . . .

6.   Particulars of the accountant or other person signing the report:

Full name. . . . .

Qualification. . . . .

Firm name. . . . .

Address. . . . .

. . . .

Date: . . . .   Signature:. . . . .

To: The Law Society
      Accountants' Reports
      Ipsley Court
      Redditch
      Worcestershire
      B98 0TD
      ENGLAND

      DX: 19114 REDDITCH

FIRST SCHEDULE

Matters in respect of which the accountant has been unable to satisfy himself/herself and the reasons for that inability:

. . . .
. . . .
. . . .
. . . .
. . . .
. . . .
. . . .
. . . .
. . . .
. . . .
. . . .
. . . .
. . . .
. . . .
. . . .
. . . .
. . . .

SECOND SCHEDULE

Matters (other than trivial breaches) in respect of which it appears to the accountant that the solicitor(s) has/have not complied with the provisions of rule 12(1) to (4) of the Solicitors' Overseas Practice Rules 1990:

....

....

....

....

....

....

....

....

....

Annex 27G

Guidance — deposit interest

Introduction

1. The rules on deposit interest ('the deposit interest provisions') appear in Part III of the Solicitors' Accounts Rules 1991 (see Annex 27B). The Society receives a number of enquiries from solicitors on two points in particular:

    A. What is the rate of interest which should be paid under the deposit interest provisions? and

    B. Is it permissible to enter into written agreements with clients to disapply the deposit interest provisions?

    It should be noted that the deposit interest provisions do not apply to money subject to a controlled trust (i.e. a trust where the solicitor is sole trustee or co-trustee only with one or more partners or employees). This guidance applies only to categories of money covered by the deposit interest provisions; i.e. money held or received on account of the firm's clients: including (i) stakeholder money; and (ii) money held or received on account of a trust where the solicitor is trustee with others outside the firm (assuming, as will normally be the case, that the solicitor holds or receives the money in his or her capacity as solicitor).

    Where the deposit interest provisions do not apply (as in the case of money subject to a controlled trust), all interest should normally be credited to the relevant trust in accordance with the general law.

A. Rates of interest

2. Rule 20(1) of the Solicitors' Accounts Rules 1991 provides that a solicitor who holds money for or on account of a client must account to that client for either:

    (i)   all interest earned (in the case of a separate designated account) or

    (ii) an equivalent sum (in the case of a general client account), based on the interest which would have been earned if the money held for that client had been kept on deposit in a separate designated account. Rule 20(1) follows section 33(1) of the Solicitors Act 1974.

3. All interest earned on a separate designated account must be paid to the client but the obligation to pay an equivalent sum for amounts held on general client account is subject to the *de minimis* provisions contained in Rule 21. It should also be noted that section 33(3) of the Solicitors Act 1974 permits solicitors to retain any interest earned on general client account over and above that which they are obliged to pay to their clients under the deposit interest provisions.

4.   Neither section 33 of the Solicitors Act 1974 nor Rule 20(1) specifies particular rates of interest. Instead, reference is made to interest actually earned on deposit in a separate designated account, or to 'a sum equivalent to the interest which would have accrued' had the money been kept on deposit in a separate designated account.

5.   In relation to the second category, the sum payable to the client is normally calculated by reference to the interest payable on a separate designated account at the bank or building society where the money is held (Rule 23(i)); i.e. the bank or building society where the solicitor keeps his or her general client account.

6.   Banks and building societies offer many different accounts with varying bands of interest. The rates of interest available for businesses may be lower than the deposit rates available to the general public, particularly for smaller deposits. Some, but not all, of the apparent difference may result from interest being credited quarterly on business accounts and only annually on accounts available to the general public.

7.   It should also be remembered that interest may be set at even lower rates for individual businesses to offset other benefits. For example, a solicitor might prefer not to be charged for telegraphic transfers or drawing cheques and this might be reflected in the rates of interest paid on the solicitor's client accounts. It is not therefore considered appropriate simply to look at the rate actually being paid to the solicitor, given that this could be kept artificially low. Rather, it would be appropriate to consider the rate or range of rates available to the bank's solicitor customers generally. *Prima facie*, separate designated accounts are business accounts. However, if the bank treats such accounts as personal accounts and pays interest accordingly, that would be the appropriate rate of interest in calculating a 'sum equivalent'.

8.   It is normal nowadays for banks and building societies to offer accounts which provide instant access to savings in conjunction with competitive rates of interest. It may, however, be relevant to consider whether the sum held on general client account would have been paid into an instant access or longer-term deposit account, had the solicitor placed it in a separate designated account. When instant access is important, this can be taken into account in assessing the appropriate rate of interest to be paid, if the solicitor's bank pays at different rates on instant access accounts. The converse applies where the money is unlikely to be required at short notice. However, a solicitor is not expected to have the benefit of hindsight.

9.   Solicitors should be aware that many banks operate deposit accounts with rates of interest as low as 1.75%, regardless of the amount deposited, and may place any sum of money earmarked for deposit in such an account, unless the solicitor stipulates otherwise. This practice is followed despite the existence of other deposit accounts which pay higher 'stepped' rates to reflect the sums invested and is obviously for the benefit of the bank concerned.

10. It would seem inconceivable that a court would consider that a solicitor had fulfilled his or her obligations to a client by placing a reasonably large sum for any length of time in a separate designated account yielding a very low rate of interest. Similarly, it is inappropriate for a solicitor to calculate the 'sum equivalent' for monies kept in a general client account by looking at accounts yielding such low rates of interest. On the other hand, solicitors would not normally be obliged to pay at a higher rate than they themselves receive on general client account, unless that rate is being kept artificially low, or unless the bank routinely pays a higher rate on separate designated accounts. Furthermore, solicitors are not required to pay the interest which the client himself or herself could have obtained.

11.   In summary, solicitors should aim to obtain a reasonable rate of interest for clients on any separate designated account and to account to their clients for a fair rate of interest on monies kept in general client account. The rate of interest may not be the highest rate obtainable but it is not acceptable simply to look at the lowest rate of interest obtainable.

B.   Contracting out of the deposit interest provisions

Partial contracting out

12.   Rule 20 is subject to Rule 26(i) which, in accordance with section 33(4) of the Solicitors Act 1974, states that:

'Nothing in Part III of these rules shall

(i)   affect any arrangement in writing, whenever made, between a solicitor and his or her client as to the application of the client's money or interest thereon;'

On the face of it therefore, it seems that a solicitor is entitled to contract out of the deposit interest provisions. However, this guidance demonstrates that caution should be exercised in this respect.

13.   Rule 21(i) contains the *de minimis* provisions relating to deposit interest. These provisions operate by way of a table setting out minimum amounts and lengths of time for which money has to be held before interest becomes payable. They should not be confused with rule 10 of the Solicitors' Practice Rules 1990, which deals with *commission* received from third parties and provides that solicitors must normally account to the client for any commission received of more than £20.

14.   When the Council looked at the deposit interest provisions on 30th April 1992, interest rates for savings between £500-£25,000 appeared to average 6%-8%. An example was given of the way in which the table contained in Rule 21(i) of the deposit interest provisions would work, using a 6% interest rate for sums below £10,000 and a 7 1/2% interest rate for sums in excess of £10,000. These figures are set out below:

Interest rate	Number of weeks	Minimum amount	Interest payable
6% x	8/52 x	£1,000 =	£ 9.23
6% x	4/52 x	£2,000 =	£ 9.23
7 1/2% x	2/52 x	£10,000 =	£28.85
7 1/2% x	1/52 x	£20,000 =	£28.85

The average of these figures is £19.04. The aim of Rule 21 is that the deposit interest provisions should provide an *average de minimis* sum of approximately £20.

15.   However, interest rates change regularly and where rates fall the sums payable at the lower end of the table may not always be high enough to justify the expense of accounting to clients. As an alternative to using the table solicitors may prefer to stipulate in standard terms of business a £20 *de minimis* exception for all sums held by them. This is acceptable.

16. Some solicitors have computerised systems which produce calculations of deposit interest due to clients. Many will, however, produce say only four bands of interest rates (whereas banks might offer 10 or more). It is acceptable to utilise a limited number of bands of interest and to stipulate in standard terms of business that those rates will be applied in the calculation of interest due to the firm's clients, provided that the firm's rates do not result overall in a materially worse position for its clients.

Contracting out altogether

17. Despite the proviso in Rule 26(i), it is considered improper for a solicitor to request a client to enter into an arrangement in writing with a view to paying no interest at all. This is because the client is then deprived of his or her entitlement under the deposit interest provisions when he or she is probably in no position to assess the merits of the request and to give informed consent.

18. It has been argued that the deposit interest provisions are similar to the commissions rule which allows a solicitor to keep commission with the client's agreement. There is however a fundamental distinction between Rule 10 of the Solicitors' Practice Rules 1990 (commissions rule) and the deposit interest provisions, in that the former only allows a solicitor to keep commission on the basis of full disclosure of the amount or method of calculation. The difficulty in seeking a client's agreement at the outset of the transaction to waive his or her rights under the deposit interest provisions is, that it will probably not be known exactly how much money the solicitor will hold or for how long and the client will thus not be in a position to give informed consent because he or she will not know precisely what rights he or she is being asked to give up. A solicitor might well be found to be in breach of his or her fiduciary duty by seeking such an agreement without affording the client an opportunity to give informed consent.

19. However, there are some cases where it might be appropriate for such an arrangement to be made where there is a *quid pro quo* for the client; for example, where a solicitor acts for a company in numerous debt collection matters, possibly with a float from the company with which to finance cases, and the rate of charge agreed with the client takes into account the fact that no interest is to be paid. There may be other acceptable cases where a special price is fixed for an individual client on the basis that the solicitor will retain interest. In seeking a client's consent to such an arrangement, solicitors will have to be aware of the differing needs of clients; for instance, a client unaccustomed to dealing with solicitors will require more by way of explanation than a commercial client who regularly instructs the firm.

20. In summary, each case should be treated on its merits. Solicitors should act fairly towards their clients and provide sufficient information to enable them to give informed consent where it is felt appropriate to depart from the deposit interest provisions. It would be considered appropriate to contract out of the deposit interest provisions where this is at the request of or for the convenience of the client, or where the client receives some compensating benefit. Contracting out would never be appropriate where it is against the client's interests.

Contracting out — stakeholder money

21. Stakeholder money is now subject to Rule 24 of the deposit interest provisions and the solicitor must pay interest in accordance with the rules to the person to whom the stake is paid. The Law Society's Standard Conditions of Sale provide at 2.2.3 that a deposit held as stakeholder is held 'on terms that on completion it is paid to the seller with accrued interest.'

22. Rule 24 is subject to Rule 26(iii) which provides:

    'Nothing in Part III of these rules shall...

    (iii) affect any agreement in writing for payment of interest on stakeholder money held by a solicitor.'

    This on the face of it seems to permit the solicitor to obtain an agreement for the solicitor to retain interest instead of paying it to the recipient of the stake. It is not however normal practice for a stakeholder in conveyancing transactions to receive remuneration in this way and solicitors must exercise caution as the following demonstrates.

23. A solicitor stakeholder is entitled to stipulate for a reasonable charge for his or her services. It may in appropriate circumstances be acceptable for solicitors to include a special provision in the contract that the solicitor stakeholder retains the interest on the deposit to cover his or her charges for acting as a stakeholder. However, this is only acceptable if it will provide fair and reasonable remuneration for the work and risk involved in holding a stake. The contract could, perhaps, stipulate a maximum charge, with any interest earned above that figure being paid to the recipient of the stake.

24. For an agreement validly to exclude the operation of the rule, three parties must assent to it — the stakeholder, the other party and the stakeholder's own client. Proper instructions must be sought from the client and no unfair advantage taken. A solicitor should be particularly careful not to take advantage of either the client or other party where the latter is unrepresented.

November 1992

Annex 27H

Tax on bank and building society interest — practice information

On 6th April 1991 the system of taxing interest paid to U.K. individuals by banks and building societies changed. Composite rate tax was abolished and replaced by deduction of basic rate tax at source. This article, which has been discussed with the Inland Revenue, explains the effect of this change on interest arising after 5th April 1991 on clients' money. The position in relation to interest arising before then is described in an article which appeared in [1987] *Gazette*, 1 July, 1960 and which was reprinted in the 1990 edition of the Guide, Appendix D18.

The Solicitors' Accounts Rules 1991, Part III

Under this part of the rules ('the deposit interest provisions'), a solicitor who is required to account for interest to a client may do so by either of two methods. He or she may:

(a)   account to the client for the interest earned on the client's money in a separate designated account; or

(b)   pay to the client a sum equivalent to the interest which would have accrued for the benefit of the client if the money had been deposited in a separate designated account pursuant to the rules. This will usually follow the deposit of the money in a general client deposit account.

These two procedures are referred to as Method A and Method B respectively. The tax position under the Solicitors' Accounts (Deposit Interest) Rules 1988, which operated prior to 1st June 1992, was identical.

Deduction of tax at source

The tax deduction at source rules apply, broadly, to designated client accounts which, before 6th April 1991, were subject to composite rate tax, e.g. accounts held for individuals who are ordinarily resident in the U.K., and, where held with a building society, clients' accounts on which the society was required to account for a sum representing basic rate tax, e.g. investments by companies, discretionary and accumulation trusts.

Interest on general client accounts, whether with a bank or (since 6th February 1989) a building society, is paid gross.

When opening any designated account the solicitor must provide the necessary information for the bank or building society to decide whether or not deduction of tax at source is appropriate.

Tax treatment of interest — Method A

Method A applies to designated accounts. Where tax is deducted at source by the bank or building society interest will be received by the solicitor net, and he or she will simply pass it on to the client net — no tax deduction certificate is required. The client, when making his or her tax return, will declare the interest as having been received under deduction of tax, and will only be liable to be assessed in relation to higher rate tax in respect of it (since he or she will have a tax credit for basic rate tax). If the client is for any reason not liable to income tax, he or she can recover any tax deducted from the interest. In those circumstances the solicitor must, on being required by the client, obtain a certificate of deduction of tax from the bank or building society and deliver this to the client. The client's position is, therefore, for practical purposes, the same as that which arises where he or she receives interest from a building society or bank on a deposit of his or her own.

Where the client is not liable to tax or is not ordinarily resident (NOR) in the U.K. the bank or building society will pay the interest gross provided that it holds the relevant declaration. Declarations of non-ordinary residence can be completed by either the solicitor or the client but declarations of non-liability by U.K. residents will normally be completed by the client. However, in view of the difficulty of obtaining complete information about an overseas client, solicitors may feel that it is more appropriate for the client concerned to make the declaration, especially since it contains an undertaking to notify the bank or building society should circumstances change.

Where the tax deduction at source rules do not apply, the solicitor will receive interest from the bank or building society gross and may account to the client for it gross, even if the client is non-resident. The client will be assessed on the gross receipt (but a non-resident client may, by concession, not be assessed) and, (unless the solicitor has been acting as the client's agent for tax purposes — see below under 'Solicitors as agents'), the solicitor himself or herself will not be assessed in respect of the interest.

Tax treatment of interest — Method B

Where Method B is used, deduction of tax at source does not apply to the solicitor's general client deposit account at either a bank or building society, and interest is therefore paid to the solicitor gross. When making a payment to the client of an equivalent sum under the deposit interest provisions the solicitor should make the payment gross even if the client is not ordinarily resident. The payment is of compensation in lieu of interest, and is not itself interest. The client will be assessed to income tax on his or her receipt, but a non-resident may, by concession, not be assessed.

Wherever payments are made by solicitors to clients under Method B they can, in practice, be set off against the solicitor's Case III assessment on gross interest received on general client account deposits; if the payments exceed the interest received, a Case II deduction can be claimed for the excess.

Stake money

(a)   Position prior to 1st June 1992

The existing law in relation to interest on stake money is generally agreed to be that the interest belongs to the stakeholder. However, at [1986] *Gazette,* 23 July, 2292, there was a recommendation by the Council that contracts should make provision for the interest on any stake held by a solicitor; the following clause was suggested:

> 'The stakeholder shall pay to the vendor/purchaser a sum equal to the interest the deposit would have earned if placed on deposit (less costs of acting as stakeholder).'

It was further recommended that, in default of such a provision, interest on stakes should normally be treated as if it were covered by the Solicitors' Accounts (Deposit Interest) Rules 1988 where the stake is paid to the stakeholder's client. The tax treatment of interest on stake money will depend on which, if either, recommendation has been followed.

Where the stake was held in a general client account interest will be paid gross by the bank or building society. The solicitor is assessable under Schedule D Case III in the normal way but any payment to the client in accordance with the Law Society's recommendation can be set-off in full. If there is insufficient available a Case II deduction would have to be claimed.

Where the stake was held in a designated client deposit account the tax position is slightly more complicated. Because in law the interest belongs to the stakeholder/solicitor it will be paid by the bank or building society under deduction of basic rate tax. But when making an equivalent payment in accordance with the Law Society's recommendation, the solicitor will have to account to the client on a gross basis since the amount received by the client will be treated by the Revenue as a taxable receipt in his or her hands. The solicitor will, however, be able to set-off the whole amount paid to the client in respect of the interest, as above. In either case the situation can arise where the solicitor is unable to make a payment to the client in the same tax year in which interest is received, for example, if stake money is held pending the outcome of litigation. Because the solicitor remains assessable throughout the period for which the stake deposit is held, there is a possible loss in terms of cashflow if the tax liability cannot be met out of the interest arising. It is essential to bear this in mind when making provision for interest in any contract or undertaking to the Court. It would not be prudent for a solicitor in such circumstances to agree a term which precluded him or her resorting to the interest arising to satisfy the taxation liability.

(b)   Position from 1st June 1992

Under the Solicitors' Accounts Rules 1991 (which came into force on 1st June 1992) stake money is expressly brought within the definition of 'client's money'. Interest will be payable to the person to whom the stake is paid using either Method A or B above. But there will still be circumstances in which payment is not possible until a later tax year. Where this situation looks likely to arise, e.g. if the stake is held pending the outcome of litigation, the deposit would normally be placed in a general client account until it is established to whom the stake is to be paid. Because, in the meantime, interest will be included in the solicitor's Case III assessment it is again important to make provision for the tax liability to be met out of the interest as it arises.

Tax treatment of interest — money paid into court

The position of monies paid into court is covered by the Supreme Court Funds Rules as amended. Where any order for payment out of monies in court is made, the order should provide for the disposal of any interest accrued to the date of the judgement or order, and for interest accruing thereafter up to the date the monies are paid out in accordance with the order. In the absence of such provision interest accruing between the date of the payment into court, and its acceptance or the judgement or order for payment out, goes to the party who made the payment in, and interest from the date of the judgement or order follows the capital payment.

Where interest is paid to a party to proceedings in respect of money held in court, it should be paid to the client gross, even if he or she is non-resident. The client will normally be assessable under Case III, but the solicitor will not, unless exceptionally he or she is assessable as the client's agent.

Solicitors as agents

Where a solicitor acts for tax purposes as agent for a non-resident client, the solicitor will remain liable to be assessed on behalf of the client in relation to interest earned in a designated deposit account, where Method A is used, unless he or she is an agent without management or control of the interest, in which case, under Extra Statutory Concession B13, no assessment will be made on him or her. Where the solicitor is assessable, the charge may, if appropriate, be to higher rate tax, so the solicitor will need to retain tax at the client's marginal rate of income tax from interest received gross from a bank or building society before remitting it to the client. This is the case even though the account would not be subject to deduction of tax at source since the client would have completed a declaration of non-liability due to his or her non-residence. No question of the solicitor being taxed as an agent will arise where the interest in question has been earned in a general client deposit account, or on stake money, but it could very exceptionally do so in relation to money held in court.

Determination of whether a solicitor has management or control for the purposes of the extra statutory concession will depend on the nature of the solicitor's relationship with the client. Under section 78 of the Taxes Management Act 1970, a person not resident in the United Kingdom is assessable and chargeable to income tax in the name of an agent if the agent has management or control of the interest. Acting as a solicitor in giving advice or in conducting a transaction on the client's instructions will not of itself give management or control nor usually would the holding of a power of attorney on behalf of the client for a specific purpose, e.g. concluding a specified purchase or sale. If a client had no fixed place of business in the U.K., and his or her solicitor had, and habitually exercised, an authority to conclude contracts on behalf of the client, this would give rise to the client having a permanent establishment in the U.K., and accordingly the client would be taxable. In essence, the solicitor would be deemed to have management and control if he or she were effectively carrying on the client's business in the U.K., rather than merely acting as a solicitor, even regularly. Therefore, in order for the agency principle to apply, the solicitor/client relationship would normally have to go beyond a solicitor's usual representative capacity. It should be noted that where interest arises in connection with the receipt of rents on behalf of the non-resident, the solicitor would be chargeable as agent in relation to the rent.

For a more detailed analysis of when solicitors can be taxed as agents, see [1991] *Gazette,* 1 May, 15 (article by John Avery Jones).

If a solicitor is assessable on behalf of the client, he or she has a general right to reimbursement, out of the monies of the client coming into his or her hands, for any tax for which the client is liable and in respect of which the solicitor has been charged. For the exercise of this right see sections 82 and 84 of the Taxes Management Act 1970.

Trusts

Deduction of tax at source may apply depending upon the type of trust and where the investment is held. But it can only apply where money is held in a designated account. The income of trusts where none of the beneficiaries is ordinarily resident in the U.K. will not be subject to deduction of tax at source, even if a designated account is used, provided that the appropriate declaration has been made.

Administration of estates

Interest on money held for U.K. resident personal representatives will, if placed in a designated account, be subject to deduction of tax at source unless a declaration is made by the solicitor or the personal representatives that the deceased was not resident in the U.K. immediately before his death.

[See also aide-memoire on page 682.]

AIDE-MEMOIRE OF NORMAL SITUATIONS

Type of account	Payment of interest by bank or building society	Consequences
A Designated — where subject to tax deduction.	Net	Pay net to client, who gets basic rate tax credit. No further tax deductions for residents (unless solicitor is assessable as an agent).
B Designated — where paid gross (client money generally).	Gross	Pay gross to client who is assessable on payment as gross income. No deduction of tax for non-residents (unless the solicitor is assessable as agent).
C Bank and building society general client account deposit — always paid gross (client money generally and stake money).	Gross	Pay gross to client who in turn is assessable on payment as gross income; in practice solicitor assessed on interest after setting-off this payment. No deduction of tax for non-residents.

4th March 1992 (updated January 1993)

Annex 27I

Treatment of VAT under the Solicitors' Accounts Rules 1991 — practice information

The 1991 Accounts Rules provide that unpaid counsel's fees should be paid into and kept in client account, rather than in office account as was possible under the previous rules.

This has raised the question of how the solicitor should deal with the VAT element on such fees.

The position with regard to VAT on counsel's fees is that by concession of the Customs and Excise, solicitors may either:

Method (i)

treat the fee as their own expense (and thus reclaim the VAT element as input tax); or

Method (ii)

cross out their own name on the receipted fee note and replace it with the name of the client. In this case the supply is deemed to be made direct to the client (who can reclaim the VAT if registered) and no VAT record need be kept in the solicitor's books.

If method (i) is used, when the solicitor delivers his own bill of costs, the value of supply for VAT purposes is the value of his own costs, plus the tax exclusive value of counsel's fees. Thus in this case the solicitor is charging output tax on a higher level of supply.

The effect of the new Accounts Rules (and in particular of the new definition of 'costs' contained in Rule 2) is best explained by example.

Assume solicitor's profit costs as £1,200 plus £210 VAT and the bill includes unpaid counsel's fees of £800, plus £140 VAT:

Method (i):

the £140 VAT on counsel's fee note is treated as the solicitor's input tax and can be reclaimed from Customs and Excise. When the solicitor's bill is delivered it must show:

Value of supply:

Costs	1,200.00
Counsel's fees	800.00
	£2,000.00
VAT	350.00
	£2,350.00

When the £2,350 is received, the effect of Rule 5 (Solicitors' Accounts Rules 1991) is that the cheque may be split sending the office element (£1,200 costs and £350 VAT) to office account and counsel's fees to client account (£800), or alternatively the entire sum of £2,350 must be paid into client account.

Because counsel's fee is being treated for VAT purposes as an expense of the solicitor and the VAT element is being reclaimed by the solicitor, payment, when it is made, must be from office account (so that the appropriate entry can be made in the Customs and Excise ledger account). At that stage the sum held in client account can be transferred.

Method (ii):

the solicitor will simply deliver a bill showing no book-keeping entries for the counsel's fees and VAT. It will simply show:

Profit costs	1,200.00
VAT	210.00
	£1,410.00
Counsel's fees (including VAT)	940.00
	£2,350.00

The effect of Rule 5 is that the cheque may be split as to £1,410 office account and £940 client account, or alternatively the entire sum of £2,350 must be paid into client account. In this case when counsel is paid, payment can be made from either client or office account (with a subsequent transfer to office account from client account).

September 1992

Chapter 28

Professional indemnity

28.01 Cover provided by the Solicitors' Indemnity Fund

Principle

'The following persons, namely

   (i)   solicitors, former solicitors, registered foreign lawyers practising in partnership with solicitors, and persons formerly practising as registered foreign lawyers in partnership with solicitors; and

   (ii) employees and former employees of the above,

shall be provided with indemnity out of the Fund against loss arising from claims in respect of civil liability incurred in Private practice in their aforesaid capacities or former capacities in the manner set out in Rule 7 and in the circumstances, to the extent and subject to the conditions set out in Part IV of these Rules and not otherwise.'

Solicitors' Indemnity Rules 1992, Rule 6

Commentary

1.   All references in this Chapter to rules are references to the Solicitors' Indemnity Rules 1992 (see Annex 28B) unless otherwise stated.

2.   Since 1976 all private practitioners have had compulsory indemnity cover. With effect from 1st September 1987 this has been by way of the Solicitors' Indemnity Fund, a statutory fund set up under section 37 of the Solicitors Act 1974 (see Annex 27A). From 1st January 1992 the Fund has covered multi-national partnerships and recognised bodies (incorporated practices). The Fund is administered by Solicitors Indemnity Fund Limited, a company limited by guarantee.

3.   Solicitors who provide services as solicitors in all or any of the following ways and none other are exempted from the obligations to provide information and make contributions to the Fund and will not be provided with indemnity out of the Fund (Rule 9):

    (a)   conduct professional business for personal friends, relatives, companies wholly owned by the solicitor's family or registered charities without remuneration; provided that the client for whom the solicitor acts is notified of the indemnity position in writing;

    (b)   administer oaths or take affidavits.

4.   Solicitors who provide services as solicitors without remuneration to persons or bodies other than those referred to in Rule 9 will be subject to the Indemnity Rules and therefore must:

    (a)   carry out the work as part of an existing practice; or

    (b)   set up a new practice and make an appropriate contribution to the Fund; or

    (c)   obtain a waiver of their obligations from the Law Society.

5.   The Indemnity Rules do not apply to private practice carried on from an office outside England and Wales by:

    (a)   a sole practitioner with no office in England and Wales;

    (b)   a firm of solicitors, if the same partnership has no office in England and Wales;

    (c)   a multi-national partnership with 75% or more solicitor principals, if the same partnership has no office in England and Wales;

    (d)   a multi-national partnership with fewer than 75% solicitor principals, whether or not the same partnership also has an office in England and Wales;

    (e)   a firm of solicitors and other lawyers practising solely outside England and Wales;

    (f)   an incorporated legal practice carried on wholly outside England and Wales;

    (g)   an assistant solicitor employed by lawyers of a jurisdiction other than England and Wales.

However, in all such cases, every solicitor who is a partner or a director in that practice, and every solicitor who works as an assistant at that office outside England and Wales, must have the indemnity cover required by Rule 17(1) of the Solicitors' Overseas Practice Rules 1990 (see Annex 9A and Commentary 7 to Principle 9.01).

6.   The overseas offices of a multi-national partnership with fewer than 75% solicitor principals are deemed to be practices separate from the practice in England and Wales and as such are outside the cover provided by the Fund.

7.   Cover is given by the Fund to the overseas offices of a solicitor's practice, or of a multi-national partnership with 75% or more solicitor principals,

provided that the overseas offices and the offices in England and Wales belong to the same practice. This means that the principals must be common to all offices of the practice and all fees must accrue to the common partnership and be returned in the annual gross fees certificate.

8. The Solicitors' Indemnity Rules allow that, if a principal or a limited number of principals represent all principals in a practice on a local basis, this shall not, of itself, cause the overseas office to be treated as a separate office and therefore be outside cover, provided that any fees or other income arising from that office accrues to the practice as a whole.

9. The indemnity provided by the Fund is against all civil liability incurred in connection with the practice of a solicitor, subject to the exclusion of certain specific items such as wrongful dismissal, trading debts and death and bodily injury. The cover is wide-ranging. As well as negligence cover it also includes defamation, the giving of undertakings and loss arising from damage to or destruction of documents. The cover even extends to a solicitor director where the solicitor's appointment arises in the course of his or her practice, provided that any fees received are paid into the partnership account for distribution under the partnership agreement. It is sometimes difficult to determine in advance of an actual claim whether a solicitor director is acting in the course of his or her practice but in most cases common sense will indicate whether or not cover will be given by the Fund or whether resort should be had to some other form of indemnity cover.

10. All members of the practice are covered. 'Member' of a practice is defined in Rule 12.6 as meaning any principal (which includes any person held out as such), any person employed in connection with the practice (including any trainee solicitor) and any solicitor or foreign lawyer who is a consultant to or associate in the practice or is working in the practice as an agent or *locum tenens* and the estate and/or the personal representatives of any such persons. Cover is, however, limited to those in private practice and does not extend to those employed elsewhere, e.g. in commerce, industry, local government or law centres.

11. Cover is provided on an each and every claim basis. This means that cover up to the current indemnity limit is available for every valid claim, subject to the payment by the practice of the appropriate deductible (otherwise called an excess). All claims against the practice arising from the same act or omission should be regarded as one claim. This does not mean, however, that where a practice uses a standard form document on a number of different occasions or loss is occasioned by theft from a general client account (where a number of different clients are affected), the losses will be aggregated and treated as one claim. In such cases, each loss will be treated as a separate claim with not only a separate indemnity limit but also a separate deductible.

12. The indemnity limit for the indemnity period 1st September 1992 to 31st

August 1993 is £1 million each and every claim (including claimants' costs).

13. The standard deductible provided by the rules is 1% of gross fees as declared in the gross fees certificate. A new practice (as defined in the rules) has a deductible equivalent to £1,000 multiplied by the number of principals. A practice in default (i.e. a practice which should have submitted a gross fees certificate and omitted to do so) has a deductible of £3,000 multiplied by the number of principals. All standard deductibles are subject to a minimum figure of £3,000 and a maximum of £150,000. Upon payment of an additional contribution to the Fund, practices can remove or reduce their deductible.

14. Further protection is given by the limit on the aggregate amount that a practice will be required to pay out in respect of claims falling within any one indemnity period (the 'aggregate' limit). For indemnity periods prior to September 1992 this limit was five times the deductible of the practice. Currently the limit is three times the deductible of the practice. Thus when a practice has contributed the figure of three times its deductible in settling claims falling within one indemnity period, the Fund will meet all further claims within that indemnity period without seeking further contribution from the practice, subject always to the indemnity limit in force. Upon payment of an additional contribution, a practice can remove or reduce its aggregate limit to one or two times its deductible, or remove it entirely.

15. Reference has been made in Commentary 11 to protection from loss occasioned by theft from a client account. Cover is given for loss arising from fraud or dishonesty of an employee or a fellow principal. The Fund does not cover the fraud or dishonesty of a sole practitioner nor of a partnership where all partners are party to the fraud or dishonesty. Such matters are for the consideration of the Compensation Fund (see Chapter 29). Furthermore the cover does not extend to the partnership assets, so it follows that loss of office monies is not covered.

28.02 Obligation to provide information — gross fees certificate

Principle

'In respect of each Indemnity Period each Principal shall by or on the preceding 31st March deliver to Solicitors Indemnity Fund Limited either

(a) a Certificate in respect of each Practice (except a New Practice or an Overseas Practice) in which he is or was at any time during the year ending on the preceding 31st March a Principal; or

(b)   **a Statement that he is a Principal in a New Practice giving the date on which the New Practice commenced.'**

Solicitors' Indemnity Rules 1992, Rule 14.1

Commentary

1.   The certificate, which is usually known as the gross fees certificate, must be in the form set out in the Schedule to the Indemnity Rules or such other form as may be approved by the Council. A form is sent out annually to each practice by Solicitors Indemnity Fund Limited.

2.   A practice which is required to deliver a certificate and which fails to do so will be treated as a practice in default and will therefore be subject to the default contribution, and the default deductible.

28.03 Obligation to provide information — notice of succession

Principle

Rule 14.2 of the Solicitors' Indemnity Rules 1992 requires the principals in a successor practice to deliver forthwith to Solicitors Indemnity Fund Limited a notice of succession containing like information and declaration in relation to the successor practice as required by a gross fees certificate (save for the questions concerning accounting period and gross fees), together with information as to the style and address of any other practice that has been formed as a result of the succession.

Commentary

1.   For definition of a successor practice see Rule 13.3.

2.   The information contained in the notice of succession will be taken into account in calculating any contribution due on 1st September, except where the notice of succession is received by Solicitors Indemnity Fund Limited after the preceeding 31st July and it relates solely to the retirement of principals or the addition of new principals.

28.04 Obligation to provide information — practice address

Principle

'A solicitor or registered foreign lawyer shall forthwith give to Solicitors Indemnity Fund Limited notice in writing of:

(i)   the address of any New Practice which he commences or of which he becomes a Principal;

(ii)   any change in the place or places of business of any other Practice of which he is or becomes a Principal.'

Solicitors' Indemnity Rules 1992, Rule 14.3

28.05 Obligation to make contributions

Principle

'Each solicitor or registered foreign lawyer shall make or cause to be made Initial and Supplementary Contributions in relation to each Indemnity Period as herein provided in respect of

(i)   each Separate Practice of which he is a Principal on 1st September;

(ii)   each Separate New Practice commencing during and in which he becomes a Principal during the Indemnity Period.'

Solicitors' Indemnity Rules 1992, Rule 15.1

Commentary

1.   The initial contribution is calculated by first calculating the basic contribution in accordance with Rule 16 by reference to relevant gross fees certificate(s) and notice(s) of succession and to Table 1 of the rules. The basic contribution is then subject to adjustment in accordance with Rule 17 to take account of number of principals, principal-staff ratio, area, low risk work, and structural surveys/formal valuations of property. The resulting figure is then subject to claims loading in accordance with Rule 18.

2.   Where a practice fails to deliver a gross fees certificate due in accordance with the rules, it is treated as a practice in default and is subject to the default initial contribution (for the indemnity period 1992/3, a rate of £10,000 per principal).

3.   The minimum contribution before claims loading is £350 for the 1992/3 indemnity period.

4.   The initial contribution in respect of a new practice is £350 for the 1992/3 indemnity period. For new practices commencing after the end of February during the indemnity period, the contribution is £175.

5.   All contributions are subject to VAT as Solicitors Indemnity Fund Limited is not an insurance company and therefore does not fall within the VAT exemption applicable to such companies.

6.   As from 1st September 1992 each practice (other than a practice in default or a successor practice to a practice in default) has a choice of payment methods, either by ten monthly instalments by direct debit commencing 1st November, or by payment in full on or before the first day of the indemnity period. Where a practice opts to pay by instalments, its contribution will be subject to a 4% charge.

7.   It is important to note that all solicitors and registered foreign lawyers who are principals in a practice on 1st September (the beginning of the indemnity period), or become principals in a new practice which commences during the indemnity period, remain jointly and severally liable to pay the full contribution due in respect of the practice, even if they leave the practice or if, during the indemnity period, the practice is the subject of a split, dissolution, merger or acquisition (Rule 15.2).

28.06 Incorporated practices

Principle

A recognised body with limited liability must take out top-up insurance over and above the indemnity limit of £1 million provided by the Solicitors' Indemnity Fund. The additional cover required is for a further £500,000 in respect of each and every claim or a further £2 million per annum on an aggregate basis.

Commentary

1.   The additional cover, which is required by Rule 13 of the Solicitors' Incorporated Practice Rules 1988, will not be provided by the Solicitors' Indemnity Fund and therefore must be obtained on the commercial market.

2.   A recognised body with unlimited liability is not subject to this requirement.

3.   The Solicitors' Indemnity Rules apply to recognised bodies (incorporated practices) as they do to any other private practice by virtue of the Solicitors' Indemnity (Incorporated) Practice Rules 1991 (see Annex 28C).

4.   When the same principals in number and identity carry on practice under more than one name or style, there is only one practice for the purpose of

the Indemnity Rules. Thus, the effect of Rule 6.3 of the Solicitors' Indemnity (Incorporated) Practice Rules 1991 is that if the owners of shares in a recognised body are the same in number and identity as the principals in a partnership, then for the purpose of the Indemnity Rules the two are treated as one and the same practice.

5. An incorporated legal practice carried on wholly outside England and Wales is outside the scope of the Solicitors' Indemnity Rules 1992 (see Commentary 5 to Principle 28.01).

28.07 Claims handling — obligation to notify claims

Principle

Where a client or third party makes a claim against a solicitor (or gives notice of an intention to make such a claim) and the claim is one in respect of which indemnity is provided by the Solicitors' Indemnity Fund, the solicitor must as soon as is practicable notify Solicitors Indemnity Fund Limited and co-operate with them or their agents in order to enable such a claim to be dealt with in the appropriate manner.

Commentary

1. A practice is required to give notice to Solicitors Indemnity Fund Limited of any claim or notice of intention to make a claim against the practice or any member thereof, including claims within the deductible which are likely to exceed £500 (Rule 30.4).

2. Although there is no obligation to give notice of circumstances that could give rise to a claim, such notice may be given to Solicitors Indemnity Fund Limited (Rule 30.5). Notification of circumstances enables consideration to be given to possible remedial action before the claim actually develops.

3. If a practice has an existing deductible amendment (i.e. has made an extra contribution to reduce its deductible) and circumstances are discovered which might give rise to a claim, then to obtain the benefit of such deductible amendment the circumstances should be notified within the indemnity period.

4. Notification of a claim or potential claim does not of itself give rise to claims loading (which only takes into account paid claims) nor would it be taken into account in the calculation of the cost of amending a practice's deductible in subsequent years, unless the claim has been paid or Solicitors Indemnity Fund Limited has placed a reserve on the claim.

5. If a practice has taken out top-up insurance (i.e. for cover over and above the £1 million indemnity limit), then the onus to notify circumstances to

top-up insurers rests with the practice although details as to any such insurance affected should be supplied to Solicitors Indemnity Fund Limited when completing the necessary report form.

6. Rules 29 and 30, impose conditions on a practice and members of that practice. These conditions include a provision that the practice or any successor practice, or any member thereof, should not admit liability for, or settle, any claim for which indemnity is provided or incur any costs or expenses in connection therewith without the prior consent of Solicitors Indemnity Fund Limited. If a breach of this or any other provision of the Indemnity Rules results in prejudice to the Fund, the solicitor may be required to reimburse the difference between the sum payable out of the Fund in respect of the claim and the sum which would have been payable in the absence of that prejudice.

28.08 Independent advice for clients

Principle

If a client makes a claim against a solicitor or notifies an intention to do so, or if the solicitor discovers an act or omission which would justify such a claim, the solicitor is under a duty to inform the client that independent advice should be sought.

Commentary

1. In cases where a client is not aware of the circumstance but the solicitor discovers an act or omission which would justify a claim, the Council recommend that the solicitor should:

    (a)   communicate the fact to Solicitors Indemnity Fund Limited;

    (b)   inform the client or third party so that independent advice may be sought;

    (c)   seek the approval of Solicitors Indemnity Fund Limited regarding the terms of any further communication to the client or third party;

    (d)   confirm any oral communication in writing.

2. If the client refuses to seek independent advice, the solicitor should decline to continue to act unless satisfied that there is no conflict of interest. See also conflict of interest, Principle 15.05.

3. In cases where the client or third party seeks independent advice and the solicitor is asked to make papers available to the new solicitor who is instructed, it is strongly recommended that the original solicitor keeps copies of these documents for reference.

28.09 Claims handling — rights of Solicitors Indemnity Fund Limited

Principle

Solicitors Indemnity Fund Limited has the right to take over the conduct of the defence or settlement of claims.

Commentary

1. Rule 30.2 gives Solicitors Indemnity Fund Limited wide powers to handle claims at its discretion.

2. Solicitors Indemnity Fund Limited shall not require any legal proceedings to be contested unless so advised by leading counsel (see Rule 30.3).

Annex 28A

Solicitors Act 1974

section 37 — professional indemnity

---

(1)   The Council, with the concurrence of the Master of the Rolls, may make rules (in this Act referred to as "indemnity rules") concerning indemnity against loss arising from claims in respect of any description of civil liability incurred -

(a)   by a solicitor or former solicitor in connection with his practice or with any trust of which he is or formerly was a trustee;

(b)   by an employee or former employee of a solicitor or former solicitor in connection with that solicitor's practice or with any trust of which that solicitor or the employee is or formerly was a trustee.

(2)   For the purpose of providing such indemnity, indemnity rules -

(a)   may authorise or require the Society to establish and maintain a fund or funds;

(b)   may authorise or require the Society to take out and maintain insurance with authorised insurers;

(c)   may require solicitors or any specified class of solicitor to take out and maintain insurance with authorised insurers.

(3)   Without prejudice to the generality of subsections (1) and (2), indemnity rules -

(a)   may specify the terms and conditions on which indemnity is to be available, and any circumstances in which the right to it is to be excluded or modified;

(b)   may provide for the management, administration and protection of any fund maintained by virtue of subsection (2)(a) and require solicitors or any class of solicitors to make payments to any such fund;

(c)   may require solicitors or any class of solicitors to make payments by way of premium on any insurance policy maintained by the Society by virtue of subsection (2)(b);

(d)   may prescribe the conditions which an insurance policy must satisfy for the purposes of subsection (2)(c);

(e)   may authorise the Society to determine the amount of any payments required by the rules, subject to such limits, or in accordance with such provisions, as may be prescribed by the rules;

(f)   may specify circumstances in which, where a solicitor for whom indemnity is provided has failed to comply with the rules, the Society or insurers may take proceedings against him in respect of sums paid by way of indemnity in connection with a matter in relation to which he has failed to comply;

(g)   may specify circumstances in which solicitors are exempt from the rules;

(h)   may empower the Council to take such steps as they consider necessary or expedient to ascertain whether or not the rules are being complied with; and

(i)   may contain incidental, procedural or supplementary provisions.

(4)   If any solicitor fails to comply with indemnity rules, any person may make a complaint in respect of that failure to the Tribunal.

(5)   The Society shall have power, without prejudice to any of its other powers, to carry into effect any arrangements which it considers necessary or expedient for the purpose of indemnity under this section.

[NOTES

1.   By virtue of section 89(3) of the Courts and Legal Services Act 1990 the power to make rules under section 37 is also exercisable in relation to registered foreign lawyers.

2.   By virtue of section 9(2)(f) of the Administration of Justice Act 1985 rules made under section 37 may be made to have effect in relation to a recognised body (i.e. an incorporated practice recognised under section 9).]

Solicitors' Indemnity (Enactment) Rules 1992 and Solicitors' Indemnity Rules 1992

SOLICITORS' INDEMNITY (ENACTMENT) RULES 1992

Rules made under section 37 of the Solicitors Act 1974 with the concurrence of the Master of the Rolls on the 9th day of June, 1992.

1. The Solicitors' Indemnity Rules 1987 as amended by the Solicitors' Indemnity Rules 1988, 1989, 1990 and 1991 shall be further amended with effect from 1st September 1992 and shall continue in force thereafter in the form annexed hereto in which form they may be known as the Solicitors' Indemnity Rules 1992.

2. The contributions payable and the indemnity available in respect of the Indemnity Periods commencing on and prior to 1st September 1991 shall remain unaltered hereby.

SOLICITORS' INDEMNITY RULES 1992

Rules made under section 37 of the Solicitors Act 1974 by the Council of the Law Society with the concurrence of the Master of the Rolls on the 4th day of May 1987, as amended subsequently, regulating indemnity provision in respect of the practices of solicitors and registered foreign lawyers carried on wholly or in part in England and Wales.

PART I

ESTABLISHMENT, PURPOSE AND OPERATION OF THE FUND

1. The Rules may be cited as the Solicitors' Indemnity Rules 1992.

2. The Society is hereby authorised to establish and maintain a Fund (hereinafter called "the Fund") in accordance with the provisions of these Rules.

3. PURPOSE OF THE FUND

3.1 The purpose of the Fund is to provide indemnity against loss as mentioned in section 37(1) of the Solicitors Act 1974 and section 89(3) of the Courts and Legal Services Act 1990 in the circumstances, to the extent and subject to the conditions and exclusions specified by the Solicitors' Indemnity Rules 1987 as the same have been and are in force and amended from time to time and by any future Rules continuing, amending, adding to or re-enacting such or other Rules to provide indemnity as mentioned in section 37(1) in respect of annual Indemnity Periods commencing on 1st September in each year (starting in 1987) unless and until otherwise determined by future Rules.

3.2   The Master Policies taken out and maintained and the Certificates issued by the Society pursuant to the Solicitors' Indemnity Rules 1975 to 1986 shall continue to provide cover subject to and in accordance with their terms in respect of their respective periods up to and including 31st August 1987. They shall not provide cover in respect of any subsequent period.

3.3   These Rules shall apply to a registered foreign lawyer who is (or at the relevant time was) practising in partnership with a solicitor, as they apply to a solicitor.

4.   CONTRIBUTIONS

4.1   The Fund shall be established and maintained by payments (hereinafter called "Contributions") which shall be made or caused to be made by solicitors and registered foreign lawyers in respect of each Indemnity Period in accordance with the provisions of Part II of these Rules.

4.2   Notwithstanding the power (if the Society so determines) to levy Supplementary Contributions in respect of any Indemnity Period, the Society may maintain the Fund as a single continuous Fund, and any deficiency in respect of one Indemnity Period may be met in whole or part from Contributions in respect of another Period or Periods and any balance in respect of one Period may be applied to the benefit of any other Period or Periods.

5.   MANAGEMENT AND ADMINISTRATION

The Fund shall be held, managed and administered in accordance with the provisions of Part III of these Rules by Solicitors Indemnity Fund Limited, a company set up by the Society for this purpose, or by such other person or persons (including the Society itself) as the Society may hereafter designate for such purpose, in place of Solicitors Indemnity Fund Limited. References in these Rules to Solicitors Indemnity Fund Limited shall include any such other person or persons.

6.   SCOPE OF INDEMNITY

The following persons, namely

(i)   solicitors, former solicitors, registered foreign lawyers practising in partnership with solicitors, and persons formerly practising as registered foreign lawyers in partnership with solicitors; and

(ii)   employees and former employees of the above,

shall be provided with indemnity out of the Fund against loss arising from claims in respect of civil liability incurred in Private practice in their aforesaid capacities or former capacities in the manner set out in Rule 7 and in the circumstances, to the extent and subject to the conditions set out in Part IV of these Rules and not otherwise.

7. MANNER OF INDEMNITY

7.1 Such indemnity shall be provided, according to the decision of Solicitors Indemnity Fund Limited as set out in Rule 7.2, in any one or any combination of the following ways:

7.1.1 by payment, in or towards satisfaction of the claim and/or claimant's costs and expenses, to or to the order of the claimant making the claim;

7.1.2 by payment, in respect of the claim and/or claimant's costs and expenses and/or costs and expenses incurred in respect of the defence or settlement or compromise of the claim, to or to the order of the person against whom the claim is made;

7.1.3 by payment, in or towards discharge of costs and expenses incurred in respect of the defence or settlement or compromise of the claim, to or to the order of the legal advisers, adjusters or other persons by whom or in respect of whose services such costs and expenses were incurred.

7.2 Solicitors Indemnity Fund Limited shall in any particular case, and notwithstanding the insolvency or bankruptcy of any person for whom indemnity is provided, have the sole and absolute right to decide in which way or combination of ways indemnity is provided.

8. SOURCE OF INDEMNITY

8.1 Such indemnity shall be provided and any claim thereto shall lie and be made exclusively out of and against the Fund.

8.2 Solicitors Indemnity Fund Limited shall have no obligation to provide indemnity save to the extent that the same can be provided out of the Fund.

8.3 In no circumstances shall any claim to indemnity lie or be made against the Society or the Council.

8.4 Save as provided in Rule 11, the Fund shall be available exclusively for the purpose specified in Rule 3.

8.5 In no circumstances shall the Fund or any part thereof be available or be treated by any person as available (whether by virtue of any claim, attachment, execution or proceeding or otherwise howsoever) for or in connection with any other purpose.

9. EXCEPTIONS

9.1 Solicitors who would otherwise be required to comply with these Rules but who provide services as solicitors in all or any of the following ways and none other shall be exempted from any obligations to provide information and make Contributions under Rule 4 and Part II of these Rules:

(a) conduct professional business for personal friends, relatives, companies wholly owned by the solicitor's family or registered charities without remuneration; PROVIDED THAT it is a condition of this exemption that every person or body for whom the solicitor acts shall be notified beforehand that the solicitor is not indemnified against professional indemnity risks by the Fund and, if such be the case, that he is not insured against professional indemnity risks or, if he is so insured to what extent and in what amount. Any such notification required by this proviso must if given orally immediately be confirmed in writing;

(b)   administer oaths or take affidavits.

9.2   Rule 9.3 applies to solicitors and former solicitors who but for Rule 9.1 or any general or individual waiver granted by the Council prior to the operation of Rule 9.1 would have been required to pay or cause to be paid premiums under any of the Master Policies or to make or cause to be made Contributions under the Solicitors' Indemnity Rules 1987 as in force and amended from time to time.

9.3   The solicitors and former solicitors referred to in Rule 9.2 shall not be entitled to be provided with indemnity hereunder against any civil liability incurred in respect of any services specified in Rule 9.1, or in any such general or individual waiver, as applying to them when providing such services.

9.4   The Society shall have power in any case or class of cases to waive in writing prospectively or retrospectively any obligation on any solicitor or registered foreign lawyer under these Rules or any provision of Part IV and to amend or revoke any such waiver.

10.   ARBITRATION

Any dispute or difference concerning any claim or the quantum of any claim to be provided with indemnity in accordance with Rules 6, 7 and 8 shall be referred to the sole arbitrament, which shall be final and binding, of a person to be appointed on the application of either party in default of agreement by the President of the Society for the time being. Any such arbitration shall take place and be conducted between, on the one hand, the person for whom indemnity is provided party to the dispute or difference and, on the other hand, Solicitors Indemnity Fund Limited for and in respect of the Fund.

11.   TERMINATION OF THE FUND

Following the expiry of the last Indemnity Period in respect of which the Fund shall provide indemnity as aforesaid, the Fund shall continue to be held, managed and administered by Solicitors Indemnity Fund Limited for so long as and to the extent that the Society, in the light of the reports made to it by Solicitors Indemnity Fund Limited, may consider necessary or appropriate for the purpose of providing indemnity in respect of any claim(s) made or intimated during any Indemnity Period and/or during or subsequent to any Indemnity Period arising out of circumstances notified during any Indemnity Period as circumstances which might give rise to such claim(s). As and when the Society no longer considers it necessary or appropriate that all or any part of the Fund should be so held, managed and administered, the Society may require all or any part of the Fund not so required to be released to the Society which shall apply the same if and to the extent the Society considers it practicable for the purpose of providing indemnity in any other way permitted by section 37(2) of the Solicitors Act 1974 and otherwise for the benefit of the solicitors' profession as a whole in such manner as it may decide.

12. DEFINITIONS

For the purposes of these Rules:

12.1 A "Certificate" means in respect of the Indemnity Period commencing 1st September 1989 and each subsequent Indemnity Period a certificate required to be delivered in respect of a Practice by the preceding 31st March under Rule 14.

12.2 A "Continuing Practice" means a Practice

(a) which commenced prior to the preceding 31st March and which was required to deliver a Certificate by that date; and

(b) in which the number and identity of the Principals has not changed since the preceding 31st March or, if a Certificate was duly delivered, from that of the Practice to which such Certificate related; and

(c) which has not since the preceding 31st March succeeded to the whole or any part of any Previous Practice.

12.3 "Foreign lawyer" and "registered foreign lawyer" have the meanings assigned to them by section 89 of the Courts and Legal Services Act 1990.

12.4 "Indemnity Period" means the period of one year commencing on 1st September in any calendar year (starting in 1987) unless and until otherwise determined by future Rules; and the "Relevant Indemnity Period" in relation to contributions or indemnity means that Indemnity Period in respect of which such contributions are payable or such indemnity is to be provided in accordance with these Rules.

12.5 "Master Policies" and "Master Policy Certificates" means the policies and certificates referred to in Rule 3.2 and "Master Policy Insurers" means the insurers thereunder.

12.6 "Member" of a practice means any principal therein, any person employed in connection therewith (including any trainee solicitor) and any solicitor or foreign lawyer who is a consultant to or associate in the practice or is working in the practice as an agent or locum tenens whether he is so working under a contract of service or contract for services and the estate and/or legal representative(s) of any such persons.

12.7 A "multi-national partnership" means a partnership whose members consist of one or more registered foreign lawyers and one or more solicitors.

12.8 A "New Practice" means a Practice commencing not more than one year prior to the preceding 31st March which has not succeeded to the whole or any part of any Previous Practice (other than another New Practice).

12.9 A "Notice of Succession" means a notice under Rule 14.2 and "succeed" and "succession" includes any taking over of the whole or any part of any Previous Practice whether as a result of any merger, acquisition, split or cession of any practice(s) or of any retirement or addition of principals.

12.10 "Overseas" means outside England and Wales.

12.11 An "Overseas Practice" means a Practice carried on wholly from an overseas office or offices, including a Practice deemed to be a Separate Practice by virtue of Rule 12.18(b).

12.12 "Practice" means a practice to the extent that it carries on Private practice providing professional services as a solicitor or solicitors or as a multi-national partnership. "Private practice" shall be deemed to include the acceptance and performance of obligations as trustees.

"Private practice" does not include:

(i)   practice to the extent that any fees or other income accruing do not accrue to the benefit of the Practice carrying on such practice;

(ii)   practice by a solicitor in the course of his employment with an employer other than a solicitor or recognised body or multi-national partnership; in which connection and for the avoidance of doubt:

     (a)   any such solicitor does not carry on Private practice when he acts in the course of his employment for persons other than his employer;

     (b)   any such solicitor does not carry on Private practice merely because he uses in the course of his employment a style of stationery or description which appears to hold him out as a principal or solicitor in Private practice;

     (c)   any practice carried on by such a solicitor outside the course of his employment will constitute Private practice.

12.13   A "Practice in Default" means any Practice required to deliver by or on the preceding 31st March a Certificate, and in respect of which no Certificate was duly delivered.

12.14   The "preceding 31st March" means the 31st March preceding the commencement on 1st September of the Relevant Indemnity Period.

12.15   "Previous Practice" means any practice which shall have ceased to exist as such (for whatever reason, including by reason of (a) any death, retirement or addition of principals or (b) any split or cession of the whole or part of its practice to another without any change of principals) prior to the commencement on 1st September of the Relevant Indemnity Period.

12.16   "Principal" means a partner or sole practitioner and includes any solicitor or registered foreign lawyer held out as a principal.

12.17   A "recognised body" means a body corporate for the time being recognised under section 9 of the Administration of Justice Act 1985.

12.18   (a)   A "Separate Practice" means a Practice in which the number and identity of the Principals is not the same as the number and identity of the Principals in any other Practice. When the same Principals in number and identity carry on practice under more than one name or style there is only one Practice.

     (b)   In the case of a multi-national partnership of which fewer than 75% of the Principals are solicitors, any overseas offices of the Practice shall be deemed to form a Separate Practice from its offices in England and Wales.

     (c)   In the case of an Overseas office of a Practice or multi-national partnership of which 75% or more of the Principals are solicitors, the fact that a Principal or a limited number of Principals represent all the Principals in the Practice on a local basis shall not of itself cause that Overseas office to be a Separate Practice provided that any fee or other income arising out of that office accrues to the benefit of the Practice or multi-national partnership.

12.19 "The Society" and "the Council" have the meanings assigned to them by the Solicitors Act 1974.

12.20 A "solicitor" means a person who has been admitted as a solicitor of the Supreme Court of England and Wales and whose name is on the roll kept by the Society under section 6 of the Solicitors Act 1974.

PART II

CONTRIBUTIONS TO THE FUND

13. DEFINITIONS

For the purposes of this Part of these Rules:

13.1 "Default Initial Contribution" bears the meaning ascribed in Rule 16.4.1.

13.2 The "Gross Fees" of a Practice include all professional fees, remuneration, retained commission and income of any sort whatsoever of the Practice excluding only:

(a) interest;

(b) the reimbursement of disbursements;

(c) any amount charged in respect of Value Added Tax;

(d) remuneration derived from any judicial office and such other offices as the Council may from time to time decide;

(e) dividends.

13.3 A "Successor Practice" means a Practice which is not a New Practice and which after the preceding 31st March succeeds (whether in consequence of any change in Principals or not) to the whole or any part of any Previous Practice in any of the following cases, or in any other case of succession not specified thereby;

Case (I):

A Practice which would be a Continuing Practice but for the retirement therefrom of one or more Principal(s) or the addition of one or more new Principal(s)

Case (II):

A Practice which would be a New Practice but for its acquisition of the whole or part of another Practice commencing prior to or on the preceding 31st March and required to deliver a Certificate by or on that date.

Case (III):

A Practice commencing prior to or on the preceding 31st March and required to deliver a Certificate by or on that date which succeeds to the whole or part of a New Practice.

Case (IV):

A Practice resulting from the merger between the whole or part of two or more Previous Practices, or the acquisition by one of the whole or part of one or more other Previous Practices, such Previous Practices having commenced prior to or on the preceding 31st March and being required to deliver a Certificate by or on that date.

Case (V):

A Practice remaining after a Previous Practice splits or cedes part of its Practice to another Practice or to a firm of foreign lawyers.

13.4   "Usual Basis of Accounting" means the basis of accounting used by a Practice, being a generally accepted basis of accounting for solicitors and applied to the Practice consistently from year to year.

14.   OBLIGATION TO PROVIDE INFORMATION

14.1   In respect of each Indemnity Period each Principal shall by or on the preceding 31st March deliver to Solicitors Indemnity Fund Limited either

(a)   a Certificate in respect of each Practice (except a New Practice or an Overseas Practice) in which he is or was at any time during the year ending on the preceding 31st March a Principal; or

(b)   a Statement that he is a Principal in a New Practice giving the date on which the New Practice commenced.

14.2   A solicitor or registered foreign lawyer who is or becomes a Principal in a Successor Practice after the preceding 31st March shall forthwith deliver to Solicitors Indemnity Fund Limited a Notice of Succession containing the like information and declaration in relation to the Successor Practice immediately after the succession as required by questions 1, 2, 5, 6, 7 or 8, 9 and (at the option of the solicitor or registered foreign lawyer) 10 and 11 of a Certificate, together with information (so far as known to him) as to the style and address of any New or other Successor Practice which any solicitor or registered foreign lawyer who was a member of his Previous Practice immediately prior to the succession referred to in the Notice of Succession commences or becomes a Principal of at or about the time of such succession.

14.3   A solicitor or registered foreign lawyer shall forthwith give to Solicitors Indemnity Fund Limited notice in writing of:

(i)   the address of any New Practice which he commences or of which he becomes a Principal;

(ii)   any change in the place or places of business of any other Practice of which he is or becomes a Principal;

(iii)   any cessation of any Practice of which he was before such cessation a Principal other than cessation involving the taking over of the whole of such Practice by one or more Successor Practices (where Notice of Succession has been delivered in accordance with Rule 14.2).

14.4   A solicitor or registered foreign lawyer shall not be required to deliver or give such a Certificate, Notice of Succession or other notice in respect of a Practice in relation to which another Principal therein delivers or gives such a Certificate, Notice of Succession or other notice as the case may be containing all of the information required in accordance with this Part of these Rules. In such case the Certificate, Notice of Succession or other notice delivered or given by that other

Principal shall be deemed to be a Certificate, Notice of Succession or other notice delivered or given by such solicitor or registered foreign lawyer and any declaration thereto signed by that other Principal shall be deemed to be a declaration signed by such solicitor or registered foreign lawyer.

14.5 A Certificate required under Rule 14.1 shall be in the form set out in the Schedule hereto or such other form as may from time to time be approved by the Council and shall

(a) state with reasonable accuracy the Gross Fees of the Practice to which it relates calculated in accordance with the Usual Basis of Accounting of the Practice in respect of an accounting period which complies with the requirements of Rule 14.7;

(b) contain the other information required by that form;

(c) contain the declaration required by that form.

14.6 The Certificate required under Rule 14.1 may also contain additional voluntary information as provided for by the form.

14.7 An accounting period complies with the requirements of this Rule if:

(a) it is of twelve months' duration or of such duration as the Council may in any case or class of cases determine;

(b) it ends not earlier than 30th September 18 months prior to the preceding 31st March; and

(c) it begins on the day after the end of the accounting period to which the last previous Certificate (if any) delivered in respect of the Practice related.

14.8 In respect of any Practice which has succeeded by succession to any Previous Practice prior to the preceding 31st March the Certificate shall state or include

(a) the Gross Fees of any such Previous Practice merged in or wholly acquired or succeeded to by the Practice;

(b) where the Practice has acquired or succeeded to a part, but not the whole, of a Previous Practice, a due proportion corresponding to the part so acquired or succeeded to of the Gross Fees of that Previous Practice;

for as much of the relevant accounting period as elapsed before such succession.

14.9 In order to ascertain whether full and accurate information has been provided in accordance with these Rules and to obtain such information so far as it may not have been, Solicitors Indemnity Fund Limited or the Secretary of the Society may appoint any person whom it or he thinks fit and may require any solicitor or Practice or any registered foreign lawyer who is or was a Principal to produce to any person so appointed at such times and places as he may request all such accounting and other records and documents, and to supply him in relation thereto with such information and explanations, as he may from time to time request.

14.10 Any solicitor, Practice or registered foreign lawyer to whom any requirement under Rule 14.9 is made by Solicitors Indemnity Fund Limited or the Secretary of the Society shall comply therewith and with such requests as may be made by the person appointed.

14.11 Any person appointed under Rule 14.9 may make to the Council and to Solicitors

Indemnity Fund Limited such report or reports as may be requested or as he may think fit.

14.12 Any such requirement under Rule 14.9 shall be made in writing and may be sent or delivered by Solicitors Indemnity Fund Limited or the Secretary of the Society to the solicitor, Practice or registered foreign lawyer at any place specified as the principal practising address or registered office of the Practice as stated in the latest Certificate, Notice of Succession or other notice delivered under these Rules (where such a certificate or notice has been delivered).

14.13 Any such requirement sent by registered post or recorded delivery to any such place so specified shall be deemed to have been received by the solicitor, Practice or registered foreign lawyer within 48 hours (excluding Saturdays, Sundays and Bank Holidays) after the time of posting.

15. OBLIGATION TO MAKE CONTRIBUTIONS

15.1 Each solicitor or registered foreign lawyer shall make or cause to be made Initial and Supplementary Contributions in relation to each Indemnity Period as herein provided in respect of

(i) each Separate Practice of which he is a Principal on 1st September;

(ii) each Separate New Practice commencing during and in which he becomes a Principal during the Indemnity Period.

15.2 Subject to Rules 15.3 and 15.4, the Initial Contribution together with any Value Added Tax payable shall be due in accordance with the provisions of Rules 16, 17, 18, 19 and 20 and also any additional Contribution payable under Rule 31.1.3 together with any Value Added Tax payable shall be due in accordance with the provisions of Rules 19 and 20 and both shall be payable as follows:

(i) in respect of a Separate Practice falling within Rule 15.1(i) other than a Practice in Default or a Successor Practice to a Practice in Default either

(a) in ten consecutive monthly instalments by direct debit on the first day of each month commencing on 1st November during the Indemnity Period; or

(b) in full on or before the first day of the Indemnity Period;

(ii) in respect of a Separate Practice falling within Rule 15.1(i) which is either a Practice in Default or a Successor Practice to a Practice in Default, in full on or before the first day of the Indemnity Period;

(iii) in respect of a Separate New Practice falling within Rule 15.1(ii) either

(a) in consecutive monthly instalments by direct debit on the first day of each month commencing on the first day of the month immediately after the date of its commencement or on 1st November during the Indemnity Period whichever is the later date and concluding on 1st August during the Indemnity Period; or

(b) in full on or before the date of its commencement.

15.3 In respect of a Separate Practice falling within Rule 15.1(i) or a Separate New Practice falling within Rule 15.1(ii) which ceases during the Relevant Indemnity Period with or without any successor in part or in whole, the amount of any monthly instalments outstanding due and to be paid during the Relevant Indemnity Period shall be payable in full immediately prior to the cessation. However, Solicitors Indemnity Fund Limited will not seek the full amount due for as long as either:

(a) the Principals in such ceased Practice shall continue to pay by direct debit as required by Rule 15.2(i)(a) or Rule 15.2(iii)(a); or

(b) the Principals in any Practices which have merged with, acquired or succeeded to part or the whole of such ceased Practice continue to pay by direct debit as required by Rule 15.2(i)(a) or Rule 15.2(iii)(a) the outstanding amounts due from the ceased Practice.

15.4 The Society or Solicitors Indemnity Fund Limited may at any time give to any Practice written notice correcting any inaccuracy in the calculation of any Initial Contribution, whether attributable to the Society or Solicitors Indemnity Fund Limited or to any failure to provide information or inaccuracy in information provided under Rule 14, or howsoever occurring; and any reimbursement or any payment of additional Contribution hereby required shall be made forthwith upon, respectively, issue or receipt of such a notice, together with any Value Added Tax applicable and (in the case of any additional Contribution payable upon correction of an inaccuracy in calculation attributable to failure to provide information or to inaccuracy in information provided under Rule 14) interest at a rate of 19% per annum with quarterly rests or at such other rate as the Society may from time to time determine and publish in the Law Society's Gazette.

15.5 Supplementary Contributions (if any) shall be made if and as the Society may at any time or times during or after the expiry of the Indemnity Period determine and in making any such determination the Society shall have complete liberty to decide whether or not all or any part of any losses or potential losses it takes into account shall consist of losses or potential losses arising from claims made or intimated or circumstances notified in the same or any previous Indemnity Period.

15.6 Without prejudice to Rule 16.4.2(b), the Society or Solicitors Indemnity Fund Limited may at any time give in respect of any Practice notice that any Initial and/or Supplementary Contributions payable in respect of that Practice shall, unless paid in full within such further period as the Society may stipulate, carry interest on any outstanding balance from time to time at a rate of 19% per annum with quarterly rests or at such other rate as the Society may from time to time determine and publish in the Law Society's Gazette.

16. CALCULATION OF INITIAL CONTRIBUTION

The Initial Contribution due in respect of any Separate Practice shall be as follows:

16.1 Continuing Practice

16.1.1 Where a Certificate was duly delivered by the preceding 31st March, the Initial Contribution in respect of a Continuing Practice shall be calculated as follows:

(a) By taking the Gross Fees stated in such Certificate and dividing them by the number of Principals stated therein in order to arrive at the Average Gross

Fee Income per Principal, then by calculating by reference to Table I set out at the end of this Part of these Rules the Average Initial Contribution per Principal (being the total of the sums calculated in respect of the relevant bands in accordance with Table I), and finally by multiplying the Average Initial Contribution per Principal so calculated by the number of Principals in the Practice as stated in the Certificate.

(b) The sum so arrived at shall be subject to adjustment in accordance with Rule 17 where appropriate and, after taking into account any such adjustment, shall in no case be less than £350.

(c) The sum arrived at after taking into account any adjustment in accordance with Rule 17 and the said minimum of £350 shall also be subject to claims loading where appropriate in accordance with Rule 18.

(d) The Initial Contribution due shall be that resulting from the calculations specified in (a), (b) and (c).

16.1.2 Where no Certificate was duly delivered by the preceding 31st March, the Continuing Practice shall be treated as a Practice in Default and the Default Initial Contribution shall be due under Rule 16.4.

16.2   New Practice

The Initial Contribution shall be £350 in respect of a New Practice commenced before the end of February during the Indemnity Period and £175 in respect of a New Practice commenced after that date subject in either case to adjustment where appropriate in accordance with Rule 17.5 (but not Rules 17.1, 17.2, 17.3 or 17.4) and Rule 18.

16.3   Successor Practice

The Initial Contribution due in respect of a Successor Practice shall be as follows:

16.3.1 In Case (I):

(a) Where a Certificate was duly delivered by the preceding 31st March and a Notice of Succession was delivered by 31st July in the same year in relation to the Successor Practice, an Initial Contribution calculated in like manner to that specified in Rule 16.1.1, by reference to information contained in such Certificate, but multiplying the Average Initial Contribution per Principal by the number of Principals in the Practice, and making any adjustments in accordance with Rule 17, by reference to the position (as disclosed by such Notice of Succession) immediately after the change in the number of Principals.

(b) Where a Certificate was duly delivered by the preceding 31st March but no such Notice of Succession was delivered by 31st July in the same year, an Initial Contribution calculated in like manner to that specified in Rule 16.1.1, treating the Practice as if it were a Continuing Practice.

(c) Where no such Certificate was delivered, a Default Initial Contribution in accordance with Rule 16.4.

16.3.2 In Case (II):

(a) Where a Certificate was duly delivered by the preceding 31st March in respect of the Practice acquired, an Initial Contribution calculated in like manner to that specified in Rule 16.1.1, by reference to information contained in such Certificate or a due proportion of such an Initial Contribution where only part of the other Practice was acquired, but multiplying the Average Initial Contribution per Principal by the number of Principals in the Practice, making any adjustments in accordance with Rule 17 by reference to the position (as disclosed by any Certificate delivered under Rule 14.2 in relation to the Successor Practice) immediately after the acquisition.

(b) Where no such Certificate was delivered in respect of the Practice acquired, a Default Initial Contribution calculated as set out in Rule 16.4 by reference to the number of Principals in the Practice acquired at the preceding 31st March or (where only part of such other Practice was acquired) a due proportion of such a Default Initial Contribution.

16.3.3 In Case (III):

(a) Where a Certificate was duly delivered by the preceding 31st March in respect of the Practice commencing prior to or on that date, an Initial Contribution calculated in like manner to that specified in Rule 16.1.1, by reference to such Certificate, but multiplying the Average Initial Contribution per Principal by the number of Principals in the Practice, and making any adjustments in accordance with Rule 17 by reference to the position (as disclosed by any Certificate delivered under Rule 14.2 in relation to the Successor Practice) immediately after the succession.

(b) Where no such Certificate was delivered in respect of the Practice commencing prior to or on the preceding 31st March, a Default Initial Contribution calculated as set out in Rule 16.4 by reference to the number of Principals in such Practice at the preceding 31st March.

16.3.4 In Case (IV):

(a) Where each Previous Practice duly delivered a Certificate by the preceding 31st March, the total Initial Contribution resulting from a composite calculation based on the information in such Certificates and made in like manner to that specified in Rule 16.1.1, or a due proportion of such an Initial Contribution reflecting the parts of the Previous Practices acquired by the Practice as a result of the merger or acquisiton, but multiplying the Average Initial Contribution per Principal by the number of Principals in the Practice, and making adjustments in accordance with Rule 17 by reference to the position (as disclosed by any Certificate delivered under Rule 14.2 in relation to the Successor Practice) immediately after the merger or acquisition.

(b) Where one or more of the Previous Practices duly delivered and the other(s) defaulted in delivery of a Certificate by the preceding 31st March, the total of:

(i) an Initial Contribution calculated in like manner to that specified in Rule16.1.1 or (where more than one of the Previous Practices delivered such Certificate) Rule 16.3.4(a) by reference to the Certificate(s) which wasor were delivered, or a due proportion thereof, and

    (ii)   a Default Initial Contribution or Contributions calculated as set out in Rule 16.4 based on the number of Principals in the Practice(s) in default at the preceding 31st March or a due proportion thereof reflecting the part of such Practice(s) merged or acquired.

(c)   Where no such Previous Practice delivered a Certificate as required by the preceding 31st March, a Default Initial Contribution based upon the total number of Principals in such Previous Practices at that date or a due proportion thereof reflecting the part of such Previous Practices merged or acquired.

16.3.5 In Case (V):

(a)   Where the Previous Practice duly delivered a Certificate by the preceding 31st March a due proportion, reflecting the part of the Previous Practice remaining after the split or cession, of an Initial Contribution calculated by reference to such Certificate in like manner to that specified in Rule 16.1.1 but multiplying the Average Initial Contribution per Principal by the number of Principals in the Practice, and making any adjustments in accordance with Rule 17 by reference to the position immediately after the split or cession;

(b)   Where the Previous Practice defaulted in delivery of a Certificate by the preceding 31st March, a due proportion of a Default Initial Contribution calculated by reference to the number of Principals in the Previous Practice at that date.

16.3.6 In any other case of succession:

an Initial Contribution calculated, and if necessary determined by the Society, as nearly as possible in accordance with the principles applicable in Cases (I) to (V).

16.3.7 For the purposes of Rules 16.3.1 to 16.3.5 the number of Principals in a Successor Practice immediately after the succession shall be that disclosed by the relevant Notice of Succession delivered under Rule 14.2. Failing any such Certificate the Society may decide the number under Rule 21.

16.4   Practice in Default

16.4.1 The Initial Contribution in respect of any Practice in Default ("the Default Initial Contribution") consists of the sum of £10,000 multiplied by the number of Principals in such Practice at the preceding 31st March or such other date as is specified in these Rules and adjusted where appropriate in accordance with Rule 18 (but not Rule 17).

16.4.2 Where subsequent to the preceding 31st March there is delivered in respect of any Practice in Default a Certificate which (apart from its lateness) complies with the requirements of Rule 14, an assessment will be made taking account of such Certificate of the Initial Contribution which would have been due under Rules 16.1 and/or 16.3 in respect of any Practice in respect of which there became due as a Practice in Default a Default Initial Contribution or as a Successor Practice to a Practice in Default an Initial Contribution which included a Default Initial Contribution or the due proportion of a Default Initial Contribution. Such Practice shall then:

(a)   be entitled to a rebate of any difference in its favour between the Initial

Contribution actually paid and the Final Contribution shown by such assessment, but any such rebate shall be paid without interest and not earlier than 15 months after the 1st September on which the relevant Indemnity Period began, or

(b)   forthwith pay any balance shown to be payable together, if the Society or Solicitors Indemnity Fund Limited shall so require in writing, with interest on any outstanding balance from time to time at the rate of 19% per annum with quarterly rests or at such other rate, for such period and with such rests as the Society may from time to time determine and publish in the Law Society's Gazette.

17.   ADJUSTMENT

17.1   The Initial Contribution in respect of any Practice shall be subject to a discount determined by reference to the number of Principals as shown in Table II, subject to a maximum discount of £225,000.

17.2   Principal — Staff Ratio

The Initial Contribution in respect of any Practice shall be subject to a 10% discount where the number of staff per Principal is 2 or less and to a 10% increase where the number of staff per Principal exceeds 5. When calculating the number of staff per Principal for the purposes of this Rule, each part-time member of staff shall only count as half (but the final total of staff shall where necessary be rounded up to the next whole number). A part-time member of staff shall mean any member of staff who is employed for 20 hours or less in the Practice's normal working week.

17.3   Area

(a)   The Initial Contribution in respect of any Practice shall be subject to a 10% discount where no office of the Practice is situated in a town with a population of 10,000 or more.

(b)   The geographical scope and population of a town for this purpose shall be determined by the Society using such sources of information as it may in its discretion decide.

17.4   Low Risk Work

(a)   The Initial Contribution in respect of any Practice shall be subject to a discount to be determined by the Society according to the proportion undertaken of work which the Society may from time to time determine should be regarded as low risk work.

(b)   Subject to any future determination by the Society, the following two classes of work, namely criminal law work and the collection of judgement debts, or debts without dispute as to liability, of not more than £7,500, shall each be regarded as low risk work, and shall each (or where this leads to a higher discount in combination) attract a discount as shown in Table III.

17.5   Practices providing structural surveys and formal valuations of property

(a)   In addition to any Contributions otherwise provided for by these Rules any Practice or Successor Practice providing structural surveys and/or formal valuations of property shall immediately pay an additional contribution of £1,000 in respect of each Member of the Practice who undertakes structural surveys and/or formal valuations of property. If the Practice commences undertaking structural surveys and/or formal valuations of property after the end of February during the Indemnity Period the additional per capita contribution immediately payable shall be £500.

(b)   Any such Practice or Successor Practice shall notify Solicitors Indemnity Fund Limited immediately of the following:

(i)   its intention to provide structural surveys and/or formal valuations of property, and

(ii)   the number, names and qualifications of all individuals who will undertake such work within the Practice and the like information in respect of any changes or additions which may occur during the Indemnity Period.

17.6   Adjustment of Initial Contribution under Rules 17.1, 17.2, 17.3 or 17.4 shall, unless the Society otherwise decides, be determined in the case of a Continuing Practice or a Successor Practice within Case (I) in accordance with the position at the preceding 31st March or earlier as disclosed by the relevant Certificate delivered under Rule 14.1 and in the case of any other Successor Practice in accordance with the position immediately after the succession as disclosed by the relevant Notice of Succession delivered under Rule 14.2.

18.   CLAIMS LOADING

18.1   For the purposes of this paragraph:

(a)   A 'Loading Claim' is any claim in respect of which the total of Indemnity Payments made by the Fund either

(i)   exceeds £5,000 where the unamended Deductible is applicable to the claim;

(ii)   exceeds the total of £5,000 and the difference between the unamended Deductible and any reduced Deductible applicable to the claim, or

(iii)   exceeds £5,000 where the Deductible has ceased to apply by virtue of any aggregate provision,

and in respect of which at least one such Indemnity Payment is made during the Relevant Period.

(b)   The 'Originating Practice' is the Practice or Previous Practice in which the act or omission giving rise to the Loading Claim occurred.

(c)   The 'Originating Principals' are the Principals in the Originating Practice at the date of the act or omission giving rise to the Loading Claim.

(d)   The 'Claims Loading Factor' is the number 'one' in respect of each Loading Claim.

(e) The 'Principal Loading Factor' is the result of dividing the Claims Loading Factor by the number of the Originating Principals and shall attach and apply to each Originating Principal in his capacity as Principal in the Originating Practice, or in any Practice which at any time succeeds to the whole or part of the Originating Practice, or in any New or Separate Practice which he may form or join upon or at any time after ceasing to be a Principal in the Originating Practice and in any such Practice succeeding thereto, or (failing any of these capacities) in his capacity as Principal in any one other Practice in which he is a Principal which the Society may decide.

(f) The 'Claims Pool' is the total of all Principal Loading Factors applying to Principals in a Practice.

(g) The 'Claims Ratio' is the value obtained by dividing the Claims Pool by the total number of Principals in a Practice.

(h) An 'Indemnity Payment' is any payment made by the Fund in respect of, arising out of or in any way in connection with any claim, other than any payments in respect of the costs of defending or investigating any such claim or the circumstances giving rise to it.

(i) A claim is deemed 'made' against a Practice when either it or notice of intention to make it was received by that Practice, or when circumstances giving rise to the claim were notified in writing to the Fund, whichever is the earlier event.

(j) The 'Relevant Period' means the four year period ending on 31st August one year previous to the commencement of the Indemnity Period for which Initial Contribution is being calculated.

18.2 The Initial Contribution calculated in respect of any Separate Practice in accordance with Rule 16 shall, where appropriate, be subject to claims loading in an amount equal to the amount shown opposite the Claims Ratio in Table IV applicable to the Practice multiplied by the number of Principals in the Practice.

19. PAYMENT BY INSTALMENTS — ADDITIONAL CHARGE

Any Contribution provided for by these Rules in respect of any Practice which is to be paid in instalments by direct debit under Rule 15.2, shall be subject to a charge of 4%.

20. VALUE ADDED TAX

Value Added Tax, to the extent chargeable on any relevant supply which takes or may be treated as taking place under or by virtue of these Rules, will be charged and payable in addition to and at the same time as the Contributions payable hereunder.

21. DECISIONS BY THE SOCIETY

For the purpose of determining the amount of any Contribution required by these Rules the Society's decision shall be final and binding on all affected on any question arising as to:

(a)   the part of any Practice merged, acquired or succeeded to;

(b)   the due proportion of any Initial Contribution or Default Initial Contribution;

(c)   the number of Principals in any Practice at any date;

(d)   the number of staff per Principal in any Practice at any date;

(e)   the geographical scope and population of any town;

(f)   the information and position (including the date) in accordance with which any adjustment of Initial Contribution (if any) is assessed under Rule 17;

(g)   the work to be regarded as low risk work and the discount(s) (if any) which such work may attract;

(h)   the calculation and/or the amount of any claims loading under Rule 18, including the capacity in which any Principal Loading Factor attaches and applies or shall attach and apply to any Originating Principal;

(i)   the Initial Contribution payable in any case of succession other than Cases I to V;

(j)   the calculation and/or amount of any Supplementary Contributions;

(k)   the gross fees to be attributed to the offices in England and Wales of a multi-national partnership whose overseas offices are deemed to form a Separate Practice by virtue of Rule 12.18(b).

TABLE I
(Rule 16.1.1(a))

Gross Fees per Partner Band		% of gross fees
Over £	Up to £	
	40,000	6.84
40,000	60,000	6.50
60,000	70,000	6.00
70,000	80,000	5.51
80,000	90,000	5.17
90,000	100,000	4.50
100,000	110,000	4.16
110,000	120,000	3.67
120,000	130,000	3.33
130,000	140,000	3.00
140,000	150,000	2.50
150,000	160,000	2.00
160,000	170,000	1.67
170,000	180,000	1.33
180,000	190,000	1.00
190,000	200,000	0.67
200,000	220,000	0.34
220,000		0.16

TABLE II
(Rule 17.1)

Number of Principals	Discount (%)
1	0
2	5
3	10
4	11
5	11
6	18
7	18
8	18
9	18
10 — 15	23
Above 15	32

TABLE III
(Rule 17.4(b))

Percentage of Gross Fees deriving from Low Risk Work	Discount %
Less than 20%	0
20% and above, but less than 40%	10
40% ,, ,, ,, ,, 60%	20
60% ,, ,, ,, ,, 80%	30
80% and above	40

TABLE IV
(Rule 18.2)

Claims Ratio				Amount per Principal £
Exceeding 0	but not exceeding		0.1	0
,,	0.1 ,,	,, ,,	0.2	200
,,	0.2 ,,	,, ,,	0.3	300
,,	0.3 ,,	,, ,,	0.4	400
,,	0.4 ,,	,, ,,	0.5	500
,,	0.5 ,,	,, ,,	0.6	600
,,	0.6 ,,	,, ,,	0.7	700
,,	0.7 ,,	,, ,,	0.8	800
,,	0.8 ,,	,, ,,	0.9	900
,,	0.9 ,,	,, ,,	1.0	1000
,,	1.0 ,,	,, ,,	1.1	1100
,,	1.1 ,,	,, ,,	1.2	1200
etc., up to:				
,,	9.4 ,,	,, ,,	9.5	9500
,,	9.5 ,,	,, ,,	9.6	9600
,,	9.6 ,,	,, ,,	9.7	9700
,,	9.7 ,,	,, ,,	9.8	9800
,,	9.8 ,,	,, ,,	9.9	9900
Exceeding 9.9				10000

PART III
ADMINISTRATION OF THE FUND

22.   POWERS OF THE SOCIETY

Solicitors Indemnity Fund Limited shall hold, and have full power to manage and administer, the Fund, subject only to

(i)   such directions, conditions and/or requirements as the Society may from time to time issue to or impose upon it expressly pursuant to this provision, and/or

(ii)   such further detailed arrangements as the Society may from time to time agree with it.

23.   POWERS OF SOLICITORS INDEMNITY FUND LIMITED

Without limiting the generality of Rule 22, the management and administration of the Fund shall include power:

(i)   to collect and recover Contributions due to the Fund in accordance with Part II of these Rules;

(ii)   to deposit or invest in such manner as Solicitors Indemnity Fund Limited may determine all or any part of the Fund, including any interest, dividends, profits, gains or other assets accruing to or acquired by the Fund;

(iii) to arrange such insurances as Solicitors Indemnity Fund Limited may determine in respect of the Fund and/or its assets and/or the Fund's liability under these Rules to afford indemnity in respect of claims and costs and expenses; and to handle all aspects of any such insurances, including the payment of premiums thereon out of the Fund and the making and recovery of claims thereunder;

(iv)   to receive, investigate and handle claims to indemnity and other notices prescribed to be given to Solicitors Indemnity Fund Limited by these Rules, including settlement and compromise and making of ex gratia payments out of the Fund in respect thereof and conduct of any dispute or difference referred to arbitration under Rule 10;

(v)   to receive, investigate and handle any claim made or intimated against any person in respect of which they are or may be entitled to be provided with indemnity out of the Fund (whether or not a claim to indemnity hereunder has been made) and/or in respect of which the conduct is by these Rules assigned to Solicitors Indemnity Fund Limited, including settlement and compromise and making of ex gratia payments and conduct of any proceedings arising in respect of such claim;

(vi)   to claim and recover reimbursement in respect of any sums paid by way of indemnity in any circumstances in which such reimbursement may under these Rules be claimed;

(vii) to exercise any right of subrogation permitted under these Rules;

(viii) to maintain full and proper records and statistics (which subject to Rule 25, shall at all reasonable times be available on request to the Society for inspection and copying) as to the Fund and all aspects of its management and administration;

(ix) to make to and review with the Council of the Society annually and at any other time that the Council may require, written and (if the Council so requires) oral reports as to the Fund and, subject to Rule 25, its management and administration, including inter alia recommendations as to the Contributions which are or may be required in respect of past, present and/or future Indemnity Periods and the circumstances in which, extent to which and conditions and exclusions subject to which indemnity should in any future Indemnity Period be afforded out of the Fund.

24. ADDITIONAL POWERS OF SOLICITORS INDEMNITY FUND LIMITED

Solicitors Indemnity Fund Limited shall further have full power:

(i)   to engage the assistance of any third party in respect of all or any aspect(s) of the management and administration of the Fund;

(ii) to delegate to any third party all or any aspect(s) of the management and administration of the Fund;

(iii) to institute and/or conduct such proceedings as it may consider necessary or appropriate for the due management and administration of the Fund in its own name or (subject to prior consent of the Society) in the name of the Society;

(iv) to disburse and/or reimburse out of the Fund all administrative and legal and other costs, overheads, fees and other expenses and liabilities incurred in respect of the Fund, including without prejudice to the generality of the foregoing any such costs, overheads, fees and other expenses and liabilities incurred by the Society in respect of the establishment or maintenance, or the management, administration or protection, of the Fund;

(v)   to disburse and/or reimburse out of the Fund payments for any educational, charitable or other useful purpose which in its opinion is likely directly or indirectly to lead to the reduction or prevention of claims on the Fund or otherwise to further the purpose or interests of the Fund;

(vi) to disburse and/or reimburse out of the Fund the costs, fees and expenses of the handling after 31st August 1987 of claims and potential claims against Assureds notified under the Master Policies and Master Policy Certificates;

(vii) to effect out of the Fund or by arrangement with third parties the funding pending reimbursement by Master Policy Insurers of such claims and potential claims and to bear out of the Fund the costs, fees and expenses incurred thereby.

25. USE OF INFORMATION

25.1 Without prejudice to the Society's power under Rule 5 to designate itself as the person responsible for holding, managing and administering the Fund, information and documents obtained by Solicitors Indemnity Fund Limited about any particular Practice or Member thereof in the course of investigating and handling any claim made or intimated or any circumstances notified as mentioned in Rule 26 may be utilised by Solicitors Indemnity Fund Limited for the purpose of preparation of general records, statistics, reports and recommendations (not identifying the particular Practice or Member) for or to the Society.

25.2 Such information and documents shall not otherwise be disclosed or available to the Society without the prior consent of the Practice (or any Successor Practice thereto) or Member concerned, except:

(i) where Solicitors Indemnity Fund Limited or the Society shall have reason to suspect dishonesty on the part of any Practice, Previous or Successor Practice or any Member or former Member thereof;

(ii) where Solicitors Indemnity Fund Limited considers that there has been any non-compliance with Rule 30.9;

(iii) where the Society has been requested by any Practice, Successor Practice or Member thereof to grant, amend or revoke any waiver under Rule 9.4 or to make a determination under Rule 21.

25.3 Solicitors Indemnity Fund Limited may give to the Council and to the Solicitors Complaints Bureau at any time and in such manner as it may determine information (whether or not obtained in the course of investigating and handling any claim made or intimated or any circumstances notified as mentioned in Rule 26) as to:

(a) the failure to provide information in respect of any Practice as required by Rule 14 or any material omission or inaccuracy in such information;

(b) the payment or non-payment in respect of any Practice of any Contribution or Value Added Tax due and payable in accordance with the provisions of Part II;

together with a copy of any relevant Certificate, Notice of Succession or other notice under Rule 14 and of any notice calculating or specifying any Contribution due or payable.

PART IV
TERMS AND CONDITIONS OF INDEMNITY

26. INDEMNITY

Upon receipt of the Initial Contribution due and any Value Added Tax payable thereon in accordance with the provisions of Part II of these Rules, the Practice and each Member thereof and any subsequent Practice which shall at any time during the Indemnity Period succeed to the whole or any part of the Practice (hereinafter "any Successor Practice") and each Member thereof, shall become entitled to be provided with indemnity out of the Fund in the manner set out in Rule 7 and to the extent and subject to conditions and exclusions set out in the following paragraphs against:-

(i) all loss (including liability for third party claimants' costs) incurred by the Practice, or any Successor Practice or any Member thereof at any time arising directly from:

(a) any claim(s) first made or intimated against the Practice or any Successor Practice or any Member thereof during the Indemnity

Period in respect of any description of civil liability whatsoever which may have been incurred in Private practice by the Practice or by a Member as a Member of such Practice or any Successor Practice or (in the case of a Principal in the Practice or any Successor Practice) by such Principal as a Principal in any Previous Practice whatever;

(b)   any claim in respect of any such description of civil liability as aforesaid made or intimated against the Practice or any Successor Practice or any Member thereof whether during or subsequent to the Indemnity Period arising out of circumstances notified to Solicitors Indemnity Fund Limited during the Indemnity Period as circumstances which might give rise to such a claim; and

(ii)   all costs and expenses incurred with the consent of Solicitors Indemnity Fund Limited (such consent not to be unreasonably withheld) in the defence or settlement or compromise of any such claim as aforesaid.

27.   MAXIMUM LIABILITY OF THE FUND

27.1   The liability of the Fund as stated in Rule 26(i) shall in no event exceed in respect of each such claim the Indemnity Limit for the Relevant Indemnity Period.

27.2   All claims arising from the same act or omission (whether or not made or intimated or arising out of circumstances notified during the same Indemnity Period and whether or not involving the same or any number of different Practices, Previous or Successor Practices and/or Members of such Practices) shall be regarded as one claim.

27.3   If a payment exceeding the Indemnity Limit is made to dispose of any such claim (or, in circumstances within Rule 27.2, claims) for loss (including claimants' costs) such as stated in Rule 26(i), then any liability of the Fund for costs and expenses under Rule 26(ii) shall be limited to such proportion of such costs and expenses as the Indemnity Limit bears to the amount of the payment so made.

28.   INDEMNITY LIMIT

The Indemnity Limit shall be £1,000,000 each and every claim (including claimants' costs).

29.   SPECIAL CONDITIONS

29.1   The Fund shall be available to provide indemnity in the circumstances, to the extent and subject only to the express conditions and exclusions set out in these Rules.

29.2   Where there has been a failure to pay any instalment of any Contribution due or any Value Added Tax payable in accordance with Part II and a claim has been made or intimated against the Practice or any Successor Practice or any Member thereof in respect of which such Practice or Member would otherwise have been entitled to be provided with indemnity, Solicitors Indemnity Fund Limited shall provide such indemnity by payment (up to the Indemnity Limit) in or towards satisfying, or enabling the Practice or Member concerned to satisfy, the claim and claimants' costs and such Practice shall thereafter upon request reimburse to

Solicitors Indemnity Fund Limited on behalf of the Fund the whole or such part as Solicitors Indemnity Fund Limited may request of any payment so made and of any costs and expenses incurred in its defence, settlement or compromise, and each Principal therein shall be jointly and severally responsible to Solicitors Indemnity Fund Limited for such reimbursement accordingly. Provided always that Solicitors Indemnity Fund Limited shall require such reimbursement only to the extent of (a) any increase which in its opinion may have occurred in the total payable out of the Fund (including costs and expenses) as a result of such failure, together with (b) such amount as may be necessary to satisfy any unpaid Contribution and Value Added Tax and interest thereon at the rate of 19% per annum with quarterly rests or at such other rate as the Society may from time to time publish in the Law Society's Gazette.

29.3   Where non-compliance with any provision of these Rules by any Practice or Successor Practice or any Member thereof claiming to be entitled to indemnity out of the Fund has resulted in substantial prejudice to the handling or settlement of any claim in respect of which such Practice or Member is entitled to indemnity hereunder, such Practice or Member shall reimburse to Solicitors Indemnity Fund Limited on behalf of the Fund the difference between the sum payable out of the Fund in respect of that claim and the sum which would have been payable in the absence of such prejudice. Provided always that it shall be a condition precedent of the right of the Fund to such reimbursement that it shall first have provided full indemnity for such Practice or Member by payment (up to the Indemnity Limit) in or towards satisfying, or enabling such Practice or Member to satisfy, the claim and claimants' costs in accordance with the terms hereof.

29.4   In respect of any loss arising from any claim or claims as described by Rule 26(i) arising out of any dishonest or fraudulent act or omission of any Member of the Practice or any Successor Practice the Fund shall nonetheless be available to afford indemnity in accordance with these Rules to the Practice or any Successor Practice and any Member thereof, other than and excluding in each case the particular Member concerned in such dishonesty or fraud; provided always that at the request of Solicitors Indemnity Fund Limited, the Practice, any Successor Practice or Member being indemnified shall:

(i)   take or procure to be taken at the Fund's expense all reasonable steps to obtain reimbursement from or from the legal representatives of any such Member concerned in such dishonesty or fraud, and

(ii)   procure that any reimbursement so obtained together with any monies which but for such fraud or dishonesty would be due to such Member concerned in such dishonesty or fraud shall be paid to the Fund up to but not exceeding the amounts paid by the Fund in respect of such claim together with any expenditure reasonably incurred by the Fund in obtaining such reimbursement.

30.   GENERAL CONDITIONS

30.1.   The Practice, any Successor Practice and each Member thereof shall not admit liability for, or settle, any claim falling within Rule 26 or incur any costs or expenses in connection therewith without the prior consent of Solicitors Indemnity Fund Limited (such consent not to be unreasonably withheld).

30.2   Subject to Rule 30.3:

(i)   the Practice, any Successor Practice and each Member thereof shall procure that Solicitors Indemnity Fund Limited shall be entitled at the Fund's own expense at any time to take over the conduct in the name of the Practice, any Successor Practice or Member of the defence or settlement of any such claim, including any claim in respect of which the Practice, any Successor Practice or Member may become entitled to partial indemnity under any insurance with any insurers and any claim which but for Rule 31.1 would have fallen within the scope of the indemnity afforded by these Rules; and

(ii) Solicitors Indemnity Fund Limited may after taking over the defence or settlement of any such claim conduct the same as it may in its absolute discretion think fit notwithstanding any dispute or difference, whether or not referred to arbitration under Rule 10, which may exist or arise between it and the Practice, Successor Practice or Member.

30.3   No Practice, Successor Practice or Member thereof shall be required to contest any legal proceedings unless a Queen's Counsel (to be mutually agreed upon or failing agreement to be appointed by the President of the Society for the time being) shall advise that such proceedings should be contested.

30.4   The Practice, any Successor Practice and each Member thereof shall procure that notice to Solicitors Indemnity Fund Limited shall be given in writing as soon as practicable of:

(a)   any claim(s) the subject of Rule 26 made during the Indemnity Period against it or him including any claim for or likely to be for more than £500 which but for Rule 31.1 would have fallen within the scope of indemnity afforded by these Rules;

(b)   the receipt by it or him of notice from any person of any intention to make any such claim(s).

30.5   The Practice, any Successor Practice and any Member thereof may also give notice in writing to Solicitors Indemnity Fund Limited of any circumstances of which it or he shall become aware during the Indemnity Period which may (whether during or after the Indemnity Period) give rise to any such claim(s).

30.6   If notice is given to Solicitors Indemnity Fund Limited under Rule 30.4(b) or 30.5, any claim subsequently made (whether during or after the Indemnity Period) pursuant to such an intention to claim or arising from circumstances so notified shall be deemed to have been made at the date when such notice was given.

30.7   The Fund waives any rights of subrogation against any Member of the Practice or any Successor Practice save where those rights arise in connection with a dishonest or criminal act by that Member and save as otherwise expressly provided in these Rules.

30.8   If the Practice, any Successor Practice or any Member thereof shall prefer any claim to indemnity out of the Fund knowing the same to be false or fraudulent as regards amount or otherwise, it or he shall forfeit any claim to any such indemnity in respect of any claim or future claim against the Practice, any Successor Practice or Member to which the false or fraudulent claim to indemnity out of the Fund may have related or relate.

30.9   Without prejudice to Rules 30.1, 30.2 and 30.3, the Practice, any Successor Practice and each Member thereof shall keep Solicitors Indemnity Fund Limited informed in writing at all times, whether or not Solicitors Indemnity Fund Limited shall specifically so request, as to the development and handling of any claim, notice or circumstances the subject of or arising subsequent to any notice given to Solicitors Indemnity Fund Limited under Rule 30.4 or 30.5; and shall consult and cooperate with Solicitors Indemnity Fund Limited in relation thereto as Solicitors Indemnity Fund Limited may request, whether or not Solicitors Indemnity Fund Limited shall take over the conduct thereof.

31. GENERAL EXCLUSIONS

31.1.1 For the purposes of these Rules:

(i) The "Deductible" means in respect of any claim

(a) in the case of a Practice in which the number and identity of the Principals have not changed since the preceding 31st March, the Deductible Proportion of the gross fees used for the purpose of calculating the Initial Contribution referred to in Rule 16 multiplied by the proportion that the number of Relevant Principals determined in accordance with Rule 31.1.4 bears to the number of Principals in the Practice at the commencement of the Indemnity Period, subject to a minimum Deductible of £3,000 and a maximum of £150,000; or

(b) in the case of a Practice which at the commencement of the Relevant Indemnity Period, has, since the preceding 31st March, succeeded in whole or any part to any Previous Practice(s), the Deductible Proportion of the gross fees used for the purpose of calculating the Initial Contribution referred to in Rule 16 multiplied by the proportion that the number of Relevant Principals determined in accordance with Rule 31.1.4 bears to the number of Principals in the Practice at the commencement of the Indemnity Period, subject to a minimum Deductible of £3,000 and a maximum of £150,000; or

(c) in the case of a Practice which, since the commencement of the Relevant Indemnity Period, has succeeded in whole or in any part to any Previous Practice(s), the Deductible Proportion of the duly apportioned or combined gross fees, as appropriate, used for the purpose of calculating the Initial Contribution of such Previous Practice(s) multiplied by the proportion that the number of Principals liable for the claim incurred as Principals in any such Successor Practice or Previous Practice(s) bears to the number of Principals in any such Successor Practice immediately after the succession, subject to a minimum Deductible of £3,000 and a maximum of £150,000.

(ii) For the purposes of calculating the Deductible

(a) each Principal in a Practice in Default shall be deemed to have gross fees of £300,000; and

(b) each Principal in a New Practice shall be deemed to have gross fees of £100,000.

(iii) The "Deductible Proportion" means 1% save as provided pursuant to Rule 31.1.3(a).

31.1.2 Each and every claim shall be subject to a Deductible in respect of which the

Fund shall not afford indemnity under Rule 26(i). Provided, however, that:

(i) this Deductible shall itself cease further to apply after the aggregate of the sums which by virtue of the Deductible the Practice (including any Successor Practice or Member) is unable to recover out of the Fund totals an amount equal to three times the Deductible;

(ii) Solicitors Indemnity Fund Limited shall disregard any Deductible when providing indemnity by any payment in respect of any claim against any insolvent or bankrupt person for whom indemnity is provided;

(iii) Solicitors Indemnity Fund Limited may pay, or include in any payment made, out of the Fund in respect of any claim the whole or any part of any Deductible applicable thereto, and in that event the Practice or Successor Practice and each Member thereof for whom indemnity was or would have been provided over and above the Deductible shall be jointly and severally responsible for reimbursing and shall forthwith reimburse to the Fund the amount of the Deductible so paid out of the Fund.

31.1.3 In respect of any claim not yet made or intimated and not arising from circumstances already known to the Practice or any Successor Practice or any Member thereof or notified to Solicitors Indemnity Fund Limited:

(a) the Deductible Proportion may be reduced to 0.5% or to nil;

(b) the aggregate provided by Rule 31.1.2(i) may be reduced or further reduced to an amount equal to one or two times the Deductible, either generally or in the event of a series of claims arising out of any dishonest or fraudulent act or omission of any past or present Member of any Practice or in the event of a series of occurrences consequent upon or attributable to one source or original cause;

in each case upon payment by the Practice or any Successor Practice to the Fund of an additional Contribution in an amount calculated on a scale approved by the Society from time to time taking into account the claims record of such Practice or any Successor Practice and of any other Practice(s) in which any Principal therein was previously a Member.

31.1.4 The number of Relevant Principals shall be as follows:

(i) where the matters giving rise to the claim occurred prior to the commencement of the Relevant Indemnity Period then:

(a) where at the commencement of the Relevant Indemnity Period there has, since the date when the matters giving rise to the claim occurred, been no change in the number and identity of Principals in, and no other Practice has succeeded in whole or substantial part to, the Practice concerned with the matters giving rise to the claim:- the number of Principals in the Practice at the commencement of the Relevant Indemnity Period;

(b) where at the commencement of the Relevant Indemnity Period the Practice or any other Practice has, since the date when the matters giving rise to the claim occurred, succeeded in whole or substantial part to the Previous Practice concerned with the matters giving rise to the claim:- the number of Principals in any such Successor Practice at the commencement of the Relevant Indemnity Period or in such

Previous Practice at the time when the matters giving rise to such claim occurred, whichever is the lesser;

(c) where at the commencement of the Relevant Indemnity Period the Practice concerned with the matters giving rise to the claim has ceased to be carried on and there exists no Successor Practice which has succeeded in whole or substantial part to its Practice:- the number of Principals shall be deemed to be one;

(ii) where the matters giving rise to the claim occurred during the Relevant Indemnity Period the number of Principals in the Practice at the commencement of the Relevant Indemnity Period or where such matters concerned any Successor Practice of the Practice which during the Relevant Indemnity Period has succeeded in whole or substantial part to its Practice then the number of Principals in any such Successor Practice immediately after the succession, whichever is the lesser.

31.2 The Fund shall not afford any indemnity in respect of any loss arising out of any claim

(i) for death, bodily injury, physical loss or physical damage to property of any kind whatsoever (other than property in the care, custody and control of the Practice, any Successor Practice or Member thereof in connection with its or his Private practice for which it or he is responsible, not being property occupied or used by it or him for the purposes of the Practice or any Successor Practice);

(ii) for any alleged breach or other relief in respect of any partnership or partnership agreement between the Principals in the Practice or in any Successor Practice or between any Principal therein and any other person as Principals in any Previous Practice;

(iii) for wrongful dismissal or termination of articles of clerkship or training contract or any other alleged breach or any other relief by either party in respect of any contract of employment by the Practice, any Successor Practice or any Member thereof; and/or for wrongful termination or any other alleged breach or any other relief by either party in respect of any contract for supply to or use by the Practice, any Successor Practice or any Member thereof of services and/or materials and/or equipment and/or other goods;

(iv) for the payment of a trading debt incurred by the Practice or any Successor Practice or any Member thereof;

(v) in respect of any undertaking given by any Principal or on his behalf (whether in his own name or in the name of the Practice or any Successor Practice) to any person in connection with the provision of finance, property, assistance or other advantage whatsoever to or for the benefit of him or any other Principal or of his or any other Principal's spouse or children or of any business, firm, company, enterprise, association or venture owned or controlled by him or any other Principal or in a beneficial capacity whether alone or in concert with others, EXCEPT to the extent that he shall establish that any such undertaking was given by him or on his behalf or on behalf of the Practice without him knowing that the undertaking was or was likely to be connected with the provision of any such finance, property, assistance or other advantage;

(vi) in respect of any dishonest or fraudulent act or omission, but nothing in this exclusion shall prevent any particular Member of the Practice or any Successor Practice who is not concerned in such dishonesty or fraud being indemnified in accordance with these Rules in respect of any loss arising out of any claim in respect of any dishonest or fraudulent act or omission by any other such Member;

(vii) in respect of any liability incurred in connection with an Overseas Practice;

(viii) in respect of any liability incurred in connection with a Practice in relation to which the obligation to pay Contribution under the Rules has been exempted under Rule 9 or waived by the Council under Rule 9.4;

(ix) arising out of any circumstances or occurrences which have been notified under the Master Policy or any certificate issued under the Master Policy or any other insurance existing prior to 1st September 1987;

(x) in the case of a multi-national partnerhip of which fewer than 75% of the Principals are solicitors, in respect of any liability incurred at an office outside of England and Wales. For this purpose a liability shall be deemed to have been incurred by a Practice at the office where or from which the major part of the work out of which the loss in respect of which indemnity is sought was being done. In the event of doubt as to which (if any) office of the Practice satisfies the requirements of this Rule, the liability shall be deemed to have been incurred at the office to which the member of the Practice who accepted the initial instructions was most closely connected.

31.3 For the avoidance of any possible doubt, any adjustment by way of claims loading which may at any future date or in respect of any future period be made by reference to any claim or claims first made or intimated during any Indemnity Period is not loss arising from any such claim or claims within the meaning of Rule 26 and shall in no event be recoverable hereunder.

32. In respect of any Previous Practice (as defined in Rule 12) no Contribution shall be due. Any Member of any Previous Practice who

(i) shall during any period of insurance or Indemnity Period have been either:

(a) an Assured as a result of the issue of a Certificate under one or more of the Master Policies, or

(b) a person entitled to be indemnified by virtue of the issue of a receipt under the Solicitors Indemnity Rules 1987-1990 or a payment of Contribution and Value Added Tax thereon as stated in Rule 26 of the Rules in their current form, and who

(ii) is not, at the time during the relevant Indemnity Period when a claim is first made or intimated against him or when circumstances which might give rise to such a claim are first notified by him to Solicitors Indemnity Fund Limited, either

(a) a person entitled to be indemnified as aforesaid, or

(b) a person who would be entitled to be indemnified but for the failure (whether by him or any other person) to pay Initial Contribution due in accordance with Part II of these Rules

shall, nevertheless, be entitled to indemnity out of the Fund in respect of any such claim first made or intimated or arising out of any such circumstances notified to the extent and subject to the conditions and exclusions (including specifically, for the avoidance of any doubt, that in Rule 31.2(viii)) set out in these Rules, mutatis mutandis. For this purpose references in these Rules to the Practice and any Member thereof shall, where appropriate, be read as referring to the Previous Practice and the Member thereof. Provided that, notwithstanding the provisions of Rule 31.1 hereof, any such claim shall be subject to:

(1) in respect of claims made or intimated or arising out of circumstances notified during all Indemnity Periods ending prior to or on 31st August 1992, the unamended (or Standard) Deductible (or excess) and any unamended aggregate provided by the Master Policy or by these Rules as the case may be in force as at the last date when he was entitled to be indemnified as result of the issue of either a Certificate or a receipt thereunder;

(2) in respect of claims (not within paragraph (1) hereof) made or intimated or arising out of circumstances notified during the Indemnity Period commencing 1st September 1992 and any subsequent Indemnity Periods, the unamended minimum Deductible and any unamended aggregate provided by these Rules in force as at the last date when he was entitled to be indemnified as the result of receipt of payment or a valid direct debit instruction in accordance with Rule 26.

SCHEDULE
(Rule 14.5)

[The Gross Fees Certificate form is sent out by Solicitors Indemnity Fund Limited and is not reproduced here.]

Annex 28C

Solicitors' Indemnity (Incorporated Practice) Rules 1991

with consolidated amendments to 1st September 1992

Rules made under section 37 of the Solicitors Act 1974 and section 9 of the Administration of Justice Act 1985 with the concurrence of the Master of the Rolls on the 16th day of July 1991.

(1) CITATION

These Rules may be cited as the Solicitors' Indemnity (Incorporated Practice) Rules 1991.

(2) INTERPRETATION

For the purposes of these rules:

    (i) "recognised body" means a body corporate for the time being recognised under section 9 of the Administration of Justice Act 1985; and

    (ii) "the Principal Rules" means the Solicitors' Indemnity Rules 1987 (as amended) as in force and amended from time to time and any future Rules continuing, amending, adding to or re-enacting such or other Rules to provide indemnity as mentioned in section 37(1) of the Solicitors Act 1974 and section 89(3) of the Courts and Legal Services Act 1990; and

    (iii) "foreign lawyer", "registered foreign lawyer" and "multi-national partnership" have the meanings assigned to them by section 89 of the Courts and Legal Services Act 1990.

(3) APPLICATION

In relation to recognised bodies the Principal Rules shall have effect with the additions, omissions and other modifications set out in Rules 4 to 10 hereof.

(4) THE FUND

4.1 The purpose of the Fund authorised by Principal Rule 2 shall include the provision of indemnity against loss arising from claims in respect of any description of civil liability incurred by the following persons:

     (i)   a recognised body or former recognised body;

    (ii)   an officer or employee or former officer or employee of a recognised body or former recognised body; and

   (iii)   a solicitor or foreign lawyer who is or was a consultant to or associate in a recognised body's practice or is or was working in such practice as an agent or locum tenens.

4.2   Indemnity shall be provided out of the Fund in respect of the persons specified in Rule 4.1 hereof in the circumstances, to the extent and subject to the like conditions and exclusions to those referred to in the Principal Rules with the additions, omissions and other modifications stated herein and in any future Rules continuing, amending, adding to or re-enacting these Rules.

4.3   Contributions shall be made or caused to be made to the Fund in relation to recognised bodies in respect of each indemnity period in accordance with the provisions of Part II of the Principal Rules as modified and applied herein.

(5) SCOPE OF INDEMNITY

5.1   Principal Rule 6 shall be read as referring to the persons specified in Rule 4.1 hereof.

5.2   For the avoidance of doubt and notwithstanding the definition of "Principal" in Rule 6.3 hereof, indemnity shall not be provided for any person in its or his capacity as a shareholder or beneficial owner of a share in a recognised body.

(6) DEFINITIONS

6.1   "Member" in Principal Rule 12.6 shall include any person specified in Rule 4.1 hereof other than in its or his capacity specified in Rule 5.2 hereof.

6.2   "Practice" in Principal Rule 12.12 shall include the business or practice carried on by a recognised body in the providing of professional services such as are provided by individuals practising in private practice as solicitors or by multi-national partnerships, whether such Practice is carried on by the recognised body alone or in partnership either with a solicitor or solicitors or with another recognised body.

6.3   "Principal" in Principal Rule 12.16 shall mean:

     (i)   in relation to a Practice carried on by a recognised body alone, (a) a member of the recognised body in whose name a share is registered and who beneficially owns the whole share; (b) where the member in whose name a share is registered does not beneficially own the whole share, the beneficial owner of the whole or any part of that share; and

    (ii)   in relation to a Practice carried on by a recognised body in partnership, (a) any such member, (b) any such beneficial owner, together in either case with (c) any individual who is or is held out as a partner in the Practice.

6.4   In relation to a Practice carried on by a recognised body alone or in partnership, any change in the number and/or identity of the Principals in the recognised body shall be ignored in determining:

     (i)   whether the Practice is a Continuing Practice within Principal Rule 12.2;

(ii) whether there has been a "succession" within Rule 12.9 thereof, and whether a Practice is a Successor Practice within Rule 13.3 thereof;

(iii) whether a Practice is a Separate Practice within Rule 12.18 thereof; and

(iv) whether a Practice shall have ceased to exist so as to be a "Previous Practice" within Principal Rule 12.15.

6.5 A recognised body which has at least one registered foreign lawyer as a director, registered member or beneficial owner of a share, shall be treated for the purpose of Principal Rule 12.18(b) as if it were a multi-national partnership.

(7) OBLIGATION TO PROVIDE INFORMATION

In relation to a Practice carried on by a recognised body alone or in partnership:

(i) the obligation to provide information under Principal Rule 14 shall rest upon each Principal in the Practice, and in addition upon the recognised body as if it were a Principal in the Practice;

(ii) the references in Principal Rule 14 to the obligations of "each Principal" and of "a solicitor or registered foreign lawyer" who is or becomes or was a Principal in any Practice shall be read accordingly, as if they referred to each of such persons;

(iii) Principal Rule 14.3 shall be read with the addition;

"(iv) any expiry or revocation of the recognition of the recognised body under the Solicitors' Incorporated Practice Rules in force from time to time, or any revocation of recognition of the recognised body under Administration of Justice Act 1985 schedule 2."

(8) OBLIGATION TO MAKE CONTRIBUTIONS

In relation to a Practice carried on by a recognised body alone or in partnership the obligation to make or cause to be made initial and Supplementary Contributions under Principal Rule 15 shall rest upon each Principal and in addition upon the recognised body.

(9) CALCULATION OF INITIAL CONTRIBUTION AND ADJUSTMENT

In relation to a Practice carried on by a recognised body alone or in partnership, a person solely acting as the company secretary of the recognised body shall not be included in the number of staff for the purposes of Principal Rule 17.

(10) WAIVER OF SUBROGATION

The waiver of subrogation in Principal Rule 30.7 shall extend to any director and the company secretary of a Practice or Successor Practice which is a recognised body.

(11) REPEAL AND COMMENCEMENT

11.1 The Solicitors' Indemnity (Incorporated Practice) Rules 1990 are hereby repealed.

11.2 These Rules shall come into force on the coming into force of section 9 of the Administration of Justice Act 1985.

Chapter 29

Compensation Fund

Introduction

29.01   The Law Society maintains the Compensation Fund pursuant to section 36 of and Schedule 2 to the Solicitors Act 1974 (see Annex 29A). The object of the Fund is to enable the Society:

(a)   to make grants to those who have suffered loss by reason of the dishonesty of a solicitor, or an employee in connection with the solicitor's practice, or in connection with any trust of which a solicitor is a trustee. Grants may also be made in the event of hardship suffered as a result of a solicitor failing to account for monies due;

(b)   to make grants in similar circumstances arising from the practice of a recognised body. For details see paragraph 6(2) and (3) of Schedule 2 to the Administration of Justice Act 1985;

(c)   to make grants in similar circumstances arising from the practice of a registered foreign lawyer as a member of a multi-national partnership. For details see paragraph 6 of Schedule 14 to the Courts and Legal Services Act 1990 and Rule 4A of the Solicitors' Compensation Fund Rules 1975.

In this Chapter references to a solicitor should be understood as including a recognised body or registered foreign lawyer where appropriate.

29.02   It should be noted that, as a general rule, a grant will be made only in respect of money or money's worth belonging to the applicant which has been misappropriated by the solicitor concerned. The Council will not approve a grant from the Fund in respect of damages or consequential losses which may flow from the act of the solicitor which gives rise to the application. In appropriate cases the Council will consider applications for grants in lieu of lost interest (see paragraph 29.21) and in respect of the applicant's solicitor's costs relating to the application (see paragraph 29.22). The Council have delegated their powers in relation to the Fund to the Adjudication and Appeals Committee.

29.03   The Solicitors' Compensation Fund Rules 1975, including the form of application for a grant, are to be found in Annex 29B.

29.04   Before the Council can consider making a grant from the Fund, the applicant must satisfy the Council that he or she qualifies for payment within section 36(2) of the Solicitors Act 1974, paragraph 6(2) of Schedule 2 to the Administration of Justice Act 1985 or paragraph 6(1) of Schedule 14 to the Courts and Legal Services Act 1990.

Interim grant in case of hardship

29.05   In an application where it appears that there is hardship, the Council may make an interim grant before the full investigation of the whole claim has been completed and without the full claim being admitted. The Council must be satisfied that there has been a loss of an amount at least equal to that to be paid out by way of an interim grant.

Applicant otherwise indemnified against loss

29.06   The Fund is administered as a fund of last resort. Thus, no grant will be made where an applicant is otherwise indemnified against loss, for example, by an insurance policy; nor will a grant be made to an applicant's insurers; nor where the loss is capable of being made good by recourse to any other person; but see paragraph 29.12.

Claims where the defaulting solicitor is or was in partnership

29.07   Since dishonesty of a partner or an employee is a risk covered by the Indemnity Fund, losses will normally be recoverable from the Solicitors' Indemnity Fund. The Council may, however, make a grant to an applicant in respect of such part of his or her claim which is not covered by the Indemnity Fund, e.g. the excess if the remaining partners are unable to pay this from their own resources.

29.08   Accordingly, the applicant should proceed with a claim against the remaining partners who, in turn, will make a claim against the Indemnity Fund. However, where there is doubt as to whether a claim should be met from the Indemnity Fund or the Compensation Fund, the Society endeavours to make suitable arrangements with Solicitors Indemnity Fund Limited to ensure that claims are paid promptly. The Society and Solicitors Indemnity Fund Limited can thereafter resolve between themselves where the ultimate liability should fall.

Institution of civil proceedings

29.09   In some cases the Council may require the applicant to institute civil proceedings, including where appropriate insolvency proceedings, against the solicitor in respect of the loss suffered. The purpose of proceedings may be to recover all or part of the alleged loss or to quantify precisely the amount of such loss. No applicant should institute proceedings unless and until the written consent of the Society has been obtained and the question of who is to be responsible for the costs has been decided, otherwise any application for a grant in respect of such costs may be rejected by the Council.

29.10 Where the defaulting solicitor is an executor, administrator or trustee of an estate or trust to which the application relates, the Council may require the applicant to take steps to have the solicitor removed from that position.

Prosecution of dishonest solicitor

29.11 In all appropriate cases the applicant will be expected to assist the police in connection with enquiries into the commission of any criminal offence by the solicitor in respect of the alleged acts giving rise to the application. However, the Council may consider an application for a grant notwithstanding that a defaulting solicitor has not been convicted of any such offence nor has been the subject of a finding of dishonesty by the Solicitors' Disciplinary Tribunal.

Action under Society's right of subrogation

29.12 Section 36(4) of the Solicitors Act 1974 gives the Society a right of subrogation to the rights and remedies of a recipient of a grant out of the Compensation Fund. The Council will require any applicant to consent to his or her name being used in any civil proceedings instituted by the Society with a view to effecting a recovery on behalf of the Fund subject to an indemnity by the Society in respect of costs.

Applications based on failure to account

29.13 Under section 36(2)(b) of the Solicitors Act 1974, paragraph 6(2)(b) of Schedule 2 to the Administration of Justice Act 1985 and paragraph 6(1)(b) of Schedule 14 to the Courts and Legal Services Act 1990, applications may be made for a grant based on the failure of a practitioner to account for money which has come into his or her hands in the course of practice. In such cases, where there is no proof of dishonesty, the Council can make a grant only if satisfied that the applicant has or is likely to suffer hardship.

Personal loans to solicitors

29.14 The Council will not normally make a grant where the application is in respect of a loan made to a solicitor personally or otherwise than in connection with his or her practice as a solicitor. If, however, the Council are satisfied that an applicant placed reliance upon the solicitor in his or her capacity as such and believed that the money was to be used for a purpose connected with the solicitor's practice, then the application may be favourably considered.

Undertakings

29.15 The Fund does not generally underwrite a solicitor's undertaking. Failure on the part of a solicitor to comply with a professional undertaking to pay a sum of money does not of itself entitle the aggrieved party to make a successful application for a grant out of the Fund. A claim will, however, be considered if the applicant can satisfy the Council that his or her claim arises out of an undertaking given with dishonest intent by a solicitor in the course of his or her practice. For undertakings generally, see Chapter 19.

Defalcations of unadmitted clerk trustees

29.16 The Council have no power to make a grant in respect of the defalcations of an unadmitted clerk who is a trustee except where the trust has been administered in the course of the clerk's employment by a solicitor and there is evidence of the passage of the trust monies through that solicitor's client account.

Claims by counsel and professional or other agents for misappropriated fees

29.17 Counsel and professional or other agents are entitled to apply for a grant out of the Fund if it can be established either that the solicitor concerned was put in funds by the client to pay counsel or the agent, or had received a sufficient sum on account of costs generally out of which the fees could have been paid, and that the solicitor had misappropriated or otherwise failed to account for the funds.

Applicant's own misconduct

29.18 When considering any application for a grant, the Council takes into account the conduct of the applicant both before and after the loss was sustained. If the Council, in their discretion, consider an applicant to have materially contributed to the circumstances of the loss, or to have failed to submit the application for a grant within a reasonable time (see also Rule 6 of the Solicitors' Compensation Fund Rules), or to have failed to pursue an application diligently, then the application may be rejected in its entirety or the amount of any grant substantially reduced.

Rejection of claim

29.19 The most common ground for rejection of claims is that they do not come within the statutory framework under which the Council are empowered to make grants. When the Council refuse to make a grant or are unable to make a grant because the application does not fall within the statutory framework, the applicant must be informed in writing of the reason for their decision. The fact that an application has been rejected does not prevent a further application being submitted or the rejected application being reconsidered, provided that substantial, new, relevant evidence or information is produced in support of the new application or request for reconsideration.

Deduction from grants

29.20 The Council may deduct from any grant the costs that would have been due to the solicitor provided that the work had been properly completed by him or her, so that the applicant will not be in a better position by reason of a grant than he or she would otherwise have been. A deduction in respect of notional costs may be made by the Council notwithstanding the fact that the defaulting solicitor may not have held a practising certificate at all material times. If the defaulting solicitor did the work so badly or did not complete it, with the result that the applicant has had to instruct another solicitor to carry out or finish the work, then the extra costs properly incurred by the applicant can be made the subject of a grant.

Payment of interest on claims

29.21 In appropriate cases the Council will consider an application for a supplementary grant in lieu of lost interest on the amount of the grant from the date of the loss until the date of authorisation of the grant (see Rule 10 of the Solicitors' Compensation Fund Rules). If paid, interest will be calculated at the Society's prescribed rates, which take into account that a grant in lieu of interest is not subject to tax.

Payment of costs of application

29.22 The Council have power to make a further grant in respect of the reasonable costs of an applicant's solicitor relating to a claim where a grant is authorised (see Rule 11 of the Solicitors' Compensation Fund Rules). The Council may not, however, be prepared to make such a further grant or may grant less than the full costs if they are of the opinion that all or part of the costs should not have been incurred or might have been saved by an earlier approach to the Society.

Annex 29A

Solicitors Act 1974

section 36 — Compensation Fund

(1)   The fund, known as the "Compenstion Fund", shall be maintained and administered in accordance with the provisions of Schedule 2.

(2)   Where the Council are satisfied -

(a)   that a person has suffered or is likely to suffer loss in consequence of dishonesty on the part of a solicitor, or of an employee of a solicitor, in connection with that solicitor's practice or purported practice or in connection with any trust of which that solicitor is or formerly was a trustee; or

(b)   that a person has suffered or is likely to suffer hardship in consequence of failure on the part of a solicitor to account for money which has come to his hands in connection with his practice or purported practice or in connection with any trust of which he is or formerly was a trustee; or

(c)   that a solicitor has suffered or is likely to suffer loss or hardship by reason of his liability to any of his or his firm's clients in consequence of some act or default of any of his partners or employees in circumstances where but for the liability of that solicitor a grant might have been made out of the Compensation Fund to some other person;

the Society may make a grant out of the Compensation Fund for the purpose of relieving that loss or hardship.

(3)   A grant under subsection (2)(c) may be made by way of a loan upon such terms and conditions (including terms and conditions as to the time and manner of repayment, the payment of interest and the giving of security for repayment) as the Council may determine, and the Society may at any time or times, upon such terms and conditions (if any) as the Council think fit, waive or refrain from enforcing the repayment of the whole or any part of the loan, the payment of any interest on the loan or any of its terms and conditions.

(4)   Where -

(a)   a grant is made otherwise than by way of loan, or

(b)   a grant is made by way of loan and a condition specified in subsection (5) is satisfied in relation to it,

the Society shall be subrogated, to the extent specified in subsection (6), to any rights and remedies of the person to whom the grant is made in relation to the act or default in respect of which it is made, and shall be entitled, upon giving him a sufficient indemnity against costs, to require him, whether before or after payment of the grant, to sue in his own name but on behalf of the Society for the purpose of giving effect to the Society's rights, and to permit the Society to have the conduct of the proceedings.

(5) The conditions mentioned in subsection (4) are -

(a) that repayment of the whole or part of the loan has been waived;

(b) that the borrower has failed to repay the whole or part of the loan in accordance with the terms and conditions of the loan.

(6) The extent to which the Society is subrogated under subsection (4) is -

(a) for a grant made by way of loan, the amount in relation to which a condition specified in subsection (5) is satisfied, and

(b) by any other grant, the amount of the grant.

(7) Where the Society refuses a grant, the Council shall state the reasons for the refusal.

(8) The Council may make rules about the Compensation Fund and the procedure for making grants from it.

[NOTES

1. For a similar provision in respect of the acts of a registered foreign lawyer in connection with the multi-national partnership of which he is or was a member see paragraph 6 of Schedule 14 to the Courts and Legal Services Act 1990.

2. By virtue of section 89(3) of the Courts and Legal Services Act 1990 the power to make rules under section 36 is also exercisable in relation to registered foreign lawyers.

3. For an analogous provision in the case of a recognised body (i.e. an incorporated practice recognised under section 9 of the Administration of Justice Act 1985) see paragraph 6(2) and (3) of Schedule 2 to the Administration of Justice Act 1985.

4. By virtue of section 9(2)(f) of the Adminsitration of Justice Act 1985 rules made under section 36 may be made to have effect in relation to a recognised body.]

Annex 29B

Solicitors' Compensation Fund Rules 1975

(with consolidated amendments to 1st January 1992)

1. These Rules may be cited as the Solicitors' Compensation Fund Rules 1975 and shall come into force on the 1st May, 1975, on which date the Solicitors' Compensation Fund Rules 1966 shall cease to have effect. These Rules are made under the power conferred by section 36(8) of the Solicitors Act 1974 and section 9 of the Administration of Justice Act 1985.

2. (a) In these Rules the following expressions have the following meanings respectively:

   'the Act' means the Solicitors Act 1974;

   'applicant' means a person applying for a grant out of the Compensation Fund under section 36 of the Act, Schedule 2 paragraph 6 of the Administration of Justice Act 1985 or Schedule 14 paragraph 6 of the Courts and Legal Services Act 1990;

   'defaulting practitioner' means:

   (i) a solicitor in respect of whose act or default, or in respect of whose employee's act or default, an application for a grant is made;

   (ii) a recognised body in respect of whose act or default, or in respect of whose officer's or employee's act or default, an application for a grant is made; or

   (iii) a registered foreign lawyer who is practising in partnership with a solicitor, and in respect of whose act or default, or in respect of whose employee's act or default, an application for a grant is made;

   and the expressions 'defaulting solicitor', 'defaulting recognised body' and 'defaulting registered foreign lawyer' shall be construed accordingly;

   'recognised body' has the meaning assigned by section 9 of the Administration of Justice Act 1985; and

   'registered foreign lawyer' has the meaning assigned by section 89 of the Courts and Legal Services Act 1990.

   (b) Other expressions in these Rules have the meaning assigned to them by the Act.

(c)   The Interpretation Act 1889 applies to these Rules as it applies to an Act of Parliament.

3. (a)   A grant may be made in respect of a defaulting solicitor notwithstanding the fact that the defaulting solicitor had not a practising certificate in force or was suspended from practice at the date of the act or default or has since such date died or ceased to practise or had his name removed from or struck off the Roll provided that in the case of a defaulting solicitor suspended from practice the Council are satisfied that at the date of the act or default the applicant was not aware of the suspension.

(b)   A grant may be made in respect of a defaulting recognised body notwithstanding the fact that the recognition of the defaulting recognised body expired by effluxion of time under Rule 18 of the Solicitors' Incorporated Practice Rules 1988 on or before the date of the act or default; or that since such date the defaulting recognised body has been dissolved or has ceased to practise or its recognition has been revoked or has expired under Rule 9 of the Solicitors' Incorporated Practice Rules 1988.

(c)   A grant may be made in respect of a defaulting registered foreign lawyer notwithstanding the fact that on or before the date of the act or default the registration of the defaulting registered foreign lawyer was suspended or was cancelled under Schedule 14 paragraph 3(4)(a) of the Courts and Legal Services Act 1990 due to non-renewal; or that since such date the defaulting registered foreign lawyer has died or ceased to practise in partnership with a solicitor or his name has been struck off the register or his registration cancelled; provided that, in the case of a defaulting registered foreign lawyer whose registration was suspended, the Council are satisfied that at the date of the act or default the applicant was not aware of the suspension.

4. (a)   No grant shall be made under section 36(2)(c) of the Act to any solicitor or under Schedule 14 paragraph 6(1)(c) of the Courts and Legal Services Act 1990 to any registered foreign lawyer, unless the Council are satisfied that no means of making good the loss are available to him and that he is fitted by reason of his conduct, age and experience to receive such a grant. No solicitor in these circumstances shall be disqualified from receiving a grant solely by reason of the fact that he had no practising certificate in force at the date of the relevant act or default of the defaulting solicitor.

(b)   No grant shall be made under Schedule 2 paragraph 6(2)(c) of the Administration of Justice Act 1985 to any solicitor, recognised body or registered foreign lawyer unless the Council are satisfied that no means of making good the loss are available to him or it, and that he is fitted by reason of his conduct, age and experience (or, in the case of a recognised body, it is fitted by reason of the conduct, age and experience of its officers and employees) to receive such a grant.

(c)   In the circumstances set out in paragraphs (a) or (b) of this rule, no solicitor or registered foreign lawyer shall be disqualified from receiving a grant solely by reason of the fact that, at the date of the relevant act or default of the defaulting practitioner, the solicitor had no practising certificate in force or the registered foreign lawyer's registration had been cancelled under Schedule 14 paragraph 3(4)(a) of the Courts and Legal Services Act 1990.

4A.   No grant shall be made under Schedule 14 paragraph 6(1) of the Courts and

Legal Services Act 1990 in respect of the act or default of a registered foreign lawyer, or of the employee or partner of a registered foreign lawyer, where such act or default took place outside England and Wales, unless the Council are satisfied that the act or default was or was closely connected with the act or default of a solicitor, or that the act or default was closely connected with practice in England and Wales.

5.   Every applicant shall complete, sign and deliver to the Secretary of the Society a Notice in the form set out in the Schedule to these Rules or in a form to the like effect approved by the Council, but where the application is for a sum of £250 or less the Council may accept a letter in lieu of such Notice.

6.   Every Notice or letter in lieu shall be delivered within six months after the loss or likelihood of loss, or failure to account, as the case may be, first came to the knowledge of the applicant.

7.   Every such Notice or letter in lieu of application under section 36(2)(b) and (c) of the Act, Schedule 2 paragraph 6(2)(b) and (c) of the Administration of Justice Act 1985 and Schedule 14 paragraph 6(1)(b) and (c) of the Courts and Legal Services Act 1990, shall contain full particulars as to the hardship suffered or likely to be suffered by the applicant.

8.   The Council may require an application to be supported by a statutory declaration made by the applicant and by the production to them of any relevant documents and may cause such enquiries to be made in relation to the application as they see fit.

9.   The Council may, before deciding whether or not to make a grant, require the pursuit of any civil remedy which may be available in respect of the loss or the institution of criminal proceedings in respect of any dishonesty leading to the loss or the making of an application to the Tribunal.

10. The Council may entertain an application for a supplementary grant by way of a sum in lieu of interest on a principal grant in respect of the period from the date of the loss until the date of the authorisation of the principal grant.

11. Where a grant is made the Council may entertain an application for a further grant for the amount of the applicant's solicitor's costs incurred wholly and exclusively in connection with the preparation, submission and proof of the application.

12. An applicant to whom a grant has been made shall be required by the Council to sign an undertaking to prove, if required, in the bankruptcy or winding up of the defaulting practitioner together with a further undertaking to comply with all proper requirements of the Council in the exercise of subrogated rights under Section 36(4) of the Act.

13. If the Council refuse to make a grant of either the whole or part of the amount applied for then the Council shall cause the applicant to be informed in writing of the reason for their decision.

14. The Council shall not make a grant unless they have caused a letter to be sent

    (i)   to the defaulting solicitor at his last known practising address;

    (ii) to the defaulting recognised body at the registered office of the recognised body last communicated to the Council or the Society under the Solicitors' Incorporated Practice Rules 1988 (or any rules for the time being replacing those rules); or

(iii) to the defaulting registered foreign lawyer at the address of the registered foreign lawyer appearing in the register kept under section 89 of the Courts and Legal Services Act 1990

informing him or it of the application and not less than eight days have elapsed since the date of the letter.

15. In these Rules, where the context so admits, reference to the applicant or to the defaulting practitioner shall include, in the event of his or its death, insolvency, liquidation or other disability, reference to his or its personal representative, trustee in bankruptcy or liquidator as the case may be.

16. Any requirements of the Council under these Rules may be communicated by a notice in writing.

17. The Council may waive any of the provisions of these Rules at the request or with the consent of the applicant, excepting Rule 14.

SCHEDULE

NOTICE OF LOSS AND APPLICATION FOR A GRANT

Name(s) of solicitor(s)/
recognised body(ies)/
registered foreign lawyer(s)
in respect of whom this
Notice is served ....

Address ....

I/We ....

(full name in block capitals)

of ....

(full name in block capitals)

....

hereby give Notice that I/(we) have sustained a loss of (or approximately of) (i) which I/(we) believe to be due to the dishonesty of the above named solicitor(s)/registered foreign lawyer(s) or his/their employee(s) or the dishonesty of the officer(s) or employee(s) of the above named registered body(ies) or (ii) which I/(we) claim is due to the failure of the said solicitor(s)/recognised body(ies)/registered foreign lawyer(s) to account to me/(us) in circumstances whereby I/(we) am (are) suffering hardship or likely to suffer hardship.

I/(We) apply to the Council of the Law Society that in the exercise of the discretion conferred upon them by the Solicitors Act 1974 that they make to me/(us) a grant in respect of my/(our) loss of any sum which they may think proper out of the Compensation Fund for the purpose of mitigating the loss and/or hardship which I/(we) have suffered in consequence of the dishonesty of or failure to account by the above named solicitor(s)/recognised body(ies)/registered foreign lawyer(s) or his/its/their employee(s) or officer(s).

Full details relative to this claim are set out in the Schedule of Particulars attached to this application.

Signed

. . . .

Compensation Fund

Schedule of Particulars

[This should contain the following information which should be given in numbered paragraphs:

1. The circumstances in which and the date or dates upon which the money or other property, in respect of which the loss has been sustained and/or hardship suffered, came into possession of the solicitor(s)/recognised body(ies)/registered foreign lawyer(s) or his/its/their employee(s) or officer(s).

2. Where relevant, particulars of the hardship suffered or likely to be suffered.

3. Full particulars of the money or property.

4. The facts relied upon in support of the allegation of dishonesty or failure to account.

5. The circumstances in and date upon which the loss or hardship first came to the knowledge of the applicant.

6. Particulars of any relevant documents which can be produced in support of this application.

7. Whether it is known that any other application is likely to be made in respect of the facts set out in this Schedule.

8. Whether any civil, criminal or disciplinary proceedings have been or will be taken in respect of the facts set out in this application. If proceedings have already been taken give the result.

9. The name and address of any solicitor instructed on behalf of the applicant.

10. Whether there are any costs due to the defaulting practitioner relating to the transaction giving rise to the loss or relating to any other transaction in which the defaulting practitioner acted for the applicant.]

(*Note*: The Council reserve the right at their discretion to require the applicant to make a statutory declaration in support of this application.)

PART VII — DISCIPLINARY PROCESS

Chapter 30

Solicitors Complaints Bureau

Introduction

30.01 The Solicitors Complaints Bureau was established by the Law Society in September 1986 to handle complaints independently. The powers exercised through the SCB are derived from the Law Society's Charter and from statute (the Solicitors Act 1974, as amended by the Administration of Justice Act 1985 and the Courts and Legal Services Act 1990). The Council of the Law Society delegated these powers to the Adjudication and Appeals Committee and some to the Director and Assistant Directors of the SCB under section 79 of the Solicitors Act 1974 (see Annex 2A).

30.02 The SCB sees its role as strengthening and maintaining the confidence of the public and the profession in the conduct and service of solicitors. It will investigate allegations of misconduct and it performs a regulatory function when, for example, solicitors are brought within the ambit of section 12 of the Solicitors Act 1974 (see paragraphs 30.23, 30.26 and 30.27). The SCB cannot give legal advice, nor can it make a finding of negligence, but the SCB will investigate allegations of poor service.

Structure

30.03 The SCB is divided into the following units, the Diagnostic Unit, the Conciliation Unit, the Professional Services Unit, the Conduct Unit and the Regulation Unit. This structure will change during 1993.

The Diagnostic Unit

30.04 This unit receives all new matters and screens them so that only matters requiring formal investigation are registered as complaints. Matters which should have been dealt with by the solicitor's own complaints handling procedure established under Rule 15 of the Solicitors' Practice Rules 1990 are either sent directly to the solicitor or to the complainant with a suggestion to contact the solicitor. See Annex 13A for a guide to setting up a complaints procedure and Annex 30E for the SCB procedure for dealing with Rule 15 matters.

The Conciliation Unit

30.05 The Conciliation Unit analyses the issues, and discusses them on the telephone with the complainant, if possible. If a face to face interview is necessary because of some communication difficulty, arrangements are made for a local conciliator to interview the complainant (for further details of local conciliators see Annex 30D). After initial evaluation, the conciliator will contact the solicitor and try to reach an agreement satisfactory to both sides. If agreement is reached the matter ends there.

30.06 If agreement cannot be reached for whatever reason, or other issues emerge during the discussions or correspondence, then the matter is either passed on to another unit for further formal investigation or the conciliator may indicate that the file is to be closed at that stage.

30.07 If the complainant is dissatisfied with this decision then the file is sent to the Assistant Director for a formal review. The case notes on which the review will be conducted are sent to both sides for comment and these case notes, together with any comments received, are reviewed by the Assistant Director. He or she may request further investigation or close the file.

30.08 There is a right of appeal against a decision to close the file which lies to the Adjudication and Appeals Committee. The appeal will be considered by a committee of at least three people, the majority being lay members. The committee consider the original case notes and comments, together with any subsequent representations.

30.09 If the complainant is still dissatisfied with the SCB's decision he or she may refer the matter to the Legal Services Ombudsman (see paragraph 30.29).

Inadequate professional services and compensation

30.10 The SCB has statutory powers to deal with complaints about the standard of service provided by solicitors to their clients. These powers are contained in the Solicitors Act 1974, section 37A and Schedule 1A. A large percentage of complaints received by the SCB fall into the category of inadequate professional services.

Definition of inadequate professional services

30.11 The Act does not specify what constitutes inadequate professional services. Therefore the SCB has to form a view of the circumstances of each particular case. To enable a complaint to be investigated fully the

SCB may excercise its statutory powers to call in the solicitor's file (see section 44B of the Solicitors Act 1974). Factors which the SCB would consider constitute *prima facie* inadequate professional services include:

(a) unreasonable delay by the solicitor in dealing with the matter overall or in taking a particular step;

(b) failure by the solicitor to seek instructions;

(c) failure by the solicitor to follow instructions;

(d) failure by the solicitor to account to the client or to account in time or making significant accounting errors;

(e) failure by the solicitor to advise the client or keep the client fully informed, or other lack of communication; and

(f) general incompetence or inefficiency (including organisational incompetence) that does not give rise to a specific legal cause of action in negligence.

Failure by the solicitor to comply with the rules or principles of professional conduct, including the written professional standards, on information on costs for clients, may amount to inadequate professional services.

The Act specifies that the SCB's powers may be exercised if a solicitor's services are inadequate 'in any respect'. The fact that the solicitor may have done a satisfactory job apart from one aspect does not preclude a finding of inadequate professional services but would be a factor which the SCB would take into account in assessing the appropriate redress.

Investigation of standard of service

30.12 If the solicitor's files have been called in, they are examined by one of the SCB's professional services officers, who will form a view upon the adequacy of the service. Both the solicitor and the complainant will see and have an opportunity to comment upon the assessment made by the professional services officer. If the matter has to proceed to a formal finding this will be made by one of the Assistant Directors.

The client's redress

30.13 The steps which the SCB may take upon a finding of inadequate professional services are:

(a) to disallow all or part of the solicitor's costs;

(b) directing the solicitor to rectify an error;

(c) directing the solicitor to pay compensation to the client;

(d) directing the solicitor to take at his or her expense such other action in the interests of the client as the SCB may specify.

These are not mutually exclusive so that, for example, the fact that the solicitor's costs were reduced would not preclude an award of compensation.

30.14 The amount of compensation the SCB may award is limited to £1,000 and applies to any matter where the solicitor's bill is dated on or after 1st April 1991. It is not necessary for the client to have a legal cause of action in negligence against the solicitor for the SCB to be able to award compensation or indeed take any of the other steps available under the Act. Where there is a finding of inadequate professional services a reduction in the solicitor's bill would in many cases be the appropriate remedy. Compensation would be considered where the client has suffered some loss or where it is clear the client has been considerably disadvantaged or inconvenienced. The amount of compensation may not necessarily equate to specific financial loss but will depend upon the overall circumstances and the seriousness of the case. A finding of inadequate professional services is not a finding of misconduct. There is a right of appeal to the Adjudication and Appeals Committee.

The Conduct Unit

30.15 The Conduct Unit deals with complaints about breaches of the Solicitors' Practice Rules and other allegations of misconduct.

30.16 When a complaint is received it is allocated to a caseworker who investigates it by a combination of telephone calls and correspondence. After investigation the caseworker may indicate that the file is to be closed because the evidence does not reveal misconduct. If the complainant does not agree with this decision the case notes will be disclosed to both sides for comment and then sent, with the comments, to the Assistant Director for a decision either to close the file or to require further investigation.

30.17 If the caseworker decides that the investigation reveals misconduct, the case notes are sent to both sides for comment. Case notes and comments are then sent either to the Conduct Committee or to the Assistant Director depending on the nature of the case.

30.18 The Conduct Committee is part of the Adjudication and Appeals Committee. It sits in panels of at least three members, the majority of whom are solicitors. The Conduct Committee would consider any case where the sanction against the solicitor could be a rebuke, severe rebuke, chairman's rebuke, institution of disciplinary proceedings, or intervention in a solicitor's practice.

30.19 An Assistant Director can:

(a)   appoint an agent to recover money and papers for the client or his or her new solicitor;

(b)   require a solicitor to co-operate or face the possibility of other disciplinary action;

(c)   warn that the powers of intervention have arisen under paragraph 1(2)(c) of Schedule 1 to the Solicitors Act 1974;

(d)   give a deposit interest certificate under Rule 25 of the Solicitors' Accounts Rules 1991;

(e)   require a solicitor to file monthly progress reports (e.g. where there is undue delay in dealing with the administration of an estate);

(f)   decline to pursue a complaint in relation to a disputed undertaking.

30.20   There is a right of appeal against the decision of the Conduct Committee or the Assistant Director to the Adjudication and Appeals Committee. Written representations are invited from both sides and any representations together with the original papers are considered by the Adjudication and Appeals Committee.

30.21   A non-solicitor, or a solicitor on the client's behalf may complain to the Legal Services Ombudsman if he or she is dissatisfied with the decision (see paragraph 30.29).

The Regulation Unit

30.22   This unit handles certain matters relating to the regulation of a solicitor's practice : applications for practising certificates such as those subject to conditions placed on them by the committee; enquiries into the late lodging of accountants' reports; and non-payment of indemnity premiums.

30.23   The Assistant Director has delegated authority to:

(a)   authorise the renewal of a practising certificate subject to a condition under section 12 of the Solicitors Act 1974;

(b)   withdraw an investment business certificate at the request of the certified firm and on the recommendation of the Society's Monitoring Unit and to withdraw a condition imposed following the failure to apply for the renewal of an investment business certificate, upon receipt by the Society of an application to renew;

(c)   refuse a waiver of a certificate of fitness under the Practising Certificate Regulations 1976;

(d)   require observations from a reporting accountant;

(e)   vest a discretion in respect of the issue of a practising certificate under section 12 of the Solicitors Act 1974;

(f)   order an inspection under Rule 27 of the Solicitors' Accounts Rules 1991.

30.24   A solicitor who has been adjudged bankrupt and whose certificate is suspended by virtue of section 15 of the Solicitors Act 1974 can apply, in writing, to the Regulation Unit for the issue of a practising certificate. The information which needs to be provided are the circumstances surrounding the bankruptcy, a copy of the order and information about proposed employment or partnership. Applications are determined by the Adjudication and Appeals Committee.

30.25 There is a right of appeal to an Appeals Committee, which will consist of three to five people, the majority of whom are solicitors.

The Adjudication and Appeals Committee

30.26 The terms of reference of the Adjudication and Appeals Committee are set out in Annex 30B. Briefly, these are to determine all matters concerning the conduct and the quality of work of solicitors and the exercise of the statutory powers of the Council in that respect. The Committee deal with matters by way of a written report prepared by the staff which will include the relevant correspondence. The committee papers are disclosed to all the parties to enable them to make further written representations. The Committee do not normally hear oral evidence. When the Committee are satisfied that the solicitor concerned is in breach of any rule of professional conduct or that his or her conduct is otherwise unbefitting a solicitor, the Committee may take one or more of the following decisions:

(a) to institute disciplinary proceedings before the Solicitors' Disciplinary Tribunal (see Chapter 31);

(b) to reduce fees and award compensation in respect of inadequate professional services pursuant to Schedule 1A of the Solicitors Act 1974;

(c) to vest a discretion with regard to a solicitor's practising certificate; this means that the provisions of the Solicitors Act 1974, section 12 apply (see Annex 2A);

(d) to impose conditions on a solicitor's current practising certificate where the solicitor is already subject to section 12;

(e) to consider applications for removal of conditions previously imposed;

(f) to rebuke the solicitor and require him or her to attend before the chairman of the Committee to be informed of the decision;

(g) to issue a written rebuke;

(h) to exercise the powers of intervention in a solicitor's practice (see paragraphs 30.32 — 30.34);

(i) to inspect a solicitor's accounts pursuant to the Solicitors' Accounts Rules 1991, and the Solicitors' Overseas Practice Rules 1990;

(j)   to require a solicitor to pay interest as certified by the Committee under Rule 25 of the Solicitors' Accounts Rules 1991;

(k)   to order production of a solicitor's file;

(l)   to require the solicitor to submit progress reports at regular intervals;

(m)   to suspend, withdraw or impose conditions with regard to the solicitor's investment business certificate.

Failure to comply with a decision of the Adjudication and Appeals Committee can result in disciplinary proceedings.

Section 12 of the Solicitors Act 1974

30.27   The text of this section is set out in Annex 2A. Where a solicitor is subject to section 12(1)(a) (first application) or (c) (application after a lapse of a year), he or she is issued with a practising certificate subject to the scrutiny of the Standards and Guidance Casework Committee. When there is evidence to suggest that the solicitor has been practising uncertificated, the matter is referred to the SCB for further investigation. The matter would then be considered by the Conduct Committee as a matter of professional misconduct. There is a right of appeal to the Adjudication and Appeals Committee.

The Policy Advisory Committee

30.28   The Policy Advisory Committee's terms of reference are:

(a)   to review generally all aspects of the policy and procedures for handling complaints against solicitors;

(b)   to advise the chairman of the Adjudication and Appeals Committee and the Council on any changes in legislation and procedure which the Committee believe to be desirable; and

(c)   to report directly to the Council as necessary and at least once a year.

The Legal Services Ombudsman

30.29   A dissatisfied lay complainant may refer his or her complaint to the Legal Services Ombudsman.

The Legal Services Ombudsman is appointed under the Courts and Legal Services Act 1990 to oversee the handling of complaints against members of the legal profession.

A lay complainant who has made a complaint to the SCB and who is dissatisfied either with the way the SCB has dealt with it or with the final decision can ask the Legal Services Ombudsman to examine the SCB's treatment of the complaint and to decide whether it was investigated fully and fairly. The Ombudsman will not accept a referral from an aggrieved solicitor who has been the subject of a complaint.

To do this the Ombudsman will ask for the SCB's file of papers dealing with the complaint. If he or she thinks that the complaint was not investigated properly, he or she can recommend further action.

The Ombudsman can by virtue of section 23 of the Courts and Legal Services Act 1990 recommend that a solicitor or the SCB pays compensation to the client. There is no limit placed on the amount that can be recommended. The Ombudsman can also publish the name of a solicitor who fails to comply with his or her recommendations.

Complaints by non-clients

30.30 The SCB can investigate complaints alleging professional misconduct from lay complainants who are not clients of the solicitor complained of, provided the complaint raises a *prima facie* issue of breach of a rule or principle of conduct. The investigation may be constrained when:

(a) the complainant and the client of the solicitor complained of are engaged in legal proceedings and the substance of the complaint cannot be distinguished from the issue before the court, or

(b) the solicitor complained of cannot answer the complaint because he or she is inhibited from doing so by reason of the duty of confidentiality owed to his or her client.

30.31 Complaints of this description are commonly misconceived. It is sometimes apparent from the outset that not only is there no breach of any rule or principle of conduct but also that the action to which the complainant refers was taken perfectly properly by the solicitor in the best interests of his or her own client.

Intervention in a solicitor's practice

30.32 The power of the Law Society contained in the Solicitors Act 1974 to intervene in a solicitor's practice may be exercised by the Adjudication and Appeals Committee in the circumstances set out in Schedule 1 (see Annex 30A). Examples of the circumstances in which these powers may be exercised are:

(a) suspicion of dishonesty on the part of the solicitor or a member of his or her staff or the personal representative of a deceased solicitor;

(b) failure to comply with the Solicitors' Accounts Rules 1991;

(c) where a solicitor is practising uncertificated; and

(d) incapacity of a sole practitioner.

Exercise of the powers requires service of the notices specified in the Schedule.

30.33 Under these provisions control over the solicitor's bank and building society accounts and documents vests in the Society. The exercise of the powers is undertaken on the authority of the Adjudication and Appeals Committee who appoint a practising solicitor as their agent for that purpose. The costs of any intervention are recoverable from the solicitor (see Annex 30F).

30.34 The Adjudication and Appeals Committee also has limited powers of intervention in a solicitor's practice where there has been a justified complaint of undue delay on the part of the solicitor in connection with any matter in which the solicitor or the firm was instructed. These powers enable the Committee to appoint a practising solicitor as their agent to take over the documents relating to the particular matter in respect of which the complaint of undue delay has been made together with any money held by the solicitor in relation to the same matter. The money is held by the Society in trust for the person beneficially entitled to it.

Defamation proceedings against complainants

30.35 Complaints to the Law Society and the SCB about the professional conduct of solicitors are protected by qualified privilege. The Council consider it is *prima facie* professional misconduct if a solicitor issues a writ claiming damages for alleged libel unless the solicitor is prepared to allege malice (see Annex 30C for the Council Statement).

Duty to answer correspondence

30.36 A solicitor is obliged to deal promptly with correspondence received from the SCB. Where a solicitor receives a letter from the SCB concerning his or her professional conduct, failure to answer it or failure to give an explanation of his or her conduct which the Council regard as sufficient and satisfactory will bring into operation the provisions of section 12(1)(e) of the Solicitors Act 1974. This gives the Law Society power to refuse to issue the solicitor's next practising certificate or to impose conditions upon the solicitor's current or next practising certificate (see Annex 2A).

Annex 30A

Solicitors Act 1974

Schedule 1 — intervention in solicitor's practice
(as amended by the Courts and Legal Services Act 1990)

Part I — Circumstances in which Society may intervene

1.   (1) Subject to sub-paragraph (2), the powers conferred by Part II of this Schedule shall be exercisable where -

(a)   the Council have reason to suspect dishonesty on the part of:

(i)   a solicitor, or

(ii)   an employee of a solicitor, or

(iii)   the personal representatives of a deceased solicitor, in connection with that solicitor's practice or in connection with any trust of which that solicitor is or formerly was a trustee;

(b)   the Council consider that there has been undue delay on the part of the personal representatives of a deceased solicitor who immediately before his death was practising as a sole solicitor in connection with that solicitor's practice or in connection with any controlled trust;

(c)   the Council are satisfied that a solicitor has failed to comply with rules made by virtue of section 32 or 37(2)(c);

(d)   a solicitor has been adjudged bankrupt or has made a composition or arrangement with his creditors;

(e)   a solicitor has been committed to prison in any civil or criminal proceedings;

(ee) the Council are satisfied that a sole solicitor is incapacitated by illness or accident to such an extent as to be unable to attend to his practice;

(f)   the powers conferred by section 104 of the Mental Health Act 1959 or section 98 of the Mental Health Act 1983 (emergency powers) or section 105 of the said Act of 1959 or section 99 of the said Act of 1983 (appointment of receiver) have been exercised in respect of a solicitor; or

(g)   the name of a solicitor has been removed from or struck off the roll or a solicitor has been suspended from practice.

(h)   the Council are satisfied that a sole solicitor has abandoned his practice;

(i)   the Council are satisfied that a sole solicitor is incapacitated by age to such an extent as to be unable to attend to his practice;

(j)   any power conferred by this Schedule has been exercised in relation to a sole solicitor by virtue of sub-paragraph (1)(a) and he has acted as a sole solicitor within the period of eighteen months beginning with the date on which it was so exercised;

(k)   the Council are satisfied that a person has acted as a solicitor at a time when he did not have a practising certificate which was in force;

(l)   the Council are satisfied that a solicitor has failed to comply with any condition, subject to which his practising certificate was granted or otherwise has effect, to the effect that he may act as a solicitor only -

(i)   in employment which is approved by the Society in connection with the imposition of that condition;

(ii)   as a member of a partnership which is so approved;

(iii)   as an officer of a body recognised by the Council of the Law Society under section 9 of the Administration of Justice Act 1985 and so approved; or

(iv)   in any specified combination of those ways.

(2)   The powers conferred by Part II of this Schedule shall only be exercisable under sub-paragraph (1)(c) if the Society has given the solicitor notice in writing that the Council are satisfied that he has failed to comply with rules specified in the notice and also (at the same or any later time) notice that the powers conferred by Part II of this Schedule are accordingly exercisable in his case.

2.   On the death of a sole solicitor paragraphs 6 to 8 shall apply to the client accounts of his practice.

3.   The powers conferred by Part II of this Schedule shall also be exercisable, subject to paragraphs 5(4) and 10(3), where -

(a)   a complaint is made to the Society that there has been undue delay on the part of a solicitor in connection with any matter in which the solicitor or his firm was instructed on behalf of a client or with any controlled trust; and

(b)   the Society by notice in writing invites the solicitor to give an explanation within a period of not less than 8 days specified in the notice; and

(c)   the solicitor fails within that period to give an explanation which the Council regard as satisfactory; and

(d)   the Society gives notice of the failure to the solicitor and (at the same or any later time) notice that the powers conferred by Part II of this Schedule are accordingly exercisable.

4.   (1) Where the powers conferred by Part II of this Schedule are exercisable in relation to a solicitor, they shall continue to be exercisable after his death or after his name has been removed from or struck off the roll.

(2)   The references to the solicitor or his firm in paragraphs 5(1), 6(2) and (3), 8, 9(1) and (5) and 10(1) include, in any case where the solicitor has died, references to his personal representatives.

Part II — Powers exercisable on intervention

Money

5.   (1) The High Court, on the application of the Society, may order that no payment shall be made without the leave of the court by any person (whether or not named in the order) of any money held by him (in whatever manner and whether it was received before or after the making of the order) on behalf of the solicitor or his firm.

(2)   No order under this paragraph shall take effect in relation to any person to whom it applies unless the Society has served a copy of the order on him (whether or not he is named in it) and, in the case of a bank or other financial institution, has indicated at which of its branches the Society believes that the money to which the order relates is held.

(3)   A person shall not be treated as having disobeyed an order under this paragraph by making a payment of money if he satisfies the court that he exercised due diligence to ascertain whether it was money to which the order related but nevertheless failed to ascertain that the order related to it.

(4)   This paragraph does not apply where the powers conferred by this Part of this Schedule are exercisable by virtue of paragraph 3.

6.   (1) Without prejudice to paragraph 5, if the Council pass a resolution to the effect that any sums of money to which this paragraph applies, and the right to recover or receive them, shall vest in the Society, all such sums shall vest accordingly (whether they were received by the person holding them before or after the Council's resolution) and shall be held by the Society on trust to exercise in relation to them the powers conferred by this Part of this Schedule and subject thereto upon trust for the persons beneficially entitled to them.

(2)   This paragraph applies -

(a)   where the powers conferred by this paragraph are exercisable by virtue of paragraph 1, to all sums of money held by or on behalf of the solicitor or his firm in connection with his practice or with any trust of which he is or formerly was a trustee;

(b)   where they are exercisable by virtue of paragraph 2, to all sums of money in any client account; and

(c)   where they are exercisable by virtue of paragraph 3, to all sums of money held by or on behalf of the solicitor or his firm in connection with the trust or other matter to which the complaint relates.

(3)   The Society shall serve on the solicitor or his firm and on any other person having possession of sums of money to which this paragraph applies a certified copy of the Council's resolution and a notice prohibiting the payment out of any such sums of money.

(4)   Within 8 days of the service of a notice under sub-paragraph (3), the person on whom it was served, on giving not less than 48 hours' notice in writing to the Society and (if the notice gives the name of the solicitor instructed by the Society) to that solicitor, may apply to the High Court for an order directing the Society to withdraw the notice.

(5)   If the court makes such an order, it shall have power also to make such other order with respect to the matter as it may think fit.

(6)   If any person on whom a notice has been served under sub-paragraph (3) pays out sums of money at a time when such payment is prohibited by the notice, he shall be guilty of an offence and liable on summary conviction to a fine not exceeding level 3 on the standard scale.

7.   (1) If the Society takes possession of any sum of money to which paragraph 6 applies, the Society shall pay it into a special account in the name of the Society or of a person nominated on behalf of the Society or into a client account of a solicitor nominated on behalf of the Society, and any such person or solicitor shall hold that sum on trust to permit the Society to exercise in relation to it the powers conferred by this Part of this Schedule and subject thereto on trust for the persons beneficially entitled to it.

(2)   A bank or other financial institution at which a special account is kept shall be under no obligation to ascertain whether it is being dealt with properly.

8.   Without prejudice to paragraphs 5 to 7, if the High Court is satisfied, on an application by the Society, that there is reason to suspect that any person holds money on behalf of the solicitor or his firm, the court may require that person to give the Society information as to any such money and the accounts in which it is held.

Documents

9.   (1) The Society may give notice to the solicitor or his firm requiring the production or delivery to any person appointed by the Society at a time and place to be fixed by the Society -

(a)   where the powers conferred by this Part of this Schedule are exercisable by virtue of paragraph 1, of all documents in the possession of the solicitor or his firm in connection with his practice or with any controlled trust; and

(b)   where they are exercisable by virtue of paragraph 3, of all documents in the possession of the solicitor or his firm in connection with the trust or other matters to which the complaint relates (whether or not they relate also to other matters).

(2)   The person appointed by the Society may take possession of any such documents on behalf of the Society.

(3)   Except in a case where an application has been made to the High Court under sub-paragraph (4), if any person having possession of any such documents refuses, neglects or otherwise fails to comply with a requirement under sub-paragraph (1), he shall be guilty of an offence and liable on summary conviction to a fine not exceeding level 3 on the standard scale.

(4)   The High Court, on the application of the Society, may order a person required to produce or deliver documents under sub-paragraph (1) to produce or deliver them to any person appointed by the Society at such time and place as may be specified in the order, and authorise him to take possession of them on behalf of the Society.

(5)   If on an application by the Society the High Court is satisfied that there is reason to suspect that documents in relation to which the powers conferred by sub-paragraph (1) are exercisable have come into the possession of some person other than the solicitor or his firm, the court may order that person to produce or deliver the documents to any person appointed by the Society at such time and place as may be specified in the order and authorise him to take possession of them on behalf of the Society.

(6)   On making an order under this paragraph, or at any later time, the court, on the

application of the Society, may authorise a person appointed by the Society to enter any premises (using such force as is reasonably necessary) to search for and take possession of any documents to which the order relates.

(7) The Society, on taking possession of any documents under this paragraph, shall serve upon the solicitor or personal representatives and upon any other person from whom they were received on the Society's behalf or from whose premises they were taken a notice that possession has been taken on the date specified in the notice.

(8) Subject to sub-paragraph (9) a person upon whom a notice under sub-paragraph (7) is served, on giving not less than 48 hours' notice to the Society and (if the notice gives the name of the solicitor instructed by the Society) to that solicitor, may apply to the High Court for an order directing the Society to deliver the documents to such person as the applicant may require.

(9) A notice under sub-paragraph (8) shall be given within 8 days of the service of the Society's notice under sub-paragraph (7).

(10) Without prejudice to the foregoing provisions of this Schedule, the Society may apply to the High Court for an order as to the disposal or destruction of any documents in its possession by virtue of this paragraph or paragraph 10.

(11) On an application under sub-paragraph (8) or (10), the court may make such order as it thinks fit.

(12) Except so far as its right to do so may be restricted by an order on an application under sub-paragraph (8) or (10), the Society may take copies of or extracts from any documents in its possession by virtue of this paragraph or paragraph 10 and require any person to whom it is proposed that such documents shall be delivered, as a condition precedent to delivery, to give a reasonable undertaking to supply copies or extracts to the Society.

Mail

10. (1) The High Court, on the application of the Society, may from time to time order that for such time not exceeding 18 months as the court thinks fit postal packets (as defined by section 87(1) of the Post Office Act 1953) addressed to the solicitor or his firm at any place or places mentioned in the order shall be directed to the Society or any person appointed by the Society at any other address there mentioned; and the Society, or that person on its behalf, may take possession of any such packets received at that address.

(2) Where such an order is made the Society shall pay to the Post Office the like charges (if any), as would have been payable for the re-direction of the packets by virtue of any scheme made under section 28 of the Post Office Act 1969, if the addressee had permanently ceased to occupy the premises to which they were addressed and had applied to the Post Office to redirect them to him at the address mentioned in the order.

(3) This paragraph does not apply where the powers conferred by this Part of this Schedule are exercisable by virtue of paragraph 3.

Trusts

11. (1) If the solicitor or his personal representative is a trustee of a controlled trust,

the Society may apply to the High Court for an order for the appointment of a new trustee in substitution for him.

(2)   The Trustee Act 1925 shall have effect in relation to an appointment of a new trustee under this paragraph as it has effect in relation to an appointment under section 41 of that Act.

General

12.   The powers in relation to sums of money and documents conferred by this Part of this Schedule shall be exercisable notwithstanding any lien on them or right to their possession.

13.   Subject to any order for the payment of costs that may be made on an application to the court under this Schedule, any costs incurred by the Society for the purposes of this Schedule, including, without prejudice to the generality of this paragraph, the costs of any person exercising powers under this Part of this Schedule on behalf of the Society, shall be paid by the solicitor or his personal representatives and shall be recoverable from him or them as a debt owing to the Society.

14.   Where an offence under this Schedule committed by a body corporate is proved to have been committed with the consent or connivance of, or to be attributable to any neglect on the part of any director, manager, secretary or other similar officer of the body corporate or any person who is purporting to act in any such capacity, he, as well as the body corporate, shall be guilty of that offence and shall be liable to be proceeded against and punished accordingly.

15.   Any application to the High Court under this Schedule may be disposed of in chambers.

16.   The Society may do all things which are reasonably necessary for the purpose of facilitating the exercise of its powers under this Schedule.

[NOTES

1.   As regards the exercise of the intervention powers in relation to a registered foreign lawyer and the practice of a multi-national partnership see paragraph 5 of Schedule 14 to the Courts and Legal Services Act 1990.

2.   As regards the exercise of the intervention powers in relation to a recognised body (i.e. an incorporated practice recognised under section 9 of the Administration of Justice Act 1985) see paragraphs 32-35 of Schedule 2 to the Administration of Justice Act 1985.]

Law Society's General Regulations 1987

regulation 34 — terms of reference of Adjudication and Appeals Committee
(with consolidated amendments to 3rd October 1991)

The terms of reference of the Adjudication and Appeals Committee are:

(1)   to determine all matters referred to the Committee concerning the following:

(a)   the conduct of solicitors, registered foreign lawyers and recognised bodies; or

(b)   the quality of work of solicitors and recognised bodies where this involves or may involve the powers conferred on the Council by the Administration of Justice Act 1985 as amended.

(2)   to exercise the powers of the Council:

(a)   under the Solicitors' Accounts Rules (excepting Rule 8(2) of the Solicitors' Accounts Rules 1986), under the Solicitors' Trust Accounts Rules, under the Accountants' Report Rules, under the Solicitors' Accounts (Deposit Interest) Rules, and under the Solicitors' Compensation Fund Rules;

(b)   under Schedule 1 Solicitors Act 1974;

(c)   under section 37A, 44A and 44B Solicitors Act 1974 and paragraph 14 of Schedule 2 to the Administration of Justice Act 1985;

(d)   under section 12 (excepting paragraphs (a) and (c) of sub-section (1)) Solicitors Act 1974 and under section 13A and section 13B Solicitors Act 1974 notifying the Standards and Guidance Committee of the imposition of any condition or the exercise of any discretion or of any other decision affecting the issue of any practising certificate in the circumstances specified in those provisions;

(e)   relating to the Compensation Fund (excepting the powers delegated to the Finance Committee under Regulation 35(8));

(f)   under any other legislation currently in force concerning the professional conduct of solicitors, registered foreign lawyers and recognised bodies;

(g)   to exercise the powers conferred by Rules 4 and 5 of the Solicitors' Investment Business Rules 1990 to issue or refuse to issue, suspend, withdraw or impose conditions on certificates of authorisation issued by the Law Society under the Financial Services Act 1986 in circumstances where it appears that there is an issue of conduct;

(h)   under sub-sections (1B) and (1C) of section 15 Solicitors Act 1974;

(i)   under paragraphs 2(3), 12(2) and 13 of Schedule 14 to the Courts and Legal Services Act 1990 to impose conditions on the registration of a registered foreign lawyer;

(j)   under paragraph 12(2) of Schedule 14 to the Courts and Legal Services Act 1990 to terminate the suspension of a foreign lawyer's registration; and

(k)   under Rule 10 of the Solicitors' Incorporated Practice Rules to revoke the recognition of a recognised body;

(3)   to deal with applications under sections 41 and 43 Solicitors Act 1974 for permission to employ persons struck off the Roll or suspended or in respect of whom a direction under section 47(2)(g) Solicitors Act 1974 has been given or certain persons who are or have been solicitors' clerks;

(4)   to deal with proceedings or proposed proceedings before the Solicitors' Disciplinary Tribunal; and

(5)   to keep under review all policy issues concerning the handling of complaints; to supervise and monitor the development of such policy issues in conjunction with the Policy Advisory Committee; and to be responsible for reporting to the Council, as appropriate, on all policy issues.

Annex 30C

Council statement on solicitors taking defamation proceedings against complainants

---

It has recently come to the attention of the Council that, in two separate instances, firms of solicitors have issued writs claiming damages for alleged libel in respect of material contained in two complaints concerning their professional conduct made to the Law Society and to the Solicitors Complaints Bureau.

Complaints to the Law Society/the Solicitors Complaints Bureau about the professional conduct of solicitors are protected by qualified privilege.

It is improper for a solicitor to issue such proceedings unless he or she is prepared to allege malice. If it comes to the attention of the Solicitors Complaints Bureau that any solicitor has acted in this way it will be treated as *prima facie* evidence of professional misconduct and dealt with accordingly.

30th August 1989

Annex 30D

SCB Local Conciliation Scheme — practice information

The Local Conciliation Scheme replaces the Interview Panel Scheme. A panel of local conciliators based in all regions of England and Wales are retained by the SCB.

Local conciliation officers are all solicitors recruited largely from the ranks of the retired or from those taking a career break. They are paid at the current legal aid rates.

A caseworker instructs a local conciliation officer when a face to face interview is required, for example:

(a)   where there are communciation difficulties through language or literacy;

(b)   where there are voluminous papers and the issues need clarifying;

(c)   when there are complex issues to identify and clarify;

(d)   where the matter can be best dealt with locally.

Practice Rule 15 — the SCB's approach — practice information

Rule 15 of the Solicitors' Practice Rules 1990 requires all firms to have an in-house complaints handling system. Failure to comply with the rule has the same effect as a breach of any other Practice Rule. However, special procedures have been developed to deal with complaints about breaches of this rule.

The Diagnostic Unit at the SCB filters out matters where it is obvious that the client has not discussed the problem with the firm concerned and where, on the face of it, the matter can be effectively sorted out by the firm involved. The SCB will usually send the matter on to the firm with a request to deal with the matter and a letter is also sent to the client explaining what has happened. Occasionally the complainant will be asked to contact the firm directly.

Dealing with complaints in this way gives the solicitor an opportunity to resolve the problem and may bridge the gulf which has arisen between the solicitor and the client. Some misunderstandings or problems are best dealt with by the firm. It also gives the firm an opportunity to learn how its services may need to be improved and to review the internal complaints handling procedure.

'Rule 15' referrals dealt with in this way are working encouragingly well and only between 10 and 15 per cent have to be formally investigated by the SCB.

To help the profession with some practical tips on avoiding complaints and to provide assistance in complying with the requirements of Rule 15 the SCB has produced an information pack which is available at £8 a copy. You should contact the Public Relations Section at the SCB for more details.

Annex 30F

Interventions — practice information

The two most common grounds for interventions by the Solicitors Complaints Bureau are where the Adjudication and Appeals Committee suspects dishonesty on the part of the solicitor and where the committee is satisfied that there have been serious breaches of the Solicitors' Accounts Rules.

Where a notice of intervention is served a member of the SCB's Legal Adviser's department will attend the solicitor's office. In the event that the factors which gave rise to the intervention cannot be remedied then, in order to persuade the committee to resolve not to intervene, the firm is invited to consider disposing of the practice to another firm. In some cases this may be with nil consideration. In the case of several partners being involved it may be appropriate to appoint a practice manager.

A notice that the Adjudication and Appeals Committee have decided to intervene has the following effects:

The firm is closed immediately.

The practising certificates of the partners or sole practitioner involved may be suspended.

Lien over documents will be lost.

A solicitor, as agent for the Law Society will be appointed to take control over all practice documents. This will usually be a local practitioner.

All the practice monies in both client and office accounts will vest in the Law Society.

The clients are notified of the intervention and their papers are distributed at their direction.

The agent does not take action to recover outstanding costs due to the solicitor concerned.

Contracts of employment and trading debts will remain the responsibility of the solicitor concerned.

The Law Society holds the solicitor involved responsible for any costs that the Law Society incurs in respect of the intervention, together with any shortfall on the client account as a result of which there are grants out of the Compensation Fund, and the Law Society will take all appropriate steps to recover such monies.

Chapter 31

The Solicitors' Disciplinary Tribunal

Introduction

31.01 The Solicitors' Disciplinary Tribunal is wholly independent of the Law Society and is established under section 46 of the Solicitors Act 1974. Its members are appointed by the Master of the Rolls and are either solicitors of not less than ten years' standing or lay members who must be neither solicitors nor barristers. There is no statutory limit on the total number of members of the Tribunal but there are normally about fourteen solicitor members and six lay members. For the purpose of hearing and determining applications, the Tribunal sits in divisions of three, comprising two solicitor members and one lay member. Pronouncements of the Tribunal, described as Findings and Orders, may be delivered by a single member.

31.02 The Tribunal is empowered to make rules governing its procedure and practice and this power is exercisable by statutory instrument with the concurrence of the Master of the Rolls. The rules are the Solicitors (Disciplinary Proceedings) Rules 1985 (see Annex 31A). New rules will come into force during 1993.

31.03 The principal function of the Tribunal is to hear and determine applications in respect of solicitors relating to allegations of unbefitting conduct or breaches of the rules of professional conduct made under the Solicitors Act 1974. The Tribunal also has jurisdiction in respect of registered foreign lawyers and persons who formerly had that status, recognised bodies (incorporated practices recognised by the Law Society), former solicitors, employees of solicitors and reporting accountants.

Applications to the Tribunal

31.04 The vast majority of applications to the Tribunal are made by the Solicitors Complaints Bureau on behalf of the Law Society but, subject to those instances under the Act where applications are limited to the Law Society alone, it is open to anyone to make an application to the Tribunal without recourse to the Society. Applications to the Tribunal made on behalf of the Law Society are conducted by solicitors in private practice instructed by the SCB. In appropriate cases, the SCB authorises the Society's solicitor to retain counsel to appear on the Society's behalf at the hearing of the application.

31.05 Whilst it is open to any person to make an application in respect of a solicitor to the Tribunal direct, it is more usual for a complainant first to approach the Solicitors Complaints Bureau for the matter to be investigated. If an application by a member of the public is made direct to the Tribunal, it may refer it to the Society for consideration and appropriate investigation. In such a case, the Society may decide to lodge its own application in respect of the solicitor who is the subject of the complaint or to undertake the conduct of the complainant's original application on his or her behalf. Subject to this, the procedure is similar, whether or not the application is made on behalf of the Society.

31.06 Applications to the Tribunal must be made in the form specified by its rules supported by a formal written statement by the applicant outlining the facts of the case. The statement also summarises the allegations of unbefitting conduct or breach of the rules which the respondent to the application is required to answer.

31.07 Applications are lodged with the clerk to the Tribunal and the Tribunal's first duty is to determine whether there is a *prima facie* case for the respondent to answer. For this purpose, members of the Tribunal do not hold a formal hearing but consider each application together with its supporting documents and, if satisfied that a *prima facie* case has been established, fix a hearing date. The respondent to the application is then notified of that date and supplied with copies of the application and the supporting documents. The Tribunal's rules prescribe the length of notice which must be given to the respondent in respect of any hearing.

The hearing

31.08 It is the current practice of the Tribunal to hear applications in private, but this may change during 1993. At the hearing itself, either party may be represented by a solicitor or counsel or may appear in person. The Tribunal might grant a right of audience to a suitable person who is neither a solicitor nor a barrister. Either party may call witnesses and the evidential procedures of the Tribunal are in virtually all respects similar to those of the High Court. Evidence before the Tribunal is given on oath and it has power to accept affidavit evidence. In the event of any party failing to appear at the hearing, the Tribunal may dispose of the case in the party's absence. It has power to order a re-hearing of the application if the respondent did not appear and was not represented at the hearing.

Findings and Orders

31.09 In practice, the Tribunal usually reserves its pronouncement upon an application and promulgates it approximately four to six weeks after the hearing. It is the practice of the Tribunal to give a written informal indication of what its Order will be within a few days of the hearing. Its pronouncements take the form of Findings and Orders. The Tribunal has power, which it exercises only occasionally, to announce its Order immediately following the hearing of an application but is then obliged to reduce its Findings to writing and promulgates them at a later date. Pronouncements of the Tribunal are delivered by one member sitting alone and the Findings and Order are then filed with the Law Society, at which stage the Tribunal's Order takes immediate effect. On application by either party at the time of pronouncement, the Tribunal may suspend the filing of its Findings and Order.

Powers of the Tribunal

31.10   The Tribunal's powers are defined by section 47 of the Solicitors Act 1974 which grants it discretion to make such Order as it thinks fit in respect of any application save one made under under section 43 (see paragraph 31.15). In particular, the Tribunal may order:

(a)   the striking off the roll of the name of the solicitor to whom the application or complaint relates;

(b)   the suspension of that solicitor from practice indefinitely or for a specified period;

(c)   the payment by that solicitor of a penalty not exceeding £5000 in respect of each and every allegation, which shall be forfeit to Her Majesty;

(d)   the exclusion of a solicitor from legal aid work (either permanently or for a specified period);

(e)   the termination of a solicitor's unspecified period of suspension from practice;

(f)   the restoration to the roll of the name of a former solicitor whose name has been struck off;

(g)   in the case of a former solicitor whose name has been removed from the roll, a direction prohibiting the restoration of his or her name to the roll except by an Order of the Tribunal;

(h)   the restoration of the name of a former solicitor (in respect of whom a direction had been made pursuant to (g) above) to the roll;

(i)   the payment by any party of costs or a contribution towards costs in such amount as the Tribunal may consider reasonable.

31.11   For the purposes of enforcement, Orders made by the Tribunal are treated as if they were Orders of the High Court. For example, the Tribunal may make an Order that a direction of the Council of the Law Society relating to the provision by a solicitor of inadequate professional services, shall be treated for the purposes of enforcement as if it were contained in an Order of the High Court. Orders imposing a penalty or requiring payment of costs are similarly enforceable.

31.12   The Tribunal may also order payment of the costs of the investigation accountant of the SCB in those cases where the application is founded on breaches by the respondent of the Solicitors' Accounts Rules which are substantiated. It is the usual practice of the Tribunal when making an Order for the payment of costs to direct that these should be taxed.

Registered foreign lawyers

31.13   In the case of a registered foreign lawyer, the Tribunal's powers which are broadly the same as in the case of a solicitor, are set out in the Courts and Legal Services Act 1990, Schedule 14, paragraph 15. The Tribunal may order that the name of a registered foreign lawyer be struck off the register or that his registration be suspended. The Tribunal may seek assistance from a member of the legal profession in the jurisdiction where the registered foreign lawyer is or was qualified.

Recognised bodies

31.14   The Tribunal's jurisdiction and powers in respect of recognised bodies (incorporated practices) are set out in the Administration of Justice Act 1985, Schedule 2, paragraph 18. Should a recognised body be convicted of a criminal offence, fail to comply with the requirement to provide an accountant's report or fail to comply with any direction given to it by the Council of the Law Society, then the Tribunal may *inter alia* order that the body's recognition by the Society be revoked or impose a financial penalty. The Tribunal may also order revocation of recognition of an incorporated practice by reason of default by a director.

Applications in respect of solicitors' clerks

31.15   The Tribunal has jurisdiction to hear applications in respect of a person who is or was a clerk to a solicitor but is not himself or herself a solicitor. This jurisdiction arises under section 43 of the Solicitors Act 1974. These applications can only be made to the Tribunal at the instance of the Law Society.

31.16   Section 43 empowers the Law Society to make an application to the Tribunal for an Order controlling the employment of a person who is or was a clerk to a solicitor and has:

(a)   been convicted of a criminal offence which discloses such dishonesty that, in the opinion of the Society, it would be undesirable for such person to be employed by a solicitor in connection with his or her practice, or

(b)   in the opinion of the Society, occasioned or been a party to with or without the connivance of the solicitor to whom he or she is or was a clerk, an act or default in relation to the solicitor's practice, which involved conduct on his or her part of such a nature that, in the opinion of the Society, it would be undesirable for him or her to be employed by a solicitor in connection with his or her practice.

31.17 A solicitor who employs (or formerly employed) a clerk convicted of dishonesty or an act or default in relation to the solicitor's practice justifying an application to the Tribunal, is under a professional duty to report these circumstances to the SCB.

31.18 Where an Order is made in respect of a clerk or former clerk to a solicitor, the Tribunal may also order payment of the costs of such application to be paid by the clerk, or his or her employer or former employer if joined as a party to the application. The Tribunal has power to revoke an Order in respect of a clerk or former clerk on his or her own application or that of the Law Society. An appeal against the making of an Order lies only at the instance of a clerk or former clerk to the Divisional Court whose decision is final.

31.19 The effect of an Order made under section 43 is to vest in the Law Society, the control of the future employment of the subject of such Order in connection with a solicitor's practice. Whilst the Order remains in force, any solicitor wishing to employ the person to whom it applies must first obtain the written consent of the Society. The Adjudication and Appeals Committee consider applications for such consent and it is their practice to seek the view of the appropriate local law society and former employers.

31.20 When a solicitor employed in local government or commerce and industry seeks to employ a clerk who is subject to an Order under section 43, the consent of the Law Society is not required as the clerk cannot be said to be employed by a solicitor in connection with his or her practice. It is, however, desirable in such cases for the SCB to be informed of the intended employment and its terms, so that the whereabouts of the clerk and his or her personal circumstances may be noted in the SCB's records.

31.21 Section 44 of the Solicitors Act 1974 provides that a clerk who acts in contravention of any Order made under section 43 is guilty of an offence triable summarily and liable to a fine. Any solicitor who knowingly contravenes the provisions of such an Order or the conditions imposed by the Law Society when application is made to employ a clerk to whom it applies, may be the subject of complaint to the Tribunal at the instance of the Society.

Application for restoration to the roll

31.22 The Tribunal has jurisdiction to restore to the roll the name of a former solicitor whose name has been struck off the roll, or where a direction has been made pursuant to section 47(2)(g) of the Solicitors Act 1974 in respect of a former solicitor. An application in such a case must be supported by an affidavit which sets out details of the original Order of the Tribunal, deals fully with the history of the applicant's employment thereafter and indicates future intentions as to employment within the profession if the application is successful. Notice of the application must be given to the Law Society which is required to publish it in the *Gazette*. As a matter of practice, the views of the appropriate local law society(ies) are invariably sought.

31.23 The Tribunal has indicated that restoration is not to be regarded as an appeal against its previous decision. Its function when considering an application for restoration is to determine whether the applicant has established that he or she is now a fit and proper person to have his or her name restored to the roll. The test of fitness and propriety is a very wide one in this context. The Tribunal must have regard to decisions made by the Master of the Rolls when hearing appeals against refused applications for restoration. Whilst such decisions relate to the individual cases in question the following principles govern the test to be applied by the Tribunal:

(a) Whilst the striking off of a solicitor may be said to punish the solicitor and protect the good name of the profession, the overriding consideration is always the protection of the public.

(b) If the need to protect the good name of the profession ultimately causes hardship to an individual whose misconduct has led to his or her being struck off, that has to be accepted as the price of maintaining the reputation of the profession and the public's confidence in it.

(c) Where an applicant has been convicted of a criminal offence — particularly one involving dishonesty — the onus falling on him or her to demonstrate that restoration to the roll could not damage the reputation of the profession as a whole, is a very heavy one.

(d) The test applied by the Tribunal is 'would any reasonable minded member of the public, knowing the facts, say "really any profession should be proud to readmit him or her as a member" '.

31.24 In practice, the Tribunal finds it helpful when considering applications for restoration to have evidence adduced which deals with the following issues:

(a) the extent of the applicant's rehabilitation and the history of his or her employment since striking off, including any consent granted by the Law Society for his or her employment within the profession under section 41 of the Solicitors Act 1974;

(b) the applicant's future intentions and whether, in the event of restoration, another solicitor would be willing to employ him or her; and

(c) whether the applicant incurred any indebtedness to the Compensation Fund or to others and, if so, the extent to which repayment has been made.

31.25 Similar considerations apply in the case of an application for restoration to the roll following the making by the Tribunal of a direction pursuant to section 47(2)(g) of the Solicitors Act 1974 and an application seeking to bring to an end an indefinite suspension.

31.26 It is established practice for a solicitor to be instructed to represent the Law Society when any application for restoration is heard by the Tribunal. In virtually every case, the Society's solicitor is instructed to oppose the application. It is the Society's policy, save in exceptional circumstances, to oppose any application made within six years of the original Order striking the applicant's name off the roll on the grounds that it is premature.

Appeals

31.27 The procedure for appeal from the Tribunal is governed by section 49 of the Solicitors Act 1974. Save as mentioned in paragraph 31.29, all appeals lie to a Divisional Court of the Queen's Bench Division and after that (except in respect of an Order under section 43) with leave, to the Court of Appeal and, again with appropriate leave, to the House of Lords. The relevant rules relating to appeals are contained in the Rules of the Supreme Court, Order 106. The appeal in these circumstances is by way of re-hearing.

31.28 At the hearing of an appeal, the Divisional Court has before it a copy of the original application to the Tribunal together with the supporting documents. It is also provided with a transcript of the proceedings before the Tribunal which it is the duty of the Law Society to bespeak when the appeal is lodged. The Tribunal is not represented before the Divisional Court at the hearing of an appeal against its Order, but may be asked for a written statement of its opinion on the instant case or on any question of fact arising from its Findings. At the hearing of an appeal, both parties to the original application have a right of audience. Where new evidence is introduced the Court may order the case to be remitted to the Tribunal for re-hearing, usually before a differently constituted division of members.

31.29 Appeals against refusals by the Tribunal to revoke an Order under section 43 in respect of a solicitor's clerk or to restore the name of a former solicitor to the roll are made to the Master of the Rolls. These are presented by way of petition, lodged with the Master of the Rolls' clerk, who fixes the date of the hearing which is held in private. At the hearing, both the petitioner and the Law Society are represented. The decision of the Master of the Rolls in these cases is final.

Annex 31A

Solicitors (Disciplinary Proceedings) Rules 1985 (S.I. 1985 no. 226)

Made 19th February 1985

Came into operation 1st April 1985

Arrangement of Rules

PART I   **Constitution of the Tribunal** (Rules 2 & 3)

PART II   **Applications against solicitors and in respect of solicitors' clerks** (Rules 4 to 10)

PART III   **Applications at the instance of a former solicitor himself** (Rules 11 to 18)

PART IV   **Applications in respect of a former solicitor's clerk** (Rules 19 to 23)

PART V   **General** (Rules 24 to 43)

SCHEDULE Forms

The Disciplinary Tribunal constituted under the Solicitors Act 1974[a] with the concurrence of the Master of the Rolls, in exercise of the Powers conferred on them by section 46 of the said Act and of all other powers them enabling hereby make the following Rules:

1.   (a) These Rules may be cited as the Solicitors (Disciplinary Proceedings) Rules 1985 and shall come into force on the 1st day of April 1985 whereupon the Solicitors (Disciplinary Proceedings) Rules 1975[b] shall cease to have effect.

   (b) (i)   In these Rules 'solicitor's clerk' means a person who is or was employed or remunerated by a solicitor or by a firm of solicitors as a clerk and is not himself a solicitor, 'the Clerk' means the Clerk to the Tribunal or any deputy or person appointed by the Tribunal temporarily to perform the duties of that office, and an 'application' includes a complaint to the Tribunal made by virtue of the provisions of the Solicitors Act 1974.

   (ii)   Other expressions in these Rules have the meanings assigned to them in the Solicitors Act 1974.

   (iii)   The Interpretation Act 1978[c] applies to these Rules in the same manner as it applies to an Act of Parliament.

---

a   1974 c.47
b   S.I. 1975 no.727
c   1978 c.30

PART I

Constitution of the Tribunal

2.   The Tribunal shall elect a solicitor member of the Tribunal to be its President.

3.   The President shall appoint a solicitor member to act as Chairman for the hearing and determination by the Tribunal of any application in accordance with the provisions of Part V of these Rules; provided that in the absence of such appointment a solicitor member of the Tribunal shall act as its Chairman.

PART II

Applications against Solicitors and in respect of Solicitors' Clerks

4.   (a) An application to the Tribunal to strike the name of a solicitor off the Roll of Solicitors, or to require a solicitor to answer allegations contained in an affidavit, shall be in writing signed by the applicant in the form numbered 1 in the Schedule hereto.

    (b) An application to the Tribunal to make an Order under section 43(2) of the Solicitors Act 1974 shall be in writing signed by the applicant in the form numbered 2 in the Schedule hereto.

    (c) In either case the application shall be supported by an affidavit by the applicant in the form set out in the Schedule hereto numbered 3 or as near thereto as the circumstances may permit, stating the matters of fact on which he relies in support of his application.

    (d) Where the application is made by the Society the application may be signed and the affidavit sworn on behalf of the Society by the Secretary or by such other person as may from time to time be instructed to do so by or on behalf of the Council.

5.   Before fixing a day for the hearing the Tribunal may require the applicant to supply such further information and documents relating to the application as they think fit and may require the applicant to supply such further copies of his affidavit and of the exhibits thereto as the Tribunal may consider requisite.

6.   In the case of an application against a solicitor where, in the opinion of the Tribunal, no *prima facie* case is shown in favour of the application, the Tribunal may dismiss the application without requiring the solicitor to answer the allegations, and without hearing the applicant. If required so to do either by the applicant or the solicitor, the Tribunal shall make a formal Order dismissing such application.

7.   In the case of an application in respect of a solicitor's clerk the parties to the proceedings shall be:

    (i)   the applicant;

    (ii)   the solicitor's clerk, and

    (iii)   if the Tribunal so direct, every solicitor by whom the solicitor's clerk was employed either at the time of the commission of any such offence as is mentioned in section 43(1) of the Solicitors Act 1974, of which it is alleged by the applicant that the solicitor's clerk has been convicted, or at the time of any such act or default as is mentioned in section 43(1)(b) of the said Act to which it is alleged that the solicitor's clerk has been party.

8.   In the case of an application against a solicitor in which, in the opinion of the Tribunal, a *prima facie* case is shown in favour of the application, and in the case of every application in respect of a solicitor's clerk, the Tribunal shall fix a day for the hearing, and the Clerk shall serve notice thereof on each party to the proceedings and shall serve on each party, other than the applicant, a copy of the application and affidavit. There shall be at least 42 days between the service of any such notice and the day fixed therein for the hearing.

9.   The notice shall be in such one of the forms set out in the Schedule hereto and numbered 4, 5, 6 and 7, as shall be appropriate and shall require the party to whom it is addressed to furnish to the Clerk and to every other party at least 14 days before the day fixed for the hearing, unless the Tribunal direct otherwise, a list of all documents on which he intends to rely.

10.   Any party may inspect the documents in the list furnished by any other party. A copy of any document mentioned in the list furnished by any party shall, on application and on payment of the proper charges therefor by the party requiring it, be furnished to that party by the other within three days after the receipt of such application.

PART III

Applications at the instance of a former Solicitor himself

11.   An application by a former solicitor whose name has been struck off the Roll to have his name restored to the Roll shall be made by way of affidavit in the form set out in the Schedule hereto and numbered 8. The affidavit shall be sent to the Clerk and a copy thereof to the Society.

12.   The Tribunal may grant an application made pursuant to Rule 11 without requiring the attendance of the applicant. In any other case the Tribunal shall fix a day for the hearing and the Clerk shall serve notice thereof on the applicant and the Society at least 56 days before the day fixed for the hearing.

13.   The notice shall be in such one of the forms set out in the Schedule hereto and numbered 9 and 10 as shall be appropriate.

14.   The Tribunal may if they think fit require the applicant or the Society to give notice of the application and of the day fixed for the hearing by advertisement or otherwise as they may direct.

15.   If any person desires to object to the application, he shall give notice in writing to the applicant, the Society and the Clerk at least seven days before the day fixed for the hearing, specifying the grounds of his objection.

16.   If the objector appears on the day fixed for the hearing, and if the Tribunal are of opinion, after hearing the parties or either of them (if they think fit so to do), that the notice discloses a *prima facie* case for inquiry of which they do not dispose on that day, they shall adjourn the hearing and shall give directions relating to the adjourned hearing, including directions as to the party on whom the burden of proof shall lie.

17.   The Rules contained in Parts II and V of these Rules shall apply *mutatis mutandis* to the hearing of any application under this Part of these Rules.

18.   In respect of any application by a solicitor to procure his name to be restored to the Roll the Tribunal shall order either that the name of the solicitor be restored to the Roll or that the application be refused and in either case may make such Order as to the costs as they think fit.

PART IV

Applications in respect of a former Solicitor's Clerk

19.   An application that an Order under section 43(2) of the Solicitors Act 1974 shall be revoked, shall be made by way of affidavit in the form set out in the Schedule hereto and numbered 11.

20.   The parties to the proceedings shall be:

   (i)   The person with respect to whom the Order under section 43(2) of the Solicitors Act 1974 was made which it is sought to revoke; and

   (ii)   The Society;

and the affidavit shall be sent to the Clerk and a copy thereof to the other party to the proceedings.

21.   The Tribunal may grant the application without requiring the attendance of the parties. In any other case the Tribunal shall fix a day for the hearing and the Clerk shall serve notice thereof on the parties to the proceedings at least 56 days before the day fixed for the hearing. The notice shall be in the form set out in the Schedule hereto and numbered 12.

22.   The Rules contained in Part II and V of these Rules shall apply *mutatis mutandis* to the hearing of any application under this Part of these Rules.

23.   In respect of any application made under this Part of these Rules the Tribunal shall order either that the previous Order be revoked or that the application be refused, and in either case they may make such Order as to the costs as they think fit.

PART V

General

24.   (a) Subject to paragraph (b) of this Rule the Tribunal shall hear all applications in private.

   (b) Any party applying that a hearing shall be in public shall notify the Clerk, and the other party or parties to the proceedings, at least 21 days before the date fixed for the hearing and unless at least 10 days before that date any other party to the proceedings objects thereto the hearing shall be in public. In the event of an objection the Tribunal shall, at the hearing, determine in private whether the hearing is to be in public.

   (c) Notwithstanding paragraph (b) of this Rule if it appears to the Tribunal that any person would suffer undue prejudice from a public hearing or that for any other reason the circumstances and nature of the case make a public hearing undesirable the Tribunal may direct that the public shall be excluded either from the whole or any part of a hearing.

25.   If any party fails to appear at the hearing the Tribunal may, upon proof of service on such party of the notice of hearing, proceed to hear and determine the application in his absence.

26.   Any party who has failed to appear at the hearing may, within one calendar month from the date of the filing of the Order of the Tribunal with the Society, and upon giving notice to every other party and to the Clerk, apply to the Tribunal for a re-hearing. The Tribunal, if satisfied that it is just that the case should be re-heard, may grant the application upon such terms as to costs or otherwise as they think fit. Upon such re-hearing the Tribunal may amend, vary, add to, or reverse their Findings, or Order, pronounced upon such previous hearing.

27.   (a) The Tribunal may, in their discretion, either as to the whole case or as to any particular fact or facts, proceed and act upon evidence given by affidavit.

(b) Every affidavit upon which any party proposes to rely shall be filed with the Clerk and served upon the opposing party not less than 21 days before the date set down for the hearing of the application, together with a notice in the form numbered 15 in the Schedule hereto.

(c) Any party on whom such a notice has been served who requires the attendance at the hearing of a deponent to any affidavit shall, not less than 10 days before such date, require in writing the other party to produce the deponent witness at the hearing.

(d) In the event of any party not requiring the attendance of a deponent witness in accordance with the provisions of these Rules the Tribunal may accept such affidavit in evidence.

(e) If a deponent witness who has been required to attend in accordance with the provisions of these Rules does not attend the hearing the onus shall be on the party seeking to rely on the affidavit evidence of that witness to show why the affidavit should be accepted in evidence.

28.   The Tribunal may at any stage of proceedings against a solicitor refer the case to the Council and may adjourn the application pending the consideration thereof by the Council in case the Council should see fit to lodge a further application against the solicitor or to undertake on behalf of the original applicant the prosecution of his application.

29.   Unless the Tribunal direct otherwise no application shall be withdrawn after it has been sent to the Clerk.

30.   The Tribunal may of their own motion, or upon the application of any party, adjourn or postpone the hearing upon such terms as the Tribunal may think fit.

31.   In the case of an application in respect of a solicitor's clerk the Tribunal may on the application of any party or on their own motion order that any such application shall be heard before, together with, or after the hearing of an application to require a solicitor by whom the clerk is or was employed to answer allegations contained in an affidavit.

32.   If upon the hearing it shall appear to the Tribunal that the allegations in the affidavit require to be amended, or added to, the Tribunal may permit such amendment, or addition, or if in the opinion of the Tribunal such amendment, or addition, shall be such as to take any party by surprise, or prejudice the conduct of his case, the Tribunal shall grant an adjournment of the hearing, upon such terms as to costs, or otherwise, as the Tribunal shall think fit.

33.   If at the conclusion of the hearing of any application the Tribunal propose to find any of the allegations made against the respondent to have been substantiated, they shall so inform the respondent and the Clerk shall then refer the Tribunal and the respondent to any previous Disciplinary Proceedings in which any allegation has been substantiated against him so that the respondent may then have the opportunity to speak in mitigation and, where appropriate, in respect of costs.

34.   Upon the hearing or determination of any application the Tribunal may, in the case of an application against a solicitor, without finding any charge of unbefitting conduct proved against the solicitor, or, in the case of an application in respect of a solicitor's clerk, without making any Order under section 43(2) of the Solicitors Act 1974 nevertheless order any party to pay the costs of the proceedings if having regard to his conduct and to all the circumstances of the case the Tribunal shall think fit.

35.   Upon the conclusion of the hearing or determination of any application the Tribunal may announce their Order while still sitting in which case the Order shall be filed immediately with the Society; or they may reserve judgment. In either case they shall pronounce their Order in public at a later date, notice whereof shall be given to the parties by the Clerk and the Clerk shall, on the day of pronouncement, file with the Society the Findings and if not already filed, the Order, and shall supply a copy thereof to each party to the proceedings and to any other person present at the pronouncement who requests one.

36.   (a) The Tribunal shall have power, upon the application of a party against or with respect to whom they have made an Order, to suspend the filing thereof with the Society.

(b) Where the filing of an Order is suspended under this Rule, the Order shall not take effect until it is filed with the Society, and if the Order is an Order that a solicitor be suspended from practice, the period of suspension shall be deemed to commence on the date of the filing of the Order with the Society or on such later date (if any) as may have been specified in the Order.

37.   Shorthand notes of proceedings may be taken by a person appointed by the Tribunal. If the Tribunal so direct, a transcript shall be made thereof and any party who appeared at the proceedings shall be entitled to inspect such transcript. The shorthand writer shall, if required, supply to the Tribunal and to any person entitled to be heard upon an appeal against an Order of the Tribunal, and to the Society, but to no other person, a copy of the transcript of such notes on payment of his charges. If no shorthand notes be taken the Chairman of the Tribunal shall take a note of the proceedings, and the provisions of this Rule as to inspection and taking of copies shall apply to such note accordingly.

38.   Service of any notice or document may be effected under these Rules by registered 'A.R.' letter or by Recorded Delivery letter addressed, in the case of a solicitor, to his last known place of business appearing in the Register (commonly known as the Practising Roll kept by the Society) or to his last known place of abode and in every other case, to the last known place of business or abode of the person to be served and such service shall be deemed to have been effected on the day when the letter is despatched.

39.   (a) Subject to the provisions of these Rules the Tribunal may regulate its own procedure.

(b) The Tribunal may dispense with any requirements of these Rules respecting notices, affidavit documents, service or time in any case where it appears to the Tribunal to be just so to do.

40. All affidavits shall be filed and kept by the Clerk. The Tribunal may order that any books, papers, or other exhibits produced or used at a hearing, shall be retained by the Clerk until the time within which an appeal may be entered has expired, and, if notice of appeal is given, until the appeal is heard or otherwise disposed of.

41. The Civil Evidence Act 1968[a] and the Evidence and Powers of Attorney Act 1940[b] shall apply in relation to proceedings before the Tribunal in the same manner as they apply in relation to civil and criminal proceedings.

42. (a) Not less than 28 days before the date fixed for the hearing of an application the applicant may require in writing the other party to indicate to the applicant within 14 days of the receipt of such requirement which of any facts set out in the affidavit submitted in support of the application are in dispute. Failure to reply to such a notice shall be material only in relation to the question of costs.

(b) Any party may by notice in writing at any time not later than nine days before the day fixed for the hearing call upon any other to admit any document saving all just exceptions and if such other party desires to challenge the authenticity of the document he shall within six days after service of such notice give notice that he does not admit the document and requires it to be proved at the hearing.

(c) If such other party refuses or neglects to give notice of non-admission within the time prescribed in the last preceding paragraph, he shall be deemed to have admitted the document unless otherwise ordered by the Tribunal.

(d) Where a party gives notice of non-admission within the time prescribed by the second paragraph of this Rule and the document is proved at the hearing, the costs of proving the document shall be paid by the party who has challenged the document, whatever the Order of the Tribunal may be, unless in their Findings the Tribunal shall find that there were reasonable grounds for not admitting the authenticity of the document.

(e) Where a party proves a document without having given notice to admit under the second paragraph of this Rule no costs of proving the document shall be allowed on taxation unless otherwise directed by the Tribunal, except where the omission to give notice to admit is in the opinion of the Taxing Master a saving of expense.

43. A subpoena issued under section 46(11) of the Solicitors Act 1974 shall be in such one of the forms set out in the Schedule hereto and numbered 13 and 14 as shall be appropriate.

Schedule

FORM 1

Form on application against a Solicitor

To the Clerk to the Disciplinary Tribunal constituted under the Solicitors Act 1974

In the Matter of C.D(1) a Solicitor

and

---

a 1968 c.64
b 1940 c.28

In the matter of the Solicitors Act 1974.

I, the undersigned A.B hereby make application that C.D(1)   of (2)   ,
solicitor, may be required to answer the allegations contained in the affidavit which
accompanies this application and that such order may be made as the Tribunal shall think
right.

In witness whereof I have hereunto set my hand

this   day of   19   .

Signature

Address

Profession, business or organisation

---

(1)   The full name must be stated. Initials are not sufficient. The names may be obtained
      by an inspection of the Roll of Solicitors at the Law Society, Chancery Lane,
      London WC2 during usual office hours.*

(2)   Last known place or places of business of the solicitor.

*   *This has changed since the rules were made and the Roll of Solicitors can now be
      inspected at the Law Society, Ipsley Court, Berrington Close, Redditch, Worcs B98
      0TD.*

FORM 2

Form of application in respect of a Solicitor's Clerk

To the Clerk to the Disciplinary Tribunal constituted under the Solicitors Act 1974

In the Matter of E.F, a Solicitor's Clerk.

and

In the Matter of the Solicitors Act 1974.

I, the undersigned A.B, of   , hereby make application on behalf of The Law
Society that an order be made by the Tribunal directing that as from a date to be specified
in such order no solicitor shall except in accordance with permission in writing granted
by The Law Society for such period and subject to such conditions as the Society may
think fit to specify in the permission, employ or remunerate in connection with the
practice as a solicitor, E.F of   , a person who is or was a clerk to a solicitor,
or that such other order may be made as the Tribunal shall think right.

In witness whereof I have hereunto set my hand

this   day of   19   .

                              Signature

FORM 3

Form of affidavit by applicant

In the matter of C.D, a Solicitor,

and

In the Matter of the Solicitors Act 1974

I, *A.B, of , make oath and say as follows:

1 +C.D, of , solicitor of the Supreme Court of Judicature in England, has been employed by me in a professional capacity for the last ten years (or as the case may be).

2 [Here state the facts concisely in numbered paragraphs, and show deponent's means of knowledge.]

Sworn etc.

*Insert full name, address and description.

+Insert full name and last known place of business.

FORM 4

Form of notice to applicant by the Clerk to the Disciplinary Tribunal

In the Matter of C.D, a solicitor, [or] a Solicitor's Clerk.

and

In the Matter of the Solicitors Act 1974.

To A.B, of

The day of , 19 , is the day fixed by the Disciplinary Tribunal constituted under the Solicitors Act 1974 for the hearing of your application in the matter of C.D, a solicitor [or] a person who is or was a clerk to a solicitor.

The Tribunal will sit at the Court Room No. 60 Carey Street, Chancery Lane, London WC2 at o'clock in the noon.

*[The parties to the application are as follows: .]

You are required by the Solicitors (Disciplinary Proceedings) Rules 1985 to furnish to every party to the application and to the Clerk to the Disciplinary Tribunal at the Court Room, No. 60 Carey Street, Chancery Lane, London WC2 at least fourteen days before the said day of , 19 , a list of all the documents on which you propose to rely.

Any party may inspect the documents included in the list furnished by the other, and a copy of any document mentioned in the list of any party must, on application and on payment by the party requiring it of the proper charges, be furnished to that party by the other within three days after receipt of such application.

If any party shall fail to appear and the Tribunal decide to proceed in his absence, any party appearing must be prepared to prove service, in accordance with the Solicitors

(Disciplinary Proceedings) Rules 1985, of the list of documents and any other notice or correspondence since the lodging of the application.

You are requested to acknowledge the receipt of this notice without delay.

Dated this   day of   , 19 .

. . . .

Clerk to the Tribunal

*To be deleted when the application is against a solicitor.

FORM 5

Form of notice to Solicitor by the Clerk to the Disciplinary Tribunal

In the Matter of C.D, a Solicitor

and

In the Matter of the Solicitors Act 1974.

To C.D, of   , Solicitor.

Application has been made by A.B, of   , to the Disciplinary Tribunal constituted under the Solicitors Act 1974 that you may be required to answer the allegations contained in the affidavit, whereof a copy accompanies this notice, and that such order may be made as the Tribunal shall think right.

The   day of   , 19   is the day fixed by the Tribunal for the hearing of the application. The Tribunal will sit at the Court Room, No. 60 Carey Street, Chancery Lane, London WC2, at   o'clock in the   noon. If you fail to appear, the Tribunal may, in accordance with the Solicitors (Disciplinary Proceedings) Rules 1985, proceed in your absence.

You are required by the said Rules to furnish to every other party to the application and to the Clerk to the Disciplinary Tribunal at the Court Room, No. 60 Carey Street, Chancery Lane, London WC2 at least fourteen days before the said   day of   , 19 , a list of all the documents on which you propose to rely.

Any party may inspect the documents included in the list furnished by any other, and a copy of any document mentioned in the list of any party must, on application and on payment by the party requiring it of the proper charges, be furnished to that party by the other within three days after receipt of such application.

In order to reduce the costs of the hearing, you are invited to inform the applicant and the Clerk to the Disciplinary Tribunal not less than fourteen days before the said day of   of any facts set out in the affidavit which are not in dispute.

You are requested to acknowledge the receipt of this notice without delay.

Dated this   day of   , 19 .

. . . .

Clerk to the Tribunal

FORM 6

Form of notice to Solicitor's Clerk by the Clerk to the Disciplinary Tribunal

In the Matter of E.F, a Solicitor's Clerk.

and

In the Matter of the Solicitors Act 1974.

To E.F, of

Application has been made by A.B, of   , on behalf of The Law Society to the Disciplinary Tribunal constituted under the Solicitors Act 1974, supported by an affidavit, a copy of which accompanies this notice, that an order may be made directing that as from a date to be specified in such order no solicitor shall except in accordance with permission in writing granted by The Law Society for such period and subject to such conditions as the Society may think fit to specify in the permission, employ or remunerate you in connection with his practice as a solicitor or that such order may be made as the Tribunal shall think right.

The parties to the proceedings are as follows:

The   day of   , 19   , is the day fixed by the Tribunal for the hearing of the application. The Tribunal will sit at the Court Room, No. 60 Carey Street, Chancery Lane, London WC2, at   o'clock in the   noon. If you fail to appear, the Tribunal may, in accordance with the Solicitors (Disciplinary Proceedings) Rules 1985, proceed in your absence.

You are required by the said Rules to furnish to every other party to the proceedings and to the Clerk to the Disciplinary Tribunal at the Court Room, No. 60 Carey Street, Chancery Lane, London WC2 at least fourteen days before the said   day of   , 19 , a list of all the documents on which you propose to rely.

Any party may inspect the documents included in the list furnished by any other party, and a copy of any document mentioned in the list of any party must, on application and on payment by the party requiring it of the proper charges, be furnished to that party by the other within three days after receipt of such application.

In order to reduce the costs of the hearing, you are invited to inform the applicant and the Clerk to the Disciplinary Tribunal not less than fourteen days before the said   day of   of any facts set out in the affidavit which are not in dispute.

You are requested to acknowledge the receipt of this notice without delay.

Dated this   day of   , 19   .

. . . .

Clerk to the Tribunal

FORM 7

Form of notice by the Clerk to the Disciplinary Tribunal to a Solicitor made party to an application in respect of a Solicitor's Clerk

In the Matter of E.F, a Solicitor's Clerk,

and

In the Matter of the Solicitors Act 1974.

To G.H, solicitor of

Application has been made by A.B, of   , on behalf of The Law Society, to the Disciplinary Tribunal constituted under the Solicitors Act 1974, that an order be made by the Tribunal directing that as from a date to be specified in such order no solicitor shall except in accordance with permission in writing granted by The Law Society for such period and subject to such conditions as the Society may think fit to specify in the permission, employ or remunerate in connection with his practice as a solicitor, and said E.F. of   , a person who is or was a clerk to a solicitor or that such other order may be made as the Tribunal shall think right.

It is alleged in the affidavit accompanying the application, a copy of which is sent herewith, that you

By virtue of Rule 7 of the Solicitors (Disciplinary Proceedings) Rules 1985, the Tribunal have directed that you be constituted a party to the application. The parties to the application are as follows:

The   day of   , 19   , is the day fixed by the Tribunal for the hearing of the application. The Tribunal will sit at the Court Room, No. 60 Carey Street, Chancery Lane, London WC2 at   o'clock in the   noon. If you fail to appear, the Tribunal may, in accordance with the Solicitors (Disciplinary Proceedings) Rules 1985, proceed in your absence.

You are required by the said Rules to furnish to every other party to the application, and to the Clerk to the Disciplinary Tribunal at the Court Room, No. 60 Carey Street, Chancery Lane, London WC2 at least fourteen days before the said   day of   , 19 , a list of all the documents on which you propose to rely.

Any party may inspect the documents included in the list furnished by any other, and a copy of any document mentioned in the list of any party must, on application and on payment by the party requiring it of the proper charges, be furnished to that party by the other within three days after receipt of such application.

You are requested to acknowledge the receipt of this notice without delay.

Dated this   day of   , 19   .

. . . .

Clerk to the Tribunal

FORM 8

Form of affidavit by an applicant being a former Solicitor whose name was struck off the Roll of Solicitors

In the Matter of C.D,

and

In the Matter of the Solicitors Act 1974.

I, C.D, of   , make oath and say as follows:

1   I was admitted a solicitor on the   day of   , 19 .

2   On the   day of   , 19 , my name was ordered to be struck off the Roll of Solicitors.

3   I hereby apply that my name be restored to the Roll of Solicitors.

4   The grounds for my application are:

Sworn, etc.

FORM 9

Form of notice by the Clerk to the Disciplinary Tribunal to the applicant, a former Solicitor

In the Matter of C.D,

and

In the Matter of the Solicitors Act 1974.

To C.D., of

The   day of   , 19 , is the day fixed by the Disciplinary Tribunal for the hearing of your application that your name be restored to the Roll of Solicitors.

The Tribunal will sit at the Court Room, No. 60 Carey Street, Chancery Lane, London WC2 at   o'clock in the   noon.

You are required by the Solicitors (Disciplinary Proceedings) Rules 1985, to furnish to The Law Society and to the Clerk to the Disciplinary Tribunal at the Court Room, No. 60 Carey Street, Chancery Lane, London WC2 at least fourteen days before the said day of   , 19 , a list of all the documents on which you propose to rely.

Any party may inspect the documents included in the list furnished by any other, and a copy of any document mentioned in the list of any party must, on application and on payment by the party requiring it of the proper charges, be furnished to that party by the other within three days after receipt of such application.

If any party shall fail to appear and the Tribunal decide to proceed in his absence, any party appearing must be prepared to prove service, in accordance with the Solicitors (Disciplinary Proceedings) Rules 1985, of the list of documents and any other notice or correspondence since the lodging of the application.

You are requested to acknowledge the receipt of this notice without delay.

Dated this   day of   , 19 .

. . . .

Clerk to the Tribunal

FORM 10

Form of notice by the Clerk to the Disciplinary Tribunal to the Law Society in relation to an application by a former Solicitor

In the Matter of C.D,

and

In the Matter of the Solicitors Act 1974.

To: The Law Society,
       Chancery Lane, London WC2

Application has been made by C.D, of   , that his name be restored to the Roll of Solicitors.

The   day of   , 19   , is the day fixed by the Disciplinary Tribunal for the hearing of this application.

The Tribunal will sit at the Court Room, No. 60 Carey Street, Chancery Lane, London WC2 at   o'clock in the   noon.

You are required by the Solicitors (Disciplinary Proceedings) Rules 1985, to furnish to the said C.D. and to the Clerk to the Disciplinary Tribunal at the Court Room, No. 60 Carey Street, Chancery Lane, London WC2 at least fourteen days before the said day of   , 19 , a list of all the documents on which you propose to rely.

Any party may inspect the documents included in the list furnished by any other, and a copy of any document mentioned in the list of any party must, on application and on payment by the party requiring it of the proper charges, be furnished to that party by the other within three days after receipt of such application.

If any party shall fail to appear and the Tribunal decide to proceed in his absence, any party appearing must be prepared to prove service, in accordance with the Solicitors (Disciplinary Proceedings) Rules 1985, of the list of documents and any other notice or correspondence since the lodging of the application.

You are requested to acknowledge the receipt of this notice without delay.

Dated this   day of   , 19 .

. . . .

Clerk to the Tribunal

FORM 11

Form of affidavit by applicant in relation to an order made under section 43 of the Solicitors Act 1974

I, the undersigned A.B,   or E.F, of   hereby make application that the Order made on the   day of   , 19 , under section 43 of the Solicitors Act 1974, in respect of E.F, be revoked.

The grounds for my application are

Sworn, etc.

FORM 12

Form of notice by the Clerk to the Disciplinary Tribunal in relation to an application in respect of a former Solicitor's Clerk

In the Matter of E.F,

and

In the Matter of the Solicitors Act 1974.

To: The Law Society,
      Chancery Lane, London WC2

and

To: E.F.

     of

Application has been made by   of   , to the Disciplinary Tribunal that the Order made on the   day of   19 , under section 43(2) of the Solicitors Act 1974, in respect of E.F. be revoked.

The   day of   , 19 , is the day fixed by the Disciplinary Tribunal for the hearing of this application.

The Tribunal will sit at the Court Room, No. 60 Carey Street, Chancery Lane, London WC2 at   o'clock in the   noon.

The parties to the application are as follows:

    (i) The Law Society

    (ii) E.F.

You are required by the Solicitors (Disciplinary Proceedings) Rules 1985, to furnish to every other party to the application and to the Clerk to the Disciplinary Tribunal at the Court Room, No. 60 Carey Street, Chancery Lane, London WC2 at least fourteen days before the said   day of   , a list of all the documents on which you propose to rely.

Any party may inspect the documents included in the list furnished by any other, and a copy of any document mentioned in the list of any party must, on application and on payment by the party requiring it of the proper charges, be furnished to that party by the other within three days after receipt of such application.

If any party shall fail to appear and the Tribunal decide to proceed in his absence, any party appearing must be prepared to prove service, in accordance with the Solicitors (Disciplinary Proceedings) Rules 1985, of the list of documents and any other notice or correspondence since the lodging of the application.

You are requested to acknowledge the receipt of this notice without delay.

Dated this   day of   , 19   .

. . . .

Clerk to the Tribunal

FORM 13

Form of Subpoena Ad Testificandum

In the Matter of C.D, a Solicitor, [or] a Solicitor's Clerk,

and

In the Matter of the Solicitors Act 1974

ELIZABETH THE SECOND, by the Grace of God, etc.

To:

greeting.

We command you to attend before the Disciplinary Tribunal constituted under the Solicitors Act 1974 at   on   day, the   day of   at the hour of   in the   noon, and so from day to day until the application in the above matter is heard, to give evidence on behalf of

WITNESS

Lord High Chancellor of Great Britain, the   day of   in the year of Our Lord

---

FORM 14

Form of Subpoena Duces Tecum

In the Matter of C.D, a Solicitor, [or] a Solicitor's Clerk,

and

In the Matter of the Solicitors Act 1974

ELIZABETH THE SECOND, by the Grace of God, etc.

To:

greeting.

We command you to attend before the Disciplinary Tribunal constituted under the Solicitors Act 1974 at　　　　　　　on　　　　　　　day, the　　　　　　　day of　　　　　　at the hour of　　　　　in the　　　　　noon, and so from day to day until the application in the above matter is heard, to give evidence on behalf of and also to bring with you and produce at the time and place aforesaid [specify documents to be produced].

WITNESS

Lord High Chancellor of Great Britain, the　　　　　　　day in the year of Our Lord

Dated this

FORM 15

Form of notice to accompany affidavit evidence

In the Matter of C.D, a Solicitor, [or] a Solicitor's Clerk,

and

In the Matter of the Solicitors Act 1974

TAKE NOTICE that the applicant/respondent proposes to rely upon the affidavits copies of which are served herewith. If you wish any witness being a deponent to one of these affidavits to be required to attend the hearing you must, not less than 10 days before the date set down for the hearing of the application, notify me and the Clerk to that effect. In the event of your failure to do so the Tribunal may accept the affidavit in question in evidence.

. . . .

Applicant/Respondent

DATED this 19th day of February 1985

J F Warren

Clerk to the Tribunal

Approved

John Donaldson

M R

EXPLANATORY NOTE

(This note is not part of the Rules)

These Rules regulate procedure for the making, hearing and determination of applications or complaints under the Solicitors Act 1974 to the Disciplinary Tribunal constituted under that Act.

The Rules re-enact the Solicitors (Disciplinary Proceedings) Rules 1975 with amendments. The changes of substance relate to hearings in public and affidavit evidence.

List of abbreviations

ABI	Association of British Insurers
ADR	Alternative dispute resolution
AJA	Administration of Justice Act
ASA	Advertising Standards Authority
BCAP	British Code of Advertising Practice
BES	Business Expansion Scheme
CAP	Committee of Advertising Practice
CCBE	Council of the Bars and Law Societies of the European Community
CML	Council of Mortgage Lenders
CPD	Continuing professional development
DIB	Discrete investment business
FIMBRA	Financial Intermediaries, Managers and Brokers Regulatory Association
FSA	Financial Services Act
IMRO	Investment Management Regulatory Organisation
IPS	Inadequate professional services
LAUTRO	Life Assurance and Unit Trust Regulatory Organisation
LCD	Lord Chancellor's Department
MNP	Multi-national practice
PACE	Police and Criminal Evidence Act 1984
PDC	Property display centre
PEP	Personal equity plan
PIA	Personal Investment Authority
PTP	Permitted third party
RFL	Registered foreign lawyer
RPB	Recognised professional body
SAS	Solicitors' Assistance Scheme
SCB	Solicitors Complaints Bureau
SFA	Securities and Futures Authority
SIB	Securities and Investments Board
SIBR	Solicitors' Investment Business Rules
SIF	Solicitors' Indemnity Fund
SIPR	Solicitors' Incorporated Practice Rules
SIP	Solicitor insolvency practitioner
SPR	Solicitors' Practice Rules
SRO	Self-regulatory organisation

Useful addresses

Set out below is a list of names and addresses of Law Society departments and external bodies whose functions are mentioned in the Guide and whom the reader may find it useful to contact.

Law Society departments

Accountants' Reports
Financial Services Section
Legal Education
Monitoring Unit
Practising Certificates Section
Professional Ethics
Professional Indemnity Section
Records Office
Transfer Unit

Ipsley Court
Berrington Close
Redditch
Worcs   B98 0TD
Tel: 071-242 1222
Local calls: 0527 517141
Fax: 0527 510213
DX: 19114 Redditch

Communications Division
Ethnic Minorities Careers Officer
Information Co-ordinator
Legal Practice
Legal Practice (International)
Practice Advice Service
Professional Adviser

Law Society House
50/52 Chancery Lane
London   WC2A 1SX
Tel: 071-242 1222
Fax: 071-405 9522
DX: 56 Lon/Chancery Ln WC2

Careers and Recruitment Service
Law Society Shop

227/228 Strand
London   WC2R 1BA
Tel: 071-242 1222
Fax: 071-583 5531
DX: 56 Lon/Chancery Ln WC2

Compensation Fund
Remuneration Certificates
Solicitors Complaints Bureau

Victoria Court
8 Dormer Place
Leamington Spa
Warwickshire   CV32 5AE
Tel: 0926 820082
Fax: 0926 431435
DX: 292320 Leamington Spa 4

External Bodies

Court of Protection

Stewart House
24 Kingsway
London   WC2B 6JX
Tel: 071-269 7000
Fax: 071-831 0060
DX: 37965 Lon/Kingsway WC2

General Council of the Bar

3 Bedford Row
London   WC1R 4DB
Tel: 071-242 0082
Fax: 071-831 9217
DX: 240 Lon/Chancery Ln WC2

Lawyers' Support Group

c/o St Giles Church
Off Wood Street
Barbican
London   EC2
Tel: 0202 734488 (Barry)
     081-870 1601 (Jonathan)
     0895 833245 (Leslie)

Legal Aid Head Office

29/37 Red Lion Street
London   WC1R 4PP
Tel: 071-831 4209
Fax: 071-831 0670
DX: 450 Lon/Chancery Ln WC2

Legal Services Ombudsman

22 Oxford Court
Oxford Street
Manchester   M2 3WQ
Tel: 061-236 9532
Fax: 061-236 2651
DX: 18569 Manchester 7

Lord Chancellor's Department

Trevelyan House
Great Peter Street
London SW1P 2BY
Tel: 071-210 8500
Fax: 071-210 8549

Master of the Rolls

Royal Courts of Justice
Strand
London   WC2A 2LL
Tel: 071-936 6000
DX: 44450 Strand WC2

Official Solicitor

81 Chancery Lane
London   WC2A 1DD
Tel: 071-911 7127
DX: 0012 Lon/Chancery Ln WC2

Solicitors' Disciplinary Tribunal

16 Bell Yard
London   WC2A 1PL
Tel: 071-242 0219
Fax: 071-831 0344
DX: 395 Lon/Chancery Ln WC2

Solicitors Indemnity Fund Limited

100 St John Street
London   EC1M 4EH
Tel: 071-566 6000
Fax: 071-566 6006 (General)
     071-566 6003 (Claims)
DX: 46601 Barbican EC1

Table of cases

All references are to pages, not paragraphs.

Table of statutes

All references are to pages, not paragraphs.

Table of statutory instruments and rules

All references are to pages, not paragraphs.

EC material

All references are to pages, not paragraphs.

List of annexes

The material in the Guide has been rearranged for the sixth edition. The purpose of this list is to help the reader to locate particular types of material which usually appear as annexes. It supplements the contents pages (see page v), the table of statutes (page 794), the table of statutory instruments and rules (page 800); the table of EC material (page 807) and the index (page 813).

References are to pages, not paragraphs.

Codes

Council direction

Council guidance

Council requirement

Council statements

Guidance

Practice information

Principles

Regulations

Rules

Statutes

Statutory instruments

Written professional standards

Index

Compiled by Elizabeth M. Moys, B.A., F.L.A., registered indexer.

Notes:
1 All references are to pages, not paragraphs.
2 References to the text of statutes, rules, etc. are in bold type.
3 Main entries for all subjects and organisations are spelt out in full but, if there is a well-known abbreviation, that is used in subheadings.

THE GUIDE TO THE PROFESSIONAL CONDUCT OF SOLICITORS 1993